# Human Sexuality

**A Text with Readings**
**Second Edition**

A student workbook has been developed to assist you in mastering the concepts presented in this text. The workbook includes a brief summary and outline of each chapter, review questions, a self-testing section to determine what areas you need to study more, and values clarification exercises. The student workbook is available from your local bookstore under the title: *Study Guide to Accompany Human Sexuality: A Text With Readings, 2nd Edition.* If you cannot locate it in the bookstore, ask your bookstore manager to order it for you.

# Human Sexuality

**A Text with Readings**
**Second Edition**

**Sam Wilson**
Indian Valley College

**Bryan Strong**
University of California
Santa Cruz

**Mina Robbins**
California State University
Sacramento

**Thomas Johns**
American River College

**West Publishing Company**
St. Paul    New York    Los Angeles    San Francisco

**Library of Congress Cataloging in Publication Data**

Main entry under title:

Human sexuality

Bibliography: p.
Includes index.
1. Sex – Addresses, essays, lectures. I. Wilson, Samuel. [DNLM: 1. Sex behavior. 2. Sex manuals. HQ21 H915]
HQ21.H738    1980      612'.6      79-27336
ISBN 0-8299-0328-3

## Acknowledgements

We would like to thank our past and present reviewers: Etta Breit and Mark Tyson, University of South Florida; Nancy Cozzens and Bud Poduska, DeAnza College; Tom Eckle, Modesto Junior College; Richard Hartley, University of Peugot Sound; Paul Weickert, Central Michigan University; Phyllis Seabolt, Western Michigan University; James Keaton, San Jose City College; Laura Schlesinger, University of Southern California; Robert Crooks, Portland Community College; Dr. Jeffrey Reichel, Stanford University Medical School; Lynn Simon, Dale Henon, Miriam Camp, Kent Bleu, who kept our trusty Smith-Corona in repair, Michele Ash, and Cathy Smith. All provided important suggestions, help and encouragement at various stages of the manuscript. We would also like to thank the staff at the Santa Cruz Planned Parenthood Office. Special thanks to Elizabeth Strong and Laurel Reseau for research and permissions. Many thanks to Joe at the post office, who always cheerfully got our manuscripts into the mail.

In particular, we would like to thank Andrew Barclay of Michigan State University, W. D. "Pete" Hardesty, Southwest Texas State University, and Nathan Liskey, California State University in Fresno, whose thorough reviews and perceptive comments helped immensely in the shaping of the second edition.

Lastly, we wish to express appreciation to the staff of West Publishing Company.

### Photo Credits

Bancroft Library, Berkley, p. 415; Culver Pictures, Inc., pp. 14, 21, 421; EKM-Nepenthe, pp. 34, 40, 42, 222, 226, 230, 232, 246, 248, 255, 276, 279, 284, 303, 338, 419, 449; Rick Grosse, pp. 388, 395; Jeroboam, pp. 391, 397; Magnum, pp. 254, 308; Stock Boston, pp. 38, 224, 250, 258, 424, 447; UPI, p. 227; Wide World, pp. 37, 423.

### Cover Art

Alloy, 1967, Helen Frankenthaller. Courtesy Collection Walker Art Center, Minneapolis.

To Lucy Autrey-Wilson, Orley and
Gina Ashenfelter, Katy, Beth,
Bruce and Ken Robbins,
and Marilyn Johns.

# Contents

Contents

Contents

# Introduction

In the years since we compiled our thoughts for the first edition, various sexual shifts have occurred. Sexual activity among adolescents, for example, increased by 30% in just five years (Zelnik and Kantner, 1977).* Two-thirds of the females in America have sexual relationships by age 19. In the year of this writing, 1978-1979, a dozen girls below the age of twelve became pregnant in a single county, Alameda, in California. Recent years have also brought venereal disease to middle class America. Types of VD which parents never knew existed (herpes genitalis and nongonorrheal urethritis, for example) are now epidemic among their children.

There have also been marked changes in abortion laws. Considered in an international perspective, the shift has been toward laws more favorable to women seeking abortions (Cook and Dickens, 1978). Yet, in our own country, the trend has been the opposite; new laws restrict the use of public monies for funding abortions of low-income women. (On the other hand, in July of 1979 the U.S. Supreme Court established that those below the age of 18 need not have parental consent to seek an abortion.) The American moral/political/legal tide also seems to be turning against people with homosexual inclinations. Anita Bryantism is rampant in many parts of the country.

The shift toward liberalism, which seemed so inevitable at the beginning of the '70s appears to have stalled, and perhaps, reversed. But, one shouldn't be surprised to see such a change; prevailing morals regarding erotica and reproduction have fluctuated widely throughout human history. Perhaps the most drastic change in moral climate came during the centuries when Christianity ascended as the religion of the West.

In its early years, Christianity found itself set in a milieu of extremes in sexual attitudes and practices. Rome was in decadence, and various sexual fetishes were rampant (Fellini, 1970). By comparison, the admittedly eclectic tastes of the Greeks of several hundred years before Christ seem tame, even playful. Curiosity over the nature of "truth", "beauty", and "love", which had characterized the age of Socrates and Plato, had given way to Roman hedonism.

Even as Nero fiddled, however, a countercurrent of asceticism was growing. Among the devotees, celibacy and virginity were exalted at the expense of marriage and children. Into these times of polarization, the early Christians introduced a middle way. It is clear in Paul's Epistle to the Romans, that the New Testament took a stern stand on libertinism. The prevailing practices of prostitution, divorce, and homosexuality came in for strong condemnation. Yet, compassion also characterized the early Christians. An adulterous woman, for example, was told to "go, and not to sin again" (John 8:11). The most harsh Christian edicts, did not come for several hundred years, perhaps culminating with the pronouncements of Augustine, who lived about as long A.D. as Socrates lived B.C.

During the Middle Ages, shifts in moral climate were relatively languid. The Church remained the dominant force, but gradually changed its point of view under pressure of the intellectual rebellion of the Renaissance. In recent centuries changes have come at a faster rate. Today one could only engage in idle speculation over what the sexual trends will be in as little as a decade from now.

It seems that change is inherent to the nature of human sexuality. Perhaps there is a parallel between the moral consciousness of our species and the curious nature of a cat which is preoccupied with the twitching of its own tail. Curiosity may even burst into a lunging attack; but, let the tail fall lifeless, and it loses its power of fascination. More likely our attitudes about sexuality are molded in many subtle ways by the changing nature of our culture at large – the economic climate, whether or not we are at war, the latest technological breakthrough in "test tube" reproduction, etc.

In establishing the tenor of our book, we have attempted to maintain academic rigor, while not masking our personal viewpoints. On the subject of sexuality, there is no such thing as an unbiased approach; and rather than couching our ideas in pedantic garble, we have chosen to state them in plain words. But, we have strived to give fair coverage to contrary viewpoints.

By including a series of pertinent readings after each chapter of text, we have tried to further broaden the coverage. Certain authors were chosen because of their areas of expertise; others for their emotional commitment. Artists as well as scientists were selected, and writings from antiquity to the present give historical perspectives. We hope you will find our approach both helpful and enjoyable.

# Readings

### *Excerpt from* Symposium

Plato

*No word is bandied about with less precision than "love". Basically, the problem is that much more is expected of it than a single syllable could possibly bear. Perhaps other words should be called in to take on some of the load. "Lust" (whose image has taken a beating over the years) would do fine for much of what is referred to as "romantic love".*

*"Love" will probably never have a very clear meaning, however, for the ironic reason that people talk about it so much. Perhaps the worst problem with the word began at a bull session over 400 years B.C. At the point of this excerpt, Socrates has the floor; and he tells of his lesson in love from Diotima of Mantineia, a wise old woman.*

... The true order of going, or being led by another, to the things of love, is to begin from the beauties of earth and mount upwards for the sake of that other beauty, using these as steps only, and from one going on to two, and from two to all fair forms, and from fair forms to fair practices, and from fair practices to fair notions, until from fair notions he arrives at the notion of absolute beauty, and at last knows what the essence of beauty is. This, "my dear Socrates," said the stranger of Mantineia, "is that life above all others which man should live, is the contemplation of beauty absolute; a beauty which if you once beheld, you would see not to be after the measure of gold, and garments, and fair boys and youths, whose presence now entrances you; and you and many an one would be content to live seeing them only and conversing with them without meat or drink, if that were possible – you only want to look at them and to be with them. But what if man had eyes to see the true beauty – the divine beauty, I mean, pure and clear and unalloyed, not clogged with the pollutions of mortality and all the colours and vanities of human life – thither looking, and holding converse with the true beauty simple and divine? Remember how in that communion only, beholding beauty with the eye of the mind, he will be enabled to bring forth, not images of beauty, but realities (for he has hold not of an image but of a reality), and bringing forth and nourishing true virtue to become the friend of God and be immortal, if mortal man may. Would that be an ignoble life?"

Such, Phaedrus – and I speak not only to you, but to all of you – were the words of Diotima, and I am persuaded of their truth. And being persuaded of them, I try to persuade others, that in the attainment of this end human nature will not easily find a helper better than love. And therefore, also, I say that every man ought to honour him as I myself honour him, and walk in his ways, and exhort others to do the same, and praise the power and spirit of love according to the measure of my ability now and ever.

The words which I have spoken, you, Phaedrus, may call an encomium of love, or anything else which you please.

---

### *Excerpts from* **the Bible**

Genesis

### *Chapter II*

15  And the Lord God took the man, and put him into the garden of Eden, to dress it, and to keep it.
16  And the Lord God commanded the man, saying, Of every tree of the garden thou mayest freely eat:
17  But of the tree of knowledge of good and evil, thou shalt not eat of it: for in the day that thou eatest thereof thou shalt surely die.
18  And the Lord God said, It is not good that the man should be alone: I will make him an help meet for him.
19  And out of the ground the Lord God formed every beast of the field, and every fowl of the air and brought them unto Adam to see what

he would call them; and whatsoever Adam called every living creature, that was the name thereof.

20  And Adam gave names to all cattle, and to the fowl of the air, and to every beast of the field: but for Adam there was not found an help meet for him.
21  And the Lord God caused a deep sleep to fall upon Adam, and he slept; and he took one of his ribs, and closed up the flesh instead thereof:
22  And the rib, which the Lord God had taken from man, made he a woman, and brought her unto the man.
23  And Adam said, This is now bone of my bones, and flesh of my flesh: she shall be called Woman, because she was taken out of man.
24  Therefore shall a man leave his father and his mother, and shall cleave unto his wife: and they shall be one flesh.
25  And they were both naked, the man and his wife, and were not ashamed.

### *Chapter III*

Now the serpent was more subtle than any beast of the field which the Lord God had made: and he said unto the woman, Yea, hath God said, Ye shall not eat of every tree of the garden?

2  And the woman said unto the serpent, We may eat of the fruit of the trees of the garden:
3  But of the fruit of the tree which is in the midst of the garden, God hath said, Ye shall not eat of it, neither shall you touch it, lest ye die.
4  And the serpent said unto the woman, Ye shall surely not die.
5  For God doth know, that in the day ye eat therof, then your eyes shall be opened; and ye shall be as gods, knowing good and evil.

6 And when the woman saw that the tree was good for food, and that it was pleasant to the eyes, and a tree to be desired to make one wise; she took of the fruit thereof, and did eat; and gave also unto her husband with her, and he did eat.

7 And the eyes of them both were opened, and they knew that they were naked: and they sewed fig leaves together, and made themselves aprons.

8 And they heard the voice of the Lord God walking in the garden in the cool of the day: and Adam and his wife hid themselves from the presence of the Lord God amongst the trees of the garden.

9 And the Lord God called unto Adam, and said unto him, Where art thou?

10 And he said, I heard thy voice in the garden: and I was afraid, because I was naked; and I hid myself.

11 And he said, Who told thee that thou wast naked? Hast thou eaten of the tree whereof I commanded thee, that thou shouldest not eat?

12 And the man said, The woman whom thou gavest to be with me, she gave me of the tree, and I did eat.

13 And the Lord God said unto the woman, What is this that thou hast done? And the woman said, The serpent beguiled me, and I did eat.

14 And the Lord said unto the serpent, Because thou has done this, thou art cursed above all cattle, and above every beast of the field: upon they belly shalt thou go, and dust shalt thou eat all the days of thy life:

15 And I will put enmity between thee and the woman and between thy seed and her seed: it shall bruise thy head, and thou shalt bruise his heel.

16 Unto the woman he said, I will greatly multiply thy sorrow and thy conception; in sorrow thou shalt bring forth children: and thy desire shall be to thy husband, and he shall rule over thee.

17 And unto Adam he said, Because thou hast hearkened unto the voice of thy wife, and has eaten of the tree of which I commanded thee saying, Thou shalt not eat of it: cursed is the ground for thy sake; in sorrow shalt thou eat of it all the days of thy life.

18 Thorns also and thistles shall it bring forth to thee; and thou shalt eat the herb of the field:

19 In the sweat of thy face shalt thou eat bread, till thou return unto the ground; for out of it wast thou taken: for dust thou art, and unto dust shalt thou return.

20 And Adam called his wife's name Eve, because she was the mother of all living.

21 Unto Adam also and to his wife did the Lord God make coats of skins, and clothed them.

22 And the Lord God said, Behold the man is become as one of us, to know good and evil: and now, lest he put forth his hand, and take also of the tree of life, and eat, and live for ever:

23 Therefore the Lord God sent him forth from the garden of Eden, to till the ground from whence he was taken.

24 So he drove out the man: and he placed at the east of the garden of Eden Cherubims, and a flaming sword which turned every way, to keep the way of the tree of life.

---

## Excerpt from The City of God

Augustine

*Augustine, who lived in Algeria around A.D. 400, had a profound influence on the development of Christianity. The following summarizes his thoughts on the rewards of lust.*

For god ordained that infants should begin the world as the young of beasts begin it, since their parents had fallen to the level of the beasts in the fashion of their life and of their death; as it is written, "Man when he was in honour understood not; he became like the beasts that have no understanding." Nay more, infants, we see, are even feebler in the use and movement of their limbs, and more infirm to choose and refuse, than the most tender offspring of other animals; as if the force that dwells in human nature were destined to surpass all other living things so much the more eminently, as its energy has been longer restrained, and the time of its exercise delayed, just as an arrow flies the higher the further back it has been drawn. To this infantine imbecility the first man did not fall by his lawless presumption . . . but human nature was in his person perverted and altered to such an extent, that he suffered in his members the warring of disobedient lust, and became subject to the necessity of dying.

### Excerpt from The Song of Roland

*The Middle Ages was a time of religious fervor, interminable wars, and chastity belts. In* The Song of Roland, *of indeterminate authorship time between A.D. 800 and 1100, news of the hero's death had more serious consequences than one might otherwise expect.*

The emperor has returned from Spain and has come to Aix, the best seat in France. He mounted the steps of the palace and went into the hall. And there came Aude, a fair damsel, and said to him: "Where is the chieftain Roland, who swore to take me for his wife?" Then Charles was filled with grief and heaviness; tears flow from his eyes and he pulls his white beard. "Sister, dear friend, thou hast asked me news of a dead man. I will give thee the best possible exchange, to wit Louis, and nothing better can I promise; he is my son, and he will hold my borders." Aude replies: "These words mean nothing to me. May it not please God nor his saints nor his angels that I remain alive after Roland." Her colour leaves her, she falls at the feet of Charlemaine and she dies straightway; may God have mercy on her soul! The French barons weep and lament for her.

# Unit I

# Sexuality in America

# The American Way of Sex:
# The Past

The American Way of Sex: The Past

**1**

S ex is a drive that is given form and direction by culture. Our social rules teach us how to channel these drives to release the physiological tensions that accompany them. We learn what to do sexually, how and when and with whom to do it, and how to feel about doing it.

The way we handle our sexual desires and feelings may seem to be innate, instinctive, and natural, but no one is born knowing how to behave sexually. Beginning in infancy, we learn about sexuality from the world around us – from parents, friends, relatives, religious leaders, communication media. Most of this learning has been acquired unconsciously, without our ever realizing that we are being taught.

The sexual code of our culture had its beginnings thousands of years ago. The main boundaries for American sexual attitudes – and confusion – are based on the Judeo-Christian tradition. Within Jewish law and tradition, great value was placed on marriage and children. The Talmud, the Jewish equivalent of the Christian Bible, places a religious obligation on both men and women to marry and produce offspring; those who remained single were considered both pitiable and immoral, because they refused to raise a family. Sexual intercourse was permitted only within marriage, and in theory was to be used only for procreation. One of the major features of the Western sexual code is this relationship between sex and procreation, a heritage from ancient Judaism. Basically it is a negative injunction, which if applied strictly would make it immoral to have sexual intercourse with any woman incapable of bearing children. (Such restrictions are not always followed in practice, however, and their major purpose was probably to prevent unmarried young people from having sexual intercourse.)

Another major legacy that has come to us from the Jewish tradition is the dominance of the male. Even today, the Orthodox Jewish male's morning ritual includes an ancient prayer that acknowledges appreciation for having been created a man rather than a woman. In earlier times, the right to own property and to obtain a divorce were held only by males. A man could divorce his wife if she committed adultery, was a poor cook, or lost her beauty. A woman could obtain a divorce only with her husband's consent.

Until recently, the sexual codes of most Western cultures retained these two aspects of ancient Jewish law – the obligation to reproduce and the domination of the male – which were incorporated into the Christian religion.

### The Christian Tradition

Although Jesus rebelled against many major aspects of Judaism, Christianity maintained the Jewish sexual tradition. Jesus died a young man, and there is no indication in his teachings that he intended celibacy to serve as a model for future generations; nevertheless, most of his pronouncements about sexuality were negative and prohibitive. (Then, as now, sex was recognized as one of the strongest of drives.)

Marriage was considered a joyful event (the first public miracle attributed to Jesus was turning water into wine for a wedding celebration). He also showed compassion toward a woman charged with adultery. For this crime the penalty (which was inflicted on the guilty woman but not the guilty man) was death by stoning. Jesus said to the woman's accusers, "He that is without sin among you, let him cast the first stone." No one felt entitled to do so, and Jesus said to the adulteress, "Neither do I condemn thee; go and sin no more." On this and other occasions, Christ displayed tolerance.

Christian sexual attitudes were greatly

He that is without sin among you,
let him cast the first stone.
*John 8*

---

changed through the influence of St. Paul. He viewed sex as something to be avoided and celibacy as the ideal (because it symbolized the triumph of will over temptation). Marriage was to be encouraged among people who could not resist sexual temptation. Paul said, "To the unmarried and the widows, I say that it is well for them to remain single as I do. But, if they cannot exercise self-control, they should marry. For it is better to marry than to burn."

**Augustine's Influence**   Paul's teachings provided the basic doctrines for Christianity until the fifth century, when they were elaborated on by St. Augustine. Augustine, as severe as Paul but more passionate (and also subject to considerable self-hatred), abandoned his beloved mistress and their son after experiencing a "revelation" from God. Thereafter, he regarded his former life with loathing. In his *Confessions*, he wrote, " ... if I was conceived in iniquity, and if my mother nourished me within her womb in sins, where, I beseech you, O Lord my God, where or when was your servant innocent?"

The strong conflict between sexual desire and the belief that sex is shameful was a personal tragedy for Augustine. He evolved a complex theology based on self-hatred, which dominated Christian thought throughout the Middle Ages. His negative views are expressed in *The City of God*, in which he wrote "of the shame which attends all sexual intercourse":

> Lust requires for its consummation darkness and secrecy; and this not only when unlawful intercourse is desired, but even such fornication as the earthly city has legalized. Where there is no fear of punishment, those permitted pleasures still shrink from the public eye ... What! Does even conjugal intercourse, sanctioned as it is by law for the propagation of children, legitimate and honorable though it be, does it not seek retirement from every eye?

Before the bridegroom fondles his bride, does he not exclude the attendants, and even the paranymphs [bridesmaids and groomsmen], and such friends as the closest ties have admitted to the bridal chamber?

Largely because of Augustine's writings, the Catholic Church took a firm stand against sexual intercourse among the unmarried, and revived the Jewish tradition that among the married it was to be used solely for procreation. The belief in the Virgin Mary's virginity became increasingly important as sexual intercourse was more and more looked down upon as the antithesis of spirituality, divine love and holiness. Her virginity became a tenet of Catholicism. Infants were baptized – and still are – to wash away symbolically the blemish of the sin their parents transmitted in conceiving them.

While the Church was devising rules, however, men and women were breaking them. Aristocrats took concubines into their manors, and peasants continued to view sex as fun. Weddings were arranged by families. By the tenth century, wedding ceremonies were held at the entrances to churches, with the father "giving" his daughter to her husband, signifying the transferral of authority over the woman. By the 1300s, however, the wedding ceremony had moved inside the church, and the father gave his daughter to the priest, who married the couple. Although the Church attempted to control marriage, the efforts were not successful; William Kephart (1961) has described the status of marriage during the Middle Ages:

> Though most people married, marriage was considered a private matter between two families, with the ceremonials being non-religious in nature; in fact, during the Middle Ages it was not unusual for "self-marriage" to take place. The bride and groom – in spite of much adverse public opinion – would simply recite the marriage ritual in the presence of

**"Whether Nocturnal Pollution
Is a Mortal Sin?"**

For every sin depends on the judgment of reason, since even the first movement of the sensuality has nothing sinful in it, except in so far as it can be suppressed by reason; wherefore in the absence of reason's judgment, there is no sin at all. Now during sleep reason has not a free judgment. For there is no one who while sleeping does not regard some of the images formed by his imagination as real . . . Wherefore what a man does while he sleeps and is deprived of reason's judgment, is not imputed to him as a sin, as neither are the actions of a maniac or an imbecile.

St. Thomas Aquinas, Summa Theologica

---

one another. The actual words – analogous to "I take thee for my lawful wedded wife" – would be spoken in the present tense *with* or *without witnesses*. This was the origin of our present common-law marriage; in fact, as it is practiced today in the United States, common-law marriage is almost identical with the *self-marriage* described.

**Thomas Aquinas**  In *Summa Theologica*, which St. Thomas Aquinas began writing in the thirteenth century, he systematically argued the Church's position on almost every conceivable question – basing his conclusions on a murky combination of "right reason," the Bible, and the writings of other theologians. From these sources, he established sets of rules covering proper behavior. Although he himself had no firsthand sexual experience, the *Summa* expounded on virtually every aspect of sexuality – from kissing to coition, from incest to bestiality, from fantasies to wet dreams. Beginning with the assumption that sex was basically animalistic, Thomas Aquinas "logically" demonstrated the superiority of celibacy, the holiness of virginity, the evil of sexual fantasy, the unnaturalness of homosexuality, the sin of fornication. In terms of sexual ethics this was not new ground; the significance of Aquinas' writings is that he systematized Church teachings and attempted to provide a rational basis for morality.

**Protestant Views**  In the sixteenth century, Martin Luther led a movement for reform, which resulted in the establishment of the Protestant Church. Luther himself struggled against strong sexual desires as a priest, concluded that celibacy is unnatural, left the monastery and married. He considered sexual desire to be natural, not sinful, and a proper (if not entirely pure) activity in marriage.

John Calvin further modified Luther's beliefs,

arguing that sex was a holy act when performed within marriage. Both Luther and Calvin, however, perpetuated the tradition of male dominance in religion, the family, and politics. (This view was not challenged in America until the mid-nineteenth century.)

**Sex in Puritan America**
The Puritans rebelled against Church of England practices, which they felt were papist and political, and settled on our continent to escape religious persecution. Their sexual ethic was basically Calvinistic; it accepted the power of human sexuality and the futility of trying to suppress it, but decreed that sexual activity should be restricted to marriage. A Puritan minister recorded in his journal that "the Use of the Marriage Bed" is "founded in man's Nature." For a man or a woman to deny this use "denies all reliefe in Wedlock unto human necessity: and sends it for supply unto Bestiality when God gives not the gift of Continency."

Among the Puritans as well as other American colonists, social and economic life centered on the family. The typical family worked together as a unit, whether on the farm or in trades, producing goods for both home and market; children were bound to obey their parents, who had complete control over them. Within marriage, sexuality was considered an important binding force – both morally and physically – and a blessing as well. Out of wedlock, sex was considered a sinful threat to both the family and the social fabric.

In the Puritan world, the two primary sexual offenses were adultery and illegitimacy, both of which threatened the family structure. Puritans were little concerned with what happened within marriage, as long as neither partner suffered from "natural incapacities, and insufficiencies, which utterly disappoint the confessed ends of marriage . . ." Such a marriage could neither produce children nor alleviate lust and could be dissolved.

Although Puritan ethics forbade premarital intercourse, the punishment was not severe if the couple had previously contracted to be married. Adultery, fornication – even rape – were viewed with a degree of tolerance; because human nature was considered to be depraved, such crimes were to be expected. But the Puritans were highly intolerant of deviation involving animals. One youth was executed for reportedly having

In the early nineteenth century minister, doctors, and writers of fiction were increasingly troubled by sexual immorality. The spread of political and social democracy reminded conservative gentlemen of the ominous predictions by European aristocrats: popular government would lead inevitably to anarchy and thus to unrestrained sexual indulgence. In the eyes of most Americans who had heard of the lascivious courts of Europe, this was obviously aristocratic prejudice. On the other hand, a nation which lacked rigid social controls and a central ecclesiastical authority had to prove that liberty was not an excuse for profligacy. The excessive prudishness of Americans was partly a manifestation of this self-mistrust.

David Brion Davis

---

had intercourse with a mare, a cow, two goats, five sheep, two calves – and a turkey. The extent to which suspicion and ignorance colored Puritan thinking is evidenced in this passage written by John Winthrop of Boston:

> . . . a sow . . . among other pigs had one [offspring] without hair, and some other human resemblances . . . also one eye was blemished, just like one eye of a loose fellow in town, which occasioning him to be suspected, he confessed . . . for which . . . they put him to death.

There are few references to homosexuality in Puritan accounts, although it was recorded that four boys who were discovered engaging in "unnatural acts" with one another were sent back to England. Homosexuality does not appear to have been as anxiety-provoking for Puritans as it is for present-day Americans, perhaps because of differences in social structure. The family structure prevailing in America during past centuries encouraged the formation of a strong male identity, which may have prevented males from feeling personally threatened by homosexuality. From the ages of six or eight, boys usually worked alongside their fathers or other males, who provided definite models of male behavior.

The sexual ethic of the Puritans did not reach present-day Americans intact, however. We are not as much their heirs in matters of sexual ethics as we are heirs of the nineteenth-century Americans whose moral views intervened.

## Victorian Sexuality

A sexual revolution occurred during the nineteenth century. This was a period of gradual change, which is reflected in the literature of the Victorian era. During the 1830s, large numbers of "marriage manuals" and books on "sexual physiology" were published, incorporating morality with the emerging concept of "scientific" thought. These popular guides were strange collections of half-truth, fantasy, and medical opinion; often, they bordered on pornography. Thousands of these books were sold – indicating that they somehow touched a responsive chord among the reading public. The medical "facts" were often appallingly erroneous. (People do not die nor become insane as a result of masturbation or frequent intercourse, and the personal experiences of readers must have provided direct proof of the fallacy of such a view.) The significance of the books is not in their content, but in the fact that their popular appeal evidenced the wide-spread anxieties, confusion, and guilt.

The guidebooks indicate that people were not learning how to behave sexually from their parents or other adults but were turning to "experts" to find out how to feel and behave. The authors – usually physicians – provided a "scientific" basis for regulating sexual behavior, often including case histories of patients whose physical or emotional difficulties were traced to masturbation or sexual excess.

The pseudo-scientific texts provided a new base for sexual morality. In earlier times, religious training had instilled people with fears that disobeying the moral code would bring eternal damnation in hell – but religion was losing its influence on behavior. Science and materialism, which formed the basis for the nineteenth-century concept of "progress," filled the breach. Medical spokesmen offered "proof" that disease and insanity were the punishment for those who broke the moral code. Consequently, medicine took on much of religion's moral flavor. Dr. Homer Bostwick, who sold thousands of copies of his *Treatise on the Nature and Treatment of*

*Seminal Diseases, Impotency, and Other Kindred Afflictions*, pointed out "the immutable character of the eternal law of retribution 'the wages of sin is death.' " Moral virtue and good health were in perfect harmony: "the sufferer is freed from the physical consequences of his crime only when his body of sin and death is deposited in the grave," wrote Bostwick.

The Victorian sexual revolution was marked by near-paranoid anxieties about masturbation and frequency of intercourse, and by increasing stress on the idea that women were sexually "pure." Purity, in fact, became a goal that also brought about changes in the English language.

**Language Taboos** Language was subjected to an extensive over-haul during the Victorian era. Bawdiness was suppressed, and words that hinted of sexuality either disappeared or were supplanted by euphemisms. Cock became "rooster," haycock became "haystack," cockroaches became "roaches" — and cockswains in the Navy were occasionally called "roosterswains." Legs were transformed into "limbs," pantaloons became "inexpressibles" or "unmentionables," and breasts became "bosoms" (except those of poultry, which were transformed into "white meat"). Women were no longer seduced, but "betrayed." The Shakespearean plays that had amused thousands of viewers were regarded as obscene, and those not banned altogether were subjected to heavy-handed censoring. Noah Webster, compiler of the first American dictionary, prepared a new version of the Bible — substituting "peculiar member" for *stones,* "to nurse" for to *give suck,* "lewdness" for *fornication,* "lewd woman" *for whore,* and "to go astray" for *whoring.*

Although these language changes may seem relatively unimportant, they had a significant ef-

fect: Americans could verbalize sexuality only in terms set forth by a repressive society. There was no longer an erotic language; thus, sex could be spoken of only in euphemisms or "scientific" terminology. The prevailing attitudes of any society, expressed through either words or the lack of words, are a powerful force in the socialization of children. During the Victorian era, the American vocabulary presented children with negative sexual values.

**Increasing Anxieties** Fears about masturbation and the frequency of coition continued to increase. The Swiss physician Tissot had first warned the public of the physical dangers of masturbation in 1758, asserting that it brought about weakness caused by the loss of semen and the draining of "nervous energy" from the brain. Benjamin Rush, prominent physician and a delegate to the Constitutional Convention, became the first American to deal with masturbation in detail. His *Medical Inquiries,* published in 1812, was one of the first major American medical treatises as well as one of the first works to link masturbation with insanity — a linkage that became a major element in society's view of sexuality. Frequent intercourse was also to be avoided; like masturbation, it involved the depletion of semen through orgasm. (Intercourse was considered dangerous, whether in or out of marriage.) The array of consequences that Rush attributed to loss of semen is considerable:

> When indulged in an undue or a promiscuous intercourse with the female sex, or in onanism [masturbation], it produces seminal weakness, impotence, dysury, tabes dorsalis, pulmonary consumption, dyspepsia, dimness of sight, vertigo, epilepsy, dypochondriasis, loss of memory, manalgia, fatuity, and death.

Such views were, of course, convenient for the

medical profession, providing a "cause" for the numerous illnesses that doctors were not yet able to diagnose. To the patient suffering from such a simple failing as "dimness of sight," however, the pronouncements were personally tragic.

And amid the increase of hostility toward sexuality, the image of woman also was subjected to changing views.

**Woman as Threat**   The Puritans had believed that human nature was depraved and sinful because of the human "Fall from Grace" that had occurred in the Garden of Eden. Woman bore a special burden of guilt, because Eve had tempted the innocent Adam with the forbidden fruit. If the forbidden fruit is interpreted to symbolize sexuality, then woman is the sensuous temptress who leads man astray. The Victorians, however, denied that sexuality is part of woman's nature; rather, her role became one of inherent purity and innocence. She had no sexual desire but only the desire to reproduce.

This denial of woman's sexuality – a major reversal in Western culture – had its roots in England in the early 1700s. The image of women it presented was initially incoherent, incomplete, and contradictory, however, and many of the old views of women's sexuality were retained. The publication in 1740 of Samual Richardson's *Pamela* provided what was needed to establish the new view – a fully developed feminine stereotype as the model for womanly behavior. Pamela was young and inexperienced, passive and passionless. Her self-definition revolved around purity before marriage and insofar as possible, purity after marriage as well.

By 1820, the "pure" woman had become the dominant stereotype in America. But, while the image of woman was acquiring "purity," the image of men had remained passionate and rather animal-like. The hostility that developed between men and women as a result of this con-

flict was to have overwhelming psychological and emotional consequences for both sexes. Our society viewed man as aggressor, woman as sexual victim. Sexuality was thus denied to half the population, resulting in untold suffering as women tried to reconcile their desires (if, indeed, they permitted themselves to experience them) with the prevailing concept of female purity. Men suffered equally, because their sexual desires resulted in acts interpreted as degrading, forced upon women who submitted only through a sense of duty. A popular cartoon depicted a young man discovering his wife unconscious from chloroform on the bed, on their wedding night, with a nearby note reading, "Momma says you can do anything you want with me."

**Victorian Sexual Ideology**   In a society where women were held to be without sexual desires, sex was fundamentally a man's problem. The theories and ethics of this period revolved around male sexuality, usually relating to women only incidentally rather than as participants.

Victorian sexual ideology stressed the idea that semen was the essential life force in the male. The "semen theory" provided a biological and materialistic explanation for growth. It stated that the testes, "through some hidden and not yet understood process . . . slowly secreted cells" into the semen. When semen was not lost through ejaculation, these cells were in some way absorbed by the blood, causing the characteristics that develop in the male at maturity: the changes in body structure, the deepening of the voice, the growth of body hair. When the mature male refrained from masturbation and "sexual excess," the seminal cells (no longer needed for growth) were carried to the brain, where they were "coined into new thoughts – perhaps new inventions – grand conceptions of the true, the beautiful, the useful, or into fresh emotions of joy

## Wealth

The counting-room maxims liberally expounded are laws of the universe. *The merchant's economy is a coarse symbol of the soul's economy. It is to spend for power and not for pleasure.* It is to invest income; that is to say, to take up particulars into generals; days into integral eras – literary, emotive, practical – of its life, and still to ascend in its investment. The *merchant has but one rule, absorb and invest*; he is to be capitalist; the scraps and filings must be gathered back into the crucible; the gas and smoke must be burned, and earnings must not go to increase expense, but to capital gain. *Well, the man must be capitalist. Will he spend his income, or will he invest? His body and every organ is under the same law. His body is a jar in which the liquor of life is stored. Will he spend for pleasure? The way to ruin is short and facile. Will he not spend but hoard for power?* It passes through the sacred fermentations, by the law of nature whereby everything climbs to higher platforms, and bodily vigor becomes mental and moral vigor. The bread he eats is first strength and animal spirits; it becomes, in higher laboratories, imagery and thought; and in still higher results, courage and endurance. This is the right compound interest; this is capital doubled, quadrupled, centupled; man raised to his highest power.

Ralph Waldo Emerson

and impulses of kindness . . . " The fallacious semen theory involves a process remarkably similar to Freud's idea of "sublimation" (for which it may have provided a basis).

Semen was not produced in unlimited amounts, however. Sexuality, like economics, was viewed as a closed system. In fact, male sexuality was often depicted in economic terminology. The words used to describe the necessity of preserving semen, for example, are those of an accountant rather than a scientist. Men were advised to take "into account" the "cost" of replacing semen "wasted" in sensual pleasure. Semen was to be "expended" only for procreation, lest a "heavy tax" be placed on the body.

Semen lost through ejaculation was viewed as a gain in personal pleasure but a loss to society – which could only progress if semen were retained, to be turned into new thoughts and inventions and kindness. The idea that sexuality should be sublimated provided a new set of values. Chastity and sexual restraint became the base upon which were pinned all other values – work, industry, good habits, piety, noble thoughts, creativity. Sexual "impurity," on the other hand, caused sloth, speculation, whiskey drinking, and loss of control. The most important quality achieved through sexual continence was self-control, which was the basis not only of sexual life but of economic life as well. Will power enables the individual to ward off temptations of the flesh, wrote one sex expert, just as it "as surely guides to success in all busines undertakings." Like Freud, the Victorian Americans believed that sexuality was the prototype of all other responses in the individual.

**Celibacy**   Nineteenth-century Americans did not embrace celibacy as an alternative to sexual activity. The deliberate rejection of marriage was closely linked with Catholicism, which was not a popular religion at that time; one political movement directed much of its hostility toward Catholics, accusing them of sexual perversities that were caused by celibacy. In 1843 a mob sacked the Ursuline Convent near Boston, because of rumors that it harbored promiscuity and perversion; there were many other violent incidents

And, if celibacy were unnatural, then what about young unmarried men? Unlike women, for whom celibacy was a "natural" state, such men obviously faced hazards. Again, theorists provided pseudo-scientific answers. Dr. Elizabeth Blackwell, the first American woman physician, pointed out that premature sexual activity diverted energy from the bodies of growing boys and diminished their future sexuality. "A permanent injury is done to the individual," she wrote, "which can never be completely repaired." The mature male should, of course, marry; the "medical" view of celibacy was based on the assumption that marriage was the proper state for men. The theory is another example of how the science of the day was applied in the attempt to enforce moral views and to encourage marriage.

**Masturbation**   Masturbation created a greater problem for moralists than did celibacy, because

**Devices to prevent masturbation**

A four-pointed penile ring and a toothed penile ring, as illustrated in J. C. Milton's *Pathology and Treatment of Spermatorrhoea* (1887)

it was practiced even among married men. (And worse yet, some women apparently engaged in it, too!) By the 1840s, masturbation was regarded as a sort of plague, which was "all around and all among us."

O.S. Fowler, eminent phrenologist and "authority" on sexuality, whose works went through more than 40 editions, urged that citizens form groups aimed at abolishing masturbation. "You must gird yourselves," he wrote, "to this disagreeable but indispensable work for philanthropy and reform, till we drive this common enemy from our midst."

The most dangerous period was said to be between the ages of eight through sixteen. Children in this age group were to be kept under constant surveillance by their parents, and were not to be allowed to play without adult supervision or to sleep with friends. But the critical period was believed to end at middle adolescence. By that time, one physician wrote, "they are apt to be frightened from the practice by reading, or hearing from friends, of the mental and physical decay which threatens to overtake them."

Masturbation was frequently blamed for deaths that could not otherwise be accounted for. A woman recounted that the practice was extensive among schoolgirls and factory workers, and that she personally knew a girl who had "just died from its effects." Frank Harris, a wellknown playboy of the nineteenth century, sadly recalled how he had warned a friend of the dangers of masturbation and nocturnal emissions. The friend tied up his "unruly organ" at night to prevent erections, but to no avail; he soon died.

Dr. Bostwick received patients who were sufffering from the "damnable effects of masturbation," recording a case history that describes the treatment:

I advised him to have 25 leeches applied to the perinaeum [base of the penis] immediately, and sit over a bucket of hot water as soon as they should drop off, so that the steam and warm bathing would keep up further bleeding. I ordered the leeches to be followed by a blister, and hot poultices, hot mustard hip baths, &c., &c. I had his bowels opened with a dose of castor oil, and confined him to a light gruel, vegetable, and fruit diet, advising him to scrupulously avoid every thing stimulating, to drink nothing but cold water and mucilaginous fluids.

The treatments continued for five weeks, until the man was pronounced "cured" and returned home. ("He was, of course, somewhat weakened and debilitated," Bostwick wrote.)

**Sexual Intercourse**    Many men assumed that if they had refrained from masturbation as boys, they were free to have intercourse as often as they pleased after marriage. Physicians, and phrenologist O.S. Fowler, challenged this idea. ("But does marriage entitle the party to kill the other or themselves?" Fowler wrote.) Coition, like masturbation, involved the loss of semen – a loss considered dangerous to a man's health. John Cowan, whose *Science of a New Life* was reprinted frequently between 1860 and 1920, warned men:

It is best to avoid marrying widows, who may have had one or more husbands, whose premature deaths were caused by other than accident, or other plainly unavoidable cause; for . . . they are likely to possess qualities in them, that in their exercise use up their husband's stock of vitality, rapidly weakening the system, and so causing premature death.

Sexual intercourse was held to be dangerous not only because of the emission of semen but also because of the orgasm. Dr. Trall wrote that "the very intensity of the sexual orgasm, when legitimately exercised [that is, for procreation] is sufficient evidence that it is not to be promiscu-

**The Ladies' Guide; 1882**

Nymphomania

This term is applied to a condition in which there is such an intense degree of sexual excitement that the passions become uncontrollable. A female suffering with this affection will sometimes commit the grossest breaches of chastity. Its *principal causes are self-abuse and a complete abondonment of the mind to lascivious thoughts*. It is sometimes produced by ovarian irritation and by various diseases of the brain. The genitals are often found in a state of great excitement and abnormal enlargement in this affection.

*Treatment*: Cool sitz baths; the cool enema; a spare diet; the application of blisters and other irritants to the sensitve parts of the sexual organs, the removal of the clitoris and nymphae, constitute the most proper treatment.

W. Kellogg

ously nor too frequently excited with impunity." Dio Lewis, another prominent sexual reformer, cautioned that a married couple should engage in intercourse "with a temperate affection, without violent transporting desires of too sensual applications."

The typical male role model, during this period, was a man who controlled his feelings and desires. Thus, the dread of orgasm expressed in writings is understandable. At the moment of orgasm, the individual experiences a reflexive action, losing control. Those with rigid ego boundaries may experience the orgasm as a loss of self, since they lose the control that is their main definition of themselves. Symbolically this loss of self is experienced as death, a major theme in men's sexuality during the past century.

**Sexual Identity**   Nineteenth-century men defined themselves largely in terms of self-control and character. The typical role model was rigid, controlled, aggressive, and chaste, albeit as the result of great inner struggle. Women were defined in terms of their roles as wife and mother, and chasteness was an important quality for both these roles. A woman who exhibited sexual desire ceased to be "feminine." Mrs. E.B. Duffy wrote that a sensual woman "is so unwomanly in all her characteristics that she seems more like a man than a woman. Certainly the preponderance of sensuality in her charcter has more of masulinity than femininity in it . . ." (The definitions of both men and women were essentially sexual, however. "Character" implied control over sexual impulses, and "chasteness" implies absence of sexual desire.)

For women, sexual desire was held to be no more than the means through which they became wives and mothers, and the term "mater-nal instinct" was sometimes used interchangeably with "sexual instinct." The popular view was that a woman who sought sex for its own sake lost all rights to husband, child, and home. People were not reluctant to label such a woman a prostitute.

It was widely accepted – at least in public – that women lacked sexuality. William Alcott wrote that in her "natural state" (whatever that may mean) the woman never makes advances based on sexual desires, for the "very plain reason that she does not feel them." After talking with many women who, although they had large families, said they had never experienced sexual desire in their lives, Alcott concluded that women who experienced strong desire were "a few exceptions amounting in all probability to *diseased cases*."

The prevailing view was that lack of sexuality was an important aspect of femininity; thus, women who experienced sexual desire often felt shame and guilt. Dr. A. J. Ingersoll, a utopian socialist, was one of the few physicians who dissented from the prevailing opinion. He described a case of hysteria in which a patient had retreated into illness to escape her own sexuality:

She had no fear, but thought in common with most women, and many men, that no wife could be pure if she had any enjoyment in sexual intercourse. Shortly before her marriage, she began to lose her health without any apparent cause . . .

I told her that the want of sexual life was the cause of her illness, that she had elevated everything except the sexual life which she thought low. She admitted the truth of my statement, saying, "That is my religion."

. . . The cause of her disease was the impression she had received from her friends, that the sexual relation in marriage was low. She said she had deter-

**Mark Twain on Polygamy**

Our stay in Salt Lake City amounted to only two days, and therefore we had no time to make the customary inquisition into the workings of polygamy and get up the usual statistics and deductions preparatory to calling the attention of the nation at large once more to the matter. I had the will to do it. With the gushing self-sufficiency of youth I was feverish to plunge in headlong and achieve a great reform here – until I saw the Mormon women. Then I was touched. My heart was wiser than my head. It warmed toward these poor, ungainly, and pathetically "homely" creatures, and as I turned to hide the generous moisture in my eyes, I said, "No – the man that marries one of them has done an act of Christian charity which entitles him to the kindly applause of mankind, not their harsh censure – and the man that marries sixty of them has done a deed of openhanded generosity so sublime that the nations should stand uncovered in his presence and worship in silence

Mark Twain, *Roughing It*

---

mined not to allow marriage to create any sexual desire, and to this determination she had religiously adhered with entire success.

Most physicians upheld the prevailing view. One described a young widow who came to him for treatment, who admitted that she had felt strong sexual desires since the age of fourteen and that she felt the conflicts this created "must soon send me to my grave." Reflecting on her case, the doctor classified it as an example of "Nymphomania, or *Furur Uterinus*." The woman agreed with his description; she herself had written, "I am sure my lascivious feelings cannot be natural – they must be the effect of disease." Although her behavior, as described, falls well within what is now accepted as normal female sexuality, the woman suffered greatly from her inability to fit into the commonly accepted pattern that had been established for her sex:

> After my marriage, this inordinate desire was in a great measure, but not entirely, subdued. I acknowledge with shame, that I practiced self-abuse [masturbation] both before and after marriage, but it was a propensity I could not possibly resist, and since his death, my passion has been more inflamed than ever, and I fear that, unless something can be done to relieve me, I shall go crazy.

The lack of sexual desire attributed to woman neatly complemented the male dread of sexuality: as long as women were not sexual beings, there was little that men had to be afraid of (save their own sexuality, which they were expected to control). But in addition, their fear of death probably affected, at least to some degree, their feelings about women. There is an air of ambiguity about the praise that women received for their sexual purity. It is not altogether clear whether this praise was offered genuinely, or in the hope that, repeated often enough, it would be true. Clearly, men needed all the help they could get in living up to their own role as controlled beings, and disinterested women meshed with this role far better than did women who admitted to sexual desires.

Mark Twain's *Letters from the Earth* included frequent references indicating that the prevailing view may have been rooted in considerable ambiguity. It is a law of God, said Twain, that there be no limit on a woman's sexual powers at any time in her life. Conversely, there are limits and restrictions on male sexual abilities through a man's entire life. Ironically – or perhaps because of this law – it is man, not woman, who regulates sexual behavior.

Few were a frank as Twain. The idea that women were not universally pure and chaste was a threat to the established male ideal; thus, when women were acknowledged as being sexual, they were usually presented in the role of seductress and temptress. The old image of woman as sensuous had not been entirely obscured; it was the underside of the belief in women's chastity. Women who engaged in sexual intercourse illicitly were held to be sexual monsters, capable of releasing some indefinable restraint that marriage puportedly imposed. Perhaps that restraint was the mutual expectation that sex in marriage was to be performed without excessive passion. Without the restraints that these expectations placed on marriage, women clearly had the potential to be even more animalistic than men.

In the prose of the day, it was held that women became sexual devourers only through seduction, which was viewed as a particularly evil crime because – through some unknown mechanism – it transformed a chaste woman into a sensual animal. Seducers were villains because they betrayed pure maidens (and perhaps also because they demonstrated that female chastity was a myth). Fowler maintained that seducers were *"THE WORST BEINGS ON EARTH,"* because they

> lay waste the whole being of pure, good girls, with all their enjoying capacities and angelic virtues; convert humanity's fairest, loveliest flowers into prostitutes, earth's worst tenants . . . ; make luscious maidens vampire fiends.

The woman whose sensuality was awakened became a temptress of men and a source of danger. In tracing the cycle of seduction, Elizabeth Blackwell presented the ambiguous view that women operate both as seducer and as victim. Young men, said Blackwell, do not initially betray women. Rather, they are led into vice by women who are older and more experienced. Once they cross the "Rubicon of chastity," however, these men rapidly become seducers of women, following young girls in the streets. They entice servant girls or go to houses of prostitution, where they meet "the unhappy fallen girls, who has become, in her turn, the seducer."

In *The Monks of Monk Hall*, America's first "best-seller," George Lippard centered his novel around seduction, combining literary cliches with middle-class pornography. In a passage that he urged his readers to note carefully, he described how a pure girl becomes a libertine. Mary, the archetypal virgin, was about to give herself up to Lorrimer, the archetypal seducer. Like all chaste women, she was willing to make this sacrifice because "him did she love with the uncalculating abandonment of self that marks the first passion of an innocent woman!"

Like man she is a combination of an animal, with an intellectual nature. Unlike man her animal nature is a passive thing, that must be roused ere it will develop itself in action. Let the intellectual nature of women be the only object of man's influence and woman will love him most holily. But let him play with her animal nature . . . let him rouse the treacherous blood, let him fan the pulse into quick, feverish throbbings, let him warm the heart with compulsive beatings, and the woman becomes like himself, but a mere animal. *Sense* rises like a vapor, and utterly darkens *Soul*.

. . . Oh, would man but learn the solemn truth – that no angel around God's throne is purer than Woman when her intellectual nature alone is stirred into development, that no devil crouching in the flames of

### Chastity

"Now," said I, "you must try the following plan, and report to me. *Fix it in your mind that a sensual idea is dangerous and harmful*; then the instant one comes it will startle you. By an effort you change the subject immediately. You can, if you are in earnest, set such an alarm in your mind, that if a lascivious thought occurs to you when asleep, it will waken you. (A number of persons have testified to this.) If when you are awake the enemy enters your mind, you will be aroused, and expel it at once without a very serious effort. If there is a moment's doubt, spring up and engage in some active exercise of the body. Each effort will be easier, until after a week or two you will have, in this particular, *complete control of your thoughts*; and that will soon make you feel a good deal more like a man.

"The fever and excitement of voluptuous revery wears out the nervous system, emasculates manhood, and shuts out all the noblest visions in this and the upper world. "

Dio Lewis

---

hell is fouler than Woman, when her animal nature alone is roused into action — would man but learn and revere this fearful truth . . .

Few nineteenth-century Americans were aware that their attitudes toward sex held implications of hostility. Rather, they felt that their views ennobled sex. Wrote Dio Lewis, whose works were immensely popular, "We maintain *the essential purity of the sexual nature*; its misuse is dishonorable, but nothing else about it should be so regarded." But sexuality was pure only when divorced from passion and sensuousness. Harriet Beecher Stowe, author of *Uncle Tom's Cabin*, said of sexuality that "it is its physicalness that is disgusting."

Middle-class Americans hoped to avoid the erotic and sensuous aspects of sex by covering them over with sentimentalities. Their hope was simply expressed by Dr. Trall, who wrote that

> by persistently affirming the nobleness of the procreative element and at the same time ignoring and denying, over and over again, the debasement usually alloted to these organs, we would live above the organic and sensual, forgetting the physical part of sex.

The way that most Americans of the past century were able to deal with sex was by swaddling it in sunny euphemisms and nobility, and by attributing reproduction to be its sole acceptable purpose.

**Sex in Twentieth-Century America** By 1900, there were indications that the confused Victorian sexual ethic was changing. Writers like Kate Chopin, Stephen Crane, and Theodore Dreiser handled sexuality with increasing frankness in their novels. The efforts of men like Anthony Comstock, who attempted to purify and censor the arts and the lives of others as well, became subjects for public ridicule.

The birthrate began to decline. This decline may have been achieved primarily through abstinence, a method that did not violate the ethic of restraint, although there is fragmentary evidence that abortion may have been fairly common. By the beginning of the twentieth century, however, reformers had begun to suggest that family size should be limited through the use of contraceptives. Contraception, with its implication that sex might be used for emotional fulfillment and pleasure, was a direct challenge to the doctrine of sexual restraint, in which the major theme was that sex should be used only for procreative purposes. And at the same time, physicians challenged the idea that sexual "excess" inevitably led to general physical debilitation; increasing scientific knowledge had provided causes for deaths that in earlier times had been attributed to sexual activity.

For the first time, marriage manuals presented sex as a means of mutual fulfillment. One physician claimed that nothing but "happy and joyous sex relations can keep the world moving and progressing." Another writer maintained that "sex relations may and should be indulged as often as they are conducive to a man's and a woman's physical, mental and spiritual health."

There was, at this time, a significant change in the self-image of men. In the nineteenth century, a man proved his worth by controlling his sexual impulses through will power; the repression of sexual activity characterized the ideal man of this century. In our century, a man demonstrates sexual integrity by being able to rise, so to speak, to every situation and circumstance. With the multiple orgasm being promoted as every woman's goal, the male has to "prove his manhood" in a manner unknown to his counterpart of the previous century.

Evidence of change in women's attitude toward sexuality after 1900 is even more definite. In the past, women often said that they were unable to experience orgasm, that they were afraid or unable to learn how to respond sexually. The difference in rates of marital orgasm, among women of different generations, is striking. In the Kinsey study, 33 percent of the women born before 1900 failed to experience orgasm in their first year of marriage, while the rate was 23 percent for those born in the following decade. The number who had achieved orgasm after ten years of marriage was also significantly larger than among those who had been married five years. By the fifteenth year of marriage, 15 percent of the women born before 1900 had still not experienced orgasm, while only 9

percent of those born between 1900 and 1910 had not.

The changes that apparently began around 1900 have by now become dominant attitudes. But the revolution is still evolving, and what additional changes lie ahead, no one knows.

## QUESTIONS

1. To what extent are traditional Christian sexual ethics practiced today? What has been modified? How?
2. What was the Puritans' attitude toward sexuality? Did they accept or reject it?
3. Imagine yourself living in the 19th Century. Which of your present sexual attitudes would remain the same and which would be different?
4. What was the significance of the semen theory in the 19th Century?
5. How did 19th Century beliefs concerning male and female sexuality affect sexual interaction?

# Readings

### Polly Baker's Speech

Ben Franklin

*Ben Franklin wrote this moving piece in the 18th century. For years his authorship was unknown and it passed as having been written by Polly Baker, defending herself for conceiving children out of wedlock. Eighteenth-century attitudes toward sex were considerably different from the next's century's attitudes.*

This is the Fifth Time, Gentlemen, that I have been dragg'd before your Court on the same

Account; twice I have paid heavy Fines, and twice have been brought to Public Punishment, for want of Money to pay those Fines. This may have been agreeable to the Laws, and I don't dispute it; but since Laws are sometimes unreasonable in themselves, and therefore repealed, and others bear too hard on the Subject in particular Circumstances; I take the Liberty to say, That I think this Law, by which I am punished, is both unreasonable in itself, and particularly severe with regard to me, who have always lived an inoffensive Life in the Neighbourhood where I

### Old American Fertility Rituals

An old gentleman in Aurora, Missouri, told me that the early settlers had a ritual for sowing flax. Just before sunup the farmer and his wife appeared in the field, both naked. The woman walked ahead of the man, and the man did the sowing. They chanted or sang a rhyme . . . Every few steps the man threw some of the seed against the woman's buttocks. Up and down the field they went, singing and scattering seed, until the planting was done. "Then," as my informant put it, "they just laid down on the ground and had a good time." Most farmers believe that cucumbers should be planted "when the sign's in the arms," which means that the moon is in Gemini. But many old-timers think that the main thing is to get the seed covered before daylight on May 1, by a naked man in the prime of life. It is believed that the quality of a cucumber depends on the virility of the planter. Cucumbers grown by women, children, or old men never amount to much.

Vance Randolph, *"Nudity and Planting Customs,"*
*Journal of American Folklore, 1953.*

---

was born, and defy my Enemies (if I have any) to say I ever wrong'd Man, Woman, or Child.

Abstracted from the Law, I cannot conceive (may it please your Honours) what the Nature of my Offense is. I have brought Five fine children into the World, at the Risque of my Life; I have maintained them well by my own Industry, without burthening the Township, and would have done it better, if it had not been for the heavy Charges and Fines I have paid. Can it be a Crime (in the Nature of Things I mean) to add to the Number of the King's Subjects, in a new Country that really wants People? I own it, I should think it a Praise-worthy, rather than a punishable Action. I have debauched no other Woman's Husband, nor enticed any Youth; these Things I never was charg'd with, nor has any one the least Cause of Complaint against me, unless, perhaps, the Minster, or Justice, because I have had Children without being married, by which they have missed a Wedding Fee.

But, can ever this be a Fault . . . I readily consented to the only Proposal of Marriage that ever was made me, which was when I was a Virgin; but too easily confiding in the Person's Sincerity that made it, I unhappily lost my own Honour, by trusting to his; for he got me with Child, and then forsook me: That very Person you all know; he is now become a Magistrate of this Country; and I had Hopes he would have appeared this Day on the Bench, and have endeavoured to moderate the Court in my Favour; then I should have scorn'd to have mention'd it; but I must now complain of it, as unjust and unequal, That my Betrayer and Undoer, the first Cause of all my Faults and Miscarriages (if they must be deemed such) should be advanc'd to Honour and Power in the Government, that punishes my Misfortunes with Stripes and Infamy.

I should be told, 'tis like, That were there no Act of Assembly in the Case, the Precepts of Religion are violated by my Transgressions. If mine, then, is a religious Offense, leave it to religious punishments. You have already exluded me from the Comforts of your Church-Communion. Is not that sufficient? You believe I have offended Heaven, and must suffer eternal Fire: Will not that be sufficient? What Need is there, then, of your additional Fines and Whipping? I own, I do not think as you do; for, if I thought what you call a Sin, was really such, I could not presumptuously commit it. But, how can it be believed, that Heaven is angry at my having Children, when to the little done by me towards it, God has been pleased to add his Divine Skill and admirable Workmanship in the Formation of their Bodies, and crown'd it, by furnishing them with rational and immortal Souls.

What must poor young Women do, whom Custom have forbid to solicit the Men, and who cannot force themselves upon Husbands, when the Laws take no Care to provide them any; and yet severely punish them if they do their Duty without them; the Duty of the first and great Command of Nature, and of Nature's God, Increase and Multiply. A Duty, from the steady Performance of which, nothing has been able to deter me; but for its Sake, I have hazarded the Loss of the Publick Esteem, and have frequently endured Publick Disgrace and Punishment; and therefore ought, in my humble Opinion, instead of a Whipping, to have a Statue erected to my Memory.

## The Unwelcome Child

Marriage and Parentage; Henry C. Wright

*Without effective contraception – and condoms declared illegal by the federal government – the "unwelcome child" was a common event in the 19th century. Unlike today, it was difficult to separate sexual intercourse from the possibility of conception, bringing untold hardship into the family.*

A father and son, in my hearing, thus addressed each other. The father was angry with his son, and said – "You have been the plague of my life; I repelled you and cursed you, before you were born, and at your birth!" "Father," said the lad of eighteen – a sad scapegoat – "am I your son?" "You are," said he, "to my shame and disgrace be it spoken. You have dishonored me, and will bring my head to the grave in sorrow," "And," said the son, "you hated and cursed me before I was born, and my mother tells me she would have killed me in the womb, if she could have done so without endangering her own life." "Yes," said the father, "from your conception to your birth, we both struggled against your existence, and when you were born, our first feeling was that of deep regret that you had come, and, on my part, a wish that your stay with us might be a short one. Your have been violent, headstrong, revengeful and vicious, from your childhood." "Where is the fault?" asked the son. "How could I be otherwise, ushered into life as you say I was? Little love and respect do I owe you for a life you have cursed from the begin-

ning. If my existence was such an offence to you, why did you give it to me?"

Are such parents deserving pity or condemnation? They gave birth to a child when they did not wish one, and they suffer the natural and necessary retribution. The momentary gratification of their sexual passion, when they were averse to having a child, had been fearfully avenged. That unwelcome child whose existence was so offensive to them, has made even their wealth, their elegantly-furnished home, and their social, political, and religious position, the source of ever-present mortification and anguish.

Not unfrequently have I heard parents, among the rich and the poor, especially mothers, bewail the conception and birth of their children. This lament is not uncommon in the heart, if not expressed in words, and it is felt and heard among all classes. What does it mean? The robber, the slaveholder, the pirate, the drunkard, the warrior, bewail the wounds and diseases, the moral indignation, obloquy and sufferings, that result to themselves, as the natural consequences of their vices and crimes; yet they go on doing the same deeds. So these parents lament the undesired conceptions and births that necessarily result from their sensual indulgence; yet persist in their right to the indulgence, and in the repetition of it. The husband demands sexual intercourse as his right, and as the great end of marriage; the wife yields, both knowing that a child may and probably will be the result, yet the hearts of both pray earnestly against it. The babe is born – the unwelcome offspring of mere sensuality; but born only to bring shame and sorrow to those who cursed its life with the curse of an undesired existence. The only apology that can be offered for such parents is that which Jesus offered for his murderers – *"They know not what they do!"* This is true, and no wonder it is true, for what has the family, the school, the church or state, done to give them light? They have, for the most part, been dumb as death.

## Solitary Vice

from J.F. Kellogg, Plain Facts for Old and Young

*Written in the 19th century, this selection suggests some of the dire consequences of "solitary vice." What are some of the myths concerning masturbation today?*

*Solitary Vice.* As a sin against nature, it has no parallel except in sodomy. It is known by the terms self-pollution, self-abuse, masturbation, onanism, voluntary pollution, and solitary or secret vice. The habit is by no means confined to boys; girls also indulge in it, though it is to be hoped, to a less fearful extent than boys, at least in this country . . . .

The sin of self-pollution is one of the vilest, the basest, and the most degrading that a human being can commit. It is worse than beastly. Those who commit it place themselves far below the meanest brute that breathes. The most loathsome reptile, rolling in the slush and slime of its stagnant pool, would not demean itself thus.

Of all the vices to which human beings are addicted, no other so rapidly undermines the constitution, and so certainly makes a complete wreck of an individual as this, especially when the habit is begun at an early age. It wastes the most precious part of the blood, uses up the vital forces, and finally leaves the poor victim a most utterly ruined and loathsome object . . . .

Upon their [masturbators'] tombstones might justly be graven, "Here lies a self-murderer . . . ."

Reader, have you ever seen an idiot? If you have, the hideous picture will never be dissipated from your memory. The vacant stare, the drool-ing, drooling mouth, the unsteady gait, the emptiness of mind – all these you well remember. Did you ever stop to think how idiots are made? It is by this very vice that the ranks of these poor daft mortals are being recruited every day. . . .

Are you guilty of this terrible sin? Have you even once yielded to the tempter's voice? Stop, consider, think of the awful results, repent, confess to God, reform. You must escape now or never. . . .

*Results of Secret Sin:* Blotched skin, tuberculosis, dyspepsia, heart disease, epilepsy, dimness of vision, paralysis, insanity, idiocy, death . . . .

*Suspicious Signs.* The following symptoms, occurring in the mental and physical character and habits of a child or young person, may well give rise to grave suspicions of evil, and should cause parents or guardians to be on the alert to root it out if possible: . . .

*Bashfulness* is not infrequently dependent upon this cause . . .

*Unnatural boldness,* in marked contrast with the preceding sign, is manifested by a certain class of victim. . . .

*Round shoulders* and a stooping position in sitting are characteristics of a young masturbator in both sexes. . . .

*Lack of development of the breasts* in females is a common result of self-pollution. . . .

*Eating chalk* is a practice to which girls who abuse themselves are especially addicted. . . .

*The use of tobacco* is good presumptive evidence that a boy is also addicted to a practice still more filthy. Exceptions to this rule are very rare indeed, if they exist, which we doubt. . . .

*Acne,* or pimples on the face, is also among the suspicious signs, especially when it appears upon the forehead. . . .

## Sex And Incest In The 19th Century Family

Bryan Strong, Journal of Marriage and the Family

*The intense concern about incest – a central theme in psychoanalysis – appears to be related to 19th century family patterns. The pseudo-incestuous relations mothers were encouraged to have with their sons brought their children many difficulties as they grew up.*

The position of women in the nineteenth century, psychologically speaking, was difficult because, on the one hand, intimate relations with their husbands both emotionally and sexually were frequently discouraged, and because, on the other hand, their roles were severely limited to those of wife and mother, permitting very little development of other aspects of their identity. While the relations between men and women were becoming more rigid and women's roles becoming more circumscribed, America was beginning to discover the child; indeed, the child was becoming the center of the family and a vast literature devoted to childrearing began to arise.

It appears unlikely that the unsatisfactory position of women in marriage and the rise of the child-centered family was simply coincidental; rather, because the relations between husband and wife were frequently strained, women turned to their children for the emotional satisfaction and sense of relation necessary for human existence. Her role as mother compensated for the emotional barrenness of her role as wife. At the same time, however, the identification with the role of mother had a quality of excessiveness to it because women frequently were trying to fulfill other areas of themselves through it, even if that led to inappropriate behavior or attitudes.

The quality of the mother's relation to her children differed significantly in accordance with the sex of the child. The mother's relation to her

daughters was more often instructor or guide. She taught her daughter how to sew and cook, wash and iron, what were correct manners, and how to make herself attractive to young men. There was an entirely different quality in the relation of the mother to her son which led, it appears, to an increased rather than decreased emotional, almost erotic, attachment of the son toward his mother as he grew older. This attachment may be described as latently incestuous, that is, it was an attachment that possessed markedly romantic and erotic components, although consciously it never was identified as incestuous or even led to actual incestuous acts.

There was a deliberate attempt made in the nineteenth century to associate sex in the minds of both boys and men with their mothers. Indeed, this was the intended effect of having mothers instruct their children. Josiah Flint wrote that there was:

> no influence to compare with that which the *mother* possesses in so remarkable a degree . . . She may shrink from so difficult and delicate a task, but there is no other to whom she can or ought to transfer her burden of responsibility . . . If she be the channel, the boy's thoughts through life will associate the subject with an ideal of womanly purity which is centered in his mother, an association which cannot fail to safeguard him.

Americans actually sought to utilize the association of sex with the mother as a means of curtailing illicit sexuality. In other words, Americans used the latent incestuous attachment with the mother to discourage relations with women outside of marriage and to limit it within marriage. The idea for this was very simple and is best articulated in a song popular in the later part of the nineteenth century

> *I want a girl, just like the girl*
> *That married dear old Dad . . .*

O. S. Fowler, the widely-read phrenologist in the nineteenth century, urged mothers to develop the manhood of their sons. "Your loving them makes them love you as a female which *chastens* as well as evolves their manhood. They must love some female as such. Say practically, by loving or chastizing them, whether it shall be you purely, or harlots sensuously." Earlier, in a book which had gone through forty editions by 1844, Fowler observed that love's "earliest promptings attach boys to their mothers most, and girls to their fathers. The *facts* of such preference are rendered certain by observation, and probably attested by the experience of every reader." He continued:

> Now it is that same faculty that attaches the son to his mother, and the husband to his wife. Hence the son who is affectionate to his mother, is generally (and always *capable* of being) devoted to his wife. Mothers, moreover, reciprocate this attachment with their sons; nor should they fail to convert to the best possible account, that tremendous influence ... Constituted to prize the masculine above *all* price, they are of course thereby fitted to develop by culture that in their sons which they love in their husbands.

Fowler made explicit the undercurrent flowing beneath the sentimental cult of motherhood. What is only suggested or intimated in middle-class sentimental literature was made explicit in his writings:

> *Every son, "Behold thy mother!"* Make love to her, and her your first sweetheart. Be courteous, gallant, and her knight-errant, and your nearest friend and bosom confident. Nestle yourself right into her heart, and her into yours. Seek her "company" and advice, and imbibe her purifying influences. Learn how to court by courting her. No other society will equally sanctify or instruct.

Fowler, unlike most writers describing motherhood, was aware of the incestuous components of the cult of motherhood, but denied its eroticism by appeal to the cult. He recalled a Mrs.

Sax who called her two sons to her side, put her arms around both, ran "her fingers through the ringlets of both; kept fondly kissing them by turns, and in like ways courted up their affections by expressing her own." To deny the implications of these acts, Fowler asks in a rhetorical manner, "*They* sin? Never. *She* impure? Then are angel loves. Wrong to *feel* or *express* this God implanted sexuo-maternal instinct? and that right out frankly?" The erotic feelings which Fowler recognized as the basis of the cult of motherhood were rationalized and put to rest whatever incipient guilt might arise in the mother by describing incestuous behavior as part of a mother's natural instinct.

If it is understood that incestuous attachments between mother and son were encouraged rather than discouraged, then one of the most striking features of nineteenth-century attitudes toward women might be explained. One of the most characteristic attitudes associated with latent or actual incestuous relations by men is the separation of women into "good" and "bad" according to whether they are sexual.

The division of women into "good" and "bad" has been explained by Freud as follows: In order for a "fully normal attitude in love" to exist, the tender, affectionate feelings must unite with sensual, erotic feelings. Affectionate feelings are the earliest feelings in the child, originating in the first years of childhood, directed toward the member of the family primarily responsible for its care, usually the mother. At the same time, however, elements of the child's sexual instinct are incorporated into this affectionate feeling. As the child becomes a man he may be unable to transfer his affectionate and erotic feelings from his mother to another woman and thereafter become impotent.

There are less severe instances, however, of what Freud called "psychical impotence" in which men may "never fail in the act but . . . perform it without special pleasure." Freud has observed that "some degree of this does in fact characterize the erotic life of civilized people." Freud's description of psychically impotent men appears to be applicable to a remarkable degree to nineteenth-century Americans.

Men protected themselves against the possibility of latently incestuous relations by *"lowering the sexual object in their own estimation, while reserving for the incestuous object and for those who represent it the overestimation normally felt for the sexual object."* Once the sexual object is degraded, erotic feeling "can have freeplay, considerable sexual capacity and a high degree of pleasure can be developed." At the same time, because there is usually little refinement or variety in sexual activity among those people who have failed to unite the affectionate and erotic feelings, men and women are able to fulfill their perverse sexual desires only with degraded sex objects, thereby creating in men a psychological necessity for degrading women.

Bryan Strong, Journal of Marriage and the Family, August, 1972. Copyright © Council of Marriage and Family Relations.

## I Sing the Body Electric

Walt Whitman

*The poet-laureate of 19th century America, Walt Whitman celebrated life in all its aspects. This selection from Leaves of Grass captures the grace, fullness, and love of "the body electric."*

I sing the body electric,
The armies of those I love engirth me and I engirth them,
They will not let me off till I go with them, respond to them,
And discorrupt them, and charge them full with the charge of the soul.
Was it doubted that those who corrupt their own bodies conceal themselves?

And if those who defile the living are as bad as they who defile the dead?
And if the body does not do fully as much as the soul?
And if the body were not the soul, what is the soul? . . .

I have perceiv'd that to be with those I like is enough,
To stop in company with the rest at evening is enough,
To be surrounded by beautiful, curious, breathing,laughing flesh is enough,
To pass among them or touch any one, or rest my arm ever so lightly round his or her neck for a moment, what is this then?
I do not ask any more delight, I swim in it as in a sea.
There is something in staying close to men and women and looking on them, and in the contact and odor of them that pleases the soul well,
All things please the soul, but these please the soul well . . . .

This is the female form,
A divine nimbus exhales from it from head to foot,
It attracts with fierce undeniable attraction,
I am drawn by its breath as if I were no more than a helpless vapor, all falls aside but myself and it,
Books, art, religion, time, the visible and solid earth, and that was expected of heaven or fear'd of hell, are now consumed,
Mad filaments, ungovernable shoots play out of it, the response likewise ungovernable,
Hair, bosom, hips, bend of legs, negligent falling hands all diffused, mine too diffused,
Ebb stung by the flow and flow stung by the ebb, love-flesh swelling and deliciously aching,
Limitless limpid jets of love hot and enormous,

quivering jelly of love, white-blow and deliri-
ous juice,
Bridegroom night of love working surely and
softly into the prostrate dawn,
Undulating into the willing and yielding day,
Lost in the cleave of the clasping and sweet-
flesh'd day.
This the nucleus — after the child is born of
woman, man is born of woman,
This the bath of birth, this the merge of small and
large, and the outlet again.

Be not ashamed women, your privilege encloses
the rest, and is the exit of the rest,
You are the gates of the body, and you are the
gates of the soul.

The female contains all qualities and tempers
them,
She is in her place and moves with perfect
balance,
She is all things duly veil'd, she is both passive
and active,
She is to conceive daughters as well as sons, and
sons as well as daughters.

As I see my soul reflected in Nature,
As I see through a mist, One with inexpressible
completeness, sanity, beauty,
See the bent head and arms folded over the
breast, the Female I see . . . .

The male is not less the soul nor more, he too is
in his place,
He too is all qualities, he is action and power,
The flush of the known universe is in him,

Scorn becomes him well, and appetite and defiance become him well,
The wildest largest passions, bliss that is utmost,
sorrow that is utmost become him well, pride
is for him,
The full-spread pride of man is calming and excellent to the soul,
Knowledge becomes him, he likes it always, he
brings every thing to the test of himself,
Whatever the survey, whatever the sea and the
sail he strikes soundings at last only here,
(Where else does he strike soundings except
here?)
The man's body is sacred and the woman's body
is sacred,
No matter who it is, it is sacred — is it the meanest
one in the laborers' gang?
Is it one of the dull-faced immigrants just landed
on the wharf?
Each belongs here or anywhere just as much as
the well-off, just as much as you,
Each has his or her place in the processsion.

(All is a procession,
The universe is a procession with measured and
perfect motion.)

Do you know so much yourself that you call the
meanest ignorant?
Do you suppose you have a right to a good sight,
and he or she has no right to a sight?
Do you think matter has cohered together from
its diffuse float, and the soil is on the surface,
and water runs and vegetation sprouts,
For you only, and not for him and her? . . .

# The American Way Of Sex:
# The Present

**2**

The sexual ethic that emerged in the nineteenth century did not last much beyond the beginning of the twentieth. By the 1950s, middle-class sexuality had become significantly different from the Victorian ideal. Sex had been accepted as a means of expressing tenderness and affection. Women were expected to enjoy sex and to be capable of orgasm. By the 1970s, women were no longer expected to retain virginity until marriage, and love making between the unmarried was no longer shocking.

These changes in attitude have not affected all people equally, however. There are significant variations according to class, age, sex, and race — categories that represent, to varying degrees, different cultures and expectations. White, middle-class, middle-aged men tend to have sexual values and roles that differ from those of black lower-class, adolescent girls, for example, and social forces do not affect middle-class and lower-class white girls in the same way. Sociologist Ira Reiss (1967) has formulated a simple hypothesis to account for the various changes that have occurred in the last several decades: *Social forces are more likely to increase individual levels of sexual permissiveness among low permissive groups than high permissive groups.*

Groups that were among the least permissive in the nineteenth century are changing at faster rates. The sexual revolution of recent times has most profoundly affected the white middle class — especially women, adolescents, and young adults. These groups, the major participants in the revolution, are the reason the older middle-class generation has become upset at the challenge of former values. Blacks and the white lower class have always been more permissive about coital experience, but this fact was no cause for alarm. Changes seem to be called "revolutions" only after people of the middle class recognize new views as affecting themselves.

The social forces that have brought about the sexual revolution are unclear. American society entered a period of enormous change shortly before World War I. Traditional belief in absolute moral values was even then being challenged by physical scientists, philosophers, and social scientists, especially psychoanalysts and anthropologists. Belief in the certainty of "right" behavior was undermined. At the same time, the economy was shifting from a system based on saving to one based on consumption, and this shift had important ramifications in the development of personality traits. Erich Fromm (1944) has pointed out the relationship between society and personality. He believes that for a society to function effectively, its members must develop the kind of personalities that will make them *want* to act in the way they *have* to act in the society; that is, they must desire the behavior considered appropriate. Human energy, then, is channeled into personality traits by inner compulsion rather than outer force.

## Abundance

During the nineteenth century, the primary values held by middle-class men were thrift, good habits, and self-control. In an economy that was saving its capital and reinvesting it, these traits were highly functional, while spontaneity was dangerous. The sexual metaphors and the behavior of this period reflected economic and social values, as noted in Chapter 1.

But the twentieth century presented a new economic picture. America had become a society of abundance rather than scarcity, and had developed an enormous potential for massproducing goods cheaply. If these goods were to be purchased, demand had to be created; the personality traits of thrift and self-control had to give

### Living With Sex

By depicting sex as a simple, uncomplicated exercise in the enjoyment of the good life, *Playboy* misleads its readers into assuming that real women are as pliable, convenient and usable as 'the play-mate of the month' – quite ready to be folded up in three sections when the next attraction comes along. And the male reader is wrongly encouraged to assume that he can approach sex in this manner without danger to his own integrity and maturity.

Richard Hettlinger

---

way to spending and, to a degree, impulsiveness and spontaneity. This economic change carried over into the sexual sphere. The colloquialism "to spend," with its negative connotations, dropped out of the sexual vocabulary. Men's physiological activities were no longer viewed as closed systems whose product was limited, and the ability to "save" semen was no longer considered proof of manliness. Instead, the male model has become an individual who gratifies whims and desires – whether for goods or for women. Abundance, of both partners and orgasms, became the proof of manhood and virility. Self-control was no longer a virtue, but an old-fashioned idea associated with the conservative element of society.

**Advertising**   The advertising industry has been assessed as one of the major institutions resulting from economic abundance. Increasingly, advertising has applied sex as a selling device. First, sex is used simply as an eye-catcher, through picturing beautiful, sensuous-looking men or women in association with various products. Women lounge on the hoods of automobiles, and an airline gained the wrath of many women with its "Fly me, I'm Jane," headlines. Second, advertising has catered to sexual or role anxieties, by indicating that certain products will increase masculinity or femininity. These ads range from "Be a man. Join the Marines," to perfumes. The merits of the products are irrelevant, the image is what is being sold to the consumer (Packard 1958).

In recent years, advertising has developed an even more sophisticated approach, with its use of subliminal techniques. These subliminal techniques, first described in Aldous Huxley's *Brave New World Revisited*, touch the consumer's mind below the threshold of awareness. One of the most important – and potentially dangerous – subliminal techniques is the use of embedding. Embedding is the hiding of emotionally-loaded words or pictures in an advertisement's background. These word stimuli are invisible to conscious perception, but are immediately picked up on an unconscious level by almost everyone. Frequently used words include sex, cunt, prick, whore, fuck, and ass, whose subliminal presence is used to trigger purchasing responses (Key, 1972).

These sexually-oriented embeddings seem to turn up everywhere. In an ad for Horsman Dolls (New York Times Magazine, December 12, 1971) a little girl is shown holding a doll. Embedded on the child's right hand and on the doll's right hand is a mosaic of SEXes. On the doll's sleeve is a large K, with only shadows or partial clues suggesting F, U, and C. The mind fills in what the four-lettered word is from the clues and associations. In the February, 1972 *Playboy* centerfold another embedding technique is used. The woman is kneeling down – presumably a fantasy of the rear-entry position – and an elaborate mosaic of SEXes cover her and the sheets. More interestingly, by holding the foldout in front of a strong light, an erect penis is seen entering her from behind. This illusion was created by shading a photograph on the opposite side, which shows through enough to be picked up unconsciously.

They have not proved to be as effective as they were predicted to be. Had the subliminal approach operated as planned, it would be used far more frequently.

The economic shift to consumption and the accompanying increase in advertising have had profound effects on the sexual landscape. We are encouraged to consume, to satisfy our every whim, to buy a car that assures masculinity or a perfume that assures femininity. Advertising has put a spotlight on sex, legitimizing it along with

For women, probably the most radical change that has ever occurred in human history is the development of modern medicine, and especially of dependable contraceptive methods. These developments have, for the first time, freed woman to a very significant degree from her biology. Never before has she been able to choose the timing and number of her children. Never has she had such assurance that the child she bears will survive to adulthood, nor run so little risk to her own life and health in the reproductive process.

Carol LeFevre

---

consumption. But advertising has not been the only change. The audience for these commercial messages, too, has changed.

## Mobility

In the late 1920s, the middle class was composed of owners and proprietors. Today's middle class is made up primarily of managers and white-collar workers, who are highly mobile economically as well as geographically. In seeking advancement, they move up and down the corporate structure, back and forth across the continent.

Increasing mobility has changed the structure of society. Lasting friendships have become more difficult to establish – people often don't know either their neighbors or their co-workers very well. As a result, men have begun to turn to their families for intimate relations, wives have become partners. Both may have to rely completely on each other for emotional and sexual fulfillment, creating new strains in marriages as well as new possibilities in relationships (Mills 1951). Often, relationships between men and women who live together do not involve marriage.

## Medical Advances

Two important medical advances have removed many former barriers to premarital intercourse – the development of effective contraceptive devices and effective treatments for venereal disease.

Contraceptive methods have been used increasingly since the Civil War, but in the past the most effective of these was the condom. This device placed responsibility primarily on the male, who may or may not have been greatly concerned about the consequences of failure. With the widespread use of birth control pills, intrauterine devices (IUDs), diaphragms, suppositories, and foam preparations (in order of decreasing effectiveness), the responsibility has passed from the man to the woman: the pill is in, the condom out. Without effective birth control methods (and the willingness to use them) sexual intercourse was closely tied to marriage and the family. Today, sex can be considered apart from procreation, instead of being inseparable from it.

The development of more effective medical

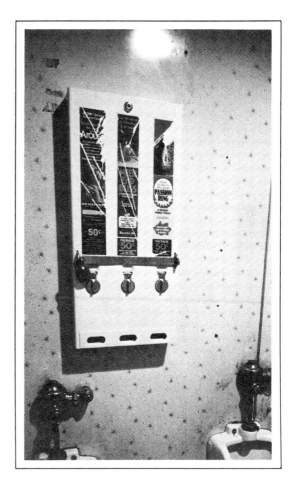

To err is human, but it feels divine.
Mae West

treatment for venereal disease has also played a part in the sexual revolution. Most of us are unaware of the terrible fears of venereal disease experienced by past generations. Campaigns against prostitution were partly related to the fear of contracting syphilis or gonorrhea, and a U.S. Public Health Service pamphlet warned, "Any girl who will give herself to you has probably given herself to others who have diseased her." Prince Morrow, an early leader of the sex-education movement, said, "Not only should these physical dangers be exposed, but the fact should be impressed that they are almost inseparable from irregular sex relations. When moral considerations would not avail, a wholesome fear of infection may act as a restraint." The old morality was supported in part by the fear of venereal disease. Although today most cases can be cured, there was no such hope 75 years ago, when paralysis, insanity, and death frequently awaited the sufferer (Strong 1972).

### The Eroticization of America

By the 1980s, the old conservative sexual ethic had been put on the defensive and the Victorian spirit put to flight. A modern sexual ethos, firmly rooted in the separation of sex from reproduction, was becoming more and more dominant. The ultimate sanction against violating sexual morality had been the *fear of pregnancy* and *illegitimacy*. As long as women might have to bear illegitimate children and suffer the social and legal consequences, they were reluctant to violate sexual norms. But, as Aldous Huxley wrote:

> The practice of birth control has robbed amorous indulgence of most of the sinfulness traditionally supposed to be inherent in it by robbing it of its socially disastrous effects. The tree shall be known

by its fruits: where there are no fruits, there is obviously no tree.

The eroticization of contemporary America is characterized by: changed sexual standards, new meanings given to sexuality, acceptance of female sexuality, and changes in sexual behavior.

**Changed Sexual Standards** Sociologist Ira Reiss (1967, 1971) has suggested that there are four moral standards regarding premarital sexuality. The first is the *abstinence standard*, which was the official sexual ideology in American culture until the 1950s and early 1960s. This belief held that it was wrong for either men or women to engage in sexual intercourse before marriage regardless of the circumstances or their feelings for each other. The *double standard*, which was widely practiced but rarely approved publicly, permitted men to engage in premarital intercourse because of their "stronger" sexual drive. Women, however, were considered "bad" if they had premarital intercourse. *Permissiveness with affection* represented a third standard. In contrast to 20 years ago, it is widely held today. Permissiveness with affection refers to sex between men and women who are involved with each other in an affectionate, stable, and loving relationship. *Permissiveness without affection* is the final standard. It holds that people may have sexual relationships with each other even if there is no affection or commitment.

**The Abstinence Standard** is rooted in the Judeo-Christian tradition, which finds sex sinful outside of marriage. Because marriage usually occurs 8 to 10 years after puberty, there is often considerable stress for those who choose to remain virgin. They have strong sexual desires but no legitimate means to express them. Religious men and women are most likely to subscribe to this standard. Indeed, one study found that the more frequently women students attended church, the less likely they were to engage in premarital intercourse; and if they did, they were more likely to feel guilty (Bell and Chaskes, Melville, 1970). When students who believed in abstinence engaged in their first premarital intercourse, they felt worried, guilty, and tense. Morton Hunt observed of these students in his study (1973):

> More than a third of our young males and close to two-thirds of our young females experienced regret and worry afterwards; and even after many experiences, a fair number continue to worry about pregnancy and VD and to be troubled by emotional and moral conflicts (Hunt, 1973)

Their moral values were reinforced by the triple threats of infection, detection, and conception. To the degree that these students abstained out of fear, to that degree their abstinence was not truly a moral statement.

**The Double Standard** is the underside of abstinence. It allows many men to publicly affirm abstinence while privately engaging in premarital or extramarital intercourse. The double standard starts from the belief that men are more sexual than women, who are believed to be without strong desires. Women are thus expected to remain virgin. With the double standard, men want to marry virgins and "nice" girls who have not had sex before marriage. In the past men resorted to prostitutes and women from lower classes or other races in exploitative relationships because women from their own backgrounds were generally unavailable. Reiss (1967) identified, however, a *transitional double standard*: if the woman is in love or engaged, then sex is permissible. Love is the critical factor determin-

ing whether or not a woman may engage in premarital intercourse.

**Permissiveness With Affection** is becoming increasingly important in today's sexual world. Among college students in may be the most widely accepted standard. It comes closer than the other standards to male – female equality in sexual relations because a woman need not keep her virginity until marriage or even engagement. Rather, if she has a stable and affectionate relationship with a man, she may make love with him. Liking replaces loving as the justification for sexual intercourse. Dating regularly or going steady, rather than engagement, is the criterion for acceptable premarital intercourse. This change is related to new patterns of mate selection in our culture.

*Patterns of Mate Selection* From colonial times to the 1950s, courtship tended to follow the "ever-narrowing-field" model (Goode: 1960; McCall 1966). Young people dated several members of the opposite sex before becoming engaged to one. There was mutual evaluation during courtship period – the girl traditionally aiming for a husband who would provide high financial status, the man for a wife who in addition to being beautiful would be a "good" wife and mother.

Once there was an engagement, however, the man and woman were expected to stop dating others. The monogamous relationship that is in our culture a characteristic of marriage began at this point. The couple sometimes engaged in petting – or even intercourse – before marriage, but sex was sometimes a battleground; many women still felt that only "bad" girls allowed sexual intimacies before the wedding night.

Concern about changing attitudes toward

sexual behavior emerged in the 1950s, when the Kinsey studies served notice that traditional beliefs were being contradicted by the behavior of sizable numbers of people of all ages. Parents became increasingly disturbed about "going steady" — which became popular even in elementary schools. Many parents, of course, had themselves engaged in premarital intercourse – but they had not done so openly. It was upsetting to most of them to be faced with the inarguable knowledge that their sons and daughters were engaging in intercourse without necessarily planning to marry.

*Premarital Intercourse* There has been a major change in attitudes toward premarital intercourse, as well as an increase in incidence, particularly among women. American men have about the same attitudes today that men in similar age groups had 15 or 20 years ago (Christensen and Green 1970). The highest increase appears to be among women attending college. (Whether this indicates an actual increase in sexual activity or merely in the willingness to respond honestly, however, is arguable. College women of the past generation tended to admit "indiscretions" only to very close friends.)

The increase in premarital intercourse seems to be related to mutual commitment between the partners involved. As emotional involvement increases, the quality of the sexual encounter may change, becoming less motivated by self-centered goals than by the needs of the partner. In one study of college students, 92 percent of the men and 90 percent of the women felt that intercourse had enhanced their relationship. Only 1.2 percent of the men and 5.4 percent of the women felt it had been a damaging experience. In all of these relationships, however, a deep and caring mutual involvement had been

established before the couple engaged in sexual intercourse. In such a situation, the previous integration of non-sexual aspects would perhaps lessen the possibility that coitus would cause hostility, aggression, anger or guilt (Kirkendall and Libby 1966).

Virginity no longer seems too important to most college students. By 1970, 75 percent of those interviewed in a Gallup poll did not think that a girl had to retain her virginity until marriage. In contrast, about 75 percent of the adults interviewed a short time before stated they considered premarital intercourse to be wrong (Swift

Alfred Kinsey

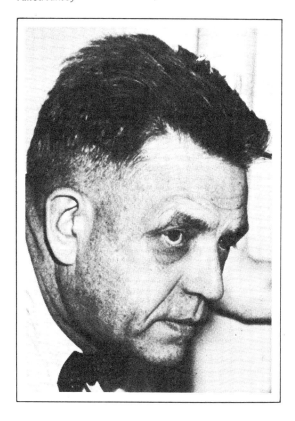

1970). In the past, great emphasis was placed on "technical" virginity. A woman was, under this interpretation, a virgin so long as she retained her hymen, or "maidenhead" – although she may have petted, spent the night nude in bed with a man, engaged in cunnilingus and fellatio. Today, however, this kind of "virginity" is no longer highly prized. In addition, it is no longer considered necessary to think of the first partner in terms of a permanent commitment.

*New Meaning to Dating*    The transition from permanent to serial commitment is basically a change in the meaning of dating. Dating was once an aspect of mate selection, it being assumed that the steady date eventually becomes the permanent mate. Today, dating has become a means by which people learn important interpersonal behavior. They develop ways of communicating, learn how to share sexual responses, often learn how to end an intimate relationship. These learning experiences involve mistakes and blunders, but they also include spontaneity, trust, and hope. In all, the experiences may help the individual to achieve maturity and a sense of identity. In the encounters, sexual drives may be modified, assuming a lesser importance than the desire for intimacy and sharing. As men and

women learn to meet the needs of their partners, they often become able to divest from sex other power-seeking motives.

The acceptance of premarital intercourse may be related to the idea that marriage should be mutually fulfilling. While dating, the partners find out whether or not their relationship is reciprocally satisfying. If a relationship provides the kind of rewards ideally associated with marriage, a couple may choose to live together in a commitment as serious as that made to marriage. Indeed the high divorce rate indicates that marriage, too, has now the role of a serial commitment.

**Permissiveness Without Affection** is basically sex for fun, sex without involement or intimacy. Its justification is that sex is for pleasure: to entangle it with emotions is to make a simple act complicated. Reiss (1971) found that only a small minority believed in recreational sex, and most who did were (not surprisingly) men. Is physical attraction, a sudden impulse or urge, or simple curiosity justification enough for most people? In the world of fantasy or grade B movies, it may be; but most people object to actually having sex for the mere pleasure of it. One study found that only 5 to 15 percent of college women would sleep with a person simply from attraction, impulse, or curiosity (David, 1971). But another study found that 27 percent of college men would sleep with a friend or casual date (Luckey and Nass, 1969). Those who engage in recreational sex tend to be older than college students. Permissiveness without affection is strongest among singles and those who were once married. Divorce strips sex of much of its innocence and romance. In fact, newly divorced men and women often express shock about the casualness with which sex is handled in what

Morton Hunt calls "the world of the formerly married." (Hunt, 1978).

**New Meanings Given to Sex**    Until this century, sex was viewed primarily as a means of reproduction. Conception was its most important and honored function. But birth control has separated sex from reproduction and given new possible meanings to sexual interaction. The most important new meaning is that of sex as a bonding force in intimate relationships, what Masters and Johnson call "the pleasure bond." The old basis for marriage lay in religion and economics; in preindustrial society marriage was a sacred institution and also a working partnership between husband and wife. But with the sanctity of marriage undermined by secularization and industrialization, what now sustains it? Increasingly, marriage is viewed in terms of its emotional structure; its bonds are the feelings between the husband and wife. Since sex is often charged with powerful feelings of love, self-esteem, and sharing, it therefore is often used as a barometer for the general health of the relationship. Sex is so wholly integrated with our personalities that it reflects our most intimate feelings and individual unique differences.

Sex is seen as one of the primary bonding forces in marriage. Unfortunately, sex in marriage is not necessarily always ideal; in fact, it is often routine, sometimes boring, sometimes exciting, sometimes frequent, sometimes rare. It goes through many adjustments and changes through the life cycle of marriage, depending on age, fatigue, stress, children, etc. In placing great importance on the significance of sex, many men and women feel thay *should* make love more frequently and have more orgasms with greater and grander fireworks. They set performance standards for themselves and when they don't meet them, feel disappointed in themselves and their partners. Whereas they should enjoy sex spontaneously, they work at it self-consciously as one more task to be accomplished. The emphasis placed on sex as a bonding force works paradoxically; if sex in a marriage is unsatisfactory, then the marriage may be judged as unsatisfactory.

The separation of sex from reproduction has made sexual pleasure a legitimate aim for people. This separation allows sexuality to be pursued as an end in itself and makes a new attitude toward sexual behavior possible. Since the purpose of sex is not necessarily procreation, premarital or extramarital sexuality no longer violates the "legitimate" purpose of sexuality, ie, reproduction. Since the purpose of sex is *also* plea-

sure, it is now acceptable to have nonmarital intercourse. Furthermore, the doctrine of sexual pleasure grants formerly forbidden behavior legitimacy. Masturbation is widely accepted as another form of sexual pleasure; previously it had been condemned because it was nonprocreative and therefore *unnatural*. Homosexuality and bisexuality have now received a certain credence; since sex is for pleasure, then what difference does it make *how* that pleasure is obtained? With the widely-held acceptance of sex as pleasure, pleasure becomes the measure of sexual morality. The sin of premarital sex is no longer the violation of religious or moral codes; the new sin is to feel guilty about the act or failing to have an orgasm. Such attitudes are becoming increasingly common in contemporary American society. The pursuit of sexual pleasure may relegate other values to secondary concerns; certainly it has called these values into question, forcing Americans to reexamine their true commitments and feelings about sex. A certain confusion continues about sexual values as a result of the sex-as-pleasure ideology.

**Women as Sexual Beings**  Perhaps the greatest discovery in recent years in America is that women are sexual. As a result of centuries of repression, many women failed to recognize their sexuality; many today are just learning to acknowledge it. In the 19th century, a sexual woman was considered deviant, without morals, more masculine than feminine. If she experienced desires, those desires were to be procreative rather than erotic. By the 1950s, however, this view had changed, but women were still believed to be less sexual than men. A woman's desires were considered dormant; she was to wait for a man to "awaken" them. Women's sexuality was thought to be less insistent, more delicate and vulnerable than men's (Gordon, 1971).

## The Feminine Mystique

Instead of fulfilling the promise of infinite orgastic bliss, sex in the America of the feminine mystique is becoming a strangely joyless national compulsion, if not a contemptuous mockery. The sex-glutted novels become increasingly explicit and increasingly dull; the sex kick of the women's magazines has a sickly sadness; the endless flow of manuals describing new sex techniques hint at an endless lack of excitement. This sexual boredom is betrayed by the evergrowing size of the Hollywood starlet's breasts, by the sudden emergence of the male phallus as an advertising "gimmick." Sex has become depersonalized, seen in terms of these exaggerated symbols. But of all the strange sexual phenomena that have appeared in the era of the feminine mystique, the most ironic are these – the frustrated sexual hunger of American women has increased, and their conflicts over femininity have intensified, as they have reverted from independent activity to search for their sole fulfillment through their sexual role in the home.

Betty Friedan

---

The 1960s assaulted the idea of women's passive sexuality. If anything, women's sexuality was more powerful and insatiable than men's. Masters and Johnson (1966) discovered that the sexual response cycle of men and women resembled each other more than they differed. Even more startling, because of the traditional concepts about women's sexuality, they scientifically showed that women had a far greater orgasmic potential than men. Mary Jane Sherfey (1972) reviewed Masters' and Johnson's work and concluded that:

> . . . the more orgasms a woman has, the stronger they become; the more orgasms she has, the more she *can* have. To all intents and purposes, *the human female is sexually insatiable in the presence of the highest degrees of sexual satiation.*

But the discovery of female sexuality has not been a simple blessing to women. For now women are expected to be highly orgasmic. The question of self worth has shifted from virginity to orgasmic adequacy; men no longer asked, writes Rollo May (1968), whether a woman will or won't, but whether she can or not. Women now have sexual performance standards and demands to live up to similar to the ones men impose on themselves. A woman's sense of self is now intimately tied to her sexual performance.

## Changes in Sexual Behaviors

A generation ago, two-thirds of the married couples interviewed by Kinsey said they always used the "missionary" position of sexual intercourse, with the woman supine and the man prone; the remaining third said they had also had intercourse with the woman on top. Today, nearly three-quarters of the people interviewed by Hunt said they had used the latter position. More than half of Hunt's respondents had engaged in coitus while lying on their sides, while only a quarter of Kinsey's respondents said they had done so. Forty percent of Hunt's sample indicated they had been involved in intercourse where the male entered the vagina from the rear.

Fewer women indicated they were sexually passive, as compared to a generation ago. In the massive survey of 100,000 women conducted for *Redbook* magazine by Robert and Amy Levin (Co-Authors with Masters and Johnson of The Pleasure Bond), 75 percent reported that they are usually or always active during intercourse. Among those who described their marriage as happy, 90 percent were in this group. In these marriages, 60 percent of the women initiate sexual intercourse about half the time, while 30 percent take the initiative occasionally (Levin and Levin 1975).

The frequency of oral-genital contact has also increased. Among young women in Kinsey's study, 57 percent said they had experimented with oral sex. In the Levin study, 91 percent of the women between 20 and 39 indicated they had experienced this form of sexual activity, and 41 percent practice it regularly; for a considerable number, oral sex is the primary means of orgasm. Approximately half the women in the survey had experimented with anal intercourse, although few practiced it regularly.

These changes reflect more than merely an increase in experimentation. They indicate a major change in attitudes toward intercourse. A generation ago, the domination of the male role was symbolized in the tendency for both sexes to consider the superior position to be the "proper" one for the man; the woman's supine position beneath him reflected her sexually passive role. During the past decade, there has been increasing acceptance of woman's sexual potential. Coitus has moved into a sphere where it is expected to be mutually satisfying (Biegel 1963.)

Sexual freedom and the expectation of pleasure, however, may include negative effects as well as positive ones. A generation ago, women were not expected to be highly orgasmic; today,

they are under the same pressure to "perform" as men are. When the woman fails to "achieve" orgasm, both partners may feel sexually inadequate. Unlike men, women are apparently subject to a wide variation of orgasmic response. It is a woman's responsibility to understand her own sexual responses, rather than to aim for some abstract standard (perhaps the "multiple orgasm") or the expectations of her partner (Boston Women's Health Collective 1972: 33).

Sexual Change in America – A Nude Beach

## QUESTIONS

1. What social forces contributed to the rise of contemporary sexual behavior?
2. What does the phrase "eroticization of America" mean? Is it a valid term describing America today?
3. What are the four sexual standards regarding premarital sexuality? To which one do you subscribe? Have your standards changed over the years? Why?
4. Discuss the manner in which sex is used in advertising. Is it used to foster a healthy attitude toward sex? What is a "healthy" sexual attitude? Is there such a thing or is "healthy" simply a disguised value judgment?
5. What is the significance of women being discovered as sexual? How does that affect the old double standard?

# Readings

### *Excerpt from* Sexual Behavior In The Human Male

Alfred C. Kinsey, W. B. Pomeroy and C. E. Martin

*In the 1940s Alfred Kinsey and his co-workers revolutionized the scientific approach to sexuality by introducing large-scale personal interviews for determining sexual habits in America. This excerpt gives the flavor of his studies. Why was his work considered revolutionary when it first came out?*

**Objectives in The Present Study**   The present study, then, represents an attempt to accumulate an objectively determined body of fact about sex which strictly avoids social or moral interpretations of the fact. Each person who reads this report will want to make interpretations in accordance with his understanding of moral values and social significances; but that is not part of the scientific method and, indeed, scientists have no special capacities for making such evaluations.

The data in this study are being secured through first-hand interviews. These, so far, have been limited to persons resident in the United States. Histories have come from every state in the Union, but more particularly from the northeastern quarter of the country, in the area bounded by Massachusetts, Michigan, Tennessee, and Kansas. It is intended that the ultimate sample shall represent a cross-section of the entire population, from all parts of the United States. The study had already included persons who belong to the following groups:

- Males, females
- Whites, Negroes, other races
- Single, married, previously married
- Ages three to ninety
- Adolescent at different ages
- Various educational ages
- Various occupational classes
- Various social levels
- Urban, rural, mixed backgrounds
- Various degrees of adherence to religious groups, or with no religion
- Various geographic origins

**Interviewing**   The quality of a case history study begins with the quality of the interviewing by which the data have been obtained. If, in lieu of direct observation and experiment, it is necessary to depend upon verbally transmitted records obtained from participants in the activities that are being studied, then it is imperative that one become a master of every scientific device and of all the arts by which any man has ever persuaded any other man into exposing his activities and his innermost thoughts. Failing to win that much from the subject, no statistical accumulation, however large, can adequately portray what the human animal is doing. However satisfactory the standard deviations may be, no statistical treatment can put validity into generalizations which are based on data that were not reasonably accurate and complete to begin with. It is unfortunate that academic departments so often offer courses on the statistical manipulation of human material to students who have little understanding of the problems involved in securing the original data. Learning how to meet people of all ranks and levels, establishing rapport, sympathetically comprehending the significances of things as others view them, learning to accept their attitudes and activities without moral, social, or esthetic evaluation, being interested in people as they are and not as someone else would have them, learning to see the reasonable bases of what at first glance may appear to be most unreasonable behavior, developing a capacity to like all kinds of people and thus to win their esteem and cooperation – these are the elements to be mastered by one who would gather human statistics. When training in these things replaces or at least precedes some of the college courses on the mathematical treatment of data, we shall come nearer to having a science of human behavior.

Problems of interviewing have been particularly important in the present study because of the long-standing taboos which make it bad form and, for most people, socially or legally dangerous to discuss one's sexual activities in public or even in the presence of one's most intimate friends. It is astounding that anyone should agree to expose himself by contributing his sex history to an interviewer whom he has never before met, and to a research project whose full significance he, in most instances, cannot begin to understand. Still more remarkable is the fact that many of the histories in the present study have come from subjects who agreed to give histories within the first few minutes after they first met the interviewer.

*Erotic Arousal and Orgasm*   Sexual contacts in the adolescent or adult male almost always involve physiologic disturbance which is recognizable as "erotic arousal." This is also true of much pre-adolescent activity, although some of the sex play of younger children seems to be devoid of erotic content. Pre-adolescent sexual stimulation in much more common among younger boys than it is among younger girls. Many younger females and, for that matter, a certain portion of the older and married female population, may engage in such specifically sexual activities as petting and even intercourse without discernible erotic reaction.

Erotic arousal is a material phenomenon which involves an extended series of physical, physiologic, and psychologic changes. Many of these could be subjected to precise instrumental measurement if objectivity among scientists and public respect for scientific research allowed such laboratory investigation. In the higher mammals, including the human, tactile stimulation is the chief mechanical source of arousal; but the higher mammal, especially the human, soon becomes so conditioned by his experience, or by the vicariously shared experiences of others, that psychologic stimulation becomes the major source of arousal for many an older person, especially if he is educated and his mental capacities are well trained. There is an occasional individual who comes to climax through psychologic stimulation alone.

Erotic stimulation, whatever its source, effects a series of physiologic changes which, as far as we yet know, appear to involve adrenal secretion, typically autonomic reactions, increased pulse rate, increased blood pressure, an increase in peripheral circulation and a consequent rise in the surface temperature of the body; a flow of blood into such distensible organs as the eyes, the lips, the lobes of the ears, the nipples of the breast, the penis of the male, and the clitoris, the genital labia and the vaginal walls of the female; a partial but often considerable loss of perceptive capacity (sight, hearing, touch, taste, smell); an increase in so-called nervous tension, some degree of rigidity of some part or of the whole of the body at the moment of maximum tension; and then a sudden release which produces local spasms or more extensive or all-consuming convulsions. The moment of sudden release is the point commonly recognized among biologists as orgasm.

The person involved in a sexual situation may be more or less conscious of some of the physiologic changes which occur although, unless he is scientifically trained, much of what is happening escapes his comprehension. Self observation may be especially inadequate because of the considerable (and usually unrecognized) loss of sensory capacities during maximum arousal. The subject's awareness of the situation is summed up in his statement that he is "emotionally aroused"; but the material sources of the emotional disturbances are rarely recognized, either by laymen or by scientists.

*Total Sexual Outlet*   The six chief sources of orgasm for the human male are masturbation, nocturnal emissions, heterosexual petting, heterosexual intercourse, homosexual relations, and intercourse with animals of other species. The sum of the orgasms derived from these several sources constitutes the individual's total sexual outlet.

There are some individuals who derive 100 per cent of their outlet from a single kind of sexual activity. Most persons regularly depend upon two or more sources of outlet; and there are some who may include all six of them in some short period of time. The mean number of outlets utilized by our more than 5000 males is between 2 and 3.

There are, both theoretically and in actuality, endless possibilities in combining these several sources of outlet and in the extent to which each of them contributes to the total picture. The record of a single sort of sexual activity, even though it be the one most frequently employed by a particular group of males, does not adequately portray the whole sexual life of the group. Published figures on the frequency of marital intercourse, for instance, cannot be taken to be the equivalent of data on the frequency of total outlet for the married male; for marital intercourse may provide as little as 62 per cent of the orgasms of certain groups of married males. Similarly, studies of masturbation among college and younger students are not the equivalents of studies of total sexual outlet for such a group. Again, many persons who are rated "homosexual" by their fellows in a school community, a prison population, or society at large, may be deriving only a small portion of their total outlet from that source. The fact that such a person may have had hundreds of heterosexual contacts will, in most cases, be completely ignored. Even psychologic studies have sometimes included, as "homosexual," persons who were not known to have had more than a single overt experience. In assaying the significance of any particular activity in an individual history, or any particular type of sexual behavior in a population as a whole, it is necessary to consider the extent to which that activity contributes to the total picture. Since all previously published rates on human sexual activity have been figures for particular outlets, such as masturbation or marital intercourse, the figures given in the present study on total outlet are higher than previous data would have led one to expect.

The average (mean) frequency of total sexual outlet for our sample of 3905 white males ranging between adolescence and 30 years of age is nearly 3.0 per week. It is precisely 2.88 for the total population of that age, or 2.94 for the sexually active males in that population. For the total population, including all persons between adolescence and 85 years of age, the mean is 2.74.

These average figures, however, are not entirely adequate, for they are based upon the particular groups of males who have contributed so far to this study. Subsequent analyses will show that there are differences in mean frequencies of sexual activity, dependent upon such factors as age, marital status, educational, religious, and rural-urban backgrounds, and on still other biologic and social factors. In order to be in-

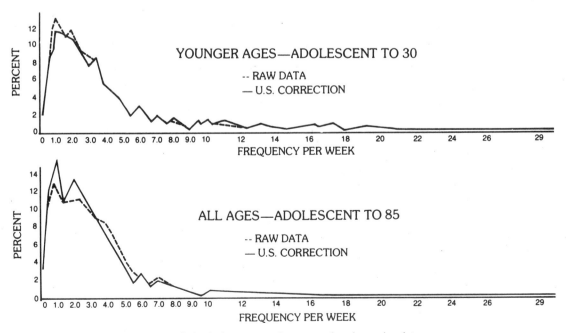

Individual variation in frequency of total sexual outlet

telligible, any discussion of sexual outlet should be confined to a particular group of persons whose biologic condition, civil status, and social origins are homogeneous. Most of the present volume is concerned with the presentation of data for such homogeneous groups. If there is any advantage in having a generalized figure for the population of the country as a whole, that figure is best calculated by determining the frequencies for a variety of these homogeneous groups, determining the relative size of each of these groups in the national census, and, then, through a process of weighting of means, reconstructing the picture for a synthetic whole.

For this synthesized population, which more nearly represents the constitution of the nation as a whole, we arrive at a figure of 3.27 per week for the total sexual outlet of the average white American male under thirty years of age. For all white males up to age 85, the corrected mean is 2.34 per week. The later figure is lower because of the inactivity of the older males.

*Individual Variation*   While approximately 3.3 is the mean frequency of total outlet for younger males, no mean or median, nor any other sort of average, can be significant unless one keeps in mind the range of the individual variation and the distribution of these variants in the population as a whole. This is particularly true in regard to human sexual behavior, because differences in behavior, even in a small group, are much greater than the variation in physical or physiologic characters. There are a few males who have gone for long periods of years without ejaculating: there is one male who, although apparently sound physically, had ejaculated only once in thirty years. There are others who have maintained average frequencies of 10, 20, or more per week for long periods of time: one male (a scholarly and skilled lawyer) has aver-

aged over 30 per week for thirty years. This is a difference of several thousand times.

Even the scientific discussions of sex show little understanding of the range of variation in human behavior. More often the conclusions are limited by the personal experience of the author. Psychologic and psychiatric literature is loaded with terms which evaluate frequencies of sexual outlet. But such designations as infantile, frigid, sexually under-developed, over-sexed, hyper-sexual, or sexually over-active, and the attempts to recognize such states as nymphomania and satyriasis as discrete entities, can, in any objective analysis, refer to nothing more than a position on a curve which is continuous. Normal and abnormal, one sometimes suspects, are terms which a particular author employs with reference to his own position on the curve.

*Positions in Intercourse*   Universally, at all social levels in our Anglo-Amercian culture, the opinion is held that there is one coital position which is biologically natural, and that all others are man-devised variants which become perversions when regularly engaged in. However, the one position which might be defended as natural because it is usual throughout the Class Mammalia, is not the one commonly used in our culture. The usual mammalian position involves, of course, rear entrance, with the female more or less prone, face down, with her legs flexed under her body, while the male is above or to the rear. Among the anthropoids this mammalian position is still the most common, but some variety of positions also occurs.

Most persons will be surprised to learn that positions in intercourse are as much a product of human cultures as languages and clothing, and that the common English-American position is rare in some other cultures. Among the several thousand portrayals of human coitus in the art left by ancient civilizations, there is hardly a single portrayal of the English-American position. It will be recalled that Malinowski (1929) records the nearly universal use of a totally different position among the Trobrianders in the Southwestern Pacfic; and that he notes that caricatures of the English-American position are performed around the communal campfires, to the great amusement of the natives who refer to the position as the "missionary position."

Alfred C. Kinsey, W. B. Pomeroy, C. E. Martin, *Sexual Behavior In The Human Male*. W. B. Saunders 1948. Reprinted by permission of Indiana University Institute For Sex Research, Inc.

## A New Kinsey Institute Report

John Barbour

*Dr. Paul Gebhard suggests that American sexual attitudes are becoming more conservative. Is this true?*

BLOOMINGTON, Ind. – Thirty years ago in this quiet college town, America took its first bite of the apple – and lost its sexual innocence.

In the three decades since, Americans have wandered through a sexual landscape that many felt bizarre and disturbing.

But a new report from Alfred Kinsey's Institute for Sex Research, due this year, [1978] indicates that some conservative bells are sounding in the American mind.

There will be continued openness in sexual discussion. The divorce rate will climb. There will be more premarital sex, until perhaps nine out of 10 will enter marriage no longer virgin.

Yet there is a strong vein of conservatism underlying all of this, says Dr. Paul Gebhard, the scholarly 60-year-old director of the institute who has been engaged in sex research since 1946.

"We asked how they (Americans) felt about different varieties of sexual behavior, and we discovered that the great majority are against extramarital intercourse. They are strongly down on prostitution. They violently disapprove of homosexuality."

Some of this is disguised. Americans questioned by the institute agree that homosexuals should have jobs. But what kind of jobs? They may be musicians, actors, florists, interior decorators – but not judges, public officials, policemen, physicians, teachers.

Marriage and the nuclear family are not threatened, but Gebhard says:

"I think society will be much more tolerant about living arrangements than they are now. Our present living-together phenomenon is for all practical purposes accepted. Who knows? Maybe even the government will accept it and allow unmarried couples to file joint tax returns.

"Most of the young people living together have ended up getting married. I've asked them why, and it's funny because they can't give you any really rational reason. The both continue working. Everything is exactly the same, except they've gotten married.

"It seems to be more a symbolic thing. They want to affirm their relationship. And what are they going to do? Take out an ad in a newspaper?"

The institute itself has hit some bad times which has made it more difficult to produce its report. The current study, for instance, was started in 1970. The staff numbers only 25, and most of that is help from Indiana University students.

This year's budget is about $200,000, down from $300,000 last year because of the loss of a federal grant which supported a national sex information bureau. The institute has changed quarters on campus a number of times and now resides with its library, the world's largest collection of erotica, in a few rooms of a gothic teaching hall. Kinsey is buried in nearby Rose Hill Cemetery. He died in 1956 of heart failure at age 63.

But the institute has had hard times before and survived. This year it issues a new report on homosexuality in San Francisco, and its work continues.

The first Kinsey report 30 years ago unhinged the American mind with such underground facts as one in three American males has at least one homosexual experience to orgasm, half of the females interviewed had premarital intercourse, one in 10 married women never had an orgasm even after 15 years of marriage.

From that year on, like a genie let out of the bottle, sex seemed to rise to any whim – something old, something new, something borrowed, something blue.

Kinsey didn't start it. Sexual habits has been getting more liberal for years. But his reports revealed the gap between the way Americans talked about sex and the way they practiced it.

What astonished Gebhard was "the rapidity with which censorship just collapsed."

There were deep forces at work on the nation's sexual consciousness, Gebhard explains. There was an increasing demand for personal freedom. There was the continuing emancipation of women demanding to be treated like human beings who had their own sexual needs and rights. There was a waning power of conventional religion with its requirement of blind, fundamentalist faith. There was greater literacy and the exposure to new ideas that transcended hometown mores. There was World War II and the social mix it created.

All of this produced change in sexual habits and sexual frankness. In 1948 when the first re-

port came out journalists complained that they couldn't use the word "masturbation" in public print. Kinsey kept most of the explicitly erotic material under lock and key. Today, the cabinets are unlocked. The same material, Gebhard says, is sold in books and magazines on Main Street.

Part of the change in the last 30 years was a rebellion to hypocrisy toward sex.

American women were told to be beautiful and sexy like a Hollywood star. Men were told to look but not touch, Gebhard remembers.

"Back in the late forties and fifties, the idea was, to put it bluntly, to be a tease. Flaunt your physical bait, but don't do anything about it until you have a marriage band on. In a way that was rather unwholesome, a kind of bartering process, not only in marriage, but in dating.

"The average male was interested in how far he could go physically, and the average female wanted to see how much of a good time she could have without having to pay too dearly . . . Today it is healthier. People marry, but not primarily for sexual reasons. You can have sex without getting married."

In his opinion, this leads to happier marriages, based on other compatibilities?

Then why the rising divorce rate?

"People expect more," Gebhard says. "Particularly women expect more from a marriage. In another day, marriage may have hung together, but they were unhappy marriages forced to stay together by social pressure, stigma and economic pressure."

There are other reasons: "People change, but not always in parallel directions. If one looks at marriage as a civil contract, rather than a religious thing, you can't conceive of anyone signing a lifetime contract without a loophole, which is what the old tradition of marriage was."

On the other hand, the divorce rate hides another trend. The vast majority of divorced people remarry. So while individual unions may break up, it may have the effect, in the end, of strengthening the institution of marriage.

Attitudes toward sex are definitely age-graded. The younger people are, the less liberal the public at large is toward their sexual behavior. But this, too, is clouded by some misconceptions.

Gebhard says most young people are not promiscuous, which implies multiple partners. Young people themselves think that is wrong. They may have a relationship that lasts a semester or until graduation or college, but in that time they are monogamous, going steady.

In the new survey, traditional ties come out strongly. The 3,000 adults queried were strongly opposed to sex between teenagers who didn't love each other, a little more liberal if they were in love, and more accepting if they were engaged.

At the other end of the age scale, most people accept it when two older people live together rather than marry and lose their individual Social Security benefits.

In a sense the last 30 years have cleared the air. Things are settling down.

Some aberrations in sexual behavior haven't worked and are being abandoned. Communes and group marriages, for instance. Jealousy has stymied so-called open marriages, and most people leave mate-swapping clubs after a couple of years.

On the other hand, Gebhard says, "We may find a greater tolerance for homosexual marriages." There may even be some sort of a civil contract to provide for property rights in such marriages. But even this will not be too widespread. Although some female marriages are lengthy and successful, male marriages rarely last 10 years.

"While there will always be a market for erotica, it won't be the large market that exists now," Gebhard predicts. "It will die down, level out."

He's convinced that erotica doesn't cause antisocial behavior any more than a pretty girl walking down the street, television or a lingerie ad in the Sears Roebuck catalog.

The reason for its demise as a modern American spectacle is presaged by the blase attitude toward it in Scandinavia where sexual free expression is older.

The half-life of pornography is rather short, so producers are always looking for something new and novel. You can exhaust heterosexuality rather quickly.

The trends toward sado-masochism and kiddy-porn are the result. And public reaction toward such kinky trends has not been favorable.

Thirty years, a generation in which so much happened – from the attitudinal studies of Alfred Kinsey to the physiological studies of Masters and Johnson.

But probably nowhere is the change so secret, and so scary, as in adolescence. Peer pressure contends with parental conservatism in the sexual arena.

"When you and I were in junior high and high school," Gebhard says, "society was on the side of virginity and inexperience. You knew that a fair number of your peers felt this way. It was just a minority that were sexually active."

But today, "the undecided or timid adolescent is in a bind. There's no pillar to cling to. They can't escape peer pressure. They can't say 'I won't do it because society says no or the church says no.' So there's a lot of heat put on them."

The answer, finally, will be growing up as a person. Gebhard tells young people, "Look, I'm all for sexual freedom. But sexual freedom allows the right to say no."

John Barbour "New Kinsey Report: Sex Trends More Conservative." *San Francisco Sunday Examiner and Chronicle* June 18, 1978. Reprinted by permission of Associated Press Newsfeatures.

## Excerpt from **The Dharma Bums**

Jack Kerouac

*Jack Kerouac lived the transition between the "beat" and the "hip" generations. "The Dharma Bums" is the story of his friendship with Japhy, a Buddhist from Oregon. In the book Kerouac calls himself Ray Smith, and Alvah is a friend with whom he shares a cottage in Berkeley. At the point of this excerpt, Japhy has just arrived at the cottage with a girl named Princess and has told her to take off her clothes. She has. Does this passage represent today's sexuality?*

This was in keeping with Japhy's theories about women and lovemaking. I forgot to mention that the day the rock artist had called on him in the late afternoon, a girl had come right after, a blonde in rubber boots and a Tibetan coat with wooden buttons, and in the general talk she'd inquired about our plan to climb Mount Matterhorn and said "Can I come with ya?" as she was a bit of a mountainclimber herself.

"Shore," said Japhy, in his funny voice he used for joking, a big loud deep imitation of a lumberjack he knew in the Northwest, a ranger actually, old Burnie Byers, "shore, come on with us and we'll all screw ya at ten thousand feet" and the way he said it was so funny and casual, and in fact serious, that the girl wasn't shocked at all but somewhat pleased. In this same spirit he'd now brought this girl Princess to our cottage, it was about eight o'clock at night, dark, Alvah and I were quietly sipping tea and reading poems or typing poems at the typewriter and two bicycles came in the yard: Japhy on his, Princess on hers. Princess had gray eyes and yellow hair and was very beautiful and only twenty. I must say one thing about her, she was sex mad and man mad, so there wasn't much of a problem in persuading her to play yabyum. "Don't you know about yabyum, Smith?" said Japhy in his big booming

voice striding in in his boots holding Princess's hand. "Princess and I come here to show ya, boy."

"Suits me," said I, "whatever it is." Also I'd known Princess before and had been mad about her, in the City, about a year ago. It was just another wild conincidence that she had happened to meet Japhy and fallen in love with him and madly too, she'd do anything he said. Whenever people dropped in to visit us at the cottage I'd always put my red bandana over the little wall lamp and put out the ceiling light to make a nice cool red dim scene to sit and drink wine and talk in. I did this, and went to get the bottle out of the kitchen and couldn't believe my eyes when I saw Japhy and Alvah taking their clothes off and throwing them every whichaway and I looked and Princess was stark naked, her skin white as snow when the red sun hits it at dusk, in the dim red light. "What the hell," I said.

"Here's what yabyum is, Smith," said Japhy, and he sat crosslegged on the pillow on the floor and motioned to Princess, who came over and sat down on him facing him with her arms about his neck and they sat like that saying nothing for while. Japhy wasn't at all nervous and embarrassed and just sat there in perfect form just as he was supposed to do. "This is what they do in the temples of Tibet. It's a holy ceremony, it's done just like this in front of chanting priests. People pray and recite Om Mani Pahdme Hum, which means Amen the Thunderbolt in the Dark Void. I'm the thunderbolt and Princess is the dark void, you see."

"But what's she thinking?" I yelled almost in despair, I'd had such idealistic longings for that girl in the past year and had conscience-stricken hours wondering if I should seduce her because she was so young and all.

"Oh this is lovely," said Princess. "Come on and try it."

"But I can't sit crosslegged like that." Japhy was sitting in the full lotus position, it's called, with both ankles over both thighs. Alvah was sitting on the mattress trying to yank his ankles over his thighs to do it. Finally Japhy's legs began to hurt and they just tumbled over on the mattress where both Alvah and Japhy began to explore the territory. I still couldn't believe it.

"Take your clothes off and join in, Smith!" But on top of all that, the feelings about Princess, I'd also gone through an entire year of celibacy based on my feeling that lust was the direct cause of birth which was the direct cause of suffering and death and I had really no lie come to a point where I regarded lust as offensive and even cruel.

"Pretty girls make graves," was my saying, whenever I'd had to turn my head around involuntarily to stare at the incomparable pretties of Indian Mexico. And the absence of active lust in me had also given me a new peaceful life that I was enjoying a great deal. But this was too much. I was still afraid to take my clothes off; also I never liked to do that in front of more than one person, especially with men around. But Japhy didn't give a goddamn hoot and holler about any of this and pretty soon he was making Princess happy and then Alvah had a turn (with his big serious eyes staring in the dim light, and him reading poems a minute ago). So I said "How about me startin to work on her arm?"

"Go ahead, great." Which I did, lying down on the floor with all my clothes on and kissing her hand, then her wrist, then up, to her body, as she laughed and almost cried with delight everybody everywhere working on her. All the peaceful celibacy of my Buddhism was going down the drain. "Smith, I distrust any kind of Buddhism or *any* kinda philosophy or social system that puts down sex," said Japhy quite scholarly now that he was done and sitting naked crosslegged rolling himself a Bull Durham cigarette (which he did as part of his "simplicity" life). It ended up

with everybody naked and finally making gay pots of coffee in the kitchen and Princess on the kitchen floor naked with her knees clasped in her arms, lying on her side, just for nothing, just to do it, then finally she and I took a warm bath together in the bathtub and could hear Alvah and Japhy discussing Zen Free Love Lunacy orgies in the other room.

"Hey Princess we'll do this every Thursday night, hey?" yelled Japhy. "It'll be a regular function."

"Yeah," yelled Princess from the bathtub. I'm telling you she was actually glad to do this and told me "You know, I feel like I'm the mother of all things and I have to take care of my little children."

"You're such a young pretty thing yourself."

"But I'm the old mother of earth. I'm a Bodhisattva." She was just a little off her nut but when I heard her say "Bodhisattva" I realized she wanted to be a big Buddhist like Japhy and being a girl the only way she could express it was this way, which had its traditional roots in the yabyum ceremony of Tibetan Buddhism, so everything was fine.

Alvah was immensely pleased and was all for the idea of "every Thursday night" and so was I by now.

"Alvah. Princess says she's a Bodhisattva."

"Of course she is."

"She says she's the mother of all of us."

"The Bodhisattva women of Tibet and part of ancient India," said Japhy, "were taken and used as holy concubines in temples and sometimes in ritual caves and would get to lay up a stock of merit and they meditated too. All of them, men, and women, they'd meditate, fast, have balls like this, go back to eating, drinking, talking, hike around, live in viharas in the rainy season and outdoors in the dry, there was no question of what to do about sex which is what I always liked about Oriental religion. And what I always dug about the Indians in our country . . . You know when I was a little kid in Oregon I didn't feel that I was an American at all, with all that suburban ideal and sex repression and general dreary newspaper gray censorship of all our real human values but and when I discovered Buddhism and all I suddenly felt that I had lived in a previous lifetime innumerable ages ago and now because of faults and sins in that lifetime I was being degraded to a more grievous domain of existence and my karma was to be born in America where nobody has any fun or believes in anything, especially freedom. That's why I was always sympathetic to freedom movements, too, like anarchism in the Northwest, the oldtime heroes of Everett Massacre and all . . . " It ended up with long earnest discussions about all these subjects and finally Princess got dressed and went home with Japhy on their bicycles and Alvah and I sat facing each other in the dim red light.

"But you know, Ray, Japhy is really sharp — he's really the wildest craziest sharpest cat we've ever met. And what I love about him is he's the big hero of the West Coast, do you realize I've been out here for two years now and hadn't met anybody worth knowing really or anybody with any truly illuminated intelligence and was giving up hope for the West Coast? Besides all the background he has, in Oriental scholarship, Pound, taking peyote and seeing visions, his mountainclimbing and bhikkuing, wow, Japhy Ryder is a great new hero of American culture."

"He's mad!" I agreed. "And other things I like about him, his quiet sad moments when he don't say much. . . ."

"Gee, I wonder what will happen to him in the end."

From *The Dharma Bums* by Jack Kerouac. Copyright © 1958 by Jack Kerouac. Reprinted by permission of The Viking Press, Inc.

## Excerpts from American Graffiti

George Lucas, Gloria Katz, and Willard Huyck

*Released in the summer of 1973, when the revolutionary fervor of the late '60s had cooled, "American Graffiti" captured the popular fancy. It would be hard to say how much the ensuing craze for '50s nostalgia was anticipated and how much was created by the film-makers. The movie spawned the most popular TV shows of the '70s, whose characters became national heroes.*

*In the following excerpts, Terry, "the Toad," catches Debbie's attention by telling her she looks just like Connie Stevens; he winds up getting something even better than the "feel" that he set out to cop.*

**DEBBIE:** You really think I look like her?

**TERRY:** No shit — excuse me, I mean I'm not just feeding you a line. You look like Connie Stevens. What's your name?

**DEBBIE:** Debbie. I always thought I looked like Sandra Dee.

**TERRY:** Oh yeah — well, you look a lot like her too.

**DEBBIE:** This your car?

**TERRY:** Yeah. I'm Terry the — they call me Terry the Tiger.

**DEBBIE:** It's really tough looking.

**TERRY:** What school do you go to?

**DEBBIE:** Dewey — can it lay rubber?

**TERRY:** Oh yeah, it's got a 327 Chevy mill with six Strombergs.

**DEBBIE:** Wow — bitchin' tuck and roll. I just love the feel of tuck and roll upholstery.

**TERRY:** You do?

**DEBBIE:** Yeah.

**TERRY:** Well, come on in — I'll let you feel it. I mean, you can touch it if you want — (realizing it's coming out wrong he gets nervous) I mean the upholstery, you know.

**DEBBIE:** Okay.

*. . . Later that Evening . . .*

**DEBBIE:** You know, I had a pretty good time
tonight.

**TERRY:** Oh come on, you're just --

**DEBBIE:** No, no, really, really. I really had a
good time. I mean, you picked me up and we
got some hard stuff and saw a hold-up, and
then we went to the Canal, you got your car
stolen, and then I got to watch you gettin'
sick, and then you got in this really bitchin'
fight . . . I really had a good time.

*Terry looks at her, starting to regain a little cool.*

**TERRY:** You think so? Yeah – well I guess I have
pretty much fun every night.

**DEBBIE:** Anyway if you're not doing anything
tomorrow night, why don't you come over?

**TERRY:** Yeah – well, I might be busy, you know.
But we could – well, I got a little Vespa I just
play around with.

**DEBBIE:** Really? Why that's almost a motorcycle. And I just love motorcycles.

**TERRY:** You do? Well, why didn't you tell
me? We wouldn't have had to go through all
that . . . fun.

*He feels his swollen lip and she touches it.
Then she leans over and kisses him.*

**DEBBIE:** I got to go.

**TERRY:** Ow.

**DEBBIE:** Goodnight.

**TERRY:** See ya.

## Federal Information Centers

Throughout the country, the federal government supports information centers which deal
with requests concerning various things, from
passports to energy conservation. The centers
acts as referral services for questions about
venereal infections, birth control; and generic
counseling.

**Alabama**

**Birmingham**
322-8591
Toll-free tieline to
Atlanta, Ga.

**Mobile**
438-1421
Toll-free tieline to
New Orleans, La.

**Arizona**

**Phoenix**
(602) 261-3313
Federal Building
230 North First Ave.
85025

**Tucson**
622-1511
Toll-free tieline to
Phoenix

**Arkansas**

**Little Rock**
378-6177
Toll-free tieline to
Memphis, Tenn.

**California**

**Los Angeles**
(213) 688-3800
Federal Building

300 North Los Angeles St.
90012

**Sacramento**
(916) 440-3344
Federal Building and
U.S. Courthouse
650 Capital Mall
95814

**San Diego**
(714) 293-6030
Federal Building
880 Front St.
Room 1S11
92188

**San Francisco**
(415) 556-6600
Federal Building and
U.S. Courthouse
450 Golden Gate Ave.
P.O. Box 36082
94102

**San Jose**
275-7422
Toll-free tieline to
San Francisco

**Santa Ana**
836-2386
Toll-free tieline to
Los Angeles

**Colorado**

**Colorado Springs**
471-9491
Toll-free tieline to
Denver

**Denver**
(303) 837-3602
Federal Building
1961 Stout St.
80294

**Pueblo**
544-9523
Toll-free tieline to
Denver

**Connecticut**

**Hartford**
527-2617
Toll-free tieline to
New York, N.Y.

**New Haven**
624-4720
Toll-free tieline to
New York, N.Y.

**District of Columbia**

**Washington**
(202) 755-8660
Seventh and D Sts., S.W.
Room 5716
20407

**Florida**

**Fort Lauderdale**
522-8531
Toll-free tieline to
Miami

**Jacksonville**
354-4756
Toll-free tieline to
St. Peterburg

**Miami**
(305) 350-4155
Federal Building
51 Southwest First Ave.
33130

**Orlando**
422-1800
Toll-free tieline to
St. Petersburg

**St. Petersburg**
(813) 893-3495
William C. Cramer
Federal Building
144 First Ave., South
33701

**Tampa**
229-7911
Toll-free tieline to
St. Petersburg

**West Palm Beach**
833-7566
Toll-free tieline to
Miami

**Georgia**

**Atlanta**
(404) 221-6891
Federal Building
275 Peachtree St., N.E.
30303

**Hawaii**

**Honolulu**
(808) 546-8620
Federal Building
300 Ala Moana Blvd.
P.O. Box 50091
96850

**Illinois**

**Chicago**
(312) 353-4242
Everett McKinley
Dirksen Building
219 South Dearborn St.
Room 250
60604

**Indiana**

**Gary/Hammond**
883-4110
Toll-free tieline to
Indianapolis

**Indianapolis**
(317) 269-7373
Federal Building
575 North Pennsylvania
46204

**Iowa**

**Des Moines**
284-4448
Toll-free tieline to
Omaha, Nebr.

**Kansas**

**Topeka**
295-2866
Toll-free tieline to
Kansas City, Mo.

**Wichita**
263-6931
Toll-free tieline to
Kansas City, Mo.

**Kentucky**

**Louisville**
(502) 582-6261
Federal Building

600 Federal Place
40202

**Louisiana**

**New Orleans**
(504) 589-6696
U.S. Postal Service
Building
701 Loyola Ave.
Room 1210
70113

**Maryland**

**Baltimore**
(301) 962-4980
Federal Building
31 Hopkins Plaza
21202

**Massachusetts**

**Boston**
(617) 223-7121
J. F. K. Federal Building
Cambridge St.
Lobby, 1st Floor
02203

**Michigan**

**Detroit**
(313) 226-7016
McNamara Federal
Building
477 Michigan Ave.
Room 103
48226

**Grand Rapids**
451-2628
Toll-free tieline to
Detroit

**Minnesota**

**Minneapolis**
(612) 725-2073
Federal Building and
U.S. Courthouse
110 South Fourth St.
55401

**Missouri**

**Kansas City**
(816) 374-2466
Federal Building
601 East Twelfth St.
64106

**St. Joseph**
233-8206
Toll-free tieline to
Kansas City

**St. Louis**
(314) 425-4106
Federal Building
1520 Market St. 63103

**Nebraska**

**Omaha**
(402) 221-3353
Federal Building
U.S. Post Office and
Courthouse
215 North 17th St.
68102

**New Jersey**

**Newark**
(201) 645-3600
Federal Building
970 Broad St.
07102

**Paterson/Passaic**
523-0717
Toll-free tieline to
Newark

**Trenton**
396-4400
Toll-free tieline to
Newark

**New Mexico**

**Albuquerque**
(505) 766-3091
Federal Building and
U.S. Courthouse
500 Gold Ave., S.W.
87102

**Santa Fe**
983-7743
Toll-free tieline to
Albuquerque

**New York**

**Albany**
463-4421
Toll-free tieline to
New York

**Buffalo**
(716) 846-4010
Federal Building
111 West Huron St.
14202

**New York**
(212) 264-4464
Federal Building
26 Federal Plaza
Room 1-114
10007

**Rochester**
546-5075
Toll-free tieline to
Buffalo

**Syracuse**
476-8545
Toll-free tieline to
Buffalo

**North Carolina**

**Charlotte**
376-3600
Toll-free tieline to
Atlanta, Ga.

**Ohio**

**Akron**
375-5638
Toll-free tieline to
Cleveland

**Cincinnati**
(513) 684-2801
Federal Building
550 Main St.
45202

**Cleveland**
(216) 522-4040
Federal Building
1240 East Ninth St.
Room 137
44199

**Columbus**
221-1014
Toll-free tieline to
Cincinnati

**Dayton**
223-7377
Toll-free tieline to
Cincinnati

**Toledo**
241-3223
Toll-free tieline to
Cleveland

**Oklahoma**

**Oklahoma City**
(405) 231-4868
U.S. Post Office and
Courthouse

201 Northwest 3rd St.
73102

**Tulsa**
584-4193
Toll-free tieline to
Oklahoma City

**Oregan**

**Portland**
(503) 221-2222
Federal Building
1220 Southwest
Third Ave.
Room 109
97204

**Pennsylvania**

**Allentown/Bethlehem**
821-7785
Toll-free tieline to
Philadelphia

**Philadelphia**
(215) 597-7042
Federal Building
600 Arch St.
Room 1232
19106

**Pittsburgh**
(412) 644-3456
Federal Building
1000 Liberty Ave.
15222

**Scranton**
346-7081
Toll-free tieline to
Philadelphia

**Rhode Island**

**Providence**
331-5565

Toll-free tieline to
Boston, Mass.

**Tennessee**

**Chattanooga**
265-8231
Toll-free tieline to
Memphis

**Memphis**
(901) 521-3285
Clifford Davis Federal
Building
167 North Main St.
38103

**Nashville**
242-5056
Toll-free tieline to
Memphis

**Texas**

**Austin**
472-5494
Toll-free tieline to
Houston

**Dallas**
749-2131
Toll-free tieline to
Fort Worth

**Fort Worth**
(817) 334-3624
Fritz Garland Lanham
Federal Building
819 Taylor St.
76102

**Houston**
(713) 226-5711
Federal Building and
U.S. Courthouse
515 Rusk Ave.
77002

**San Antonio**
224-4471
Toll-free tieline to
Houston

**Utah**

**Ogden**
399-1347

Toll-free tieline to
Salt Lake City

**Salt Lake City**
(801) 524-5353
Federal Building
125 South State St.
Room 1205
84138

**Virginia**

**Newport News**
244-0480
Toll-free tieline to
Norfolk

**Norfolk**
(804) 441-6723
Stanwick Building
3661 East Virginia
Beach Blvd., Room 106
23502

**Richmond**
643-4928
Toll-free tieline to
Norfolk

**Roanoke**
982-8591
Toll-free tieline to
Norfolk

**Washington**

**Seattle**
(206) 442-0570
Federal Building
915 Second Ave.
98174

**Tacoma**
383-5230
Toll-free tieline to
Seattle

**Wisconsin**

**Milwaukee**
271-2273
Toll-free tieline to
Chicago, Ill.

# Unit 2

## Sexual Systems

# Sexual Structure and Function

"**A**natomy is destiny," Sigmund Freud presumptuously claimed a half century ago when he argued that women somehow were physiologically incomplete because they lacked a penis. Psychologically they experienced that "lack" as a sign of inferiority. The penis was erect and aggressive; the vagina was hidden and receptive. These anatomical differences implied, within the Freudian framework, that men would be active or aggressive and that women would be passive or submissive. That was Freud's fantasy – and much of our own – about women and men.

In one sense, anatomy *is* destiny, because people's genitals label them as either male or female. This labeling gives the individual his or her gender identity, and influences the way that person will be treated. In the socialization of a child, certain activities are favored or frowned upon, depending on gender. It is a major influence – if not the prime factor – in determining such disparate decisions as career choice and hair style. Certain behavior patterns have long been linked with gender – women cry, men should not; men curse, women should not, and so·on.

Ironically, the genitals that determine our gender are the parts of our body that are the most taboo; they are often a source of shame or embarrassment. Outside of specified sexual situations, people are discouraged from looking at or touching their genitals or those of other people. From childhood throughout life, discussion of the genitals is discouraged or accompanied by nervous laughter or other expressions of embarrassment. It is common to hear slang terms for sex organs used as insults.

The taboo surrounding our genitals is related to the fact that they serve both erotic and excretory functions, the two bodily functions about which our culture feels most ambiguous. Men urinate through the urethral opening at the tip of the penis; the semen which they ejaculate also passes through the urethra. The urethral opening for a women lies in the vulva between her clitoris and vaginal opening. For both sexes, the genitals lie close to the anus.

Our culture has endowed the genitals with powerful connotations. The erect penis is a symbol of power and potency, virility, manliness, and fertility; a flaccid penis represents impotency, weakness, and sterility. The vagina is usually not viewed in terms of potency; rather it is a symbol of mystery; it is seen as a receptacle, hence the presumption that women are receptive or passive in their sexuality. Historically genitals have been regarded with negativity. The power of the penis was thought to be rooted in sin. The old name for vulva, still used occasionally, was *pudendum*, meaning "thing of shame".

Today, the prevailing outlook regarding sexuality is far more lighthearted. As indicated by the very existence of the course for which this book was written (a course that was unheard of a couple of decades ago) people are now questioning traditional dogma on eroticism and reproduction. The reasons for this new attitude are not clear, but the advent of effective birth control techniques and relatively liberal legal and social trends are two significant factors that have profoundly altered the nature of human sexuality. Perhaps because of the efficacy of modern methods of birth control, eroticism has come to be viewed as a type of communication not necessarily connected with reproduction.

However, like many products of technological progress, modern methods of birth control are a mixed blessing. They provide a way to avoid the emotional and physical drain of unwanted pregnancy, but they also involve a certain amount of risk. We live in an age of contraceptive experimentation, and some of the methods that have been tried have proved to involve more risk than many people would like to take. Some have opted for relatively safe but less effective methods of contraception, while others have turned to modes of sexual activity other than *intromission* – insertion of a penis into a vagina. Oral-genital stimulation and mutual masturbation were once considered perverse and obscene, but these and certain other forms of *sodomy* – all modes of sexual intercourse except intromission – are now considered by sexologists to be both physically and psychologically healthy, among consenting partners.

**The Male Genitals**

When a man is sexually unaroused his genitals loosely hang from his *pubic area*, the lower abdomen. The *scrotum*, a pouch of wrinkled, elastic skin, is located behind the shaft of the *penis*. Pubic hair, which is sparse on the scrotum, grows dense on the pubic area.

**The Penis**   The penis contains muscles, blood vessels, nerves, and three parallel tubes of spongy tissue (Figure 3.2). The two relatively large tubes, the *corpora cavernosa*, lie above the third, the *corpus spongiosum*. During sexual arousal, these three corpora fill with blood by a rapid influx through the many arteries permeating the penis. Simultaneously the penis's veins constrict, and it becomes rigid and erect as it fills with trapped blood. Unlike the erect penises of many other animals, the human erection does not contain a bone.

In external structure the penis has two distinct parts, the *shaft*, and the *glans penis*. The shaft is covered with thin, loose skin through which several blood vessels are visible when the penis is flaccid. During erection these vessels bulge as they become engorged with blood.

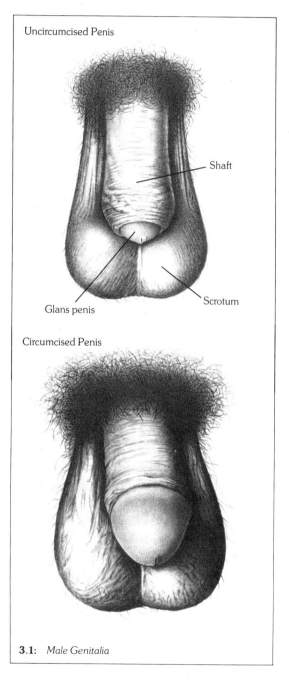

Uncircumcised Penis

Shaft

Glans penis

Scrotum

Circumcised Penis

**3.1:**  *Male Genitalia*

At the end of the penis is the glans penis, or head, a smooth acorn-shaped tip. All males are born with a fold of skin, called a *prepuce*, or foreskin, that extends from the shaft over the glans. This flap of skin is routinely removed from over 90 percent of the males born in hospitals in the United States. The surgical removal of the foreskin is called *circumcision*. In an uncircumcised penis a moist, curdlike substance called *smegma* accumulates beneath the foreskin. Without frequent bathing, smegma can develop a foul odor and can cause irritations or infections of the glans penis. However, frequent attention to cleanliness eliminates the hygienic disadvantages of not being circumcised.

Statistical studies have indicated that uncircumcised males are more prone to cancer of the glans penis than are circumcised males. Also, a type of cervical cancer has been reported in the female sex partners of uncircumcised males. But correlations between intercourse with uncircumcised males and cervical cancer are conflicting and far from conclusive.

The age-old debate between circumcised and uncircumcised men over the relative erotic advantages of their anatomical states remains unresolved.

*Penis Size*    The average flaccid penis is between three and four inches long, and the average erect length is about six inches. No correlation exists between the size of a man's body and the size of his penis, and differences in lengths during the flaccid state are not necessarily reflected during erection. In fact, a study by William Masters and Virginia Johnson indicates that short penises expand more during erection than do long ones:

> Forty men whose penises measured 7.5-9 cm. in length in the flaccid state were compared to a similar number of study subjects whose penises in the flaccid state measured 10-11.5 cm. Measurement was crudely clinical at best and can only be presumed suggestive and certainly not specific in character. The length of the smaller penises increased by an average of 7.5-8 cm. at full erection. This full erection essentially doubled the smaller organs in length over flaccid-size standards. In constrast, in the men whose organs were significantly larger in a flaccid state (10-11.5 cm.), penile length increased by an average of 7-7.5 cm. in the fully erect state (Masters and Johnson, 1966).

*Erogenous Zones*:    The penis is the most erotically sensitive part of the male body. In response to tactile stimuli, touch-sensitive nerves within it set off impulses to pleasure centers in the brain. Other nerves, which are pressure-sensitive, communicate erotic sensations because of the pressure within an erection. Thus, contact with

**3.2:**  *Cross section of a penis. During erection the porous tissues of the corpora cavernosa and corpus spongiosum fill with blood.*

the penis is not necessary in order for a man to have erogenous feelings centered in it. Nerve endings are most concentrated in the glans penis and *frenulum*, the ridge on the underside of the shaft immediately behind the glans penis; hence these are the most erotically responsive areas.

Most men prefer delicate stimulation to the penis; however there is certainly no established norm as to what is erotically pleasing and what is not. Some males enjoy a level of stimulation that others would find excruciatingly harsh. But because the male sex organs are external, one should never assume that the penis and its accessory organs are tough. They are hypersensitive to touch and pressure and the penis and scrotum should never be grabbed, pinched, or bitten (unless such treatment is expressly requested).

Although the penis is the primary male erogenous organ, it is by no means the only one. Stimulation to many parts of the body such as the ears, mouth, breasts, anus, and scrotum may initiate erogenous sensations. However, sensual preferences are highly individulized – what is pleasurable for one man may be painful, annoying, or aesthetically displeasing to another.

**The Path of Sperm: Part I**  The scrotum contains a male's primary reproductive organs, the paired *testicles* (Figure 3.3). Their name derives from the Latin verb meaning "to testify." (In Roman civilization, oaths were sworn to while cupping the testicles in the right hand.) By gently squeezing the scrotum, the testicles can be felt to be egg-shaped bodies, about two inches long. They are similar in firmness to a flexed muscle. Like muscles, testicles become less firm with age.

*Sperm Production*  The testicles produce the male reproductive cells, called *sperm*, by the process of *spermatogenesis*. In each of the paired

testicles is a mass of tiny, convoluted tubes called *seminiferous tubules* along whose walls sperm are prolifically produced. A normal pair of testicles generates over 100 million sperm each day.

Seminiferous tubules of each testicle converge and empty into a single duct, the *epididymis*. The extended length of an epididymis is several yards, but it is folded back and forth against itself many times to form a compact structure adhering to the surface of the testicle. It can be felt through the skin of the scrotum, as a bump; but it tends to be extremely tender to the touch. Between ejaculations sperm are stored within the epididymises.

Each epididymis straightens into a thin tube, the *vas deferens*, that ascends into the abdomen. They loop over the bladder and form *ampullae*,

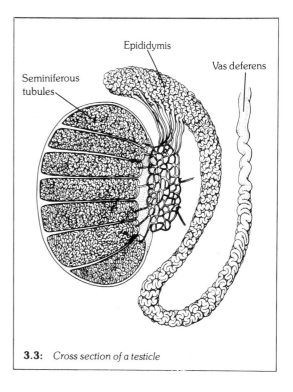

**3.3:**  *Cross section of a testicle*

which are convoluted ducts somewhat like epididymises. Toward the ends of the ampullae, the sperm combine with fluid from the paired *seminal vesicles*. This fluid activates sperm, stimulating their whip-like tails into rhythmic swimming movements. After merging with the seminal vesicles, the ampullae enter the *prostate gland*, a muscular organ, via two tiny *ejaculatory ducts*. Secretion from the prostate adds to the *semen* (spem plus the fluid bathing them). In fact, the prostate gland produces most of the semen – a fluid with a characteristic milky hue and a slightly gelatinous consistency.

In addition to producing semen, the prostate gland also plays a function in the elimination of urine. Within it, the *urinary duct* joins the bladder with the ejaculatory ducts, forming a single tube, the *urethra*. The urethra passes through the penis and performs the dual function of eliminating urine and transporting semen. The musculature within the prostate is such that a man cannot normally urinate with a full erection.

Beyond the prostate are the paired *Cowper's glands*, the final organs of secretion along the path of the urethra. These glands are each about the size of a pea, and the liquid they produce is clear and sticky. It commonly oozes from the urethral meatus of the erect penis prior to ejacu-

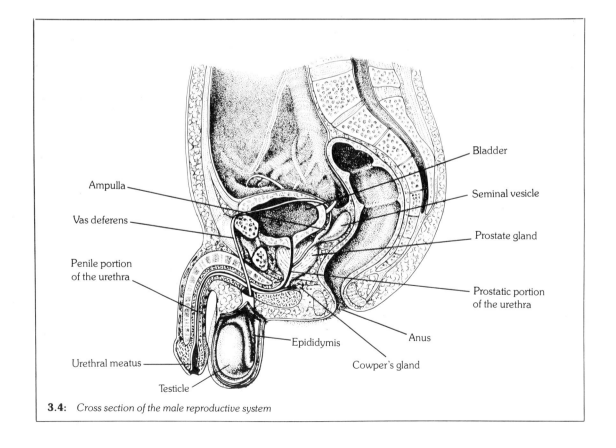

**3.4:** *Cross section of the male reproductive system*

lation. The alkalinity of the secretion from Cowper's glands protects sperm by neutralizing acids in the male urethra and in the vagina. For persons who practice the withdrawal method of birth control, the fluid from the Cowper's glands has an ominous property – it often contains tens of thousands of sperm. Thus, fertiliaztion may result even without ejaculation.

*Ejaculation of Semen*   *Ejaculation*, the forceful expulsion of about a teaspoon of semen, involves contractions of the vasa deferentia, seminal vesicles, prostate, and penis.

Ejaculation occurs in two distinct phases, the first of which is accumulation of semen within the prostate, where it is held back for two to three seconds by a sphincter muscle surrounding the prostate portion of the urethra. During this brief interval, the man is aware that ejaculation (and orgasm) is imminent and there is nothing he can do to stop it. In the second stage the sphincter opens, and rhythmic muscle contractions along the urethra and at the base of the penis eject the semen. The first few contractions occur at about one-second intervals and may be forceful enough to propel semen over a foot beyond the tip of an uncontained penis. Within three to four seconds, however, the contractions taper off to slow, weak pulsations of the penis muscles. Expulsions of semen consequently taper off and cease within a maximum of fifteen seconds.

Ejaculation into the bladder via the urinary duct, or *retrograde ejaculation* is rare but may occur because of prostate infection, certain illnesses, or as a side-effect of tranquilizers. Retrograde ejaculation happens when the sphincter muscle that normally closes the urinary duct during erection remains open; consequently, the muscle contractions of ejaculation force semen up into the bladder rather than out through the urethra. The sensation of orgasm during retro-grade ejaculation is about the same as it is during a normal ejaculation, but little or no semen appears at the *urethral meatus* (orifice of the urethra). Obviously, retrograde ejaculation comes as quite a surprise the first time it happens, but it causes no harm. However, it might indicate the existence of an underlying health problem. If a man experiences repeated retrograde ejaculations, he should seek medical attention.

**The Female Genitals**

The external genitals of the female are known collectively as the *vulva*. Women who wish to examine their genitals can use a hand mirror to clearly view all the external structures.

The fatty mound approximately six inches below the navel is the *mons veneris*, which at puberty develops a covering of hair.

The *labia majora* (literally, "major lips") are two mounds of flesh that extend from the mons veneris along the midline between the legs. The

outer sides of the labia majora are darkly pigmented and covered with hair; the inner labia majora are smooth, hairless, and tender. Between the labia majora lie the labia minora, clitoris, and the urethral and vaginal openings (Figure 3.5b).

**The Labia Minora and Clitoris**   Within the fold of the labia majora are the *labia minora*, ("minor lips"). During sexual arousal, the labia minora engorge with blood, and as they swell two to three times their unstimulated size, they protrude from the labia majora. The labia minora contain nerve endings connected to pleasure centers in the brain and with heightened sexual tension, they become increasingly sensitive.

Somewhat analogous to the penis, the *clitoris*, is the center of female erotic arousal. Unlike the penis, however, the clitoris serves no direct reproductive function. In the absence of sexual arousal, the clitoris is almost hidden by a hood of flesh at the peak of the labia minora.

The clitoris is composed of two corpora cavernosa, which engorge with blood during sexual arousal. It also contains high densities of touch- and pressure-sensitive nerve endings, which are most concentrated in the tip, or *glans clitoris*. The overall length of the glans clitoris plus shaft is usually between one-quarter of an inch and one inch.

Visible enlargement and engorgement of the glans and labia minora occur late in the excitement phase of sexual arousal. Immediately before and during orgasm, the clitoris withdraws beneath the clitoral hood and may flatten and recede to half its unstimulated length (See Figure 3.11). Although initial enlargement of the organ indicates sexual excitement, its subsequent retraction should not be interpreted as a loss of sexual tension or arousal. The clitoris is so often compared to the penis that its normal response is

misinterpreted. On the contrary, what seems like a lost "erection" may indeed be a preorgasmic or orgasmic clitoris. In some women, an attempt to directly contact the clitoris when orgasm is imminent may create more pain than pleasure. But, indirect stimulation of it by rhythmically applied pressure on the labia majora and the mons veneris usually enhances erogenous sensations. Also, stroking or licking the labia minora may indirectly stimulate the clitoris by pulling the clitoral hood back and forth along it.

**Urethral and Vaginal Orifices**   The orifices of the urethra and vagina lie between the labia minora. The urethral orifice (or, *meatus*) is between the clitoris and vagina, and is barely visible. Unlike the male urethra, the sole function of the female urethra is elimination of urine.

The vaginal orifice lies at the rear juncture of the labia minora and in some women, may be partially closed by a thin membrane, the *hymen*. If the hymen is intact at the time of first intercourse (it often is not), the experience can be painful. However, the pain which some women feel during their first intercourse is due more to tension, fear, and anxiety than to torn flesh. In anticipation of intercourse, a woman can gently stretch the hymen with her fingers, or a doctor can do it by a simple surgical technique during an office call.

The vaginal opening is separated from the anus (the orifice of solid elimination) by a band of erotically sensitive muscular tissue, the *perineum*.

On either side of the vaginal opening are two small organs that produce a secretion during sexual arousal. Called *Bartholin's glands*, these organs were once thought to play a role in vaginal lubrication, but research by Masters and Johnson refuted this persumption. By using an "artificial coital" machine, it was discovered that most of the lubrication comes from the walls of the vagina, itself:

> The artificial coital equipment was created by radiophysicists. The penises are plastic and were developed with the same optics as plate glass. Cold-light illumination allows observation and recording without distortion. The equipment can be adjusted for physical variations in size, weight, and vaginal development. The rate and depth of penile thrust is initiated and controlled completely by the responding individual. As tension elevates, rapidity and depth of thrust are increased voluntarily, paralleling subjective demand. The equipment is powered electrically.
>
> . . . Neither the healthy cervix nor the Bartholin's glands make any essential contribution to the total of vaginal lubrication. . . . As sexual tensions rise, a "sweating" phenomenon may be observed developing on the walls of the vaginal barrel. Individual

droplets of transudation-like, mucoid material appear scattered throughout the rugal folds of the normal vaginal architecture. These individual droplets present a picture somewhat akin to that of the perspiration-beaded forehead (Masters and Johnson, 1966).

**The Inner Vagina**    The *vagina* is a collapsible, tubular organ, which extends up and toward the back of the abdomen. Located between the bladder and *rectum* (the terminal portion of the large intestine), the vagina is lined with a wrinkled, elastic mucous membrane.

As described in the preceding excerpt from *Human Sexual Response*, the vagina's first reaction to sexual arousal is the secretion ("sweating") of a mucous-like lubricating fluid. As sexual tension heightens, the vagina develops a second physiological response – the inner two-thirds of it

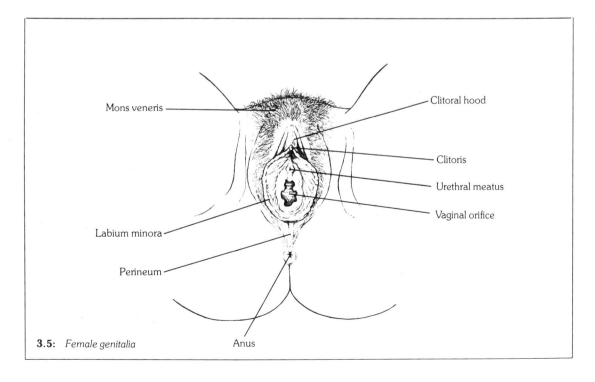

Mons veneris

Clitoral hood

Clitoris

Urethral meatus

Vaginal orifice

Labium minora

Perineum

**3.5:** *Female genitalia*        Anus

expands. Referred to as tenting, this phenomenon results when the muscles that normally hold the vagina closed begin to relax, and the ligaments between the vagina and the pelvic bone contract. Elevation of the uterus, which is connected to the upper end of the vagina, also adds to tenting. According to Masters and Johnson, sweating and tenting indicate a level of female sexual arousal comparable to that indicated by a male's erection.

As a source of erotic sensation, the vagina is less sensitive than the clitoris. However, the outer third of the vagina, the *orgasmic platform*, responds to stimulation at a level similar to that of the labia minora and the other tissues immediately surrounding the vaginal orifice. During orgasm the orgasmic platform undergoes a series of rhythmic contractions similar to those of the urethra of an ejaculating male.

**The Uterus, Fallopian Tubes, and Ovaries**
Located behind the bladder, the *uterus*, or womb, is a muscular receptacle with a size and shape similar to a pear. The small end of it, the *cervix*, can be felt as the smooth, firm knob at the end of the vagina. A narrow opening through the cervix, the *os*, joins the uterine cavity with the vagina.

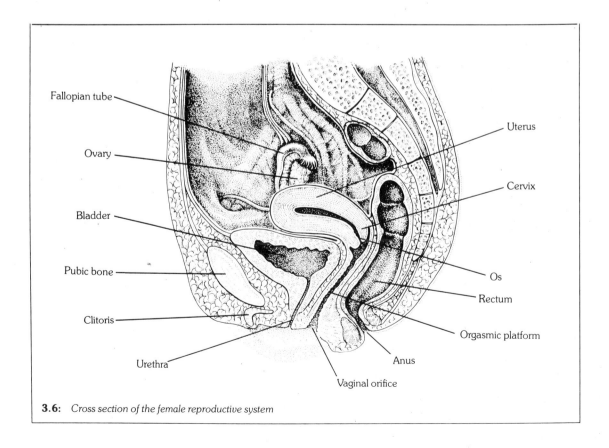

**3.6:** *Cross section of the female reproductive system*

The inner lining of the uterus, the *endometrium*, is a delicate tissue, permeated with tiny blood vessels. If fertilization occurs, the embryo settles into the endometrium and receives nourishment from it. When a woman is not pregnant, the endometrium cyclically thickens and degenerates in monthly periods of menstrual bleeding, which are expulsions of endometrial blood and tissue. (See Chapter 4 for further discussion of the menstrual cycle.)

The uterus is held in place by two *broad ligaments* that stretch to opposite sides of the pelvic bone (Figure 3.7). Within the upper edge of each broad ligament is a narrow duct, the *Fallopian tube*, which is about four inches long. These soft tubes, which resemble miniature saxophones, are attached to the sides of the uterus and enter it through small pores, approximately one-sixteenth inch wide.

The *ovaries* are female *gonads* (a synonym for primary reproductive organs). They produce *ova* (eggs) and the female hormones, *estrogen* and *progesterone*. Ovaries are similar in shape to the male gonads, or testicles. They are suspended from the broad ligaments, and stalk-like ligaments containing blood vessels connect them to the uterus. Near the ovaries Fallopian tubes open into delicate *infundibula* which sometimes

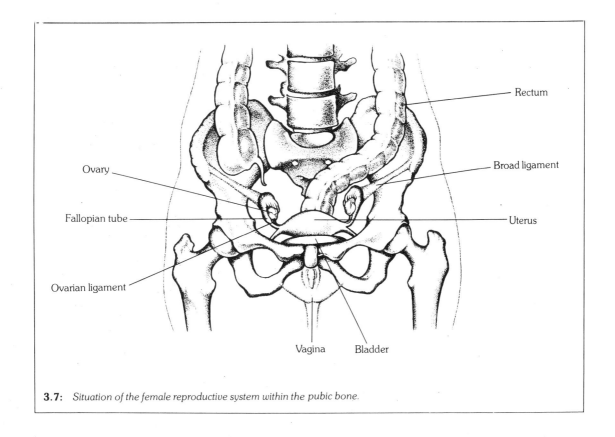

**3.7:** *Situation of the female reproductive system within the pubic bone.*

cling to ovaries but are not attached. Ova are embedded in capsules, or follicles, near the surfaces of ovaries. Each follicle contains only one ovum.

A female infant is born with about 400,000 immature follicles, but unlike testicles, which continually produce new sperm throughout the years of a man's sexual maturity, ovaries do not generate new follicles after birth. A female's birthright is more than enough, however, since only about 400 ova reach maturity over the course of her fertile years.

Each month one or the other ovary (not both) releases an egg on a day approximately midway between the menstrual periods. The moment of release, or *ovulation*, is preceded by a period of follicle growth. As it expands from a microscopic speck to a fluid-filled pocket with a half-inch span, the follicle dwarfs its egg (which only reaches a diameter of about .005 inch). Ultimately the surface of the follicle bursts, and the egg floats outward.

Following ovulation an egg drifts (it has no apparent means of locomotion) into the infundibulum of a Fallopian tube. There are no ducts between the ovaries and Fallopian tubes, so, for a brief time, the egg hangs suspended in abdominal fluid. It has been suggested that the hairlike

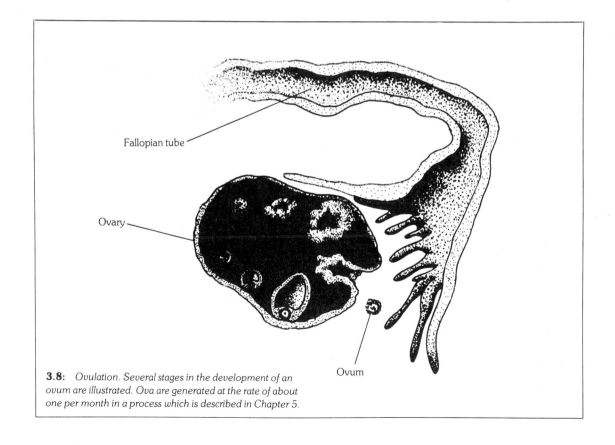

Fallopian tube

Ovary

Ovum

**3.8:**  *Ovulation. Several stages in the development of an ovum are illustrated. Ova are generated at the rate of about one per month in a process which is described in Chapter 5.*

projections that form velvety linings along Fallopian tubes, set up currents with rhythmic lashing movements to draw eggs inward; however, the actual process is not known. Undoubtedly some eggs never make it into a Fallopian tube, in which case they are probably absorbed into the abdominal fluid.

An unfertilized egg has a short life. If is isn't fertilized within twenty-four hours following ovulation, it ceases to be viable. Therefore, because it travels only an inch per day along a Fallopian tube, an egg must be fertilized long before it reaches the uterus.

**The Path of Sperm: Part II**    An average ejaculation deposits one to four hundred million sperm within the vagina. Because only one of them can fertilize an egg, this number seems excessive. However, if the ejaculate contains less than 20,000,000 sperm, it is unlikely that fertilization will occur.

There are several reasons why so many sperm are necessary to fertilize one egg. To begin with, in the ejaculates of even the most healthy men, a small percentage of sperm are "dead on arrival" – they lack the whiplike tail movements necessary to propel them though the uterus and Fallopian tube. Furthermore, the vagina is a hostile environment for sperm. Its secretions are acidic, and sperm survive best in slightly alkaline surroundings. Although semen is a powerful buffer, many sperm are immobilized by the acidity of the vagina within a few minutes. Only a small fraction of the sperm live long enough to find their way through the os, into the uterus. Masters and Johnson found that female orgasm widens the os slightly, thus increasing accessibility to the uterus by sperm. The effect is not significant enough, however, to give credence to the myth that a woman's restraint from orgasm is an effective method of contraception.

Uterine fluid is more alkaline than vaginal fluid, so once sperm make it through the cervical os, conditions are more favorable for their survival. Nevertheless, their difficulties are not over. They must find their way into the correct Fallopian tube. It is theorized that the egg gives off a guiding chemical that seeps into the uterus and helps sperm to "home in."

Fertilization usually occurs in the portion of the Fallopian tube closest to an ovary, and only one sperm combines with the egg to form the first cell of the embryo. However, several sperm participate in the process.

Prior to fertilization the egg is surrounded by a layer of small cells, left clinging to it by the follicle. Sperm gather around the egg and prod or bump against it. At the same time, the sperm release a chemical (similar to a digestive enzyme) that dissolves the surrounding cell mass. One sperm eventually breaks through and surges into the interior of the egg. Simultaneously a membrane forms around the egg, preventing entrance by other sperm. The cell wall of the fertilizing sperm dissolves, and its contents merge with the contents of the egg.

**Infertility**

About 10% of American couples are involuntarily childless, and the percentage is rising, primarily because people are delaying having children till after the optimum years of fertility, the mid-twenties. Damage to reproductive organs from venereal disease (which is epidemic throughout the nation), and complications arising from birth control pills, abortion, and IUDs also contribute to infertility.

Approximately 40% of the cases of infertility in America have been attributed to problems with the male reproductive structures and most of the remainder to problems with the female organs

(Speroff, et. al., 1973). However, infertility is a relative affair; a male who cannot achieve fertilization with one woman may be capable of it with another, and vice versa. Some people are more fertile than others. Moreover, psychological factors come into play. In cases of *erectile dysfunction* (also known as "impotence"), the male's inability to achieve erection is generally a problem of the mind. Other types of infertility may have less obvious psychological roots.

In certain cases, infertility is temporary; a woman may be rendered infertile for a few months by a uterine infection, for example. In other cases, the deficiency is more permanent. It might involve congenitally deficient reproductive organs or genetic/hormonal shortcomings. Various surgical and hormonal techniques have been devised to treat infertility, all with attendant risks.

In certain cases "infertility" can be "cured" simply by modifying the frequency or position of intercourse (Masters and Johnson, 1975). The couple should have intercourse every 24 to 48 hours during the most fertile time of the month (midway between menstrual cycles). The "missionary" position (with the woman flat on her back) is generally the most conducive for fertilization; but this might not be the case, depending on the way the uterus is oriented in the abdomen. If, after six months to a year, fertilization has not occurred, the advice of a fertility expert might be helpful.

**Male Infertility**   In the male, causes of infertility include insufficient sperm production, inactivity of the sperm, and obstructions along the sperm ducts. The problem may begin with infections or injury to the testicles, insufficient hormone production by the thyroid or pituitary gland, or prostate disease. *Varicoceles*, which are varicose veins in the scrotum, are thought to con-

tribute to infertility by blocking the flow of blood to the developing sperm.

Certain hormonal treatments for infertility are now in development; anyone considering such treatments should realize that they are experimental. The treatments focus on improving an existing, but low, sperm count. If there are no sperm present, there is no effective drug treatment.

If an obstruction of the sperm ducts is the cause of infertility, microsurgical techniques are sometimes applied. Varicoceles can also be removed surgically. A success rate of 50% for such surgery has been claimed (Kaercher, 1979).

**Female Infertility**   Women may be infertile because of a failure to ovulate, blockage of the Fallopian tubes, or *hostile mucus*. The latter is an aptly termed secretion by the cervix which mires the sperm, keeping them from passing through to the uterus. A gonorrheal infection which has progressed to the Fallopian tubes can cause irreversible blockage. Recent developments in "test tube" fertilization offer hope for women with blocked tubes. Such techniques, however, are not widely available at present (see Chapter 4). More commonly, an attempt is made to open the tubes surgically. The success rate is low, however; estimates range from 10% to 50%.

When failure to ovulate is the problem, treatment with the drug *clomid* is a common measure. This works in about 70% of the women to whom it is applied. Sometimes, however, it work too well, resulting in multiple births.

Other treatments include antibiotics to control infections, and douching with solutions designed to neutralize acidic vaginal secretions. For women with hostile mucus, the physician may recommend artificial insemination by injecting sperm directly into the uterus, via the cervix.

**Allergic Infertility**   Certain relatively rare forms of infertility result from bizarre allergic reactions. The woman may have an allergic response to sperm, and produce antibodies which kill them. Or the male may be autoimmune, producing both sperm and the antibodies which kill them at the same time. In certain cases, an allergic incompatability exists only with certain partners, and not with others.

**Erotic Stimulation**

For most people, a day never passes without some thought of sexual activity. Sometimes a passing erotic fantasy is enough to assuage sexual urges; other times the desire for orgasm is so compelling that total psychic and physical energies are directed toward it.

There are as many ways to find sexual satisfaction as there are people seeking it. From those who are confirmed abstainers from sexual activities to those whose total creative energies are focused on finding new ways to "do it" – every individual has his or her own way of experiencing eroticism.

Everyone has unique sexual preferences: What is pleasurably stimulating for one person may be irritating, repulsive, or painful to another. Thus, preoccupation with technique can be self-defeating if it detracts from awareness of the desires of a partner. Fondling, caressing, kissing, rubbing, probing, sucking, licking, and so forth of the genitals and other parts of the body are potentially pleasing activities; but if they are done without sensitivity, the effect is likely to be ludicrous rather than sensuous. Partners should open their eyes (at least once in a while) to keep in touch with the desires that only facial expressions, not words, can reveal. Of course, partners should also feel free to speak their desires.

To some extent deliberate control over one's sexual characteristics is impossible. Conscious control may be contradicted by physical capacities, innate urges, or deeply ingrained psychological hang-ups. Thus, both physical and mental factors contribute to the overall pattern of an individual's sexual being. Each individual is sexually unique, yet certain physiological characteristics of sexual stimulation are the same for everyone.

**Sensory Stimulation**   Sensory stimulation – such as the sight of a potential sex partner, the touch of a kiss, or the smell of sexual secretions – set off impulses to the brain and spinal cord via neurons (Figure 3.9). Some of the impulses initiate thoughts and emotions; others trigger responses that do not enter the realm of consciousness. Even an unconscious man can be aroused to erection by gentle stroking of his glans penis.

The mechanism of erection involves nerve paths between the penis and the lower portion of the spinal cord. Stimulation of the penis or the surrounding area (particularly the inner thighs) sends impulses to the spinal cord along touch-sensitive nerves. Within the spinal cord the impulses are transferred to neurons which extend to the base of the penis. These neurons control dilation of the arteries that enter the penis. The arteries are stimulated to expand and a rush of blood fills the spongy tissue of the penis. Men who are paralyzed from the waist down and have no feeling in their lower bodies will react in the same way, if the *reflex arc* of nerve cells between the lower spinal column and penis is intact.

However, this simple reflex arc can be prevented from functioning by uncontrollable signals from the brain. This condition, which is called *erectile dysfunction*, or *impotency*, is usually temporary; but it obviously is the source of great frustration. Even when he consciously wills an erection, the man who is experiencing impotency is prevented from achieving it by "unconscious" messages from his mind. (The nature of "unconscious" mental activity is not precisely known, but theories relating to it are discussed later in this chapter.) However, some men are able to consciously direct their sexual functions, including erection and ejaculation. Like erection, ejaculation involves a spinal reflex arc and can be

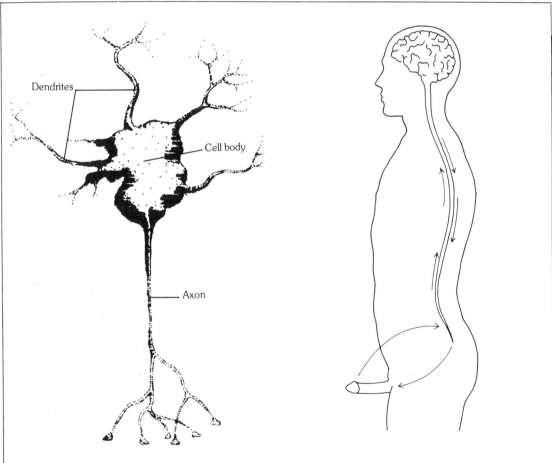

**3.9:**  *A neuron – the basic unit of the nervous system. An axon carries impulses toward the cell body; dendrites carry impulses away from the cell body. An axon may receive impulses from an organ of sensation or from a dendrite of another neuron.*

**3.10:**  *The reflex of ejaculation . . . impulses from the brain impinge via the spinal cord.*

consciously delayed if it will enhance either partner's sexual satisfaction (Figure 3.10).

Similar reflex arcs and mental modifiers are involved in the female sexual system. Inability to achieve orgasm and *vaginismus* (tightening of the vaginal musculature to the point that it is impenetrable) are problems that may arise if the female mental/physiological concert is out of tune.

Sexual arousal, therefore, is a complex and individually unique phenomenon involving both conscious and unconscious reactions to sensory stimulation.

**Touch**   Touch is the most basic and direct means of sexual stimulation. Ultimately it is though touch that orgasm is usually achieved (although there are reports, that some people arrive at orgasm through fantasy alone). For most people orgasm occurs only after direct, rhythmically applied pressure to the genitals, but stimulation to other parts of the body can also be orgasmic. For example, some women can achieve orgasm through stimulation of their breasts.

There are many other areas of the body that respond to touch, including the lips and interior of the mouth, the ears, buttocks, thighs, and many others. Known as erogenous zones, these areas vary from person to person — what is sexually arousing to one person may not be for another. Some men, for instance, find massaging of their nipples to be pleasurable, while others find it unpleasant.

**Sight**   The visual world is a strong source of sexual stimulation and gratification. Currently, the pornography industry is booming — spurred on by a seemingly insatiable desire by the public for new and different depictions of sexual fantasy. For many people visual stimuli (a 'Playboy' or 'Playgirl' magazine foldout, for instance) furnish inspiration for masturbatory fantasies. Often, however, a momentary rush of nonorgasmic sensation is all that is wanted from a visual stimuli.

**Taste and Smell**   Responses to these closely related senses vary widely. For example, some people find the odors and tastes associated with *cunnilingus* (oral stimulation of the female genitals) and *fellatio* (oral stimulation of the male genitals) are exciting, while others find them repulsive.

Many species of animals (including most mammals) produce odiferous substances, called *pheromones*, that stimulate sexual responses by the opposite sex. Whether or not pheromones are involved in human sexual response is not known. If they are, however, conscious recognition of the effects of them has been suppressed. Although the makers of deodorants and mouthwashes perpetuate the American obsession with body and mouth odors, it is important to realize that certain odors that some might find offensive could be erotically stimulating to others.

**Sound**   Sound is transmitted through air as a series of pressure waves, and it stimulates the sense of hearing by setting the eardrums in vibration. If the volume is great enough, other parts within the body can also react in a similar way; however, the effects of sound on sexual response are subtle. For example, the sound of high volume music is not only perceived through the sense of hearing, but the vibrations also stimulate other internal membranes and organs. The almost primitive rhythms of some modern music seems to have been influenced by the rhythmic pelvic thrusts of sexual intercourse. Many people find that music enhances lovemaking.

Sensory stimulation is a basic element of a sexual encounter, but no less important is the context. Unusual surroundings or circumstances, for instance, can contribute to the enjoyment of an erotic encounter.

### Erotic Response

The last few decades have brought an increase of scientific interest in sex as a physical phenomenon. Foremost among contemporary researchers of sexual physiology are William Masters and Virginia Johnson, who analyzed orgasmic responses of several hundred individuals and reported their findings in the landmark book, *Human Sexual Response*. Through their work they have revealed striking similarities and subtle differences in the sexual responses of men and women.

Masters and Johnson describe the sexual response patterns of both sexes as occurring in four phases: *excitement*, *plateau*, *orgasm*, and *resolution*. These "phases" flow into one another during a sexual experience; there are no abrupt shifts. The "phases" are generalizations from which every individual has unique deviations. (See the excerpt from *Human Sexual Response* that follows this chapter.)

**Excitement Phase** For people of both sexes, a general rise in body tension accompanies the anticipation of a sexual experience. This response, termed *myotonia*, is centered in the nerves and muscles and becomes more intense during succeeding stages of the response cycle. Also during the excitement phase the rate of heartbeat quickens, with a consequent rise in blood pressure. By a process called *vasocongestion*, blood rushes to the spongy tissues within and nearby the genitals. For women (who have more congestive tissue in the pubic area than do men) there is an accumulation of blood in the clitoris, labia minora, and the entrance of the vagina. Pressure within vasocongested tissues

sets off impulses along neurons leading to pleasure centers in the brain, and the caresses of sex play stimulate more frequent impulses. Vasocongestion may also develop in the tiny blood vessels just beneath the surface of the skin of the breasts, abdomen and shoulders, where a *sex flush* may appear, particularly on hot days. For most women and a smaller number of men, the nipples become congested and erect.

The definitive signs of the excitement phase are penile erection and vaginal lubrication, both primarily vasocongestive phenomena. The penis becomes erect as the congestive tissues within it (the corpora cavernosa and corpus spongiosum) fill with blood. Within the vaginal wall vasocongestion causes mucoid secretions to "sweat" from many small pores.

As the excitement phase blends into the plateau phase, muscular contractions cause shifts

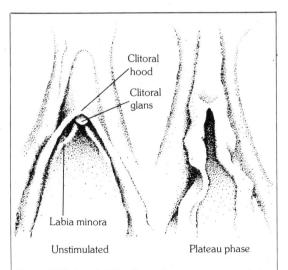

Clitoral hood

Clitoral glans

Labia minora

Unstimulated                    Plateau phase

**3.11:** *Withdrawal of the clitoris during sexual arousal. As the labia minora and clitoral hood engorge with blood, the clitoris retracts. Direct stimulation at the peak of arousal may be painful.*

of the internal sex organs. In women, contractions within the pelvis expand the inner two-thirds of the vagina (tenting), and the uterus rises up and back toward the spine. The vaginal barrel increases about an inch in length and expands to more than double its unstimulated width. In men, tightening of the muscles around the vasa deferentia draw the testicles upward. In fact the testicles may ultimately be drawn into the abdominal cavity before the response cycle is over. As they rise, the testicles become larger due to vasocongestion.

**Plateau Phase**  Transitions between the excitement and the plateau phases are not distinct. Rather, one phase merges into the other, and the intensity of sexual arousal rises and falls, particularly during the plateau stage. The plateau is the delicate balance between the peak of excitement and the release of orgasm, and much of the joy of sex is the titillation of the balance at this borderline.

As was previously discussed, a striking difference exists between the responses of the penis and clitoris at the pleateau of sexual response. For men, the glans penis continues to swell, and increasingly intense stimulation is usually desired (the urge to thrust more vigorously can be consciously suppressed, however, in order to delay ejaculation). For women, however, the clitoral glans withdraws beneath the clitoral hood at the peak of the labia minora, and direct stimulation of it may be painful. However, stimulating the clitoris indirectly (by licking or stroking the labia and mons veneris) may be extremely pleasurable. Futhermore, the erotic sensitivity of the labia minora, themselves, heightens as they become more congested with blood. The same is true for the first third of the vaginal barrel (the *orgasmic platform*), which constricts with increasing vasocongestion.

For both sexes myotonia and vasocongestion increase during the plateau phase. Myotonia is commonly manifested as spastic twitching and clutching movements of the hands and feet (*carpopedal spasms*). Intense vasocongestion is manifested in the red to burgundy hues of the labia minora. For males, a similar vasocongestive effect sometimes results in a purplish cast to the ridge of the glans penis.

Mucoid secretions also characterize the plateau phase for both sexes. In the female the Bartholin's glands, which are imbedded in the folds of the labia minora near the entrance of the vagina, secrete a small amount of fluid, the function of which is unknown. In males, Cowper's glands secrete a few drops of a clear mucoid fluid that oozes from the urethral meatus at the tip of the penis. This secretion is basic, and it neutralizes the acidity of the traces of urine in the urethra which would otherwise be harmful to the sperm.

As the level of excitation increases, the rates of breathing and heartbeat become more rapid. Vasocongestion and myotonia become more intense, as does erotic sensitivity.

**Orgasmic Phase**  For both sexes orgasm involves rhythmic contractions of the pelvic muscles accompanied by sensations of pleasurable release, which last from three to ten seconds. During orgasm there are overt demonstrations, including twisting, thrusting, screaming, laughing, or other expression of enjoyment, which differ from individual to individual and from situation to situation.

Male orgasm is initiated by contractions of the seminal vesicles, the vasa deferentia, and the prostate gland that compress seminal fluid behind the sphincter muscle surrounding the prostatic urethra. The sensation of this pre-ejaculatory phase, which lasts two to three sec-

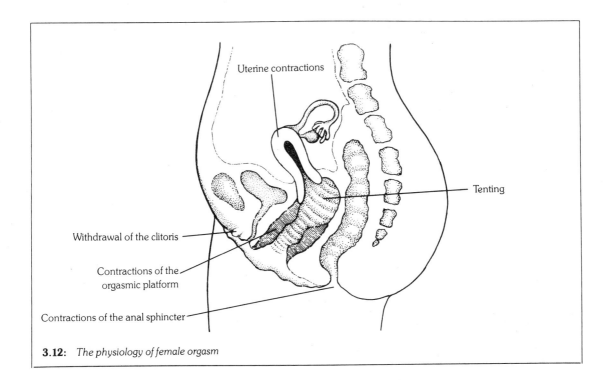

Uterine contractions

Tenting

Withdrawal of the clitoris

Contractions of the orgasmic platform

Contractions of the anal sphincter

**3.12:**  *The physiology of female orgasm*

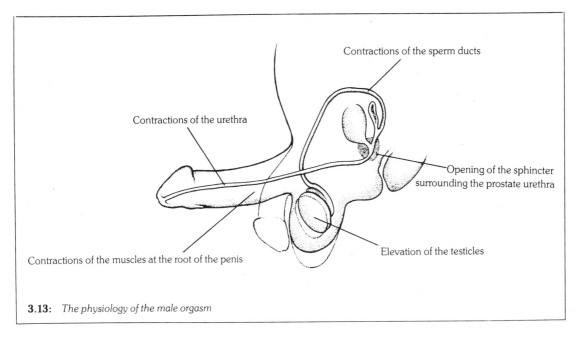

Contractions of the sperm ducts

Contractions of the urethra

Opening of the sphincter surrounding the prostate urethra

Contractions of the muscles at the root of the penis

Elevation of the testicles

**3.13:**  *The physiology of the male orgasm*

onds, is one of inevitability – the man knows that he is about to ejaculate, and he can do nothing to stop it. Ultimately the sphincter opens, and semen is pumped outward by pleasurable pulsating contractions of the muscles at the base of the penis. The contractions first occur at 0.8 second intervals but soon taper off – two or three expulsions are followed by a couple of slower, less forceful ones.

Female orgasm involves pleasurable, rhythmic contractions of the clitoris, uterus, and orgasmic platform. For a duration that, on the average, lasts about twice as long as male orgasm, the female sex organs throb – four to eight highly stimulating pulsations (at 0.8 second intervals) are followed by a few weaker ones.

For people of both sexes rhythmic contractions of the rectal sphincter synchronize with the pulsations of the reproductive organs. Rectal contractions are normally weak, but it is possible to consciously ·enhance them by forcefully contracting the muscles of the buttocks and thighs.

**Resolution Phase**    Following orgasm, men pass into a *refractory period* that begins when the nonexpulsive contractions of the penile urethra subside, and lasts until sexual tension is reduced to excitement-phase levels. During the refractory period, which may last less than ten minutes for young men but gradually increases with age, rearousal is impossible. Females have no refractory lapse and are capable of immediate rearousal to orgasm. Given continued stimulation, multiple orgasms in rapid succession are possible for women. Although some men prefer bringing a quick end to erotic play following orgasm, prolonged sensuous (if not orgasmic) pleasures are also possible for them.

After orgasm, the physiological characteristics of erotic arousal usually disappear more quickly for men than for women. Blood recedes from the penis more rapidly than it leaves the clitoris, orgasmic platform, and labia minora.

For people of both sexes, loss of vasocongestion and myotonia are slower when orgasm has not been achieved. When sexual arousal has been maintained at plateau levels without orgasm for extended periods (as is common for prostitutes), loss of vasocongestion may take an hour or more. In such cases the pressure can be highly irritating, but it can be relieved by masturbation to orgasm. When orgasm has been achieved, vasocongestion and myotonia may be lost within a matter of minutes after stimulation ceases, particularly if the duration of the encounter – from excitement to resolution – has been brief.

Sensitivity to the unique sensual desires of one's mate is particularly important during the resolution phase. When a woman might prefer continued stroking of her genitals, her mate might like having his back massaged. The sensual desires of both partners cannot always be satisfied at the same time; but with a little ingenuity, and honest communication, a couple should have no trouble finding a mutually satisfying give-and-take of sensual pleasures.

### The Kaplan Model

In the years since Masters and Johnson first published their interpertation of the human sexual response cycle, other researchers have published what they feel are the physiological highlights of the phenomenon.

Helen Singer Kaplan suggests that the four-phase formulation of Masters and Johnson obscures what is basically a two-phase process (Kaplan, 1974). Kaplan's first phase is the "vasocongestive reaction" during which a male's penis becomes erect and a female's vagina begins to lubricate. In the second phase, reflex muscular contractions result in the sensation of orgasm for both sexes. Although Kaplan's model of erotic response embodies little that is new in the way of physiological revelations, her ideas have significant psychosexual implications. For instance, Kaplan concludes that the male vasocongestive response is more vulnerable to psychic influences than is the female vasocongestive response. Hence inability to achieve erection is a common problem for men, but inhibition of lubrication is relatively rare for women. On the other hand, female orgasm seems more vulnerable to inhibition than male orgasm — inability to achieve orgasm is more common among women than men.

### "Recreational" Drugs

Among the remaining hieroglyphs of ancient Egypt is evidence that at least one person of the age believed the radish to be an *aphrodisiac* (a substance which is said to enhance sex drive). Perhaps he was mistaking heart burn for ardor; at any rate, the idea didn't catch on. In view of the many persistent myths about aphrodisiacs, however, it is surprising that would-be satyrs aren't still popping radishes.

Oysters still have a following as an aphrodisiac (it's been suggested that their vague resemblance to the vulva started the story), as do sheep's testicles (Rocky Mountain oysters). To date, however, no substance has been shown to consistently enhance sex drive, or otherwise make sexual intercourse more pleasuable. Some of them, including the infamous "Spanish fly," are poisonous.

The most widely accepted beliefs in drugs as sexual stimulants concern those substances which alter perceptions and moods, such as alcohol and marijuana. A poll of 500 psychiatrists showed that over half of them believed that "small dosages of alcohol and marijuana enhance lovemaking" (Gallant, 1978). According to Gallant, however, "A combination of sexual dsyfunction and feelings of sexual inadequacy are bound to develop after prolonged dependence upon alcohol or drugs to enhance the sexual performance or satisfaction."

### Health Implications

Aversions to certain sexual activities are sometimes based purely on sensual grounds (some people might not like the taste of semen, for example), but questions of health may also be inhibiting. For example, many people worry about the hygienics of oral-genital contact. In general, both cunnilingus and fellatio are harmless. But, if the male gets carried away during felatio, and thrusts too deeply, he can cause his partner to choke — a momentary problem, perhaps, but certainly one that tends to cool passions.

Anal intercourse may cause somewhat more serious health problems. When done frequently or too vigorously it can cause hemorrhoids or otherwise damage the tissues of the anus. If a heterosexual couple switches orifices in mid-intercourse, there is danger of infecting the vagina with microbes from the anus. Risks to the male who is on the giving end of anal intercourse include *urethritis* (infection of the urethra) and *cystitis* (infection of the bladder) from the common bacteria of the anus, *E. Coli*. If, in spite of the risks, a couple feels moved to perform anal intercourse, certain precautions may be taken. Wearing a condom gives protection from the infections just mentioned, as well as certain of the venereal diseases which are discussed in Chapter 7. Penetration should be gentle; otherwise there is danger of tearing the sphincter muscle of the anus. Lubrication with saliva or K-Y jelly (available at any drugstore) is advisable.

State law can be a factor that limits the variety of sexual interaction between consenting adults. However, there are probably no laws that are more flagrantly violated. In recent years some states have repealed restrictive sex laws and others are expected to follow suit.

## Eroticism and Aging

Erotic capability and desire change with time; nevertheless, many older people enjoy active sex lives into and beyond their seventies. For some, however, poor health requires a (usually temporary) curtailment of sexual activities. For example, the elevation of blood pressures that accompanies erotic arousal can be dangerous for people who have suffered heart attacks. But, most older people (including those who have recovered from heart attacks) can safely experience sexual intercourse.

Contrary to what many believe, people don't play themselves out with "too much" sex when they are younger; in fact, people who are highly sexually active in youth tend to be relatively active in old age. With an end to the possibility of pregnancy and an abundance of leisure time, old age can be a time of renewed interest in sex and other satisfying endeavors.

For men, aging is characterized by a decrease in virility – erections occur less often and it takes more direct manual or oral stimulation for them to become firm. But, once achieved, erection can be maintained longer. Hence, men who were "premature" ejaculators in younger years may not be troubled with the problem as they grow older. However, there may be somewhat of a tendency to lose what control one has managed to achieve over orgasm. In general, there is less of a sensation when orgasm is imminent (so, it may come as a surprise). At other times, no

matter how hard the male tries, he cannot achieve orgasm. At such times one should learn when to call it quits (prolonged intercourse may become painful or even boring for the female), and look forward to the next time. As a rule, the desire for erotic activity will return sooner when a male has not come to orgasm.

In women, following the drop in hormonal output by the ovaries during menopause, the vagina lubricates less and its tissues lose suppleness. Consequently, intercourse can be painful for some older women. However, artificially lubricating (with saliva or lubricating jelly) loosens and soothes the vagina. Hormone substitution therapy has also been successfully used to rejuvenate tissues and restore lubrication; however, presently there is much debate over the advisability of long-term hormone therapy. For many older people sexual relations diminish or stop because of reasons other than the physiological changes of the aging process. After many years with the same partner, for example, monotony may set in. Sometimes preoccupations with hobbies, art, or religious activities add to an older person's indifference to sex. Whatever the reason, many senior citizens find a disparity growing between themselves and their mates over how much sexual activity to have.

Ours is not an easy culture in which to grow old. Americans are obsessed with sex, and with that goes a preoccupation with youth and a fear of aging. Older people, who once might not have considered a diminishing sex drive problematical, are now being deluged with the presumption that sex is the ultimate experience. Realistically, sex is a lovely form of communication, but it must be emphasized that it is only one of many. If anyone, no matter the age, finds that intercourse fails to satisfy his or her needs, it should not always be construed as a danger signal. For many, especially older people, love and affection are often given and received in nonsexual ways.

## Sexual Dysfunctions – Physical Roots

Because erotic experience is unique for every individual, it is difficult to apply precise definitions to sexual problems, or *dysfunctions*. Nevertheless, certain problems occur with sufficient frequency to warrant generalized descriptions. For men the most common problems are *erectile dysfunction* (failure to achieve or maintain an erection, also called "impotence"), *premature ejaculation* (inability to delay ejaculation), and *ejaculatory incompetence* (inability to ejaculate within a vagina). Women's most frequent difficulties are *orgasmic dysfunction* (failure to attain orgasm), *vaginismus* (tightening of the muscle surrounding the vagina to the point that it is impenetrable by a penis) and *dyspareunia* (painful intercourse).

Again, it must be emphasized that word "dysfunction" when applied to something as subjective as sexual experience is imprecise at best. For example, what one woman considers "premature" ejaculation may be perfectly timed for another. Similarly, a woman who suffers "orgasmic dysfunction" with one partner may find that she has no problem achieving orgasm with another. Furthermore, when a couple has a long history of sexual dissatisfaction it is difficult (if not impossible) to trace the problem to the origin. For example, a woman may develop vaginismus who has had a long relationship of frustrating sexuality with an impotent male, whose problems, in turn, may date back to his early childhood. Many contemporary psychologists believe it is more fruitful to concentrate on treating the problem in the here and now, rather than looking for its antecedents.

The majority of sexual malfunctions are psychologically rooted; however, there are also physical disturbances that can cause problems with sexual performance. Some diseases (including prostatitis, hepatitis, cirrhosis, diabetes, and epilepsy) can hamper or prevent sexual activities. In males spinal abnormalities, including spinal cord tumors, fractured vertebra, and multiple sclerosis can damage the neural reflex arcs of erection and ejaculation.

Certain surgical procedures may injure the genitals. In cases of advanced cancer of the prostate, for example, surgery may result in destruction of the neuromuscular mechanism of ejaculation. Poorly repaired *episiotomies* (incisions made during childbirth to widen the vaginal orifice) may result in vaginal pain during intercourse.

Hormonal deficiencies may also be at the root of sexual dysfunctions. Several of the endocrine glands secrete hormones which are involved in erotic functioning. The ovaries and testicles are the primary sources of sex hormones, but the adrenal glands produce them in lesser amounts. Hormones secreted by the pituitary and thyroid glands are also involved in sexual functioning. As discussed in Chapter 5, the endocrine glands are involved in complex (little understood) hormonal feedback systems, mediated by the bloodstream. Successes have been reported in treating certain cases of sexual dysfunction with hormonal therapy (Greenblatt, 1978). But, as discussed in later chapters, hormones administered to cure one problem may cause other health problems.

In spite of the many possible physical causes of sexual dysfunctions, most experts agree that the vast majority of cases have psychological rather than physiological roots. Consider, for example, an instance reported by Sarrel and Sarrel (1978):

A 24-year-old graduate student came to see us because he had difficulty maintaining an erection with his fiancee. Along with other relevant information we learned that when they lay naked together he usually kept his eyes closed. He felt somewhat embarrassed by the nudity, although in his upbringing his mother and sisters often were naked in his presence – skinny-dipping, using the bathroom, and so on. When asked for the specifics of his reactions to these nude at-home scenes, he recalled that he was always worried that he might have an erection; therefore he had concentrated on focusing his eyes from the neck up or tried to avoid the situations altogether.

He still felt self-conscious in the presence of a naked woman, including his fiancee. Now the conflict was that if he had an erection, he was concerned that she might feel pressured to have intercourse, and if he didn't have an erection, she might feel he was not a real man. After tracing back his reaction to nudity to the conditioning of his preadolescent and teen-aged years, he found he could look at his fiancee, and he had no further difficulty responding in her presence.

The literature of psychology abounds with such stories of early traumas and therapeutic successes in later life. This is the subject of Chapter 13.

## QUESTIONS

1. Eroticism and reproduction are biologically intertwined, but humans have found ways to separate them. What are your opinions on the morality of such separation?
2. Do you think there is a good hygienic rationale for circumcision, or do you believe it to be a hold-over of ritualized mutilation of genitals? Are you glad that you are "un"-circumcized? Circumcized?
3. What are your favorite erogenous zones? Have you let your sexual partner(s) know where they are?
4. If an ejaculation contains less than 20 million sperm, it is unlikely that fertilization will occur. Why are so many sperm necessary?

# Readings

## The Differentiation Between Men and Women

*Sigmund Freud*

*No one has had more influence on modern thought about human sexuality than Sigmund Freud, and no one's thoughts have raised greater controversy. The following excerpt is Freud at his most ire-provoking, discussing his theory of the development of libido (sex drive) during adolescence. His definitions of "masculine" and "feminine" are widely considered as erroneous, and his belief that the center of female erotic arousal must shift from the clitoris to the vagina during adolescence has been refuted.*

As we all know, it is not until puberty that the sharp distinction is established between the masculine and feminine characters. From that time on, this contrast has a more decisive influence than any other upon the shaping of human life. It is true that the masculine and feminine dispositions are already easily recognizable in childhood. The development of the inhibitions of sexuality (shame, disgust, pity, etc.) takes place in little girls earlier and in the face of less resistance than in boys; the tendency to sexual repression seems in general to be greater; and, where the component instincts of sexuality appear, they prefer the passive form. The autoerotic activity of the erotogenic zones is, however, the same in both sexes, and owing to this uniformity there is no possibility of a distinction between the two sexes such as arises after puberty. So far as the autoerotic and masturbatory manifestations of sexuality are concerned, we might lay it down that the sexuality of little girls is of a wholly masculine character. Indeed, if we were able to give a more definite connotation to the concepts of 'masculine' and 'feminine', it would even be possible to maintain that libido is invariably and necessarily of masculine nature, whether it occurs in men or in women and irrespectively of whether its object is a man or a woman.[1]

Since I have become acquainted with the notion of bisexuality I have regarded it as the decisive factor, and without taking bisexuality into account I think it would scarcely be possible to arrive at an understanding of the sexual manifestations that are actually to be observed in men and women.

**Leading Zones in Men and Women**    Apart from this I have only the following to add. The leading erotogenic zone in female children is located at the clitoris, and is thus homologous to the masculine genital zone of the glans penis. All my experience concerning masturbation in little girls has related to the clitoris and not to the regions of the external genitalia that are important in later sexual functioning. I am even doubtful whether a female child can be led by the influence of seduction to anything other than clitoridal masturbation. If such a thing occurs, it is quite exceptional. The spontaneous discharges of sexual excitement which occur so often precisely in little girls are expressed in spasms of the clitoris. Frequent erections of the organ make it possible for girls to form a correct judgment, even without any instruction, of the sexual manifestations of the other sex: they merely transfer on to boys the sensations derived from their own sexual processes.

If we are to understand how a little girl turns into a woman, we must follow the further vicissitudes of this excitability of the clitoris. Puberty, which brings about so great an accession of libido in boys, is marked in girls by a fresh wave

---

[1] It is essential to understand clearly that the concepts of 'masculine' and 'feminine', whose meaning seems so unambiguous to ordinary people, are among the most confused that occur in science. It is possible to distinguish at least three uses. 'Masculine' and 'feminine' are used sometimes in the sense of activity and passivity, sometimes in a biological, and sometimes, again, in a sociological sense. The first of these three meanings is the essential one and the most serviceable in psycho-analysis. When, for instance, libido was described in the text above as being 'masculine', the word was being used in this sense, for an instinct is always active even when it has a passive aim in view. The second, or biological, meaning of 'masculine' and 'feminine' is the one whose applicability can be determined most easily. Here 'masculine' and 'feminine' are characterized by the presence of spermatozoa or ova respectively and by the functions proceeding from them. Activity and its concomitant phenomena (more powerful muscular development, aggressiveness, greater intensity of libido) are as a rule linked with biological masculinity; but they are not necessarily so, for there are animal species in which these qualities are on the contrary assigned to the female. The third, or sociological, meaning receives its connotation from the observation of actually existing masculine and feminine individuals. Such observation shows that in human beings pure masculinity or femininity is not to be found either in a psychological or a biological sense. Every individual on the contrary displays a mixture of the character-traits belonging to his own and to the opposite sex; and he shows a combination of activity and passivity whether or not these last character-traits tally with his biological ones.

of *repression*, in which it is precisely clitoridal sexuality that is affected. What is thus overtaken by repression is a piece of masculine sexuality. The intensification of the brake upon sexuality brought about by pubertal repression in women serves as a stimulus to the libido in men and causes an increase of its activity. Along with this heightening of libido there is also an increase of sexual over-valuation which only emerges in full force in relation to a woman who holds herself back and who denies her sexuality. When at last the sexual act is permitted and the clitoris itself becomes excited, it still retains a function: the task, namely, of transmitting the excitation to the adjacent female sexual parts, just as – to use a simile – pine shavings can be kindled in order to set a log of harder wood on fire. Before this transference can be effected, a certain interval of time must often elapse, during which the young woman is anaesthetic. This anaesthesia may become permanent if the clitoridal zone refuses to abandon its excitability, an event for which the way is prepared precisely by an extensive activity of that zone in childhood. Anaesthesia in women, as is well known, is often only apparent and local. They are anaesthetic at the vaginal orifice but are by no means incapable of excitement originating in the clitoris or even in other zones. Alongside these erotogenic determinants of anaesthesia must also be set the psychical determinants, which equally arise from repression.

When erotogenic susceptibility to stimulation has been successfully transferred by a woman from the clitoris to the vaginal orifice, it implies that she has adopted a new leading zone for the purpose of her later sexual activity. A man, on the other hand, retains his leading zone unchanged from childhood. The fact that women change their leading erotogenic zone in this way, together with the wave of repression at puberty, which, as it were, puts aside their childish mascu-

linity, are the chief determinants of the greater proneness of women to neurosis and especially to hysteria. These determinants, therefore, are intimately related to the essence of femininity.

### Excerpt from Human Sexual Response

William H. Masters and Virginia E. Johnson

*Within recent years the work of Masters and Johnson has become the preeminent model for researchers of human sexuality. Their influence has been felt in disciplines as disparate as experimental biology and clinical psychology. Among other things their physiological findings showed that Freud's concept of vaginal orgasm was off the mark. The following excerpt summarizes their well known model of human sexual response.*

The techniques of defining and describing the gross physical changes which develop during the human male's and female's sexual response cycles have been primarily those of direct observation and physical measurement. Since the integrity of human observation for specific detail varies significantly, regardless of the observer's training and considered objectivity, reliability of reporting has been supported by many of the accepted techniques of physiologic measurement and the frequent use of color cinematographic recording in all phases of the sexual response cycle.

A more concise picture of physiologic reaction to sexual stimuli may be presented by dividing the human male's and female's cycles of sexual response into four separate phases. Progressively, the four phases are: (1) the excitement phase; (2) the plateau phase; (3) the orgasmic phase; and (4) the resolution phase. This arbitrary four-part division of the sexual response cycle provides an effective framework for detailed description of physiologic variants in sexual reaction, some of which are frequently so transient in character as to appear in only one phase of the total orgasmic cycle.

Only one sexual response pattern has been diagrammed for the human male (Fig. 3-14). Admittedly, there are many identifiable variations in the male sexual reaction. However, since these variants are usually related to duration rather than intensity of response, multiple diagrams would be more repetitive than informative. Comparably, three different sexual response patterns have been diagrammed for the human female (Fig. 3-15). It should be emphasized that

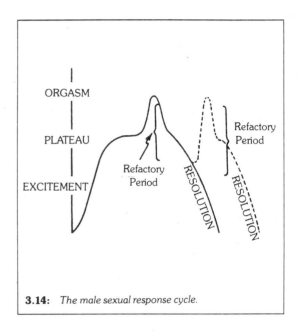

**3.14:**    *The male sexual response cycle.*

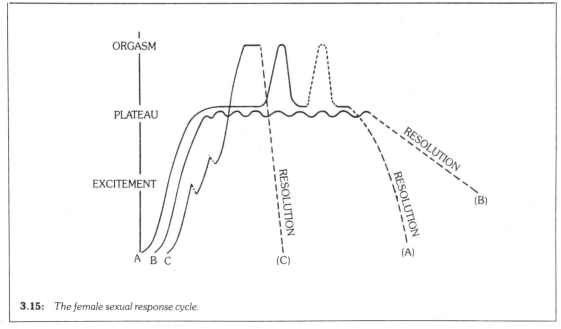

**3.15:**    *The female sexual response cycle.*

these patterns are simplifications of those most frequently observed and are only representative of the infinite variety in female sexual response. Here, intensity as well as duration of response are factors that must be considered when evaluating sexual reaction in the human female.

The first or excitement phase of the human cycle of sexual response develops from any source of somatogenic or psychogenic stimulation. The stimulative factor is of major import in establishing sufficient increment of sexual tension to extend the cycle. If the stimulation remains adequate to individual demand, the intensity of response usually increases rapidly. In this manner the excitement phase is accelerated or shortened. If the stimulative approach is physically or psychologically objectionable, or is interrupted, the excitement phase may be prolonged greatly or even aborted. This first segment and the final segment (resolution phase) consume most of the time expended in the complete cycle of human sexual response.

From excitement phase the human male or female enters the second or plateau phase of the sexual cycle, if effective sexual stimulation is continued. In this phase sexual tensions are intensified and subsequently reach the extreme level from which the individual ultimately may move to orgasm. The duration of the plateau phase is largely dependent upon the effectiveness of the stimuli employed, combined with the factor of individual drive for culmination of sex tension increment. If either the stimuli or the drive is inadequate or if all stimuli are withdrawn, the individual will not achieve orgasmic release and will drop slowly from plateau-phase tension levels into an excessively prolonged resolution phase.

The orgasmic phase is limited to those few seconds during which the vasoconcentration and myotonia developed from sexual stimuli are re-

leased. This involuntary climax is reached at any level that represents maximum sexual tension increment for the particular occasion. Subjective (sensual) awareness of orgasm is pelvic in focus, specifically concentrated in the clitoral body, vagina, and uterus of the female and in the penis, prostate, and seminal vesicles of the male. Total-body involvement in the response to sexual tensions, although physiologically well-defined, is experienced subjectively on the basis of individual reaction patterns. There is great variation in both the intensity and the duration of female orgasmic experience, while the male tends to follow standard patterns of ejaculatory reaction with less individual variation.

The human male and female resolve from the height of their orgasmic expressions into the last or resolution phase of the sexual cycle. This involuntary period of tension loss develops as a reverse reaction pattern that returns the individual through plateau and excitement levels to an unstimulated state. Women have the response potential of returning to another orgasmic experience from any point in the resolution phase if they submit to the reapplication of effective stimulation. This facility for multiple orgasmic expression is evident particularly if reversal is instituted at plateau tension level. For the man the resolution phase includes a superimposed refractory period which may extend during the involuntary phase as far as a lower excitement level of response. Effective restimulation to higher levels of sexual tension is possible only upon termination of this refractory period. With few exceptions, the physiologic ability of the male to respond to restimulation is much slower than that of the female.

Physiologic residuals of sexual tension usually are dissipated slowly in both the male and female unless an overwhelming orgasmic release has been experienced. Total involution is completed only after all manner of sexual stimuli have been withdrawn.

It always should be borne in mind that there is wide individual variation in the duration and intensity of every specific physiologic response to sexual stimulation. Those that occur early in the response cycle and continue without interruption during several phases are obvious (penile erection or vaginal lubrication). However, some physiologic reactions are fleeting in character and may be confined to one particular phase of the cycle. Examples are the plateau-phase color changes of the minor labia in the female and the coronal engorgement of the penis in the male.

In brief, the division of the human male's or female's cycle of sexual response into four specific phases admittedly is inadequate for evaluation of finite psychogenic aspects of elevated sexual tensions. However, the establishment of this purely arbitrary design provides anatomic structuring and assures inclusion and correct placement of specifics of physiologic response within the sequential continuum of human response to effective sexual stimulation.

Masters and Johnson, *Human Sexual Response.* Copyright © Little, Brown, and Company, Boston, 1966. Reprinted by permission.

### Excerpt from The Female Eunuch

Germaine Greer

*As Germaine Greer points out, the findings of Masters and Johnson were a step in the right direction, but they have, by no means, done away with erotic insensitivity.*

The banishment of the fantasy of the vaginal orgasm is ultimately a service, but the substitution of the clitoral spasm for genuine gratification

may turn out to be a disaster for sexuality. Masters and Johnson's conclusions have produced some unlooked for side-effects, like the veritable clitoromania which infects Mette Eiljersen's book, *I accuse!* While speaking of women's orgasms as resulting from the "right touches in the button," she condemns sexologists who

> recommend . . . the stimulation of the clitoris as part of the prelude to intercourse, to that which most men consider to be the "real thing." What is in fact the "real thing" for them is *completely devoid of sensation* for the woman.
>
> This is the heart of the matter! Concealed for hundreds of years by humble, shy and subservient women.

Not all the women in history have been humble and subservient to such an extent. It is nonsense to say that a woman feels nothing when a man is moving his penis in her vagina: the orgasm is qualitatively different when the vagina can undulate around the penis instead of vacancy. The differentiation between the simple inevitable pleasure of men and the tricky responses of women is not altogether valid. If ejaculation meant release for all men, given the constant manufacture of sperm and the resultant pressure to have intercourse, men could copulate without transport or disappointment with anyone. The process described by the experts, in which man dutifully does the rounds of the erogenous zones, spends an equal amount of time on each nipple, turns his attention to the clitoris (usually too directly), leads through the stages of digital or lingual stimulation and then politely lets himself into the vagina, perhaps waiting until the retraction of the clitoris tells him that he is welcome, is laborious and inhumanly computerized. The implication that there is a statistically ideal fuck which will always result in satisfaction if the right procedures are followed is depressing and misleading.

There is no substitute for excitement; not all the massage in the world will insure satisfaction, for it is a matter of psychosexual release. Real satisfaction is not enshrined in a tiny cluster of nerves but in the sexual involvement of the whole person. Women's continued high enjoyment of sex, which continues after orgasm, observed by men with wonder, is not based on the clitoris, which does not respond particularly well to continued stimulus, but in a general sensual response. If we localize female response in the clitoris we impose upon women the same limitation of sex which has stunted the male's response. The male sexual idea of virility without languor or amorousness is profoundly desolating: when the release is expressed in mechanical terms it is sought mechanically. Sex becomes masturbation in the vagina.

Many women who greeted the conclusions of Masters and Johnson with cries of "I told you so!" and "I am normal!" will feel that this criticism is a betrayal. They have discovered sexual pleasure after being denied it but the fact that they have only ever experienced gratification from clitoral stimulation is evidence for my case, because it is the index of the desexualization of the whole body, the substitution of genitality for sexuality. The ideal marriage as measured by the electronic equipment in the Reproductive Biology Research Foundation laboratories is enfeebled – dull sex for dull people. The sexual personality is basically antiauthoritarian. If the system wishes to enforce complete suggestibility in its subjects, it will have to tame sex. Masters and Johnson supplied the blueprint for standard, low-agitation, cool-out monogamy. If women are to avoid this last reduction of their humanity, they must hold out – not just for orgasm but for ecstasy.

From Greer, *The Female Eunuch*. Copyright © McGraw-Hill, New York. Reprinted by permission.

## Excerpt from **The Kama Sutra**

*This excerpt from the classic Indian treatise on social grace and erotica (which is thought to have originated several centuries B.C.) gives a curious opinion on female sensuality.*

Auddalika says, "Females do not emit as males do. The males simply remove their desire, while the females, from their consciousness of desire, feel a certain kind of pleasure, which gives them satisfaction, but it is impossible for them to tell you what kind of pleasure they feel. The fact from which this becomes evident is that males, when engaged in coition, cease of themselves after emission, and are satisfied, but it is not so with females."

This opinion is, however, objected to on the grounds, that if a male be long-timed, the female loves him the more, but if he be short-timed she is dissatisfied with him. And this circumstance, some say, would prove that the female emits also.

But this opinion does not hold good, for if it takes a long time to allay a woman's desire, and during this time she is enjoying great pleasure, it is quite natural then that she should wish for its continuation. And on this subject there is a verse as follows:

"By union with men the lust, desire, or passion of women is satisfied, and the pleasure derived from the consciousness of it is called their satisfaction."

Pregnancy is a profound event for any woman, but it is often experienced ambiguously. Simone de Beauvoir writes in the *Second Sex*:

> ... pregnancy is above all a drama that is acted out within the woman herself. She feels it as at once an enrichment and an injury; the fetus is part of her body, and it is a parasite that feeds upon it, she possesses it, and she is possessed by it; it represents the future and, carrying it, she feels herself vast as the world; but this very opulence annihilates her, she feels that she herself is no longer anything. A new life is going to manifest itself and justify its own separate existence, she is proud of it; but she also feels herself tossed and driven, the plaything of obscure forces.

### Women and Pregnancy:
### The Crisis Experience

Pregnancy is ordinarily a crisis point for women; but it is a crisis in the sense that it is a turning point. The Chinese orthographic character for "crisis" is a combination of two simpler characters, one meaning "danger" and the other meaning "opportunity." There is *danger*, the old habits and relations are no longer adequate or relevent. A woman's body is changing, and she is more likely to respond with more intense feelings; she may experience old conflicts and feelings that she thought had been resolved years ago. There is also *opportunity*: She must begin to evaluate how she will be as a mother; she must establish a parenting relation with her partner.

The three essential tasks that a woman usually has to deal with during pregnancy include altered relationships to herself, her partner, and her mother (Bibring, 1975).

Before a woman becomes pregnant, she is what Grete Bibring calls "a single, self-contained organism, whose self-image coincides normally with the boundaries of her own existence." When she becomes pregnant, she nourishes within her body first an embryo, then a fetus, and ultimately, upon birth, a child, *her* child. That child was once a part of her, then, when she gave birth, it separated from her. That she carried the child within her for nine months gives her a special relationship with it that no one else – neither the child's father nor siblings, nor later its partner, lover, or friend – can duplicate. The mother will experience the child as an individual, urging and supporting its growth and independence. But she will also continue to see the child as part of herself and her body; she will want to hold on to her child, protect and guard it from others – from strangers, friends, and lovers – and from the world itself.

After its birth, each woman must struggle with the realization that her child is no longer part of her flesh, even though it once was. Her task is to permit the child to mature according to its needs while giving it support and love. At the same time, she must be careful not to cut herself off from the child or reject it as someone who has violated her body, her freedom, or her independence.

A second influence on a woman's emotional response to pregnancy and childbirth is her relationship to her partner and the circumstances under which she became pregnant. Did she want to become pregnant? Does she want to bear *his* child? She must consider her relationship with her sexual partner. Does she love him? Does he love her? Is he an emotional partner as well? How will they assist each other in the rearing of the child? Will the child enhance or detract from their relationship? Will he accept responsibilities as a father? Can they relate to each other as parents as well as partners? Is she willing to share *her* child with her partner? Does she want to be – or is she – a single parent?

The third area of significance revolves around the pregnant woman's relationship with her mother. Her relationship with her mother has been a changing one from the moment she was born, moving from dependency in childhood, increasing self-reliance before adolescence, and often an explosive struggle for independence through adolescence. It is often assumed that a level of stability has been reached between mother and daughter after the woman has left home. But pregnancy appears to introduce further changes in the mother-daughter bond.

Among those women in Bibring's study who appeared above average in their dependence on their mothers – turning to them for advice on every detail of their life from diet to maternity clothes – there was a growing independence and self-esteem as pregnancy progressed. Among those women who expressed alienation, hostility, or distance from their mothers, a growing acceptance and toleration developed when the daughter became pregnant. Many remarked, "I understand mother much better now. . . ." These women began to identify with the difficulty their mothers experienced and to resolve many of the residual conflicts left over from growing up.

Most of this chapter is a practical discussion of pregnancy and childbirth, the central topic of which include the physical and emotional changes of pregnancy, prenatal health precautions, and techniques of childbirth. Before getting into these subjects, however, the discussion briefly returns to the level of reproductive cells for summaries of the mechanisms of

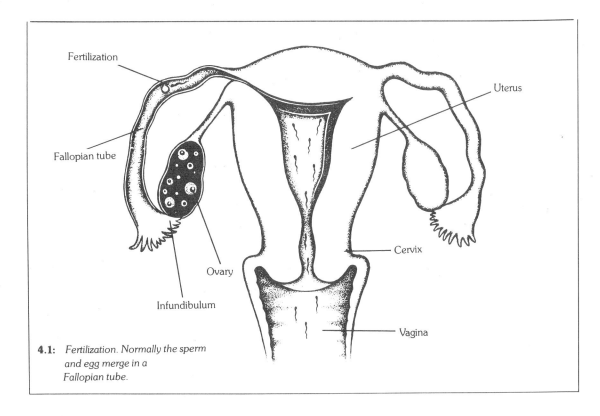

**4.1:** *Fertilization. Normally the sperm and egg merge in a Fallopian tube.*

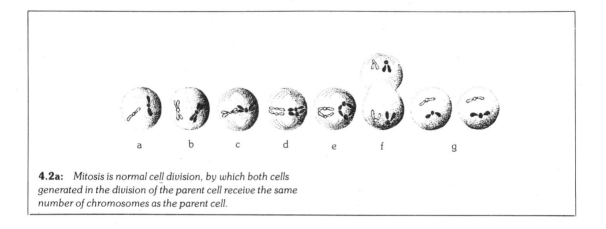

a   b   c   d   e   f   g

**4.2a:** *Mitosis is normal cell division, by which both cells generated in the division of the parent cell receive the same number of chromosomes as the parent cell.*

heredity and *prenatal* (before birth) human development.

## Mechanisms of Heredity

When an egg and sperm merge they bring together hereditary "codes," or *genes,* of the parents. Genes are conglomerates of biochemical compounds that determine (or, at least, influence) the characteristics of an individual. They affect many levels of existence – including traits as diverse as eye color, intelligence, and psychological health. But how? Although biochemical properties of genes are fairly well understood, the ways in which genes exert their influences, particularly on mental characteristics, are among the deepest of biological mysteries.

Genes are located on tiny bits of matter called chromosomes, each of which carries several thousand genes. Normal human eggs and sperm have twenty-three chromosomes each. Therefore, a fertilized egg, or *zygote,* has forty-six chromosomes.

The cells of a human body are produced through a sequence of cell divisions beginning with the zygote. In the original division the zygote

forms two cells, these become four, which then produce eight, and so on. By the time a human infant is born, it consists of many billions of cells.

In normal cell division, *mitosis,* each new cell receives all forty-six chromosomes. This seeming impossibility is possible because the chromosomes duplicate between divisions (Figure 4.2a). All of the body's cells are produced by mitosis, except for sperm and egg. Cell divisions in seminifereous tubules and ovarian follicles occur by a unique kind of division, *meiosis,* which halves the number of chromosomes (Figure 4.2b).

Chromosomes function in pairs (paired chromosomes carry genes influencing the same traits), and meiosis generates cells with one member of each pair. Twenty-two of the twenty-three pairs of human chromosomes are matched in structure. For women the remaining pair is also matched, but for men it is not (Figure 4.3). Men have one chromosome which is identical in shape to those of the female pair and another which is smaller and of a different shape. Female and male chromosomal constitutions are abbreviated as XX and XY, respectively. Since all female cells contain only X-chromosomes,

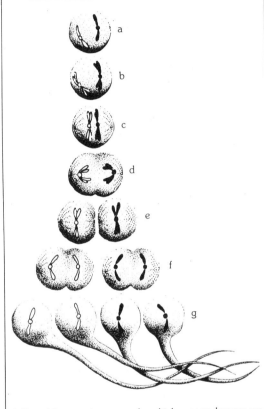

**4.2b:** *Meiosos, the process by which eggs and sperm are generated, halves the number of chromosomes. Spermatogenisis is illustrated.*

meiosis produces only X-bearing eggs. On the other hand, since male cells contain both X-and Y-chromosomes, a sperm cell may have either an X or a Y. Thus, the chromosomal constitution of the fertilizing sperm determines the sex of the human-to-be.

## Assisted Fertilization

In cases of male or female infertility (discussed in the preceeding chapter) there are techniques which can assist the union of a sperm and egg or the successful implanting of the embryo in the uterus. At present the technology of dealing with male infertility is much further advanced than the methods of circumventing malfunctions of the female reproductive system. However, we are currently in an age of rapid advances.

**Artificial Insemination** Artificial insemination simply involves the placing of healthy sperm in the vagina through means other than sexual intercourse. Artificial insemination has been a method for breeding cattle for hundreds of years, but it is only recently that it has become socially acceptable for humans. At present, artificial insemination results in about 10,000 births per year in the U.S.

The primary reason for artificial insemination is infertility of the male. This accounts for 95% of all instances of sperm transfers from donors, who are generally anonymous. It has also been done in cases where the couple feared a transfer of genetic disease from the father. Curie-Cohen (1979) has reported that the third most common reason for artificial insemination by donor is to provide women without a male partner with an offspring. In a survey of physicians likely to perform artificial insemination, 36 respondents had effected this procedure for unmarried women.

Though the technique of artificial insemination is simple, it can bring about some thorny legal problems. For example, the majority of states do not recongnize the husband of a woman who conceived a child by artificial insemination as the child's legitimate father. Thus, adoption proceedings can be an absurd necessity. Far more difficult problems arise when the offspring of artificial insemination want information concerning their biological fathers.

When the nature of a husband's infertility in-

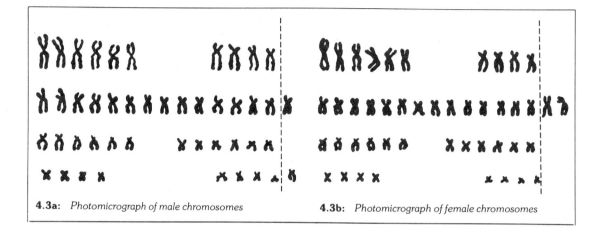

**4.3a:** *Photomicrograph of male chromosomes*     **4.3b:** *Photomicrograph of female chromosomes*

volves only a low sperm count, artificial insemination with his sperm may be accomplished by pooling the products of several ejaculations. Since sperm cells are short-lived, this involves freezing the ejaculates until a "critical mass" has been accumulated.

The fact that sperm may be frozen without demonstrable damage has opened various other possibilities for artificial insemination. For example, if a male is contemplating having a vasectomy, he could provide for a change of mind by having a sample of his semen frozen at one of the many "sperm banks" located throughout the country. Couples should be aware, however, that insemination with sperm which has been frozen is not always successful. Sperm cells that have been frozen, then thawed, suffer a significant loss of motility. Fertility capacity is 12-15% lower for frozen than for fresh sperm (Population Reports, 1976).

**"Test-tube" Fertilization**   In 1978 British scientists Dr. Patrick Steptoe and Robert Edwards shook the world with their announcement that they had succeeded in fertilizing a human egg in a laboratory culture, and implanting the embryo

in the uterus of the woman from whom the egg was taken. Since she suffered from blocked Fallopian tubes, a common form of female infertility, Lesley Brown had not been able to conceive through intercourse.

Although Steptoe and Edwards have been slow to give precise information on their techniques, they are well established in their fields of gynecology (Steptoe) and physiology (Edwards); their reported success came at a time when it had been anticipated by other researchers. Figure 4.4 summarizes available information on the operation ("Medical Aspects of Human Sexuality", 1978).

The first clinic in the United States to perform *in vitro* ("test tube") fertilization is scheduled to open in January, 1980, at Eastern Virginia Medical School in Norfolk. To be considered at the clinic the woman must have a fertile husband and have a healthy uterus and ova.

**Embryo Transfer**   Chronic miscarriage is undoubtedly the most tragic form of infertility. Women who suffer from this are capable of conceiving, but the embryo inevitably fails to remain attached to the endometrium. However, help

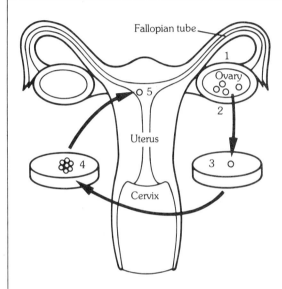

**4.4 Test Tube Fertilization**

. . . it was necessary to obtain eggs that were ready for fertilization, but before they were released by the ovary and lost to retrieval. A hormone, *human chorionic gonadotropin* (HCG), was administered to control the exact time of ovulation. The hormonal treatment also stimulated the maturation of several eggs.

. . . approximately 33 to 34 hours after HCG was administered, Mrs. Brown was put under general anesthesia; a thin periscope-like device, a laparoscope, was inserted into an incision in her abdomen, one or more eggs were removed with a suction device, inserted alongside the laparoscope.

. . . sperm from Mr. Brown were placed in a nurturing medium to simulate condtions in the female reproductive tract. The egg was transferred to the sperm solution.

. . . some hours after fertilization occurred, the embryo was transferred to a more supportive fluid environment, where cell division proceeded for 2 to 4 days.

. . . at some point around the *blastocyst* stage of development, when the embryo was a tiny sphere of cells, it was transferred into the uterus with a plastic tube (like a miniature pea-shooter). The embryo settled into Mrs. Brown's endometrium, and proceeded to develop into Louise, who was born on July 25, 1978.

may be forthcoming.

In 1975 a baboon gave birth to a healthy infant after the embryo had been transferred from another female (Kraemer, et. al., 1976). This was the first successful transfer of a *primate* (a biological grouping which includes humans). Although no successful human embryo transfer have been reported, researchers believe that it is likely that success will be forthcoming during the 1980s.

Perhaps research into embryo transfer has lagged behind "test tube" fertilizaton more because of social/legal implications than technological hang-ups. There are no precedents, for example, for dealing with a case in which both

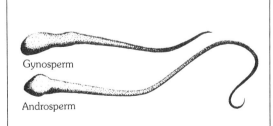

**4.5:** *X-bearing sperm (gynosperm) have larger heads and shorter tails the Y-bearing sperm (androsperm).*

the donor and the host might claim legal parenthood. In cases of birth defects, both parties might refuse to take responsibility for the child.

**Choosing a Baby's Sex**

In the early 1960's Landrum B. Shettles discovered that characteristics observable with a microscope revealed the sexual identities of sperm (Figure 4.5). After examining more than 500 specimens, he was convinced that the relatively small, but long-tailed sperm carried male-producing Y-chromosomes and that a larger, short-tailed type carried the female-producing X-chromosomes. He noticed that in most cases the long-tailed sperm far outnumbered those with short tails. Dr. Shettles concluded that male-producing sperm are more likely to die before fertilizing an egg and claims to have devised several techniques by which prospective parents can play a part in determining the sex of their baby. According to Shettles his methods will result in an infant having the sex of the parents' choice in about 80 percent of the attempts (Rorvik and Shettles, 1970). This may be an overstatement, but, if nothing else, the following descriptions give some interesting sidelights on the nature of fertilization.

**To Conceive a Male:** Y-bearing sperm (androsperm) are generally less hardy than X-bearing sperm (gynosperm). Once they have been ejaculated into the vagina, most androsperm die within twenty-four hours, while gynosperm live for a couple of days. Therefore, parents desiring a male child should use condoms or a diaphragm for most of the month and have non-contracepted intercourse only for a few days, beginning with the day of ovulation. (See discussion of the "Rhythm" method in Chapter 6 for instruction on determining the time of ovulation.)

The normal chemical environment of the vagina is slightly acidic, and androsperm are more sensitive to acid than gynosperm. Neutralizing the acidity before intercourse, therefore, enhances the odds for fertilization by an androsperm. Thus, douching with a solution of two tablespoons of baking soda in a quart of warm water will, according to Shettles, optimize the chances for conceiving a male.

Shettles also claims that if a woman experiences orgasm before the partner ejaculates, the chances are better for a male conception. A possible reason for this is that the cervix and uterus produce alkaline secretions that are forced into the vagina during orgasm. Rhythmic contractions of the uterus pump the alkaline fluids into the vagina, giving androsperm a more hospitable greeting than if no orgasm were achieved.

Because the chances for survival of male-producing androsperm are better within the uterus than in the vagina, a position that deposits sperm close to the cervix should be used. The belly-to-belly, "missionary", approach is one such position. (See Chapter 12 for illustrations of various positions for intercourse.)

Finally, if a couple wants a boy, the man should refrain from ejaculation for a few days prior to the woman's anticipated date of ovulation. This period of abstinence helps ensure a maximum sperm count, a factor favoring androsperm. An average of about three days is required for the sperm count to reach a maximum level.

**To Conceive a Female:** Within the female reproductive system, a gynosperm can survive up to five days, but an androsperm rarely lasts longer than one day. Thus, a couple desiring to have a girl should abstain from intercourse or use contraception for a few days prior to ovulation. Since a low sperm count is associated with a high ratio of gynosperm to androsperm, frequent ejaculation also ups the odds for conceiving a female.

Because gynosperm are less sensitive to acidity than androsperm, intercourse four days before ovulation (when vaginal secretions are at their most acidic) is particularly likely to yield female offspring. However, this must be the last non-contracepted intercourse before the expected day of ovulation. Another technique favoring a female conception is a slightly acid douche prior to intercourse. A solution of two tablespoons of vinegar in a quart of water will raise the vaginal acidity to the point where a large proportion of androsperm are immobilized, while most gynosperm keep swimming.

Also, intercourse should be shallow in order to deposit sperm away from the cervix, thus leaving them with a long swim in the acidic secretions of the vagina. The rear-entry position, which allows for less penetration than most other positions, is said to be a good way to go about conceiving a female.

### Prenatal Development: Between Conception and Birth

The fertilized egg, or *zygote*, begins dividing soon after the moment of fertilization, as it is gently drawn toward the uterus by the wafting cilia and slow peristaltic contractions of the Fallopian tube. By the time the cell mass reaches the uterus (it moves about an inch per day and arrives four to seven days after conception) it is a fluid-filled sphere, the *blastocyst*. It is composed of approximately 100 cells, most of which are concentrated in a patch that covers a small portion of its inner wall.

Soon after reaching the uterus, the blastocyst settles into the membranous uterine lining, the *endometrium*. At this stage it is less than 0.05 inch in diameter, but it grows rapidly.

**The Embryo**    The patch of cells within the blastocyst soon develops characteristics of a living organism, although its outward appearance does not look human for approximately two months. During the interim it is called an *embryo*. While the embryo develops, the remaining cells of the blastocyst evolve into external tissues, including the *placenta*, the *amnion*, and the *yolk sac*.

The *placenta* is an organ of exchange between the embryo and mother. It is formed of tissues from both uterus and the blastocyst. Within the

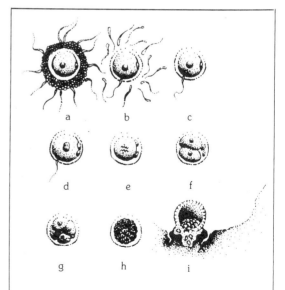

**4.6:**   *Development from an egg which is about to be fertilized to a blastocyst, during passage from the Fallopian tube to the endometrium.*

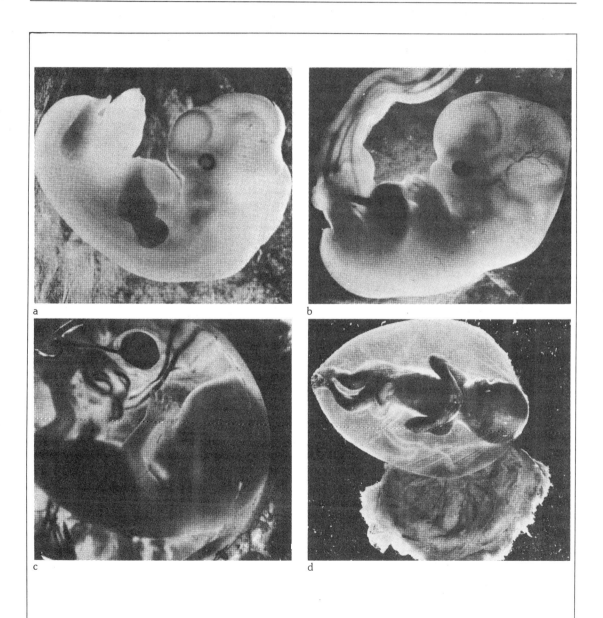

**4.7:**  *Development of the human embryo and fetus at five weeks (a), six and half weeks (b), eleven weeks (c), and sixteen weeks (d).*

placenta the mother's blood circulates around tiny, thin-walled pockets (*chorionic villi*), which contain the baby's blood. Materials pass through the villi, but the circulatory systems of the developing embryo and the mother do not normally mix. Vital nutrients and oxygen are passed to the embryo through the placenta, but certain harmful substances also make it through. Most drugs, viruses, and the microorganism which causes syphilis can reach the embryo via the placenta.

The *amnion* is a fluid-filled, membranous pouch surrounding the embryo. It equalizes pressure around the embryo and absorbs physical shocks. The *yolk sac* is an evolutionary vestige of an organ that stores nutrients for animals that hatch from eggs. It seems to serve little purpose for human embryos.

During the first few weeks of development, the human embryo bears close resemblances to those of other vertebrate animals (Figure 4.8). Traces of gills, for instance, are found in the embryos of humans and other land-dwelling animals. But they become functioning organs only in fish and certain other species that live in the water. As a human embryo develops, it loses its gills and most other vestigial organs. However, it retains others – the appendix, for example, is an organ of digestion for some mammals but has no apparent function in humans.

**The Fetus** Nine weeks after conception most basic human features have appeared. At this stage the early *fetus* (this name applies from the ninth week until birth) is only about one inch in length. Hands, facial features, and internal structures are recognizably human but lack refinement.

The sexual system is the slowest organ system to develop. Rudiments of sex organs are usually present by the seventh week, but they do not become discernible as male or female for another month or so.

Sex organs develop in a process that involves degeneration of certain structures and growth of others. For example, early male and female fetuses both have *Mullerian ducts* (forerunners of Fallopian tubes) and *Wolffian ducts* (potential sperm ducts). In female fetuses Mullerian ducts develop while Wolffian ducts degenerate; the reverse is true for males (Figure 4.9).

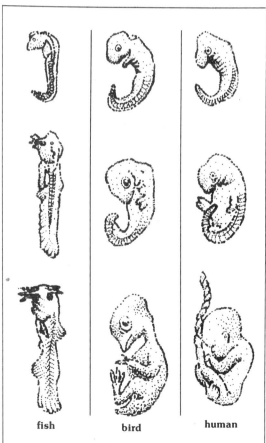

    **fish**      **bird**      **human**

**4.8:** *Comparison of development from embryo to fetus of a fish, bird and human.*

From the time that the fertilized human egg imbeds itself into the lining of the uterus at the age of six or seven days until its birth sometime between 265 and 280 days after conception, the human individual grows far more than in any other comparable time span during life. The one cell which was created at the time of conception turns into over two billion cells at the time of birth.

Paul Bohannan, *Lover, Sex and Being Human*

A related process results in the formation of *homologous organs* (male and female organs that develop from common embryonic structures). For instance, early in the fetal phase, the undifferentiated organs that may become ovaries or testicles are situated high in the abdomen. In women, these structures shift downward to the level of the upper edge of the pelvis. For men, however, they settle into the scrotum, trailing the Wolffian ducts, which are developing into the two vasa deferentia and epididymises. Other female-male homologies include the labia majora-scrotum and clitoris-penis.

In recent years significant advances have been made in the sciences exploring genetic, biochemical, and physiological interrelationships during early sexual development. Most of the evidence has come from experiments with mammals other than humans (including rats, rabbits, hamsters, monkeys, and dogs). But, the mechanisms of sexual differentiation appear essentially the same for all mammals.

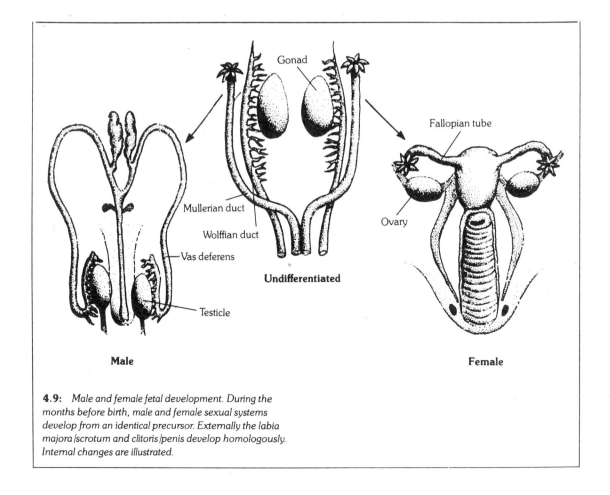

**4.9:** *Male and female fetal development. During the months before birth, male and female sexual systems develop from an identical precursor. Externally the labia majora/scrotum and clitoris/penis develop homologously. Internal changes are illustrated.*

With delicate surgery, gonads have been removed from embryos before sexual differentiation (approximately six weeks after fertilization). All such embryos, even those with XY chromosomes, subsequently developed into anatomical females. In other experiments, testosterone has been injected into the bloodstreams of XX fetuses, with subsequent masculinization of their anatomical features. A female fetus may develop an oversized clitoris or a scrotum-like pouch of skin, for example. The conclusion to such experiments has been that testosterone secreted by the developing gonads of an XY fetus stimulates development of male reproductive organs. There is no corresponding need for self-stimulation by gonadal hormones in order for an XX fetus to become anatomically female (Money and Ehrhardt, 1972). Perhaps, however, hormones produced elsewhere than the embryonic gonads (the placenta, for example, produces estrogen and progesterone during pregnancy) stimulate development of female sex organs.

Between the third month of pregnancy and the moment of birth, the fetus increases from a couple inches in length and a fraction of an ounce in weight to an average of twenty inches and over seven pounds. This explosive growth is supported by continued nourishment from the mother via the placenta. Nutrients and oxygen are carried inward and wastes are removed through blood vessels within the *umbilical cord*, which attaches the placenta to the infant's abdomen.

## Experiencing Pregnancy:

**The First Trimester**   A pregnancy lasts about nine calendar months, although variations of a couple weeks either way are not unusual. A common convention for describing this nine

month gestation period is the division of the overall span into three equal *trimesters*.

*Indications of Pregnancy*   A missed menstrual period may indicate that a woman is pregnant, but it is by no means a sure sign. Missed periods of menstrual bleeding are commonly experienced by women who are not pregnant, and some women who are pregnant have uterine bleeding during the first few months.

If a woman is actually pregnant there are early physical signs other than a missed menstrual period. For example, the breasts usually swell slightly and become tender, the need to urinate becomes more frequent, and feelings of nausea may develop. Such signs should not, of course, be interpreted as absolute indications of pregnancy.

Nausea (and sometimes vomiting) is experienced by about half of all pregnant women. When it occurs, it is usually most severe in the morning – hence the term, *morning sickness*. The exact cause(s) of morning sickness are not known. However, some authorities believe it is a side-effect of the hormonal changes of early pregnancy — particularly outpourings by the placenta of the female hormones, estrogen and progesterone.

*Pregnancy Tests*   Arrangements for a pregnancy test ought to be made soon after a woman is sure she has missed a menstrual period. Immediate testing is of particular importance if termination of pregnancy is contemplated, because the sooner the abortion is performed, the smaller the risk. Early detection is also important if the pregnancy is to be carried through, since certain health precautions (considered in later sections) are necessary to safeguard the health of the embryo during the first months of pregnancy.

There are several ways of examining for pregnancy, including certain methods based on anatomical observations. *Hegar's sign*, for instance, is softening of the uterus just above the cervix, which can be felt through the vagina. A visual sign is a slight purple hue that develops in the labia minora.

Today's most sensitive pregnancy tests involve monitoring hormones produced by the developing embryo. During its journey to the uterus, the embryo secretes *human chorionic gonadotropin*, HCG. This hormone is also produced in relatively small amounts by the endocrine system of the mature female, and was mentioned earlier as a stimulator of ovulation (in the section on "test tube" fertilization). HCG has several effects in preparing the female body for nurturing an embryo.

As early as the sixth to eighth day after ovulation, the level of HCG is sufficient to be detected by *radioreceptorassay* (RRA), a technique which appears to be replacing a similar method developed a few years earlier, *radioimmunoassay* (RIA). According to a report concerning the first 1,000 RRA's the test was correct in 100% of the cases at the time of the first missed menses (Landesman and Sazena, 1976). Since the test requires a blood sample, one must arrange for it with a doctor.

HCG is also excreted in the urine, in which it can be detected as early as 21-28 days after fertilization (Hatcher, et. al., 1978). Testing the urine for HCG is currently the most common pregnancy test. By the *agglutination test*, HCG in the urine prevents coagulation of a test solution.

A variation of the agglutination test has been developed for women to apply to themselves. Manufacturers of "in-home" test kits claim accuracy as early as nine days after missed menstrual bleeding (*San Francisco Chronicle / Examiner*, 1978). As one might expect, however, the accuracy of the test varies from person to person,

depending both on skill and individual hormonal variations. Experts on pregnancy caution that women should not be lulled by the in-home test into being lax about seeking professional attention during the crucial early weeks of pregnancy (Hatcher, et. al., 1978). The cost of an in-home test, $10-12 at the time of this writing, may be more than one would have to pay to have the testing done by a clinic.

HCG can also be detected by injecting certain animals (including rabbits and frogs) with the woman's urine and then examining the animals for tell-tale physical reactions. Male frogs, for instance, ejaculate as a positive sign for pregnancy, and the ovaries of female rabbits become congested with blood. Unfortunately the "rabbit test" involves killing the rabbit. Such tests are not commonly used anymore.

Properly done, modern pregnancy tests are nearly 100% accurate. If they err, it is generally by giving false negative results early in pregnancy. So, re-testing might be necessary. Proof does not come until late in the first trimester when fetal heartbeats and movements can be detected.

***Seeing a Doctor***    A woman should be in the best possible general health before starting pregnancy; thus, the ideal time for the first prenatal visit to the physician is *before* pregnancy. She should have a physical examination that can help her answer the question: "Shall I have a baby now?" Among other things the possibility of genetic problems (usually remote) ought to be discussed. If the complete examination has not been done before the start of the pregnancy, it should be accomplished in the early weeks. Conditions that might result in complications of pregnancy, obstructed labor or difficult delivery can often be detected and corrected before they cause problems. The individual plan of prenatal care will be based on the results of this examination. Needs for special diet or exercise can be determined at this time.

*Spontaneous Abortion*    Commonly called "miscarriage," *spontaneous abortion* is noninduced loss of an embryo or fetus. The percentage of pregnancies that end in spontaneous abortion is not known. Estimates range from 10 to over 50 percent – the former figure considers only fetuses, while the latter takes all stages of development into account. Sometimes a small discharge of blood from the vagina is the only evidence of miscarriage, but in other cases bleeding is profuse. Although a miscarriage often has emotional consequences, especially for women who have had difficulty conceiving, there is rarely any physical damage to the woman. Most spontaneous abortions occur before the twelfth week of pregnancy, and in many cases are "benevolent" natural phenomena. Miscarried fetuses often have serious physical or genetic defects.

Some women are prone to *chronic* spontaneous abortion. If a woman has miscarried three or more times, it is possible that she has a physical and/or psychological problem. In some cases, therapeutic techniques can help make a future pregnancy successful.

In the 1950s progestins were successfully administered to women who were chronic spontaneous aborters. But, although, pregnancies were saved, female infants born to these women occasionally had masculinized genitalia, including penises and scrotums. Also, follow-up studies on progestin-masculinized females revealed a higher than average incidence of cancer of the cervix and vagina.

**The DES Problem**    *Diethylstilbestrol* (DES) is a synthetic form of a estrogen which was used to prevent miscarriages. It is estimated that between 1941 and 1971 several million women were given the drug during pregnancy, especially if they had a history of previous miscarriage. A large proportion of daughters born to women who took DES have been found to have abnormalities in their vagina or cervix. Most of these are not dangerous. The most common is *adenosis* – the presence of a type of glandular tissue in the vagina which usually occurs in the cervix. In some DES daughters, the vagina and cervix also show structural changes. None of these changes interfere with normal erotic or reproductive functions.

However, a small number of DES daughters have cancer of the vagina or cervix. The risk of getting this cancer is rare, probably less than 1 in 1,000. If found early, the cancer can be treated. DES daughters should discuss the problem of whether or not they have any abnormal symptoms with their physicians.

Little is known about the effects on DES sons. But on going studies indicate the possibility of non-cancerous effects on the penis and testicles, including cysts, undescended testicles, and lowered sperm counts.

Studies of the women to whom DES was administered suggest a possible increase in cancer of the reproductive organs or breasts. Before taking any estrogens, such as birth control pills, the morning-after pill, or estrogens for menopausal symptoms, DES mothers should discuss the benefits and risks with their doctor.

*Tubal Pregnancy*    A rare phenomenon, which has potentially serious physical consequences, tubal pregnancy is the implantation and initial development of an embryo in a Fallopian tube. It occurs in about 4 out of every 1,000 pregnancies. Tubal pregnancy begins similarly to a normal pregnancy – a placenta forms, and the embryo starts to grow. But a Fallopian tube lacks the

*Author's note: As this edition goes to press, word comes that intercourse during pregnancy may be a significant cause of infection and death. The following is the abstract of an article in the bellwether journal, 'New England Journal of Medicine'. (The statistical notation, P<0.001, means that the probability of the discrepancy in question happening by pure chance is less than one in one thousand.):*

**Abstract.** Data were analyzed from 26,886 pregnancies to determine whether coitus is involved in the genesis of amniotic-fluid infections. The frequency of infection was 156 per thousand births when mothers reported coitus once or more per week during the month before delivery, versus 117 per thousand when no coitus was reported (P<0.001). The percentage of infected infants who died

uterus's capacity for expansion, and it bursts during the latter half of the first trimester.

Because the initial symptoms of tubal pregnancy are essentially the same as the first sign of pregnancy, early diagnosis is difficult. Usually the first sign that something is wrong is sharp pain in the lower abdomen. If undetected, the Fallopian tube will rupture. Afterward, the pain may become dull or may disappear for a while. In either case, cramps in the abdomen and chest develop as the body reacts to internal bleeding. Without immediate medical attention a victim of a ruptured tubal pregnancy may go into shock and die.

Treatment of tubal pregnancy usually involves removal of the damaged Fallopian tube. The operation reduces the chance for future fertilization by half, but otherwise does not affect a woman's ability to have a baby.

*Erotic Activity During Pregnancy*    In general, erotic activity during pregnancy is not detrimental to the health of the mother or child. Some authorities suggest that women with histories of chronic spontaneous abortion should refrain from all types of orgasmic activity (including mas-

turbation) during pregnancy. But, an obstetrician should be consulted before curtailing erotic activity. For the vast majority of women, there is no physical danger in having erotic activity during pregnancy.

However, some women find that their sex drives diminish during early pregnancy. Breast tenderness, morning sickness, and fatigue are among the reasons why sexual activity may not be enjoyable.

**The Second Trimester**    By the end of the first trimester the worst of the negative aspects of early pregnancy is over. As the first trimester blends into the second, morning sickness and fatigue subside and erotic interest is usually renewed.

*Erotic Activity*    Many women experience high levels of sensual excitation during the second trimester. Feelings of physical and psychological well-being are commonly expressed, and erotic desires may even be enhanced over pre-pregnancy levels. The reason for this rise is not precisely known, but changes in the levels of sex hormones and pressure in the pubic area from the growing fetus have been suggested as physical causes. Acceptance of the pregnancy and eager anticipation of its outcome may also contribute to heightened erotic interests.

*Physical Changes*    Pregnancy becomes increasingly obvious during the second trimester. The abdomen expands and a faint line of brown pigmentation usually forms between the naval and pubis. Similar pigmentation darkens the *areolas* surrounding the nipples and sometimes appears on the face. Facial color usually returns to normal after pregnancy, but the line of the abdomen and darkening of the areolas remain.

Breasts enlarge during the second trimester in

**4.10:**   *Tubal pregnancy*

was 11.0 when there was coitus versus 2.4 when there was no coitus (P<0.001). The frequencies of low Apgar scores, neonatal respiratory distress, and hyperbilirubinemia were about doubled when mothers reported coitus. The coitus-associated effects were greater in preterm than in full-term infants. The pregnancies in the study took place between 1959 and 1966, when national perinatal mortality rates were higher than they are now. Deaths from coitus-associated infections may be less frequent today. (N Engl J Med 301:1198-1200, 1979)

---

response to hormonal stimulation. They also begin producing a sticky substance called *colostrum*, which oozes from the nipples and should be washed away daily with warm water.

Fetal movements (*quickening*) become obvious during the second trimester. At first, twisting and kicking of the fetus can only be felt internally by the mother, but later movements ripple the skin of her abdomen. Toward the end of pregnancy some babies are rambunctious enough to keep their mother awake at night.

**The Third Trimester**    The physical and emotional exhilaration of the second trimester may fade in the final weeks of pregnancy. Physical discomforts (including backache and fatigue) and feelings of anxiety and irritability sometimes occur.

*Erotic Activity*    For some women in the third trimester, physical discomforts and emotional demands impair erotic interests. But, late pregnancy is by no means a time of physical or emotional incapacitation; for some couples erotic activity is a source of mutual enjoyment, even in the final days before delivery.

There is a possible occurrence in the last few weeks of pregnancy, however, which should be taken as a sign to limit sexual activities. It is a phenomenon called *lightening*, in which the baby's head engages in the cervix; and dips down into the vagina. Although the head remains encased, the swollen cervix is subject to abrasion, and intercourse should be curtailed until after the baby is born. However, this prohibition does not apply to other erotic activities such as masturbation or oral stimulation. Apart from lightening, the attending physician may discover other physical complications that limit certain types of erotic activity in late pregnancy. But, in most cases intercourse is safe.

Although intercourse, per se, need not be prohibited during the final trimester, certain positions are unsafe, uncomfortable, or simply impossible. Obviously, the "missionary" position must be abandoned when the pregnant woman's abdomen is too large. It is possible, however, for the man to approach from behind while she, on her knees, rests her head and arms on the edge of a couch or bed. Deep penile thrusts may be painful for a woman during late pregnancy, and, for some women, contractions of the uterus during orgasm are painful. Of course, anything that hurts or causes bleeding should be avoided. The third trimester could be looked upon as a good time for gentle erotic exploration.

*Physical Changes*    As the abdomen grows larger, reddish striations ("stretch marks") may appear on it. They are often aggravated by skin dryness, which is characteristic of late pregnancy. Bath and baby oils or cocoa butter help relieve the itching and minimize traces that may remain after pregnancy. Striations that can appear on the breasts can be minimized or prevented if the breasts are supported by a properly fitted bra.

As uterus expands, the other internal organs must shift to accommodate it. The stomach and intestines, for instance, are compressed, which often causes indigestion and constipation.

Water retention (*edema*) is another frequent and potentially painful problem in late pregnancy. It sometimes causes swelling in the face, hands, ankles, and feet. Controlling the amounts of salt and carbohydrates in the diet may relieve the edema. But if the problem is not alleviated by dietary controls, medical treatment is necessary. A doctor may prescribe *diuretics*, which are drugs that increase urination, thus eliminating excess fluid retention. Diuretics may also inhibit lubrication of the vagina, however, making intercourse painful.

**Precautions During Pregnancy**
In preparing for birth, a certain amount of help can come from a clinician, but ultimately it is the woman who must be responsible for the well-being of herself and her baby. Responsibility begins with an increased awareness of the various factors that can contribute to a trouble-free pregnancy.

**Diet** Each individual has unique nutritional needs. Nevertheless, a few generalizations can be made about diet. First, a person (pregnant or not) should eat protein every day. Protein is the basic building material of the body. Every part of the body – from hair to skin to muscle to toenails – requires protein as its primary structural mater-

ial. Certain hormones and other compounds vital to maintaining the chemical reactions of life are also formed from proteins.

Animal sources of protein include eggs, fish, chicken, red meat, milk, and milk by-products (including hard cheese, cottage cheese, and yogurt). Plant sources include nuts, rice, beans, and corn; however, it is extremely difficult to get enough of the right kinds of protein by eating just plant foods. Generally, it is best to have more than one source of protein at any given meal – chicken with beans and corn, for example is better than a big chunk of steak. The wider the range of foods, the more varied the nutrients from which the body can choose.

A variety of fresh fruits and vegetables are important as sources of vitamins and minerals. The coarse texture also keeps the digestive system functioning smoothly, which is especially important during pregnancy because of the tendencies toward indigestion and constipation.

Whether vitamins and minerals taken in pill form are desirable during pregnancy is a matter of debate. Most obstetricians prescribe supplemental iron, but there are mixed opinions on whether vitamin supplements are beneficial. The decision whether or not to use vitamin supplements is best made in consultation with a physician familiar with the unique characteristics of the individual woman. Some women may benefit from extra vitamins, while others may not.

In addition to protein, vitamins, and minerals, the body requires food containing carbohydrates and fats. The average American, however, has little problem getting enough of these – for most of us, the problem is getting too much. The term, carbohydrate, refers to both sugars and starches (starches are chain-like molecules formed of many bonded sugar molecules). Sources of sugar include honey, sugar cane, fruits, and milk.

Starches are included in all plants and are particularly concentrated in potatoes, corn, rice and wheat. Fats enter the body in foods and are also formed within the body from carbohydrates eaten in excess of immediate energy needs.

**Weight Gain** During pregnancy women are particularly prone to weight gain, and most authorities agree that gains over twenty-five pounds are excessive. However, exactly where to set the upper level is a matter of dispute. Some obstetricians limit their patients to less than fifteen pounds. They point out that deliveries are more difficult for heavy women, excess weight puts added strain on the heart, and flabbiness often persists after delivery. Also, a complication of pregnancy, *toxemia* (retention of toxic body wastes, which sometimes develops in late pregnancy) is aggravated by excessive weight. On the other hand, excessively restrictive diets have been linked with fetal malnutrition and death (Life and Health, 1972; Shaw, 1974).

Restrictive dieting is not the major cause of fetal malnutrition, however. In many cases the problem is attributable to poor nutritional balance. For many peole (especially those living on limited incomes) diets are too high in carbohydrates and fats in proportion to protein. People on limited incomes should remember that relatively cheap protein is still available in foods such as peanut butter, soybeans, dry milk, chicken, animal organs, and the lean portions of cheaper cuts of meat. Fruits and vegetables are also relatively cheap and easy to grow.

**Drugs** Whatever a pregnant woman eats or drinks is eventually received in some proportion by her baby. The same is true of injections, which enter the blood stream directly and reach the fetus without being diluted or detoxified by the mother's digestive system. Researchers are finding that many commonly used drugs have damaging effects on unborn infants.

Sometimes the detrimental effects of drugs are obvious; such was the case with the body deformities caused by the tranquilizer, thalidomide, which was used in the early 1960s. Other drugs are more subtle in their effects. A study of the offspring of mothers who were heavy alcohol drinkers during pregnancy, for instance, produced evidence linking chronic drinking with congenital heart defects, defective joints and smaller than average head size. Mothers who regularly used the opiate drugs (heroin, morphine, codeine, and opium) will likely bear infants who are addicted at birth.

Tetracycline must not be taken by pregnant women. During pregnancy a woman is highly susceptible to tetracycline-induced liver damage, which in some cases is fatal. Furthermore, tetracycline crosses the placenta and damages the delicate teeth and bones of the growing fetus. Infants may be born with permanent discoloration of the teeth or stunted growth.

Babies born to women who smoke cigarettes during pregnancy are one-forth to one-half pound lighter than babies born to non-smokers. British physicians calculated in one study that one out of five babies that died at birth would have lived had their mothers been nonsmokers. The Surgeon General has calculated that about 5,000 such deaths occur annually in the United States (Fielding and Yankauer, 1978). The mechanism by which tobacco affects the fetus is not known; it has been suggested that the oxygen supply to the fetus may be reduced by carbon monoxide (one of the gases in cigarette smoke) poisoning the red blood cells, or by nicotine constricting the arteries and reducing placental blood flow.

An expectant mother should keep in mind that her fetus is at a very fragile stage of life, and all drugs, including such widely used ones as to-bacco, marijuana, sleeping pills, and aspirin should be used with medical supervision, or preferably not at all.

**Diseases**    During pregnancy all infectious diseases should be carefully avoided, but one common disease, *rubella*, can be particularly damaging to the unborn child. To most people, rubella (also called three-day German measles) involves a rash, sore throat, temperature, and a few days in bed. However, if a woman contracts it in the first trimester of pregnancy it can cause permanent debilitation for her child. In the last major out-break of rubella in the 1960s, it caused congenital defects including limb deformities, blindness, deafness, and mental retardation in over 20,000 babies. An immunization against rubella is available; but, women planning to have children must be inoculated *before* they become pregnant, because the injection is as harmful as the disease to an early fetus.

The sexually transmissible diseases, *syphilis* and *gonorrhea*, also pose threats to fetuses. A baby born to a gonorrhea-infected woman may be blind. Syphilis can cause spontaneous abortions and still-births. If the baby is born alive, it may be blind, deaf or deformed. It may also have contracted the disease from the mother.

If discovered early, syphilis or gonorrhea can be stopped in a pregnant woman by antibiotic treatments, and no harm will come to the child. As a second line of defense against infant blindness, a bacteria-killing agent (such as silver nitrate or penicillin) is administered as eyedrops to newborns.

**Blood Tests**    Soon after confirmation of pregnancy several blood tests are routinely performed. Among them are a syphilis test, a red cell count, and an Rh-factor analysis. In many states a syphilis test is prescribed by law. Red cell counts are done to see if the oxygen-carrying capacity of the blood is sufficient to fulfill the needs of the mother and child.

The *Rh-test* is a comparison of a woman's blood with that of her mate. It checks for a genetic difference which may lead to destruction of a fetus's red blood cells. A person inherits either "Rh-positive" or "Rh-negative" blood (in the United States the positives outnumber the negatives by five to one). Trouble develops if a mother is Rh-negative, her mate is Rh-positive, and the unborn child inherits the positive trait from her father. In this case, the small amount of baby's blood which inevitably passes through ruptures in the placenta, causes the mother to produce certain *antibodies* (proteins which destroy foreign substances). In a chemical mechanism similar to the way a vaccination creates immunity to smallpox, the child's blood causes the mother's blood to produce antibodies which destroy Rh-positive red blood cells. There is usually no danger to the first infant, because ruptures in the placenta usually don't develop before labor. But, if another Rh-positive child is conceived, its life is in danger unless steps have been taken to prevent antibodies from forming. This is possible by administering the drug, *rhogam*, to the mother within three days following the birth of the first Rh-positive child. In cases of abortion, rhogam is administered if there is an Rh-incompatability between the woman and the fetus.

**Genetic Counseling**    Parents can inadvertently endow their offspring with genetic defects, including *Tay-Sachs disease* (an enzyme deficiency common to Jews of Russian and Polish descent, which results in a build-up of toxins in the brain); *sickle cell anemia* (a deformity of red blood cells occurring frequently among blacks); *PKU* (short for phenylketonuria – an enzyme deficiency that leads to severe mental retardation); *muscular dystrophy* (a slow deterioration of the muscles, characterized by spastic convulsions); and *Trisomy-21* (in which a zygote with one chromosome too many develops into a child with mental retardation and stunted growth).

Trisomy-21, (also called "Down's Syndrome" and "Mongolism"), is of particular concern because it is the most common genetic disease. The risk of bearing a child with trisomy-21 increases rapidly with age. A woman of 30 has approximately a 1-in-1,500 to 2,000 chance. When she reaches 35, the odds approach 1-in-100 to 150. After the age of 40, the risks jumps to 1-in-30 to 50. Babies born with this irreversible genetic anomaly develop a larger than normal tongue, slanting eyes, and short hands, feet, and trunk. They tend to have heart defects, and are more susceptible to respiratory infections than most people. The physical processes of aging occur at a mysteriously rapid rate; hence, people with trisomy-21 may "die of old age" when they are only 40.

Genetic disorders (as well as sex of a fetus) can be detected before birth. By a surgical technique called *amniocentesis*, a needle is inserted through the mother's abdomen, and a small portion of the amniotic fluid surrounding the fetus is withdrawn. This liquid contains cells that have been expelled from the fetus, which can be microscopically examined and chemically analyzed. Depending on the outcome, the parents may decide to continue or discontinue the pregnancy. There are presently no cures for genetic diseases, although the symptoms of some – especially PKU – can sometimes be alleviated by medication and special diets.

Amniocentesis should not presently be considered a routine test. The genetic disorders for which it examines are rare, and the procedure involves a certain amount of risk to the mother and fetus. In some cases spontaneous abortion is brought on by the operation (Golbus, et. al., 1979). Thus, it should be applied only in special cases, including: when a woman has alread had a child with a genetic affliction, if a woman or her mate is a known carrier of a dangerous gene, or if the woman is of advanced age. Amniocentesis is advisable in the later case, because of the increased possibility of trisomy-21. Prospective parents who are merely interested in the sex of their fetus should not use amniocentesis.

Obviously, preventative medicine is the best way of dealing with genetic diseases. If family history or chromosomal analysis of either parent (which can be performed simply by swabbing loose cells from underneath the tongue) indicates the possibility of a disorder, an amniocentesis may be indicated. It should certainly be performed if both parents are carriers of the same recessive defect.

Unfortunately, not all people anticipating birth in America are given the rudiments of genetic counseling. In a study of one children's hospital, a review of the charts of patients with any of ten specified types of genetic or congenital disorders were studied to document whether genetic counseling had been: "given"; "offered only"; or "considered only." Of the 478 charts studied, genetic counseling had been "given" in five cases, "offered only" twice, and "considered only" by none in the sample. The study is particularly alarming when one considers that the children's hospital is affiliated with a medical school (Riccardi, et. al., 1978).

Women should make sure that the subject of genetic counseling comes up at their *first* meeting with the specialist who will see them through delivery.

## Labor and Delivery

The sensations of birth usually begin with sporadic spasms of the uterus. Prelabor contractions last only a few seconds and may come at irregular intervals for several days, or the first one may be followed within a matter of minutes by a "true" labor contraction. True *labor* begins when uterine contractions become regular. Although the processes of labor are not fully understood, the secretion of a hormone-like substance, *prostaglandin*, is thought to be an early step. Prostaglandin is known to stimulate contractions by the uterus, and therefore may initiate the contractions of labor. As labor progresses, *oxytocin* (a hormone produced by the pituitary gland) is released, and causes the powerful contractions which ultimately expel the fetus. Labor is commonly described as occurring in three stages:

**First-Stage**    This phase is the longest of the three, usually lasting about ten to sixteen hours for women having their first babies and four to eight hours in subsequent births. The contractions (which are felt as gradual tightenings of the uterine muscles) cannot be controlled by the mother, and become increasingly intense and tiring. At the onset, labor contractions are about fifteen to twenty minutes apart and last approximately one minute.

One early sign of first-stage labor is expulsion from the vagina of the plug of slightly bloody mucus that has been blocking the cervix ("bloody show"). Either concurrently or later, a second fluid discharge comes from the vagina ("breaking of the waters"). This is the amnionic fluid, which pours from the ruptured amnionic membrane. Because the infant is susceptible to infection after this protective membrane breaks, the mother should be given medical attention soon thereafter, if not before. The amnion sometimes bursts before the onset of labor. If it does not, however, women are usually advised to wait until contractions are definitely periodic before entering the hospital or being attended at home.

Concurrent with first-stage contractions the cervix undergoes an amazing expansion that ultimately enlarges the opening through it, the *os*, to a diameter of about four inches. As labor proceeds, uterine contractions become more frequent. Just before birth, they may be almost constant. First-stage labor ends when the baby's head passes into the vagina.

**Second-Stage**    During second-stage labor the baby passes through the vagina. This phase may last only a matter of minutes or extend for several hours. The second-stage is frequently the most difficult phase for the mother. It involves the exhausting effort of bearing down with the muscles of the upper abdomen during contractions. Some women find second stage labor to be extremely painful. However, other women find that the contractions and the effort of bearing down produce a euphoria. Anesthetics are commonly administered prior to or during the second stage, but routine use of them is a matter of debate.

**Third-Stage**    After the baby has been delivered, the uterus continues to contract. The placenta dislodges from the uterus and is expelled along with the fetal membranes. Expulsion of this "afterbirth" may take a few minutes to a half hour. The umbilical cord is tied, then cut, leaving the navel as a scar.

**Premature Births**    If a newborn weighs less than five and a half pounds, it is considered premature. About 8 percent of the births in the

United States are premature, and of these some end in fetal death. However, the chances for survival are fairly good for infants who weigh over three pounds, which roughly corresponds to an age of seven months. Immediately after delivery a premature infant is placed in an *incubator*, where sterility and controls on oxygen, temperature, and humidity create an optimum environment.

Approximately half the cases of premature birth are unexplained; for the remainder there are several known causes. Among them are maternal diseases (including toxemia, diabetes, and syphilis), poor nutrition, fetal abnormalities, and multiple pregnancy. Prematurity is also common for teenage mothers, who may not be physically ready to carry a pregnancy to term.

**Obstetric Techniques**
About 90 percent of fetuses approach birth with their heads in the cervix and their arms and legs crossed (the *cephalic* position). This is the optimum position for birth. In most other cases the baby has its buttocks in the cervix (the *breech* position) or it is situated crosswise. If so, a physician can usually rotate it into the head first position during the last month of pregnancy. Many fetuses develop up to the third trimester in the breech position, but make an unassisted 180-degree turn before the last month of pregnancy. In about 0.5 percent of all pregnancies the baby develops with an arm, foot or shoulder lodged in the cervix. In these cases a doctor may not be able to manipulate it into the headfirst position.

**The Enema and Shave** Standard procedure in many obstetrics wards is to give the woman an enema and shave her pubic hair soon after she is admitted. Neither procedure is absolutely necessary, and if they aren't wanted, the woman

should discuss it with her physician long before her due date.

**Caesarean Section** If the baby is awkardly lodged in the cervix, or if the mother's birth canal is too small to accommodate delivery, a *Caesarean section* may be necessary. In this operation the infant is removed through an incision into the uterus. About 10 percent of the deliveries in the United States are performed by Caesarean section.

A Caearean section does not necessarily make future births through the vagina impossible. If it is done because a woman's pelvic opening is too small to admit the infant's head, then, subsequent births will probably also require this procedure. However, if a Caesarean is done because of malpresentation or because of an unforeseen emergency, then future babies can generally be delivered through the birth canal.

**Induction of Labor** Labor is sometimes artificially hastened if the pregnant woman has diabetes or heart disease, or if she exhibits symptoms of toxemia. It may also be induced for convenience of the obstetrician (who may be late for a golf date). But, induction of labor under any circumstances involves risk, thus it should never be done just for convenience – in fact some hospitals do not allow it unless it is done for medical reasons.

There are two ways in which labor can be induced. Usually a drug, *pitocin*, is administered that mimics the natural labor-inducing hormone, *oxytocin*. Oxytocin is a hormone released by the pituitary gland during late labor. Besides stimulating the most powerful contractions of labor, it also plays a role in *lactation*, the secretion of milk from the breasts. Mechanical rupturing of the amniotic membrane with a metal probe is the second technique for inducing labor.

**Episiotomy**  When the baby's head first appears, the physician often makes an incision across the perineum from the vagina toward the anus. Episiotomy is performed routinely by many doctors. The justifications for it include minimization of pressure on the infant's head and prevention of ragged tearing of the skin and muscle around the vagina. Also, by sugically enlarging the vaginal opening and then stitching it up after delivery, some doctors claim that the vagina is returned to its original size and muscle tone. Other obstetricians, however, believe that the advantages of episiotomy are not sufficient to warrant its routine use. Healing of the incision is commonly painful, and, if the vaginal opening is repaired and left too small, chronic painful intercourse can result.

**Forceps**  Occasionally forceps are used to pull the baby from the vagina. The most common type has spoonlike metal tongs that cup the baby's head (Figure 4.11). Most obstetricians use forceps only in cases of emergency. They are used when the infant's passage through the vagina is abnormally slow, for instance, or if its heartbeat is erratic and medical attention must be administered as quickly as possible. Certain types of anesthesia eliminate the mother's ability to bear down and force the baby out thus making a forceps delivery mandatory.

**Anesthesia and Childbirth**  The value of anesthesia for complicated deliveries (particularly Caesarean sections) is indisputable. However, drugs to eliminate the sensations of labor and delivery are routinely used in many American hospitals. Many doctors and the women they serve are questioning the wisdom and safety of such blanket policies on anesthesia. Doctors are debating whether the dangers of anesthetics are inherent in the drugs or whether lack of skilled technicians is the main problem. An active field of research is considering the dangers to infants born under anesthesia.

The following discussion considers the pros and cons of common obstetric anesthetics.

*General Anesthetics*  Drugs of this category are applied during the second stage of labor to produce a state of unconsciousness. Some are inhaled (including nitrous oxide, halothane, and ether) and others are injected (sodium pentothal).

General anesthesia is the oldest method known to Western medicine for deadening the pain of birth – and it is also the most dangerous. Chloroform was the first general anesthetic to come into wide use in the mid-nineteenth century. It was frequently applied by soaking a handkerchief and placing it over the nose and mouth. Chloroform reached its peak of popularity within a few decades, but fell into disfavor when doctors realized that some of their patients were dying from its side effects. The three major problems were heart stoppage, inhalation of

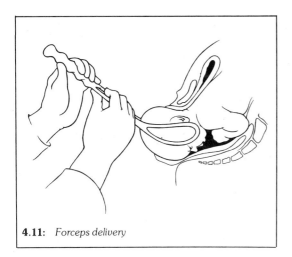

**4.11:**  *Forceps delivery*

vomit (with subsequent suffocation), and massive blood loss.

Today's commonly used general anesthetics are safer than chloroform, but the same problems persist. For example, of the eighty-five maternal deaths reported to result from anesthetics in North Carolina between 1946 and 1965, approximately 80 percent were caused by general anesthetics (mostly due to inhalation of vomit).

General anesthetics also have adverse effects on infants, by passing through the placenta and depressing metabolic and cognitive functions. In *Apgar tests* (a series of examinations designed to rate vital physical and mental activities of newborns), children born to women under general anesthesia score lower on the average than infants delivered with any other type of anesthetic.

*Spinal Injection*    In this procedure, an anesthetic is injected directly into the spinal column; it numbs the body, but it does not produce unconsciousness. Depending on where and how much of the drug is used, the woman can be numbed as extensively as from the shoulders to the feet or as minimally as the part of the body that would touch a saddle (hence the term *saddle block*). Injections that are made low on the spine numb less of the body than those that are made higher up.

Spinal anesthetic temporarily destroys a woman's ability to bear down during labor contractions. Thus, her doctor must take a more active role than he would if she were not anesthetized; usually this includes using forceps to extract the infant from the vagina.

Headaches and low back pain are commonly felt by women following delivery with spinal anesthesia, and the activities of their infants are depressed for a short time after delivery. Occasionally maternal death results from heart or respiratory complications.

*Epidural Injection*    This injection of anesthetic is made near, but outside, the spinal cord. *Epidural* means "upon the *dura*", which is a tough, fibrous sheath that surrounds the spinal cord. The procedure is currently one of the most popular techniques among doctors and mothers who have compared it with other methods. However, high cost and the shortage of people skilled in its use limit availability.

An epidural is continuously administered with a catheter from late in the first stage throughout the second. The woman does not feel her uterine contractions, but she can bear down when told to do so – an important advantage over spinal anesthesia.

Considering its effects on mothers, epidural anesthesia has a good record of safety, and it is widely accepted as an excellent method for performing Caesarean sections. However, infants delivered of women anesthetized by the epidural method are reported to have low Apgar scores.

*Paracervical Block*    This procedure involves an injection of anesthetic into the cervix by way of the vagina. Paracervical blocks are frequently administered during labor before the cervix has reached its maximum dilation. Unfortunately, they are known to slow fetal heart rates and consequently have been banned by some hospitals.

*Narcotics*    This group of drugs includes the opium-derivatives as well as synthetics; all of them relieve pain, dull senses and induce sleep. Some of the most commonly used obstetric drugs are narcotics, among them: morphine, Demerol, and Nisentil. Nisentil is perhaps the least harmful, since its effects are relatively shortlived (usually less than 2 hours). It is injected toward the end of first stage labor, as the cervix stretches to maximum dilation and contractions reach crescendo.

In taking narcotics to relieve pain, the woman sacrifices a certain amount of awareness and ability to respond to the demands of labor (some women, however, are thankful for the induced aloofness from the fantastic physical reality). Nausea, vomiting and hallucinations are possible side effects. For the fetus breathing and heartrate are depressed, and the oxygen supply from the mother is restricted.

As with other types of anesthetics, pitocin may be administered at the same time to induce contractions and speed delivery. Otherwise the infant might suffer irreversible brain damage from oxygen deprivation.

**Tranquilizers**    Drugs such as Valium, Librium, Equanil, and Miltown are the mildest pain killers for labor. They relax tension and cause drowsiness. Like other anesthetics, tranquilizers cross the placenta, but their effect on the fetus is relatively slight.

**Barbiturates**    Drugs including Secobarbital, Nembutal, Luminal, and Seconal induce sleep, thus when used in labor they slow breathing and depress the mental activity of both mother and child. Barbiturates are selectively stored by the tissue of the brain, and behavioral researchers have found that they muddle the mental centers that direct a baby's physical activities for a week or more after birth. Studies have revealed, for instance, that an infant's sucking response is depressed by barbiturates. The effect is not severe enough to prevent the child from getting sufficient nutrition, but, behaviorists caution that disruptions of such things as sucking behavior may only be overt symptoms of damage done to the mother-child relationship.

### Prepared Childbirth

In recent years there has been growing criticism of the control of childbirth by the medical profession. A woman who would prefer to have her baby without anesthetics, for instance, often has a hard time finding a doctor and hospital willing to comply. If she would like to have her baby at home rather than in a hospital, she usually finds even more resistance. Nevertheless, more and more of America's obstetricians are becoming sensitive to women wanting a less surgical approach to childbirth. Doctors inevitably caution, however, that someone wanting to deviate from standard obstetric procedures must take extra care to prepare herself mentally and physically.

*Natural childbirth* has become a popular term in recent years – so much so that it has lost most of its original meaning. When it was coined several decades ago, however, "natural childbirth" was used in the context of some valuable ideas for women anticipating birth. In a book of lasting value, *Childbirth Without Fear* (published in 1944). Dr. Grantly Dick-Read pointed out that the pain of childbirth could be minimized by first overcoming the fear of it. He stressed that fear causes muscle tension, which in turn causes pain. A vicious circle is completed when pain intensifies fear. Dick-Read advocated education about pregnancy and birth for both parents, and suggested that the father could have a positive influence in the delivery room. He also devised techniques to help relieve muscle tension.

In the 1950s a French doctor, Bernard Lamaze, introduced a more complex series of physical and mental procedures to alleviate the pain of labor and delivery. A woman practicing the Lamaze method responds to the accelerating rushes of uterine contractions with a prelearned set of physical postures and breathing techniques. The Lamaze method also stresses the value of encouragement and support from the husband and other participants, including the physician, in the birth experience. Some couples have found their relationships strengthened as the result of sharing the intense emotional experience of childbirth.

Frederick Leboyer is a more contemporary questioner of Western civilization's techniques of delivery (Leboyer, 1975). He wonders, for instance, why a new human being, entering the world from the dark warmth of its mother's body must be greeted with the glare of operating room lights and loud voices. He asks why, when the vulnerable spines of newborns have always been curved, do obstetricians insist on holding them upside down and jerking their backs straight. Leboyer's techniques of delivery are designed to ease the transition from the womb to the world by placing the infant on its mother's stomach after it is born and by gently massaging it. The umbilical cord is not cut until after it has stopped pulsating.

**Midwifery**  At a time when some hospitals have closed their obstetrics wards because of the depressed birth rate, midwife clinics across the country are having boom times. Not many years ago, when someone said "midwife," images of a ham-handed matron in a blood-stained frock came to mind. Midwives were for people who could not afford a doctor, and the lack of training common in the profession sometimes justified the skepticism with which midwives were reviewed.

But, today's midwife is a far cry from the archaic image. She is a *certified nurse-midwife* (C.N.M.) with the knowledge to justify the faith that more and more people are placing in her. (The gender of the term should not be taken to imply that midwives must be women; in fact, there are male midwives now in practice.) Modern midwives have a professional organization (the American College of Nurse-Midwives, ACNM ), and they must put in years of training

to be licensed. Being a registered nurse is one of the requirements, which also includes experience as an obstetric nurse. In 1977 all but three states allowed practice by C.N.M.s (Michigan, Wisconsin, and Massachusetts being the exceptions).

Regarding the limits of the modern midwife, the ACNM guidelines are as follows: ". . . the area of management of care of mothers and babies throughout the maternity cycle so long as progress meets criteria accepted as normal." C.N.M.s are licensed for managing pregnancies and deliveries except in situations of medical complications, as determined by state law. Midwives are also trained to counsel women in family planning, to give gynecologic examinations, and to help new mothers learn how to care for their babies. However, C.N.M.s are not independent practitioners. Rather they are members of an obstetric team, with back-up by physicians who are available if their skills are needed. As stated by one midwife: "Our excitement comes not from performing intricate Caesarean sections or from deftly wielding a pair of forceps, but from helping a woman do a job her body was beautifully designed to do" (Brennan and Heilman, 1977).

**The Birth Environment**  Some women believe it is wiser to choose the location for birth before picking the professional attendant (Paulsen and Kuhn, 1976). This is particularly true if what one wants is a family-oriented hospital environment or a home delivery. More and more hospitals are adopting plans which invite the fathers participation in the delivery. Characteristically the plans offer "rooming in" whereby the baby rooms with the mother for most or all of the day, and visitation by the newborn's siblings. To be sure what services are available, one should call the hospital, or, better yet, visit before the time of birth.

If one has found a satisfactory doctor but not a suitable hospital, and if the pregnancy is proceeding without complications, giving birth at home might be the best alternative. At present, only a small fraction of obstetricians are willing to attend home deliveries, primarily because they fear unanticipated troubles. This is no problem in some areas, however, where mobile maternity units wait outside the home during a delivery; then emergency facilities are on hand, whether or not they are needed.

### Postpartum

The *postpartum period* (the month or so immediately following birth) is a phase of physical stabilization and emotional adjustment. During the postpartum period the mother and her family must begin dealing with the new responsibilities of child care. Sometimes there are moments of emotional turmoil as she and those close to her make adjustments to the new infant. It is not surprising, therefore, that many women have brief spells of physical and emotional letdown. Common complaints include fatigue, sudden outbursts of crying, fear of failure as a parent, and disinterest in sexual activity. Not everyone experiences these symptoms, known as "postpartum blues," and only about half of the women who give birth feel unusually low more than a couple weeks afterward.

Sometimes there are obvious circumstances for postpartum blues (neglect by the husband, for instance). But, it is so common that psychologists have begun looking for physiological and biochemical causes. One line of research has produced evidence linking depression with hormonal changes following birth. Immediately after a child is born, a woman loses an important hormone-producing organ, the placenta. In addition to serving as the structure through which nutrients pass from mother to fetus, the placenta is a source of estrogen and progesterone during pregnancy. When it is lost as afterbirth, the concentrations of sex hormones in the bloodstream rapidly decline. There is evience that this sudden loss may touch off a sequence of chemical interactions leading to psychological depression.

### Breast Feeding

*Lactation* is production of milk, and it usually begins within three days after childbirth. Prior to lactation the breasts produce a yellowish liquid

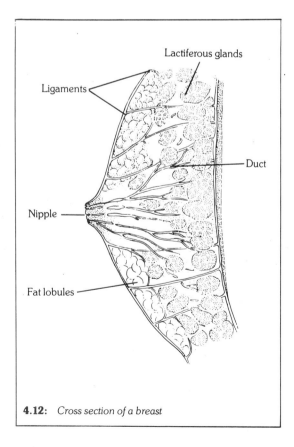

**4.12:** *Cross section of a breast*

**Sources of Information**

MATERNITY CENTER ASSOCIATION
(48 East 92nd Street, New York, N.Y. 10028).

The MCA is a progressive training center for good obstetrics, dispersing timely information on methods and research, and frequently sponsoring cross-disciplinary workshops and seminars for improving the quality of maternity care.

ICEA SUPPLIES CENTER
(208 Ditty Building, Bellevue, Wash. 98004).

The Supplies Center makes available a wide range of books, pamphlets, films, and teaching aids on every aspect of family life for both lay and professional people.

LA LECHE LEAGUE INTERNATIONAL
(9616 Minneapolis Avenue, Franklin Park, Ill. 60131
[telephone 312 455-7730]).

The LLL offers help to women who want to breastfeed their babies, through literature, member groups in many communities, and a medical board of consultants for counsel in unusual breastfeeding problems.

AMERICAN COLLEGE OF NURSE-MIDWIVES
Suite 500, 1000 Vermont Ave., N.W.
Washington, D.C. 20005
202-628-4642

Write for information on midwifery services in your area.

---

called *colostrum*, which may appear at the nipples as early in pregnancy as the second trimester. Colostrum is high in protein and contains antibodies that protect a baby from infectious diseases.

The switch from colostrum to milk happens in conjunction with hormonal changes that begin during labor. Two hormones from the pituitary gland, *prolactin* and *oxytocin*, are released into the bloodstream. Upon reaching the breasts they stimulate lactation. Unless a mother nurses her baby, however, her breasts cease to produce milk. If a woman does not want to breast-feed, lactation can be quickly stopped with an injection of estrogen soon after the child is delivered. In some hospitals this may be done routinely. So, women who do wish to breast feed should make this clear to the attending physician and staff.

Today, fewer than 50 percent of American women choose to breastfeed. But, if she is healthy and maintains a good diet, a mother's milk will give her child the best nutrition available. Even after her colostrum is gone, a woman's milk will give her child the best nutrition available and provide antibodies that protect against infectious diseases. Furthermore, breastfed babies are less likely to become constipated, contract skin disease, or develop respiratory infections.

There are psychological as well as physical benefits of breastfeeding. Both mother and child derive a sense of emotional well-being from the close physical contact. Also, stimulation to the breasts can be sensually satisfying.

There are several reasons why most contemporary American woman choose not to breast-feed, among them are inconvenience, messiness, tenderness of the nipples (which usually lasts only a few days), and modesty. Many women balk at the prospect of having to nurse their babies in public. However, concern over nutrition (and, balancing the budget) has increased, and shame over physical exposure has diminished in recent years. Concurrently there has been a resurgence in the proportion of women who nurse their infants.

If a woman chooses to breastfeed, she must keep in mind that what she eats or drinks will eventually reach her baby. Although a newborn is less susceptible to toxic substances than it was while it received nourishment through the placenta, it can still be harmed by impurities (such as antibiotics and other drugs) in its mother's milk.

## Sexual Activity after Childbirth

Women usually become fertile within a few months after they have had a baby. However, some women go for more than a year before their ovaries resume egg production, while others can become pregnant after less than a month. Women who are breastfeeding generally remain infertile longer than those who are not, because the hormonal activity of lactation suppresses the menstrual cycle. But, breastfeeding shouldn't be counted on as a method of contraception. The absence of menstrual bleeding should not be taken as an indication that ovulation has yet to begin. If another pregnancy is not wanted, a method of contraception should be used as soon as intercourse is resumed.

AMERICAN SOCIETY FOR
PSYCHOPROPHYLAXIS IN OBSTETRICS
(36 West 96 Street, New York, N.Y. 10025).

This organization is dedicated to furthering the teaching of the Lamaze-Pavlov approach as it has been adapted to this country, training couples for childbirth in education classes throughout the country. It also accredits teachers in this method of childbirth preparation.

INTERNATIONAL CHILDBIRTH EDUCATION
ASSOCIATION, INC.
(P.O. Box 5852, Milwaukee, Wis. 53220).

The ICEA is a federation of individuals and of community childbirth education groups throughout the United States and other countries. Because of its wide contacts, it is a valuable resource agency for all those who want information concerning childbirth education opportunities in various areas, or current trends in childbirth literature and practice.

AMERICAN INSTITUTE OF FAMILY RELATIONS
(5287 Sunset Boulevard, Los Angeles, Calif. 90277).

The AIFR has been a responsible resource center for all aspects of family life for many years, including materials on sex education and education for childbirth. A wide range of publications are available on request.

---

But, in the period immediately following birth, most methods of contraception cannot be used. Oral contraceptives must not be used by women who are breastfeeding, for example, because the active ingredients, estrogen and progesterone, could be harmful to the baby. An IUD cannot be used for a least a few weeks, until the uterus contracts to a stable size. A diaphragm used prior to the pregnancy will no longer fit properly. The rhythm method cannot be used until predictable cycles of menstrual bleeding are reestablished (which is usually several months following birth). This leaves the condom, foams and jellies, and withdrawal as the only commonly used means of contraception. The condom in combination with foam or jelly will give nearly 100 percent protection from pregnancy. The failure rate of withdrawal is infamous. Intercourse is physically safe by about three weeks after delivery, providing the episiotomy incision or tears around the vagina have completely healed.

### The Cycle of Life – Why Bother?

Why bother going through the cycle of human reproduction, with its frustrating cycle of being dependent and depended upon? Perhaps the main reason is that we are depended upon only once in our lives, while dependency comes twice – when we are very young and very old. There is reassurance in knowing that someone will be there to take care of us as we become frail. That is, there used to be.

The contemporary decay of the stable family with the ascendancy of the mania for "self-fulfillment" (which too often translates as "wealth") has added loneliness to the uncertainty of old age. Ironically, the more profound self-fulfillment motives for raising a new human have been ignored. But rewards come even at the price of stinking diapers, shrieks in the night, temper tantrums, goofing off, and "how bout five bucks for Saturday night? . . . uh, maybe make that ten."

One must acknowledge before having children that the future is going to take time, energy, and money. In the traditional scheme of things women are charged with the former responsibility, while men come up with the latter. But the most successful couples of today seem to be crossing the boundaries. Breastfeeding, for example, may be offered in exchange for diaper duty.

Of course, finding enough time is tricky if both partners are working. Moreover, during the early months of life, infants crave their mothers for more than their milk; there seems to be a psychological need for reassurance. But, if three months (plus or minus a few weeks) of near undivided attention can be given by the mother to the infant, the need seems to be fulfilled. Then both partners can return to their money-making roles. (It is helpful if the male can also devote most of his attention to the infant during the crucial early months.)

Obviously, the problem of having enough time is still there. The solution, as more and more young parents are finding, is to take on several surrogate parents; day care centers and cooperative sharing of child-care responsibilities among friends can help immensely. Neighborhood co-ops are viable economic options if all the parents have saleable skills. One such skill could be the full-time directorship of the operation (a worthy and demanding position). Others within the co-op could arrange to take off a day of the normal work week to get in on the fun.

If one acknowledges that child-rearing is going to take time and energy, then forgives one's self for being human, hence imperfect, then one is in a better frame of mind for enjoying the amazingly rapid unfolding of conscious life. To a certain extent, seeing one's child develop is to see one's self begin again. With half of each parent's genes, and in an environment which the parents largely dominate, the developing individual is much the product of the parents' selves. When the demands are viewed as the price of the "ticket," then the development of new life can be enjoyed for the wondrously revealing journey into the self which it is. If love for the child is found along the way (don't expect it to always glow, and certainly don't snuff it out when it only glimmers), then love of self will likely be there too.

## QUESTIONS

1. "Natural childbirth" is a frequently used term. Do you think it is used with validity?
2. Has information on the physiology of the embryonic and fetal phases of human life in this chapter affected your opinion on abortion?
3. Do you think the government should have the right to make abortions mandatory in cases of known genetic defects? Which, if any, genetic defects do you believe necessitate abortion?
4. If you are a male, do you feel cheated by nature in not being able to experience pregnancy and childbirth? If you are female, do you feel pressured into having babies?
5. Once labor has started, do you believe obstetricians should have total latitude in determining how the baby is delivered?

# Readings

## Excerpt from Childbirth Without Fear

Grantly Dick-Read

*The originator of "natural childbirth" summarizes the highlights of labor:*

. . . even if efficient relaxation is practiced, there is always the possibility of a few relatively painful contractions at the end of the first stage — the final dilation of the cervical canal. On many occasions I have formed the opinion that the only true pains of normal labor, if present at all, are the last few contractions that completely dilate the cervix. When this discomfort is recognized and its significance appreciated, a woman may confidently be asked to put up with about six or eight such contractions. The reaction to such a request is almost invariably an easy compliance. "If it is only six or eight, I don't mind, but I thought it might be going on and getting worse all the time now." And so it proves true; this short phase passes into the more definite but completely different second stage. The discomfort of the end of the first stage lifts, either gradually or suddenly, depending upon the mode of onset of the bearing-down reflex.

I have in mind a nurse who attended cases with me until she herself was seven months pregnant. About two weeks after her baby boy was born I had an opportunity to ask her in detail what she thought about the whole process. We discussed at length everything that had happened during her pregnancy and labor. She had closely followed my teaching, which she had seen practiced in the maternity home, and her final judgment was that she could not understand why some women made such a fuss about having a baby. At one point only – and then for a very few contractions – she was in discomfort, but other than that the whole thing, as she put it, was an exciting and marvelous experience.

As the second stage becomes fully established, acquired social habits and manners are thrown off. The woman becomes aware of the conscious effort demanded of her to help, so far as possible, in the expulsion of her child. She is engrossed in the task, concentrating upon the all-important occupation of the moment. When the muscular effort ceases, her mind and body relax and she passes into a restful, sleepy state, sometimes into a deep, snoring slumber. This condition of complete alienation from other thoughts and associations either causes or passes into a state of amnesia and partial anesthesia; the perception is dulled and the interpretation of stimuli through the normal channels is clouded. She rests peacefully, arousing only to work with each contraction.

I cannot lay too much stress upon the necessity for recognizing this *amnesiac state*, and the changes in perception, interpretation, and reaction that accompany it. If control is removed from a mind that is undisturbed and confident, a quiet peace remains, a fact best demonstrated by the relative absence of discomfort when a woman retains both confidence and courage.

"Hard work, yes – the hardest work I have ever known," was the comment of a fearless woman. The physical reactions to the emotional state in the second stage must be more clearly understood if interference is to be avoided in normal labor.

Take, for another example, the grunting moans during a second-stage contraction. In a natural, uncomplicated labor they vary, not only according to the strength of the woman's muscular activity, but according to her emotional state, and they have no association with physical pain. The large majority of undrugged and fully informed women have very little if any discomfort with second-stage contractions, but a deal of hard work. Their grunts and moans are like those of a man who pulls successfully upon a rope, the physical strain at the utmost. His determination adds to the violence of his effort; when he relaxes, it is with a groan of satisfaction and relief that he may rest in preparation for the next pull, and having rested he is ready for a renewal of his exertion. So he struggles in the sure confidence of victory until at last his objective is attained, and according to his valuation of the prize, so is the joy with which he hails success. His contortions have not been accompanied by physical agony, though his facial expression may well have represented it. His groans have been physiological, for our bodies abhor a sudden change of tension and most of all a sudden drop of intra-abdominal pressure. The diaphragm must be gradually released and the muscles of the chest slowly relaxed from the strain of their rigidity. There is nothing to cause purely physical pain, but the partial closure of the larynx, which produces the grunt, groan, or long-drawn-out moan, is a part of the design for safety after effort.

There is yet one more observation upon the natural anesthesia and analgesia of the second stage. The stretching of the *vulva* (external genitals) just befor the baby is born is felt as a burning sensation. But this is temporary, and the actual passage of the baby through the vulva is often accomplished with so little sensation that the woman is with difficulty persuaded her baby has arrived; until she sees or hears it she is unwilling to believe it is born. In a natural labor the *perineum*, the area between the vulva and the anus, is practically insensitive.

It is my custom to lift up the crying child, even before the cord is cut, so that the mother may see "with her own eyes" the reality of her dreams. I have been told that no woman should see the baby until it has been bathed and dressed; my patients, however, are the first to grasp the small fingers and touch gingerly the soft skin of the infant's cheek. They are the first to marvel at the miracle of their own performance; to them indeed is due the inspiring reward of full and conscious realization. That there is anything unsightly in the appearance of a newborn babe is nonsense; that a mother might be shocked at her own baby is fantastic. Its first cry remains an indelible memory on the mind of a mother; this is the song that carried her upon its wings to an ecstasy mere man seems quite unable to comprehend. But like all other natural emotional states, it is part of a great design; its magnitude is significant of its important purpose. No mother and no child should be denied that great mystical association. It is not only advantageous for the immediate present, to perfect the restoration of the muscles and tissues involved in the birth to their nonpregnant state, as we shall see in a moment, but it lays a foundation of unity of both body and spirit upon which the whole edifice of mother love will stand.

From *Childbirth Without Fear*, 4th Edition by Grantly Dick-Read. Copyright © 1959, 1972 by Jessica Dick-Read. Reprinted by permission of Harper and Row, Publishers, Inc.

## Limbering and Posture Exercises

Marjorie Karmel

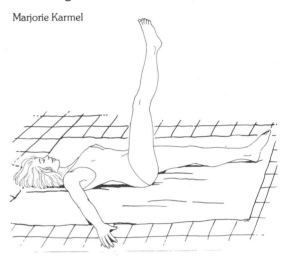

*The following exercise for keeping in shape during pregnancy are part of the Lamaze regimen.*

As pregnancy progresses, the growing uterus exerts pressure on the bones of the pelvis, occasionally to the extent of interfering with the functioning of its joints. At the same time it presses on the blood vessels more than usual, which often leads to leg cramps and varicose veins. The following exercises will help prevent the development of these complaints, release tensions, and be an aid later on, during the delivery, as they lead to limberness and better muscle tone in the pelvic region, and a greater elasticity of the pelvic floor.

The first two exercise should be done while lying on the back on a firm surface (a mat or carpet on the floor), with a pillow under the knees, and the arms stretched out on each side.

1. Slowly raise the right leg until it is vertical (at right angles to the floor), while inhaling deeply through the nose. Then slowly lower the leg again, while exhaling through the mouth. Then do the same with the left leg.

Repeat this exercise five or ten times, alternating legs.

2.  Raise the right leg and swing it out to the side and toward the right hand, spreading the thighs as far as possible, while inhaling deeply through the nose. Then drop the leg slowly to its starting position while exhaling through the mouth. Repeat this exercise five or ten times, alternating legs.

3.  Sitting tailor position: Sit on a firm suface, legs bent, knees spread apart, the back rounded and the body bent slightly forward. By pressing on the knees spread the thighs and limber the joints. Try to spend ten to fifteen minutes, several times a day, sitting in this position. It is extremely helpful in relaxing the back and preventing fatigue, as the weight of the uterus usually pulls the spine forward and tires the muscles of the back by forcing it to a concave position.

Unless your doctor forbids it for some medical reason, do these exercises every day, several times a day if possible. Don't overstrain yourself. Regulate the amount of exercise according to your physical condition. Begin slowly, and you will soon notice with pleasure a delightful increase in your general well-being that will serve you also at the time of your delivery.

*From Thank You, Dr. Lamaze: A Mother's Experience in Painless Childbirth* by Marjorie Karmel. Copyright © 1959 by Marjorie Karmel. Reprinted by permission of J. B. Lippincott Company.

### *Excerpt from* Birth Without Violence

Frederick Le Boyer

*Frederick LeBoyer's sensitivity to the nature of childbirth is reflected in his poetic statement on delivery.*

Now is the moment.

The baby emerges . . . first the head, and then the arms; we help to free them by sliding a finger under each armpit. Supporting the baby in this way, we lift the little body up, as if pulling someone out of the well. We *never* touch the head. And we settle the child immediately on its mother's belly.

What better place could there be? Her belly has the infant's exact shape and dimensions. Swelling a moment before, hollow now, the belly seems to lie there waiting, like a nest.

And its warmth and suppleness as it rises and falls with the rhythm of her breathing, its softness, the glowing life of its skin, all work together to create the best possible resting place for the child.

Finally — and this is crucial — the very closeness of contact permits the umbilical cord to be left intact.

To sever the umbilicus when the child has scarcely left the mother's womb is an act of cruelty whose ill effects are immeasurable. To conserve it intact while it still pulses is to transform the act of birth.

First, this forces the physician to be patient; it is an invitation to both the doctor and the mother to respect the baby's own life-rhythm.

And it does more.

When air rushes into the baby's lungs, it feels like burning fire.

Before he was born, the infant made no distinction between the world and himself, since "outside" and "inside" were all one. He knew nothing of the tension of opposites — nothing was cold, since cold can only be known by contrast with what is warm. An infant's body temperature and its mother's are always identical; how could there be any separation between them?

For the newborn infant to enter our world is to enter a universe of opposites, where everything is good or bad, pleasant or unpleasant, dry or wet . . . it is to discover these contradictions that cannot exist apart from one another.

And how does the infant enter this kingdom of opposites?

Through breathing. In taking its first breath, it crosses a threshold. And it is here.

## Natural Childbirth (as if it happened any other way)

Susan Schwartz McDonald

*Not everyone is sold on natural childbirth.*

In recent months I have spent many long hours with pregnant friends (it's that time of our lives) who talk inevitably and tediously about the impending event. I am always surprised by the number of these young women who have chosen natural childbirth – and I have been piqued, on occasion, by the arrogance with which they transform a personal decision into a belligerent crusade.

Like the manufacture of natural food and old-fashioned crafts, our recent idealization of natural childbirth represents one more contrived attempt to get in touch with the way life used to be – to free ourselves from the artifice of modern society with some equally artful and selfconscious simulations of nature. Natural childbirth is becoming an unassailable middle-class institution, and its practitioners are humbling the rest of us with their stoicism.

Decisions related to modes of delivery are highly personal ones, and I see nothing wrong with foregoing anesthesia if that sort of abstinence makes childbirth more rewarding for a woman. What irks me is our uncritical acceptance of natural childbirth (and nearly every other manifestation of back-to-naturism) as rugged and ingenuous virtue. It's time we stopped confusing delivery with deliverance.

Now, pregnant women tend to make tiresome company under any circumstances. They are enamored of their own girth, preoccupied with the symptoms of pregnancy, and slightly beatific in their maternity couture. But flamboyant gestation was tolerable until natural childbirth came into vogue and its advocates felt free to narrate their transcendental deliveries at dinner. Now they insist on taking the rest of us to task for our timid decision to deliver under local anesthesia – which is, as one pregnant friend put it, the forfeiture of "essential womanhood" (a phrase to watch) and an abnegation of maternal responsibility. Never has the old adage about reformed sinners seemed more appropriate.

Ironically, the very naturalness of pregnancy is undermined by months of self-conscious training for male and female and the unreasonable emphasis on participatory delivery. A woman planning natural childbirth generally enlists the services of her husband, who may share months of preparation so that eventually he can coach and inspire her through the discomforts of labor. (David Carradine, star of *Kung Fu*, reportedly played piano through the six-hour natural delivery of his son, Free.) To me, the demand that one's husband be implicated in every ceremonious step of pregnancy, beyond intercourse to afterbirth, seems an unreasonable and unjustified division of labor. Child-rearing is a joint responsibility but childbirth is not, no matter how empathetic we train our husbands to be. The time would be better invested if men were trained for fatherhood in that period, rather than midwifery.

Some husbands are reluctant at first to serve as deputies or even witnesses to their wives labor but it is a responsibility not easily avoided once a woman chooses natural delivery. Many men report afterward that they are glad they participated. But what, after all, can we expect of new fathers except relief, enthusiasm, and a manly pride in their endurance? Helping a wife deliver has become a form of *machismo*.

If one judges natural childbirth by its various adherents – a mixed bag of aggressively liberated women and rather ordinary housewives – it is difficult to find any common motivation, save a susceptibility to whatever is trendy and new. Perhaps the most defiant of today's liberated young – the sort who are wed after seven months of pregnancy, then deliver at home with the husband superintending and a friend photographing – are making a profound statment about women, nature, and childbirth. I don't pretend to understand all of my "sisters." But certainly the more conventional young mothers who marry and conceive in the usual sequence are telling us nothing through natural delivery, except that it has caught on in suburbia, along with granola and vitamin E. For such women, natural childbirth may be a dramatic way of initiating men into new domestic responsibilities, at the same time serving as a vivid illustration that women are able to do what men cannot. So, too, it becomes a demonstration of continued female dominance in the realm of childbearing and rearing. We're wiping out all distinctions between the sexes but can't resist the temptation to manipulate men by idealizing every physiological experience from *Mittelschmerz* to menopause.

Natural childbirth may also reflect a subliminal resentment of men for their insulation from the pains of childbirth, and their freedom from the constraints which childbearing traditionally imposes on females. Or, like other manifestations of the new feminine consciousness, it may signal some of the hostility and frustration many women feel because they are unable to achieve sexual satisfaction as easily as most men. It is,

after all, the drive for equal-opportunity orgasm that inspires so much strident man-baiting in the orthodox women's movement.

What concerns me most about the natural-childbirth craze is the sense of failure and the loss of self-esteem a woman may experience when she is unable to complete a natural delivery as planned. The conviction that this is an especially meaningful way to launch one's career as a mother can make any other mode of delivery a somber disappointment. At least one obstetrician I know tries to prepare his patients for the possibility that natural delivery may be impossible, but he still finds it difficult to relieve the disappointment, and sometimes even humiliation, some mothers feel when, for one reason or another, they must deliver under anesthesia.

Natural childbirth is a fine idea, if you want it, and no one can dispute that it is safer for the infant than general (but usually not local) anesthesia. What I resent is the new pantheism in this country which emphasizes the *trappings* of nature – sometimes at the expense of its spirit. Obstetrics, like nearly everything else in our "gotta-have-a-gimmick" society, has been infected by this pretentious striving for a state of natural grace. Having a child is such a lovely event – one of the most important things a woman, and a man, ever do; there should be little need to orchestrate or rehearse the hours of delivery beyond what is medically required. All the really important responsibilities, like preparing a person to live happily and productively in society, come later. We might just as well celebrate the toilet training. That's where most problems begin.

## Practical Hints on Breast Feeding

Most women find that a good nursing bra, one that provides good uplift and that opens easily for nursing, makes nursing easier and more comfortable. Many wear such a bra day and night during the months they are nursing.

Use the first few days, when there is little milk in the breast, to get your nipples used to your baby's nursing. Let him suck for only two minutes at each breast at each feeding the first day, three minutes the second day, and five minutes the third day. If your nipples get sore at any time later, you can limit nursing time to five minutes at each breast. Even a slow nursing infant gets at least four-fifths of the milk in his first five minutes at breast.

Find a position that is comfortable for you and your baby; a foot stool, a pillow and a chair with arms are often helpful.

Touch the baby's cheek with the nipple to start. He will turn his head to grasp the nipple. (If you try to push him to the nipple with a finger touching his other cheek or chin he will turn away from the nipple toward the finger.)

Allow him to grasp the entire darkly colored part of the breast in his month. He gets the milk by squeezing it from the nipple, not by actually sucking. His grasp on your nipple may hurt for the first few seconds, but the pain should disappear once he is nursing in a good rhythm. When you want to remove his mouth from your breast, first break the suction by inserting your finger in the corner of his mouth. This will save sore nipples. If your entire breast becomes sore, you may be able to relieve the painfulness simply by lifting and supporting the breast with one hand during nursing.

A small amount of milk may come out of your nipples between feedings. A small nursing pad or piece of sanitary napkin inserted in the bra over the nipple will absorb this milk, keeping the bra clean and preventing irritaiton of the nipple.

Wash your nipples with mild soap and water at least once a day, and rinse off any messiness with clean water before or after most feedings.

If you notice a spot of tenderness or redness on your breast or nipple that persists for more than two feedings be sure to seek medical advice promptly.

From *Infant Care*, 1973, Department of Health, Education and Welfare.

## Make Your Own Baby Foods

The Editors of *Consumer Reports*

Preparing baby foods at home is really a simple operation. You'll need either a food mill, a strainer, or an electric blender. A food mill will puree fruits and vegetables and separate out seeds, cores, and skins as it does so. A strainer can be used to puree soft fruits and vegetables. A good blender will puree meats, vegetables, and fruits. (Before pureeing fruit in strainer or blender, peel, core, and remove seeds.)

Once your baby is old enough to eat strained solids, you can adapt foods prepared for family meals. Simply take out the baby's portion after the food is cooked but before you add seasonings and spices, then puree. Prepared this way, homemade baby foods should cost less overall than commercial foods. Use fresh foods only. Canned foods may contain added salt and other undesirable additives; frozen foods, though a bit better, often contain added salt.

Here are some basics for preparing baby foods:

*Fruits*. A baby's first fruit is usually bananas,

which you need only mash with a fork. All other fruits should be cut up into small pieces, steamed until soft, and pureed.

*Vegetables*. Babies usually like carrots, zucchini, peas, and sweet potatoes. Cut vegetables into small pieces, cook, then puree. Avoid spinach and beets, since they may contain an excess of harmful nitrates. Cabbage, broccoli, and cauliflower may produce gas, and corn is difficult for an infant to digest.

*Meats, poultry, fish*. These can be baked, broiled, poached, stewed, or braised, but not fried. It's probably best to start with chicken, since it is easily digested. Simply cook it, remove the skin and any bones, cut up, and puree. Fish is also easy to digest. When you prepare any fish, even fillet, go through it carefully for bones before pureeing. Cooked, cut-up lamb, veal, beef, and pork can be pureed in a blender.

*Eggs*. Some pediatricians feel that infants shouldn't eat egg whites. Others disagree. Consult your own doctor on the matter. But whether your baby eats both the white and the yolk or just the yolk alone, hard-boil the egg, then mash what you need with a fork to make a smooth paste. Custard is an egg-rich food. To make it, simply follow a standard recipe, omitting sugar, nutmeg, cloves, and similar spices.

*Other foods*. Cottage cheese is an easily digested food for babies. Puree it first and add a little pureed fruit, if you like. Soup is another good choice. When you fix a pot of soup for the family, take out a cup for the baby before you add spices, puree if necessary.

Prepare baby food with clean hands (to prevent any spread of harmful bacteria) and clean, freshly washed utensils. When the food is ready, cover and refrigerate the unused portions immediately; they'll keep for three days. Or better, cover a tray with foil, drop on spoonfuls of the prepared foods, then freeze and individually wrap the portions. They'll keep for one month in the freezer. Once you've started the baby on a portion, do not keep it for more than a day.

Almost any food can touch off an allergic reaction, so introduce strained solids one at a time. If the baby has an unfavorable reaction – diarrhea, a rash, spitting up – discontinue the food, then check with your doctor.

Following the extremely active phase of sexual differentiation during fetal life is a decade or so when sexual development hangs in limbo. Most people do not become fertile until the teens or early twenties. (Although, there are records of girls as young as nine giving birth). Nevertheless, many infants have what appear to be erotic experiences. Some male infants have erections and babies of both sexes appear to masturbate to orgasm. However, for most babies the ability to have erotic sensations is soon lost.

What happens to eroticism in the years after infancy is not known. Some sexologists believe that social constraints against sexual activity cause psychological repression of the capacity for orgasm, while others believe that depressed eroticism is a natural biological safeguard against pregnancy at an age when it would be physically harmful. Whatever the cause of this shift away from erotic pleasure during the first decade of life; if all goes well, erotic drives and activity return as the sexual structures mature.

Maturation of the genitals and reproductive systems occurs during *puberty* and involves complex hormonal and physiological changes. The first section of this chapter considers puberty as it occurs for the majority of adolescents. Following sections give added perspectives to the unique cyclical nature of female sexuality. The final sections consider genetic abnormalities and aging.

### Puberty

In females, *menarche*, the onset of menstrual bleeding, initiates puberty, but it is by no means an indication of total sexual maturity. In general, ovulation is infrequent or nonexistent during the months immediately following menarche, and periods of menstrual bleeding are commonly sporadic.

For males, the first ejaculation bears a biological significance similar to menarche. It indicates that sexual maturation is underway but not that a male is reproductively potent. Sperm capable of effecting fertilization may not be included in the semen of a male for a year or more after his first ejaculation.

The changes of puberty generally happen over several years for people of both sexes. However, adolescents should not interpret this as meaning they can have sexual intercourse without taking contraceptive precautions, because the timetable of sexual maturation is highly variable.

Puberty is a significant event in each person's life, not only because it marks the beginning of one's reproductive years but also because it is the beginning of a new stage of life. Puberty marks the end of childhood and entrance into adulthood. For the first time, our culture acknowledges the sexuality of its children. Many cultures mark this change with initiation rites which symbolize the individual's change in status. Among the Arapesh a special hut is built for the newly menstruating girl; among the Manus the village girls come and sleep in the young girl's hut, then great feasts and splashing parties in the lagoon take place. There are no elaborate ceremonies in America for a girl's first menstruation, but it is nevertheless regarded as a particularly unique event. One woman recalled:

> I used to worry about having my period. It seemed that all my friends had gotten it already, or were just having it. I felt left out. I began to think of it as a symbol. When I got my period, I would become a woman. (Our Bodies, Ourselves, 1973)

At present there is no satisfactory explanation for why puberty happens when it does. According to one hypothesis, a "biological clock" triggers it, but attempts to find a physiological timing mechanism within the human body have failed.

**The Decreasing Age of Puberty**  In Western civilization, the age at which puberty begins has been steadily decreasing for at least the last century and a half. A century ago, for example, the average age of menarche in Europe was about sixteen; today it is approximately thirteen. While there is no well established explanation for this phenomenon, there are several theories. The most commonly suggested one is that improved nutrition in recent history has made people more healthy and, hence, more quick to mature. Evidence substantiating this belief has come from studies of the age of puberty as related to economic class. Children of relatively poor families generally mature a year or so slower than children of the same race but from wealthy families.

Some sex researchers believe that a person's psychological environment influences the age of sexual maturation. Within recent history (as Western life has become increasingly protected from concerns of starvation, disease, and environmental disaster) people have come to devote increasing attention to sexual activity. It is possible that social atmospheres with powerful sexual messages (we are constantly bombarded, for instance, by advertisements with sexual overtones) accelerate the onset of puberty.

The mystery of the declining age of puberty is made deeper by evidence that a few centuries ago, in Shakespeare's time, the onset of adolescence may even have occurred earlier than it does today.

> Capulet: My child is yet a stranger in the world
> She hath not seen the change of fourteen years;
> Let two more summers wither in their pride
> Ere we may think her ripe to be a bride.
> Paris: Younger than she are happy mothers made.
>
> *Romeo and Juliet, (Act 1, Sc. ii)*

**Puberty: The Role of the Pituitary**  Although there is no satisfactory explanation for what triggers puberty, early steps in the sequence of events leading to reproductive maturity occur in the brain. Prior to puberty, a child's body produces both male and female hormones, in approximately equal amounts. Sex hormones help to regulate growth at all ages, but it is only when a child reaches puberty that the brain signals the pituitary gland to begin the production of hormonal levels found in adult men and women.

Around the age of ten, the *hypothalamus* (an interior portion of the brain, which is connected by nerves and blood vessels to the pituitary gland) produces secretions that cause the pituitary to release certain hormones, the *gonadotropins* (gonad-stimulators). The gonadotropins of men and women are identical.

Gonadotropins were first discovered in females, and they were originally named for their female functions, *follicle-stimulating hormone* (FSH) and *luteinizing hormone* (LH). In men the former is also termed FSH (although, of course, males have no ovarian follicles), but the latter is named for its male function, *interstitial cell-stimulating hormone* (ICSH). There is no apparent reason why one name has been changed for males and the other has not.

**Male Puberty**  Within the testicles, ICSH stimulates *interstitial cells* to produce testosterone (Figure 5.1). At the onset of puberty the effects of testosterone are manifested close to its centers of production — it causes the penis and scrotum to enlarge. Rapid growth of the external genitalia usually begins around age twelve, but variations of a couple of years either way from this average are common. Appearance of pubic hair is another early sign of puberty. At first pubic hair is fine and silky, but in a few years it becomes coarse and curly. With the appearance of pubic hair, erections become more frequent and firm. Intense orgasms may be experienced several months before ejaculation ever occurs.

The changes of puberty accelerate as the testicles increase their output of testosterone. Approximately a year after the appearance of puberty's first signs, the external genitalia go

Hypothalamus and other centers

FSH and LG–releasing factors

Pituitary

FSH

Spermatogenisis

ICSH

Negative feedback

Testosterone secretion from interstitial cells

Development and maintenance of secondary sexual characteristics

5.1

through a phase of rapid growth during which the first ejaculation usually occurs.

Concurrent with the effects of testosterone in puberty, the pituitary hormone FSH stimulates development of sperm. Between the ages of eleven and seventeen, FSH affects the seminiferous tubules of the testicles, prompting them to produce viable sperm. Because sperm require an environment with a temperature lower than that of the body, the testicles must descend from their original position in the lower abdomen and hang loosely in the scrotum. Sometimes one or both of the testicles does not descend, but this can usually be corrected surgically. If it is not corrected before puberty, there is a high risk of infertility.

At the same time these developments are occurring in the genitalia, hormone-stimulated changes occur elsewhere in the body. These signs of maturation are collectively termed the *secondary sex characteristics*. Among them is the testosterone-stimulated development of the male physique – skeletal muscles enlarge and the rib cage broadens.

Testosterone is also related to body height, but in an inverse way. During puberty height increases rapidly due to stimulation by the *growth hormone*, which is produced in the pituitary gland. This hormone causes growth of the long bones (the bones of the arms and legs). Testosterone retards the increase in height by counteracting the influence of growth hormone. But, it is not until a man matures into his late teens or early twenties that the effects of testosterone outweigh the influences of the growth hormone, and bone elongation slows to a halt.

There are influences on body height in addition to the interplay of testosterone and growth hormone. Nutrition, other hormones (particularly those of the thyroid gland), and genetic factors as yet unexplained all affect one's maximum height. As with the dynamics of the development of all secondary sex characteristics, the factors affecting height are only superficially understood.

Another secondary sex characteristic is the sprouting of body hair, which begins early in puberty but does not reach its full extent for several years. Pubic hair generally appears first, followed by *axillary* (underarm) hair. Hair on the forearms and legs may get darker and more coarse. Fuzz and eventually coarse facial hair develops on the upper lip and gradually spreads to the chin and cheeks. Other secondary sex characteristics include deepening of the voice, which occurs as a result of testosterone-stimulated enlargement of the *larynx* (voice box) and Adam's apple. In the fairly recent past, drastic measures were sometimes taken to prevent voice change. *Castration* (removal of the testicles) was performed on some European choir boys as late as the eighteenth century, in order to maintain their angelic voices into adulthood.

Acne, which is caused by increased activity of oil-secreting glands of the face, neck, and back, is a universally despised characteristic of puberty. Some young males experience certain other unwanted physical changes during puberty. A pad of fatty tissue may develop around the root of the penis, making the organ look smaller, particularly when viewed from above (the owner's point of view). *Gynecomastia* (enlargement of the breasts) is another transient characteristic of puberty. It is estimated that 75 percent of pubescent boys experience at least a small amount of breast enlargement. Studies have indicated that chronic marijuana-smoking by a pubescent male might aggravate gynecomastia. The cause-and-effect relationship between marijuana smoking and gynecomastia is not well understood (or even well established), but research has indicated that heavy use of the drug depresses the amount of testosterone in the blood (Kolodny, et al, 1974).

Totally deprived of testosterone, a *eunuch* (a male who is castrated) develops quite differently than a normal male. His arms and legs become disproportionately long relative to his trunk, and fat deposits develop with a feminine distribution. No beard grows but pubic and axillary hair do appear. Growth of pubic and axillary hair is presumably stimulated in eunuchs by sex hormones produced by the *adrenal glands*, which lie atop the kidneys and produce minute amounts of sex hormones in all men and women. Sex drive varies widely among eunuchs; some are extremely sexually active. If castration occurs before puberty, the penis remains full-sized and capable of erection. Eunuchs have at least one advantage over non-castrated men – they are less prone to balding, which is aggravated by testosterone in the years of maturity.

**Female Puberty** On the average, puberty starts about a year earlier for girls than for boys. The first signs of it often appear around age eleven; yet, it is not unusual for women in their early twenties to be unable to conceive. Thus, like puberty in the male, female puberty is a gradual process and one that varies from individual to individual.

Female puberty begins when the pituitary produces FSH, which subsequently stimulates production of estrogen by ovarian follicles. Estrogen, in turn, promotes changes in reproductive organs and development of secondary sex characteristics.

Estrogen stimulates growth of the nipples and initiates deposition of fat in the female breasts. As maturation proceeds, more fat deposits are induced in the breasts, buttocks, and thighs. A fully mature form develops over the course of several years.

Like testosterone in the male, estrogen affects the growth hormone of the pituitary in a similar manner as testosterone – it slows growth of the long bones. The effect of estrogen, however, is even more pronounced than that of testosterone – on the average, women are shorter than men and usually reach their maximum height before men.

Estrogen also affects other aspects of skeletal growth. For instance, it influences development of the pelvic bone, widening the opening through it in preparation for childbirth.

At the genitals estrogen stimulates swelling of the labia and growth of the reproductive organs. The muscles of the uterus thicken and become more firm. The vaginal lining also thickens and increases its output of mucus.

The clitoris grows during puberty, but estrogen plays little or no role in its development. Instead it responds to stimulation from hormones produced by the adrenal glands. These hormones are classified as *androgens* (a structurally similar group of hormones, with masculinizing influences). Testosterone is a member of the androgen family, and is produced in small quantities by female adrenal glands. Testosterone influences female sexuality in several ways. It stimulates sex drive, for instance, and prompts growth of axillary and pubic hair.

In the course of female maturation, yet another hormone comes into play, *progesterone*. Ovaries produce progesterone in response to stimulation by LH from the pituitary gland. In turn, progesterone stimulates development of the endometrium, which lines the uterus. Progesterone, estrogen, FSH, and LH are involved in a cyclical build-up and break-down of the endometrium of a mature woman.

**The Menstrual Cycle**

Women experience a cyclical series of physical changes, with approximately a monthly frequency. Underlying these changes is a periodic fluctuation in the productions of sex hormones. At the time of menarche, a girl is not necessarily sexually mature; her production of eggs and her periods of menstruation may remain erratic for several years. Usually by age twenty, however, a regular menstrual cycle is established. Vaginal bleeding lasts from three to seven days and is the most obvious characteristic of the underlying physical changes that are repeated every month. The span of the menstrual cycle is highly variable, and fluctuations several days either way from the average of around twenty-nine days are common.

**Attitudes Toward Menstruation**    Attitudes toward menstruation are immensely varied, but a central theme that has prevailed in many cultures is that women possess magical power at that time. To curtail that power, taboos have

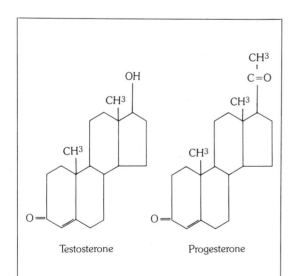

**5.2**  *Chemical structures of testosterone and progesterone. They differ by a single side group.*

been established; in particular, these taboos protect men from contact with menstrual blood. Throughout the world it is not unusual for menstruating women to be prohibited from cooking food for men, participating in religious activities, and having sexual intercourse. Among the Arapesh in New Guinea, menstruating women are isolated in small huts and men are forbidden from approaching them for fear of death. The Saux tribes in America prohibit a menstruating woman from taking part in tribal ceremonies because her power at that time is greater than that of the medicine man or shaman. Our own heritage expresses fear of menstruating women. In Leviticus (XV, 19), the Bible says: "And if a woman shall have an issue, and her issue in her flesh be blood, she shall be separated seven days; and whosoever touches her shall be unclean." Occasionally, one still hears menstruation referred to as "the curse."

In America the taboo still lingers, although less obviously than in some other cultures. Out of anxiety over menstrual blood, many couples abstain from sexual intercourse while the woman is menstruating. Women go to great lengths to hide the fact that they are menstruating, fearing embarrassment or shame. Advertisements, in particular, perpetuate that fear, by promising the woman who purchases a particular tampon or sanitary napkin (note the word "sanitary") absolute safety from detection. Some women bathe constantly during this time and use special powder and deodorants to avoid "unpleasant" odors. The anxiety or depression that some women experience during their period – "the menstrual blues" – may possibly be traceable not so much to hormonal changes as to cultural conditioning.

**Ovulation**    Between periods of menstrual bleeding an egg is released from one of the ovaries, and travels down a Fallopian tube to the uterus. If fertilization does not occur, the uterus expels the tissues that were formed to receive the embryo. Ovulation usually occurs two weeks before the onset of menstrual bleeding. In a twenty-eight day cycle, for instance, it occurs on about the fourteenth day following the beginning of the last menstrual flow.

The development and release of an egg usually happens only once during a menstrual cycle. Sometimes, however, two or more eggs are released and multiple pregnancies may result. *Fraternal twins* are conceived if two eggs are fertilized simultaneously (*identical twins*, who are genetic duplicates, result from the splitting of a single zygote). About one percent of the pregnancies in America lead to multiple births. However, a product of hormone technology has slightly increased this rate. Treatments with drugs containing synthetic gonadotropins ("Clomid," for example) have been successfully used to stimulate ovulation in women unable to conceive due to abnormalities of the output of gonadotropins by the pituitary gland. Sometimes these synthetic hormones work too well, causing several eggs to leave the ovaries simultaneously. The incidence of twins for women who have taken fertility drugs is several times higher than the national average. In certain unfortunate cases, as many as six or more eggs are fertilized and begin development; the fetuses rarely survive.

**Phases of the Menstrual Cycle**    By its nature, the menstrual cycle has no beginning or end, but, by convention, the day on which menstrual bleeding begins is designated as the "first" day of a cycle.

The menstrual cycle is commonly described as occurring in three phases: *menstrual, proliferative*, and *secretory*. The menstrual phase is the period of discharge, when a flow of blood, mucus, and bits of tissue leave the wall of the uterus (where they had formed the endometrium). The volume of an average monthly discharge is about a quarter cup. The amount varies, however, and a woman having heavy menstrual bleeding may develop anemia as a result of excessive loss of minerals (particularly iron).

Following the menstrual phase a new endometrium develops during the proliferative phase. Ovulation marks the end of the proliferative phase and the beginning of the secretory phase. During this phase, which lasts about a week, the endometrium reaches its peak of development and begins to deteriorate.

**Hormonal Feedback** Inherent in the physiological changes of the menstrual cycle are a series of hormonal interactions that are repeated from month to month. These biochemical-physiological processes form a self-perpetuating system of reactions. It is a *negative feedback system* in that the presence of any one of the hormones retards the mechanism of its own production. The system is a dynamic one, constantly changing in response to itself. The primary roles in these changes are played by the ovaries, uterus, and pituitary gland. The chain of events described in this section is complex, so a summary of the major points is included at the end.

All the influences on the menstrual cycle are not known, but it apparently will operate with or without input from the brain (Figure 5.4). Via the hypothalamus, (which is known to respond to erotic situations as well as various other stimuli), the brain "communicates" with the portion of the pituitary gland which produces FSH and LH, the *anterior lobe*. There are no neural connections to the anterior lobe of the pituitary, but blood vessels carry at least two compounds, *FSH-and LH-releasing factors*, which do just as their names imply – stimulate the release of FSH and

LH. No mention of the releasing factors is made in the following discussion, but keep in mind that certain (little understood) conditions bring them into the menstrual cycle.

During the proliferative phase the pituitary gland accelerates production of FSH, which, in turn, stimulates a maturing ovarian follicle to produce estrogen. At the site of its production, estrogen promotes development of an egg, while in the uterus it stimulates development of the endometrium.

At the same time that estrogen is affecting the uterus and ovaries, it is also circulating to other parts of the body. When its concentration

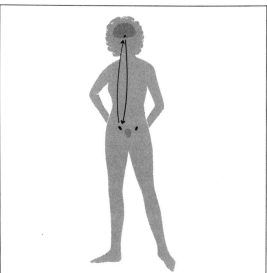

**5.3** *The menstrual cycle involves a cyclic interplay of hormones between the pituitary and the ovaries. The pituitary secretes gonadotropins (FSH and LH) into the blood stream. These affect production of sex hormones by the ovaries. The uterus responds to varying levels of the sex hormones by cyclically preparing to receive an embryo. All of this is observed, and perhaps affected, by feedbacks with various portions of the brain, which communicate with the pituitary via the hypothalamus.*

reaches a critical level at the pituitary gland it depresses the release of FSH. This is negative feedback, in that FSH is the hormone which stimulates production of estrogen in the first place. The result is that release of estrogen from the follicle declines over the next few days. However, before the concentration of estrogen in the blood begins to diminish, it perpetuates the cyclic changes of menstruation by stimulating production of the second gonadotropin of the pituitary, LH.

Upon arriving at the active follicle (the one that the egg left a few days before), LH initiates a renewed production of estrogen and also promotes secretion of progesterone. In the days following the departure of the egg, the follicle continues to develop as it produces the primary sex hormones. Although its size remains microscopic, the follicle plays a central role in the rest of the changes of the menstrual cycle.

Gradually the follicle loses its cuplike shape, and becomes a tiny blob of yellow cells, the *corpus luteum* (Latin for "yellow body"). As the corpus luteum develops, the endometrium responds to the new peak of estrogen and the added influence of progesterone. During the secretory phase (which extends from the point of ovulation to the beginning of the new menstrual cycle) the endometrium reaches full development and begins to secrete nutrients that an implanted embryo would need.

If fertilization occurs, it is usually within a Fallopian tube, and the embryo reaches the uterus on about the twentieth day of a menstrual cycle, where it comes to rest in the delicate membranes of the endometrium. If fertilization has not occurred, the egg degenerates.

Also, if there is no fertilization, the pituitary

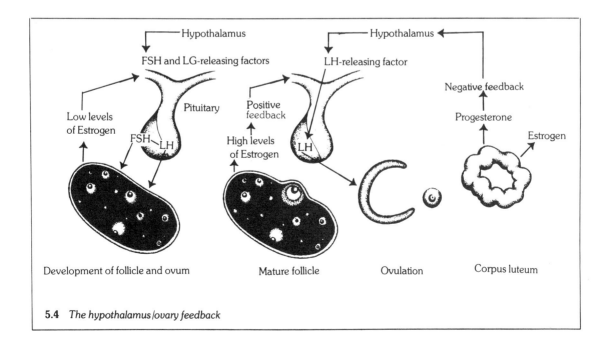

Development of follicle and ovum     Mature follicle     Ovulation     Corpus luteum

**5.4**  *The hypothalamus/ovary feedback*

gland responds to the high blood level of progesterone by slowing production of LH. However, because stimulation by LH is needed to maintain secretion of estrogen and progesterone by the corpus luteum, the ultimate effect is a depression in the production of both hormones. They decline to minimal concentrations in the blood by about the twenty-fifth day of the menstrual cycle.

Because estrogen and progesterone are necessary to maintain the endometrium, the ultimate physiological consequence of their lowered concentrations is breakdown of the endometrium. On about the twenty-eighth day, the cycle comes full swing, and a discharge of menstrual fluid passes out of the vagina. At the same time the pituitary gland responds to the lowered levels of estrogen in the blood, and steps up production of FSH. Thus, the cycle begins again, with maturation of a new follicle as the old corpus luteum withers away.

*Summary*   There is no beginning or end to the menstrual cycle but starting with its most obvious physical characteristic, menstrual bleeding, the following hormonal and physiological interactions occur (**Figure 5.5**). Menstrual bleeding begins when the endometrium breaks down because of depressed levels of estrogen and progesterone in the bloodstream. The pituitary responds to the low estrogen concentration by producing FSH. Upon reaching an egg-producing follicle, FSH stimulates production of estrogen that, in turn, prompts development of the endometrium. At the pituitary gland, estrogen depresses production of FSH but stimulates production of LH, which reaches the follicle at about the same time the mature egg leaves the surface of the ovary. A post-ovulatory follicle is called a corpus luteum, and under stimulation by LH, it produces estrogen and progesterone. In the uterus these hormones promote development of the endometrium, but in the pituitary gland progesterone depresses production of LH. Because LH is needed to maintain secretion of the sex hormones at the corpus luteum, the result is that the concentrations of estrogen and progesterone begin to subside. If you go back to the second sentence of this paragraph, you will see that this is where we came in.

**The Menstrual Cycle: A Behavioral, Social, and Cosmic Phenomenon?**   At this point, the menstrual cycle may seem quite self-contained -- an interplay of hormones to and from the pituitary and the ovaries, with the state of development of the uterus hanging in the balance. However, it is not that simple, and it is, by no means, completely understood. There are other influences on the menstrual cycle – both internal and external – and their subtleties and implications are subjects for study by contemporary researchers. For one thing, the period of menstruation appears to be influenced by a woman's psychological state. During times of emotional upheaval, for example, menstruation may lose its regular periodicity or cease temporarily.

Social interactions can also influence menstrual cycles. For instance, statistical studies of women living together in close relationships have revealed that their menstrual cycles tend to coincide. One study has shown that college women living together in dormitories often have synchronized periods. When they are no longer living together, however, their menstrual synchronization usually ceases (McClintoch, 1971).

The records of early explorers and anthropologists reveal another interesting social characteristic of menstruation. The original travelers from Western civilizations to isolated cultures in Africa, Polynesia, and South America often reported that women lacked periodicity in their vaginal bleeding and, in general, menstruated less frequently. One explorer to Tierra del Fuego claimed that the women experienced menstrual bleeding only about once a year.

For those who are looking for extraterrestrial influences on human existence, the monthly periodicity of menstruation is of particular interest. The average span of the menstrual cycle too closely aligns with the monthly periodicity of the moon to overlook the similarity. However, although lunar influences have frequently been suggested, no mechanism of interaction has ever been conclusively shown.

In an evolutionary sense menstruation is of interest in that it appears to have come relatively late in the history of life on earth. Certain female apes and monkeys have a menstrual cycle similar to that of human females, but other mammals do not.

Human females are unique in the degree to which sexual desire lacks periodicity. The females of other primates, for example, have al-

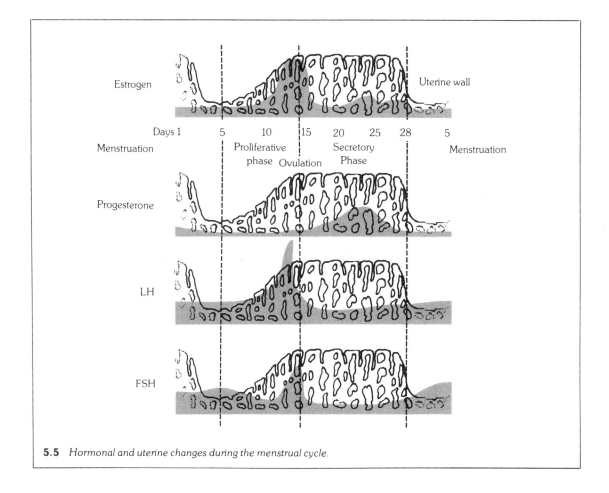

**5.5** *Hormonal and uterine changes during the menstrual cycle.*

ternating periods of rejection and reception of sexual advances from males. During phases of "heat" they may encourage the sexual advances of many males, but in between these receptive periods show little interest in sex (and, likewise, the males often have little interest in them). Most human females, however, have relatively slight fluctuations in sex drive, and those changes that do occur are opposite to those of other animals. Most animals that experience heat are at the height of passion at the time of ovulation, when the level of estrogen is at its highest. However, sex drive in human females is frequently strongest at about the time of menstruation when estrogen is at its *lowest* level in the blood. Some researchers of human sexual behavior believe that estrogen depresses human sexual desires; but whether or not it does, it is evident that both male and female sex drive is more dependent on higher centers of mental activity than on concentrations of sex hormones. Males' sex drive appears to be more influenced by hormones than is the female sex drive. Attempts to use estrogen as a male contraceptive, for example, have resulted in depressed levels of sexual responsiveness. Estrogen is thought to stifle the female sex drive too, but not to the extent that it does the males'.

**Menstrual Problems** *Dysmenorrhea:* Some women experience pain in association with the menstrual cycle. Though the symptoms vary from individual to individual, menstrual pain has been given the catch-all name, *dysmenorrhea*. For most younger women, the major complaint is cramps in the lower abdomen, but they may also experience headaches, backaches, and nausea. Some women experience emotional depression during one or more phases of the menstrual cycle; depression or irritability may accompany the physical complaints, it may occur at a separate part of the cycle, or may be experi-

enced in the absence of any physical complaints.

The symptoms of dysmenorrhea often begin a few days before menstrual bleeding, and are usually relieved with the heaviest menstrual flow. Many women find that orgasms also help to relieve distress possibly because orgasmic contractions of the uterus facilitate release of the menstrual discharge. For this reason, masturbation and intercourse are two of the best treatments for menstrual discomforts. Other remedies that may help relieve dysmenorrhea include aspirin, a heating pad or hot-water bottle held to the abdomen and curling up in the fetal position with the knees pulled to the chest.

Some women (especially those who have not been menstruating long) experience a pain that occurs midway between menstrual periods. *Mittelschmerz* (German for "middle pain") is associated with ovulation, and is felt as a cramp in either or both sides of the abdomen. Occasionally it is mistaken (even by doctors) for appendicitis.

*Amenorrhea:* The absence of menstrual bleeding, *amenorrhea*, has several possible causes, including pregnancy, cysts or tumors in the reproductive organs and emotional distress. "Pregnancy scares" sometimes initiate self-perpetuating cases of amenorrhea that last for several months. Rather than worry, a woman who fears she is pregnant should arrange for a pregnancy test.

A second type of amenorrhea, *primary amenorrhea*, is indicated in women who have not begun to menstruate. Although relatively rare, this condition may indicate a hereditary hormonal imbalance or some other congenital malfunction of the reproductive system.

*Vicarious menstruation:* This is a relatively rare problem, which involves bleeding from places other than the uterus during the menstrual periods. The most common type is bleeding from the nose. Apparently mucus membranes outside the reproductive system react to the sex hormones in a similar fashion as the lining of the uterus.

*Disposing of Menstrual Discharge:* In our cosmetic conscious Western culture, a large industry has developed to deal with menstrual bleeding, and several methods are now available. The most popular are *tampons* (which are cylinders of cotton inserted into the vagina) and *sanitary napkins* (which are highly absorbent pads of cotton).

It is often said (usually by over-protective mothers) that tampons should not be used by young women who have not yet had intercourse but it is a false assumption. There is usually enough of an opening in the hymen to allow for insertion of tampons. If there is not, this is a sign that the hymen should be stretched before first intercourse. The repeated use of tampons might provide the mechanical stretching, which may prevent a woman from having to have the procedure done in a doctor's office.

## The Mature Male

It is a basic difference between the biochemistries of men and women in that there is no cycling of male hormones analogous to the hormonal shifts in the female menstrual cycle. Testosterone is secreted at a fairly constant rate from the testicles and if there are periodic changes in masculine physiological and emotional states, they are not obvious, given current standards of evaluation. The word "obvious" must be stressed here because some research has indicated that men may experience subtle physical or psychological cycles with close to a monthly periodicity. Statistical studies of industrial accidents, for instance, have shown that some men have phases during the month when they are accident prone. As yet, however, behavioral scientists have formulated no well-founded generalizations about male cycles.

Changes in the male sexual system are less dramatic than those of the female; certainly there is no male equivalent of the physiological revolution of childbearing. For the male, things tend to run relatively smoothly into the fifties (and, for many men, well beyond the fifties). If problems develop, they usually involve the prostate gland. Two common prostate maladies are bacterial infections and cancer, which are considered in chapter 7.

## Genetic, Hormonal and Physiological Abnormalities

Occasionally people are born with ill-defined sexual physiologies. In some cases neither male nor female sex organs are properly developed. Other infants are born with sexual anatomies intermediate between male and female – a condition termed *hermaphroditism*. In "true" hermaphroditism (which is extremely rare) gonads have both ovarian and testicular components. People with *pseudohermaphroditism* possess either male or female gonads but are otherwise ambiguous in sexual anatomy. For example, a pseudohermaphrodite may have a complete set of female organs plus an empty scrotal sac.

Most abnormalities of sexual physiology are rooted in genetic defects. However, as described later in this section, sex hormones administered for medical reasons have inadvertently resulted in cases of pseudohermaphroditism.

**Chromosomal Abnormalities**  Sometimes zygotes are formed with too many or too few sex chromosomes. In *monosomy-X*, also called "Turner's Syndrome", (which occurs in about one out of 6000 births) the sperm or the egg lacks a sex chromosome. Thus, a fetus develops with only forty-five chromosomes in each cell rather than the normal forty-six. An embryo with a single Y chromosome does not survive, and a single X chromosome gives rise to a female with a stunted physiology. However, the effects do not become obvious until the age when puberty is expected.

A girl with monosomy-X has no ovaries, thus her body produces little estrogen. Consequently she does not menstruate, and she is sterile. She is also shorter than average (usually between four and one-half and five feet tall) and is otherwise stunted in physique – a puzzling characteristic in view of estrogen's depressing effect on growth of normal women. Women with monosomy-X tend to be naive and childlike, as if their emotional growths were arrested at pre-puberty levels.

In recent decades, estrogen has been administered by pill and injection to puberty-age girls having monosomy-X with physiological benefits. For example, their breasts have been stimulated to grow slightly, and an inch or so can be added to height.

There are three other chromosomal abnormalities that occur at about the same frequency as monosomy-X. Trisomy-X, for example, is a syndrome resulting in cells containing three X chromosomes (XXX). The effects of trisomy-X vary from individual to individual. Some women who have it are fertile and appear quite normal. Others have symptoms similar to those of monosomy-X. In some cases there is severe mental retardation. The XXY syndrome (also called "Klinefelter's syndrome") results when a normal egg is fertilized by an XY sperm. A person with this genetic constitution appears more male than female but is sterile and otherwise sexually underdeveloped. Sometimes there is

mental retardation. The XYY syndrome results when a YY sperm fertilizes a normal egg. While men with an extra Y chromosome tend to be above average in height, they are often normal in their physical, mental, and sexual characteristics. Some behavioral scientists believe that an XYY genetic endowment predisposes a man to acts of violence, citing as evidence the high proportion of the syndrome among prison inmates relative to the general population. However, because there has been no indisputable estimate of the syndrome in the general population, the correlation with violence is not well-established. Moreover, even if there is a relatively large population of men in prison with the XYY syndrome, it could be that they are just easier to track down and apprehend because of their unusually massive physiques.

**Androgen-Insensitivity Syndrome**    There are genetic defects other than abnormalities of chromosome number that give rise to unusual sexual physiologies. In the androgen-insensitivity syndrome, for instance, the individual is chromosomally male (XY) but has cells that are unresponsive to testosterone. Consequently the fetus develops with partially feminized sex organs.

During the crucial weeks of sexual differentiation the gonads of an androgen-insensitive fetus produce testosterone, but the cells that should react to it fail to do so. Thus, for example, Wolffian ducts do not form internal male reproductive organs. However, internal female reproductive organs do not develop either. In external anatomy the fetus usually appears female, and in most cases the newborn is mistakenly thought to be a normal girl. Sometimes, however, the clitoris is enlarged and the testicles descended somewhat to form lumps in the labia majora.

People who have the androgen-insensitivity syndrome can never become reproductively male or female. However, it is possible to feminize their external anatomies. When necessary, underdeveloped traces of external male genitals can be removed by surgery. On the other hand, attempts to masculinize children with the syndrome have been unsuccessful because their bodies remain unresponsive to androgen throughout life. Attempts to stimulate penis growth with artificially applied testosterone, for instance, have failed. In general, people with the androgen-insensitivity syndrome who are raised as females are more satisfied with their sex roles than those who are raised as males.

**Adrenogenital Syndrome** This genetic anomaly results in the development of a chromosomally female person (XX) with masculinized external anatomy and female internal anatomy. People with the adrenogental syndrome have a malfunction of the adrenal glands that causes abnormally large amounts of androgens to be produced. During fetal life, these hormones induce growth of the clitoris to penis-like dimensions and development of a scrotal sac. Internally, however, a uterus and vagina develop rather than male organs.

Masculinization of the external anatomies of infants with the adrenogenital syndrome is often so complete that they would be considered male were it not for nonsexual side effects. Salt-fluid balances are disrupted, with consequent physical illness. When the abnormality is diagnosed, the child can be treated with *cortisone* (the hormone that the adrenal glands should produce instead of excess androgens). Sometimes, however, the adrenogenital syndrome is not diagnosed at birth, and the child is unwittingly raised as if it were a boy.

Surgery on the external genitals of children

with the adrenogenital syndrome can feminize their appearances, and treatments with cortisone throughout life can help them to lead fairly normal lives as women. In many cases it is possible for them to conceive and bear children. Without cortisone treatments, however, their bodies develop physiological characteristics of male puberty (deepening of voice, growth of body hair, and so on) around the age of five.

**Progestin-Induced Hermaphroditism** As described in the preceding paragraphs, hormone therapy has been invaluable for treating congenital sex defects. However, in certain cases, medically administered hormones have triggered unexpected sexual disorders. In the 1950s, for example, progestins (synthetic progesterone) were used to prevent miscarriages by women who had histories of chronic spontaneous abor-

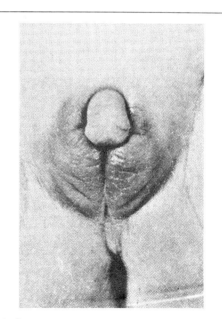

5.6 *Progestin-induced hermaphroditism.*

tions. The drugs were administered during pregnancy and inadvertently the sexual development of female fetuses was disrupted. Girls were born with scrotal sacs, fusion of the labia majora or penis-like clitorises. The effects were similar to the adrenogenital syndrome in that internal anatomy developed as female in spite of external masculinization. In most cases, surgical and hormonal techniques have been used for feminization.

Studies of the lives of girls with the adrenogenital syndrome and progestin-induced hermaphroditism have revealed several effects (Money and Ehrhardt, 1972; Ehrhardt, et al 1968). For example, young study subjects often show unusual characteristics – boys rather than girls are preferentially sought as playmates and strenuous activities are chosen over the relatively docile play of most pre-pubertal girls. In some cases, study subjects have expressed desires to be boys rather than girls, but most of them are happy with their gender. When asked about their hopes for the future, a relatively high proportion of the fetally "androgenized" girls expressed desires to pursue careers in addition to (or instead of) living as housewives.

## Is There a Biological Basis for Homosexuality?

Leon Speroff (1978) poses again a question which has come up several times in the '70s. The answer still seems to be inconclusive.

Speroff cites research by Charles Phoenix and his associates at the Oregon Regional Primate Research Center, who studied female monkeys which were masculinized by the administration of testosterone to their mothers during pregnancy. These "masculinized" females showed male-like social behavior, including increased mounting of other females. However, they were fully capable of reproducing, after a somewhat delayed menarche.

Human counterparts to these experiments can be found in the accidental phenomena of adrenogenital syndrome and progestin-induced hermaphroditism. But, in the studies cited in the last section, John Money and his associates found no indications of lesbianism in subjects followed through adolescence (Money, et. al., 1972). The girls were, however, slow to reach the "boyfriend" stage. Money postulates that "the biological clock for falling in love was in arrears, but not ... set to respond to a member of the same sex."

Speroff (1978) points to reverse evidence for a hormonal link to homosexuality in the conspicuous absence of homosexuality in males with precocious (early) puberty, "a situation in which one would expect a profound androgen influence."

But, at this writing, the authors of this text are not aware of direct evidence for a hormonal cause of homosexuality.

## Aging

Styles and frequency of erotic activity change throughout life. Frequency of orgasm, for instance, generally reaches a peak early in adulthood, then gradually tapers off. For men, this peak occurs in the teens or early twenties; for women, it may not arrive until the thirties.

This difference in average age of maximum orgasmic activity may be due to differences in the dynamics of physical maturation, but social influences enforce the disparity and may be causally related. The relatively severe moral restrictions with which young women are indoctrinated, for instance, could be a significant factor in depressing their sexual interests below the intensity felt by young men. Because societal pressures against early female sexual activity are less restrictive now than several years ago there may be a lowering in the average age of the peak female sex drive in future decades.

From age forty and beyond, sexual activity generally diminishes, but the effects of aging vary widely from person to person. People who are happy with their lives and preserve their health usually can continue to have satisfying sexual relationships, even in old age. The following sections consider the physical and emotional changes of aging.

**Female Aging**    Sometime around the age of fifty, women pass through a phase of relatively rapid change that ultimately leads to the end of fertility. Chemically these changes are due to a decrease in the production of estrogen. For an unknown reason, a break in the reproductive hormone cycle happens at the ovaries, which quit responding to FSH. The activity of the pituitary ceases to influence the primary reproductive organs.

The most obvious result of the depletion of estrogen is the end of menstrual bleeding. For most women, *menopause* (also termed the *climacteric* or "change of life") progresses over the course of several years, with menstrual periods becoming increasingly erratic and widely spaced. For some women, however, menstruation goes on regularly, then abruptly discontinues, and never returns.

Although many women pass through menopause with little or no feeling of physical or emotional upset, others experience moments of distress. One symptom known as the *hot flash* may come on intermittently and without warning. The sensation has been described as being similar to looking into a hot oven or of having stayed in a hot shower too long. Hot flashes are thought to be caused by erratic responses of the circulatory system to diminished estrogen.

Because estrogen is necessary to maintain secretion by the uterus and vagina, these organs begin to deteriorate with the onset of menopause. The vaginal wall becomes thinner and less elastic, and lubrication during sexual stimulation diminishes. As a result, intercourse may bcome painful. However, lubricating substances (including saliva and K-Y jelly) can be used to relieve the problem.

In addition to the changes of the vagina and uterus, several other characteristics of aging may be aggravated by depletion of estrogen. Rates of heart disease and cancer, for instance, both increase dramatically among menopausal and postmenopausal women. (However, a cause-and-effect relationship has not been established between estrogen depletion and these afflictions.) Also, because estrogen is linked to the processes that maintain healthy bones they tend to break down and lose their shape. The spine is particularly susceptible and, as life continues into old age, vertebrae tend to compress. Several other physical ills have been attributed to menopause, including headaches, backaches, insomnia, and loss of muscle tone.

Sometimes the physiological changes of menopause are accompanied by emotional depression. However, it is by no means inevitable. Just as the emotional changes of the menstrual cycle are influenced by cultural and psychological factors, so, too, are the characteristics of menopause. The more fulfilled and secure a woman is prior to the climacteric, the more likely she is to be happy during and after it. Similarly, the more compatible and fulfilling her relationships with associates, friends, and lovers, the more likely she is to pass through the changes with minimal emotional distress. Maintenance of close relationships with children is particularly important for women whose major role in life has been motherhood.

Within recent years discoveries in hormonal research have added powerful tools to medical treatment of the side effects of menopause. Doctors have found, for example, that estrogen taken in controlled amounts can alleviate some of the physical and emotional problems. Additionally, estrogen creams applied to the vagina can restore some of the vitality to its tissues. However, estrogen therapy is relatively new and involves certain risks. Women considering estrogen therapy should first look into its potential dangers, which include increased risk or aggravation of several types of cancer, especially cancer of the breast, uterus, cervix, and vagina.

Some doctors consider the risks of estrogen-induced cancer to be a trade-off against the protection it may give against heart disease. Research reported by Barrett-Connor, et. al. (1979) has shown that postmenopausal estrogen therapy tends to reduce levels of cholesterol in the blood. Blood pressure also tends to be lower. The authors point out, however, that a conclusive demonstration of reduced cardiovascular disease is yet to come.

Once the drastic changes of menopause have passed and sexual characteristics again become relatively stable, women often find renewed interest in erotic activity. With the end of the menstrual cycle comes the end of the need for contraception, and many women understandably feel more freedom in their sexual relations. By nine months after the last period of menstrual bleeding, it is unlikely that a woman can become pregnant. However, it would be wise to consult a gynecologist before dispensing with contraception.

**Male Aging**    For men there is no absolute end to fertility as there is in women, but production of testosterone and sperm gradually slacken following a peak in the late teens or early twenties. Nevertheless, some males well over eighty produce viable sperm and have fathered children.

With a drop in the level of testosterone, male reproductive organs gradually undergo changes. The testicles grow smaller and semen gets thinner and less plentiful. From the mid-twenties onward, the abilities to arouse an erection and reach orgasm gradually diminish. Therapists have had a certain amount of success in renewing male sex drive with testosterone replacement therapy, but there is evidence that the power of suggestion plays more of a role than the hormone itself. Men given *placebos* (medically inert substances) often develop elevated sex drives if they are convinced they are taking testosterone.

By far, the most common sexual maladies of aging men are troubles with the prostate gland. Malfunctions of the prostate plague about 10 percent of the male population at age forty, and 50 percent of those who are eighty. Problems are of two major types, bacterial infections and tumors. The latter can be either cancerous or benign, and both types may be removed surgically. More is said about prostate disease in Chapter 7.

Erotic activity may be impaired by prostate surgery, but if problems are detected early, chances are excellent for maintenance of sexual functions. Hence, symptoms of possible problems (pains or a burning sensation in the lower abdomen, particularly during urination or intercourse) should receive immediate medical attention.

In general, the psychological changes of aging develop more slowly for men than women. For some men, however, there is a phase of marked emotional change that, on the average, happens about ten years later than female menopause. As with menopause there is a question as to the relative effects of physical changes and socio-psychological influences. Mandatory retirement, for example, may be the major cause of depression among older men.

Old age is often looked upon as a dirty trick played on humanity. In America old people are no longer revered and sought after for advise as they are in many other societies. Thus, medical science has treatments for the changes that accompany menopause but would not think of medicating young women for the changes inherent in menarche. The message seems to be: entering youth is normal, acceptable, but passing beyond youth should be treated and medicated away. Kinder, less fearful attitudes toward aging might provide relief for some of the most damaging feelings of this phase of life.

## QUESTIONS

1. Some infants appear to have erotic experiences. Why does their erotic sense usually disappear in early childhood??

2. If you are a male, do you believe you have experienced cyclical changes comparable to the menstrual cycle? If you are female, do you notice changes in the males you know? If any, what are the changes?

3. Do you notice any changes in your (or your mate's) erotic desires during the menstrual cycle?

4. Do you think the "problems" connected with menstruation are as bad as they are commonly said to be?

# Readings

### The Hormone Connections

Ruth Winter

*Thoughts and emotions ebb and flow under the constant influence of the endocrine system. The translation of chemical activity into the dynamics of human existence is a deep mystery, but the infinitesimal amounts of hormones that circulate in the blood play vital roles.*

During the period I was nursing our youngest son, I awoke one night to hear his cry in another room and immediately the milk in my breasts began to flow. It suddenly struck me that something very primitive and involuntary was at work. The sound of my son's voice had been instantly interpreted as a cry of hunger by my brain and an automatic hormonal signal had been sent to my breasts to release the milk and to prepare me for the baby's feeding. And yet, there had been no physical contact between my baby and me when I heard the cry that had aroused me from sleep.

This interaction between stimuli, brain, hormones and behavior has intrigued me ever since. There are many who say we are controlled by "the establishment" or by our environment but more and more evidence is accumulating that our hormones and our mothers' hormones predetermine our adult behavior even before we leave the womb. The great lovers in our society, the impotent, the criminals, geniuses, feminists, soldiers and homosexuals may all behave the way they do not so much because of their past experiences or present situations but because of the minute secretions of their endocrine glands.

The word "hormone" for the substance secreted by the endocrine glands is derived from the Greek word "hormao" meaning "I arouse to activity."

The largest of the hormone secreters, the pancreas, has an average weight of less than three ounces. The smallest, the mysterious pineal, is about the size a grape seed. All the others together – the thyroid, the four parathyroids, the twin adrenals, the pituitary, the thymus and the paired ovaries of women or testes of men – total between four and seven ounces.

Of all the endocrines, the ones which have intrigued man most have been the sex glands which determine not only fertility, but sexual desire and personality.

As any woman who has suffered from premenstrual tension and any man who has viewed the body of a desirable female knows, hormones greatly affect our outlook on life. The degreee to which they control our behavior, however, is controversial to say the least. One has only to remember the outcry when Hubert Humphrey's personal physician remarked several years ago that women were unfit for high political office because of the emotional effects of the menstrual cycle. And there is a heated scientific debate now current about how much is learned and how much hormonal when it comes to masculine or feminine behavior.

For instance, Dr. John Money of Johns Hopkins University has reported that a prenatal excess of the male sex hormone, androgen, significantly increased the IQs of females, even when the overproduction was corrected shortly after birth.

"The relationship is intriguing," Dr. Money reported, "For it suggests the existence of a contributory factor which has received little or no previous recognition. The intelligence-stimulating factor in males is androgen. In women, it is progesterone, a female hormone that has a strong male hormone component."

Dr. Money believes that hormones may one day be altered prenatally to increase intelligence, particularly in cases of mental deficiency related to low levels of hormones.

Dr. Lynwood G. Clemens, a Michigan State University zoologist, reported that when female rodents share the womb with male rodents, the females act more masculine when adult. He said the same thing occurred when he injected male hormone into female hamsters one day after birth. Although no further male hormone was administered, the girl hamsters acted masculine when they reached adulthood. Yet, when male hamsters received female hormone, nothing happened.

Dr. Clemens explained this phenomena by pointing out that female hormones don't become very active until puberty. "Most psychologists attribute tomboy traits of females who are twins of males as an effect of being raised with a brother," Dr. Clemens said, "But we now know there is a potential hormonal influence."

Oregon researchers as far back as 1964 proposed that the strength of a person's sexual drive in adulthood was the result of prenatal gonadal (sex) hormones which superseded psychological factors, social level, cultural background and tradition.

Drs. William C. Young, Robert Goy and Charles Phoenix of the Oregon Regional Primate Research Center pointed out that in an early stage in the unborn child, the gonads of both sexes have the same structure. Hormones then determine the sexual differentiation of the genitals and the developing brain.

The Oregonians produced female monkeys, guinea pigs and rats with male organs by injecting them in the womb with male hormones. When researchers administered more male hormones after birth, the females acted as if they were really males in adulthood.

The Oregonians maintain that homosexuality or "incongruities between sexual behavior and physique" may be attributed to predetermined psychosexuality created by hormonal imbalances before birh. Lending weight to such theories are the reports of such studies as the one showing that sons of diabetic mothers given estrogen during pregnancy behaved in a more feminine manner than sons of diabetic mothers who did not receive the female hormone.

Researchers at Masters and Johnson's Reproductive Biology Research Foundation in St. Louis reported lower levels of male hormone in the blood of young men who are predominantly homosexual, and Los Angeles scientists have found they could correctly identify the homosexuals in a group of males merely by measuring the traces of the male hormone, testosterone in human samples.

Such findings are particularly significant today when the psychiatric world is still reeling from the American Psychiatric Association's Board of Directors ruling that homosexuality is not abnormal behavior but merely a variant of sexual expression.

Villanova University's Dr. Ingebord Ward goes so far as to maintain that pregnant animals exposed to stress will have male offspring that behave in a more feminine manner in adulthood. The Pennsylvania psychologist "stressed" mother rats by placing them in tiny plexiglass tubes under direct light, a situation frightening to them. She then found that the male offspring of such mothers behaved in a feminine manner in adulthood.

Does male hormone given after birth make a male more aggressive and more successful? Feminists notwithstanding, many researchers have reported that castration reduces aggressiveness in males. Females do not ordinarily attack other females and when males are given ovarian hormones, it decreases their aggressiveness. It can also cause maternal behavior in them. On the other hand, early injections of testosterones have been shown to accelerate the development of aggressiveness in juvenile male animals.

Dr. Alan I. Leshner of Bucknell is studying hormones and aggressiveness. He and his associates can predict which monkey will eventually dominate a colony merely by determining the level of hormone in urine.

Other researchers have reported that dominant male rats have increased male hormones in their urine and that they spread that urine all around the cage while less dominant males urinate in just a corner.

The male dominant rats secrete a hormonal pheromone in their urine, a substance which stimulates the sex glands of the female rats. When a female rat is placed in a cage with a strange male rat, it is believed that the male's pheromones turn off her ability to implant an ovum in her womb, even if she has been previously fertilized. This might explain how animal populations become self-limiting when there is overcrowding. The females become "infertile" because something turns off their hormonal balance.

Can any of these intriquing animal studies be applied to human behavior?

The United States government is financing a study of testosterone and aggressive behavior by Dr. Robert Rose of the Boston School of Medicine and Dr. Irwin Bernstein of the Yerkes Regional Primate Research Center to find out.

Drs. Rose and Irwin maintain that it is possible that testosterone may be inhibited in subordinate males by the stress of living in a social group. This diminished level of male hormone could, in turn, result in decreased aggressive behavior which would be appropriate for a low ranking male.

From a previous study, Dr. Rose found evidence to support this theory. He found that soldiers under the increased stress of combat training usually had lower testosterone levels than soldiers attending officers candidate school. Furthermore, in studies of prisoners at a Maryland institution for defective delinquents, he found that inmates arrested before the age of 18 years for violent or aggressive crimes secreted more testosterone than other prisoners.

That hormones may play a significant part in encouraging people to commit crimes is given a great deal of weight by endocrinologists. A number of studies have shown that women are more prone to commit infractions of the law during premenstrual tension and in fact, in one prison study, 64 percent of the female prisoners were in jail for offenses committed during the menstrual periods. Other studies have shown that suicides occur more often in women just before menstruation.

The severe depression and irritability which sometimes occurs during menopause is well known, even to the lay public. However, as much as a woman may be subject to mood swings due to her hormonal cycle throughout her reproductive years, she will probably live longer than her contemporary males because of her sex hormones.

In her entire lifetime, a woman produces barely two tablespoonfuls of the female hormones estrogen and progesterone and yet the survival of the human race depends upon the release and perfect synchronization of tiny amounts of these substances.

There is a great deal of evidence which points to these hormones as shields against life-shortening illnesses. A woman who still maintains her menstrual cycle has far less heart disease than her male contemporaries and she lives

an average of 12 years longer than they do.

But Dr. James Hamilton of New York Down State Medical Center believes that it may be male hormone which is damaging to men rather than the female hormone which is beneficial to women. Dr. Hamilton has long been fascinated with the difference between the life spans of men and women.

"Some years ago," Dr. Hamilton said, "I discovered that acne and baldness were dependent upon male hormones. If these common conditions are associated with maleness, I began to wonder what else was.

"There are three possible explanations to the difference in survival rate between men and women. Stress, sex chromosomes and sex hormones.

"As for the first, despite popular opinion, I doubt that bigger stresses are applied to males. I think males just can't withstand many of the stresses as well as females. I say this because if you compare statistics on obesity and smoking, you will find the males are much worse off. That is, a higher percentage of males who are heavy smokers suffer from cancer than females who are heavy smokers. Likewise, the decrease in the life period as a result of obesity is greater for men than for women.

The second explanation, the sex chromosomes, becomes intimately tied up with the sex hormones theory, according to Dr. Hamilton. A chromosome is a unit of a cell which carries genetic information. In mammals, a female has two X chromosomes, while a male has only one X and a much smaller Y chromosome.

Some believe that second X protects women. Dr. Hamilton believes that it is the small Y chromosome which is detrimental to the male. In both the human species and in lower forms of life, there are certain "supermales" who have two Y chromosomes instead of an X and a Y. A number of these supermales have been found in prison. Scientists theorize it is because of their innate aggressiveness.

Dr. Hamilton has demonstrated in his laboratory that male animals with YY chromosomes have shorter life expectancies than normal XY males. This has confirmed his belief that genetic and hormonal factors are involved in male life expectancy.

As for the third factors on Dr. Hamilton's list, sex hormones, he and his co-workers have found that castrated males live significantly longer than normal males, especially if the castration takes place before puberty.

In contrast to former centuries when castration was performed on singers in churches and opera houses, as well as on personnel in harems and imperial palaces, the operation is now done chiefly in cases of prostatic cancer (kwhich is linked to male sex hormone) and on mentally retarded or psychotic males.

Dr. Hamilton and his colleagues have been conducting a long term study of institutionalized mentally retarded males. The subjects are 735 intact males and 297 eunuchs. Each eunuch has been matched closely with one or more intact males for such characteristics as year of birth and length of hospitalization.

The results so far show that the average life span for intact males is 55.7 years and for eunuchs, 69.3 years. The younger the males are castrated, the longer they live.

One fact in the study which must be taken into consideration is that mentally retarded subjects have only a vague idea of the effects of castration which reduces any adverse psychological effects of the operation.

Evidence is accumulating that the more virile a man, the younger he dies. Statistics show that ambitious aggressive men – men with high levels of testosterone – die sooner than their less hor-

monally endowed brothers. Despite this fact, most men would choose virility over a long life.

In fact, men will do anything, it seems, to enhance sexual potency. A French professor at the Sorbonne, Charles Brown-Sequard, in 1969 injected semen into the blood of old men in an effort to restore potency. He then injected extract of dog testicle in himself and claimed it made him virile and vigorous. He reputedly died some time later of a venereal disease after he had set the infant science of endocrinology back years.

Doctors today know that the male hormones, do, indeed, play a part in sexual prowess. However, the results of giving doses of male hormone to shore up flagging potency have been equivocal. There have been reputed successes with the implantation of from 12 to 15 pellets of testosterone in about 50 percent of the patients, but such reports are highly controversial.

Giving male hormones to females has reportedly increased their susceptibility to psychic and somatic sexual stimulation, produced increased sensitivity of the external genitalia and induced greater intensity of sexual gratification. In fact, the administration of male hormone to desperately ill female cancer patients has reportedly rekindled their sex drives despite severe physical and emotional debilitation.

Just as hormones deeply affect our behavior, so too does our behavior affect our hormones. One has only to think of the way our hearts beat faster as we secrete hormones during fright or during lovemaking.

Many cases of cessation of menses have been reported in medical literature when fear of pregnancy or other stresses such as the London Blitz of World War II occurred. There have also been a number of reports of infertile women who suddenly conceived after adopting a child and there are multiple instances of men who are impotent only with certain women.

## Does Menopause or Hysterectomy Terminate a Woman's Sex Life?

James Leslie MCary

It is understandable that in the relatively unenlightened medical world of the 1800s, physicians would reason that since the ovaries dwindle in their production of female sex hormones at and after the climacteric, women's sex drive would accordingly decrease. It is now known that women's sex drive often does not diminish even when the ovaries are surgically removed. Hormones are only one of many factors affecting the capacity for sexual response; more crucial factors are the woman's emotional stability and attitude toward sex.

Total hysterectomy is the removal of the uterus;

---

We are all prisoners of our hormones to some extent. The debate is over the extent. Dr. Robert Kolodny, director of endocrinology at the Reproductive Biology Research Foundation in St. Louis, concedes that hormonal as well as other factors play a part in behavior but choices such as homosexuality, he contends, are primarily learned. "But whether hormonal factors set the stage for learned behavior is still an open question," he emphasized.

Ruth Winter, "Are You a Prisoner of Your Own Sex Hormones?" *Science Digest*, Copyright © 1974. Toni Mendez Inc., New York. Reprinted by permission.

---

*Excerpt from*
## Letters From The Earth

Mark Twain

*Mark Twain didn't mince words about his perception of the relative erotic capabilities of males and females.*

The law of God, as quite plainly expressed in woman's construction, is this: There shall be no limit put upon your intercourse with the other sex sexually, at any time of life.

The law of God, as quite plainly expressed in man's construction, is this: During your entire life you shall be under inflexible limits and restrictions, sexually.

During twenty-three days in every month (in the absence of pregnancy) from the time a woman is seven years old till she dies of old age, she is ready for action, and competent. As competent as the candlestick is to receive the candle. Competent every day, competent every night. Also, she wants that candle — yearns for it, longs for it, hankers after it, as commanded by the law

of God in her heart.

But man is only briefly competent, and only then in the moderate measure applicable to the word in his sex's case. He is competent from the age of sixteen or seventeen thenceforward for thirty-five years. After fifty his performance is of poor quality. The intervals between are wide, and its satisfactions of no great value to either party; whereas his great-grandmother is as good as new. There is nothing the matter with her plant. Her candlestick is as firm as ever, whereas his candle is increasingly softened and weakened by the weather of age, as the years go by, until at last it can no longer stand, and is mournfully laid to rest in the hope of a blessed resurrection which is never to come.

By the woman's make, her plant has to be out of service three days in the month and during a part of her pregnancy. These are times of discomfort, often of suffering. For fair and just compensation she has the high privilege of unlimited adultery all the other days of her life.

That is the law of God, as revealed in her make. What becomes of this high privilege? Does she live in the free enjoyment of it? No. Nowhere in the whole world. She is robbed of it everywhere. Who does this? Man. Man's statutes — if the Bible is the Word of God.

Now there you have a sample of man's "reasoning powers," as he calls them. He observes certain facts. For instance, that in all his life he never sees the day that he can satisfy one woman; also, that no woman ever sees the day that she can't overwork, and defeat, and put out of commission any ten masculine plants that can be put to bed to her. He puts those strikingly suggestive and luminous facts together, and from them draws this astonishing conclusion: The Creator intended the woman to be restricted to panhysterectomy is removal of uterus, Fallopian tubes, and ovaries. In the first instance, there would not even be the reason of hormonal imbalance to account for loss of sex drive; if the woman's surgeon carefully explains the effects of the operation, neither should she have any diminution of sex drive because of psychological factors. If any change does occur, in fact, it might be in the direction of increased drive, since fear of pregnancy is now

removed. If ovaries and tubes are also removed, some hormonal changes will occur, although medication can make up any deficiencies.

Considering all the factors, a woman can expect to maintain her sex drive at approximately the same level between the ages of about thirty to sixty years, despite menopause or hysterectomy.

---

one man.

So he concretes that singular conclusion into a law, for good and all.

And he does it without consulting the woman, although she has a thousand times more at stake in the matter than he has. His procreative competency is limited to an average of a hundred exercises per year for fifty years, hers is good for three thousand a year for that whole time – and as many years longer as she may live. Thus his life interest in the matter is five thousand refreshments, while hers is a hundred and fifty thousand; yet instead of fairly and honorably leaving the making of the law to the person who has an overwhelming interest at stake in it, this immeasurable hog, who has nothing at stake in it worth considering, makes it himself!

You have heretofore found out, by my teachings, that man is a fool; you are now aware that woman is a damned fool.

From pp 39-41 in Mark Twain *Letters From The Earth*, edited by Bernard DeVoto. Copyright © 1962 by The Mark Twain Company. Reprinted by permission of Harper and Row, Publishers, Inc.

---

### Excerpt from
### The Second Sex

Simone De Beauvoir

*Freud believed that "penis envy" was a significant part of female sexual development. The following are the thoughts of the matriarch of feminism, Simone De Beauvoir, on the subject.*

There are few questions more extensively discussed by psychoanalysts than the celebrated feminine "castration complex." Most would admit today that penis envy is manifested in very

diverse ways in different cases. To begin with there are many little girls who remain ignorant of the male anatomy for some years. Such a child finds it quite natural that there should be men and women, just as there is a sun and a moon: she believes in essences contained in words and her curiosity is not analytic at first. For many others this tiny bit of flesh hanging between boys' legs is insignificant or even laughable; it is a peculiarity that merges with that of clothes or haircut. Often it is first seen on a small newborn brother and, as Helene Deutsch puts it, "when the little girl is very young she is not impressed by the penis of her little brother." She cites the case of a girl of eighteen months who remained quite indifferent to the discovery of the penis and attached no importance to it until much later, in accordance with her personal interests. It may even happen that the penis is considered to be an anomaly: an outgrowth, something vague that hangs, like wens, breasts, or warts; it can inspire disgust. Finally, the fact is that there are numerous cases where the little girl does take an interest in the penis of a brother or playmate, but that does not mean that she experiences jealousy of it in a really sexual way, still less that she feels deeply affected by the absence of that organ; she wants to get it for herself as she wants to get any and every object, but this desire can remain superficial.

There is no doubt that the excretory functions, and in particular the urinary functions, are of passionate interest to children; indeed, to wet the bed is often a form of protest against a marked preference of the parents for another child. There are countries where the men urinate while seated, and there are cases of women who urinate standing as is customary with many peasants, among others; but in contemporary Western society, custom generally demands that women sit or crouch, while the erect position is reserved for males. This difference constitutes for the little girl the most striking sexual differentiation. To urinate, she is required to crouch, uncover herself, and therefore hide: a shameful and inconvenient procedure. The shame is intensified in the frequent cases in which the girl suffers from involuntary discharge of urine, as for instance when laughing immoderately; in general her control is not so good as that of the boys.

To boys the urinary function seems like a free game, with the charm of all games that offer liberty of action; the penis can be manipulated, it gives opportunity for action, which is one of the deep interests of the child. A little girl on seeing a boy urinating exclaimed admiringly: "How convenient"! The stream can be directed at will and to a considerable distance, which gives the boy a feeling of omnipotence. Freud spoke of "the burning ambition of early diuretics"; Stekel has discussed this formula sensibly, but it is true, as Karen Horney says, that the "fantasies of omnipotence, especially those of sadistic character, are frequently associated with the male urinary stream"; these fantasies, which are lasting in certain men, are important in the child. Abraham speaks of the "great pleasure women derive from watering the garden with a hose"; I believe, in agreement with the theories of Sartre and of Bachelard, that identifying the hose with the penis is not necessarily the source of this pleasure though it is clearly so in certain cases. Every stream of water in the air seems like a miracle, a defiance of gravity: to direct, to govern it is to win a small victory over the laws of nature; and in any case the small boy finds here a daily amusement that is denied his sisters. It permits the establishment through the urinary stream of many relations with things such as water, earth, moss, snow, and the like. There are little girls

who in their wish to share these experiences lie on their backs and try to make the urine spurt upward or practice urinating while standing. According to Karen Horney, they envy also the possibility of exhibiting which the boy has. She reports that the patient, upon seeing a man urinating in the street, suddenly exclaimed: "If I could ask one gift from Providence, it would be to have for once in my life the power of urinating like a man." To many little girls it seems that the boy, having the right to touch his penis can make use of it as a plaything, whereas their organs are taboo.

That all the factors combine to make possession of a male sex organ seem desirable to many girls is a fact attested by numerous inquiries made and confidences received by psychiatrists. Havelock Ellis cited these remarks made by a patient of Dr. S. E. Jelliffe, called Zenia. "The gushing of water in a jet or spray especially from a long garden hose, has always been highly suggestive to me, recalling the act of urination as witnessed in childhood in my brothers or even in other boys." A correspondent, Mrs. R. S., told Ellis that as a child she greatly desired to handle a boy's penis and imagined scenes involving such behavior with urination, one day she was allowed to hold a garden hose. "It seemed delightfully like holding a penis." She asserted that the penis had no sexual significance for her, she knew about the urinary function only.

## On Human Cloning

Laurence E. Karp

*Cloning is the regeneration of an organism from a single one of its cells. It is a theoretical possibility for all creatures, and has been achieved with certain organisms, including plants and frogs.*

*In 1978 a writer of questionable ethics claimed in a book called "In His Image" that a baby boy had been cloned from a 67-year-old millionaire. But the book did not identify the clone, and offered no evidence that the state of the art had advanced to the point at which mice, let alone men, could be cloned. Nevertheless, the national huff over cloning that had first flared earlier in the decade was rekindled.*

*Even if the claim were true, however, anyone who gives the subject much thought must see the folly in fears of cloned armies of supermen or an endless succession of the same dictator.*

\* \* \*

Cloning might, in theory, be used to create large numbers of people to different specifications. In this way, clones of dull, unintelligent persons might be created to do tedious, unpleasant tasks. Large armies of soldiers could be cloned from the nastiest thirty-year master sergeants in the country. It has even been suggested that clones might be established from genetically legless persons, to create astronauts who would fit better into space capsules. However, these schemes all presuppose a nationally directed reproductive program, where having children is no longer an individual prerogative, and where a person's destiny is foreordained. Insistence upon freedom of individuality probably is the best safeguard in this area. Such insistence will be far more valuable than any laws that might be passed to forbid the practice of cloning — bans that no self-respecting dictator would feel compelled to obey, anyway.

A problem for our hypothetical dictator would be that cloning is an inefficient technique. Just like any other babies, clonees have to grow up, and an army of cloned master sergeants in diapers would not be helpful in doing battle with the

Chinese next week. To obtain his armies, his morons, or his astronauts, a dictator would be far more likely to resort to more immediate techniques, such as brainwashing, drug treatments, surgery, or even good old-fashioned orders at the point of a gun.

H. J. Muller foresaw great possible use for cloning in his positive eugenics ventures. Whether by governmental edict or by individual parental choice, this would involve the cloning of geniuses in accordance with need in different areas of human endeavor. We would create teams of Einsteins, Newtons, Mozarts. or Chaucers.

Even if we pay no attention to the arguable question of whether genius by committee would in fact constitute a blessing, there still exist strong objections to such a plan. For one thing, it ignores the considerable contribution to a person's functioning made by environment. Although members of a common clone would be genetically identical (except for mutations), it is unlikely that the overall resemblance between themselves and their genetic parent would be any greater than that which normally exists between identical twins. Twins do bear strong resemblances to each other, but they are not "carbon copies," even when they are brought up together, and therefore presumably share an identical postnatal environment. Even prenatal environment is important: it is usually assumed that twins are exposed to identical intrauterine conditions, but this is not so. For example, in identical twins — with identical genes — one twin may be born normal and the other anencephalic. This may be explained by differential placental blood supplies, which, in turn, would cause one fetus to receive less oxygen, or more environmental teratogen, than the other. Clearly, no men are truly created equal. The extreme difficulty of producing exact copies of human beings is explained with grace and wit by Dr. Lewis Thomas in his article "On Cloning a Human Being," which is included in the reference list at the end of the book (refer to the bibliography).

Another problem with cloning for positive eugenic purposes is based on the observation that greatness so often seems to be simply a matter of the right man happening to be in the right place at the right time. It could even be argued that environmental and social conditions continually select for genius, and so, by limiting our genetic diversity through cloning (as would also occur with parthenogenesis), we might find ourselves with fewer, not greater, numbers of geniuses, being saddled instead with groups of Xeroxed has-beens. Limitation of genetic diversity generally seems unwise.

Another serious potential problem related to cloning concerns the psyche of the clonee. Whether he were cloned from his de jure parent or from a particularly illustrious person, a cloned individual would be very likely to have his performance measured in the light of unreasonable expectations. In fact, I would wonder whether any sort of comfortable parent-child relationship could be formed under these circumstances. In this context, it might be appropriate to recall an aspect of the early life of Vincent van Gogh. His parents had had an older son, whom they also had named Vincent. This boy had died before the birth of the future artist. The second Vincent later described the discomfort and anxiety he had felt each day while walking to school, because his path led through the graveyard, where he could see his brother's tombstone with his own name on it. Whether this experience contributed to van Gogh's famous psychosis is problematic, but the possibility should give pause to would-be cloners of humans.

It has been suggested that cloning would present us with the ability to keep genetically identical copies of ourselves deep-frozen, so that we would have available a ready supply of "spare parts" that could be transplanted to ourselves whenever necessary. Certainly, this situation would present a raft of novel legal and ethical dilemmas, which, as usual, can be scarcely imagined let alone solved, at this time. I suspect that most persons at present would find such an arrangement highly repugnant, at least until such time as they were to find themselves in mortal need of a compatible organ for transplantation.

# Unit 3

## Sexual Systems— Under Control and Out of Control

Not many years ago, birth control wasn't a polite topic of conversation; but today it's a favorite subject of small talk. For many people it has even become a matter of pride, since global overpopulation now looms as a threat in the popular consciousness. Also, in recent years, many men and women of Western countries have concluded that having children would restrict their lifestyles, and they have chosen one or more of the various methods to prevent conception – abstention, abortion, contraception, and sterilization.

Birth control has not gone unopposed, and objectors are forceful. The U.S. Supreme Court has ruled that states cannot restrict sale of nonprescription contraceptives (condoms and spermacides) to people of any age. Of course, this does not stop individual "moral" judgments. Minors should be aware that the law is behind them if they are obstructed in their attempts to procure contraceptives.

Policies of state governments may prevent or encourage the use of certain methods of birth control. In some states sterilization and abortion are legal (even mandatory) for people who have committed rape or incest, or are mentally retarded.

At the other end of the legal spectrum are the rights of women who would like to terminate pregnancy but who are prevented from doing so by the state. The state quo of this question was suddenly upset early in 1973 when the Supreme Court ruled that up to the end of the third month of pregnancy the decision whether or not to terminate the pregnancy is entirely left to the woman and her physician. However, after *viability* (when the fetus is capable of living outside the womb) a state government may prevent abortion unless it is done to protect the health of the mother. This decision (based on the "due process" clause of the Fourteenth Amendment of

the Constitution) reversed the anti-abortion policies that existed in many states. In July of 1979 the Supreme Court ruled that female minors need not have parental consent to seek an abortion.

Moral objections to birth control have come from several religious groups and other sociopolitical groups. At the individual level, attitudes toward birth control vary markedly and are influenced by many factors. For example, children's ideas about the use of birth control are shaped by parent's views, which can range from a strict refusal to even discuss contraception (or anything else concerning sex) to an anxious sales pitch for it.

Many contemporary men and women utilize contraceptives. The more drastic measures of abortion and sterilization are becoming more commonly used, but they are usually turned to only as a last resort. Information on birth control can be obtained from Planned Parenthood, which has offices in many cities and is listed in the phone books.

**Birth Control in America**

Throughout the nineteenth and much of the twentieth centuries, the moral standard of sex solely for reproduction was predominant in America. The government sought to enforce that morality by suppressing information about birth control, regardless of the consequences to women and their families. The result was abstinence and anxiety in sexual relations, larger families, poverty, abortions, and the deaths of thousands of women from the burden of continuous childbearing or the slaughter of illicit abortions. By the beginning of the twentieth century, however, out of a desire for a higher standard of living, the birth rate began to drop. The birth control technique, *coitus interruptus*, was

I want to remind young women that motherhood is the vocation of women. It was that way in the past. It is that way now, and it will always be that way. It is woman's eternal vocation.

Pope John Paul II

widely practiced, contraceptive devices and information were sold on the black market, and more and more women were not getting married.

The key to limiting family size lay in the dissemination of contraceptive information, information that had been banned by federal law as obscene. But in 1914, Margaret Sanger, began publishing a newspaper called *The Woman Rebel*, in which she asserted that women should have the right to decide whether or not to bear children. In her newspaper Sanger coined the term "birth control" to describe contraception. She began her movement to permit open birth control after having witnessed the death of a young woman who had tried to abort herself. She was determined "to do something to change the destiny of mothers whose miseries were as vast as the skies." But everywhere she met government resistance. The Post Office Department refused to mail five issues of her newspaper, and in August, 1914, two government agents appeared at her home and handed her a summons for violating the federal Comstock Law against obscenity. She took the summons but refused to let the agents leave; instead, she spent two hours explaining the righteousness of her cause, converting them into advocates of birth control.

She was arraigned, but rather than endure a long trial and certain conviction, she fled the country, returning the next year to renew her fight. The government, the churches, and the medical profession — all traditional bastions of conservatism — argued that the only acceptable form of birth control was abstinence. They believed any other form would open the door to immorality, licentiousness, and degradation, endangering not only the individual but the nation.

In the fifty years following Sanger's fight for a new approach to contraception, the federal Comstock law (which had declared *Lady Chat-*terly's Lover, Ulysses, and *Tropic of Cancer* obscene) and twenty-two state "Little Comstock" laws were repealed or ruled unconstitutional. All had prohibited the mailing, transporting, or disseminating of contraceptive devices or information. The last major law prohibiting the sale of contraceptive devices was struck down in 1966. And, in 1973 the U.S. Supreme Court established the right of women to obtain an abortion in the first trimester of pregnancy.

## Contraception: A Matter of Conviction

Over a million unwanted pregnancies occur annually in the United States. (National Center for Health Statistics, 1977). Consequences of the roughly 700,000 unwanted adolescent pregnancies in 1977 included 300,000 abortions, 200,000 out-of wedlock births, 100,000 hasty marriages, and 100,000 miscarriages. Beneath those cold statistics is a lot of human suffering, most of which could have been prevented by contraception.

In spite of the revolutionary shift in American attitudes toward birth control in recent years, many people remain uninformed about the contraceptive techniques available to them. Yet, even among those to whom information and the means of contraception are readily available, there is a puzzlingly high rate of unwanted pregnancy. A professor of human sexuality at a midwestern university tells of two unwanted pregnancies among the teaching assistants in his sexuality course!

Perhaps there is a reproductive urge at work, which drives us to procreate in spite of expressed desires to the contrary. Even discounting such an urge, there are psychological forces at work which act to prevent people from using contraception. Among these, religious and/or moral injunctions are the most obvious. The edicts of

There are 190 local branches of Planned Parenthood located throughout the nation. The address of the one nearest you can be obtained by contacting the national headquarters in New York. Planned parenthood provides counseling in family planning, birth control, and pregnancy testing.

Planned Parenthood Federation of America
810 7th Avenue
New York, New York 10019
phone: 212-541-7800

---

the Catholic Church remain firmly against most methods of contraception; new, even more strict constraints have come with the spate of Eastern religious movements which have swept the country.

But, religious dogma may not be the main psychological stumbling block of contraception. One can describe the way to contraception as fourfold. First an individual must acknowledge to her/himself that intercourse is a possibility. We all come into life as virgins, and the choice to become sexual with others is achieved with more or less anxiety and uncertainty, depending primarily on the experiences of youth. The experience of rape when one was very young, parents who

disapprove of the erotic nature of sexuality, or any number of other negative experiences can instill negative feelings about erotic desires. Probably none of the adults reading this book made it through adolescence without at least a twinge of guilt over the early libidinous fantasies which exploded into consciousness whether we wanted them to or not. For nearly everyone, (particularly adolescent males), the "itch" is undeniable and might demand being "scratched" without much warning.

Given that one has acknowledged that intercourse is a possibility, one must have time to get the paraphernalia of contraception. This second step in the fourfold way is obviously most difficult

---

**Table 6.1**    Failure Rates of the Most Common Methods of Birth Control

Number of pregnancies during the first year of use per 100 non-sterile women initiating the method.

| Method | Theoretical Failure Rate (Used correctly and consistently) | Actual Failure Rate Among U.S. Women |
|---|---|---|
| Abortion | 0 | 0+ |
| Abstinence | 0 | ? |
| Hysterectomy | 0.0001 | 0.0001 |
| Tubal Ligation | 0.04 | 0.04 |
| Vasectomy | 0.15 | 0.15+ |
| Oral Contraceptive (combined) | 0.34 | 4-10 |
| I.M. Long-Acting Progestin | 0.25 | 5-10 |
| Condom plus Spermicidal Agent | less than 1 | 5 |
| Low Dose Oral Progestin | 1-1.5 | 5-10 |
| IUD | 1-3 | 5 |
| Condom | 3 | 10 |
| Diaphragm (with Spermicide) | 3 | 17 |
| Spermicidal Foam | 3 | 22 |
| Coitus Interruptus (withdrawal) | 9 | 20-25 |
| Rhythm (Calendar) | 13 | 21 |
| Douche | ? | 40 |
| Chance (Sexually active) | 90 | 90 |

for those who feel socially shaky. A matronly drugstore clerk, arranging the shelves near the condom display, can look formidable as one imagines her disapproval; more than one well-meaning young fellow has shuffled back out the door, empty-handed. Similar fears plague young women when they consider purchasing a spermacide.

But, if the prospective sex partners can pluck up the courage to put together a condom/spermacide combination, they will have a safe, highly effective method of contraception, as well as somewhat of a defense against most sexually transmissible diseases (STD's better known as VD). Such a pact would involve the third step: communication. But, this is often the hardest part of all. Fears of appearing "uncool," a desire to make the experience as "natural" as possible (someone once said that the only unnatural act is one that can't be done), and just plain timidity may stand in the way of taking contraceptive precautions. This is a problem even among married couples.

The final step, of course, is actually using the contraceptive. This may not sound like much of a problem, but the statistics show that this is where many people fail. One must resolve to use the contraceptives in spite of one's own or a partner's protests. The theoretical failure rate for "the Pill," for example, is about 0.3 percent per year. That is, of 1000 women who are using the Pill correctly and consistently, chances should be that 3 of them will become pregnant. In actuality, however, annual failure rates have been recorded in the range of 4-10 percent. That is, 40-100 out of every 1000 women who are on the Pill become pregnant during one year of use. (Hatcher, et al., 1978)

The following sections consider the commonly used methods of contraception in order of effectiveness. One should not interpret this as the order of desirability, however. The most effective ones, oral contraceptives and IUDs, are also the ones with the highest rate of associated health problems (Table 6.1). Condoms and spermacides are available without prescription, and if used conscientiously (which they often are not) they give sufficient protection against pregnancy and VD to be well worth the bother.

## Oral Contraceptives

The increasing popularity of contraception may be as much a product of hormonal technology as of changes in moral attitudes. Birth control pills have added a new dimension of freedom to human sexuality, but they have also brought with them associated health problems. Although both men and women benefit from the freedom, women take all the risks of oral contraception, because all the currently used pills are designed for them. This onesidedness has prompted charges of "sexism" against the predominately male researchers of contraception. The charges are strengthened by the fact that most research in oral contraception is directed toward finding new pills for women. However, in recent years, the search for contraceptives for males has been stepped up.

**The Various Kinds of Pills and How They Work**    The most common oral contraceptives contain combinations of female sex hormones. When sex hormones were first isolated and synthesized in the 1930s and '40s, physiologists realized that they might work as contraceptives, if administered out of phase with the menstrual cycle. By the mid-1950s scientists had finished preliminary contraceptive experiments in animals and considered using hormonal contraception in human females. Early tests were conducted in San Juan, Puerto Rico, (which, when first re-

**Absolute Contraindications to the Pill**

A woman with any of the following *contraindications* (signs of trouble) *must not take oral contraceptives under any circumstances, with no exception.* If you develop any of these conditions while taking the Pill, you must stop at once:

**Blood-clotting, now or in the past, such as thrombophlebitis, pulmonary embolism (clots in the lung), heart attack, stroke, or angina (heart pain).**

Impaired liver functions, including active or recent hepatitis, alcohol liver damage, severe mononucleosis, or liver tumor in the past.

**Known or suspected cancer of any type**

**Current pregnancy or current suspected pregnancy.**

adapted from:
Stewart, F., F. Guest, G. Stewart, R. Hatcher,
*My Body My Health*, p. 190 John Wiley & Sons,
1979

---

vealed, brought criticisms of secrecy and racism). Around the turn of the decade the Food and Drug Administration (FDA) approved the use of oral contraceptives in the U.S.

The active ingredients in the early oral contraceptives were *progestins*, a group of hormones of which progesterone is a member. Although there are several progestins, the singular term "progestin" is often used to refer to all of them. Progestin has two contraceptive effects. First, it depresses production of LH by the pituitary gland, creating a break in the normal hormonal cycle; ovulation ceases. Second, progestin causes the mucus produced at the cervix to thicken, thereby impeding penetration by sperm.

Progestin accomplishes contraception, but using it alone causes problems, including nausea, vomiting, and abnormal uterine bleeding. Today's most popular oral contraceptives contain less progestin than the original ones plus a small amount of estrogen. Health problems and side effects have been partially alleviated by this adjustment, but pills still carry potential hazards, which are discussed later in this chapter.

*Combination pills* popularly known as "the Pill", contain about one milligram of progestin and a fraction of a microgram of estrogen in each tablet. Like progestin, estrogen administered out of phase with the normal menstrual cycle inhibits the usual interplay of hormones between the pituitary and the ovaries. In fact, estrogen alone works well to inhibit ovulation, and *sequential pills* contain larger amounts of estrogen than progestin. Sequential pills were developed after combination pills and were distributed for several years. They were banned in early 1976, however, when the FDA determined that they caused severe health problems, particularly circulatory disruptions.

Low-dose progestin pills, known as *mini-pills*, have been marketed in the United States since 1973. Each mini-pill contains a small dose of progestin (with no estrogen), which must be taken every day of the month.

Unlike combination and sequential pills, mini-pills do not always prevent ovulation. Instead, their contraceptive effect comes mainly from thickening of the mucous secretions of the cervix, which makes it difficult for sperm to pass through to the uterus. Some sperm manage to make it through, but the mini-pill provides a second line of defense. By causing changes in the secretions of the uterine lining, it makes the uterus unreceptive to implantation by an embryo. Despite the barriers to fertilization and implantation, however, the mini-pill has about a 3 per cent theoretical failure rate, making it less effective than combination or sequential pills. Gynecologists have been watching for adverse side effects of the mini-pill for several years. It seems to be relatively safe, but it may cause abnormal uterine bleeding.

**The Risks and Side Effects of Oral Contraceptives** Opponents of oral contraception stress that artificially administered hormones disrupt normal hormonal balances. Proponents of oral contraception counter by claiming that taking the Pill is somewhat like being pregnant. During pregnancy the placenta and fetus produce sex hormones, thus preventing ovulation.

Because of the hormonal parallels between pregnancy and the Pill, it is not surprising that some of the side effects of oral contraceptives are similar to those of pregnancy. For example, nausea and vomiting (similar to "morning sickness") are experienced by some women starting the Pill. About 20 per cent of new users experience nausea during the first few weeks. Unfortunately, not all of the side effects of oral contraceptives described in the following sections are as innocuous as nausea.

*Heart Attack* A study published by the *British Medical Journal* in May, 1975 established that the Pill increases a woman's chance for having a heart attack. According to the study, users of the Pill in the 30-39 age bracket have fatal heart attacks at the rate of about 0.005 per cent (the rate for non-users is 0.002 per cent). For Pill users, ages 40-44 the rate of fatal heart attack is over 0.05 per cent (versus about 0.03 per cent for non-users). Thus, the chance in this country for Pill-induced heart attack increases with age. The U.S. Food and Drug Administration (FDA) has released a bulletin suggesting that women over forty should choose a form of contraception other than the Pill.

More recent British research (Beral, 1977) indicated an excess death rate of 20/100,000 among women who had ever used oral contraceptives. This is a far greater excess risk than previous reports that surveyed vascular disease as a Pill-related cause of death. Harm to the vascular system appears to persist after the Pill is discontinued. Risk is especially high if the pills contain more that 50 micrograms of estrogen, if they are used longer than 5 years, if the woman smokes, or if she is over 35 years of age.

*Blood Clots* Formation of blood clots in the legs (*thrombophlebitis*) and lodging of blood clots in the lungs (*pulmonary embolism*) are potentially fatal side effects of the Pill. A British study has revealed that about 0.05 per cent (1 out of every 2000) of women using oral con-

traceptives develops thrombophlebitis serious enough for hospitialization every year. For women not using the Pill, the annual rate of thrombophlebitis is about 0.005% (1 out of every 20,000). All oral contraceptives add to a woman's chance of developing internal clotting, but sequential pills and high-estrogen combination pills are particularly dangerous. Primarily for this reason, the FDA banned sequentials.

The mortality rate from internal clotting by women using the Pill is about 0.004 per cent, which is considered by some women to be more risk than they would like to take. Proponents of oral contraception have pointed out, however, that the danger is a good deal less than the chance of dying from complications of pregnancy (about 0.02 per cent).

*Problems with the Breasts* Breasts are extremely sensitive to sex hormones, and breast pains and size changes are common side-effects of oral contraception. Pain and tenderness are most common with contraceptive pills high in estrogen, while high-progestin pills tend to cause enlargement. Changes in the type of pill can usually alleviate problems, but for a small fraction of women breast troubles prohibit oral contraception altogether. Statistical studies have indicated that the Pill aggravates existing cases of breast cancer, but it has not been shown to initiate the disease in cancer-free users.

Nursing mothers should be aware that their milk can pass on hormones to their infants. The effects of extraneous hormones on childhood development have not been extensively studied. But, estrogen is known to inhibit bone growth in infants of both sexes, and progestins have caused masculinization of female fetuses (see Chapter 7).

*Changes in the Menstrual Cycle* In general, the menstrual discharge is lighter for women taking the Pill, and instances of missed periods are common. Many women find that their menstrual flow is not only lighter, but that it is regular when they are taking oral contraceptives. If the Pill is taken at the same time every day, the onset of menstrual bleeding may be predictable not only to the day, but to the hour.

*Water Retention and Weight Gain* Women who have a tendency to be overweight sometimes find the problem aggravated by the Pill. Because added weight can result from hormone-induced water retention and/or fat deposits caused by overeating, and because sex hormones stimulate the appetite, women who are watching their weight have to watch even harder while taking oral contraceptives. The best solution is a diet low in calories and salt (the latter increases water retention).

*Vaginitis* This vaginal infection can be caused by fungus, yeast or bacteria. All women are susceptible to these itching infections, but birth control pills may cause them to occur more frequently (pregnancy also increases the incidence of vaginitis).

*Breakthrough Bleeding* Estrogen and progesterone stimulate growth of the uterine lining, which sometimes breaks away between periods of menstrual bleeding. This causes "spotting" and is particularly a problem for women just beginning oral contraception. "Spotting" is not necessarily cause for worry, but a physician should be consulted.

*Vaginal Discharge* A small discharge of a clear, moist mucous from the vagina is normal, but oral contraceptives tend to increase the volume of the discharge. It may be copious enough to require a tampon or a sanitary napkin. Switching to pills with a different blend of estrogen and progestin may help reduce the discharge, but the switch should never be to stop it completely – a certain amount of discharge is an important part of the body's self-cleansing process.

*Hair Loss* In rare cases, pills cause a loss of hair similar to that sometimes experienced during pregnancy. The problem is reversible, however.

*Psychosomatic Side Effects* Obviously, the foregoing physical side effects of the Pill can bring on psychological trauma. And, there appear to be even more direct influences on the taker's psyche. Fatigue, for example, is common with women first starting oral contraceptives, and seems to be associated with the body's adjustment to increased levels of hormones. Similar mental and physical lethargy is experienced by women adjusting to the hormonal changes of early pregnancy. In both cases, normal energy generally returns after a few weeks.

Fluctuations of emotions are linked with changes in the body's level of sex hormones; thus oral contraceptives can alter emotional states. For example, some women find that the Pill alleviates premenstrual depression. On the other hand, there are women for whom pills aggravate depression – sometimes to the point that they have to stop using them. The influence of sex hormones on emotions is still a subject of extensive research and to date there is no well-established biological explanation for the variability in emotional side effects among women using oral contraception.

*The Pill and Sex Drive* In light of the emotional influences of sex hormones, it is not surprising that women starting oral contraception sometimes experience changes in sex drive. Among some women, the Pill increases sexual desire, and for others, sexual urges are diminished.

Both physiological and psychological reactions are involved in the effects of the Pill on sex drive. Some women find that certain types of pills (particularly those that are high in progestin and low in estrogen) diminish the degree of vaginal lubrication – sometimes to the extent that intercourse may be painful. On the other hand, high-estrogen pills have been known to stimulate a sense of well-being and enhance the desire for sex. It should be noted, however, that these same pills effect other women in the opposite manner, depressing their sex drives. Obviously there is a great deal of variability in women's reactions to oral contraception.

**Getting and Using Pills**   For a woman who has decided to use oral contraceptives, the best basic advice is to see a doctor first. A medical examination should include a breast check, a *Pap smear* (a test for cancer of the cervix), and a check for varicose veins or other signs of circulatory trouble. Certain chronic illnesses (particularly severe diabetes) preclude use of oral contraceptives.

Although choosing the proper pill is somewhat a matter of guesswork, there are certain physical signs that can help a woman and her doctor make the right decision. If, for example, she has relatively small menstrual discharges and more than average body hair, her body chemistry is probably progesterone-dominant. This means that her ovaries produce unusually large amounts of progesterone and/or her physical reactions to it are abnormally pronounced. Such women tend to be susceptible to the adverse side-effects of progestin and generally have the

best luck with low-progestin pills.

On the other hand, if a woman usually has heavy periods of menstrual bleeding and if her breasts become tender before her period, she is probably estrogen-dominant. For her, low-estrogen pills are probably the best choice. If the pills she is using have too much estrogen, she will probably have chronic trouble with one or more of the following symptoms: leg cramps, breast pain, nausea, and headaches. There is no easy formula for determining the proper pill, and a woman should seek the help of a professional in choosing one. There are a myriad of brands on the market already and more are now in a state of testing and development.

Pregnancies among women who are taking the Pill are more often due to forgetfulness than to failure of the contraceptive itself. A strict schedule must be followed. However, if only one pill has been missed, there is still relatively little chance of pregnancy compared to the risk with the other popular methods of contraception. Some doctors suggest that if one pill is forgotten, two of them should be taken the following day. Planned Parenthood suggests that if one of the first seven pills is missed by someone just starting oral contraception, back-up techniques should be used. If two or more days are missed in succession, the chance for pregnancy rapidly increases; it would be wise to contact a gynecologist about back-up methods.

## IUDs

IUDs (*intrauterine devices*) are objects inserted into the uterus via the cervix and they are second only to the Pill in contraceptive effectiveness. (This statement must be qualified in that condoms used with spermicides have a better record of effectiveness than IUDs. Condoms and spermicides are discussed in later sections.) Nobody has the last word on how IUDs work, but their constant irritation of the endometrium is thought to inhibit implantations of embryos. Other effects have also been suggested, including inhibition of sperm movement and speeding of passage by eggs. No matter how they work, however, gynecologists agree that their effects are much more localized than those of the Pill, and this forms the basis of the strongest argument for choosing an IUD rather than oral contraceptives.

**Side Effects**    Although IUDs do not have widespread side effects comparable to those of the Pill, they may cause direct physiological damage. The three major dangers are pregnancy, infections of the reproductive organs, and perforation of the uterus. Researchers have looked for a link between IUDs and cancer of the reproductive organs, but as yet none has been found.

Pregnancy may cause serious problems in two ways: tubal pregnancy and spontaneous abortion (see Chapter 4). Miscarriage most often occurs during the first three months of pregnancy, but with an IUD in place, it can happen even after six or more months of pregnancy (Stewart, et. al., p. 145). If such is the case, the attending physician may have to make the heart-breaking decision of whether or not to take the infant's life. It is with regard to such cases that the "pro-life" or "anti-abortion" (depending on your point of view) movement makes its strongest case.

Tubal pregnancy poses the most subtle threat to the mother. If allowed to proceed undetected it may lead to death due to massive internal bleeding from the ruptured Fallopain tube.

Infection of the uterus and Fallopain tubes occurs in about 1 per cent of the women who use IUDs. The risk of uterine infection is doubled by an IUD, and though it is usually controllable, it

can get out of hand and lead to sterility. Women who contract gonorrhea while using an IUD should be quick to have the device removed. An IUD may aggravate the disease, causing it to spread up the Fallopian tubes where it can do permanent damage.

In about 5 women out of 1,000 an indelicate insertion results in perforation or tearing of the uterus. In most cases the wound heals with relatively minor medication, but occasionally surgery is required and a few instances of death from internal hemorrhaging have been reported. Because of the threat of uterine perforation, only a clinician trained in the technique should attempt to insert an IUD.

Not everyone can use an IUD. About 15 per cent of those inserted must be removed because of severe cramping in the abdomen, backache, or unusual bleeding. In general, IUDs are more easily tolerated by women who have already had a baby; however, this is not a prerequisite for their use.

**Kinds, Use, and Effectiveness**    At the time of this writing, IUDs come in five types (Figure 6.1). They are made of flexible plastic, and are inserted through the os into the uterus with a plunger device that works somewhat like a hypodermic needle. One or two fine threads hang from the base of an IUD, protruding through the cervix. These threads enable the user to determine whether the device is still in place. She (or her mate) should feel for the threads prior to intercourse.

There is good reason to check an IUD regularly, since about one-third of the pregnancies among women using them result from "fall-out." Sometimes (especially during menstruation) an IUD can slip through the vagina unnoticed. A second insertion may be more successful, but

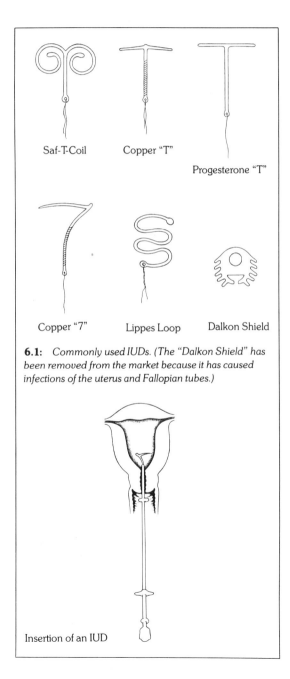

Saf-T-Coil

Copper "T"

Progesterone "T"

Copper "7"

Lippes Loop

Dalkon Shield

**6.1:** *Commonly used IUDs. (The "Dalkon Shield" has been removed from the market because it has caused infections of the uterus and Fallopian tubes.)*

Insertion of an IUD

some women chronically void them. A physician should examine a woman using an IUD at least once a year.

A few years ago, the "Lippes Loop" and "Saf-T-Coil" were the most commonly used models; but, at the time of this writing, the relatively new "copper" IUDs have replaced them. The "Copper-T" and "Copper-7" are nearly 100 per cent effective. A "copper" IUD actually consists of a plastic core, wrapped with a fine copper filament. This filament slowly dissolves, creating a toxic enviroment. It must be replaced every 2 years.

A still newer IUD is impregnated with progesterone, which is slowly released within the uterus, hence mimicking the conditions immediately prior to menstruation and preventing implantation. Since this involves a direct application of lesser amounts of hormones than in the Pill, it is hoped that it will provide *effectiveness* while minimizing the risks associated with artificially administered hormones. However, this "Progesterone 'T' " (also known as "Progestasert") has given at least one sign of being inferior to the "copper" IUDs. Tubal pregnancies account for about 1 out of every 5 pregnancies that occur with a Progestasert. With the plain plastic IUDs the proportion is lower: 1 out of 20. And with the "copper" IUDs the proportion is 1 out of 60.

## Condoms

Otherwise known as "rubbers" and "prophylactics," condoms are tubes of thin, flexible material that fit tightly over an erect penis. Condoms are the veterans of contraception in the Western world. In relatively crude forms they were used by the ancient Romans and were rediscovered in England early in the eighteenth century. The first condoms were made of animal intestines, but today most of them are latex rubber (although a few connoisseurs still prefer natural "skins").

A condom's closed tip may either be blunt or have a nipple to trap semen, and the open end is surrounded by a thick rubber ring to hold firmly around the base of the penis. Condoms can withstand quite a beating, but sometimes they do break. The ones without the nipple ends must be used with particular caution; a half inch or so should be left at the end to catch the ejaculate. This can be accomplished by pinching the tip of the condom with one hand while it is unrolled on the penis with the other hand.

Condoms can slip off as the erection withers, so one of the partners should hold on to the rim until the penis is withdrawn from the vagina. (Keep in mind that the erection may wax and wane during an erotic experience.)

If used without any other contraceptive technique, condoms are less effective than IUDs. In combination with spermicidal foams, however, they are nearly 100 per cent effective. Thus, the condom/spermicide combination is even better at preventing pregnancy than an IUD.

The major argument against condoms is that they thwart sexual arousal. However, what some couples find to be a drag, others enjoy. When the woman takes charge of slipping it on, it can be very erotic for the man. Another "disadvantage" of condoms is that they diminish the stimulation of stroking in the vagina. Depending on the erotic sensitivity of the male, however, decreased stimulation can be a blessing in disguise. For men who normally ejaculate before they want to, a condom can add to staying power.

If used without lubrication, a condom can make penetration of the vagina difficult and even painful for the woman. Pre-lubricated condoms cost a bit more, but are certainly worth it. There is no reason why a woman couldn't purchase a brand that suits her, and bring it along in her purse. This is certainly a better place to keep a condom than a man's wallet, where pressure and repeated jostling render it useless in a few months. If the moment arrives, and the only condom available is a dry one, spermacidal foam, K-Y jelly, or saliva will ease penetration. Petroleum jelly should *not* be used as a lubricant, because it is not water-soluable, and it causes latex to deteriorate.

The most favorable characteristic of condoms is that they help protect against venereal disease, particularly when used with a spermicidal foam (which not only kills sperm but also kills certain disease-causing organisms). Condoms do not give complete protection against venereal disease but they are far better than nothing.

### The Diaphragm
Diaphragms are thin, flexible rubber cups placed over the cervix to prevent sperm from entering the uterus. From Victorian times until the 1960s (when it was supplanted by improved IUDs and

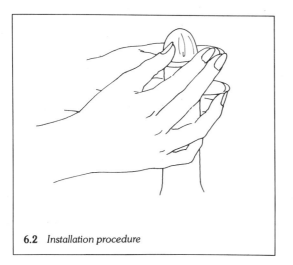

6.2   *Installation procedure*

the Pill) the diaphragm was the most effective method of birth control available to women of Western societies. Even today there is still a very good reason for giving this method of contraception serious consideration; that is, there is far less chance of physical harm from a diaphragm than from either the Pill or an IUD. However, there is also a good case against them; they are significantly less effective than the other two devices. Depending on how she uses it, a woman takes 3-25 per cent chance of becoming pregnant. To have even 90 per cent assurance that pregnancy will not happen, diaphragms must be used with about a teaspoon of spermicidal cream or jelly (Figure 6.3).

A thin spring is embedded in the edge of a diaphragm, which snaps into place behind the pubic bone and presses into the back of the vagina. Diaphragms range in diameter from about two to four inches, and must be fitted by a clinician. The size of the vagina and cervix change throughout life (particularly as the result of first intercourse, pregnancy and fluctuations in weight of ten or more pounds), so a woman using a diaphragm should frequently check to make sure it is still fitting snugly. An annual examination by a gynecologist decreases the likelihood of continued use of an ill-fitting diaphragm.

Besides improper fit, certain styles of intercourse can also lead to disengagement of a diaphragm. Positions with the woman on top are the most risky, and repeated removals and reinsertions of the penis also increase the chance of sperm seeping around the rim.

Problems with the diaphragm-spermacide combination include: allergy to latex or spermicide, cramping due to pressure from the diaphragm rim, chronic bladder infections, vaginal infection, and poor taste (most spermacides taste somewhat worse than gasoline – making cunnilingus a masochistic activity). A relatively new

type, the "cervical cap" is smaller than the conventional diaphragm; it is designed to fit more snugly over the cervix. This refinement seems to relieve some of the problems of cramping. There are no known life-threatening risks directly related to the diaphragm, other than the health risks of pregnancy or abortion should the user become pregnant.

Cream or jelly

Spring (coil-spring type)

Dome of soft rubber

**6.3:** *Using a diaphragm. Spermacidal cream is squeezed into cup and around the rim before insertion.*

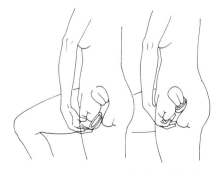

Insertion of diaphragm        Checking of diaphragm

A diaphragm may be put in as long as six hours before intercourse. However, since the chance for it slipping out of place increases with time, it is best to have as short a lapse as possible between insertion and intercourse.

After intercourse the diaphragm must be left in for at least six hours for the spermicide to protect against diehard sperm. The woman should not douche. More spermicide should be used if intercourse is repeated. In this case the diaphragm can be left in place and the spermicide applied to its underside.

Unfortunately, the diaphragm has a reputation for being a "turn-off." If it is inserted at the last minute, it may disrupt the delicate state of sexual arousal. However, couples who have had long-term relationships have found that they can become comfortable about including insertion of the diaphragm as part of foreplay.

Because of the relatively low protection from pregnancy the diaphragms afford when used alone, some couples use them in combination with other techniques. Rhythm, for instance, can significantly decrease the chances of fertilization.

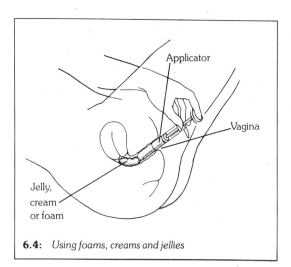

**6.4:**  *Using foams, creams and jellies*

### Spermacides

Spermicidal creams, foams, and jellies are available at drugstores without prescription. They are all intended to be inserted into the vagina before intercourse and come with instructions and an applicator.

A relatively new form of spermacidal contraception involves the insertion of a suppository (about as big as the tip of an index finger) at least ten minutes prior to intercourse. Somewhat more effective than other forms of spermacide, these "silver bullets" are designed for slow release of spermacide by gentle effervescence.

If used alone, none of the spermicides are totally effective, but they are excellent auxiliaries to condoms, and mandatory with diaphragms. There are no long-lasting health problems caused by spermicides, but they may cause temporary irritation to the penis or vagina. If this persists, some other form of contraception should be used. Spermacides have traditionally been the bane of those who fancy cunnilingus; but one may take heart in knowing that fruit flavors are now on the market.

### Rhythm

The success or failure of the rhythm method depends on the regularity of the menstrual cycle and the practitioners' skill in determining the phase of the cycle when fertilization is least likely to occur. Also, it leans heavily on the will power of both partners to refrain from intromission for a span of a week or more each month.

A woman is most fertile around the time of ovulation, which fairly consistently occurs fourteen days before the next menstrual period begins. For a woman with a 32-day cycle, for example, ovulation usually occurs about eighteen days after the beginning of the last period of menstrual bleeding. While the above is the general rule, there are certain exceptions. Ovulation may occur more than once during a given menstrual cycle, or it could be brought on at an unusual time by erotic arousal. These are not the norm, however.

Used alone, rhythm is not a dependable method of contraception. The average failure rate of 35 per cent indicates that it is a poor choice for most couples. However, for those who have intercourse infrequently and who do not limit their orgasmic activities to intromission, rhythm may be a satisfactory technique.

A personal rhythm chart can be roughly calculated by keeping track of the lengths of menstrual periods for several months (an entire year is preferable) and doing some simple arithmetic. In the following calculations, day #1 of the menstrual cycle is the first day of bleeding. Subtracting 18 from the length of the shortest menstrual cycle yields the first "unsafe" day (the day on which abstinence should start). Subtracting 10 from the length of the longest menstrual cycle gives the first "safe" day (the day on which intercourse can

begin again). For instance, if 27 and 31 are the shortest and longest periods, the first "unsafe" day is 27 − 18 = 9, and the first "safe" day is 31 − 10 = 21. This means that intromission should cease before the 9th day following the start of a menstrual period and may begin again on the 21st day and continue until the 9th day of the following menstrual cycle. According to this example, abstention would last for 12 successive days in each menstrual cycle.

In cases of highly irregular menstrual cycles (with fluctuations of ten days or more), the failure rate for rhythm is over 35 per cent, even for people capable of long abstention. Obviously, rhythm is not for everyone, and if a woman is considering it she must take the time to familiarize herself with her menstrual rhythm. After she has accumulated a year's worth of data on the length of her menstrual cycle, the oldest listing should be deleted as the newest is added.

Further assurance that the timing of ovulation is being correctly estimated can come from monitoring daily *basal body temperature* (the

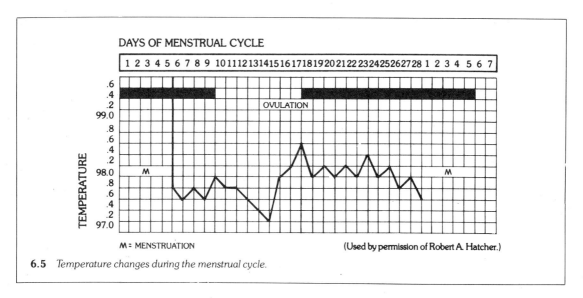

**6.5** *Temperature changes during the menstrual cycle.*

**Abstinence sows sand all over
the ruddy limbs and flaming hair.**

William Blake

temperature taken immediately after waking in the morning, when the body is rested and operating at a minimum level of activity). Following ovulation, body temperature generally rises slightly, by a few tenths of a degree (Figure 6.5). The change is not well defined, however, and can be obscured by the effects of minor illnesses (such as colds), a restless night, or even getting up to go to the bathroom. Since the temperature change is so slight, a thermometer that can be easily read down to 0.1 degree gradations should be used.

For women using a chemical or mechanical method of contraception, rhythm can give added assurance that fertilization will not happen. The average failure rates for popluar contraceptive techniques are given in Table 6.1. For those who are not satisfied with the protection afforded by their method of birth control, a few days of abstinence at the peak of fertility will provide additional assurance.

**Rhythm with a Different Beat**    A relatively new, potentially more accurate, method of rhythm involves analyzing the natural secretions from the woman's cervix. As a woman nears ovulation, the glands of the cervix secrete a thin, watery mucus. Following ovulation the mucus becomes thick and opaque. To avoid conception women should abstain from intercourse from the time thin mucus appears until four days after it is replaced by the opaque mucus. As an alternative, condoms plus spermacide could be used during the fertile period.

During ovulation the cervical mucus contains an unusually high proportion of sugar, which can be measured with a fertility test kit or "Tes-Tape", both available without prescription at drugstores. According to Shapiro (1977) a woman can also use a speculum (available from a doctor or surgical supply store) to directly observe her own pattern of cervical mucus secretion. Shapiro believes that committed couples, with proper clinical training, can achieve 97% annual success by rhythm, based on cervical observations. He asks the question: "Why does sex have to be spontaneous?"

**Withdrawal**
The success of withdrawal depends on the agility and the honesty of the male partner. It is one of the most common techniques of birth control, and some people who practice it in combination with the rhythm method find that it works quite successfully. Expert practitioners of withdrawal have failure rates of 10 per cent. For unprepared novices, however, the rate is closer to 50 per cent.

There are several causes of failure of withdrawal. First, the few drops of fluid from Cowper's glands, which often appear immediately after erection, may contain active sperm. Since there is only a very small chance that any given sperm will fertilize the egg, however, the relatively few in the pre-ejaculatory fluid (tens of thousands) are much less likely to effect fertilization than are the hoards of them in an average ejaculation (hundreds of millions). However, the actual incidence of pregnancy caused by sperm from the Cowper's glands is not precisely known.

One common fallacy (which perhaps accounts for part of the failure rate of this method) is that penetration is necessary to achieve fertilization. This is not true, because even sperm deposited on the moist labia minora may find its way to the egg. Thus, the penis must be pointed well away from the vagina during (and after) ejaculation.

Some couples find that no matter how hard they try, they cannot quite make it apart in time. In other cases, the male partner satisfies his desire for orgasm at the expense of his partner, who is left at the plateau of sexual arousal when he rapidly pulls out. Nevertheless, some couples can successfully practice withdrawal and still achieve mutual satisfaction. Practiced in combination with rhythm it is far less than perfect but better than nothing.

**Douching**
Of all the common methods of contraception, douching is the worst. In fact, it is so ineffective that it has been called a non-method. Douching involves spraying water or other cleansing solutions into the vagina. Certain commercially prepared douching solutions act as spermicides, although mild solutions of vinegar, lemon juice and salt do just as well. However, frequent or strong douches will irritate the delicate tissues of the vagina. Futhermore, even the best douche is less effective than the worst of the other methods of contraception.

Within a minute or two after ejaculation, a few sperm are on their way through the cervix to the uterus – well out of the way of a douche's spray. Even if a woman is able to jump from the bed and sprint to the bathroom in less than a minute, she still runs a high risk of pregnancy. The rush of water inevitably forces a few sperm up into the cervix just as it washes others out of the vagina.

**Contraceptive Research**
It appears that contraceptive research has stalled somewhat from the boom times of the '60s and early '70s. Sensitive observers of trends in contraception point out that: "Glowing descriptions of research breakthroughs often appear in the news, but remember as you read that initial research reports are often the most promising; realistic effectiveness rates and complication

rates are usually discovered somewhat later" (Stewart, et. al., page 268). For the media, no news is bad news.

What we are seeing should not be surprising, however. The astounding success of the past decade – the Pill – is not likely to be matched in the near future.

At present, revising the Pill is still the "main road" of contraceptive research ('*Contemporary OB/GYN*', 1978), with investigators concentrating on making it safer. Research into hormonal contraceptives for males, which lagged during the '60s and '70s, is still lagging.

The hypothetical "rhythm pill" has low concentrations of hormones and seems promising as an alternative for those women who are unusually sensitive to the higher concentrations of commonly used brands (Wilson, 1977, pers. com.). In addition to its contraceptive effects (which are somewhat less than perfect), the rhythm-pill renders the menstrual cycle highly predictable. Thus, in combination with a few days of abstention each month, the "rhythm-pill" is theoretically 99 per cent effective.

**Hormonal Contraceptives – New Techniques of Administration** The only widely available hormonal contraceptives are designed to be taken by mouth, but new modes of introduction are currently under clinical study. Injections of long-lasting hormonal preparations (which are taken up by fat deposits and slowly released), for instance, have proved highly effective in preventing pregnancy. One of the methods is a solid silicon rod, inserted under the skin either in the forearm or buttock. However, the return to fertility once injections have been stopped is sometimes slow. They also cause irregular menstrual bleeding.

Hormone-releasing devices that are inserted into the vagina, cervix, or uterus seem to have more promise than injectibles. Since they are placed within the reproductive organs, their effect is direct and the amounts of hormones they release can be far less than the amounts needed with injections. The "vaginal ring," for example is inserted like a diaphragm, and slowly releases progestin. Gynecologists are also experimenting with hormone-impregnated IUDs (such as the "Progesterone-T") and much smaller devices to be placed in the cervix.

Hormone-releasing devices inhibit ovulation, cause sperm-stopping mucous secretion by the cervix, and make the uterus unfit to nurture an embryo. Unfortunately, they may cause abnormal uterine bleeding. Also, since sex hormones are easily absorbed into the walls of the vagina and uterus, a small proportion of them ultimately enter the bloodstream. Thus, the "vaginal ring," for instance, can cause hormonal side effects (although less pronounced than those caused by the Pill) at points as far removed from the vagina as the breasts and the brain.

**New Biochemical Techniques**   Because of the problems inherent with using sex hormones as contraceptives, scientists are searching for new chemical methods to stop fertilization. Some researchers have had success in "vaccinating" women against sperm. Just as immunity to certain diseases (such as small pox) develops after injections of weak strains of disease-causing organisms, an "immunity" to pregnancy can be achieved through injections of semen. Once immunized, however, some experimental subjects have stayed that way.

Presently there are no chemcial agents of contraception proven to be as safe, effective, and reversible as the Pill. Within the past few years, however, a family of compounds different from the female sex hormones has been found to safely induce abortions early in pregnancy, and may eventually be adaptable as contraceptives. These *prostaglandins* are described in the section on abortion.

**Male Contraception**   Contraceptive techniques for men are conspicuous in their relative absence. Among all commonly used birth-control techniques, the condom is the only one that requires the male to play an active role. As yet, no medically acceptable contraceptive pill for men has been found. According to Sheldon J. Segal, director of the population division of the Rockefeller Foundation, "We know less about the male reproductive system, and the intervention points are not as numerous."

Nevertheless, a few methods have been tried, including various brands commonly used by women. The chemical mechanism by which the Pill blocks fertility in men is similar to the way it works in women; that is, it inhibits secretion of FSH and ICSH from the pituitary. Inhibition of gonadotropin-secretion makes a break in the hormonal support system of sperm, and production of them diminishes. Unfortunately, female sex hormones tend to inhibit male sex drive and cause *gynecomastia* (enlargement of the breasts).

The male hormone, testosterone, has shown some promise as a contraceptive, but it too has drawbacks. Among them is a potential for causing prostate cancer.

Mechanical blocks to the passage of sperm along the vasa deferentia have been tried. One technique involves the insertion of tiny valves, which would be turned on or off at the user's discretion. The surgical techniques, however, are presently too complex for the method to have general applicability. Vasectomy (the simple cutting of the vasa deferentia) is more feasible, but it is usually permanent. The pros and cons of vasectomy are discussed in the final section in this chapter, "Sterilization."

### Abortion

Prior to the Supreme Court decision of January 1973, abortion was generally prohibited by state law. It is now legal if performed before the fetus becomes viable, which occcurs sometime between the 20th and 30th week of pregnancy (wide individual variation has made this a heated point of debate). Thus, pregnant women who do not want to have a baby need no longer seek dangerous alternatives for terminating their pregnancies.

**Vacuum Aspiration and D & C**    The method for abortion depends primarily on the state of development of pregnancy. If performed before the second trimester, it is often done by a procedure termed *vacuum aspiration*, by which the fetus is literally sucked from the uterus. A plastic tube, through which a vacuum attachment is inserted, is gently manipulated within the uterus until the fetal tissue is removed.

*Dilation and Curettage* (D & C) is another method for terminating pregnancy in the first trimester. In the first phase of D & C the opening through the cervix is expanded either by insertion of a thin, porous rod that swells as it absorbs fluid, or by insertions of successively thicker non-expanding rods. Once the cervix is dilated, the uterus is scraped with a sharp instrument (a curet) and forceps are used to remove the fetal tissue. Vacuum aspiration generally causes less damage to the uterine lining than does a D & C. Complications during either procedure, however, are uncommon when performed by a skilled physician. Nevertheless, there are occa-

sional instances of harm to the woman, including perforation of the uterus, hemorrhaging, and uterine infection. In most clinics a local anesthetic is applied during both D & C and vacuum aspiration.

**Menstrual Extraction**    If action is taken within the first weeks of pregnancy (on the basis perhaps of a positive RRA pregnancy test) the relatively gentle procedure, *menstrual extraction*, may be applied. This is performed with a flexible vacuum tube, whose diameter is small enough that the cervix need not be dilated to admit it; hence no anesthetic is required.

**Saline Injection**    If pregnancy progresses into the second trimester, abortion becomes more difficult. In this instance, a technique called *saline injection* is used to induce delivery of the immature fetus. The procedure involves the introduction of a concentrated salt solution into the amniotic fluid (see chapter 4 for a discussion of amniocentesis). This irritates the uterine musculature, causing contractions and subsequent expulsion of the fetus within three days. In recent years prostoglandims and urea have begun to replace salt in this procedure.

The dangers of saline injection are similar to those of vacuum aspiration and D & C, but there is the added possibility of drug reactions (salt poisoning, for example, can lead to brain damage if it is not detected quickly). The woman is fully awake during this procedure, because the physician relies on her to report any unusual sensations.

**The "Morning-After Pill"**    In recent years several hormonal techniques have been developed for inducing abortion. The "morning-after pill," for one, is a large dose of estrogen (actually,

### Menstrual Extraction

An Interview with Marcia L. Storch, M.D.

Menstrual extraction is the term applied to the removal of the contents of the uterus by a process that can be used either for very early abortions or for removal of the menstrual period. It is performed with a device called a flexible cannula, which is small enough so that the cervix need not be dilated to admit it; hence, no anesthetic is required.

*Q: Do you know whether many members of the self-help groups are doing menstrual extraction on each other?*

A: There were never very many groups doing extraction, and I doubt whether more than a very few, if any, are still doing it.

*Q: What do you think of the practice of using extraction for removal of the menstrual period, either occasionally or regularly?*

A: Considering that all you gain is not having a period, it's unduly dangerous. There is a risk of introducing infection into the uterus.

---

a series of doses given over several days), which renders the uterus inhospitable to embryonic settlement. Treatment with the "morning-after pill" must be started within 24-72 hours following intercourse, and it may cause severe nausea and vomiting. Some doctors suggest that women use it one time *only*. It has not been in use long enough for physicians to know its long-term effects.

**Prostaglandins**    Prostaglandins are hormone-like substances secreted by several organs, including – in particularly large amounts – the prostate gland. Although the normal function of prostaglandins in the human body are not known, they have been discovered to cause contractions of certain kinds of muscles, including those of the uterus.

In the 1960s prostaglandins were first tested as abortive agents, and have since become approved by the FDA. As with the "morning-after pill," long term side-effects are not known.

### Sterilization

Sterilization is the ultimate form of birth control; it is the closest to being 100 per cent effective. The surgical procedures are safe (although they are usually irreversible), and the after-effects appear to be negligible.

Until recently, sterilization was considered an extremely undesirable form of birth control, to be avoided whenever possible. Today, however, it is the fastest growing contraceptive technique used by married couples in America. By 1973, according to a national fertility study conducted by Princeton's Population Research Center, a quar-

ter of all married couples using contraception had chosen sterilization of the husband or wife. In fact, sterilization is second only to the Pill as the most popular form of contraception.

**Male Sterilization**    *Vasectomy* is simpler to perform than any of the methods for female sterilization. After small injections of local anesthetics into each side of the scrotum, the vasa deferentia are withdrawn through small incisions, tied at two points, and snipped in between. The entire operation may take only a quarter of an hour, and its immediate after-effects for healthy men allow almost immediate return to non-sexual activities. It may, however, be a month or more before the subject feels up to intercourse. Approximately 5 million American men have had vasectomies in the past 10 years.

Owing to sperm that has been stored in the sperm ducts inside the abdomen, a man may remain fertile for a few weeks following a vasectomy. Thus, a contraceptive technique should be used until a laboratory examination indicates that the semen is free of sperm. Sometimes the operation is a failure because of spontaneous rejoining of the severed ends or because of the presence of more than two vasa deferentia. However, failures occur in only a small fraction of one per cent of vasectomies.

Sexual performance is generally little changed by a vasectomy. Since sperm and fluid from the testicles account for less than 10 per cent of the volume of a fertile man's semen, the physical characteristics of ejaculation are essentially unaltered by a vasectomy. Some men even find their sex drives enhanced (presumably because there is no longer apprehension about unwanted

*Q: What about the use of menstrual extraction for abortion?*

*A:* Menstrual extraction for abortion must be done very soon after a missed period, and many women have it done before they know whether they're actually pregnant. I'd recommend waiting for a positive pregnancy test for the following reasons:

First, obviously a number of women who have extraction without knowing they're pregnant turn out not to have been pregnant. These women are undergoing an unnecessary procedure that has some risk attached that

there's no need for them to run.

When menstrual extraction is done on a pregnant woman within a week of what would have been the first day of the first missed period, there's a greater likelihood that the pregnancy site will be missed, since the fetus is still so small, at best the size of a pea. Then the woman just has to have an abortion later anyhow.

from The Health Advisor

---

pregnancy). Nevertheless, a small fraction of men find their sexual capabilities depressed by vasectomy. This is particularly the case for those who expect the operation to dramatically enhance the quality of their sex lives.

At present, it appears that the side effects of vasectomy are mild. However, evidence from experiments with rats indicates that it may result in depressed outputs of testosterone. Furthermore, there have been reports that it causes upsets in the immunological system resulting from

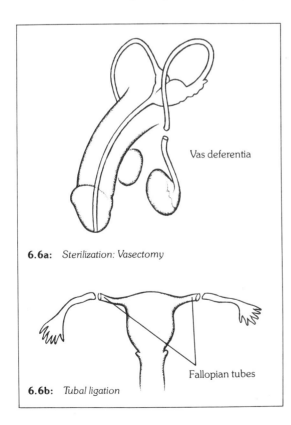

**6.6a:** *Sterilization: Vasectomy*

Vas deferentia

Fallopian tubes

**6.6b:** *Tubal ligation*

the body's reaction to retained sperm. The sperm cells, which are still produced by the testicles following vasectomy, are eventually destroyed and absorbed into the surrounding fluids. Consequently, the body reacts as if it were being attacked by a disease organism and produces sperm-destroying antibodies. Preliminary studies have indicated that this triggering of the immunological system may lead to auto-immune diseases, which include rheumatoid arthritis. Research aimed at determining the severity (if any) of this side effect is now in progress.

Vasectomy is the only commonly used technique for male sterilization, but removal of the testicles, *castration*, has been done to sex offenders in this country to prevent further offenses. (Men who are castrated are still capable of having erections.)

**Female Sterilization** The techniques for female sterilization are somewhat more complex than vasectomy. Nevertheless, the operations have been refined to safe and quick routines.

The most common female sterilization operations involve severing the egg-bearing ducts. In *tubal ligation* (more commonly known as "getting the tubes tied") the Fallopain tubes are approached through an incision in the abdomen. They are either tied and cut or cauterized (sealed by burning).

The surgical procedures for tubal ligation are now in a state of change. The traditional procedure is done with general anesthesia, involves a two-inch-long incision in the abdomen, and requires a hospital stay of several days (and, hence, a hospital bill of several hundred dollars). Recently developed techniques, however, can be performed under local anesthesia in an outpatient clinic. In *laparoscopy*, for instance, the Fallopian tubes are reached through two small incisions in the abdòmen. They are precisely located with a laparoscope (a periscope-like viewing tube, about the same diameter as a pencil). Laparoscopy is a simple operation, which may be performed in a gynecologist's office. In *culdoscopy* the tubes are cauterized through incisions in the cul-de-sac at the back of the vagina.

## Abstention

On this subject, very little needs to be said. It is perfectly safe. Keep in mind that abstention from intromission need not preclude other orgasmic activities.

## QUESTIONS

1. Which methods of birth control (if any) do you believe to be morally permissible?
2. Do you believe oral contraceptives are as safe as you thought they were five years ago?
3. What are the criteria that a method of birth control must satisfy, for you? If you practice birth control, are you happy with the method you use?
4. Why should you use KY jelly instead of a petroleum jelly to lubricate a condom?
5. How do you feel about sodomy as a method of birth control?

# Readings

## *Excerpt from* An Essay On The Principle Of Population

Thomas Robert Malthus

*Concern about global population didn't become widespread until recent years, but the potential for it was revealed in an essay written shortly after the American revolution. It's of historical interest that Malthus' thoughts were stimulated by an observation of America's greatest genius, Benjamin Franklin, and the essay, in turn, sparked Charles Darwin's concept of "natural selection" which is the cutting edge of evolution.*

The cause to which I allude is the constant tendency in all animated life to increase beyond the nourishment prepared for it.

It is observed by Dr. Franklin that there is no bound to the prolific nature of plants or animals but what is made by their crowding and interfering with each other's means of subsistence. Were the face of the earth, he says, vacant of other plants, it might be gradually sowed and overspread with one kind only, as for instance, with fennel: and were it empty of other inhabitants, it might in a few ages be replenished from one nation only, as for instance with Englishmen.

This is incontrovertibly true. Through the animal and vegetable kingdoms Nature has scattered the seeds of life abroad with the most profuse and liberal hand; but has been comparatively sparing in the room and the nourishment necessary to rear them. The germs of existence contained in this earth, if they could freely develop themselves, would fill millions of worlds in the course of a few thousand years. Necessity, that imperious, all pervading law of nature, restrains them within the prescribed bounds. The race of plants and the race of animals shrink under this great restrictive law; and man cannot by any efforts of reason escape from it.

In plants and irrational animals, the view of the subject is simple. They are all impelled by a powerful instinct to the increase of their species; and this instinct is interrupted by no doubts about providing for their offspring. Wherever therefore there is liberty, the power of increase is exerted; and the superabundant effects are repressed afterwards by want of room and nourishment.

The effects of this check on man are more complicated. Impelled to the increase of his species by an equally powerful instinct, reason interrupts his areer, and asks him whether he may not bring beings into the world for whom he cannot provide the means of support. If he attend to this natural suggestion, the restriction too frequently produces vice. If he hear it not, the human race will be constantly endeavouring to increase beyond the means of subsistence. But as, by the law of our nature which makes food necessary to the life of man, population can never actually increase beyond the lowest nourishment capable of supporting it, a strong check on population, from the difficulty of acquiring food, must be constantly in operation. This difficulty must fall somewhere, and must necessarily be severely felt in some or other of the various forms of misery, or the fear of misery, by a large portion of mankind.

## Older Than History

Birth Control; Garrett Hardin

*Effective methods of birth control are relatively new, but people have been trying since time immemorial.*

Why birth control? There are two reasons. The first is a personal reason: one simply does not want to have a child (or another child) at this time, under these conditions. The second reason we might call a community reason: birth control is needed to achieve population control.

Population control has been talked about a great deal in recent years. It is not an ancient topic of discussion; it all started less than two hundred years ago. Before then, before Louis Pasteur and the germ theory of disease, before penicillin, before all of modern medicine, there didn't seem to be any population problem. "Nature" took care of things. Every time people became too numerous, an epidemic thinned the population. Several times during the Middle Ages and the Renaissance, the population of Europe was decreased by twenty-five per cent in a single year. Think of it! The next time you are surrounded by a group of your friends, stop and think what it would be like to live in such a world. Suppose that of the two dozen people you are with at the moment, six of them should be dead two weeks later. That would be an experience you would not easily forget! Living in such a world it would be quite natural for your thoughts to turn often to sudden death, and to the reasons proposed to account for it — sin and transgression. In such a world, if you thought of population at all, you would probably think only of the threat of *under*population. You would not, for the good of the community, be "pushing" birth control. You might even be bitterly opposed to it, knowing how tenuous life was.

But all of that is changed now. How many of your friends died of disease last week? Or, indeed, during the last year? How many people have you seen die — *seen with your own eyes*? Millions die of starvation some place in the world each year, but the people who are starving don't read books, and the readers of books like this don't see the people who are starving. Since the beginning of time, malnutrition has been a reality for one-third to two-thirds of the world's population during some period of their lives. The fraction is no less now, and the total number of people is the greatest it has ever been – 3.5 billion. One-third of 3.5 billion is a lot of people to have to suffer from malnutrition and starvation. Worse: the rate of increase of the population at risk is also greater than it has ever been before; each year there are 70 million more people on the limited space ship we call Earth. No wonder that pollution, a by-product of overpopulation, increasingly threatens the survival of the too-numerous inhabitants of our space ship.

Concern with the personal anguish of being burdened with an unwanted child is at least as old as recorded history. We do not know when man discovered where babies come from, but we do know that almost as soon as he learned how to write he started recording his worries about having unwanted children. Some of the papyruses from ancient Egypt, dating back almost four thousand years, include recipes for not having children. From that day to this, birth control has been an abiding concern of men and women throughout the world.

There are basically two kinds of birth control: abortion and contraception. In abortion, the not yet formed human creature (*embryo or fetus*) is detached from the wall of the mother's *uterus* ("womb"), following which it is expelled. In contraception (literally, *against* conception), "conception" is prevented by killing the reproductive cells beforehand, or interfering with their coming together in the act of fertilization.

It is incredible what human beings have used for this purpose. An incomplete list of the astonishing things used at one time or another would include: okra seed pod, tannic acid, various seaweeds, lemon juice, the root of spotted cowbane, castor beans (quite poisonous), marjoram, thyme, parsely, lavender, rosemary.

Crocus, myrtle, camphor, black hellebore, a small ball of opium, elephant dung, crocodile dung, camel dung.

Olive oil, cedar oil, copper sulphate, willow, fern root, cabbage blossoms, a piece of bark tied in three knots, tea made from gunpowder and foam from a camel's mouth.

The last item on the list was popular for many centuries. Did it work? You might think that our research scientists would leave no stone uncovered in their investigations; but as far as I know there are no scientific reports on the contraceptive efficacy of camel's foam. Who knows, it might be good. It would be rather embarrassing if we discovered it was the best of all contraceptives! Considering the present state of the camel population, however, it would be a bit difficult to supply the 900 million fertile women in the world with enough of this kind of foam.

Other methods of controlling birth depended on procedures rather than substances. One highly recommended method was this: after intercourse, a woman should go to the nearest graveyard and step three times over a grave. Needless to say, the stepping always had to be done in the same direction (otherwise one step might negate another). It was especially desirable to do this at night, if possible in the dark of the moon.

If a graveyard wasn't handy, some other procedures might do the trick. For instance, if the woman carefully held her breath at the moment of climax in sexual intercourse this was supposed to help. If she failed in doing that, it was recommended that she sneeze immediately afterward. Many times.

How much confidence did people have in these methods? Probably not much. The fact that there were so many methods indicates a lack of confidence in all of them. There was probably only one method that enjoyed the complete confidence of all who heard about it. This was one that a physician recorded almost a hundred years ago as his advice to any woman who asked what she should do to avoid having children. "My dear," he said, "before going to bed, drink a glass of cold water and *don't touch another thing all night*."

## The Origins Of The Birth Control Movement

Autobiography; Margaret Sanger

*Margaret Sanger, who was a nurse, recounts her decision to begin the movement for birth control in America. Birth control information as well as contraceptive devices were illegal throughout most of the United States well into the 1920s.*

During these years in New York trained nurses were in great demand. Few people wanted to enter hospitals; they were afraid they might be "practiced" upon, and consented to go only in desperate emergencies. Sentiment was especially vehement in the matter of having babies. A woman's own bedroom, no matter how inconveniently arranged, was the usual place for her lying-in. I was not sufficiently free from domestic duties to be a general nurse, but I could ordinarily manage obstetrical cases because I was notified far enough ahead to plan my schedule. And after serving my two weeks I could get home again.

As soon as the neighbors learned that a nurse was in the building they came in a friendly way to visit, often carrying fruit, jellies, or gefüllter fish made after a cherished recipe. It was infinitely pathetic to me that they, so poor themselves, should bring me food. Later they drifted in again with the excuse of getting the plate, and sat down for a nice talk; there was no hurry. Always back of the little gift was the question, "I am pregnant (or my daughter, or my sister is). Tell me something to keep from having another baby. We cannot afford another yet."

I tried to explain the only two methods I had ever heard of among the middle classes, both of which were invariably brushed aside as unacceptable. They were of no certain avail to the wife because they placed the burden of responsibility solely upon the husband – a burden which he seldom assumed. What she was seeking was self-protection she could herself use, and there was none.

Each time I returned to this district, which was becoming a recurrent nightmare, I used to hear that Mrs. Cohen "had been carried to a hospital, but had never come back," or that Mrs. Kelly "had sent the children to a neighbor and had put her head into the gas oven." Day after day such tales were poured into my ears – a baby born dead, great relief – the death of an older child, sorrow but again relief of a sort – the story told a thousand times of death from abortion and children going into institutions. I shuddered with horror as I listened to the details and studied the reasons back of them – destitution linked with excessive childbearing. The waste of life seemed utterly senseless. One by one worried, sad, pensive, and aging faces marshaled themselves before me in my dreams, sometimes appealingly, sometimes accusingly.

Then one stifling mid-July day of 1912 I was summoned to a Grand Street tenement. My patient was a small, slight Russian Jewess, about twenty-eight years old, of the special cast of feature to which suffering lends a madonna-like expression. The cramped three-room apartment was in a sorry state of turmoil. Jake Sachs, a truck driver scarcely older than his wife, had come home to find the three children crying and her unconscious from the effects of a self-induced abortion.

The doctor and I settled ourselves to the task of fighting the opticemia. Never had I worked so fast, never so concentratedly. The sultry days and nights were melted into a torpid inferno. It did not seem possible there could be such heat, and every bit of food, ice and drugs had to be carried up three flights of stairs.

After a fortnight Mrs. Sachs' recovery was in sight. Neighbors, ordinarily fatalisitc as to the results of abortion, were genuinely pleased that she had survived. She smiled wanly at all who came to see her and thanked them gently, but she could not respond to their hearty congratulations. She appeared to be more despondent and anxious than she should have been, and spent too much time in meditation.

At the end of three weeks, I was preparing to leave the fragile patient to take up her difficult life once more, she finally voiced her fears, "Another baby will finish me, I suppose?"

"It's too early to talk about that," I temporized.

But when the doctor came to make his last call, I drew him aside. "Mrs. Sachs is terribly worried about having another baby."

"She well may be," replied the doctor, and then he stood before her and said, "Any more such capers, young woman, and there'll be no need to send for me."

"I know, doctor," she replied timidly, "but," and she hesitated as though it took all her courage to say it, "what can I do to prevent it?"

The doctor was a kindly man, and he had worked hard to save her, but such incidents had become so familiar to him that he had long since lost whatever delicacy he might once have had. He laughed good-naturedly. "You want to have your cake and eat it too, do you? Well, it can't be done."

Then picking up his hat and bag to depart he said, "Tell Jake to sleep on the roof."

I glanced quickly at Mrs. Sachs. Even through my sudden tears I could see stamped on her face an expression of absolute despair. We simply looked at each other, saying no word until the door had closed behind the doctor. Then she lifted her thin, blue-veined hands and clasped them beseechingly. "He can't understand. He's only a man. But you do, don't you? Please tell me the secret, and I'll never breathe it to a soul. *Please!*"

What was I to do? I could not speak the conventionally comforting phrases which would be of no comfort. Instead, I made her as physically easy as I could and promised to come back in a few days to talk with her again. A little later, when she slept, I tiptoed away.

Night after night the wistful image of Mrs. Sachs appeared before me. I made all sorts of excuses to myself for not going back. I was busy on other cases; I really did not know what to say to her or how to convince her of my own ignorance; I was helpless to avert such monstrous atrocities. Time rolled by and I did nothing.

The telephone rang one evening three months later, and Jake Sachs' agitated voice begged me to come at once; his wife was sick again and from the same cause. I turned into the dingy doorway and climbed the familiar stairs once more. The children were there, young little things.

Mrs. Sachs was in a coma and died within ten minutes. I folded her still hands across her breast, remembering how they had pleaded with me, begging so humbly for the knowledge which was her right. I drew a sheet over her pallid face. Jake was sobbing, running his hands through his hair and pulling it out like an insane person. Over and over again he wailed, "My God! My God! My God!"

I left him pacing desperately back and forth, and for hours I myself walked and walked and walked through the hushed streets. When I finally arrived home and let myself quietly in, all the household was sleeping. I looked out my window and down upon the dimly lighted city. Its pains and griefs crowded in upon me, a moving picture rolled before my eyes with photographic clearness: women writhing in travail to bring forth little babies; the babies themselves naked and hungry, wrapped in newspapers to keep them from the cold; six-year-old children with pinched, pale, wrinkled faces, old in concentrated wretchedness, pushed into gray and fetid cellars, crouching on stone floors, their small scrawny hands scuttling through rags, making lamp shades, artificial flowers; white coffins, black coffins, coffins, coffins interminably passing in never-ending succession. The scenes piled one upon another on another. I could bear it no longer.

As I stood there the darkness faded. The sun came up and threw its reflection over the house tops. It was the dawn of a new day in my life also. The doubt and questioning, the experimenting and trying, were not to be put behind me. I know I could not go back merely to keeping people alive.

I went to bed knowing that no matter what it might cost, I was finished with palliatives and superficial cures; I was resolved to seek out the root of evil, to do something to change the destiny of mothers whose miseries were vast as the sky.

*Margaret Sanger Autobiography*. Reprinted by permission of Grant Sanger, M.D.

## Excerpt from A Barefoot Doctor's Manual

*Installed by the government of the People's Republic of China in the 1950s, the "chijiao yisheng" (barefoot doctor) program now includes some two million medical workers who are stationed in the thousands of agricultural communes and hundreds of thousands of villages throughout the immense Chinese countryside. Their title is misleading, since "barefoot doctors" neither go about barefoot, nor are they doctors. The government defines them as citizens who have had basic medical training and can, among other things, see to the peoples' birth control needs.*

## BIRTH CONTROL PLANNING

*Section 1. Significance of Birth Control Planning*  Birth control planning is a momentous measure of national import and interest. It uses the scientific method to suitably determine the timing and frequency of human reproduction.

*Section 2. Promoting Late Marriage*  If the young people talk about love, marriage and having children at too early an age, their energies will be dissipated, affecting their work and their study. Futhermore, from the standpoint of physical development, most young people do not attain all-round maturity until after 25 years of age. Premature marriage and procreation are not beneficial for the young and succeeding generations.

*Section 3. Contraception*  Contraception is a technique employing scientific methods to prevent union of the spermatazoa and the ovum, so that conception is not possible within a certain time span. Several simple yet safe methods of contraception are as follows:

*Chinese Herbs* (effective to a certain extent)

1. Decoction prepared from tender sprouts of *Pinus massoniana*, 9 stalks (each about 5 inches (ts'un) long), and roots of white stipa, 1 liang, to be taken once after conclusion of menstrual period, for 5 months in succession. Effective as contraceptive for 3 years.

*Use of Condoms*

A contraceptive device used by the male, it is simple to use, with good results. Its selection depends on the size of the erect penis. Before intercourse, the condom should be blown up to test for leaks. Then air at the tip should be expelled before fitting it on the penis. After ejaculation, and before the penis becomes completely soft, the condom should be removed by pulling at the opening, to prevent its retention in the vagina. Wash and clean after use. Dry, and check for breaks. Dust with talc, wrap and put away for later use.

Other devices, such as the diaphragm and the loop, are also effective. However they must be fitted for appropriate use.

*Oral Contraceptives*

At present, western contraceptive medicines are based primarily on hormones used to control ovulation. Their use follows a regimen described as follows:

1. Progesterone, 1 tablet taken nightly beginning on 5th day of menstrual period, for a total of 22 days, as one cycle.

2. Duosterone, used in the same manner as progesterone.

Note: Precautions while on oral contraceptives.

(1) Be sure to follow regimen prescribed for the cycle by taking a pill daily, for this approach to be effective.

(2) Be aware that uncomfortable symptoms such as nausea, dizziness, weakness and distended breasts may be experienced upon first taking the drug, but will subside later on.

3. If a small amount of vaginal bleeding occurs after taking the drug, take another 1-2 tablets of ethinyl estradiol each evening. If bleeding is heavy, discontinue the pill, but use another method of contraception.

4. If menstruation does not occur after 22 days on the pill, begin the next cycle of pill-taking 7 days later.

5. Do not use such medications in the presence of liver disease or nephritis.

**Section 4. Sterilization**    Oral contraception or some other measure may be used by those who have had too many children too closely, or by those whose health does not recommend having more children, to terminate their reproductive capacity. This is called *sterilization*, that is, no more children born for the rest of their lives. Some of the more common sterilization measures are described below:

*Chinese Herbs*: of certain value

1. Fresh roots from the date palm, 3-5 liang, and hog large intestines, half chin.

First cook the date palm roots in water. Bring to boil. After 20 minutes add the hog large intestines. Continue cooking until the ingredients are tender, then remove roots and season with a small amount of sugar or salt. Eat the hog intestines and take the herb juices in one sitting after a menstrual period.

*Surgery*

Sterilization accomplished through surgical technique hardly affects the health and working capability in those who undertake the operation. It is equally satisfactory for males and females. In particular, vasectomy, performed on men, is a simple technique that should be given greater promotion.

1. *Vasectomy*. This surgical technique is simple and quick to perform. There is very little bleeding, and does not affect the individual working ability. Its practice should be widened.

However, for a 3-month period following surgery, other contraceptive measures should still be taken during sexual intercourse, as some sperm are still retained in the seminal vesicle. (Consult section on "Therapeutics" for surgical procedure).

2. *Tube Ligation* (ligation of fallopain tubes). This technique can be done anytime after 24 hours post-partum, after artificial abortion, or after end of menstrual period.

When Christopher Columbus discovered America, he found not only a New World, but a new disease as well. Columbus had never heard of syphilis – it was unknown in Europe – and so he never knew that the sores on his body and his increasing blindness were the results of sexual intercourse with infected native Americans. Eventually he died of syphilis; as did hundreds of thousands of other Europeans in the next century.

It was the age of discovery and exploration, and as the Europeans explored, conquered, and destroyed new lands, they spread syphilis along with their culture. Vasco da Gama, heralded for his exploration, took syphilis along with him to India; from India it was transmitted to China; and then to Japan. The slavers moving into Africa introduced syphilis there, and those who were captured and enslaved returned it to America. Within a century syphilis was spread to most parts of the world.

Gonorrhea has an older known history than syphilis; accounts of this disease can be traced back to the ancient Egyptians and Chinese. It has been among the Europeans from the beginning of their history. Many of the plagues described in the Bible may have been descriptions of gonorrhea. It was not until the nineteenth century, however, that gonorrhea and syphilis were isolated as separate and distinct diseases.

This chapter is predominantly concerned with sexually transmissible diseases in America today. But, there are also certain diseases of the sexual organs that are not necessarily transmitted during intercourse. Among these are cystitis, vaginitis, and cancer, which are considered in later sections.

## The Sexually Transmissible Diseases

Until the present century – specifically until the development of penicillin – there were no effective treatments for what are now termed *sexually transmissible diseases*, STDs (Yarber, 1978). In fact, clear distinctions had not been made between the various types of maladies, which were collectively termed *venereal* (from 'Venus', the goddess of love and beauty) *disease*. The less poetic term has been adopted among doctors, and 'STD' may come into popular usage as more and more people seek medical help for this rampant health problem. However, 'VD' is still the best known designation, and is used in this chapter.

The VD problem is truly epidemic. Americans are contracting the diseases at a rate of 10 million per year, and the variety of the infections is as mind-boggling as the frequency. Among the common VDs are herpes genitalis, nongonococcal urethritis, cytomegalovirus, trichomoniasis, hepatitis, scabies, venereal warts, pubic lice and lympho-granuloma venereum.

VDs are not, as popular fantasy have it, the sole problems of prostitutes and other "low life" types. College campuses are as much their domain as the ghetto. Wherever they occur, they bring psychological trauma, as well as physical damage.

VDs are infections, just as pneumonia and the flu are infections. Unfortunately, though, getting one is still loaded with "moral" implications.

**Preventive Measures** There are many ways one can avoid STD infections:

- □ *the condom*: This is a barrier to most, but not all, types of STD organisms. It does not offer much protection against parasites (such as "crabs").
- □ *spermacides:* The common, over-the-counter contraceptive foams, creams, and jellies designed for intravaginal use have been found to prevent more than conception. They also pro-

vide some protection against gonorrhea, syphilis, and herpes virus.

□ *washing:* Even though there is no scientific proof that washing prevents STD infections, it may provide some protection.

□ *urination:* This may flush out STD organisms.

□ *douching:* Douching with a mild germ-killing solution may give protection against STDs, but it should not be used on a regular basis. Frequent douchings irritate the vagina, and may lead to infection. One should consult a gynecologist before using this method.

□ *inspection of partner:* Unusual discharges, or sores on or near genitals or mouth should be taken as a sign to refrain from intimate activities involving those areas. *But, visual inspection cannot be relied upon.* Many infections are out of sight, within the internal sex organs.

□ *communication:* This is potentially the most effective form of protection, and it is obviously lacking in today's culture.

**Venereal Disease and Interpersonal Relationships** Venereal disease always involves at least two people. And any person who has a venereal infection must assume the responsibility of informing those with whom he or she has had sexual contact. Some people may feel embarrassed to talk about it, others may fear its impact on a relationship. There are countless reasons people can give themselves for not telling their partners about their infection, but there is not one that is valid. The consequences of undetected infection are potentially so harmful that there is no legitimate excuse for withholding the information. For people who are unwilling to tell their partners directly, there are local public health services that will do it for them, preserving anonymity.

**Where To Get Help** Free diagnosis and treatments for venereal diseases are available at public health centers throughout the country. But victims must take the initiative by reporting the earliest symptoms. Ignoring any sign of trouble, hoping that it will disappear, is a foolish risk. Sometimes a symptom will disappear – such as a chancre sore in the first stage of syphilis – but this does not necessarily mean that the disease is cured. It may simply mean – as with syphilis – that the infection is entering a new or dormant stage.

Upon entering a clinic for diagnosis, patients will be asked to describe their symptoms and to recall whether they had sexual contact with anyone who is known to have, or who might have, VD. Patients will then be examined and laboratory tests made to determine if a disease is actually present.

Tests will be conducted both for syphilis and gonorrhea. For the syphilis test, a blood sample is taken from the arm. The smears and cultures that indicate gonorrhea are taken with a cotton swab from the urethra, cervix, or rectum. Both tests are painless. If the penis, vulva, or mouth have ulcers on them, the physician will use a capillary tube to obtain some of the serum, which will then be examined under a microscope. It generally takes only ten or fifteen minutes to obtain the result. (These examinations are discussed in more detail later in this chapter.)

Once the specific disease has been determined and treatment given – usually an oral antibiotic or an injection into the buttocks – the infected person must return for further examination and tests to make sure the disease has been arrested. The examinations and tests vary with the disease. For gonorrhea, a clinic typically requires two negative cultures for men at three-to five-day intervals and three negative cultures at three–to five-day intervals for women. For syphilis, retesting depends on the stage the disease reached. Usually blood tests are taken every month for six months and then every three to six months for the next five years. For *herpes* the patients are seen each week until the lesions are healed; for *lympho-granuloma venereum* the infected person is seen every one to two months for one year.

Following diagnosis and treatment in a VD clinic, the infected person is usually interviewed by an epidemiologist so that other infected people may be discovered and contacted. Patients will be asked who may have infected them and whom they may have infected. This information is confidential and the contacts will not be informed of the source of identification unless permission is given to do so. The contacts will generally receive a form letter informing them that they have been exposed to venereal disease and that they are required to go to a doctor or clinic within a certain period of time, usually 48 hours. These people must be examined and treated, if necessary, before they in turn spread the disease to others.

**Where to Call**

Following is a list of health clinics of Venereal Disease Control Centers in some of the leading cities in the United States. (Also, "Operation Venus" is a toll-free hot line in Philadelphia which will refer you between 9 A.M. and 9 P.M. to the nearest help in your area. Call 800-523-1885.

Atlanta, Ga.
(404) 572-2201

Baltimore, Md.
(301) 494-2713

Berkeley, Calif.
(415) 845-0197

Milwaukee, Wis.
(414) 278-3631

Minneapolis, Minn.
(612) 822-3186

Nashville, Tenn.
(615) 327-9313

Birmingham, Ala.
(205) 324-9571

Boston, Mass.
(617) 727-2688

Buffalo, N.Y.
(716) 846-7687

Chicago, Ill.
(312) 842-0222

Cleveland, Ohio
(216) 249-4100

Concord, N.H.
(603) 271-2101

Dallas, Tex.
(214) 528-4084

Denver, Colo.
(303) 893-7232

Hartford, Conn.
(203) 566-6116

Houston, Tex.
(713) 222-4201

Indianapolis, Ind.
(317) 630-7192

Kansas City, Kan.
(913) 321-4803

Los Angeles, Calif.
(213) 564-6801

Louisville, Ky.
(502) 584-5281

Memphis, Tenn.
(901) 522-2987

Miami, Fla.
(305) 325-2557

Newark, N.J.
(201) 733-7584

New Orleans, La.
(504) 523-6409

New York, N.Y.:
English:
(212) 269-5300
Spanish:
(212) 691-8733

Philadelphia, Pa.
(215) 546-0141

Phoenix, Ariz.
(602) 258-6381

Pittsburgh, Pa.
(412) 355-5781

Richmond, Va.
(804) 649-4365

San Francisco, Calif.
(415) 558-3804

Seattle, Wash.
(206) 583-2590

St. Louis, Mo.
(314) 453-3523

Syracuse, N.Y.
(315) 477-7889
(315) 477-7658
(4 p.m. to 8 p.m.)

Washington, D.C.
(202) 629-7578

Wilmington, Del.
(302) 571-3400

**Gonorrhea**

In 1977 the reported case rate for gonorrhea was 469 per 100,000 people in the United States. (V.D. Fact Sheet, 1977, Joseph H. Blount, ed., pg. 365). The bacteria that causes gonorrhea, *Neisseria gonorrhea*, is one of the most delicate of all disease-causing organisms. Outside the human body it dies within a few seconds. Thus, contrary to popular belief, it is almost impossible to catch gonorrhea from toilet seats, cups, towels, and so on that have been used by an infected person. *N. gonorrhea* grows well only in mucous membranes, such as the moist linings of the vagina, penis, anus, mouth, and throat.

Bacteria may be transferred from the mucous membranes of an infected person's sexual organs to the membranes of a sexual partner; but sexual relations with someone who is infected do not always result in transmission of the disease. In a single instance of vaginal intercourse with an infected partner, for example, an uninfected man has about a 60 percent chance of escaping the disease; however, an uninfected woman has less than a 50 percent chance of avoiding it. If she is using the Pill without other contraceptives, she is almost certain to contract it. Obviously, the chance of avoiding the disease decreases as the number of sexual encounters with the infected individual increases. Taking the Pill increases the probability of contracting gonorrhea, presumably because changes in vaginal and cervical secretions create a more hospitable environment for the gonorrheal bacteria.

**Gonorrhea in Females — Early Symptoms**   Gonorrhea is particularly threatening to women. Over 70 percent of female cases occur without obvious early symptoms. For this reason, women may discover the disease in themselves only through reports from male partners (for whom the early symptoms are more obvious). If left undetected, female gonorrhea can lead to permanently damaging internal infections. (A recent trial in Wyoming put teeth in the injunction that a man with VD should inform his sexual partners. The jury ordered a man who infected a woman and did not tell her to pay $1.3 million in damages.)

Gonorrheal infection in women usually begins in the cervix, and, within a few days following the infecting intercourse, pus is discharged through the cervical opening. But, since the cervix lies high in the vagina, the pus may not reach the vaginal opening. If it does, however, it usually appears yellow-green and is irritating to the vulva. Some infected women (or their sexual partners) notice a distinctive, mushroom-like odor coming from the vagina. It should be remembered, however, that a healthy vagina also has a distinctive odor.

As a gonorrheal infection progresses, some women begin to feel a persistent low backache or pains in the abdomen. For some women the urethra becomes infected, and a burning sensation is felt during urination. In about half the cases of female gonorrhea, the disease organisms infect the anus, which may occur either as a result of anal intercourse with an infected male, or when menstrual bleeding carries the disease organisms to the anus from the cervix. Symptoms of anal gonorrhea may include a burning sensation in the anus (particularly during bowel movements) and pus in the feces. Even in cases of combined cervical and anal gonorrhea, however, the victim may not realize she has the disease.

If a thick discharge is seen coming from the urethral meatus or vagina, and/or if an unusual mushroom-like odor exudes from the genitals, it would be wise to refrain from further sexual activity. It should be remembered, however, that healthy genitals normally have distinctive odors and that thin, clear fluids are emitted from the vagina and from a male's urethral meatus during periods of erotic arousal.

*Advanced Symptoms*   Although early female gonorrhea usually has no obvious symptoms, the invading bacteria steadily advance deeper into the reproductive organs. Progressing along the delicate membranes of the endometrium, they eventually (about two to three months following the original infection) reach the Fallopian tubes. Gonorrheal infection of the Fallopian tubes is termed *salpingitis*.

During salpingitis, bacteria attack the inner walls of the Fallopian tubes. Pus forms within the tubes and eventually leaks through the open, funnel-like ends onto the ovaries and other pelvic organs. The resultant infections are often extremely painful.

Symptoms of salpingitis can be "acute" or "subacute." In women for whom they are subacute, a feeling of heaviness or a dull aching pain develops in their lower abdomen. There may also be sharp pains during and/or after sexual intercourse. Backache, a fever, and general feelings of illness sometimes develop. In some cases the symptoms steadily get worse; other times they temporarily disappear after a few days. Because the symptoms of subacute salpingitis are mild (and similar to the symptoms of certain other gynecological disorders), it is difficult to diagnose the disease.

Symptoms of acute salpingitis often begin with disruption of a menstrual period (which may be longer or more painful than usual). Menstrual disorders occur concurrently with bacterial invasion of the uterine lining. In acute salpingitis, pelvic pain becomes increasingly intense during the days following menstruation. Simultaneously the victim's temperature rises and she may experience headache, nausea, and vomiting.

Symptoms of acute salpingitis eventually become so severe that sufferers seek emergency medical attention. Unfortunately, symptoms of certain diseases (such as acute appendicitis and tubal pregnancy) resemble those of salpingitis, and sometimes exploratory surgery is necessary to correctly identify the malady.

**Long-term Damage** Antibiotic treatments are capable of killing gonorrhea bacteria and arresting its physiological effects, but occasionally salpingitis leads to irreversible damage of the Fal-

liopian tubes. If the tubes are blocked, pus is not able to escape. Normal secretions subsequently accumulate within them, and they become grossly enlarged. In some cases the internal reproductive organs are misshapened and pulled out of place by thick growths of scar tissue. By completely and permanently closing both Fallopian tubes, salpingitis sterilizes about 25 percent of its victims.

Sometimes salpingitis causes only partial block-age of the Fallopian tubes, leaving narrow, convoluted passages. In such cases a fertilized egg is likely to lodge in a tube and begin embryonic development. This condition, *tubal pregnancy* (which is described more completely in Chapter 4), can result in a ruptured Fallopian tube with subsequent severe internal bleeding. Without prompt medical attention the victim may go into shock and die.

Salpingitis does not necessarily preclude a future pregnancy. But, unless a pregnancy is desired, women who have had the disease should use highly effective contraceptives, such as the Pill or the condom/spermicide combination. However, IUDs should *not* be used. IUD's prevent implantations of embryos in the uterus, but they do not prevent fertilization or implantation within a Fallopian tube.

**The Examination** In an examination for gonorrhea, a gynecologist begins by checking the vulva for inflamation and discharge, and feeling the lower abdomen for enlarged or tender lymph glands. Using a *speculum* (a metal or plastic, pliers-like device which opens the vagina for observation), the doctor examines the walls of the vagina and cervix for discharge. Bacteria samples are taken from the cervix and anus with cotton swabs, and, as described later in this chapter, these samples are analyzed after laboratory culturing.

## Gonorrhea in Males — Early Symptoms

In males the penile urethra is usually the first point of attack by gonorrhea bacteria, and the symptoms are first noticed within two weeks after the infecting intercourse. At first, a clear, mucoid discharge seeps from the urethral meatus. Within a day or two, however, the discharge becomes thick and creamy. It is often white, but may be yellow or yellow-green. It contains bacteria, dead urethral cells, and white blood cells, and is irritating to the urethral meatus. Often the delicate tissues at the tip of the penis swell and become inflamed. Most victims feel a burning sensation in the penis, particularly when they are urinating. The urine itself becomes cloudy with pus and sometimes contains traces of blood. In uncircumcised men the entire glans penis may become red and sore as the infection spreads to the inside of the foreskin.

*Advanced Symptoms* If treatment of a gonorrheal infection is delayed for more than a few days after symptoms first appear, bacteria spread further up the urethra and pain during urination becomes increasingly intense. However, after about two weeks the symptoms begin to fade and may disappear. Nevertheless, bacteria are still spreading into the reproductive organs.

Within three weeks the bacteria reach the prostate gland, where an abscess may form. Symptoms of a prostate abscess include sensations of heat, pain, or swelling in the lower abdomen. The enlarged, infected prostate gland presses into the bladder and rectum, making it painfully difficult to urinate and defecate. Ultimately the abscess breaks, releasing pus through the urethra.

Since an abscess develops in only about 10 percent of the men in whom the bacteria have reached the prostate, the bacteria often spread for several months with only moderate side effects. For some men, however, severe pains occur within the scrotum as the bacteria infect the epididymis of one or both testicles. This affliction, terms *epididymitis*, results in a hard, painful swelling at the bottom of the testicle(s). Even when cured with antibiotics, epididymitis leaves scar tissue which prevents passage of sperm from the testicles into the vasa deferentia. However, since the disease usually first develops on one side, the victim is not necessarily left sterile if he seeks medical attention before the second epididymis becomes infected.

*The Examination* Because the early symptoms of gonorrhea are almost always obvious in males, antibiotic treatments can usually be applied soon enough to stop the infection before it causes permanent damage. Thus, if a man finds an unusual discharge coming from his urethral meatus and/or experiences a burning sensation upon urination, he should seek immediate medical attention. Because women have the misfortune of lacking early symptoms of gonorrhea, infected men should not only seek medical attention for themselves, but also inform recent sexual partners of their possible problem.

In a gonorrheal examination each testicle is gently squeezed to check for epididymitis, and a bacterial specimen is taken from the urethral meatus with a cotton swab. Most cases of male gonorrhea of the genitals can be diagnosed with superficial observations, but the bacterial sample is taken for confirmation. In men who have recently performed oral-genital sex acts, a bacterial specimen is also taken from the throat, and for those who have had anal intercourse a sample is taken from the anus.

## Oral Gonorrhea

Gonorrheal infections are usually restricted to the genitals, but they can develop in several other places within the body. In oral gonorrhea the bacteria thrive in the mucoid tissues of the mouth and throat. Oral gonorrhea often has no symptoms, but sometimes a victim develops a sore throat or a low fever, which begins a few days after the infecting contact.

**Septicemia**    A relatively rare condition, septicemia, affects only about one percent of people (both males and females) with untreated gonorrhea. However, it may lead to death if its early symptoms do not prompt the victim to seek medical attention. Septicemia occurs when bacteria break into the bloodstream from the genitals or from other centers of infection. Among the symptoms are a high fever, chills, and pain in the joints. The most severely affected areas include the wrists, knees, fingers, and ankles. In some cases a skin rash develops in the regions of the affected joints. Antibiotic treatments must be given immediately to avoid permanent damage to the joints.

**Fetal Infections**    Certainly the most tragic of the possible side effects of gonorrhea is infant blindness. If a birthing woman has the disease, she will pass it to her infant. Unless there is damage to the placenta, a gonorrheal infection in a pregnant woman is not transmitted to the fetal blood; rather the infant becomes infected during birth, when the protective amniotic membrane has broken. The newborn's eyes are most vulnerable to attack.

About 5 percent of pregnant American women have gonorrhea. Thus, at least one test for the disease should be done during pregnancy.

If detected early in pregnancy, gonorrhea can easily be stopped with antibiotic injections. As a second-line defense, however, a bacteriacidal agent (either silver nitrate or penicillin) is administered to the eyes of newborns. In most obstetrics wards, eye drops are routinely given to all infants.

**Tests**    Microscopic analysis of specimens taken with cotton swabs is the quickest way to test for gonorrhea. However, immediate examinations of the specimens give "false negative" results (that is, the disease is not detected when it actually is present) for about 20 percent of infected males and 50 percent of infected females. "False positive" results are sometimes obtained as the result of the presence of harmless bacteria that resemble the disease-causing organism.

For a reliable analysis the bacteria must first be grown on a culture medium (a high-protein, "jello-like" substance made from seaweed). The bacteria reproduce by the billions, forming tiny gray mounds on the surface of the medium (which is carefully protected from contamination by bacteria from anywhere apart from the sampled area). In a day or two there are sufficient bacteria to perform highly accurate chemical tests. Thus, the results are available within a few days after taking the specimen.

**Treatments**    Antibiotics are highly successful in treating gonorrhea. Penicillin, given by injection into a buttock, is the oldest (and still the best). From the muscle within the buttock, penicillin is absorbed into the bloodstream and is distributed throughout the body, killing gonorrheal bacteria wherever they have settled. If caught early, within a week following the initial infection, the disease will usually be eradicated within two or three days.

Although penicillin is the preferable treatment for gonorrhea, there are cases for which it cannot be used: some people are allergic to it, and in certain geographic areas (including many large cities and Vietnam) strains of gonorrheal bacteria have become resistant to penicillin.

Approximately 5 percent of the North American population is allergic to penicillin. In most cases of allergy there is a delayed reaction, that is, the symptomatic skin rash does not appear for a week or two. Usually the reaction is no more serious than a fever and/or a slight, temporary blistering of the skin. Nevertheless, any allergic reaction should be remembered and described to unfamiliar physicians prior to antibiotic treatments. Allergic reactions to penicillin tend to become worse with repeated treatments. In cases in which the patient has a history of allergy to penicillin, or if the infection is resistant to it, another drug, *tetracycline*, may be used to stop gonorrhea. Tetracycline is given orally, and it is routinely prescribed by some doctors as the first-line of defense against gonorrhea. This policy is criticized by some physicians, however, on the grounds that undesirable side effects (which may include nausea, vomiting, diarrhea, and heartburn) are more common with tetracycline than penicillin. Furthermore, routine use of tetracycline has caused certain strains of gonorrheal bacteria to become resistant to it.

### Non-Gonorrheal Urethritis

*Non-gonnorheal urethritis* (NGU) is a disease that resembles gonorrhea in symptoms and mode of transmission. It has only been recognized as a distinct disease in recent times, hence it still goes by several names, including *nongonococcal urethritis* and *nonspecific urethritis* (NSU). For men, the primary symptom of NGU is a gonorrheal-like discharge from the urethra. There are no obvious symptoms of NGU in women; however, women can be carriers of it. In

parts of Europe NGU accounts for as many cases of abnormal urethral discharge as does gonorrhea. In America it is not nearly so common, but the incidence is increasing. The cause(s) of NGU are not known, but it is generally thought to result from the presence of infectious microorganisms (although, it has also been suggested that NGU is an allergic reaction to vaginal secretions). Treatments with tetracycline and erythromycin hasten recovery. Recent findings indicate that NGU may even be more common than gonorrhea, for which it is often mistaken by physicians.

### Syphilis

The incidence of gonorrhea is far greater than that of syphilis (over 2 million people currently have gonorrhea, whereas 100,000 have syphilis). But syphilis is more often fatal.

**The Disease Organism and its Transmission**    Syphilis is caused by the microorganism *Treponema pallidum*, which looks like a corkscrew when seen under high magnification (it is only about 0.00004 of an inch long). Warmth and moisture are essential to the survival of *T. pallidum* (it dies within seconds on surfaces such as toilet seats), thus making it highly unlikely for the disease to be transmitted by any means other than sexual contact.

During sexual intercourse, *T. pallidum* is given ideal conditions for transmission – close contact and moist interfaces. Within minutes it can burrow through the thin skin and membranes of the genitals.

**Protection**    Condoms give partial protection against syphilis, but during heated sexual activity, the disease organism can slip around the open end. Since *T. pallidum* is highly susceptible to soap and water, thorough washing of the male genitals before intercourse or immediately afterward also provides some protection. Even a combination of condoms and thorough washing, however does not necessarily offer absolute protection.

**Primary Syphilis**  The symptoms of syphilis are similar for men and women, and they develop in a slow but devastating sequence.

In *primary syphilis*, which appears between a week and three months after the infecting contact, one or more chancres (pronounced "shankers") appear on the body. Chancres are syphilitic sores, and they develop at the site of the disease organisms' invasion. In men this is usually somewhere on the surface of the penis or scrotum. In women the chancre generally develops along the vagina or on the cervix (though it may also appear on the vulva). Since chancres are painless, female victims who have them internally may be unaware they are infected. As with gonorrhea, anyone who discovers the presence of syphilis should immediately inform his or her sex partner.

A chancre first appears as a dull red bump, about the size of a pea. Within a few days its surface breaks and it becomes a sore, which may be covered by a crusty scab. The edge of a chancre is often raised and hard, and the immediately surrounding skin may become hard and rubbery. If people have had anal intercourse, a chancre may develop in or around the anus. If the infection is transmitted through cunnilingus or fellatio, the chancre may develop on the tongue, lips, or in the throat.

If left untreated, chancres play themselves out within a few weeks after they first appear. In some cases a faint scar is left, but usually there is no trace. For a while syphilis is symptomless,

but it continues to spread and to remain communicable.

**Secondary Syphilis**  Within a few months after the disappearance of the chancre, new symptoms of syphilis develop. A nonitching rash appears, which, in some cases is isolated in small patches and in other instances nearly covers the body. The rash may develop as flat pink spots, or bumps may raise from the skin. The rash commonly appears on such places as the abdomen, chest, shoulders, back, and upper arms and legs. In some cases it develops on the scalp, where it causes hair loss.

Within and around the genitals, reddish patches may form, which ooze a clear fluid. This liquid contains high concentrations of the disease organism; hence syphilis is extremely contagious during this phase.

Other symptoms of secondary syphilis include swelling of the lymph glands (particularly in the armpits and neck), sore throat, headache, nausea, constipation, muscle pain, and a low fever. Few people experience all of these symptoms, but the skin rash almost always appears.

Even if untreated, the symptoms of second stage syphilis disappear within about a month. A long latent phase begins, but if left untreated the disease progresses to its final, sometimes deadly, stages.

**Tertiary Syphilis**  The latent phase following secondary syphilis sometimes lasts for many years, even decades. In the first or second year there may be a brief recurrence of the skin rash, but, in general, there are no symptoms for a long time.

Syphilis may ultimately reappear in several ways. In about 20 percent of its victims, ulcers develop in one or more areas, including the lungs, eyes, liver, and digestive tract. This is the mildest form of tertiary syphilis, and if treated with antibiotics the ulcers can usually be cured.

For about 10 percent of the sufferers of late-phase syphilis, injury is done to the heart and major blood vessels. In some cases, cardiovascular damage leads to death.

*Neurosyphilis* – a deterioration of the brain and spinal cord – develops in an undetermined fraction of untreated cases of syphilis. Sometimes it is a horrifying disease, which causes paralysis and/or insanity, eventually ending in death. In other cases, neurosyphilis is insidious, developing so slowly that it is impossible to discriminate between the effects of the disease and the results of aging.

Approximately 60 percent of the people with tertiary syphilis complete their lives with no obvious symptoms. However, since the earlier stages of syphilis are quickly cured with antibiotics, it is senseless to allow it to go unchecked after the first symptoms appear.

**Syphilis and Pregnancy** Children born to women with untreated syphilis almost always have the disease congenitally. If the mother's infection is in the primary or secondary stage during pregnancy, the infant is often born dead or dies soon after birth. Infants who live may be blind, deaf and/or have deformed bones and teeth.

If a woman has tertiary-stage syphilis during pregnancy, the infant may escape the disease entirely or be born with a latent phase of it. In such cases, the child may mature and live its entire life with no overt symptoms of the disease; or it might live several decades before one or more of the symptoms previously described for tertiary syphilis develops.

*T. pallidum* reaches the fetus of an infected woman through the placenta. But, before the placenta is well developed (before the second trimester) the disease organism cannot cross it. Thus, if it is treated before the fourth month of pregnancy, syphilis will not infect the fetus.

**Diagnosis** Syphilis is a difficult disease to diagnose because its early symptoms are similar to several other diseases. Thus, samples of blood and the secretions from chancres must be taken for laboratory analysis.

People who suspect that they have syphilis should *not* put any type of medication on their sores before they are examined. *T. pallidum* is highly sensitive, and the bacteria that are near the surface will be killed and destroyed. Thus, subsequent microscopic examinations of fluid taken from treated chancres may give "false negative" results.

Examinations for syphilis generally include the taking of blood for chemical tests. In fact, blood tests for syphilis are part of the routine of many physical examinations, including those taken when going into the army, applying for a marriage license, and checking on early pregnancies. Chemical analyses of the blood samples are aimed at detecting the antibodies that form within the blood to ward off the disease organism. Because no test is 100 percent accurate, usually two or more analytic techniques are used. In addition to giving occasional "false negative" results, the tests are sometimes "false positive," especially if the patient has recently had measles, mononucleosis, or another infectious disease. Even a recent vaccination for smallpox may lead to a "false positive" result.

**Treatment** Penicillin is the preferred drug for treating syphilis. If syphilis is in the primary or secondary phase, it may be cured with a single injection of penicillin. Tertiary syphilis also responds to penicillin, but treatment over an ex-

## Sweet Success

Authors' note: The important word in this story is "symptoms."

Of all the forms of venereal disease in the U.S. one of the most troublesome is that caused by the common *herpes simplex* virus. Comprising about 13% of VD cases, the contagious infection produces painful sores in the genital area and discomfort while urinating. It is particularly dangerous in women: during delivery it can be transmitted to the infant; it is also linked to cervical cancer. For years, doctors have searched for a cure. Now researchers at the University of Pennsylvania may have achieved that goal. In the *Journal of the American Medical Association*, Drs. Herbert Blough and Robert Guintoli report testing a cream containing the sugar 2-deoxy-D-glucose on 36 women with genital herpes infections. Within four days, it cleared up symptoms in 90% of the women with first infections. For women with recurring infections, improvement was almost as dramatic. A next step: to see if this magic bullet works equally well in infected men.

*Time* magazine, July 9, 1979

---

tended period may be necessary.

Following a penicillin injection, recovery from early-phase syphilis is often rapid. In fact, there may be brief physical side effects from the quick destruction of the disease organisms. For example, soon after injection of the antibiotic, the infecting microorganisms die en masse. As they rapidly decompose, they release their toxic contents into the bloodstream causing such physical reactions as fevers of 100° + and inflamation of any chancres that are present. These symptoms are temporary, however, generally passing after only a few hours.

Not all cases of primary and secondary syphilis are cured with single injections of penicillin, however, and follow-up examinations are highly advisable. Three or four examinations are routinely made at intervals during the year following the initial treatment. A period of abstinence from sexual intercourse should precede the first follow-up examination, which is usually scheduled about one month after the injection..

As mentioned earlier, in cases of allergy to penicillin, other antibiotics can be used; tetracycline and erythromycin are the most common substitutes.

## Herpes Genitalis

*Herpes Genitalis* is a viral infection of the genital areas of both men and women. It is caused by the virus, *herpes simplex II*, and may affect the genitals or mouth. A similar virus, *herpes simplex I*, causes cold sores or fever blisters around the mouth, which are not sexually contracted. However, *herpes simplex I* can be transmitted to the genital area by oral-genital contact.

All the ways in which the herpes simplex viruses are transmitted are not precisely known; however, statistical data indicates that sexual intercourse is a common mode of infection by *herpes simplex II*. Nevertheless, there are cases of herpes genitalis in people whose only sexual partner shows no trace of the disease.

Before going into specifics on this particular disease, it is worth considering the general nature of viruses which are entities at the border of life and nonlife. In structure they are more like large molecules than living cells, and they must be in contact with a more complex organism before they show any signs of "life." Once established, however, viruses are extremely hard to stop. In taking over the nuclei of the host's cells, they direct their own replication by the millions. Consequently, infected cells are no longer functional units of the host organisms, but "factories" for viruses.

The first symptom of a herpes infection is a tingling, burning sensation, followed by blistering on the sexual organs. In women, the blisters commonly develop on the labia minora, clitoris, anus, or cervix (where they may not be detected). Occasionally the vaginal wall, buttocks, and thighs are infected. For men, the sores most commonly appear on the head, shaft, and foreskin of the penis; sometimes they develop on the scrotum, perineum, buttocks, anus, thighs, and in the urethra. When the urethra is the only site of infection, a man may be a carrier of the disease and not know it. The same is true for a woman who is infected only on the cervix.

The blisters eventually rupture, forming open sores. Sometimes a secondary bacterial infection causes pus to form. In most areas of infection, the sores are painful; however, on the cervix, where there are few nerve endings, there is no sensation to reveal the infection. Where pain occurs, it may range from a dull ache and tenderness in the entire genital area to a sharp, tingling or burning pain, especially after the blisters break open. A burning sensation while urinating is common, and sometimes the pain radiates into the legs. The latter is particularly severe for women, who may be rendered incapable of walking.

Within a week, herpes sores begin to disappear (even without medical treatment), and by six weeks they are usually healed, with little or no scarring. But, the virus is still present, and blistering may sporadically reappear. Tension and stressful situations, as well as excessive exposure to sunlight have been cited as causes of recurrence.

As with syphilis and gonorrhea, the most severe effects of herpes genitalis are suffered by offspring of women who become infected while pregnant. Brain damage, blindness, and death are among the possibilities. In general, if the mother has a primary infection during pregnancy the effects are more severe than if she is suffering a recurrence.

Most commonly, the infection is passed to the infant at the time of birth. But, it is possible for the virus to reach the fetus through the placenta. If sores are present at the time of birth, a Caesarean section is recommended.

A statistical link between the incidence of herpes genitalis and cancer of the cervix in women has been interpreted as indicating that *herpes simplex II* may cause cervical cancer. But, as yet, no direct cause and effect relationship has been discovered. Cancer of the cervix is a disease which is usually not associated with sexual activity, and is discussed later in this chapter.

The test for herpes simplex is essentially the same as a *Pap smear* (the test for cancer of the cervix). A specimen from the cervix is taken with a cotton swab and smeared on a microscope slide. The slide is then treated with a dye and examined under high magnification. If the virus is present there will be abnormalities in the structures of infected cells.

Unfortunately herpes genitalis is sometimes misdiagnosed as syphilis and treated with penicillin. But, penicillin has no effect; indeed there is no known cure. Although the virus is usually in an inactive state, causing no known permanent damage, the victim carries it for life.

However, there are certain treatments which have been successful for treating the symptoms of the sores. Ultraviolet light, sulfa creams, ether, chloroform, adrenaline, and vitamin therapy have been medically prescribed. Sufferers of the disease have applied certain non-prescription remedies with varying success. Among these are baking soda, cornstarch, witch hazel, and Aloe vera. (Santa Cruz Women's Health Collective, 1978)

**Venereal Warts**
Like herpes genitalis, veneral warts are caused by a virus. They may be contracted without sexual intercourse, but there is a 60 to 70 percent chance of developing them after regular sexual intercourse with an infected partner.

Venereal warts appear within a couple of months after the infecting intercourse. For men, the most commonly affected areas are the glans penis and foreskin (there is a relatively high incidence of the disease among men who are uncircumcised). The shaft, scrotum, and anus may also become infected. In women venereal warts commonly develop near the entrance to the vagina. But the innermost vagina, cervix, and vaginal lips are also susceptible.

*Pubic Lice*

When they develop in moist areas venereal warts are usually reddish and soft, with a cauliflower-like surface. Several warts may grow together, forming a patch of infected tissue. On skin that is not normally lubricated, such as the labia majora, venereal warts are similar to ordinary skin warts.

If venereal warts are treated when small, they can be easily removed with a surface application of *podophyllin*, the dark red resin of the mandrake plant. An application of podophyllin is left on the warts for six hours, after which it must be thoroughly washed with soap and water. If it is left on for more than six hours, it will cause painful chemical burns. If the treatment is successful, the warts dry and fall off within a few days. If they are allowed to become large, venereal warts must be surgically removed.

## Pubic Lice

Commonly called "crabs," pubic lice are the largest agents of VD. With three pairs of claws, a louse is a fearsome monster when seen under magnification, but it is no larger than the head of a pin. Clinging to the base of a pubic hair, a louse pierces the flesh with its mouth parts and feeds from small blood vessels.

Pubic lice are most frequently contracted during sexual intercourse. But because they can survive for a day apart from a host, they may be transmitted through recently infested bedding or clothing. People react differently to pubic lice; to some the itching is unbearable, but others hardly seem to notice them.

Excellent techniques exist for treating pubic lice – creams or shampoos containing toxic compounds are applied to the infected areas. Creams must be left on for up to twenty-four hours, but the shampoos can be rinsed off within a few minutes. The lice are almost always destroyed with one treatment.

## Lympho-granuloma Venereum

Abbreviated as LGV, this disease of Asian origin occurs at the rate of a few thousand cases per year in the United States. Before the Vietnamese War it was almost nonexistent in the United States. LGV is caused by a microorganism (midway in structure between a virus and a bacteria), which invades the lymph system. The lymph system is a network of vessels in close contact with blood vessels. Lymph fluid is similar to blood, but contains few red blood cells. Concentrations of lymph vessels (lymph nodes) occur in the armpits, neck and groin. Within the lymph nodes foreign substances (such as bacteria) are destroyed.

The first symptom of LGV is a whitish, boil-like sore, which usually appears on the external genitals. Sometimes, however, the sore is internal (within the urethra or vagina). The sore usually disappears within a few days, but the disease organisms move on to the lymph vessels. Here a "battle" ensues between the microorganisms and white blood cells, and dead "combatants" collect in the lymph nodes. The nodes in the groin are the first to show the effects, they swell to form a painful sausage-shaped mass, which lodges within the fold of the groin. Other symptoms include fever, chills, and pains in the joints.

LGV is a difficult disease to treat. It responds slowly to antibiotics, and treatment may take several weeks. Sometimes it is necessary to drain the swollen lymph nodes with a sterile needle inserted through the abdomen.

## Chancroid

Also called "soft chancre," this bacterial disease is common in tropical countries, but rarely occurs in temperate parts of the world. Like LGV, only a few thousand cases of chancroid occur in North America per year.

Chancroid is usually transmitted by sexual intercourse, but it is sometimes passed by less intimate contact. It is particularly contagious if there are cuts or other breaks in the skin.

If passed by sexual intercourse, the first symptom of chancroid is one or more sores on the genitals. They first form as pimple-like bumps, which eventually burst into painful open sores that bleed easily. In some cases, the sores form narrow rows, or they may spread to cover the entire genital area. If left untreated chancroid sometimes results in swelling of the lymph nodes in the groin, similar to the effects of LGV. The disease can be cured within a couple of weeks with tetracycline or sulfa drugs.

### Cystitis

*Cystitis* is a bacterial infection of the bladder, which may develop in men or women. Between puberty and the mid-forties, however, it occurs almost exclusively in women. There are a variety of bacteria that can cause cystitis, but most commonly, it results from a particular bacteria that is present in the intestines of all healthy people, *Escherichia coli* (E. coli). The symptoms include a burning sensation during urination, made worse by an almost constant desire to urinate. The urine may be hazy or reddish with blood from the infected bladder.

Cystitis may be transmitted in several ways; by wiping from back to front instead of from front to back after elimination, for example. Sexual intercourse is another common mode of transmission. In fact the disease used to be known as "honeymoon cystitis," because it commonly develops as the result of vigorous and frequent sexual intercourse with a new partner. The term is now somewhat archaic.

Cystitis is usually treated with sulfa drugs. However, other antibiotics may also be used. If the disease becomes chronic, treatments for several months may be necessary to achieve a lasting cure. Such prolonged exposure to antibiotics should be avoided by everyone, because they destroy the normal balance of microbial life in the body. Hence, cystitis and all other venereal diseases should be treated as soon as possible after the first symptoms appear.

### Vaginitis

*Vaginitis* is the most common disease of the female genitals. It is an uncomfortable inflamation that can be caused by various microorganisms, including parasites, fungi, and bacteria. Although the common types of vaginitis all have similar symptoms, they must be treated differently. Thus, a microscopic examination of the vaginal secretion is necessary in order to determine the proper medication.

**Trichomonal Vaginitis** The parasite *Trichomonas vaginalis* (also called trichomonad) can survive for several hours on moist objects. Hence, this form of vaginitis may be passed via a public toilet, a shared towel, and so on. Men as well as women are susceptible to trichomonad infection, but in males it is usually without symptoms and is essentially harmless. Some infected males notice a slight discharge and tickling sensation in the penis. In most men, trichomonads quickly die, but they may survive for several days beneath the foreskin of an uncircumcised penis.

Certain men are potential carriers of trichomonads. Rather than dying, as in most men, the parasites swim (with lashing motions of whip-like flagella) up the urethra and enter the prostate gland. When an infected man ejaculates during intromission, he then inoculates the vagina.

Women who harbor trichomonads have an itchy inflamation of the vagina and frothy, white or yellow vaginal discharge. If the infection is not treated, the symptoms become less severe but do not disappear completely. If the infection persists for several months, cells of the cervix may become damaged. Statistical evidence indicates that chronic trichomonad infection may lead to cervical cancer.

Examination for trichomonads in women involves sampling vaginal secretions. Women should not douche immediately prior to an examination, since douching reduces the number of trichomonads in the vagina. Males are examined for trichomonads by swabbing fluid from beneath the foreskin or the urethral meatus. In people of both sexes the disease can be successfully treated with *metronidazole*, which is taken in pill form for about ten days. If the disease is contracted during pregnancy, metronidazole suppositories should be used instead. Thus, the drug is kept out of the bloodstream where it might do harm to the fetus. To keep the drug out of milk, nursing mothers should also use suppositories. Metronidazole will not cure any form of vaginitis other than a trichomonal infection.

**Monilial Vaginitis** This is another disease that is caused by a fungus that is present on the skin of most healthy people. Why it sometimes causes disease is not known. Women who have diabetes, who are taking birth control pills, or who are pregnant are unusually susceptible to monilial vaginitis. Symptons include intense vaginal itching and a white discharge, which resembles cottage cheese. The vagina becomes inflamed and dry, and intercourse becomes painful.

Monilial vaginitis is treated with the antibiotic *nystatin*, which is administered by vaginal sup-

positories and/or oral tablets. If the disease is mistakenly diagnosed as a bacterial infection and treated with tetracycline it may actually become worse. Tetracycline does not harm the monilial fungus but by killing competing microorganisms, it allows the monilial populations to "explode."

**Bacterial Vaginitis** A variety of bacteria may infect the vagina, some of which produce symptoms similar to those of early gonorrhea. Treatments are similar to those for gonorrhea.

**Prostatitis**

Inflammation of the prostate is called prostatitis. Normally it is the result of bacterial or viral invasion (*infectious prostatitis*), but occasionally it is caused merely by a disruption of the prostatic function due to changes in patterns of sexual behavior (congestive prostatitis).

The most common invading bacterium is the gonococcus, transmitted through sexual contact. But, NGU organisms may also cause it. They first invade the urethra than move upward into the prostate, which becomes inflamed.

A word about sexual irregularity (Rowan and Gillette, 1973):

The prostate, as has been noted, secretes in response to sexual arousal. Like most other glands that are responsive to behavioral or emotional stimuli, it develops patterns of response based upon the frequency with which it is routinely stimulated; and it manufactures its secretions in anticipation that the pattern will be continued. Thus, if a man establishes a routine of masturbation or coitus three times a day, then abruptly cuts back to no sexual activity, the prostate is caught unprepared — rather like the merchant who has stocked his warehouse in anticipation of continued brisk business, only to find that his customers have suddenly stopped buying. Secretions accumulate in the gland, and the result is congestive prostatitis, characterized by pain in the rectum, burning on urination, and a urethral discharge which, when examined microscopically, is found to be free of the normal disease bacteria. The process works in reverse as well; the man who goes abruptly from a schedule of zero orgasmic experiences to several experiences per day makes demands on his prostate that it cannot comfortably meet. Thus he who would avoid congestive prostatis must avoid abrupt changes of sexual frequency in either direction.

Symptoms of prostatitis include swelling in the genital area, a sensation of heat, and pain. Penicillin is the choice drug to use, since there is no easy way of telling the difference between the infectious and congestive types. What doctors do is to treat the symptoms as if they indicated the infectious variety, which is the case approximately 85 percent of the time, then deal with the problem if it turns out to be congestive.

For congestive prostatitis, prostatic massage is performed by inserting a finger in the anus, then rhythmically pressing against the prostate. This works out any congestion which is present. Restricting one's diet to non-spicy foods and avoiding certain drugs (including alcohol and marijuana) may also relieve the symptoms.

### Cancer

The cause(s) of cancer remain among the most elusive mysteries of medical science. And such a mystery is appropriate to consider in this book because cancer of the reproductive systems are the most common forms of the disease in people of both sexes.

**Cancer in Men**   Cancer of the prostate is the predominate form of the disease in men. It is rare before middle age, but the incidence drastically increases during the later years. Twenty-five percent of the men who reach the age of 90 have cancer of the prostate.

Removal of part or all of the prostate gland is the primary treatment for this type of cancer. The operation results in decreased erotic capabilities for some men, but others experience little or no long-term disruption. A curious characteristic of prostate cancer (when contrasted with breast cancer in women) is that it is aggravated by testosterone and somewhat alleviated by estrogen.

**Cancer in Women**   Cancer of the breast is the most common form of the disease in women. It rarely develops prior to the age of 30, but as a woman ages her chances of getting breast cancer increase. Ultimately, about 5 percent of women in the United States develop breast cancer.

Technically, the breasts are not part of the female reproductive system. But, they are highly sensitive to sex hormones. In women with existing cases of breast cancer, artificially administered sex hormones are known to accelerate spread of the disease. For this reason, women with breast cancer are advised not to take birth control pills, and hormone replacement therapy may be dangerous for post-menopausal women with the disease. As yet, there is no conclusive evidence either way on the question of whether the Pill actually causes breast cancer.

Treatment of breast cancer usually involves removing the infected breast. A certain amount of success has been had in treating the disease by removing the ovaries (the source of female sex hormones). Treatments with the male sex hormone, testosterone, have also been somewhat successful. For an unknown reason, testosterone slows the spread of breast cancer.

Cancer of the cervix is the second most common type of cancer in women. It develops in about half as many women as breast cancer. Since apparent symptoms of cervical cancer do not develop for several years, women are advised to have a routine annual Pap smear, which is made from a specimen swabbed from the cervix. Statistical studies of cervical cancer have revealed a low incidence of the disease among Jewish women relative to the general population. From this bit of evidence sexologists have

hypothesized that smegma from beneath the foreskins of uncircumcised penises (Jewish males are routinely circumcised) may cause cancer of the cervix. This hypothesis is contradicted, however, by studies of European males (many of whom are uncircumcised, regardless of religious beliefs) which indicate no such correlation. Cancer of the cervix can be fatal, but is curable if detected early.

# Readings

### Excerpt from **Candide**

Francois Voltaire

*Voltaire, a French writer of the 18th century, satirized the ways of Western life. In this excerpt, the hapless Pangloss tells of his receipt of a roundabout gift from the New World. What he refers to as "the pox" is now known as syphilis.*

'My dear Candide, you knew Paquette who was lady's-maid to our respected baroness. I enjoyed in her arms the heavenly bliss which produced these hellish torments with which I am now consumed. She was infected with it, and has probably died of it. She received this gift from a most learned Franciscan who had traced it back to source. He caught it from an old countess who caught it from a cavalry captain who had it from a marchioness who got it from a page who had caught it from a Jesuit who, during his novitiate, had contracted it in direct line from one of Christopher Columbus's companions. But I shall not pass it on to anybody; I shan't last much longer.'

'Oh, Pangloss!' cried Candide, 'what an extraordinary genealogy! Surely it must trace back to the devil?'

'Not at all,' the great man replied. 'It was an

indispensable part, an essential ingredient, of the best of all possible worlds. You see, if Columbus had never contracted, in a Caribbean island, this disease which infects the reproductive organs and often actually prevents reproduction, thus running directly counter to nature's great design, we should not have chocolate or cochineal. It is worth noting that in present-day Europe the disease is specific to us, as is theological controversy. The Turks, the Indians, The Persians, the Chinese, the Siamese, the Japanese, are still free from it, but there is a sufficient reason why they will experience it in their turn in the next few hundred years. In the meantime it has made astonishing headway over here, particularly in those vast armies composed of honest, decent mercenaries who decide the fate of the nations of the world. Depend upon it, when thirty thousand men engage in pitched battle against an equal number of the enemy, about twenty thousand on each side have the pox.'

'You amaze me,' said Candide, 'but you must go and be cured.'

'How can I do that?' asked Pangloss. 'My dear fellow, I haven't a farthing, and there's nowhere in the whole wide world where you can be bled or purged without paying, or without some other person paying for you.'

These words finally decided Candide. He threw himself at the feet of his charitable Anabaptist, Jacques, and drew such a touching picture of his friend's plight that the good fellow did not hesitate to take Dr. Pangloss in and have him treated at his own expense. In the course of the cure Pangloss lost only an eye and an ear.

## "NGU – Spreading Like Wildfire"

*Sexual Medicine Today*, May, 1979.

*According to a recent report, nongonococcal urethritis is, by far, the nation's most common venereal disease. Outnumbering gonorrhea by two or three to one, NGU has now reached epidemic proportions among the affluent white populations most often seen in private medical practice. It is thought that more than one disease organism might cause NGU; however, the bacteria Chlamydia trachomatis is thought to be the primary cause. NGU is often indistinguishable from gonorrhea on clinical examination, and is unresponsive to penicillin therapy. It can lead to serious complications for patient, partner, and offspring if ignored.*

Nongonococcal urethritis (NGU), a venereal disease found increasingly among middle-class teenagers and adults, is "spreading like wildfire," says Dr. Nicholas J. Fiumara, Director of the Massachusetts Division of Communicable Diseases.

NGU is now the number one venereal disease at 22 Massachusetts hospital clinics. And in England, NGU cases in men alone exceed the number of gonorrhea cases in both sexes.

About 600,000 U.S. males will contract NGU this year, according to Paul J. Wiesner, Director of the Venereal Disease Division of the Center for Disease Control in Atlanta. An equal number of men will get gonorrhea, he said, with a total number of gonorrhea cases for men and women this year of 1 million, about the same as last year. Dr. Wiesner had no figure for NGU incidence in women because of the extreme difficulty of diagnosis. At VD clinics, however, NGU has generally pulled ahead of gonorrhea, with 55% of urethritis cases being NGU, the rest gonorrhea.

NGU "cannot be dismissed as a trivial problem," says Dr. Fiumara, since it can lead to systematic complications, including inflammation of the pelvic organs in women, leading to sterility; and eye infections and pneumonia in infants.

One of the primary reasons for the rapid spread and severe consequences of NGU has been the failure of some physicians to treat NGU as a venereal disease and make an attempt to

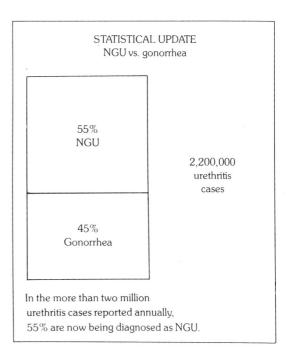

STATISTICAL UPDATE
NGU vs. gonorrhea

55% NGU

45% Gonorrhea

2,200,000 urethritis cases

In the more than two million urethritis cases reported annually, 55% are now being diagnosed as NGU.

### Breast Reconstruction

*After mastectomy* it is important for the wife to come to terms with the absence of a breast. To help her, the husband should encourage her not to wear a prosthesis (padded bra) during intercourse. However, the husband should not press the issue if the wife is very reluctant.

Reconstructive breast surgery is an option increasingly sought. At this writing, the technique is relatively new; there is also some evidence that the implants may cause or mask new tumors. Thus, there are contraindications to the procedure which should be considered. Desire for breast reconstruction is strongest in the period immediately following the mastectomy, and with a good adjustment diminishes sharply or disappears

---

treat the sexual partners of their patients as well as the patients.

Summed up Dr. Oriel: "It really is important to get rid of the idea that nongonococcal urethritis is just a matter of a patient getting a drip. Beyond that patient is his contact who is in line for pelvic inflammatory disease, and beyond her is a baby at risk."

---

### Breast Cancer -- the Dilemma of Diagnosis

*Medical technology is a mixed blessing. Sometimes a "cure" brings on problems worse than the original disease. The first of the following articles describes how the X-ray technique for detecting breast tumors (mammography), may actually cause the disease it is testing for. The second of the two readings describes a newer technique, which, although less accurate than mammography, is absolutely safe because it measures radiation produced by the body itself.*

*Mammogram Muddle* More than 250,000 women 35 years old and older have taken part over the past three years in a breast-cancer detection program conducted by the American Cancer Society and the National Cancer Institute. Because any cancerous tumors they may have are detected early, say the sponsors, these women presumably will have a lower-than-average rate of mortality from breast cancer, which will kill some 32,000 in the U.S. this year. Last week the screening program became the center of a major medical storm stirred by a group of doctors who warned that X-rays used in

the screening might actually increase the risk of breast cancer.

*Low Dose.* Besides having her breasts examined manually and photographed by a heat-sensitive technique called thermography, every participant in the screening program is annually subjected to mammography, or breast X-rays. Although only an extremely low dose of radiation is required, a team of scientists under the leadership of Dr. Lester Breslow, a U.C.L.A. epidemiologist, nonetheless argues that it may well be enough to cause cancer. Mammography, Breslow insists, is "a striking example of a situation where the very disease may be caused by the technology."

As evidence, Breslow cited a seven-year breast-cancer detection program, involving 62,000 women, undertaken in the 1960s by New York's Health Insurance Plan (H.I.P.). Analysis of the H.I.P. statistics showed that while mammography was of significant value in women over 50, the screening program did not reduce the mortality rate in those under that age. Breslow also noted studies showing increased breast-cancer rates among women exposed to higher radiation levels — those subjected to X-rays in treatment of tuberculosis, patients receiving radiotherapy for acute breast infection, and survivors of A-blasts in Japan. Extrapolating from these data, he concluded that "there is no absolutely safe dose" for X-rays and urged prompt discontinuation of mammography in routine screening of women under 50.

To allay fears of women alerted by press accounts of Breslow's criticism, the National Cancer Institute (NCI) hastily called a meeting in Bethesda, Md., last week. The directors of the screening program noted that mammography techniques have improved considerably since the H.I.P. study began 12-1/2 years ago and that completely as time passes. It is recommended that the recent mastectomy patient seeking breast reconstruction be encouraged to wait at least one year, to allow time to help her integrate her loss into her psychological functioning. Counseling for the woman may also be suggested. If at the end of the year the woman still avidly desires breast reconstruction, then of course her decision should be respected and proper arrangements should be made. If she has begun to vacillate, she should be encouraged to wait another year.

from: Medical Aspects of Human Sexuality, October, 1978.

---

the radiation doses now used have been reduced to about a third of their old level. More important, they said that about two-thirds of the cases detected were in an early, curable stage – and only about half these cancers could have been detected without X-rays. Said Dr. Philip Strax, director of the New York detection center: "The real risk is in not doing mammography." Added Dr. Barbara Ward of Boise, Idaho: "These reports are doing more damage than good by scaring women away."

Whether mass mammography will continue is to be decided in the next weeks, after further study by the National Cancer Institute that will include a poll of women Government workers in Bethesda. Asked how he would advise a patient if he were still in medical practice, Dr. Guy R. Newell, NCI's deputy director, said that he would have no hesitation recommending mammography for any woman over 50. "For a woman under 50," he added, "I would tell her that there is a risk attached to the X-ray technique, a small risk that she might get breast cancer 15 to 30 years from now. But I would also state that by then there is a good chance there will be better treatment and a possible cure."

*Time, The Weekly News Magazine,* copyright © August, 1976, Time Inc. Reprinted by permission.

---

***Tuning in to Breast Tumors***   "Did I understand that you cooked my breast with microwaves?" the woman angrily asked Dr. Norman Sadowsky, chief radiologist at Boston's Faulkner Hospital. Sadowsky reassured her that he had not. Yet her concern is typical of the initial response to the hospital's breast-cancer detection program. To help in the all-important early discovery of a disease that has reached epidemic levels in the U.S.

(90,000 cases a year), Faulkner radiologists are using microwaves to spot breast cancers.

Microwaves, though they are being employed for everything from sending telephone messages to cooking steaks, would seem to be a highly unlikely medical tool. Like other electromagnetic radiation – notably X-rays – they damage tissue at high enough energies. But the Faulkner microwaves are perfectly safe. Reason: the radiation involved is emitted not by the detector, as in conventional breast X-rays (mammography), but by the body itself.

The idea comes from M.I.T. Astrophysicist Alan Barrett, who decided that the same electronic wizardry that was enabling him to tune in to microwaves from free-floating molecules in interstellar space could have a down-to-earth application. If they were reduced in size, he reasoned, the sensitive antennas could even pick up the weak microwave (or heat) emissions from a tumor.

Because of the rapid rate of growth and increased blood supply, a tumor is hotter than normal tissue and hence gives off more radiant energy. Thermography, or heat scanning, concentrates on looking for infra-red radiation to find tumors. But such waves are rapidly absorbed by bodily tissue, thus tumors that lie any distance below the skin's surface cannot be readily picked up by infra-red sensors. By contrast, microwaves – which are much longer and more penetrating – can locate tumors up to 10 cm. (4 in.) below the surface.

Not much larger than a stethoscope and used somewhat like it, the little antenna built by Barrett and an M.I.T. colleague, Philip Myers, is placed against nine different sites on the breast and held at each for about 10 seconds. If one spot turns out to be significantly hotter than a comparable area on the other breast, the super-

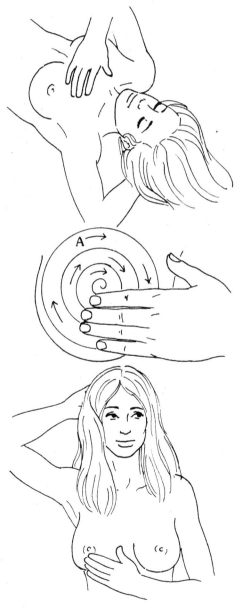

**After the shower, do a more thorough check.**
*Follow these simple steps*

**1**  Lie down. Put one hand behind your head. With the other hand, fingers flattened, gently feel your breast. Press ever so lightly.
*Now examine the other breast.*

**2**  This illustration shows you how to check each breast. Begin where you see the A and follow the arrows, feeling gently for a lump or thickening.
*Remember to feel all parts of each breast.*

**3**  Now repeat the same procedure sitting up, with the hand still behind your head.

*How to Examine Your Breasts,* © 1971, American Cancer Society, Inc., New York, Reprinted by permission.

vising radiologist is alerted and can make other checks for a tumor, including X-rays.

About 70% accurate, the gadget is admittedly less precise than mammography (90%) and only on a par statistically with infra-red thermography. But since there is no radiation risk and no need for a skilled X-ray interpreter to make an initial judgment, Sadowsky points out, the microwave detector could at the very least be used for pre-screening women – especially those under 35 who are ordinarily not encouraged to have mammograms unless they have a family history of breast cancer or symptoms of the disease.

*Time, The Weekly News Magazine*, Copyright © June 1977, Time Inc. Reprinted by permission.

## A Breast Check

*So Simple... So Important*

Bathing. Showering. Your moment to take care of yourself. Time to begin your breast examination.

Your fingers slide easily. As you wash you can do a simple check that will require practically no time. Examine your breasts. Keep your fingers flat and touch *every* part of each breast. Feel gently for a lump or thickening. The fact that your skin is slippery makes it easy.

Why should you do this? It can save your life. After all, it's what you don't know that can hurt you.

## Facts on Prostate Cancer

Here are the facts about cancer of the prostate – signs and symptoms, progress in diagnosis and treatment, prognosis and hope for the future.

Next to lung cancer, prostatic cancer has the highest incidence of any form of male cancer.

About 57,000 new cases are diagnosed in the United States each year, and more than 20,000 men die of the disease annually. The risk of developing cancer of the prostate increases with age. It causes few deaths under 40. But in the age group 55 to 74 it becomes the third highest cause of male cancer deaths, and after the age of 75 it is the second greatest cause.

***The Function Of The Prostate***   The prostate is a male genital gland about the size of a chestnut. It lies just below the urinary bladder and surrounds the first inch of the urethra, the canal that carries urine from the bladder (see sketch). The secretion of the prostate provides part of the fluid for ejaculation.

***Tumors In The Prostate Gland***   The commonest tumors found in the prostate gland are

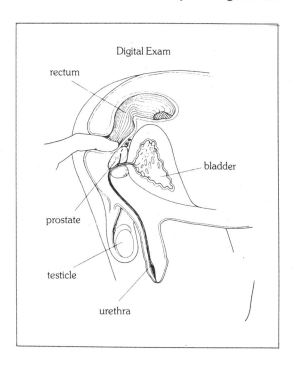

Digital Exam

rectum

bladder

prostate

testicle

urethra

not malignant. The most common tumor in this area is called benign prostatic hypertrophy, which causes enlargement of the gland. More than 50 percent of men in the United States over 50 years of age have some degree of prostatic hypertrophy. At times this enlargement obstructs the urethra and interferes with urination and makes it difficult to empty the bladder.

**Prostate Cancer Risk Factors**   The typical prostatic cancer patient is aged 55 or older. The incidence rate increases with aging. In the United States, both incidence and death rates of prostatic cancer are considerably higher among black men than white. The disease also appears to occur more frequently among married men than among single men. The American Cancer Society and the National Prostatic Cancer Project of the National Institutes of Health are supporting research to identify other high risk factors that might exist.

**Signs and Symptoms**   The signs and symptoms of prostatic cancer include a variety of urinary difficulties:

- Weak or interrupted flow of urine
- Inability to urinate or difficulty in starting urination
- Need to urinate frequently, especially at night
- Blood in the urine
- Urine flow that is not easily stopped
- Painful or burning urination
- Continuing pain in lower back, pelvis or upper thighs.

It must be emphasized that these signs and symptoms are more likely to indicate prostatic enlargement, or other conditions, rather than cancer – but such signs and symptoms should never be ignored.

**Diagnosis Of Prostatic Cancer**   The initial step in diagnosing this condition is palpation, or digital examination of the gland through the rectum. By palpation, the physician can feel an irregular or unusually firm area that may indicate a tumor. Fortunately, almost all prostatic cancers begin in the part of the prostate that can be felt by rectal examination (see sketch).

If the physician finds a suspicious area, he will perform a battery of tests. These tests usually include X-ray, urine and blood analyses.

The only way to determine conclusively if a tumor is malignant is by biopsy, which is the surgical removal of a small piece of tissue from the suspected growth for microscopic examination.

In some cases, prostatic cancers go undiagnosed, or they are diagnosed as benign prostatic hypertrophy. Most of these tumors are in elderly men, and progress so slowly that no signs or symptoms are noticed.

**Treatment**   Depending on the state of the cancer and on the patient's age, treatment will include one or more of the following therapies:

**Surgery**   A cancer that is completely confined to the prostate can usually be successfully treated by surgical removal of the gland (total prostatectomy). This usually results in impotence and, in 5-15 percent of cases it results in incontinence.

**Hormone Treatment**   If the cancer has spread, it can often be checked for long periods of time by controlling the body's supply of male hormone which stimulates the growth of prostatic cancer.

This is done by surgical removal of the testes (orchiectomy) or injections of female hormone to suppress the manufacture of male hormone. Sometimes a form of cortisone is used to suppress the adrenal glands which also contribute to the body's supply of male hormone. Although hormone therapy may also cause impotence, some hormones now are controlling the disease effectively while preserving sexual function.

*Radiation Therapy*  The basic principle of radiation therapy is to bombard a cancer with rays at doses which damage or destroy the cancer yet produce only minimum damage to surrounding tissues. When radiation is used to treat prostatic cancer, it is administered either externally or internally, depending on the stage and characteristics of the growth.

A recent study of 405 patients treated only with external radiation therapy for cancer confined to the prostate showed a five-year survival rate of 72 percent, and a ten-year survival rate of 44 percent.

When internal radiation is the treatment of choice, tiny pellets of radioactive isotopes are inserted into the prostate while the patient is anesthetized. The pellets, too small to cause discomfort, give off their curative rays for about a year. By then they have become inert and can safely remain in place for the rest of the patient's life. Sexual potency is unaffected. In many cases, radioactive implants have proved effective in decreasing the size of the tumor and greatly relieving pain.

Skin reactions, nausea, vomiting, a feeling of tiredness can be side effects of radiation. Rest and good nutrition help the body recover more quickly.

*Chemotherapy*  Chemotherapy may be used alone, or in combination with surgery or radiation, to cure some cancers, to retard spread of the tumor, or reduce patient discomfort.

The special drugs used in chemotherapy produce more extensive injury to cancer cells than to normal cells and the physician must maintain a delicate balance between dose and frequency by giving enough chemotherapy to kill cancer cells without destroying too many healthy ones. Chemotherapeutic drugs work in several different ways but they usually interfere with cell division or growth. Rapidly growing cells, both normal and cancer, are most vulnerable to chemotherapeutic drugs.

Several drugs now being used, singly or in combination, are proving effective in relieving many of the painful symptoms of advanced prostatic cancer. Drugs in use are 5-FU (5-fluorouracil) and Cytoxan, two potent antifolic medications, and Estracyt, a derivative of nitrogen mustard. In addition, six other chemicals of possible value are being tested under the direction of the National Prostatic Cancer program in a number of cancer centers. Patients being given chemotherapy for prostatic cancer are usually hospitalized during the early stages of treatment.

During treatment, there are certain common side effects. These include nausea and vomiting; diarrhea; hair loss; anemia; reduced blood-clotting ability, susceptibility to infections, and mouth sores. Individuals tolerate drugs differently and when treatment is stopped, side effects disappear; hair grows back, for example, or anemia is corrected. Any unexpected side effect should be reported to the physician.

*Prognosis*  More than half of all prostatic cancers are discovered while still localized within the general region of the prostate. Recent studies show that about 68 percent of patients whose tumors are diagnosed at that stage are alive five years after treatment.

For all stages of prostatic cancer combined, including early and advanced, the five-year survival rate is 56 percent. And an encouraging fact is that survival rates have gradually increased since 1940.

*Hope For The Future*    The real hope for the future is in earlier detection. Cancer specialists all over the world are working to improve diagnostic techniques, to learn more about the nature of "early" or "minimal" cancer, to develop more effective combinations of treatments and better drugs with lowered toxicity, to activate the body's own immune system.

The public and medical profession must be alerted to the need for earlier detection by better identification of those men at high risk of developing prostatic cancer.

*How To Help Protect Against Cancer Of The Prostate*    Every man over 40 should have a rectal exam as part of his regular physical checkup. Be alert to changes such as urinary difficulties, continuing pain in lower back, pelvis or upper thighs and if any occur, see your physician. The key to saving lives from cancer of the prostate is early detection and treatment.

*Facts on Prostate Cancer* Copyright © American Cancer Society, Inc. New York. Reprinted by permission.

# Unit 4

---

# The Sexual Person

# Learning to be Sexual:
# Sex and Sex Roles

8

*and women*

All men are created equal.

---

Each of us is born with an unorganized array of sensations, impulses, and possibilities. Then, immediately after birth, someone looks at our genitals and pronounces us "Boy" or "Girl" – a pronouncement that directs and limits those sensations and impulses and possibilities throughout the rests of our lives. The crucial decision that determines our destiny rests entirely on whether we have a penis or vagina. It is the basis for a lifetime of responses – made both by us and to us. Yet occasionally the decision is erroneous. A boy with an under-developed penis and testicles that have not descended into the scrotum may be mistakenly identified as a large "girl." A girl with an enlarged, penis-like clitoris may be labeled a "boy." Such individuals often assume the psychological and emotional traits associated with the sex to which they have erroneously been assigned.

## Gender Identity

It is difficult to analyze the relationship between biology and personality, for learning begins immediately at birth. There is evidence, however, that infant females are more sensitive to pain and to sudden changes of environment, while infant males are more active in gross motor movement. The influence of biology is apparently indirect. Although it does not determine behavior, it predisposes a male or female to certain responses.

The learning that directs these responses begins immediately after birth. In our culture, infant girls are usually held more gently and treated more tenderly than are boys, who are ordinarily subjected to rougher forms of play. By the time children are three, they have already learned what kinds of behavior are considered appropriate for their own sex.

## Learning Sex Roles

Children learn their sex roles by *identifying* with the parenting adult of their own sex, whose movements, gestures, actions, and emotions they observe and imitate. They may identify either personally or positionally. In *personal identification*, children identify with their role model because of love and affection. They apparently feel that if they were like the loved adult, in a sense they would have this person with them all the time. Thus, they would love themselves as much as they do the admired person.

Conversely, *positional identification* is based not on love and empathy but on fantasy projections. The child wants to be in the adult's position, and apparently believes that by acting like the adult, he or she will have that person's power. Positional identification is usually a response to the lack of parental warmth and affection but may also result from oedipal desires. ("My mother or father will love *me* instead of *you*.") Positional identification often causes individuals to be rigid and unspontaneous in their later sex roles. Most often, children identify both personally and positionally, identifying positionally to the degree that they fail to identify personally.

In addition to identifying, children also learn their proper sex role by *complementing* the parenting adult of the opposite sex. Children usually respond to the expectations of both parenting adults, seeking approval and love through their own behavior. As single-parent households become more common in our society, however, complementing is obviously becoming less accessible as a means of learning sex roles.

## The Learning Process

Many parents are not aware that their words and

**Fascinating Womanhood**

A good definition of Feminine Dependency is *a woman's need for masculine care and protection*. Women were designed to be wives, mothers and homemakers and therefore in need of masculine help to make their way through life. The men were assigned to fill this need for women by serving as their guide, protector and provider. Feminine dependency is very attractive to men.

Do not think that protecting a dependent woman is an imposition on a man. *One of the most pleasant sensations a real man can experience is his consciousness of the power to give his manly care and protection. Rob him of this sensation of superior strength and ability and you rob him of his manliness.* It is a delight to him to protect and shelter a dependent woman. The bigger, manlier and more sensible a man is, the more he seems to be attracted by this quality.

Helen Andelin

---

actions contribute to their children's socialization. Although parents may recognize that they respond differently to sons and daughters, they usually have a ready explanation – there are "natural" differences in the temperament and behavior of girls and boys. Parents may also believe that they adjust their responses to each particular child's personality. In an every-day living situation that involves changing diapers, feeding babies, stopping fights, and playing with dolls or with cars, it is difficult for the harassed parents to perceive that their own actions may be largely responsible for the differences they attribute to nature.

Children are socialized in sex roles through four very subtle processes: manipulation, channeling, verbal appellation and activity exposure (Oakley, 1972).

Parents *manipulate* their children from infancy onward. They treat a daughter gently, tell her she is pretty, and advise her that nice girls don't fight. They treat a son roughly, tell him he is strong, and advise him that big boys don't cry. Eventually children accept the parental view of themselves as being integral parts of their personalities.

Children are *channeled* by directing their attention to specific objects. Toys, for example, are sex differentiated. Dolls are considered appropriate for girls, guns for boys. Such toys represent pleasurable "rehearsals" for adult life. (Girls grow up to be mothers, boys grow up to be soldiers.)

*Verbal appellations* are also important in the socialization process. Girls are "sweet," boys are not. Boys are "strong," but girls are not. Different words are often used in describing the same behavior. A boy who pushes others may be described as "active," while a girl who does so is usually called "aggressive."

The *activity exposure* of boys and girls differs widely. Although both are usually exposed to feminine activities early in life, boys are discouraged from imitating their mothers, while girls are encouraged to be "mother's little helper." In some homes, even the chores children do are categorized according to sex. Girls may wash dishes, make beds, and set the table, with boys assigned to carry out trash, rake the yard, and sweep the walk. (The boy's domestic chores take him outside the house, the girl's keep her in it – another rehearsal for traditional adult life.)

For young children, the visible and behavioral aspects of sex identity are most important. By the time they are two, children firmly know which sex they are. They rarely relate this identity to the possession of a penis or a vagina, but know they are a boy or a girl because of the way others treat them. They also know that, in general, people treat boys and girls differently and that boys and girls dress differently. Only when they reach five or so do children begin to understand that what really identifies a boy is a penis and that what really identifies a girl is a vagina. (Bardwick, 1971).

**Learning "Appropriate" Behavior**

The activities considered "appropriate" for males and for females vary in different cultures, and per se do not define a person as a "man" or a "woman." A man in our society is no less male if he does housework, likes to knit, and cooks. A woman is no less a female if she is a banker, plays poker, and builds a table.

It is important for children to learn that, although they have a free choice of activities in today's world, their gender identity is not optional. A child who has a penis is a boy; one who has a vagina is a girl. A boy may engage in activities that are traditionally assigned to women — sewing, playing with dolls, cooking — but must maintain his gender identity as a boy. A girl may also engage in any activity she likes, but must know that she is a girl. Sex-role activities depend on the culture, but gender identity is determined by biology.

Until the child reaches three or four, parental expectations of proper behavior are generally related to age rather than sex. Parents usually think in terms of what is appropriate for a three-month-old infant, not what is appropriate for a three-month-old girl or boy. Yet parents also respond to their infants with subtle differences, according to the child's sex. Infant girls are touched more frequently by their mothers. Mothers breast-feed their daughters significantly more than they do sons (Goldberg and Lewis, 1969) perhaps fearful of the erotic sensations accompanying breast feeding, leading to incestuous feelings in the case of male infants. Unlike girls, boys receive little tenderness on which to build their own gentleness in later years.

By the time children are three or four, tasks and responses are no longer related to age but are based on sex. This presents particular problems for little boys. Because they have little contact with their fathers, boys generally identify with an abstract idea of what it is to be a man. They may gain their ideas from television stereotypes. Even more significantly, they learn about masculinity from mothers and women teachers, who may instill masculine values in boys by telling them not to act like girls or sissies.

In our society, being masculine is often defined in terms of being *not* like a girl. Bardwick *(1971)* has found that human traits such as compassion and tenderness become polarized into sex-linked

traits that are identified as being "female," and boys are discouraged from expressing these aspects of their personalities. Boys seem to have a difficult time developing masculine identity. They turn toward their peers and older boys for positive role models, pooling anxieties and misinformation, and over-emphasizing physical strength and aggression. (Bardwick, 1971).

Girls, in contrast, have a positive role model. If they imitate what their mothers are doing, they know they are being feminine. In general, parents do not focus as much attention on making girls "feminine" as they do making boys "masculine." Until they reach the teen years, girls are not expected to behave in an exclusively

Better a Socrates dissatisfied than a pig satisfied.

John Stuart Mill

feminine manner.

As children emerge from infancy, both sexes exhibit dependent behavior, which in our culture is considered acceptable for females but not for males. Because girls are not required to be independent, parents can merely support a continuation of dependency. At the same time that she is permitted to be competitive and achievement-oriented, a girl is also learning to become passive. But female passivity is in terms of a male model of physical activity and aggression. A girl does not hit and does not play war games. She learns to be aggressive verbally, she learns interaction skills and actively mediates conflicts, and she learns maternal behavior that requires unbounded skill and activity.

Both boys and girls feel that there is a distinct and exclusive division in sex roles. But the division is not as rigid with young girls, who are free to engage in behaviors assigned to the opposite sex (although their brothers are not). Many girls, particularly those of the middle class, know that it is permissible to compete in sports and for leadership positions – activities that later in life will be defined as "masculine." (Girls may experience critical role conflict as adolescents, however, when they discover that achievement is adversely affecting their social relationships with boys.)

Because boys and girls are exposed to both male and female models while they are growing up, in theory they observe both *instrumental* (goal-directed) and *expressive* (affection-oriented) behaviors. But many parents experience the vague fear that if they allow boys to engage in expressive behaviors, their sons will become homosexual. Beneath this fear lies the cultural definition of a boy as a *not*-girl.

In a study by Van Gelder and Carmichael *(1975)*, this anxiety is revealed even among women who identify themselves as feminists.

These women felt it easier to free daughters from sex stereotypes than they do sons. They want sons to be both liberated *and* masculine (even though they themselves find the traditional masculine model oppressive). Only a few feminists have raised sons who have successfully escaped the male stereotype; most of the mothers feel that they lose the battle once their sons enter school, where stereotypes predominate.

Many of the feminists admitted that they find themselves actively discouraging "feminine" behavior in their sons. They do not, for example, allow young sons to wear lipstick or dresses when playing "dress up" with other children. They feel uncomfortable when sons imitate female body movements or mannerisms, or express a liking for frilly clothes or flowers. Feminists were also to be numbered among the many parents who insist that small boys ride a "boy's" bicycle (although the "girl's" model is much easier to get on and off when you are learning, and it is less likely to injure genitals in a fall).

Paradoxically, feminists do not have similar anxieties when daughters engage in behaviors traditionally considered "masculine." Their daughters are encouraged to play with toy trucks and to learn carpentry skills, and the fear that they may become lesbian apparently does not arise.

Mussen's investigations *(1961, 1962)* indicate that boys are 20 percent more likely than are girls to maintain traditional sex-role behavior in later life. Girls may be more flexible in later years because they have already participated in male behaviors earlier, or because they are drawn to the rewards and status that accrue to "male" activities.

The fear that many men have of displaying the expressive traits associated with women may be evidence of an identity anxiety based on a simple

## Amoretti

My love is like to ice, and I to fire,
How comes it then that this her cold so great
Is not dissolv'd through my so hot desire,
But harder grows the more I her entreat?
Or how comes it that my exceeding heat
Is not allayed by her heart frozen cold,
But that I burn much more in boiling sweat,
And feel my flames augmented manifold?

What more miraculous thing may be told,
That fire, which all things melts, should harden ice,
And ice, which is congealed with senseless cold,
Should kindle fire by wonderful device?
Such is the power of love in gentle mind,
That it can alter all the course of kind.

Edmund Spenser

and relatively recent historical phenomenon. Until the present century, most boys grew up with frequent contact with their fathers or other men, working on farms or in trades as apprentices. Industrialization did not alter this pattern significantly – many children worked in factories, often alongside other family members. Eventually, however, compulsory schooling and the abolition of child labor removed the boys from close contact with males, placing them under the supervision of teachers who are usually women.

As changing sex-role patterns allow men to take on greater responsibilities in child rearing

and homemaking, it is possible that boys will not experience as much difficulty in creating a masculine identity. The emerging family structure, although unlike that of earlier times, may strengthen the identification process among males to a considerable degree.

### Adolescence

Adolescence, a major turning point for both boys and girls, signifies that society recognizes them as sexual beings. (Although they may have had sexual play during earlier years, adults usually

prefer to ignore this fact.) With adolescence, the quality of sexual experience changes: young people become unambiguously erotic, but at the same time break abruptly with previous types of sex play. During this period (discussed more specifically in the following chapter), boys become more aggressive in their sexual behavior, while girls give the appearance of being reticent. Traditionally, boys are expected to be sexually active and girls are expected to be virgins (a situation that has never been based on logic). Nevertheless, it is in adolescence that sexuality is decisively formed.

Adolescence is also a period of diminishing parental influence, particularly for boys. Boys tend to be more combative and rebellious than girls, who until recently have been more receptive to the standards set by parents. Parents of girls are usually concerned with limiting the occasions for sexual experience. In order for a girl to have extensive experience, she usually has to either deceive or reject her parents.

Boys, beginning very early, are expected to be active, aggressive, athletic, and independent. With adolescence, "making it" with a girl becomes an additional symbol of masculinity. Feelings of tenderness and love are often abandoned or repressed in the pursuit of sexual conquests. In a sense, adolescent boys are as much victims of their roles as are the girls they seek. Young males who remain sensitive to their own human needs and to those of their girlfriends may be ridiculed by their more stereotypical peers as lacking "masculinity."

Adolescence is no less complex for girls. Upon reaching puberty, they are expected to retreat from competitive sports, to become followers rather than leaders, and to be unequivocally "feminine." In a girl's adolescent development, the emphasis is on acquiring social skills rather then mastery skills. The latter — mechanics, building, debate, mathematics, leadership – suddenly become reserved for males. As a result of this shift, girls are usually more mature than boys in social relationships. They learn interpersonal skills: listening, caring, loving. Traditionally, the girl's future identity is dependent on marrying and having children; with marriage as the major goal, she must make herself attractive without being overtly sexual. Often, however, women have created identities for themselves that are totally dependent on a man's love or approval (a situation that is not common among men).

For adolescents of both sexes, the cost of not meeting sex-role expectations is great. There is confusion and considerable peer pressure – and young people who fail to exhibit the expected behaviors may face rejection and be mislabeled as "sisses" or "queers," or as "tomboys" or "dykes."

## Traditional Adult Sex Roles

Adolescence is the training ground for adult identity. The man's world is instrumental, conquering, non-emotional. The woman's world is expressive, dependent, and passive. Both sexes have much the same motivations, although these may be expressed in different ways.

To the male, particularly those who believe in the male mystique, heterosexual success is an important element of his personality. He may pride himself on sexual prowess. The word *potency* is an indication that this attitude has a long history – it is derived from the Latin term for "being able." Significantly, women are not described in terms of being "potent." They are almost always "able" to have sexual intercourse (although not necessarily orgasmically), while a man's ability to perform is not so consistent.

Occupational success is a second major element in a man's identity, and striving to attain it affects relationships with others. To be successful, for example, he must usually compete with others and render them *unsuccessful*. For this reason, men are often unable to form close and open relationships with other men after leaving school. Some males are able to escape the competitive aspects of work and to find genuine enjoyment in their occupations; other (perhaps most) men escape the competitiveness inherent in work by means of routine jobs that offer little involvement for their egos.

Both sexual success and occupational success are often subject to great variation throughout a lifetime. Men who build their self-worth around these two values are likely to experience disap-

pointments at various periods. Aging, for example, obviously affects a man's sexual activity. Sexual potency usually declines with age, and most men make love less often than they did in earlier years. If they have based their identity and self-esteem on sexual performances instead of satisfaction, with frequency of intercourse the major goal, sexual anxieties will increase with age. They find themselves unable to achieve the results that made them feel "manly" in youth, yet their standard of performance remains that of a young Don Juan. Falling short of this unrealistic goal, they feel inadequate and depressed. They may withdraw from their wives both physically and emotionally in the belief that their spouses share their own self-expectations.

Despite the myth that anyone who is capable can succeed by really trying, occupational success often lies beyond an individual's control. The nature of the economy, for example, is cyclical, and employment is often determined by outside influences. When recessions and depressions occur, people may lose their jobs and, although the forces causing unemployment are usually remote, they ask themselves: Why me? What did I do wrong? Was I not good enough?

There is a high level of unemployment even in times of relative prosperity, particularly among the young, minorities, and women. Teenage unemployment averages 13.5 percent in times of prosperity, for example; it averaged 20 percent during the recession of 1973, with unemployment among minorities rising to 40 percent.

For a young man leaving high school or college, the economic uncertainties affect his identity as a male, often causing stress and anxiety. Having spent several years preparing for work, he is inexperienced but eager. He has been looking forward to proving himself a "man" and to being independent, with a job. But unemployment hits his age group hard, and it hits at a time when he is seeking to establish an important part of his masculine identity. The inability to find a job is often taken as personal failure.

***Traditional Female Sex Roles***   Although a woman usually works before she marries or has children, her identity as she leaves adolescence traditionally revolves around the expectations of becoming a wife and mother. Until recently, sterility was considered the only acceptable reason for the failure of a woman to bear children, and women with children were not expected to

*Smile, a 1975 film by Michael Ritchie, satirized the institution of the beauty contest (as well as small town America). Perhaps because it cut too deeply, the film never gained much popularity. Its title, however, seems apropos this photograph.*

*At the climax of the recent Miss Universe contest, when photographers rushed to catch the image of the victorious Miss Venezuela, the stage fell in. Seeming to respond more to their training as beauty queens than to the immediate danger, the contestants plunged to the floor with impeccable smiles.*

I have always been convinced that if a woman once made up her mind to marry a man, nothing but instant flight could save him.

W. Somerset Maugham

work outside the home. Although attitudes are changing, the feeling that work is incompatible with a woman's roles as wife and mother still prevails.

As a consequence of traditional role expectations, many women live vicariously, finding identity only through husband and children. The roles of wife and mother can provide a woman with great satisfaction, but carried to excess they can also be used to disguise unsatisfactory relationships and a lack of intimacy. Some women become the "perfect" wife and mother, the slave who is imposed on by other members of the family. Unlike women who have successfully integrated the roles of wife and mother into the rest of their lives, who live first of all as human beings, the "perfect little woman" is often disengaged from her own emotions.

Women are trained from childhood onward to look forward to becoming mothers. The prevalent method of instilling such feelings – providing dolls for "little mothers" – is perhaps the worst of all possible preparations. Flesh-and-blood infants and children are loud, messy, argumentative, and in many other ways exceedingly unlike dolls. Children can bring great fulfillment to a mother, but they also bring frustration, anger, helplessness, and confusion. A woman who is not prepared with the expectation of being angry with her children and sometimes yelling at them will feel guilty. (This is *not* how mothers are supposed to feel, ever.) The desire to carry out her role expectations as a mother may lead a woman to repress genuine feelings of anger or helplessness. Those who modify the traditional image, who do not attempt to function only as a full-time mother but find opportunities to take part in other activities, are more likely to find fulfillment.

When children leave home, an important element of a woman's identity is lost. She must redefine herself. Many marriages are subjected to a major crisis at this point, for the presence of children has served to conceal the fact that their parents have been enduring a relationship that is not basically satisfactory either to one or both of them. Divorces are a rather common consequence of the dispersal of children, with women often re-entering the job market as a means of finding new identities.

As women enter middle age, the feminine beauty that has been an important part of their sex role since childhood begins to fade. Although standards of beauty vary throughout history, in our current culture, youth is one of its essential aspects. Being attractive is the hallmark of being feminine, as potency is the symbol of masculinity; the woman who views sagging cheeks and jowls in the mirror faces a crisis similar to that experienced by the man whose sexual prowess is waning.

**Sex Roles and Sexual Expression**

People learn to express themselves sexually by means of sex roles, which involve specific expectations. Among past generations, for example, men usually had far more sexual experience than did women, because society expected the two sexes to behave differently in sexual matters. Sex roles form the general outlines of each individual's sexuality, and are more influential than is biology in establishing sexual behavior, frequency, and drive.

The basic pattern of an individual's sex role is developed by the end of adolescence. Traditionally, these roles divide the world neatly into categories. The human traits of love, aggression, tenderness, affection, assertiveness, compassion, and dominance are rigidly assessed as being either "male" or "female." Men are assigned instrumental traits, women the expressive ones. Because of these cultural definitions, the

## Cows, Pigs, Wars, and Witches

If I had knowledge only of the anatomy and cultural capacities of men and women, I would predict that women rather than men would be more likely to gain control over the technology of defense and aggression, and that if one sex were going to subordinate the other, it would be female over male. While I would be impressed with the physical dimorphism—the greater height, weight, and strength of the males—I would be even more impressed by something which the females have and which the males cannot get—namely, control over the birth, care, and feeding of babies. Women, in other words, control the nursery, and because they control the nursery, they can potentially modify any lifestyle that threatens them.

Marvin Harris

spectrum of possibilities are restricted for both sexes.

Men who like flowers may be labeled "feminine" and women who actively engage in sports may be called "masculine." But men and women vary as greatly among themselves as they do in relation to the opposite sex. Think of how you and friends of the same sex differ. You often prefer different colors, different foods, different books, different recreational activities – yet you may find someone of the opposite sex who shares your own preferences.

Even though sex roles do not tell us much about specific individuals, they partly determine our personalities by drawing broad general limits. They help direct our personal behavior and to provide us with appropriate ways of expressing sexual behavior.

Depending upon the individual, sex roles may be an integral part of personal identity or a superficial convenience. The significance of the sex role to any individual depends on the content of the role. Does it allow individual variation and expression? Does it fit the needs, temperament, and personality of the individual? And finally, does it allow the individual to find conplementary experiences outside the sex role? People are more than the total of their roles: they are integrated human beings. But if individuals have low self-esteem, they are likely to confuse role with self. Then their roles become rigid and inflexible; spontaneity disappears, leaving them with feelings that may seem hollow or alien.

The most likely candidates for involvement in sexual power games are people of low self-esteem, who need to demonstrate their masculinity or femininity for all to see. Their sexual behavior, psychologist Abraham Maslow (1942) has pointed out, is related less to sexual drive than it is to the need for self-esteem. The more secure individuals are in their identities, the less the need to dominate enters their sexual lives. It is the insecure people who, to assuage their fears, seek to dominate and control sexual relationships. Maslow observes that "hasty copulations" are not so much sexual affairs as "dominance affairs" or "insecurity affairs."

A crucial point in the traditional relationship between men and women involves power and dominance. Henry Kissinger, when Secretary of State, revealed the connection between sex and dominance very plainly. When asked how he accounted for his "success" with starlets and society beauties, he replied that power was the most effective aphrodisiac ever invented by *man* (italics added).

Maslow has also pointed out that psychologically healthy people can share love without making inflexible distinctions between their roles and their personalities. Neither partner assumes that the male must be aggressive, the female always passive; and both feel free to either initiate or receive love-making. Because activity and passivity have their own unique meanings, this kind of flexibility allows both partners to share a wide range of experiences.

### Toward New Sex Roles

Maslow's study, made more than thirty year ago, raised questions about whether sex roles result in our becoming *more* human, or *less*. Do traditional sex roles limit or expand our individual potential? Whatever the answer, it is obvious that new sex roles are evolving, providing a challenge to stereotypes.

The open questioning of traditional sex roles began in the 1960s, with the rise of the women's

### The Natural Superiority of Women

Since greater size and physical power are overt evidences of masculinity, boys are in most cultures encouraged to demonstrate their "superior" masculinity by indulging in games, sports, and other activities that are at the same time calculated to underscore the inferiority in power of the girls. And this is done at a time when the girls may be, at the same chronologic ages, larger in size and physically more powerful than the boys! Boys are encouraged to be tough and rough, to play with guns and other weapons of destruction, and to go in for sports that are "rugged." In addition, because boys are supposed to be able to endure more than girls, boys may be corporeally punished (and so unconsciously encouraged in the development of additional hostilities), whereas girls are usually punished by deprivation or by the assignment of unpleasant chores.

Ashley Montague

---

liberation movement, which asked whether there are alternatives for women other than roles as wife and mother. (Obviously there are, because millions of women have joined the work force; despite this, in the 1960s work was not considered an "acceptable" alternative to motherhood).

The questioning of tradition by women has, in turn, had enormous impact on men. Because sex roles operate reciprocally, the female rebellion affected the male sex role. Traditionally, for example, a man opens doors for a woman. It caused understandable consternation among men, when women for whom they tried to open doors suddenly snarled at them that they were perfectly capable of opening doors for themselves. Capability has never been the issue — rather, our sex roles had provided an established means of deciding who was going to enter doorways first. When such a pattern is destroyed, a new one must be developed.

Much of the change is occurring within the context of humanistic psychology, which stresses human potential and fulfillment as appropriate goals. The *humanness* of individuals is emphasized, rather than "maleness" or "femaleness." Paradoxically, however, the move away from sex-role stereotypes enables people to become more "male" or "female," in accordance with their biological drives. Sex differences are no longer concealed beneath stereotypical myths, and an essential sexuality may emerge. Men who once felt that sexual activity validates their maleness may no longer feel "compelled" to have intercourse with women they are not genuinely attracted to, and greater numbers of women may feel free to initiate sexual encounters instead of waiting for males to do so.

### New Directions for Women

The movement away from tradition may be rooted not in individuals so much as in the social environment. Sex roles, which reflect a compromise between social needs and individual needs, are reciprocal. As a society changes, sex roles and expectations also change. With the structural changes that have been made in the family and in work over the last several decades, former sources of fulfillment are declining. In the early part of the twentieth century, for example, the average woman had time-consuming house-

Advertising can become an extension of the "locker-room" effect . . . in which unrealistic goals are set for boys who know they can never fully meet those goals, fearing at the same time that most other men have achieved them. By presenting a consistent, unattainable myth of what every man should be, the advertiser hopes that the consumer will identify with the product that is associated with this image, settling for a vicarious realization of this standard. Men are therefore manipulated into purchasing (via desultory products) a myth that leaves them with ulcers if they attain it and defense mechanisms if they do not.

Warren Farrell, *The Liberated Man*

---

hold responsibilities, including doing the laundry and cleaning without powered equipment, processing and preserving foods, and caring for children. Today, housework is simplified by efficient equipment, foods are readily available and quickly prepared, and most families are smaller. The traditional roles of women no longer have the same content – indeed, in many respects they are lacking in any content at all. The movement away from traditional roles thus represents a search for new substance, reflecting the new reality of contemporary women.

The two main thrusts of the current search for new sex roles are concerned with equality and options. *Equality* is part of the American political tradition, but women have long realized that they have never been treated as equals. Women do not receive equal pay for equal work; they are seldom promoted to high levels but remain for the most part in clerical or secretarial positions. In addition to economic equality, women are demanding social equality. Rejecting roles of dependency, they want to be able to be assertive without being labeled as "castrating" (a sex-linked term for assertiveness), to be able to behave as they feel, instead of as a "woman" is traditionally supposed to act.

The emerging sex roles involve *options*, or a choice of acceptable alternatives. Traditionally, women have not had the option of seeking a career, because the only roles considered appropriate for females were those of wife and mother. Today, it is becoming less unusual for a woman to openly decide not to become a wife or mother at all, or to become a wife and mother *and* whatever else she wants to become. Effective contraception and the legalization of abortion have made motherhood a voluntary act, giving women choices they have not previously had. Women who are wives may prefer a more egalitarian marriage, with husbands sharing in household chores and child rearing (participation that has also been welcomed by men). Perhaps most of all, women don't want to feel guilty for selecting alternatives to the traditional roles. They want to feel it is appropriate and acceptable for them to make their own choices, instead of fulfilling a pattern that was established in times when our society was far different.

**New Directions for Men**

Sex roles are reciprocal. It is impossible for men not to be affected when women begin to challenge their own traditional sex roles. A man's first response to the idea of revising roles is often defensiveness. His traditional role, after all, has been one of dominance. His second response is usually confusion. New roles require new sets of rules – and no one yet knows what the rules will be. Meanwhile, the transition from old to new can cause anxiety in the male. What is he to do if a woman initiates a sexual encounter? What if he is unable to "perform"? If his wife takes a job, will this make him less of a "man"?

Because men seem to have more difficulty in developing their male identity, they cling to traditional sex roles more tenaciously. Nevertheless, change is occurring in several areas. First, men are attempting to relate to women not as sex objects, or even specifically as women, but as human beings. Within relationships – whether dating, living together, or marriage – men are seeking partnerships instead of dominance. The result is a wider scope of possible relationships.

Second, men are attempting to develop in themselves a new series of traits, including gentleness, tenderness, expressiveness, child-rearing capabilities, and others that have been tabooed in the past as being "feminine." They are seeking to become human beings first, then men.

Third, men are attempting to escape from the

traditional work-and-success ethic, which puts achievement and competition before all other things. Competition makes every other person a potential rival rather than a friend, and the isolation and repression of feelings accompanying competition are being closely examined. The overall result of the traditional male sex role seems to be a fundamental fear, which Joseph Heller has expressed vividly in *Something Happened:*

> I get the willies when I see closed doors. Even at work, where I am doing so well now, the sight of a closed door is sometimes enough to make me dread that something horrible is happening behind it. Something that is going to affect me adversely

...My hands may perspire, and my voice may come out strange. I wonder why.

In the office in which I work there are five people of whom I am afraid. Each of these five people is afraid of four people . . . for a total of twenty, and each of these twenty people is afraid of six people, making a total of one hundred and twenty people who are feared by at least one person. Each of these one hundred and twenty people is afraid of the other one hundred and nineteen.

Most of us like working here, even though we are afraid, and do not long to leave for jobs with other companies. We make money and have fun. We read books and go to plays. And somehow the time passes.

Changing traditional sex roles is not easy, because they are established so early in life. Self-evaluation is intimately linked to sex role, and a sense of adequacy is linked to sex-role performance as defined by parents and peers in childhood. ("You're a good boy/girl.") The sex role is so much a part of an individual's personality that it seems to be a part of "human nature"; hence, individuals sometimes defend the role as being "natural," even when it is dysfunctional or destructive. To threaten an individual's sex role is to threaten his or her sexual identity. "Such threats," writes Barbara Polk (1974), "are a major mechanism for psychologically locking people into traditional roles."

Obviously, the time to begin replacing traditional sex roles with more satisfying ones is in childhood. But even then it is difficult, not only because of peer pressure but also because parents have ambivalent attitudes about proper behavior. Parenting adults may retain many traditional behaviors, and often give their children mixed messages. Parents may tell a child that girls can be anything they want to be — yet the mother is at home doing dishes and cleaning house while the father is at work. Parents may

**Sexpionage**

With an international reputation as a ladies' man, the president seemed like an obvious target for a sex trap during a visit to Moscow. A number of beautiful women were introduced to him and they usually ended up in his bedroom where the hidden cameras filmed the proceedings. Towards the end of his visit the president was escorted to KGB headquarters where the films were played back to him as the prelude to blackmail. Dr.

Sukarno beamed as the movies unrolled. When the show was over and the lights came up, he asked astounded KGB officials if it would be possible to have copies of the film made to take home with him for public showing. He is reported to have said: "My people are going to be so proud of me!"

David Lewis

---

feel apprehensive if their sons play with dolls or if they ask if they can learn to sew. It will be many years before the traditional roles are supplanted or even appreciably altered, but they will not remain static as society changes.

And as sex roles change, so will sexual behavior.

## QUESTIONS

1. How are children socialized into their respective sex roles?
2. What is the relationship between sexuality and sex roles? What is the impact of sex roles on our sexual development?
3. Do traditional American sex roles polarize human traits into male/female traits? What are other possible ways of being male and female?
4. Compare and contrast traditional sex roles with non-traditional sex roles. What are the advantages of traditional sex roles? Non-traditional sex roles? How do you live your life?
5. If you were a member of the opposite sex, which of your personality traits would be encouraged and which discouraged? What would remain the same in your life and what would be different?

---

# Readings

### *Excerpt from* Feminine Personality and Conflict

J. Bardwick, Wadsworth Publishing, 1970

*Where do women's sex roles come from? Are they biologically rooted, socially learned, or both?*

It is fairly obvious that a woman's self-esteem and self-concept are more closely linked to the appearance and functioning of her body than is true of the man. Whereas masculinity is at least partially defined by success in marketplace achievements, femininity is largely defined by success in establishing and maintaining love relationships and by maternity. A woman's attractiveness is clearly instrumental in attracting men, and her self-evaluation as a woman will largely depend on her sexual and maternal success.

The menstrual cycle and pregnancy reinforce an awareness of internal reproductive functions. The obstetric and gynecological literature strongly supports the idea that women have a close psychological relationship to their reproductive system, which is a frequent site for the acting out of impulses, especially aggression and its derivatives, sex anxiety, and maternity-pregnancy fears. When we examine the dynamics of these psychosomatic behaviors, we find that they are closely linked to the level of the woman's self-esteem. There is, in women, a common psychological vulnerability that comes from low feelings of self-esteem, a strong and persistent need for respect from others in order to support self-esteem, and the fear of loss of love that could destroy self-esteem. A vulnerable sense of self-esteem – one that is dependent on appraisals from others – implies that there is no independent sense of self.

How can we understand this apparently curtailed development of independence in the female? I believe that the tendency of little girls to be less motorically impulsive, less physically aggressive, and less sexually active than little boys means that girls tend generally to get into less trouble than boys, tend not to engage in physical fighting, and tend not to masturbate. They are as a result less likely to perceive parents as people who thwart impulses. To the extent that girls are not separated from their parents as sources of support and nurturance, they are not forced to develop internal controls and an independent sense of self. In addition, girls can remain dependent and infantile longer than boys because the dependency, fears, and affection-seeking that are normal in early childhood for both sexes are defined as feminine in older children. Girls are, then, not pressed, by virtue of intense impulses, and by the culture's definition of "sissy" after the age of 2½, to become independent as early as boys. When the boy can no longer depend on continuous, nondemanding approval from his parents, he is pushed to develop internal, independent sources for good feeling about his self.

Unlike the boy, girls tend to continue in the affectionate, dependent relationships that are characteristic of all young children. More than boys, they will continue for an extended period of their lives to value the self as a function of reflected appraisals. This means, in a very pervasive and significant way, that unless something intervenes, the girl and then the woman will continue to have a great need for approval from others and that her behavior will be guided by a fear of rejection, or the fear of a loss of love. Although the prepubertal girl had a bisexual rearing in the sense that individual achievements, especially academic, were important resources for feelings of self-esteem, the emphasis changes at puberty. Our societal definition of successful

femininity requires interpersonal success, especially with males; and at puberty the pressure on the girl increases to be successful in heterosexual relations. For the boy there is a parallel pressure to achieve esteem through individual academic or occupational successes.

What I am suggesting is that young girls are more dependent on others for feelings of self-esteem than boys are and that this dependency is increased at puberty because of our definition of femininity and successful role performance.

From *Feminine Personality* and *Conflict* by J. Bardwick, E. Douvan, M. Horner, and D. Gutmann. Copyright 1970 by Wadsworth Publishing Company, Inc. Reprinted by permission of the publisher, Brooks/Cole Publishing Company, Monterey, California.

## On Male Liberation

Jack Sawyer, *Liberation Magazine*

Male liberation calls for men to free themselves of the sex-role stereotypes that limit their ability to be human. Sex-role stereotypes say that men should be dominant; achieving and enacting a dominant role in relations with others is often taken as an indicator of success. "Success," for a man, often involves influence over the lives of other persons. But success in achieving positions of dominance and influence is necessarily not open to every man, since dominance is relative and hence scarce by definition. Most men in fact fail to achieve the positions of dominance that sex-role stereotypes ideally call for. Stereotypes tend to identify such men as greater or lesser failures, and in extreme cases, men who fail to be dominant are the object of jokes, scorn, and sympathy from wives, peers, and society generally.

One avenue of dominance is potentially open to any man, however — dominance over a

Kent wanted Lois, Superman didn't – thus marking the
difference between a sissy and a man. A sissy wanted girls
who scorned him; a man scorned girls who wanted him.

Jules Feiffer, *The Great
Comic Book Heroes*

woman. As society generally teaches men they
should dominate, it teaches women they should
be submissive, and so men have the opportunity
to dominate women. More and more, however,
women are reacting against the ill effects of being
dominated. But the battle of women to be free
need not be a battle against men as oppressors.
The choice about whether men are the enemy is
up to men themselves.

Male liberation seeks to aid in destroying the
sex-role stereotypes that regard "being a man"
and "being a woman" as statuses that must be
achieved through proper behavior. People need
not take on restrictive roles to establish their sexual identity.

A major male sex-role restriction occurs
through the acceptance of a stereotypic view of
men's sexual relation to women. Whether or not
men consciously admire the Playboy image, they
are still influenced by the implicit sex-role demands to be thoroughly competent and self-
assured – in short, to be "manly." But since self-
assurance is part of the stereotype, men who
believe they fall short don't admit it, and each
can think he is the only one. Stereotypes limit
men's perception of women as well as of themselves. Men learn to be highly aware of a woman's body, face, clothes – and this interferes with
their ability to relate to her as a whole person.
Advertising and consumer orientations are
among the societal forces that both reflect and
encourage these sex stereotypes. Women spend
to makes themselves more "feminine," and men
are exhorted to buy cigarettes, clothes, and cars
to show their manliness.

The popular image of a successful man combines dominance both over women, in social relations, and over other men, in the occupational
world. But being a master has its burdens. It is
not really possible for two persons to have a free
relationship when one holds the balance of

power over the other. The more powerful person
can never be sure of full candor from the other,
though he may receive the kind of respect that
comes from dependence. Moreover, people who
have been dependent are coming to recognize
more clearly the potentialities of freedom, and it
is becoming harder for those who have enjoyed
dominance to maintain this position. Persons
bent on maintaining dominance are inhibited
from developing themselves. Part of the price
most men pay for being dominant in one situation is subscribing to a system in which they
themselves are subordinated in another situation. The alternative is a system in which men
share, among themselves and with women,
rather than strive for a dominant role.

In addition to the dehumanization of being (or
trying to be) a master, there is another severe, if
less noticed, restriction from conventional male
sex roles in the area of affection, play, and ex-
pressivity. Essentially, men are forbidden to play
and show emotion. This restriction is often not
even recognized as a limitation, because emotional behavior is so far outside the usual range
of male activity.

Men are breadwinners, and are defined first
and foremost by their performances in this area.
This is a serious business and results in an end
product – bringing home the bacon. The process
area of life – activities that are enjoyed for the
immediate satisfaction they bring – are not part
of the central definition of men's role. Yet the
failure of men to be aware of this potential part of
their lives leads them to be alienated from themselves and from others. Because men are not
permitted to play freely, or show affection, they
are prevented from really coming in touch with
their own emotions.

If men cannot play freely, neither can they
freely cry, be gentle, nor show weakness – because these are "feminine," not "masculine." But

The great question . . .
which I have not been able
to answer, despite my thirty
years of research into the
feminine soul, is "What does
a woman want?"

Sigmund Freud

---

a fuller concept of humanity recognizes that all men and women are potentially both strong and weak, both active and passive, and that these and other human characteristics are not the province of one sex.

The acceptance of sex-role stereotypes not only limits the individual but also has bad effects on society generally. The apparent attractions of a male sex role are strong, and many males are necessarily caught up with this image. Education from early years calls upon boys to be brave, not to cry, and to fight for what is theirs. The day when these were virtues, if it ever existed, is long past. The main effect now is to help sustain a system in which private "virtues" become public vices. Competitiveness helps promote exploitation of people all over the world, as men strive to achieve "success." If success requires competitive achievement, then an unlimited drive to acquire money, possessions, power, and prestige is only seeking to be successful.

The affairs of the world have always been run nearly exclusively by men, at all levels. It is not accidental that the ways that elements of society have related to each other has been disastrously competitive, to the point of oppressing large segments of the world's population. Most societies operate on authoritarian bases – in government, industry, education, religion, the family, and other institutions. It has been generally assumed that these are the only bases on which to operate, because those who have run the world have been reared to know no other. But women, being deprived of power, have also been more free of the role of dominator and oppressor; women have been denied the opportunity to become as competitive and ruthless as men.

In the increasing recognition of the right of women to participate equally in the affairs of the world, then, there is both a danger and a prom-

ise. The danger is that women might end up simply with an equal share of the action in the competitive, dehumanizing, exploitative system that men have created. The promise is that women and men might work together to create a system that provides equality to all and dominates no one. The women's liberation movement has stressed that women are looking for a better model for human behavior than has so far been created. Women are trying to become human, and men can do the same. Neither men nor women need be limited by sex-role stereotypes that define "appropriate" behavior. The present models for men and women fail to furnish adequate opportunities for human development. That one-half of the human race should be dominant and the other half submissive is incompatible with a notion of freedom. Freedom requires that there not be dominance and submission, but that all individuals be free to determine their own lives as equals.

Jack Sawyer, "On Male Liberation." Liberation Magazine. Copyright 1970. Reprinted by permission of the Liberation Collective.

---

### Excerpt from The Taming of The Shrew

William Shakespeare

*William Shakespeare portrayed the battle of the sexes more eloquently than anyone before or since him.*

*Petruchio.* Good morrow, Kate – for that's your name, I hear.
*Katharina.* Well have you heard, but something hard of hearing;
They call me Katharine that do talk of me.
*Petruchio.* You lie, in faith, for you are called plain Kate,

And bonny Kate, and sometimes Kate the curst:
But Kate, the prettiest Kate in Christendom,
Kate of Kate Hall, my super-dainty Kate,
For dainties are all cates, and therefore, Kate,
Take this of me, Kate of my consolation --
Hearing thy mildness praised in every town,
Thy virtues spoke of, and thy beauty sounded,
Yet not so deeply as to thee belongs,
Myself am moved to woo thee for my wife.
   *Katharina.* Moved! in good time! let him that
   moved you hither.
Remove you hence: I know you at the first
You were a moveable.
   *Petruchio.* Why, whats a moveable?
   *Katharina.* A joint-stool.
   *Petruchio.* Thou hast hit it: come, sit on me.
   *Katharina.* Assess are made to bear; and so are
   you.
   *Petruchio.* Women are made to bear; and so
   are you.
   *Katharina.* No such a jade as you, if me you
   mean.
   *Petruchio,* Alas, good Kate! I will not burden
   thee,
For knowing thee to be but young and light --
   *Katharina.* Too light for such a swain as you to
   catch,
And yet as heavy as my weight should be.
   *Petruchio.* Should be! should – buzz!
   *Katharina.* Well ta'en, and like a buzzard.
   *Petruchio.* O, slow-winged turtle! shall a buz-
   zard take thee?
   *Katharina.* Ay, for a turtle, as he takes a buz-
   zard.
   *Petruchio.* Come, come, you wasp, i'faith, you
   are too angry.
   *Katharina.* If I be waspish, best beware my
   sting.
   *Petruchio.* My remedy is then, to pluck it out.
   *Katharina.* Ay, if the fool could find where it
lies.

   *Petruchio.* Who knows not where a wasp doth
   wear his sting?
In his tail.
   *Katharina.* In his tongue.
   *Petruchio.* Whose tongue?
   *Katharina.* Yours, if you talk of tales, and so
   farewell.
                  [she turns to go]
   *Petruchio.* What, with my tongue in your tail?
   nay, come again. [he seizes her in his arms]
Good Kate, I am a gentleman --
   *Katharina.* That I'll try.
                  ['she strikes him']
   *Petruchio.* I swear I'll cuff you, if you strike
   again.
   *Katharina.* So may you loose your arms!
If you strike me, you are no gentleman,
And if no gentleman, why then no arms.
   *Petruchio.* A herald, Kate? O, put me in thy
   books!
   *Katharina.* What is your crest? A coxcomb?
   *Petruchio.* A combless cock, so Kate will be
   my hen.
   *Katharina.* No cock of mine, you crow too like
   a craven.
   *Petruchio.* Nay, come, Kate, come; you must
   not look so sour.
   *Katharina.* It is my fashion, when I see a crab.
   *Petruchio.* Why, here's a crab, and therefore
   look not sour.
   *Katharina.* There is, there is.
   *Petruchio.* Then show it me.
   *Katharina.* Had I glass, I would.
   *Petruchio.* What, you mean my face?
   *Katharina* Well aimed of such a young one.
                  [she struggles]
   *Petruchio.* Now, by S. George, I am too young
   for you.
   *Katharina.* Yet you are withered.
              [touches his forehead]
   *Petruchio.* [kisses her hand]. 'Tis with cares.

*Katharina*. [she slips from him]. I care not!

*Petruchio*. Nay, hear you, Kate . . . In sooth,
you scape not so. [he catches her once more]

*Katharina*. I chafe you, if I tarry . . . Let me go!
[she struggles again, biting and scratching as he
speaks]

*Petrucio*. No, not a whit – I find you passing
gentle

'Twas told me you were rough and coy and sullen,

And now I find report a very liar;

For thou art pleasant, gamesome, passing
courteous,

But slow in speech . . . yet sweet as spring-time
flowers.

Thou canst not frown, thou canst not look
askance,

Nor bite the lip, as angry wenches will,

Nor hast thou pleasure to be cross in talk;

Be thou with mildness entertain'st thy wooers,

With gentle conference, soft and affable . . .

[he releases her]

Why does the world report that Kate doth limp?

O slan'rous world! Kate like the hazel-twig

Is straight and slender, and as brown in hue

As hazel-nuts and sweeter than the the kernels . .

O, let me see thee walk: thou doest not halt.

*Katharina*. Go, fool, and whom thou keep'st
command.

*Petruchio*. Did ever Dian so become a grove

As Kate this chamber with her princely gait?

O, be thou Dian and let her be Kate,

And then let Kate be chaste and Dian sportful!

*Katharina*. Where did you study all this goodly
speech?

*Petruchio*. It is extempore, from my mother-
wit.

*Katharina*. A witty mother! witless else her son.

*Petruchio*. Am I not wise?

*Katharina*. Yes, keep you warm.

*Petruchio*. Marry, so I mean, sweet Katharine,
in thy bed.

And therefore, setting all this chat aside,

Thus in plain terms: your father hath consented

That you shall be my wife; your dowry 'greed
on;

And, will you, nill you, I will marry you . . .

Now, Kate, I am a husband for your turn,

For by this light whereby I see thy beauty,

Thy beauty that doth make me like thee well,

Thou, must be married to no man but me.

For I am he am borne to tame you, Kate,

And bring you from a wild Kate to a Kate

Conformable as other household Kates. . .

### Excerpt from **Memories, Dreams, Reflections**

C. G. Jung, Random House, 1962

*Throughout the course of his emotionally charged relationship with Sigmund Freud, C. G. Jung was successively an awe-struck student, a secret detractor, and a bitter opponent. The ultimate schism between them centered on Jung's unwillingness to accept Freud's theory that the sexual drive lay at the root of all human thought and action. Jung admired the genius in Freud that illuminated the unconscious psyche; but he came to believe that Freud was hiding from personally painful truths behind the rhetoric of his sexual dogma.*

*As he developed as an independent thinker, Jung came to envision human existence on a more mystical level than Freud. The following is an excerpt from a unique book in which Jung created a soul-searching self-portrait. Written in collaboration with Aniela Jaffe, Memories, Dreams, Reflections is Jung's attempt, in old age, at a personal psychic evaluation.*

. . . When I was writing down these fantasies, I once asked myself, "What am I really doing? Certainly this has nothing to do with science. But then what is it?" Whereupon a voice within me said, "It is art." I was astonished. It had never entered my head that what I was writing had any connection with art. Then I thought, "Perhaps my unconscious is forming a personality that is not me, but which is insisting on coming through to expression." I knew for a certainly that the voice had come from a woman. I recognized it as the voice of a patient, a talented psychopath who has a strong transference to me. She had become a living figure within my mind.

Obviously what I was doing wasn't science. What then could it be but art? It was as though these were the only alternatives in the world. That is the way a woman's mind works.

I said very emphatically to this voice that my fantasies had nothing to do with art, and I felt a great inner resistance. No voice came through, however, and I kept on writing. Then came the next assault, and again the same assertion: "That is art." This time I caught her and said, "No, it is not art! On the contary, it is nature," and prepared myself for an argument. When nothing of the sort occurred, I reflected that the "woman within me" did not have the speech centers I had. And so I suggested that she use mine. She did so and came through with a long statement.

I was greatly intrigued by the fact that a woman should interfere with me from within. My conclusion was that she must be the "soul," in the primitive sense, and I began to speculate on the reasons why the name "anima" was given to the soul. Why was it thought of as feminine? Later I came to see that this inner feminine figure plays a typical, archetypal, role in the unconscious of a man, and I called her the "anima." The corresponding figure in the unconscious of

woman I called the "animus."

At first it was the negative aspect of the anima that most impressed me. I felt a little awed by her. It was like the feeling of an invisible presence in the room. Then a new idea came to me: in putting down all this material for analysis I was in effect writing letters to the anima, that is, to a part of myself with a different viewpoint from my conscious one. I got remarks of an unusual and unexpected character. I was like a patient in analysis with a ghost and a woman! Every evening I wrote very conscientiously, for I thought if I did not write, there would be no way for the anima to get at my fantasies. Also, by writing them out I gave her no chance to twist them into intrigues. There is a tremendous difference between intending to tell something and actually telling it. In order to be as honest as possible with myself, I wrote everything down very carefully, following the old Greek maxim: "Give away all that thou hast, then shalt thou receive."

Often, as I was writing, I would have peculiar reactions that threw me off. Slowly I learned to distinguish between myself and the interruption. When something emotionally vulgar or banal came up, I would say to myself, "It is perfectly true that I have thought and felt this way at some time or other, but I don't have to think and feel that way now. I need not accept this banality of mine in perpetuity; that is an unnecessary humiliation."

The essential thing is to differentiate oneself from these unconscious contents by personifying them, and at the same time to bring them into relationship with consciousness. That is the technique for stripping them of their power. It is not too difficult to personify them, as they always possess a certain degree of autonomy, a separate identify of their own. Their autonomy is a most uncomfortable thing to reconcile oneself to, and yet the very fact that the unconscious presents itself in that way gives us the best means of handling it.

What the anima said seemed to me full of a deep cunning. If I had taken these fantasies of the unconscious as art, they would have carried no more conviction than visual perceptions, as if I were watching a movie. I would have felt no moral obligation toward them. The anima might then have easily seduced me into believing that I was a misunderstood artist, and that my so-called artistic nature gave me the right to neglect reality. If I had followed her voice, she would in all probability have said to me one day, "Do you imagine the nonsense you're engaged in is really art? Not a bit." Thus the insinuations of the anima, the mouthpiece of the unconscious, can utterly destroy a man. In the final analysis the decisive factor is always consciousness, which can understand the manifestations of the unconscious and take up a position toward them.

But the anima has a positive aspect as well. It is she who communicates the images of the unconscious to the conscious mind, and that is what I chiefly valued her for. For decades I always turned to the anima when I felt that my emotional behavior was disturbed, and that something had been constellated in the unconscious. I would then ask the anima: "Now what are you up to? What do you see? I should like to know." After some resistance she regularly produced an image. As soon as the image was there, the unrest or the sense of oppression vanished. The whole energy of these emotions was transformed into interest in and curiosity about the image. I would speak with the anima about the images she communicated to me, for I had to try to understand them as best I could, just like a dream.

Today I no longer need these conversations with the anima, for I no longer have such emotions. But if I did have them, I would deal with them in the same way. Today I am directly conscious of the anima's ideas because I have learned to accept the contents of the unconscious and to understand them. I know how I must behave toward the inner images. I can read their meaning directly from my dreams, and therefore no longer need a mediator to communicate them.

# Becoming Sexual:
# Psycho-Sexual Development
# and Change

## 9

Many people think of sex in terms of churning bodies and pulsating, throbbing, uncontrollable drives and instincts. Sex seems to be a strong natural drive seeking natural outlets: penises seek vaginas, vaginas seek penises, both seek orgasms. Nothing could be simpler, nothing could be more natural. But beneath this apparent naturalness lies a profound learning, beginning with childhood and ending with death. (Burgess 1949).

Both Sigmund Freud and Alfred Kinsey believed that sexuality is a biologically determined drive. They believed that innate sexual impulses, rooted in biology, constantly seek outlets. Usually these drives are repressed or channeled by society or the individual. If they were not, there would be ungovernable levels of sexual activity and no one would be safe – the minister's daughter, the barber's son, the police chief's wife, the police chief himself. The world would be overwhelmed in an orgy of sex and copulation, and fantasies would become reality.

But sexual drives are not always as powerful as we think. What may actually be more powerful are the feelings that accompany them. We feel love, guilt, tenderness, anxiety, aggression, and security in association with our sexual drives. Because we experience these feelings at the same time we may be masturbating, kissing, or making love, we misread the physiological event, identifying the emotional intensity with the physical act.

## Sexual Scripting

Sexual behavior and feelings depend more on learning than on biological drives. Sexual drives are malleable and can be molded in almost any direction. What is "natural" is what society chooses to decree is natural; there is very little spontaneous and unlearned behavior (Gagnon and Simon 1973). Our sexual impulses are organized and directed through a script, which we learn and act out. These scripts define the sexual sensations, events, objects, situations, and people, and all the elements must occur together to lead to sexual behavior. If certain elements are missing, then there will be no sexual activity. For example, a man arrives at his class in anthropology 30 minutes early, so he will have a chance to review the assignment. He walks toward his usual seat, thinking about northern Borneo. Suddenly he notices a naked woman sitting in his seat. Startled, he drops his book on the floor, asking himself, "Am I in the wrong classroom? Maybe I'm in Art 102 by mistake." He goes back outside and checks the classroom. Right classroom. He is confused. What is a naked woman doing in Anthropology 409? He checks with the office. Right room, the class hasn't been cancelled. He waits outside the classroom, confused and clutching his book. Unconsciously, he has defined the woman and the setting as nonsexual; thus he has not experienced sexual feelings.

Another example of the importance of sexual scripts in initiating sexual behavior is that of a woman going to her gynecologist – a man – for a check-up. The doctor touches her breasts, then inserts a finger into her vagina. If all you knew about sex was that touching breasts and genitals is arousing, you would expect the woman to become excited. But unless there are mixed signals, neither patient nor doctor is sexually aroused. Sexual excitation requires not merely manipulation, but a script that defines the setting, the touching and the actors as potentially erotic.

The scripts that facilitate sexual activity have two major components. The *intrapersonal* component deals with the internal and physiological states that lead to sexual arousal. The *interpersonal* component deals with the externally shared conventions and signals that enable two mutually dependent people to engage in sexual acts.

**Intrapersonal Scripting** On the intrapersonal level, sexual scripts enable individuals to give meaning to their physiological responses. The meanings depend largely on the situations. Erections, for example, do not always mean sexual excitement. Young boys sometimes have erections when they are frightened, anxious, or worried. In the morning men may experience erections that are not accompanied by arousal. Adolescent girls sometimes experience sexual arousal without knowing what their feelings mean, reporting them as a funny, weird kind of feeling; at other times, they may be reported as anxiety, fear, or an upset stomach. The sensations are not linked to a sexual script until the girl becomes older and physiological states acquire a definite erotic meaning. Many erections and vaginal lubrications are simply physiological.

The internal script also determines what physiological events our minds will become aware of. During masturbation or intercourse an enormous number of physiological events occur simultaneously, but we are only aware of a few of them. These are the events we associate with sexual arousal, such as increasing heartbeat and tensing or contracting muscles. Others – such as curling toes – may not filter through to one's consciousness.

Finally, internal scripts provide a sequence of body movements, by acting as mechanisms that activate biological events and release tension. In our culture, for example, a definite script of body movement leads to sexual intercourse. First a couple embrace each other and kiss. They pet above the waist, then below, finally they make love. This sequence of movements is learned, with each movement leading to the next in a certain order, and with little variation. People with little experience, especially young adolescents, are often unfamiliar with sexual scripts. What do they do after kissing? Do they embrace? Pet above the waist? Below? Or what? They learn the sequence, eventually. The sexual script is also related to age and sex. Young adolescents often limit their scripts to kissing, holding hands, and embracing, yet feel completely satisfied. Kissing for them may be as exciting as sexual intercourse for more experienced people. When the range of their script increases, the earlier stages lose some of their sexual intensity. Remember the first time you touched someone's hand erotically, after you first became aware of sex? The intensity of the act was probably as high, in some ways, as your strongest sexual responses are now.

The interpersonal is the area of shared conventions, which make sexual intercourse possible. Very little of our public lives are sexual. We live in a world where we are men and women, parents and workers, husbands and wives and partners; most of our interaction is nonsexual. Yet there are signs or gestures – verbal or nonverbal – that define encounters as sexual. We make our sexual motives clear to each other by the way we look at each other, the tone of our voices, the movements of our bodies, and other culturally shared phenomena. A bedroom or a motel room ordinarily are potentially erotic locations. Classrooms, offices, and factories are not. The sequence of movements we use in arousing ourselves or others are erotic activators. A person touching another's genitals is a sure sign of erotic potential in some settings, but not all (remember the gynecologist, the army physical). All these factors help define actors and situations as potentially erotic for both people. They are learned over long periods of time, beginning in childhood.

If large numbers of people did not share these conventions, there would be sexual chaos. Imagine that two people came together, one with our culture script (which calls for petting before coitus), the other from a society where people customarily pet after intercourse rather than before. They would be unable to get their act together, and each would consider the other weird.

This kind of confusion occurs fairly often. There is not necessarily a direct relation between what our culture calls erotic and what any particular individual calls erotic. Culture sets the general contours, but there is too much diversity in terms of personality, class, and sex for each person to have exactly the same erotic script. Thus, sexual scripts can be ambiguous. We may believe that everyone shares our own particular script, but that is because we are projecting our experiences on others, assuming that all people share our erotic definitions of objects, gestures, and situations. Although people usually expect their partner to share a sexual script that is similar to or complementary to their own, often they initially do not. The partner may have come from a different class or religious background, and may have had far different learning experiences. Each has to learn the other's sexual script and be able to complement and adjust to it. They must make their needs known through words, gestures, or movements, if their scripts are to be integrated.

## Psychosexual Development in Childhood

People do not develop sexual identities in isolation, but by interacting with people and situations. At the same time they are finding sexual identity, they are also developing other aspects of a larger social identity. Children learn trust, au-

tonomy, initiative, and industry from infancy on, experimenting with different roles. They try to achieve self-confidence in their interactions with parents, adults, and peers. The development of these characteristics is crucial to the development of their sexuality. Children who grow up feeling self-confident in other aspects of their personalities are likely to also be confident about sexuality. Children who are flexible in other areas are likely to be more spontaneous in their later sexual relations and to experience a wider range; women will be active as well as receptive; men will be receptive as well as active (Erikson 1968).

## Early Childhood

Traumatic experiences in early childhood do not usually lead to specific fixations in later years, but may contribute to faulty personality development. The first major identity task for an infant is to develop trust. If parents are rejecting, hurtful, and uncaring, the child may fail to develop trust. Subsequent experiences may reflect this basis. After trust, the young child's subsequent tasks are to develop autonomy instead of shame, initiative instead of guilt, industry instead of inferiority. There is a general development from one stage to the next, and a failure to develop at any one stage will distort further development.

The earliest experiences influence later sexuality, even though they are not fundamentally sexual but are general influences that affect our entire identity. Thus, if trust becomes a major part of a person's identity, he or she will be trustful rather than suspicious in general relations, and sexual relations will probably be open, trustful, and spontaneous. The development of mistrust also affects sexuality. Mistrustful people may hide behind rigid sex roles and become aggressive, defensive, and ungiving. Mistrust may not affect the frequency of their sexual performance, but it will probably affect the quality.

Infant boys may have erections soon after birth, and four-month old infants may respond in an apparently erotic manner when their genitals are rubbed. But these infants do not seem to be any more interested in their genitals than any other part of their bodies. By the time children turn two or three years old, however, they begin exploring each others bodies, touching and playing with their own and each other's genitals. When children are around five, about 10 percent begin what is called "sex play" (a misnomer that should probably be called "genital play," because the children don't associate the sensations with erotic meanings.) As boys get older, they engage in more sex play than do girls. Kinsey (1953) reported that the rate for boys, who are expected to be sexual, increases from 10 percent at age five (3 percent less than girls) to 35 percent at age thirteen (five times as much as girls). These patterns, however, may be changing as the generations that came to maturity in the 1960s begin to raise children. These parents may pass on to their children less restricted attitudes toward sex. To date, unfortunately, no major studies have investigated the impact of the sexual revolution on children's sex play.

After children become verbal, two important experiences dominate the development of their sexual identities. The first is the reaction of adults to what they believe are children's sexual activities. The second is the child's continuous development of his or her sex role. *The sex role determines the nature, frequency, and intensity of sexual drive, within the limits of personality.* It provides children with their sexual script. The third is the children's observation of their parent's interaction with each other.

## Sex Play

When adults see children touching their own genitals, they usually respond to this as if it were a sexual activity. Playing with the genitals is normal for the child, but it may trigger various responses in the parent. The adult may feel anxious that the child is masturbating so young. Does that mean the child is going to become sexually precocious? Many adults tell the child to stop, that such play is "nasty." Often adults mislabel the activity as "masturbation"; then they either ignore it or make a judgment about it. What is significant is that the behavior means different things to the child and to the adult. Children do not view playing with their bodies as having moral or erotic significance, nor do they have any complex moral and emotional associations with what adults call masturbation. But the child senses that sex play is forbidden.

Adults often place adult motives on children's sex play, although these motives are not relevant to the child's world. When a small boy climbs atop the back of a kneeling girl, the appearance resembles a form of sexual intercourse. Does the mounting signify dominance for him and submission for her? Does it mean the children desire to make love? It might mean these things for adults, but not for young children. They are merely playing. But adults may communicate negative feelings to the children in their responses to this particular play behavior, giving the children a sense that they are doing something morally wrong. So they sense the difference. Experiences are cumulative and play begins to take on special meanings. The feelings are vague, undefined, unformed and misinformed. But they are strong (Sears, Maccoby, and Levin, 1957).

Parental judgments which are usually primitive "yes" or "no" injunctions, may be very difficult for children to deal with later, when they are older. They stay with the child at least through adolescence, and often they are internalized for a lifetime. The judgments may be rigidly black-and-white, and children are in no position either to determine that there may be gray areas or to challenge their parents' authority. Such injunctions may become part of the individual – without any interpretive nuances. Girls are told in early years not to let boys or men "touch" them, for example, and are expected to turn away or turn off from touching. Their bodies have built the injunction into automatic responses; their muscles tighten, their senses freeze. On becoming adolescents, however, girls are told that it is all right to let husbands touch them; and more progressive families even accept touching without marriage. But by that time, the girl's body has been trained otherwise, and does not distinguish immediately between legitimate and illegitimate touching. A boyfriend's or husband's touch – which is legitimate – may still cause a woman's body to tense. Eventually the response can be unlearned, but this is often a trying task

for both the woman and the man.

While children are receiving a vague sense of adult judgments about unnamed things, they are also learning a special sexual vocabulary, which at first they do not associate with sexual activity. For example, "fuck," "screw," "cocksucker," "queer," and "fairy" are sexual terms, although they are used, hostilely and aggressively, as slang words or epithets. By the time a child understands their sexual meaning, the words have acquired powerful negative connotations. Yet such words help shape the child's sexual feelings. To say "I fucked someone" implies a host of aggressive, dehumanizing associations; thus, power, aggression, anger and hostility may unconsciously enter into what children understand "fucking" to be.

Adults speak in a language children cannot understand, and often answer questions that children have not asked. When children want to know how babies are made, they don't want to be told about sperm wiggling up mommy's tubes looking for an egg. They want to know about "doing it." What's it like? Can they watch? Why not? Because adults usually turn aside this type of question, children turn to their peers for answers. Unfortunately, peers seldom have real information. Some may know that penises enter vaginas ("Yuk," they often say when they find out) but most know little more than this.

But probably more important than what children learn or mislearn is the setting in which they exchange information. They know that you have to be careful about talking about these things, so that your parents or teachers will not find out. So children get the feeling that they are sharing secret knowledge, a feeling that has a profound effect on us as we get older. There are certain things you learn not to share with people you love, and you learn to keep sex a secret. Children develop a sense of guilty knowledge that they often carry throughout their lives.

Children go through various forms of sex play during early years. They play "doctor," looking at and feeling each other's genitals. They engage in mutual genital stimulation and play with themselves in front of friends. Many have orgasms, although boys do not yet ejaculate.

Kinsey found that sex play with members of the same sex is slightly greater than with members of the other sex. The level of sex play is high for boys, both with girls and with other boys. At age 12, 30 percent of the boys had some form of sex play with other boys; after puberty, the percentage declined significantly.

There seems to be little relation between preadolescent sex play and adolescent sexuality; rather, the real determinant of children's sexuality is their sex role. Pressure to conform to a sex role becomes very strong with puberty and adolescence, in large part channeling, directing and regulating sexual frequency. In most cultures, puberty marks the beginning of adulthood. The concept of "adolescence" is a recent historical phenomenon which developed in the nineteenth century. Adolescence is the psychological state occurring during puberty, which is a biological period. The traits of adolescence – dependency, identity crisis, role anxiety – are cultural. Adolescents are sexually mature in a physical sense, yet they are still learning their sexual scripts.

At adolescence a person's sexuality is publicly recognized for the first time, but it is not permitted expression. Masturbation, petting, and sexual intercourse are discouraged, especially among girls. Boys are not exactly encouraged by their parents, but neither are they exactly discouraged. Public or parental disapproval does not prevent all sexual expression, but it does set the stage for guilt and conflict between adults and children.

During adolescence, sex play takes on new

The years of adolescence were to me very lonely and very unhappy. Both in the life of the emotions and in the life of the intellect, I was obliged to preserve an impenetrable secrecy towards my people. My interests were divided between sex, religion, and mathematics. I find the recollection of my sexual preoccupation in adolescence unpleasant. I do not like to remember how I felt in those years. The facts of sex first became known to me when I was twelve years old, through a boy named Ernest Logan who had been one of my kindergarten companions at an earlier age. He and I slept in the same room one night and he explained the nature of copulation and its part in the generation of children, illustrating his remarks by funny stories. I found what he said extremely interesting although I had as yet no physical response.

Bertrand Russell

---

significance. Once simply exploration, it now is explicitly and unambiguously defined as sexual. Touching each other's genitals is thus very different from before, for sexual feelings and arousals are involved. The "strange" feelings centered in clitoris and penis are now defined as sexual.

## Sex Roles and Adolescence

In adolescence, socialization along sex lines becomes more intense, further separating boys and girls from each other. They no longer have as many common experiences and activities, but develop separate spheres of feeling and acting.

They begin to experience their sexuality in radically different ways according to the patterns set forth by their sex roles.

Boys begin overt heterosexual activities very early. Their sexual activities, however, are tied very closely to their needs for status among other boys. They want to be recognized as "men" by the people with whom they spend most of their time. Girls, in contrast, have very few overt sexual experiences. Although they spend most of their time with other girls, they are also encouraged to associate with boys in romantic, nonsexual relations. Adolescence, for girls, centers around romance and preparation for marriage. "Nice" girls — that is, girls with little sexual experience — are the kind of girls boys want to marry. So the traditional pattern is that girls control their sexuality during adolescence, instead of becoming sexually active.

For boys, adolescence is a time of rapid increase in sexuality. They are not preparing to be husbands and fathers but are learning to be sexually active and aggressive. (It is assumed they will be good husbands and fathers if they are occupationally successful.) Men are not traditionally expected to be extensively involved in their families and marriages to be successful; all they have to do is "take care" of their families (that is, provide financial support). Thus, men enter marriage with sexual experience but without the degree of emotional maturity and interpersonal experience that women have acquired.

## Sexual Behavior Among Adolescents

**Psychosexual Development**    The most difficult problem facing adolescents in their psychosexual development is that they are confronted with many conflicting demands. In earlier decades, adolescents were reared in a generally restrictive social environment. By contrast today, the world in which they live is highly sexualized; unfortunately, they have not yet attained the maturity they need to deal with the pervasive sexual freedom to which they are exposed. Nor do their parents or society help them achieve this maturity. Because parents tend to be more conservative than their children, their children feel unable to turn to them for information about sex, although the majority of children want this information from them (Johns, 1975). The larger social institutions, especially public schools, do not permit the free discussion of sexuality in the classroom; if they do have sex education courses, these classes rarely discuss contraception because of parents' fears that such discussion will encourage premarital intercourse. Churches continue to teach sexuality through their traditional "Thou Shalt Not..." approach. All the while, society at large teaches "Thou Shalt." The basic problem confronting American adolescents is developing a solid emotional understanding of sexuality in the face of such conflicting values.

**Masturbation** Masturbation is a powerful influence creating genital priority in the body by directing sexual sensations toward the genitals. The relatively small amount of masturbatory experience among adolescent girls creates a non-sexual period in their lives, before their genitals become a major source of sexual pleasure.

It is possible that the lack of experience makes many women dependent on men for genital pleasure. Women do not experience the same degree of sexual autonomy. While men learn that they can receive genital pleasure from either women or themselves, women are taught that genital pleasure should be provided by a male. Men feel no such dependency, particularly in relations that are not satisfactory in non-sexual

ways. Thus a man may say to himself, "I don't need her. I can do it just as well myself, with a lot less hassle." Masturbation makes men's sexuality less dependent on women; the lack of it ties women more strongly to men (Gagnon and Simon, 1973).

### Sexual Intercourse

The rates of premarital sexual intercourse vary significantly in adolescence. According to Kinsey, 24.3 percent of the boys have had premarital sexual intercourse by age 15, 52.4 percent by 20. The most striking variable is in terms of social class, as determined by educational level. By age 20, 76 percent of the men who did not complete high school said they had had premarital sexual intercourse, while the rate was 44 percent among men with a college background. Morton Hunt's recent study indicates an important change in sexual behavior among men who have gone to college, however. By age 17, approximately half of them have had premarital intercourse (more than twice as many as Kinsey's comparable group). Among those without any college, almost three-fourths had been involved in premarital intercourse by age 17 (Hunt 1974).

There was very little premarital sexual intercourse among adolescent girls, according to Kinsey, but there have been major changes since his investigations. In a study published in *Family Planning Perspectives* (July, 1979), research by Melvin Zelnick found that in 1976, 63.3 percent of American girls had sexual intercourse by age 19. The sharpest increase in rates of premarital intercourse was among white adolescent girls, where the average jumped 10 percent in a five year period. Age of first intercourse for white adolescent girls was 18.4 years and for black adolescent girls first intercourse was age 16.6 years.

Unfortunately, this increase in adolescent sexual intercourse has resulted in a startling increase in teen-age pregnancy, which is reaching almost epidemic proportions. The statistics are startling:

▫ Almost one in five births is to a teen-age mother.
▫ Only one in five sexually active teen-age women uses contraception consistently.
▫ Among sexually active teen-age women who do not use contraceptives, seven in ten think that they cannot become pregnant.
▫ Most births by teen-age mothers result from unplanned pregnancies.

Sexual activity is increasing, but there is a woeful lack of responsibility and knowledge concerning

its consequences. Yet the larger society does little to prepare its youth with such knowledge, preferring to believe against all evidence that adolescents are not sexual. One result is that teen-age pregnancies cost taxpayers approximately $8.3 billion a year in welfare and related costs.

**Homosociality**    More important than sexual intercourse *per se* is the context in which it occurs. For boys, especially those with working-class backgrounds, adolescence is characterized by *homosociality; that is, self-esteem and status are more closely linked to evaluations from people of the same sex than the opposite sex.* Homosociality has important consequences, in

Does this long period of relative sexual inactivity among girls come from repression of an elemental drive or merely from a failure to learn how to be sexual? The answers have important implications for their later sexual development. If it is repression, the path to a fuller sexuality must pass through processes of loss of inhibitions, during which the girl unlearns, in varying degrees, attitudes and values that block the expression of natural internal feelings.

On the other hand, the "learning" answer suggests that women create or invent a capacity for sexual behavior, learning how and when to be aroused and how and when to respond. This approach implies greater flexibility: unlike the repression view, it makes sexuality both more and less than a basic force that may break loose at any time in strange or costly ways. The learning approach also lessens the power of sexuality altogether; all at once, particular kinds of sex activities need no longer be defined as either "healthy" or "sick."

William Simon and John Gagnon

---

terms of relations with girls. A girlfriend's importance may lie in giving a boy status among other boys, with his relationship with her being secondary. Adolescents begin to distinguish between "good" girls and "bad" girls (although in recent years this distinction has obviously been declining in importance). Good girls have had little or no sexual experience; bad girls have "gone all the way," either in terms of sexual intercourse or extensive petting. Boys often relate to bad girls in purely sexual terms, regarding them as sex objects and feeling that they are "dirty" (a projection of how the *boys* feel about sex).

The generalized role expectations of males — that they must be competitive, aggressive, and achievement-oriented — carry over into sexual activities. They receive recognition for "scoring" with a girl, much as they would for scoring a touchdown or home run. Sexual encounters, as opposed to sexual relationships, function in large part to confer status among peers. (Zelnick and Kanter 1972; Levin 1975).

A 1969 study by Kanin has suggested that almost 25 percent of the men interviewed had tried to have sexual intercourse with a woman against her wishes. Another report (Christensen 1971) has indicated that a quarter of the women interviewed had their first sexual intercourse because of force or a sense of obligation, rather than from their own desire.

Among middle-class boys, the homosocial element is moderated by the desire to seek emotionally satisfying relations with their partners. Today, youths are more likely to have premarital intercourse with a girl for whom they feel affection, although the boy's commitment may not be as strong as that of the girl's. One study indicated that among its respondents, 60 percent of the girls planned to marry the boy they first had intercourse with, while only 14 percent of the boys had similar feelings. Despite this inconsistency, middle-class youth no longer associate sex with a degraded female to the degree they did a generation ago.

**Heterosociality**    The almost predatory activities of boys, however, often limits the range of their later heterosexual relations. In adolescence, they learn to relate to women in terms of their own status needs, rather than relating to women as people. Their later experiences are built on this basis. Some men, as a result, find it difficult to develop *heterosocial* relations, or those in which sexual activities involve respect or love for the woman. Heterosocial relationships bind men and women together, in striking contrast to homosocial relationships, in which women are used to bind men together.

**Ambiguity Toward Female Sexuality**    During adolescence substantially fewer girls than boys experience premarital sexual intercourse. The relationships of most girls are characterized by a commitment to love and romance, not to sexuality. Their relations with men are fundamentally heterosocial. If they are known to have had sexual experiences, they may be labeled "bad". Some boys still seek "bad" girls for their own sexual and status needs, and such girls often form the "pool" from which boys find sexual partners (Gebhard 1967).

But even those girls who do not have overt sexual experience are still learning sexual behavior. Teaching is often prohibitory ("Sit with your legs crossed; don't let anyone touch you; be

It is written. A daughter is a vain treasure to her father. From anxiety about her he does not sleep at night; during her early years lest she be seduced, in her adolescence lest she go astray, in her marriageable years lest she does not find a husband, when she is married lest she be childless, and when she is old lest she practice witchcraft.

The Talmud

---

home by ten.") but also takes the form of preparation for marriage. They learn that pursuing the traditional woman's goal of marriage requires them to make themselves sexually attractive without being sexual. (You want to be alluring, but you don't want to be "bad," because men marry only "nice" girls.) This conflict causes considerable confusion among males. Women dress to be sexually attractive, but resent whistles or leers. A woman's manner may give off sexual signals, according to a man's sexual script, but her manner or dress may not have overt sexual meanings for her. Nevertheless, being attractive does have sexual undertones, although these may not be obvious to the woman or even especially important to her.

## Adolescent/Parent Conflict

During this time, tensions generally increase between adolescents and their parents as the children move toward greater independence. Adolescents tend to be more experimental toward sexuality if they communicate less and feel less intimate with their parents; their experimentation is also related to the degree of their commitment to their parents' religious values (Gagnon and Greenblat, 1978). The more they fear their parents' moral judgments, the more secretive they will be. With the growing separation from their parents, adolescents become increasingly influenced by their peer group. One researcher observed, "a student who perceives his friends to act in a sexually permissive manner and to have 'lots of sex' will also be sexually permissive and engage in coitus. If he perceives his friends as having little sexual experience, then he is much more likely to remain a virgin" (Teevan, 1972). Yet because close friends do not necessarily reveal their actual sexual experience (boys tend to exaggerate while girls tend to minimize) for fear

of censure, friends often do not know how each other are *really* acting. As a result, media images become more important in providing models of behavior.

Much of the conflict between parents and adolescent children about sexuality is not the result of changing sexual standards. Value conflict results in part from different roles and role expectations (Reiss, 1968; Fell, 1966). Adolescents are often more experimental, and more permissive about sexuality than are their parents. Parents, in contrast, tend to have well-defined sexual standards and are expected to restrict the sexual activities of their children as part of the parental role. The parental refrain, "We-did-all-the-things-you-kids-are-doing-now — but-that-doesn't-make-it-right", does not necessarily indicate hypocrisy. Rather, it reflects a change in roles and role expectations. Parents may internalize their own peer standards in terms of restrictiveness, feeling they would be judged as lax by friends and associates if they were sexually permissive with their children.

Although older people tend to be less permissive about sex than adolescents or college youth, the difference is not very great. Significantly, couples without children are much more willing to accept premarital intercourse than are couples with the same background who have adolescent children. The more responsible parents feel about their children's sex lives the less permissive they tend to be.

A recent study (Levin, 1975) of women's attitudes suggests that there may be change in this area. Only 24 percent of the women said they would object to their daughters having premarital intercourse; in a significant example of the double standard, only 12 percent would object to such a relationship on the part of their sons. Most responses, however, came from women who do not have adolescent children; they may become

"I can't tell you just now what the moral of that is, but I shall remember it in a bit."

"Perhaps it hasn't one," Alice ventured to remark.

"Tut, tut, child!" said the Duchess. "Everything's got a moral, if only you can find it."

Lewis Caroll, *Alice in Wonderland*

---

less permissive as their children grow older. The data does indicate that premarital intercourse appears to be becoming the accepted norm, however. If this is true, it is possible that in the future there will be less generational conflict concerning sexual behavior.

For girls, the conflict appears to intensify in relation to increasing family size. It decreases for boys, as the family exceeds five children. Girls are traditionally more restricted than boys in their social life, but the difference becomes greater in larger families. It is easier to restrict a girl socially than to deal with the feared consequences of freedom (that is, premarital pregnancy). Because boys have been socialized to be independent, it is easier to let them go their own ways than to try to restrict them. Finally, if a girl becomes pregnant, family members are disgraced and may have to raise an illegitimate child. They do not have to worry about raising the illegitimate child of a son, because that responsibility traditionally falls on his sexual partner and her family. No shame is associated with a boy who gets a girl pregnant. (In fact, some families may find it amusing, supporting the boy's masculinity. "You're not a man until you've knocked a girl up!")

### Adult Psychosexual Development.

It seems quite remarkable that any of us survived adolescence. This period of life is charged with development, change, growth, and crises. Adolescents must achieve intimacy instead of isolation. Their sexuality must become more than simply sexual discharge. They must learn to have deep feelings in relationships and love. They must be able to experience their bodies erotically. If their basic needs are satisfied, in adult life they will be able to seek goals higher than the simple need for gratification. After establishing a

sense of intimacy, they must go on to establish their *generativity*, which is the ability to nurture and guide children, the ability to be creative, productive, and altruistic. Failing to establish generativity results in stagnation, boredom, and a sense of emptiness. Finally, as old age approaches, people need to develop a sense of integrity about their lives; to feel that they have lived fully, that they developed their own potentialities, that they have not fallen victim to life's circumstances. The alternative is the despair that comes from the knowledge that one's life has been meaningless (Erikson 1968).

Although adulthood is the beginning of profound new experiences, not much is known about the psychosexual development of the adult. The intensive study of children's developing sexuality may be derived in part from our anxieties about childhood sexuality: We want to know about children in order to control and channel their sexuality. What we do know about adult sexuality is that it seems to decline in importance to many people, both physically and psychologically. Adulthood is a time in which most people marry or form alternative associations, and no longer need to struggle to find a sexual partner. People who live alone are able to find others of their own age who also have experience and fewer prohibitions. Work, children, personal relations, a sense of security – all of these offer non-sexual means of acquiring self-esteem. People also seem to have less physical energy for sexual relations: Men and women work all day at offices, homes, or factories. Sex is also a means of mate selection, and it loses its importance once a partner is found.

Frequency of sexual intercourse declines. This decline is generally related to lessening interest on the part of men, however, for the erotic responsiveness of women increases as they get older. As women acquire more experience, they learn to develop their erotic capabilities. The irony is that, as women become more sexual, the frequency of intercourse may decline in marriage. Many women consequently never have the opportunity to explore their full erotic potential, which is limited in youth because they are unmarried, and is limited in later life because of a partner's declining interest in sex.

The decline in men's interest may be only partially related to aging. As adolescents, they classified women into "good" and "bad," and most of them married "good" women. But part of their attraction to "good" women was that such women were either non-sexual or sexually inexperienced. Often men do not have the same strong sexual feelings for "good" women that they do for the "bad" ones, however. Thus, they may have married women with whom they did not have a particularly strong sexual bond. If they allow themselves to be fully sexual with their wives, that would make their wives "bad." So they may hold both themselves and their wives back sexually.

A second reason for declining sexuality, particularly among men from a lower socio-economic background, is related to homosociality. These men had patterned their adolescent sexual experiences in homosocial terms, but they no longer receive status from "the boys" for their sexual relations. (No one wins any points for

"scoring" with a wife.) In earlier years, they had sexual intercourse in part for peer approval, and now that support is gone. They have to go it on their own now: relations are between the man and woman alone.

This pattern of declining sexual interest may be changing, however, as a result of alterations in sexual attitudes and behavior during the last decade. Sexuality and affection are becoming more united, and some of the psychosexual problems related to aging may diminish as the present generation gets older.

Recent studies indicate that there has been an increase in the frequency of marital intercourse. Among Kinsey's respondents, the median weekly frequency of marital intercourse was 2.45 for those aged 16-25, declining to .50 for those aged 56-60. Hunt's shows a dramatic increase, ranging from 25 to 50 percent in some cases. His range moves from 3.25 for those 18-24, to 1.00 for those 55 and over. This change reflects a marked alteration in sexual attitudes among married couples. Whereas a generation ago sex was viewed as enjoyable only for the husband, today the increased sexual responsiveness of married women is being recognized within marriage, raising the frequency of coitus. A woman's sexual desire has become legitimate rather than being regarded as shameful or unnatural. (Hunt 1974).

Within marriage there is also the fluctuation of

Anyone who fails to go along with life remains suspended, stiff, and rigid in mid-air. That is why so many people get wooden in their old age; they look back and cling to the past with a secret fear of death in their hearts. From the middle of life onward, only he remains vitally alive who is ready to die with life, for in the secret hour of life's midday the parabola is reversed, death is born. We grant goal and purpose to the ascent of life, why not to the descent?

Carl Jung

interest when partners have extra-marital affairs, which may be motivated less by sexual dissatisfactions per se than other factors. For men it may be a way of "scoring" again and filling ego needs. For both partners, extramarital relations may be a means of letting go sexually with someone else or of fulfilling intimacy or relational needs. For women, affairs may be a way of discovering sexual potential or the means of affirming attractiveness.

As people go through middle age, there are further changes, especially for women. Physically, there is a menopause. This may be very disturbing if most of a woman's identity is tied in with her reproductive capability. But menopause can also be liberating, especially if a woman has never used contraception because of religious beliefs, for she is now able to make love without worrying about pregnancy. A woman may also be disturbed by the loss of the mothering functions. Her children are leaving home; those who remain, if they are teenagers, don't want to be mothered. So she must search for new definitions for herself and new activities for her life.

## Aging

In a society that esteems youth, it is understandable that aging is widely dreaded. Old age is the final period of the life cycle that begins with infancy and proceeds to youth and maturity. Because most of us eventually become old, it is better to understand this part of life than to fear it as so many people do.

One of the least understood aspects of life in old age is sexuality. Those of us who are young seldom think about becoming old; we use our own standards to judge and measure everyone else. Thus, many older people continue to adhere to the standards of activity or physical attraction they held when they were young.

Comparing themselves to the young or to their own youth, they fall short, and may experience a sense of loss and despair. But there is no need for such comparison. Each age has its own integrity, each age has its own abilities and its own beauties.

Twenty-five hundred years ago, the Sphinx presented her riddle to Oedipus; if he failed to answer — as had the others before him — he would die. The riddle was deceptively simple: What walks on four legs in the morning, two legs at noon, and three legs at night. The answer is man, but the symbolism of the riddle — which Oedipus comprehended — was the acceptance of our human condition; the change from one age to another. The Sphinx's "riddling song constrained us to leave the unknown unknown and to face the present." Not to accept the human condition of aging was, in a metaphorical sense, to die.

Fear of unknown things that *might* happen produces anxiety. Among men, anxiety as much as any biological change can cause problems of impotence. The lessening frequency of intercourse and the increasing time required to attain erection produce anxieties in many older men, making them fear they are becoming impotent. This fear may very well lead to impotence. "It is a curious but not generally recognized fact," wrote Dr. A. L. Wolbarst, "that the physician cannot and does not make the diagnosis of impotence. The patient brings the diagnosis with him" (Rubin, 1965). When the natural slowing down of sexual responses is interpreted as the beginning of impotence, this self-diagnosis triggers a vicious spiral of fears and anxiety.

But, as Masters and Johnson have pointed out, "Inevitably all physical responses are slowed down...A man can't run around the block as fast as he could 20 or 30 years previously. Yet the simple fact that sexual functioning is but one more element in his total physiologic functioning has never occurred to him".

Women do not face fear of being impotent, because they are sexually capable throughout their lives. "Biologically, men are at the greater disadvantage," writes Simone de Beauvoir. "Socially, it is the women who are worse off, because of their condition as erotic objects." (De Beauvoir 1972).

To a large extent, women are viewed by potential partners in terms of their attractiveness. Yet in our culture, beauty is equated with youth. Thus, as women grow older, they lose one of the major aspects of their femininity. Although they have more sexual desire than they had in youth, older women usually have increasing doubts of their sexual appeal. The double standard of aging places women in a difficult position. They outnumber men of their own age – and many of these men seek younger women, a situation that is considered acceptable socially, although the union of an older woman with a young man is not.

Both men and women may experience a lessening of sexual desire as they grow older. Some experience the desire to desire, wishing for a return of the sexual longings of their youth. Still attached to the erotic world of their youth, they feel a renewal of sexual desire would somehow renew their youth. But this "desire to desire" is not the same as the desire of youth. It is tinged with regret and a sense of loss (DeBeauvoir, 1972).

Of course, not all old people regret a declining libido; those who have not considered their sexuality to be a positive force do not regret its decline. Neither do those who would be saints, nor those who – because of fears of inadequacy, their upbringing, their morality – participated in sex begrudgingly or as a destasteful duty. These people use increasing age as a reason to withdraw from sexual activities, often without attempting to understand their true motivation. A frigid woman may use the traditional image of sexless old age as a reason to refrain from intercourse claiming that it is not "proper for people our age to do such things." Men who are worried about becoming impotent may be happily relieved when old age provides them with a convenient excuse to stop sexual activities.

An older person may suspect that a partner's coolness or lack of responsiveness results from an extramarital affair. A husband or wife may imagine that a partner's impotence is caused by reckless bouts of lovemaking with someone else. Conversations with members of the other sex may be mistaken as the beginning of intrigue. All that these suspicions indicate, however, is a lowered sense of self-esteem in the aged individual, caused by a sense of diminished sexual attraction. To the person experiencing these suspicions, however, they are real and vivid; they should be dealt with by the partner.

In terms of actual sexual behavior, the greatest determinant of an older individual's heterosexual activity is the availability of a partner. Those who do not have partners may turn to masturbation as an alternative. In one study of older people, only 7 percent of those who were single, divorced, or widowed were sexually active, yet 54 percent of those living with a partner were. Frequency for this group – average age 70 years – ranged from three times a week to once every two months. Those who described their sexual activities strong in youth reported them moderate in old age. Those whose sexual feelings had been weak or moderate in youth described themselves as without sexual feelings. Apparently the best preparation for sexual activity in old age is a happy, healthy sexuality in youth and middle age.

After age 75, however, there is a significant

So we'll go no more a-roving
  So late into the night,
Though the heart be still as loving
  And the moon be still as bright.

For the sword outwears its sheath,
  And the soul wears out the breast,
And the heart must pause to breathe,
  And love itself have rest.

Though the night was made for loving,
  And the day returns too soon,
Yet we'll go no more a-roving
  By the light of the moon.

Lord Byron

---

decrease in sexual activity. These seem to be related to health problems, such as heart disease, arthritis, and diabetes. But often these people indicated that they continued to feel sexual desires; they simply lacked the ability to express them because of their health.

Social attitudes toward the aged discourage the expression of sexual desires. Such desires may be labeled abnormal, dirty, or inappropriate. The old may incorporate these attitudes into their own perception of themselves, fearing ridicule or disapproval. Pressure to conform may also come from younger family members. In Florida, two families recently tried to have an elderly couple committed to an institution, because they were living together.

The greatest distortion of the sexuality of old age occurs in the nursing homes where hundreds of thousands of the elderly spend the remaining days of their lives. The American Nursing Home Association, which includes 7,000 facilities as members, has yet to discuss sexuality and the aged at any of its meetings. Physicians, nurses, and attendants at these homes often stereotype the aged as being without sexual desires or needs, and are horrified or disgusted at discover-

For everything there is a season, and a time to every purpose under heaven:
a time to be born and a time to die;
a time to plant, and a time to pluck up what is planted;
a time to kill, and a time to heal;

a time to break down, and a time to build up;
a time to weep, and a time to laugh;
a time to mourn, and a time to dance;
a time to cast away stones, and a time to gather stones together;

a time to embrace, and a time to refrain from embracing;
a time to seek, and a time to lose;
a time to keep, and a time to cast away;
a time to rend, and a time to sew;

a time to keep silence, and a time to speak;
a time to love, and a time to hate;
a time for war, and a time for peace.

Ecclesiastes 3:1-8

---

ing that residents are taking part in sexual activities. For example, a nurse who came upon a couple making love at a large nursing home ran to the director's office and frantically asked "What should I do?" The enlightened director responded, "Tiptoe gently out so you don't disturb them" (Lobsenz 1974).

The environment of most nursing homes is totally desexualized with the sexes segregated and no opportunities for privacy. Few institutions provide areas where couples can even be alone together for conversational intercourse, much less intercourse that is sexual. Frequently, married couples are separated and some state institutions allow the sexes to mix only under supervision. A 70-year-old woman complained of a nursing home where there was no place to be alone with her husband, who was in the home only to convalesce from an eye operation. She said poignantly, "… there is nothing else wrong with him, no reason why we can't make love. Yet when I come to visit him we must meet only in 'public' areas. Even if we could be alone in his room, there's only a narrow hospital bed there. When I suggested to the home's director that he put at least a three-quarters bed in my husband's room, the man looked at me as if I were some sort of sexual monster." (Lobsenz 1974).

The erotic life of the aged is only beginning to be understood and accepted by the public and — in some instances — by the aged themselves. But many people continue to find it totally incomprehensible that their older parents or grandparents still desire sexual intercourse. The traditional labeling of the elderly person who is still interested in sex as a "dirty old" man or lady prevails. This is unfortunate, for the sexuality of old people is as much a part of them as it is with

adolescents. Unfortunately, society doesn't yet know how to deal effectively with either.

## QUESTIONS

1. Discuss the significance of *sexual scripting* in learning to become sexual.
2. Why is masturbation an important aspect of psychosexual development? Is masturbation normal? Why is it discouraged by the Catholic Church and some Protestant churches?
3. What are the characteristics of adolescent psychosexual development? Why is there an epidemic of teen pregnancies? What does this epidemic reveal about adolescent sexuality and maturity?
4. What is the significance of homosocial relations during adolescence in the development of later heterosexual relationships?
5. Discuss adult psychosexual development. Why does growing older often lead to a crisis for many people concerning their sexuality?

# Readings

## Learning About Sex in Mangaia

Donald S. Marshall

*The Mangaians live on one of the Cook Islands in the geographical center of Polynesia. As the reading illustrates, their children learn about sex quite differently than do American children and adolescents.*

*Circle.* The Mangaian is born, as he lives and loves and dies, in the midst of his clustered kinsmen. To bring forth her child, the mother labors in a circle formed by family members; the grandmother, the husband or father and the midwife all help her. Social warmth and approval envelop a newborn child; he is an added source of strength and power — his birth has strengthened the ties of sexual affection between his parents and extended the web of kinship.

Boys and girls may play together until three or four. Between four and five they separate into sex-age groups that will distinguish them socially for the rest of their lives. Brother and sister, sweethearts, lovers, husband and wife, mother and father, old man and old woman — except for economic activities, such pairs rarely mix socially in public, despite their intense private relationships. A six-year-old Mangaian brother and his three-year-old sister would not think of walking hand-in-hand in town, nor would the dignified Mangaian deacon and his wife walk to church together.

*Play.* The preschool Mangaian boy's bottom and penis rarely are covered except for church. There is no real shame associated with a child's genitalia (except for uncovering the glans of the penis) until he is about 12.

Small children may play at copulation, but only in private. In a somewhat different sense adult copulation never is socially acknowledged. The Mangaian enjoys an extraordinary sense of "public-privacy." He may copulate at any age in the single room of a hut that contains five to 15 family members of all ages – as have his ancestors before him. His daughter may receive and make love with a succession of nightly visitors in the same room. (This is motoro – the sleep-crawling tradition of Polynesian courtship in which a young man tests and socially demonstrates his courage and ardor by slipping into the family sleeping room soundlessly and copulating with the girl. Her parents and others in the room are theoretically asleep. But the mother and father may listen anxiously for the sound of laughter as a sign that their daughter will be happy with her new partner. They "sleep soundly," say my informants with a smile. Parental over-vigilance might cost the daughter a husband. But under most conditions all of this takes place without social notice; everyone seems to be looking in another direction.)

A Mangaian boy first hears of masturbation when he is about seven. He discusses it with his friends and eventually, between his eighth and ninth years, he experiments with himself while off feeding the pigs or fishing.

Although parents may try to stop children's masturbation, their efforts and their punishments are both light. A traveling husband or an older boy without a girl may also masturbate, using only his hand, thinking of girls or of orgasm.

*Cut.* Some Mangaian boys experiment early with sexual intercourse. Such "new boys" must go to sexually promiscuous older women and widows; the younger girls won't cooperate. Most boys do not commence their sexual adventures until they are 13 or 14 and have undergone superincision. (In superincision the skin on the top of the penis is cut down through the cartilaginous tissue for almost the full length of the organ, and the skin folded back and covered with a herbal powder. Nothing is cut off or removed; the skin is rearranged so that the scar tissue will leave the glans of the penis permanently exposed.) Girls learn about sex and develop the appetite for it at 12 or 14, about the time they start to menstruate.

When a boy reaches 12 or 13 his male peers begin to press him to undergo superincision. Since he may be taunted publicly for a lack of courage or be said to have a stinking penis (the ultimate Polynesian insult), it is not long before he or his father or an uncle decides that he must submit. It is usually a kinsman who gives the idea to the boy and finds an expert to perform the operation.

The superincision expert is the most important source of the boy's formal schooling in sexual behavior – what to do with women, and how to do it. He may also arrange for a woman to undertake the practical exercises when the boy's cut has healed, to provide more direct sex instruction.

Superincisions of one boy or a group of them takes place in a secluded spot, preferably on the seashore or beside a mountain stream. The cut used to be made with a flake of a flintlike local stone. Most experts now prefer a straight razor. An anvil is whittled from a coconut shell to the size and shape of a tablespoon bowl, and used to protect the glans of the penis and to provide a firm working surface. When the extremely painful operation is complete the youth runs into the sea or the stream for relief, exultantly proclaiming "Now I am really a man!"

*Rite.* More culturally interesting than the superincision, more important to the youth than physiological treatment, is the sexual knowledge and training that the boy gets from the expert. He learns the techniques of coitus and the means of locating a "good girl." He is taught to perform cunnilingus, to kiss and suck breasts, to bring his partner to climax several times before he reaches his own climax, and to achieve mutual orgasm.

Copulation with an experienced partner follows this period of instruction. The goal in this rite of passage, some two weeks after the operation, is to remove the superincision scab by actual sexual intercourse. Obviously, an experienced woman is required. In the past she was a kinswoman, but now she may be any mature and experienced woman, perhaps the village trollop.

There is said to be a special thrill for the woman in removing the scab this way, but there are indications that some women find it objectionable. More significant to the youth, his instructress practices various acts and positions with him, and trains him to hold back until he can achieve orgasm in unison with his partner.

The newly cut penis gives a youth the cleanliness he must have to be accepted and bolsters his confidence that he can thrill his partner, make the sexual act more vigorous, and bring his partner thrice to orgasm. And, if the cut has been properly made and the scab properly removed by an experienced partner, the organ in itself is thought to be beautiful.

Thus endowed, a boy leaves off masturbation. He aggressively seeks out girls or they seek him out. Soon copulation becomes an every-night affair.

The Mangaian girl, who also has been instructed in the ways of sex by an older woman, demands instant demonstration of sexual virility as the first test of her partner's desire for her and as a reflection of her own desirability. In one virility test, a girl requires her lover to have sexual intercourse with her while in contact with only her genitals.

Chapter 5, "Sexual Behavior on Mangaia" by Donald S. Marshall, from *HUMAN SEXUAL BEHAVIOR: Variations in the Ethnographic Spectrum*, edited by Donald S. Marshall and Robert C. Suggs. © 1971 by The Institute for Sex Research, Inc., Basic Books, Inc., Publishers, New York. This is an adaptation of the above mentioned chapter as it appeared in *Psychology Today*, February 1971, "Sexuality – Two Anthropological Studies: Too Much in Mangaia." Reprinted by permission.

## Learning and Un-learning About Sex

Andrew M. Barclay, Michigan State University

*What are the difficulties we face in our culture in learning about sex as a wholistic experience?*

Learning to regard sexuality as a positive *human* force has been difficult throughout the history of Western culture. Books on the subject traditionally have been biased or based on misinformation regarding the origins and expression of human feelings. Often, the books have had a religious or moralistic bias, emphasizing shame or guilt. More recently, they have sought to present sexuality objectively, but have lost the sense of humanness about it, making sex cold, distant, and alienated. Many college courses on sexuality have failed to integrate sex as part of the total person because there has been no adequate textbook. Teachers have often bravely tried, but their efforts have not always succeeded. Sexuality is a hard course to teach.

In recent years we have begun to realize that sexual ignorance creates not only unwanted pregnancies, but also feelings of low self-esteem. Many colleges and universities teach courses in human sexuality as part of the biologi-

cal sciences, the social sciences, or the liberal arts depending upon the loyalties of the individuals offering the course and which area of sexuality is stressed. Biologically-oriented courses emphasize physical aspects of sex, the anatomy of sex organs, and their physiology, venereal diseases and so on. Socially-oriented courses may include descriptions of physical processes such as positions of sexual intercourse, but their major emphasis is on how sex is acted out in society, the norms and rules governing our sex roles, and the various relationships existing within and between roles. Many courses try to bridge the gap, but many more choose the safe course of presenting one side or the other.

Similarly, textbooks focus on physical aspects or responses because these are the easiest aspects of sexuality to discuss. Our physical selves are fairly well-defined and have been defined for more than 300 years. Sex norms have been stretched to allow us to talk about sex so long as we maintain our objectivity; medical science makes it easy to be objective about sex. Kinsey and Masters and Johnson's research broke the early ground for discussing physical sexual activity. Teaching about sex organs, nomenclature, and positions of sexual intercourse is much easier than taking on the more complex aspects of sexuality such as sex roles, sex norms, and the mind-body split.

Many so-called "primitve" societies train their children to experience sexual feelings *as* they act them out. Parents and children discuss sexual nomenclature just as they discuss nonsexual areas of the body, that is, directly and without shame. Young girls are often taken aside by older women and taught sexual responsiveness because, in their "primitive" wisdom, they know it does not come naturally. Girls are taught how to reach satisfaction through masturbation, sexual intercourse, and how to associate sexual feelings in their bodies with their sex organs so they can have an orgasm as easily as the men do.

Compare their child-rearing practices with ours: little direct discussion and naming of sex organs, children told not to touch their sex organs, at any time for any reason except elimination, little girls taught to avoid sexual feelings, thoughts and contacts, and on and on.

Psychologists are now finding out that training children to look at sex in this way has profound effects on adult behavior and these effects are not limited to sexuality alone. Human beings cannot control just one aspect of their emotional response; if you try to control your sexual feelings, for example, all feeling ultimately is inhibited. The most frequent means of controlling feelings it *repression*, a defense where we pretend we are not feeling what we are feeling and then forget we are pretending. This is very effective, from the individual's point of view, because the feelings we are afraid to experience appear to go away. Unfortunately, life is real, not pretend; the feelings are still present and have to show up somewhere.

A much more subtle effect of this type of learning is the feeling of separation between the mind and the body. This incorrect form of thought is so prevalent these days, many readers will be unable to think of the alternative to a split mind-body. In this respect we have not advanced beyond 17th century Cartesian logic which held the mind and body separate meeting at the pineal body or the thymus gland. No one ever suspects that feeling mind-body split arises from cultural learning.

Many contemporary philosophers and theologians have realized that the mind and body cannot be separated either physically or philosophically. The mind is the imaginary aspect of the body and the body is the real aspect of the mind; both are necessary to exist in the world. Obviously you could not be here reading this without a body to create and interpret primitive sensation, nor could you do this creative act without a mind to animate your body and intellectually interpret the real meaning hiding behind these words. Most Westerners learn to use their minds for body control in much the same way that a rider controls a horse. Perhaps the most frequent form of sexual conflict is a person's body saying, "Yes," with the mind saying, "No" to sexual expression, be it masturbation, petting or sexual intercourse; sometimes it is the other way around.

Everthing we do, even definitions of self, suffers from this split. Men are taught to consider themselves as solely masculine, to seek action to strive for accomplishment, to achieve power every day. Women are taught to think of themselves as solely feminine, to be, to exist in purity of thought and form without being defiled by the world. Since these are *roles* in the society, it is impossible for people to be all one way or the other. A role is just another act we do in public; we pretend we are all one way or the other which, once again, means denying true aspects of the self. Men have to pretend they are strong, unemotional, and rational; women have to pretend they are weak and dependent on men.

The catch is that every person is a complete entity, a whole being. How can whole beings, who are complete unto themselves, be split into a mind-component and a body-component? How can people be so dichotomized in male/female sex roles?

What we must work for is a re-integration of the mind and body. A good place to start is with our sexuality so that we can act as whole, healthy individuals.

## Sex-Related Problems:
## Reflections of Emotional Growth

By Bruce A. Baldwin, Ph.D.

In our society, various standards are used to gauge adulthood. On the objective side, educational level, employment stability, and family status are reference points for maturity. There are also a number of emotional criteria for assessing maturity — a series of developmental tasks that must be confronted and resolved adaptively by the adolescent in order to be deemed emotionally mature. This emotional development occurs primarily between the onset of puberty and age thirty, although the struggle with specific maturational issues may continue much longer for some.

These developmental issues are distinct for each culture. For example, in this country stress is placed on attaining emotional autonomy by adulthood. Yet, in other cultures where extended families are part of the social structure, emotional dependence on one's elders is quite common and does not conflict with standards for adulthood.

The process of becoming emotionally mature in our culture causes difficulties for most adolescents. Confronting developmental tasks necessarily involves struggle, problems, and personal difficulty. It is not surprising, then, that conflicts reflecting these long-term developmental issues often underlie the immediate problems presented to health professionals by young people. Detecting these developmental issues in sex-related problems is helpful in using the problem as a maturing experience while resolving the immediate problem as well.

**The Developmental Framework**    Six major areas of conflict comprise the basic maturational issues of our culture.

1.  *Becoming Emotionally Autonomous.*    This issue involves struggle between one's needs for emotional dependence and one's needs for emotional autonomy. The choice is between remaining emotionally dependent on one's parents (or on a parent-like partner) in order to be taken care of, or becoming emotionally autonomous and attaining reasonably independent emotional functioning at an adult level. Adequate resolution of this conflict entails confronting the process of emotional separation and developing a comfortable blend of independent emotional functioning while retaining the capacity for emotional interdependence with others.

*Amy.* Struggling for emotional independence and the need to make her own choices, Amy began to engage in many casual sexual encounters with a variety of males in her high school. She believed that closer relationships were unimportant to her. Just below the surface, however, lay strong dependency needs that she was unable to acknowledge or deal with effectively. To control these needs she became excessively "independent" and very fearful of needing others emotionally. After her growing reputation at school came to the attention of several of her teachers, her school counselor helped her become aware of these needs and begin developing true emotional autonomy.

*John.* As a young man midway through junior college, John had a pattern of becoming excessively dependent in relationships with females after initially presenting himself to them as quite independent. He was passive in most areas of his life, including his sex life. His relationships with the women he dated quickly took on aspects of a parent-child relationship, which inevitably caused difficulties for both partners. Continued feelings of depression and occasional sexual impotence brought him to the Student Counseling Center for help. His counselor helped him see that he had not adequately separated from his parents, whom he continued to need desperately to give him security.

2. *Attaining an Adequate Sexual Identity.* Conflict over sexual identity is triggered by the rapid physical changes occurring at puberty. Maturity requires acceptance of oneself as sexually adequate. Often this sense is not achieved comfortably until the mid-twenties, and for many it requires a much longer period. There is a tendency for both males and females to over-sexualize their identity. Some, however, take the opposite route by masking their sexuality. Both extremes are somewhat maladaptive. For a healthy resolution of this issue, the individual develops several means in addition to a sexual relationship (e.g., non-sexual friendships, social activities, and – later – in being an effective parent) by which to express his identity as male or female.

*Allen.* Presenting himself as a very "macho" young man, Allen boasted of his many sexual conquests and led his friends to believe that he was a sexual athlete. Beneath this facade he felt very insecure about himself and his sexual identity. By convincing others (and consequently himself) of his success with women, he was able to bolster a rather inadequately developed sense of masculinity. He noticed early V.D. symptoms following a series of one-night sexual encounters. He called his local Switchboard for V.D. treatment referral. In talking with a peer counselor about V.D. prevention, he began to see clearly his sexual behavior pattern and to acknowledge his insecurity.

*Brenda.* A bright and articulate high school senior, Brenda was a strong achiever with high grades and many scholastic honors. Those around her, however, noticed that she consistently wore ill-fitting clothes that minimized her femininity. She was not socially involved at school; she dated very little; and she became very anxious in any but platonic relationships with the young men in her class. Her behavior was confusing to these young men, as she was both attractive and well-liked. Behind her deliberately constructed drab exterior and her over-reliance on achieving to maintain her self-esteem, she had a poor body image and an underdeveloped sexual identity. Discussing her feelings about her lack of social activities with her minister (a trained counselor), she became aware of the roots of her difficulty.

3. *Defining a Personal Value System.* For this part of the maturing process, the young adult attempts to define personal values as contrasted to the values of significant others, particularly those of parents and peers. Commonly encountered among youth is a total rejection of parental values and a complete acceptance of peer values. An adaptive resolution to this developmental task entails defining and accepting a personal set of values rather than blindly rejecting or embracing an externally defined set (i.e., the values of one's parents or peers). The confusions, the behavioral inconsistency, and the stress of this process often produce sex-related problems.

*Sue.* Throughout her teens Sue completely rejected her parents' values as "too old-fashioned" and "too rigid." Soon after puberty she began a series of transient sexual encounters. Her behavior was supported by her peer group of young women also striving for "freedom." In completely dismissing her parents' sexual values and embracing those of her peers, she never worked out what was right for her. Her parents' inability to understand this aspect of her growth made her rebellion more intense and longer lasting, as they made futile attempts to help her see her behavior from their perspective. Currently, as a young woman of 19, she finds it difficult to maintain a satisfying relationship, and she is uncomfortable with her pattern of short-term relationships centered solely around sex. After talking with a young social worker who consults in a day care center where she works, Sue accepts a referral to a group for young adults struggling with similar issues in development.

*Harry.*    As a junior at a large state university, Harry recently became sexually involved with a young woman he had been dating for about a year. He soon appeared at the university's Psychological Clinic suffering from extreme guilt over this sexual activity. Coming from a deeply religious background, sex before marriage conflicted with his own religious values as well as those of his family. Yet, he was deeply in love with this young woman, and they planned to be married within a year. With the help of a staff psychologist, Harry began to explore his values and to define those areas where his values conflicted with his behavior.

4.  *Accepting Emotional Intimacy: Learning to Trust.*   This issue is particularly difficult for young adults during the maturing process when self-image is often quite tenuous, when personal security is just developing, and when identity is in the formative stages. Some choose isolation and the security it provides rather than emotional intimacy and the vulnerability that goes with it. Others develop maladaptive ways to create some form of emotional closeness without risk or vulnerability. All maladaptive solutions result in loneliness and feelings of emptiness that inevitably come when basic emotional needs are not being met.

*Andy.*    Andy was a young craftsman several years out of high school. During his school years he had been involved with several women who

had rejected him. He never resolved the hurt and betrayal he felt, but instead developed a pattern of deceiving himself by substituting sex for emotional intimacy. He began to seek sexual intimacy without giving of himself, with little expression of caring and without developing trust and openness with his partner. Now he feels that "something is missing" from his relationships, and the women he dates agree with him. He is seeking help at his local mental health center because he is lonely and he recognizes the pattern in his relationships, which he is unable to change by himself.

*Sally.*    Deprived of adequate nurturance in her childhood, Sally was again deeply hurt by a critical, rejecting man she met as a college freshman and who later left her for another woman. Rather than resolve her feelings of abandonment, she – like Andy – developed a substitute for emotional intimacy. She typically chose a man who had some problems of his own and who initially enjoyed dependency. Then she "gave herself" sexually to him, began to mother him, and fostered his dependency on her so that he would not leave her. The relationship inevitably turned sour as she overplayed the mothering role, which she misinterpreted as emotional intimacy. Sally feels increasingly victimized as men continue to withdraw from her after initial involvement. While attending a rap group on sex in her residence hall, she begins to talk with her Resident Advisor about her feelings and is referred to the College Mental Health Service for further help.

5.  *Dealing With Authority.*   Dealing with power issues in relationships involves struggle for many adolescents. The conflict is experienced either as difficulty in accepting the power and influence of others (e.g., parents, teachers), or as problems in developing a realistic sense of per-

sonal power. At one extreme, the inability to accept the legitimate authority or power of others leads to excessive rebelliousness. Conversely, the inability to develop a sense of personal power to influence others leads to a lack of self-assertiveness. Learning to negotiate compromise, and to give and take in relationships are the marks of adaptive resolution of this maturational issue.

*Tom*.  Recently graduated from technical school and now working, Tom consistently feels that others are attempting to control his actions and establish their power over him. At work he resents the authority of his foreman. In his social relationships he has become controlling and dominating to insure that others do not control him. Recently he has begun to have problems in his marriage. His wife, Pam, whose submissiveness he has always taken for granted, has begun to demand a more active part in marital decision-making. As she has become more assertive and more active sexually, Tom has begun to experience sexual insecurity and frequent impotence. In marital counseling with a local professional, power issues and the inability to feel secure when not in control of a relationship or a situation were identified as major unresolved causes.

*Pam*.  Throughout childhood and adolescence, Pam was not allowed to make her own decisions, since all decisions were made for her by her parents. As a teenager she found herself unable to express an opinion or to disagree, unable to say no to men when sex was suggested, and unable to make even simple decisions for herself. She never enjoyed sex and was inorgasmic, perceiving sex primarily as a way to please the man she was involved with at the time. She married Tom because he was assertive and he made decisions for them both. Through

his control of their relationship, he provided the security she sought. However, she became progressively unhappy in the marriage and after several years became involved in a consciousness-raising group sponsored by the local YMCA. She began to take tentative steps to assert herself in her marriage. After reading a book on the fulfillment of female sexuality, Pam became acutely aware of what she was missing in her sexual relationship with Tom. She consulted a therapist about her inability to experience orgasm, and she began to work on her submissiveness as well.

*6.  Developing Reasonable Self-Discipline*.  Reaching a reasonable balance between achievement-oriented activities and leisure activities is essential to emotional health. Our society is competitive and success-oriented, yet at the same time leisure time is increasing. Adolescents often have difficulty integrating the two adequately. Some become excessively leisure-oriented, impulsive, and unable to meet their responsibilities for the present or the future. On the other hand, there are those who become excessively achievement-oriented, always focused on the future, delaying leisure today to achieve for tomorrow, and becoming progressively unable to relax and enjoy the time for relaxation that is available.

*Elaine*.  A career woman at age 20, Elaine has always been pushed by her parents to achieve. She has always looked ahead to the next goal and has created increasingly high expectations for herself. As time has passed, she has become less and less able to relax in her infrequent free moments. One result is that she has become almost unaware of her sexual feelings and sex has little appeal other than as a brief diversion fitted into her busy schedule. She is engaged to marry a young lawyer but is worried because she has become inorgasmic and has difficulty becoming aroused at all. With encouragement from her fiance, she has contacted the local Family Planning Clinic to see if her diminished sexual feelings might be caused by the birth control pills she is using. However, the problem is soon defined to be the result of her achievement-orientation and inability to relax.

*Ken.* A sometime college student, Ken has few aspirations for the future. His motto is: "if it feels good, let's do it." He works or attends college sporadically, and his interest in activities quickly wanes as the novelty wears off and he is faced with the work involved. There is a growing recognition within him that most of his peers are passing him by as they develop personally satisfying careers, lifestyles, and relationships.

He is living with a young woman and the child that resulted – at least in part – from his impulsivity and failure to use contraception consistently. Recently, he has found it difficult to relate effectively to his partner because he is constantly distracted by other women. His last fling with another woman has triggered a confrontation with his partner. The threatened loss of the woman he loves, due to his impulsivity and irresponsibility, prompts him to contact the Crisis Counseling Center in a nearby town for help.

*Sex Related Problems: Reflections of Emotional Growth*, Bruce A. Baldwin. Copyright ©. Reprinted by permission.

---

## Sexuality and the Aged

Georgia Barrow

*Why is the sexuality of the aged hidden or ignored? What are the reasons for this?*

***Sexual Invisibility*** A term that corresponds with sexual invisibility is "asexual." The term "asexual" means nonsexual or lacking sexuality.

Old people are often stereotyped as asexual. If a sexual relationship between two old people is revealed, the resulting view is that it is perverted or morally shocking. The widely used phrase "dirty old man" indicates the unacceptability of sexual interests on the part of older men. It suggests that what is appropriate behavior for a young man becomes wrong or "dirty" at an older age. No parallel phrase is applied to women probably because the sexuality of old women is considered to be nonexistent. She is a "dried-up old woman." No one suspects her of being interested in sex. Old men are apparently seen as deviating from their asexual image often enough to warrant the censure of being a "dirty old man."

When NBC aired a special program *Of Men and Women* (1975) which included an interview with a couple in their seventies who had an active sex life, the results were quite revealing. The elderly woman was asked to comment on the stereotype that older people are not interested in sex. She replied, "That's a bunch of baloney. That's a bunch of bunk!" She went on to describe in very positive terms her active sexual relationship with the 78-year-old man she was living with saying that if all she had to live for was three meals a day and sleep, she'd rather be dead. Students in a marriage and family class which viewed the program expressed surprise that old people are sexually active. One student said, "Although no one had ever told me, I had assumed that people phased sex out of their lives around their sixties." This response was typical of many students who had either not thought much about whether older people were interested in sex, or had concluded they were not. When old people marry, many people tend to view the happening as an oddity or with amusement. They make comments like, "Isn't that cute?" or "I'm surprised they bothered at their age."

People tend not to impute a sexual motive. But, of course, only the newly married couple knows the real truth!

Even old people themselves sometimes accept the stereotype of asexuality. If we can believe the accuracy of Ann Landers' column, many an older person has married and been surprised to find that the new spouse expects more than companionship and a bridge or checkers partner.

The reasons for sexual invisibility of the aged are basically rooted in the youth culture of our society. Three cultural themes stand out as playing a major role. (1) the idea that sexual attraction is much stronger for the young with "good-looking" bodies; (2) the idea that romance is for the young; and (3) the idea that sex is for procreation. Feldstein (1970) covers these themes in his book *Sex in Later Life*, and the discussion of them here is partially based on his work. In the final analysis, old people may be sexually invisible because they keep their sex lives "in the closet."

*Physical Attraction and Youth.* The idea is wiespread that sexual tension is built mainly on physical attraction between the sexes and that very young men and women are the most physically or sexually attractive. The theme that good looks, youth, and sex go together is perpetuated through advertising, film, television, and stage. Models are generally young and beauty contests are sometimes held for the "junior miss" and even children. But who has ever heard of a beauty contest for the aged? In advertising, products are promoted by presenting the idea that their use preserves a youthful and beautiful look and makes one sexier. It is the young in television and film who are portrayed as attractive and sexually desirable. Because of the promotion of glamorous youth, older people seen on films, TV, or in real life, find their physi-

cal appearance less highly regarded than younger people's.

Even the middle aged in our society suffer from the narrow definition of physical beauty, especially those who do not have beautiful bodies. A study in a sociology class examined student attitudes toward the physical appearance of a middle-to-older-aged couple. Students were shown a picture of a somewhat overweight nude couple seated comfortably in their living room. The picture, one of a collection taken by Diane Arbus, appears in a copy of *Ms* magazine. The students were asked to look at the picture and then write down neutral comments such as "mom and dad," "beautiful," and "free," many more supplied negative responses. Some of the negative words used were "gross," "repulsive," "ugly," "shocking," "sick," "grotesque," "absurd," "slobbish." Words used to describe the physical appearance were "sagging," "overweight," and "loose." Several students with negative views added written comments pertaining to the sexuality of the couple. One said:

> Even though it's a nude picture it doesn't seem to deal with sex because they are both so old, fat, and saggy.

Another said:

> In this case a woman with boobs to her waist and a man with several rolls around the middle does not turn me on. If you've got it, flaunt it. But if it's offensive or gross, get rid of it or cover up.

Many people consider only the young, perfectly proportioned body to be sexually attractive. If the factor of age is combined with overweight or some other physically detracting feature, negative attitudes result.

When people view aged bodies as neither sexually stimulating nor desirable, the next step is to assume that no interest in sex or sexual activity occurs in old age. This assumption, if shared by the aged, can produce a self-fulfilling prophecy in which old people feel devalued sexually and thus lose interest in sex. (The media and society as a whole make it difficult for middle-aged and old people to accept their wrinkled and sagging skin and other physical declines.) Old people need self-confidence to avoid the frustration and disappointment that our society fosters.

*The Idea That Romantic Love Is Only for the Young.* While romantic love has been variously defined, it has a number of generally accepted characteristics: idealization of mate, consuming interest and passion, fantasy, and desire for a blissful state of togetherness. Love at first sight and the idea that love conquers all are often elements of romantic love. Eric Fromm (1956) describes romantic love as "falling" in love as opposed to the more mature "standing" in love. There is no inherent reason why only young people should have exclusive access to romantic love. Yet in all forms of media, romantic love is predominantly an emotion for young people. From Shakespeare's *Romeo and Juliet* to Eric Segal's *Love Story* passion and romance is for young lovers. Perhaps the concept came to be associated with young people because they are the ones most often involved in mate selection. However, with the increasing divorce rate and with increasing life expectancy, mate selection often continues throughout the life span. When only young people are viewed as being capable of strong passionate feeling, this view adds to the stereotype of the asexuality of the aged.

*Sexual Function Is Purely for Procreation.* This concept disassociates the aged and sex and is embodied in the Christian religion by the teachings of St. Augustine. Accordingly, a woman's femininity is measured by her child-bearing and mother role; a man's masculinity is measured by the number of offspring he produces. Because of the association between sexuality and procreation, men and women beyond the usual child-bearing years are therefore seen as being less sexual. More and more, however, the sex act is being viewed as an expression of love and happiness with the reward being pleasure instead of children. But deep-seated ideas take a long time to vanish, as evidenced by the still present fear on the part of some men that a vasectomy would rob them of virility and manhood and the fear on the part of some women that a hysterectomy would rob them of femininity. Because of the traditional idea that sex is only for procreation, people continue to make the mistaken assumption that the inability to bear children means the absence of sexuality and sexual desire. Aged men and women suffer from this idea, especially aged women. Many do not know that aged men can impregnate a woman as long as they have active sperm. While some decline in fertility occurs with age, many men do not become infertile until they reach their '70s or '80s.

Finally, a major factor involved in the perpetuation of the idea that sex is the prerogative of the young might be lack of open display on the part of the aged. Older people are not as candid in revealing an interest in sex as younger people. A survey of college students by the authors bears on this point. The students were asked if their grandparents openly discussed their own sex life or displayed any show of sexual interest in their partner in the student's presence. The first question was "Have you ever heard either set of grandparents discuss their own sexual relationship in any way no matter how casual?"

Of fifty students who had two sets of living grandparents, 65% had never heard their grandparents discuss their own sexual relationship. The second question was "Have you ever seen your grandparents show any sexual interest in one another?" Fifty percent of the students had never seen either set of grandparents show any sexual interest, and an additional 30% had rarely seen either set of grandparents show any sexual interest in one another. Sexual interest was not defined but left open to the student's individual imagination or definition.

The study leaves a lot of questions unanswered: How did the student define sexual interest? What goes on that grandchildren don't see? How much sexual interest is present on the part of the aged? But the study does point up one fact: Old people don't typically imply through their talk or behavior that they have active sex lives.

The apparent absence of open interest in sex may be in part based on the conservative sexual values of older people regarding the privacy of sexual matters. In part it may also be due to the taboos against sex for old people. Some old people are worried about reported cases of children asking that their parents be committed to mental institutions because they suddenly moved in with an elderly person of the opposite sex. Whatever the reasons for the lack of openness about their own interest in sex, the secrecy perpetuates the sexual invisibility of the aged.

Overriding the entire discussion of the strong association made between youth and sex in this society is the fact that little has been understood or made known about the sexuality of the aged. However, changes will occur as more and more research in this area yields information that will be available to the public. Recent findings help clarify the myths and misconceptions.

*Aging, Ageism and Society.* Georgia M. Barrow, Patricia A. Smith. Copyright © West Publishing Co., St. Paul, 1979.

# Intimate Relationships

Whatever a person's age, an integal part of his or her life is the ability to love and receive love. Learning to love and be loved is a crucial task a person must accomplish in his or her psychosexual development. Daniels and Horowitz (1976) write:

> When I love, I'm more likely to find love around me. For when I am loving toward you, you're more likely to touch your own ability to love, and meet me from that place. And when you can feel that I really care for you, that I'm not trying to exploit you, you're more likely to work out our difficulties, instead of making little conflicts into big ones.

Loving is expansive, a way of giving and receiving, a source of growth and intimacy. Failure to successfully learn how to love leaves the individual disconnected and isolated in the world, a rootless Steppenwolf.

Fortunately, most of us have experienced love at some time in our lives, beginning with our parents. This love (and sometimes *not*-love) that we received from our parents (especially the parent, who held and nurtured us when we were infants) sets the model for our love for others. If we had little love and affection and holding as children, then it will be harder for us to learn to give and receive love as adults. If we had an abundance of love as children, then we are likely to have an abundance of love as adults.

Regardless of whether or not our parents (or parenting adults) loved us, the people we seek out in adult life are likely to resemble them in significant ways. Sometimes, however, the resemblance (which is usually unconscious) is only in our mind. We *project* onto other people qualities or traits we want (or do not want) them to have. Then we react to these persons *as though* they actually possessed those qualities, whether they do or not. Such projections prevent us from relating to them as unique individuals in themselves.

## Romantic Love

Projection forms a large part of our love life, especially in adolescence and young adulthood. Projection is the basis for romantic love, an illusory love that is richest and most passionate when it is unattained, when it is beyond our reach. If we do reach it and attain the ones we love, then the love may soon disappear. Tales of romance do not begin with marriage but end with it. Its essence is yearning. It differs from admiration, Woody Allen writes, because when you admire someone you admire them from a distance; when you are in love with someone, you want to be in the same room with them, hiding behind a couch.

Falling in love with someone usually prevents us from seeing the person as he or she really is. What we usually love is the *image* we have formed of that person. And, when that image dissolves as we get to know the other person, our love may dissolve as well because we feel disappointed. The image that we have of the person is really an image we have of an *ideal* person projected onto them. That image often contains elements of our parents.

The ultimate basis for romantic love is alienation from self. There are aspects of ourselves that do not fit our image of what it is to be a man or a woman in our culture. Out traditional sex roles severely limit the range of feelings and activities that we may "legitimately" experience. Men, for example, are discouraged from expressing tenderness, dependence, and tears; women are discouraged from expressing intelligence, independence, and strength. We deny those aspects in ourselves and then project them onto the person of the opposite sex, calling them masculine traits or feminine traits. We polarize our being human into being male and being female.

Often, the person we project these traits onto may not have them or not have them in the

Individuals do not always feel passionate about the person who provides the most rewards with the greatest consistency. Passion sometimes develops under conditions that would be more likely to provoke aggression and hatred than love.

E. Walster

---

same way we want them to have them. Whatever the case, we are often asking the person with whom we are in love to fill those empty spaces in ourselves. It is an impossible demand because no one can fill those holes except ourselves; but we will blame the other for not filling the holes.

Ultimately, romantic love relationships begin to fall apart. Each person relates to the image of the other and tries to maintain his or her own image at the same time. It is a heavy burden that few people can carry very long. Each begins to feel disappointed in the other because he or she does not really fit the projected image; the other does not fill the holes. It is at this point that relationships change or break apart. The relationship can simply fade away, without anyone knowing why or even really caring. It can become like a poison, each person poisoning the other so badly in words and deeds that the relationship becomes unendurable and ends in a final explosion. No one honestly has said what has been really happening, they simply fight or argue or withdraw, accumulating poison and resentment. Or the relationship can end honestly with each recognizing the images, demands, needs, and disappointments. The two might even be able to become friends after the hurt has ended. Or, finally, they might be able to change the relationship with a lot of love, work, and commitment. If each discovers they care enough about the other as he or she really is (minus projections), each can change and evolve new ways of loving. This is the beginning of conscious love.

## Conscious Love

When we love someone consciously, we are aware of who that person really is. We do not relate to their image but to their reality. We are aware of who we are, what our needs are, our

dependence as well as our independence. We do not expect the other to give us what we lack; we give it to ourselves, although we may have their help. We love the ordinary qualities in the other and appreciate their ordinariness. We fight with caring, we get angry with each other but work things out. We do not hurt.

Sidney Jourard (1971) described this kind of loving:

> If I love her, I love her projects, since she is their source and origin. I may help her if she wants my help; or let her struggle with them unaided if this is meaningful to her. I respect her wishes in this manner.
>
> If I love myself, I love my projects since they are my life. If she loves me, she confirms me in my projects, helps me with them, even if the help consists in leaving me alone. If she tries to control me, she doesn't love me. If I try to control her, I don't love her. I experience her as free and treasure her freedom. I experience myself as free and treasure my freedom.

Conscious love is not an abstraction or an idea or a state of being. It is an activity. A person loves by actively loving through both words *and* deeds. You cannot "always hurt the one you love" and really love. A person who always hurts does not really love: that is merely their image of themselves. Their actions speak otherwise. The existentialist philosopher Jean Paul Sartre described conscious love when he wrote: "There is no love apart from the deeds of love; no potentiality of love other than that which is manifested in loving" (Jean Paul Sartre, 1956). A person is what his or her actions are. If a person does not act lovingly, then he or she does not love.

In conscious love, sex often takes on a different meaning than in romantic love, and sex is used as a means of communicating strong, deep feelings; its range goes far beyond the mystical orgasms of romantic love. It becomes a means of

**Marriage is neither heaven nor hell; it is simply purgatory.**
Abraham Lincoln

touching and sharing, of giving pleasure and receiving pleasure, of having fun. Sometimes, it is highly erotic, sometimes not; sometimes, it even may be boring. But what could be more natural than this spectrum of experience? We are human and sex is a very human activity. It is the way that we regard our sexuality in the ordinary, everyday life that gives it its meaning in conscious love.

There is a Zen poem that gives light to the ordinariness of sex:

I draw water.
I gather wood.
How beautiful!
How miraculous!

In conscious love, sex takes its proper place in human relationships: something ordinary and special at the same time. We make it what it is.

### Living Together

In cultures of poverty, it has never been unusual for unmarried couples to live together. Only recently, however, has this kind of relationship become a significant alternative to marriage for the middle class. It has become an important element in the lives of both young adults and the elderly. Although these two groups may seem at opposite ends of the spectrum, they share an

important characteristic: they are usually childless at the time.

### The Young

Few people appear willing to subject their children to the social discrimination that arises from giving birth when unmarried. This is especially true for young adults. Through the stigma associated with illegtimate birth, society maintains its rules among the middle class. The increasingly common decision of youths to live together is a result of changing sexual standards and marital ideals. The middle-class ideal of love and mutual-

---

## THE TWELVE GIFTS OF SELF

1. **The Gift of Time**
   "Just 'being' with someone can be a great comfort to them."
2. **The Gift of a Good Example**
   "Most people learn fundamental attitudes of feeling by observing other people."
3. **The Gift of Acceptance**
   "People *begin* to change when they know they are accepted for what they are."
4. **The Gift of Seeing the Best of People**
   "When we expect others to respond in a positive way, they usually come through for us."
5. **The Gift of Privacy**
   "Too frequently, we tend to 'smother' people with questions and demands on their time."
6. **The Gift of Self-Esteem**
   "We sometimes cripple those we love by criticizing too much."
7. **The Gift of Giving Up a Bad Habit**
   "It's love when you strike that vital balance between your own needs and the needs of your partner."
8. **The Gift of Self-Disclosure**
   "Bottling up feelings and resentments deprives the other person of truly knowing who you are."
9. **The Gift of Helping Someone Learn Something New**
   "Helping someone learn something new is an important investment in *their* future happiness."
10. **The Gift of Really Listening**
    "Few of us know how to listen in an effective manner."
11. **The Gift of Fun**
    "It's important when you can help those close to you find fun in ordinary, small events."
12. **The Gift of Letting Others Give to Us**
    "When we let others give to us, and when we can accept their gifts in a gracious and mature manner, we may be giving *them* one of the most important gifts of all."

## Property-sharing Rights for Unmarried Couples

The fact that a man and woman live together without marriage, and engage in a sexual relationship, does not in itself invalidate agreements between them relating to their earnings, property or expenses.

Agreements between nonmarital partners fail only to the extent that they rest upon consideration of meritricious sexual services.

California Supreme Court, Marvin v. Marvin, 1976

ity has, ironically, rendered marriage unnecessary for many, for both may exist independently of marriage. With sexual intimacy becoming an increasingly important aspect of courtship and a means of testing emotional and sexual interaction, marriage offers little except security and respectability. And to many people, this is unimportant.

Couples may find advantages in living together. First, they do not have to deal with identity problems of integrating the new roles of hus-

band and wife into their personalities. In addition, the type of commitment and the pressures are different. Living together usually signifies a commitment to care for each other — if caring ceases, the commitment ends. In marriage, however, couples may feel they are together not because they care about each other but because they are married. Marriage itself has the role of a third participant. A couple may work together to save its marriage, rather than to relate more fully, while couples living together seldom strive to

save "living together." Marriage exists as an independent structure; living together does not. Finally, couples living together do not have to deal with complex relations of raising a family, because their commitment usually excludes the idea of having children. Should they decide to have children, they usually marry.

There are disadvantages as well. Couples who live together lack the social and legal supports given married people. In many areas, landlords do not readily rent to unmarried couples, and businesses are reluctant to hire at middle and upper management levels a person living "immorally." Parents may oppose the living arrangement vigorously, cutting off both financial support and emotional ties. Finally, living together is viewed by many as merely a temporary arrangement; it does not always offer the security of long-term commitment that marriage implies and which some people need.

There are no accurate figures on how many unmarried people are living together, partly because this state tends to be more transient than marriage. The Levins (1975) found that 3 percent of their respondents reported that they were living with a man. Most of these women were young and had lived with the same partner for less than five years. (The median length of marriage is 7 years.) Three-quarters of the women worked full- or part-time, and they were likely to be in the lower income bracket. Their sex lives are similar to women who had been married less than one year (that is, those women who are most satisfied with marital intercourse). Both groups described themselves as happy most of the time and had sexual intercourse an average of nine times a month. But there are also striking differences. Unmarried women living with men are more likely than are newlyweds to experiment with new sexual techniques. They are more

likely to masturbate, try anal intercourse, use vibrators, and have lesbian experience. They are more likely than any other group to mix sex and marijuana, with three-quarters indicating they have tried it.

Living together has become another mode of premarital commitment. For most people, it is not a permanent alternative to marriage but a relationship that prepares for marriage, by providing experience in relating sexually and emotionally in a similar situation. For those who marry after experiences of living together, marriage signifies more than simply love and mutuality. It is a commitment to children, security, and respectability – a movement back into the mainstream.

**The Middle Aged**

Although the largest percentage of people living together are under thirty, living together is becoming increasingly accepted among those over thirty as well. Generally, these unmarried couples are divorced or single people who have decided not to have children. Among the divorced, many are not willing to marry again (at least for a while) because of their unhappy experiences during marriage. Many women especially do not want to be identified as wives because of the limitations and expectations such roles imply. They want intimate relationships, but not the roles and the sense that their freedom is curtailed. They may be deeply committed to careers which provide more meaning to them than a career as a housewife. For them, living together satisfies many of their intimacy needs without the necessity of dealing with roles found in marriage. Divorced men are often wary of the legal problems involved with marriage, especially if they are paying alimony or support. The recent Mar-

## The Mirages of Marriage

Unsatisfactory sexual relations are a symptom of marital discord, not the cause of it. It is difficult for the victims to see this because of the mass of progaganda about sex that attacks them day and night, on the street, in the home, in the office.

John Jones, for example, is dissatisfied with his marriage. On his way to work he may look up and see a billboard with a picture of a nearly nude, beautiful woman, advertising a brand of stockings. John is stimulated sexually and says to himself, "Boy, I'd like to have an affair with something like that." He knows this is wishful thinking, and may even recognize that the

---

vin decision in California in 1979 provided a relief for many of these men. The decision (Marvin v. Marvin) favored actor Lee Marvin whose former live-in mate sued him for support after they broke up. Michele Marvin contended she should receive support from him for their long term living arrangement which *implied* a marriage contract. The court ruled against her.

Divorced couples may or may not have children living with them from an earlier marriage. Unless the couple plans to marry, they themselves usually choose not to have children of their own. In part, this is because they do not want to start another family after they themselves have reached their thirties. But living with other people's children is usually stressful, and many relationships break up because of the difficulties which many blended families experience (Strong, 1979).

Among single people over thirty, an important reason for marrying is to have children. But among those who are living together, the decision has usually been made not to have children. Thus a primary reason for marriage, to legitimize children, is absent. Such persons are usually more committed to a partner-type relationship than to a family one. They are generally more committed to their work or careers and would find marriage and family too demanding.

## The Elderly

Among people of 50 and 60, the death rate increases significantly, breaking up lifelong patterns of relating to a mate. Widows and widowers experience a great sense of loss and disorientation, having structured their lives around the presence of another person. They raised children together, laughed together, slept together. Death breaks this pattern. How do they learn to laugh again, to sleep alone? The partner's absence may even be experienced as a presence: Joe used to walk along this same path each day; Mary's eggs tasted so much better.

Women, who outnumber men four-to-one in the over-65 age group, most commonly have to make the adjustment necessary on the death of a mate. They have to cope with loneliness and despair, fears of growing sick, and senility. Companionship is what old people seem to miss the most. Given a community, they will seek it; but often there is no community, just the isolation of run-down hotels or slum neighborhoods.

It is becoming increasingly common for older people to live together without marrying. Often, they simply cannot economically afford marriage. Almost half the income of the elderly comes from pensions, and for many, pensions and Social Security are the only income. If a widow remarries, she often loses half or all of her pension, but if she lives with and does not marry a man, then the two can pool their incomes without any cut. (The pooled income is higher than that permitted a couple receiving Social Security.) More than 25 percent of the elderly live below the poverty level, with an even larger number living marginally.

Elderly people generally refer to their partners as "companions," rather than lovers or mates. Companionship in a sense is the core of their relationship, meeting needs for intimacy and sharing, but it may have a sexual dimension as well. Their relationships often include affection, touching, kissing, and making love. Younger people often find it difficult to accept the extent of their sexual activities (perhaps because old people remind us of our parents, whom we may find it difficult to imagine as sexual).

beautiful model might be incompatible with him. Next he retreats from the daydream and his thoughts turn toward his wife. But the sexual fantasy he has had about the girl in the ad colors his reflections about his marriage relationship, and he thinks, "Golly, Mary's legs might look better in that kind of hosiery." What he means if, "If Mary were a better sexpot we'd both have a happier marriage." He is caught in a double error: the appearance of Mary's legs has nothing to do with the couple's sexual satisfaction, *and* he has forgotten his *own* function in achieving a successful union.

William Lederer and Don Jackson

---

## Marriage

The moment people marry, their relationship and their world changes, sometimes abruptly and without apparent warning. Although they knew their lives would be different, they are often unprepared for the magnitude of difference. They are confronted with a new set of role expectations: a man becomes a husband, a woman becomes a wife. Romance may be suddenly replaced by reality, new roles, and stress from role adjustments. If partners have not worked out a satisfactory manner of relating before, they must do so now. In marriage there is no separate home; each must create personal space without cutting the other off. Children futher complicate marriage. Now the man becomes man/husband/father/parent; the woman becomes the woman/wife/mother/parent. Each must relate not only to their children but also to each other as partners.

Adjustment to these new roles may be accompanied by stress and alienation. People may be legally married without actually *feeling* married. The roles in marriage are socially defined and are generally understood. The husband is expected to be the economic provider and decision-maker; the wife (with some modification) to be the housewife, dependent on her husband, and supportive of his needs and decisions (Laing 1967; Strong 1973; Lidz 1963). But the temperaments and personalities of many people do not fit these role expectations, and integration is difficult. There has to be experimentation, innovation, and change in role definitions on the part of both. No role can be totally accepted as it is socially defined; it must be modified by the individual (Erickson, 1968).

Men usually do not experience as radical a change in identity with marriage as do women.

The male role is a continuation of his participation in the larger world outside the home. His roles as provider and worker merge, and are mutually supporting; he can feel that he is a good husband, even if he has little contact with his wife or children. The concept of a "good husband" does not necessarily work toward fulfillment in marriage.

The woman who marries faces a radical break with past experiences. Courtship ends with marriage, and often romance ends as well. Yet love and romance have been two of the primary goals for a young woman. Often she may feel disillusioned with marriage. Her old identity – even her name – is radically altered by marriage. Her status no longer depends as much on her occupation or class background as it does on that of her husband (Parsons, 1942). Depending on her husband's background, people will say, "Mary married a doctor and he'll make a pile of money. She's really done well." Or, "I don't know what got into Mary, marrying a garbage collector. Imagine what her family must think – her father's a doctor, you know."

If the woman accepts the traditional role in marriage, she may suddenly be cut from the larger world around her, especially if she has children. Part of her husband's status comes from her *not* having to work. She may quit work, or may have to move, if her husband is transferred in his job. Although many women have consciously chosen traditional roles, it may be difficult for them to function as well in them as they expected. For those women who wish to maintain independent status, adjusting to their new role expectations is extremely difficult. There must be flexibility within the marriage, to allow women to adjust their roles to their personalities. Otherwise they may experience extreme stress and alienation.

**Prisoner of Sex**

Still he had not answered the question with which he began. Who finally would do the dishes? And passed in his reading through an Agreement drawn between husband and wife where evey piece of housework was divided, and duty-shifts to baby-sit were divided, and weekends where the man worked to compensate the wife for chores of weekday transportation. Shopping was balanced, cooking was split, so was the transportation of children. It was a crystal of a contract bound to serve as model for many another.

---

**Peer Relationships**    Marriage also alters relationships to peer groups. Changes began when the couple became romantically involved with each other – each probably spent less time with friends. They may make new friends as a couple, rather than as individuals. Each may feel threatened or jealous of the other's old friends. New forms of interaction are necessary.

The change in peer relationships may affect the sexual interaction of the couple, especially if the man's past sexual experience has been based on gaining status among his friends, rather than on genuine interaction with a woman; he may become confused, even impotent. He has to learn to relate emotionally and to give sexually, to meet his partner's needs as well as his own (Erickson, 1968).

**New Sexual Meanings**    Within this evolving and complex pattern, the man and woman must also establish a satisfying sexual relationship. This is often quite different from their premarital sexual relationship, even though both may include coitus. The motivation must often change. Sexuality as a form of ego gratification – conquest, aggression, or power, for example – must evolve into mutual personal gratification.

Before marriage, sexual relations often take place secretly and are associated with a sense of guilt. The automobile, often the only means of escaping the watchful eyes of parents, becomes not only a symbol of virility but also the means by which people literally move out of their parents' sphere. It becomes literally the vehicle by which sexual experience may be obtained. But this setting is inadequate for developing the mature sense of sexuality required in marriage. There is greater emphasis on kissing and petting than on intercourse, which is usually performed as swiftly as possible. As soon as the man climaxes, in this kind of setting, intercourse is over. The couple must rearrange clothing quickly in order not to be compromised if they are discovered.

This aura of secrecy leads to men – and women – learning to center sexual intercourse on the man's response. There is little sexual activity after the man's orgasm, because the woman's might take too long. As a result, women may not have the opportunity in their premarital affairs to learn to be orgasmic; they may also lack masturbatory experience. Women tend to learn how to have orgasms after marriage, because this setting is legitimate and socially supported (Kinsey, 1953). But even after marriage, couples may continue the pattern of sexual responses they learned while their behavior was considered "immoral." If they both desire orgasms and afterplay, they may have to learn new ways of responding. But bodily and emotional responses do not change overnight merely because of marriage. It often takes consciously directed effort to change old patterns.

**Sex and Marital Happiness**    Within marriage, sexual satisfaction seems to depend in part on marital happiness, and marital happiness is fostered by – but is not dependent on – a mutually fulfilling sex life. Gebhards's studies found that in extremely happy marriages, only 4.4 percent of the women did not experience orgasm during intercourse. Well over half experienced orgasm 90 to 100 percent of the time. Those women who describe themselves as being moderately happy to very unhappy do not differ significantly in orgasmic frequency, yet there is a significant percentage of women in these categories who never experience orgasm (ranging from 9 percent for the moderately happy, to 15.8 percent for the moderately unhappy, to 19 percent for the very unhappy).

This sample of 1026 women suggests that

No, he would not be married to such a woman. If he were obliged to have a roommate, he would pick a man. The question had been answered. He could love a woman and she might even sprain her back before a hundred sinks of dishes in a month, but he would not be happy to help her if his work should suffer, no, not unless her work was as valuable as his own. But he was complacent with the importance of respecting his work – what an agony for a man if work were meaningless: then all such rights were lost before a woman.

By Norman Mailer

---

there is a definite correlation between marital happiness and female orgasm. Among happily married women, sexual responsiveness is apparently greater; it may be significantly deadened among some unhappily married women. The remaining women may be able to respond sexually independently of their feelings toward their husband (Gebhard, 1966).

**Communication, Family Size, Roles**  What factors help determine marital happiness? Although this question ultlimately can be answered only by each individual, a number of factors do seem to generally encourage or support a happy marriage. The three that appear to be most important – communication, family size, and flexible marital roles – are interrelated. For example, there is evidence that small families facilitate marital happiness, but a small family requires communication between husband and wife about desired size and contraception. Roles detemine whether there will be communication within the marriage: a man may demand a large family, with no questioning his decision. Roles determine whether a woman wants children: does she feel that she wants to be a mother or a career woman? Family size affects the patterns of communication between partners: if there are too many children, the mother may be too tired or resentful to discuss problems with her husband. Thus, communication, family size, and marital roles are inseparable.

*Communication*  Communication (see Chapter 11) enables people to fulfill their needs for union with others, and at the same time to maintain the boundaries that prevent their sense of individuality from being violated. Sexual communication cannot be separated from other types of communication, because neither our lives nor our feelings can be compartmentalized.

For example, a person cannot discuss love meaningfully without discussing its sexual aspects, while parents cannot discuss child-rearing adequately without including their children's sexuality. Couples cannot fulfill themselves sexually without communicating their needs to their partners.

There can be no open discussion in which certain elements, by definition, are not allowed. For example, imagine that a society has established that "nice" people eat only steak and potatoes, and never discuss food. When they are hungry, they do not tell anyone, because talking about food is improper. And imagine a couple that has lived together properly for 20 years without ever discussing food. Every night they eat steak and mashed potatoes, because these are what "nice" people eat – yet both prefer fried chicken. But, because nice people do not discuss food, neither knows that the other secretly likes chicken. They continue to eat their food, without telling the other of the "perverse" desire for chicken. Substitute "sex" for "food" and you will have an idea of the results of poor sexual communication.

The Levins' survey of 100,000 women suggests that communication is crucial to sexual satisfaction in marriage. Of these women who *always* discuss their sexual feelings with their partner, 58 percent describe their sex lives as very good; 30 percent as good. Among women who *never* discuss sex with their partners, only 9 percent describe their sex lives as very good; 21 percent as good.

*Family Size*  Family size depends largely on the decision to use birth control. Generally, it appears that *the larger the family, the greater the tendency for strain between husband and wife.* (Nye, Carlson and Garrett, 1970; Bossard and Ball, 1956; Campbell and Frederick, 1970). Strain increases after two children, and even

**Principle of Least Interest**

That person is able to dictate the conditions of association whose interest in the continuation of the affair is least.

W. Waller and R. Hill

---

more greatly after four. A large number of children frequently makes it difficult for the parents to fulfill role expectations. For example, if a woman is often pregnant and already has many children to care for, much of her emotional and physical resources must go to the children. She will not have surplus energy to meet her husband's emotional needs, and may even resent him for her constant pregnancies. She may not respond to him sexually, either from fatigue or hostility. If they do not use contraception, for her, every sexual encounter is a potential pregnancy.

Her husband is likely to feel tension and anger toward her, believing that she is not fulfilling her role as a wife: He feels rejected. And the numerous children make it difficult for him to fulfill his role as family provider. The more children *she* has, the more difficult it is for him to earn enough money to support his family.

In large families, the pattern of relationships may shift from mutuality to authoritarian, simply because this shift seems the most expedient way of coping with seemingly unmanageable numbers. The parents cannot discuss each situation with their partners or children, and instead go by rules. One parent may dominate. Authoritarian parents do not encourage communication, but rely on corporal punishment to enforce authority. (Sears, Maccoby, and Levin, 1957; Clausen, 1966).

I should say that the relation between any two decently married people changes profoundly every few years, often without their knowing anything about it; though every change causes pain, even if it brings a certain joy. The long course of marriage is a long event of perpetual change, in which a man and a woman mutually build up their souls and make themselves whole. It is like rivers flowing on, through new country, always unknown.

D.H. Lawrence, *Phoenix*

*Role Flexibility*  The marital role relationships in marriage include both reciprocal role expectations and the activities of husband and wife in relation to each other. Those relationships range from jointly organized to intermediately separated to highly segregated. In *joint organized role relations*, the partners either share activities or carry them out separately at different times. They plan family activities together and make decisions jointly, stressing the value of sharing and mutual concern. Although there is a division of labor – the husband is the provider and the woman is the housewife – each is interested in the understanding of the other's tasks. In *segregated role relations*, the activities of husband and wife are separate and different, but fit together functionally. The husband works outside the home; the woman keeps house, cooks, cares for the children. They formally divide labor along traditional sex-role lines instead of emphasizing family unity by sharing activities, and seldom express interest or concern in the partner's activities. In *intermediate role relations*, the couple may value shared activities, but does not share and exchange tasks as much as jointly organized marriages. The partners have a more formally defined and traditional division of labor than do jointly organized couples. Fathers in this group want to share in child-rearing activities more than do male parents among segregated couples, however (Bott, 1957; Rainwater, 1965).

Scattered data suggest that among middle-class marriages, segregated roles may be an obstacle to marital success, perhaps because of expectations that marriage would be a joint concern. Among lower-class marriages, role segregation is more widely expected and accepted. Those who are usually unhappy are the wives in such marriages (Rainwater, 1965, 1966; Rainwater and Handel, 1966; Komarovsky, 1964).

There is definite data correlating class and role relations with sexual satisfaction, especially for women. Women experienced a greater range of responses to sex than did their husbands, but most men expressed a high interest in sex. Only 6 percent in one study said that they found no pleasure in intercourse. This general consistency of response suggests that sexual enjoyment or interest may be a core element in men's definition of themselves.

Among women, almost twice as many middle-and upper-lower-class wives found sexual intercourse gratifying as did lower-lower class women. Sexual indifference and rejection steadily increase as women move from middle to lower-lower class. Only lower-lower class women frequently rejected sexual intercourse strongly. The low value placed on sexual relations reflects the segregation of their marital roles in general. Neither husband nor wife is used to relating to others intimately; neither is happy about their sexual lives. They do little to change the situation, however. Half the men in highly segregated role relationships believed their wives enjoyed sex more than the wives themselves indicated.

Similarly, lower-class men in highly segregated role relationships make few efforts to help their wives experience sexual satisfaction, placing little value on mutual gratification. Among the wives, 40 percent believe their husbands are inconsiderate of them sexually; 30 percent believed sex was primarily a duty that women perform.

A major difference between the middle class and the lower class – and in the lower class between relationships that are intermediately and highly segregated – is the degree to which sexual relations are integrated with the rest of the marital life. Among the middle class and lower class with intermediate role segregation, sex is a continuation of mutuality. Among lower-class couples who have highly segregated roles, sex is isolated from husband-wife interaction. Sex requires cooperation, and highly segregated couples are often unable to act together cooperatively.

## Extramarital Sexuality

This material is adapted from Strong, et, al., *The Marriage and Family Experience*, Copyright © 1979 West Publishing Co., St. Paul.

Two great themes of literature have been love and infidelity. But actually, infidelity is simply a variation on the theme of love. Novels employing the theme of love usually end with the lovers marrying. Readers are left to imagine that the lovers will live happily ever-after. But when novelists write about love within marriage they usually describe it within the context of infidelity. Two of the world's greatest novels – Flaubert's *Madame Bovary* and Tolstoy's *Anna Karenina* – take up the theme of love, yet the protagonists Emma Bovary and Anna Karenina are not in love with their husbands, but with their "lovers," a term which takes on particular significance since a person's spouse is rarely regarded as one's lover. Husbands and wives are infrequently spoken of as lovers, yet the root of the word "lover" is "love." Is language revealing some secret about love and its relationship to marriage?

Oscar Wilde has an interesting dialogue on love and marriage in his play *A Woman of No Importance* which helps illuminate some of the motivations underlying extramarital affairs.

*Gerald:*    You have never been married, Lord Illingworth, have you?

*Illingworth:*    Men marry because they are tired; women because they are curious. Both are disappointed.

*Gerald:*    But don't you think one can be happy when one is married?

*Illingworth:*    Perfectly happy. But the happiness of a married man, my dear Gerald, depends on the people he has not married.

*Gerald:*    But if one is in love?

*Illingworth:*    One should always be in love. That is the reason one should never marry.

*Gerald:*    Love is a very wonderful thing, isn't it?

*Illingworth:*    When one is in love one begins by deceiving oneself. And one ends by deceiving others. . . .

Extramarital involvements may assume many forms. The most important factor, however, is whether these involvements are strictly sexual or are emotional as well. One sociologist quite rightly notes that "there is an important qualitative difference between the sexual act which constitutes virtually the sum total of the interaction and coital behavior which takes place in the course of a more or less continuous, affectionately meaningful, totally companionable relationship" (Cuber, 1969). In other words, a significant difference exisits between extramarital intercourse during one-night stands and extramarital intercourse that happens in an intense, emotional involvement. Cuber suggests that these companionable relationships are much more frequent than the mythology of extramarital affairs indicates. There is no one single kind of extramarital (or adulterous) relationship. Instead, extramarital affairs are quite varied, come from a number of different motivations, and satisfy a number of different needs.

The majority of extramarital sexual involvements are sporadic. Most people involved in extramarital sex probably do not have extramarital sexual intercourse more than five times a year (Gagnon, 1977). It is not clear how many people

Oh, I don't know that I love him [explains George's wife to her new lover]. He's my husband, you know. But if I get anxious about George's health, and if I thought it would nourish him, I would fry you with onions for his breakfast and think nothing of it. George and I are good friends. George belongs to me. Other men may come and go; but George goes on forever.

George Bernard Shaw, *Getting Married*

---

become involved in extramarital sex. Kinsey's studies found that by age forty, one-half of the married men and one-quarter of the married women had had extramarital sex at least once.

The Levins' 1975 study showed amazing increases in extramarital sex among women. Among women aged twenty to twenty-five, twenty-five percent had extramarital sex compared to nine percent in Kinsey's study. Among women in the thirty-five to thirty-nine age bracket, thirty-eight percent had extramarital sex in contrast to twenty-six percent among Kinsey's respondents. It is important to remember, however, that the significance of extramarital sex depends on its context. How many of these women had meaningful involvements as opposed to one-time-only experiments is not known.

Whatever the case, men tend to have their extramarital sex when they are younger; women tend to have theirs when they are older. Women in their late thirties tend to be more interested in sex then when they were younger. This difference in their sexual life cycle may account for women's increasing involvement in extramarital sex.

Most extramarital sex does not take place as a love affair, but is generally self-contained and more sexual than emotional (Gagnon, 1977). It is difficult for most extramarital encounters to grow into affairs for a number of reasons. Most important is the limited time each person has available to spend with the other. If the lover is married, it may be difficult to get away from his or her partner and responsibilities. Married people usually do not have much free time at their disposal — the husband or wife usually knows what their spouse is doing. If spouses change their routine — come home later, have to go out — then they usually are expected to explain their comings and goings. There is a doggedness to routine in marriage and, as a re-

sult of these routines, most extramarital sex happens when there is open time: during vacations, travel, or conventions.

Most extramarital encounters do not become affairs (meaningful emotional relationships) because there is so little free time. Affairs involve getting together, having lunch or dinner, going out. This arrangement is especially difficult if the man is married and the women is single because the woman expects to have some of the life she would have if her lover were single: she wants to go out, spend time together, be intimate.

The marital status of each person is crucial in extramarital affairs. When both participants are married, it is difficult for the affair to escalate. Both are restrained from spending substantial time together because of their marital obligations and responsibilities. Both are aware of being found out, so they may tend not to make strong demands on each other's time. The greatest danger rises when one wants a divorce, breaking the symmetry of the relationship.

Affairs between married men and single women are also common, usually involving an older man and younger woman. These relationships tend to be very unstable because the woman often wants to increase the emotional involvement and commitment. For the single woman, this kind of relationship is not emotionally satisfying because she must wait for the married man to have the time to see her. She cannot communicate with him when she wishes to or needs to.

Most people become involved with extramarital sex because they feel that something is missing in their own marriage. Something may or may not be wrong with their marital relationship but, for some reason, they have judged their marriage defective, but not defective enough to consider divorce. Extramarital relationships act as a compensation or substitute for the deficien-

They knew each other too well to feel those mutual revelations of possession that multiply its joys a hundredfold. She was as sated with him as he was tired of her. Emma was finding in adultery all the banalities of marriage.

Gustave Flaubert, *Madame Bovary*

cies in a marriage (Cuber, 1969). They help maintain the status quo by giving emotional satisfaction to the unhappy partner. In a certain sense, some affairs prevent people from taking responsibility for their marriages for fundamental marital problems may then be ignored.

Affairs may even become like a second, simultaneous marriage, kept separate from the first, a secret from the spouse. Cuber notes that long-term extramarital relationships are "strikingly similar to good marriages in their psychological dimensions." Such relationships may have strong emotional and erotic bonds as well as shared feelings and activities. They also tend to be monogamous and the partners mutually supporting.

William Gagnon describes some of the attraction that brings people into extramarital affairs:

Most people find their extra-marital relationships highly exciting, especially in the early stages. This is a result of psychological compression: the couple get together; they are both very aroused (desire, guilt, expectation); they have only three hours to be together . . . Another source of attraction is that the other person is always seen when he or she looks good and is on best behavior, never when feeling tired or grubby, or when taking care of children, or when cooking dinner. . . . Each time, all the minutes that the couple has together are special because they have been stolen from all these other relationships. The resulting combination of guilt and excitement has a heightening effect, which tends to

*"Do I satisfy your needs?"*

Koren, *The New Yorker*

Seldom, or perhaps never, does a marriage develop into
an individual relationship smoothly and without crises;
there is no coming to consciousness without pain.

Carl Jung

explain why people may claim that extramarital sex
and orgasms are more intense. (Gagnon, 1977)

Oftentimes, extramarital affairs are discovered
if one of the lovers tells his or her own marriage
partner out of a sense of guilt. Whereas the person involved in the affair may not feel that he or
she has broken an important bond, his or her
partner almost always experiences the affair as a
betrayal. Infidelity is usually experienced as betrayal for several reasons.

Most married people feel that a basic trust has
been broken by the spouse who is unfaithful.
Sexual accessibility implies emotional accessibility. When a person learns that his or her spouse
is having an affair, the emotional commitment of
that spouse is brought into question. Commitment is no longer a given in the relationship – it
now has to be proven. But how do you prove
that you still have a commitment? You cannot.
That's the Catch-22 about commitment. Commitment is assumed – it can never be proven.
Furthermore, an affair implies indifference to the
feelings of the marriage partner. And finally, it
may imply to that partner (rightly or wrongly)
that he or she is sexually inadequate or
uninteresting.

All of these implications may or may not be
true, but that is of little consequence. What is
important is whether they are *believed* to be
true, for beliefs ar difficult to change. "How can I
ever trust you again?" is a common question in
soap operas, but it may also be common in the
everday drama of life. Situations of marital infidelity may be tragic in real life. One woman
recalled her loss of trust in her husband:

> After my husband left I screamed and yelled that I
> wanted him back. "I don't care what you do, just
> don't go see her. Come back. Everthing will be
> fine." So there was a whole year of lies, terrible,
> terrible lies. Then finally I said, "Please, just tell me

the truth." Everytime he left the house he left me in
hysterics, crying.
> I still love him. But I have decided that if he ever
> decided to come back, it can't be. I can't take him
> back, even if he came back, and start over again.
> Who knows, after being lied to for so long, whether
> I could ever believe him again. (Weiss, 1975)

This sense of lost trust is intensified because of
the duplicity usually involved. A husband or wife
may say that the day was spent at the library or
the laundromat, when in fact it was spent in bed
with someone else. A secret affair is itself a major
deception, requiring complex and tangled lies to
keep hidden.

However, one's revealing the truth of an affair
to one's marriage partner is not much better. A
person having an affair is caught two ways: if he
or she does not tell the spouse, deception causes
a burden of guilt; if he or she does tell the partner, the guilt of hurting the spouse must be
borne. It is a no-win situation. As Simone de
Beauvoir observes of pseudohonesty:

> There is a certain type of supposed loyalty which I
> have often observed, and which in fact constitutes
> the most flagrant hypocrisy: it is limited to the
> sphere of sexual relations, and its purpose, far from
> aiming at any intimate understanding between a
> man and woman, is to supply one of them – more
> often the male partner – with a soothing alibi. He
> nurses the illusion that by confessing his infidelities
> he somehow redeems them; whereas actually he
> inflicts a double hurt on his partner. (Beauvoir,
> 1968)

A spouse's response to learning about an affair
is usually intense shock and disbelief. "But how
could you do it? How could you do it? I always
trusted you?" In Ingmar Bergman's *Scenes from
a Marriage*, Johan finally tells Marianne that he is
in love with someone else. She is deeply shaken,
she had never even been suspicious or noticed
anything. She says she feels like a blind, unsus-

pecting fool. And Johan replies: "No you haven't noticed anything. But then you were never very clear-sighted. Especially where our personal relations were concerned."

And that is often cruelly true: everything seemed perfectly normal, nothing appeared especially suspicious. But then the deceived person begins to remember little incidents which until that moment seemed unimportant: the spouse's working or studying late, long errands, trips to the library. Everthing is seen in new perspective. The wronged mates feel angry, hurt, and as if they have been made a fool of.

## Postmarital Sex

Separation and divorce are times of turmoil, change, and adjustment. New responsibilities, roles, experiences, and relationships mark the transition from marriage to separation. Sadness, trauma, and relief are common — but new opportunities and possibilities also present themselves. In terms of sexual life, a renewed interest often develops with an intensity that was lacking in marriage. Sexual interest apparently declined as a result of the conflicts endured in unsatisfactory marriages ("Who wants to make love with someone who causes so much trouble?"). The transitions and anxieties of unhappily married people affect their sexual responsiveness to each other.

But after divorce, new desires and satisfactions lead people to rate their sex lives appreciably higher. Hunt found that over five-sixths of divorced men and two-thirds of divorced women describe their sex lives as significantly better. They had gained knowledge and experience in marriage that they may have lacked before. Women who are divorced reach orgasm in

three-fourths of the sexual contacts in Hunt's sample.

The Levins discovered other interesting characteristics about divorced women. Divorced women tend to be sexually more assertive than married women; they are active in intercourse, initiating it at least half the time. Approximately 45 percent of divorced women combine sex and marijuana, a surprising number for women who tend to be older. Only those married women 24 years and younger were more likely to smoke marijuana and make love.

**Separation**    Most startling to a newly-separated person is the new world of what Morton Hunt (1977) calls "the formerly married." In this world, sex is more casual than it was before a person got married; the formerly married are more highly sexually experienced . Hunt found that about half of his newly-divorced respondents were surprised, even shocked, by the fast paced, less inhibited and experimental nature of post-marital sex. Many people are playing out sexual fantasies they had while in marriage but felt unable to act out; frequent partners, bondage, anal intercourse, etc., are some of these.

In the end, however, most find the sexual mores of this world alienating, especially women who are viewed simply as bodies, their personhood ignored. After a while, sex loses its exaggerated significance in dating and generally finds a more suitable perspective in a relationship. After all, people who were once married have a matured attitude toward relationships; they know that good relationships need intimacy, companionship, love, loyalty, and trust. When they separate, they may feel the physical loss of sex, but usually they find that they miss the emotion, tenderness, and intimacy that accompany it. They begin to seek again those qualities in a dating partner and to affirm their needs. Although the vast majority of divorced people in Hunt's study had casual sex at least once, most expressed a desire for something more meaningful.

**Widowhood**  People who are widowed may have very different responses. Their marriages ended through death rather than choice, and many widowed people feel a deep loss. They are likely to fear or resent experiences that might devalue memories of their partners. Others retain a sense that the dead partner is still present — almost like a conscience — inhibiting them from sexual involvement; they may view a new marriage or relationship as if they were cheating their dead spouse. Consequently, widowed persons have less postmarital experiences than their divorced peers of any age group. Divorced people often need new relationships and experiences in order to restore their self-esteem and image, which had been damaged by marriage and divorce. Widows and widowers generally do not have these needs (Bohannan, 1972).

## QUESTIONS

1.  What is the differences between romantic love and conscious love? Is this a valid description of love?
2.  What are the advantages of living together? The disadvantages? How is the experience different depending on whether the people are young, middle-aged, or old? Is there any time in your life in which living together would be more advantageous than marriage and vice-versa? What are the criteria that one needs to examine in making a decision to live together? What role does sex play in such a decision?
3.  Discuss the impact of marriage on sex roles. On sexual behavior. Does marital happiness depend on good sex, or does good sex depend on a good marriage?
4.  What is the impact of family size on marital happiness? Why?
5.  What are the dynamics of extra-marital relationships? What meaning does sex have in such relationships? Are extramarital relationships basically sexual . . . or what?

# Readings

*Excerpt from* Women In Love

D.H. Lawrence

*D.H. Lawrence was a philosopher of love and sexuality whose ideas find more favor now than they did in 1921, when he published* Women in Love. *In this novel, Ursula Brangwen and Rupert Birkin, and Gerald Crich and Gudrun Brangwen are lovers.*

Gerald waited for the Ursula-Birkin marriage. It was something crucial to him.

"Shall we make it a double-barrelled affair?" he said to Birkin one day.

"Who for the second shot?" asked Birkin.

"Gudrun and me," said Gerald, the venturesome twinkle in his eyes.

Birkin looked at him steadily, as if somewhat taken aback.

"Serious — or joking?" he asked.

"Oh, serious. Shall I? Shall Gudrun and I rush in along with you?"

"Do by all means," said Birkin. "I didn't know

you'd go that length."

"What length?" said Gerald, looking at the other man, and laughing.

"Oh, yes, we've gone all the lengths."

"There remains to put it on a broad social basis, and to achieve a high moral purpose," said Birkin.

"Something like that: the length and breadth and height of it," replied Gerald, smiling.

"Oh, well," said Birkin, "it's a very admirable step to take, I should say."

Gerald looked at him closely.

"Why aren't you enthusiastic?" he asked. "I thought you were such dead nuts on marriage."

Birkin lifted his shoulders.

"One might as well be dead nuts on noses. There are all sorts of noses, snub and otherwise—"

Gerald laughed.

"And all sorts of marriage, also snub and otherwise?" he said.

"That's it."

"And you think if I marry, it will be snub?" asked Gerald quizzically, his head a little on one side.

Birkin laughed quickly.

"How do I know what it will be!" he said. "Don't lambaste me with my own parallels—"

Gerald pondered a while.

"But I should like to know your opinion, exactly," he said.

"On your marriage? — or marrying? Why should you want my opinion? I've got no opinions. I'm not interested in legal marriage, one way or another. It's a mere question of convenience."

From *Women in Love* by D.H. Lawrence. Copyright 1920, 1922 by David Herbert Lawrence. Copyright renewed 1948, 1950 by Frieda Lawrence. Reprinted by permission of The Viking Press, Inc.

## The Art of Loving

Erich Fromm

*What is the relationship between love and sexuality as Fromm described it? Are there other ways to see erotic love?*

Brotherly love is love among equals; motherly love is love for the helpness. Different as they are from each other, they have in common that they are by their very nature not restricted to one person. If I love my brother, I love all my brothers; If I love my child, I love all my children; no, beyond that I love all children, all that are in need of my help. In contrast to both types of love is *erotic love*; it is the craving for complete fusion, for union with one other person. It is by its very nature exclusive and not universal; it is also pehaps the most deceptive form of love there is.

First of all, it is often confused with the explosive experience of "falling" in love, the sudden collapse of the barriers which existed until that moment between two strangers. But, as was pointed out before, this experience of sudden intimacy is by its very nature short-lived. After the stranger has become an intimately known person there are no more barriers to be overcome, there is no more sudden closeness to be achieved. The "loved" person becomes as well known as oneself. Or, perhaps I should better say as little known. If there were more depth in the experience of the other person, if one could experience the infiniteness of his personality, the other person would never be so familiar — and the miracle of overcoming the barriers might occur every day anew. But for most people their own person, as well as others, is soon explored and soon exhausted. For them intimacy is established primarily through sexual contact. Since they experience the separateness of the other person primarily as physical separateness, physical union means overcoming separateness.

Beyond that, there are other factors which to many people denote the overcoming of separateness. To speak of one's own personal life, one's hopes and anxieties, to show oneself with one's childlike or childish aspects, to establish a common interest vis-a-vis the world – all this is taken as overcoming separateness. Even to show one's anger, one's hate, one's complete lack of inhibition is taken for intimacy, and this may explain the perverted attraction married couples often have for each other, who seem intimate only when they are in bed or when they give vent to their mutual hate and rage. But all these types of closeness tend to become reduced more and more as time goes on. The consequence is one seeks love with a new person, with a new stranger. Again the stranger is transformed into an "intimate" person, again the experience of falling in love is exhilarating and intense, and again it slowly becomes less and less intense, and ends in the wish for a new conquest, a new love – always with the illusion that the new love will be different from the earlier ones. These illusions are greatly helped by the deceptive character of sexual desire.

Sexual desire aims at fusion – and is by no means only a physical appetite, the relief of a painful tension. But sexual desire can be stimulated by the anxiety of aloneness, by the wish to conquer or be conquered, by vanity, by the wish to hurt and even to destroy, as much as it can be stimulated by love. It seems that sexual desire can easily blend with and be stimulated by any strong emotion, of which love is only one. Because sexual desire is in the minds of most people coupled with the idea of love, they are easily misled to conclude that they love each other when they want each other physically.

Love can inspire the wish for sexual union; in this case the physical relationship is lacking in greediness, in a wish to conquer or to be conquered, but is blended with tenderness. If the desire for physical union is not stimulated by love, if erotic love is not also brotherly love, it never leads to union in more than an orgiastic, transitory sense. Sexual attraction creates, for the moment, the illusion of union, yet without love this "union" leaves strangers as far apart as they were before – sometimes it makes them ashamed of each other, or even makes them hate each other, because when the illusion has gone they feel their estrangement even more markedly than before. Tenderness is by no means, as Freud believed, a sublimation of the sexual instinct; it is the direct outcome of brotherly love, and exists in physical as well as in non-physical forms of love.

In erotic love there is an exclusiveness which is lacking in brotherly love and motherly love. This exclusive character of erotic love warrants some further discussion. Frequently the exclusiveness of erotic love is misinterpreted as meaning possessive attachment. One can often find two people "in love" with each other who feel no love for anybody else. Their love is, in fact, an egotism *a deux*; they are two people who identify themselves with each other, and who solve the problem of separateness by enlarging the single individual into two. They have the experience of overcoming aloneness, yet, since they are separated form the rest of mankind, they remain separated from each other and alienated from themselves; their experience of union is an illusion. Erotic love is exclusive, but it loves in the other person all of mankind, all that is alive. It is exclusive only in the sense that I can fuse myself fully and intensely with one person only. Erotic love excludes the love for others only in the sense of erotic fusion, full commitment in all aspects of life – but not in the sense of deep brotherly love.

Erotic love, if it is love, has one premise. That I love from the essence of my being – and experience the other person in the essence of his or her being. In essence, all human beings are identical. We are all part of One; we are One. This being so, it should not make any difference whom we love. Love should be essentially an act of will, of decision to commit my life completely to that of one other person. This is, indeed, the rationale behind the idea of the insolubility of marriage, as it is behind the many forms of traditional marriage in which the two partners never choose each other, but are chosen for each other – and yet are expected to love each other. In contemporary Western culture this idea appears altogether false. Love is supposed to be the outcome of a spontaneous, emotional reaction, of suddenly being gripped by an irresistible feeling. In this view, one sees only the peculiarities of the two individuals involved – and not the fact that all men are part of Adam, and all women part of Eve. One neglects to see an important factor in erotic love, that of *will*. To love somebody is not just a strong feeling – it is a decision, it is a judgment, it is a promise. If love were only a feeling, there would be no basis for the promise to love each other forever. A feeling comes and it may go. How can I judge that it will stay forever, when my act does not involve judgment and decision?

Taking these views into account one may arrive at the position that love is exclusively an act of will and commitment, and that therefore fundamentally it does not matter who the two persons are. Whether the marriage was arranged by others, or the result of individual choice, once the marriage is concluded, the act of will should guarantee the continuation of love. This view seems to neglect the paradoxical character of human nature and of erotic love. We are all One

– yet every one of us is a unique, unduplicable entity. In our relationships to others the same paradox is repeated. Inasmuch as we are all one, we can love everybody in the same way in the sense of brotherly love. But inasmuch as we are all also different, erotic love requires certain specific, highly individual elements which exist between some people but not between all.

Both views then, that of erotic love as completely individual attraction, unique between two specific persons, as well as the other view that erotic love is nothing but an act of will, are true – or, as it may be put more aptly, the truth is neither this nor that. Hence the idea of a relationship which can be easily dissolved if one is not successful with it is as erroneous as the idea that under no circumstances must the relationship be dissolved.

### How the Famous Feel About Love
Kate Shelley

*Those who seek fame as entertainers seem characteristically prone to a narcissism which gets in the way of stable, loving, relationships. Yet, these are the people to whom many Americans turn as romantic models.*

Many people fantasize that, with fame and riches, their lives, loves and marriages would all suddenly shimmer with perfection.

But here the super-famous put the lie to that illusion. Mankind's oldest commonplace, love between the sexes, still befuddles the most stellar personalities of our time:

Glenda Jackson, winner of two Academy Awards, recently divorced Roy Hughes, a British theatrical director and actor, after 18 years of marriage.

"There's no reason any more for any woman

to support a fragile male ego at the expense of her own happiness and fulfillment. Marriage inevitably comes to that since all men who marry have some need of psychological reinforcement; if they didn't, why on earth would they marry in the first place? This is a definite no from me for marriage—future tense."

Lillian Gish has been a movie star for 65 years and recently completed her 100th film. Now in her 80s, Miss Gish has never married.

"I saved a lot of men a lot of unhappiness. I would have been a dreadful wife. I don't think actresses have the right to marry and ruin a man's life. If you're going to marry, give up the theater or be like the Lunts and never take an engagement apart.

"My mother's marriage was not a success and to me she is still the most perfect human being I've ever met. I thought if she couldn't make it work, how on earth could I?"

Muhammad Ali is, arguably, the most famous living person in the world. He has been married three times.

"I believe in marriage. If a man's got a good woman behind him, he can handle anything.

"But inside marriage, there ain't going to be no equality. I'm a man. I'm known for being a man. Someone's got to wear the pants and someone's got to wear the dress. There ain't going to be no equality.

"If you want to be equal with me, you can get your own Rolls-Royce, your own house and your own million dollars."

Woody Allen has perhaps the best comic mind of his generation.

"From my childhood I was told never to marry a Gentile woman, never to shave on Saturday and, most especially, never to shave a Gentile woman on Saturday.

"The only love I care about is the love between a man and a woman. I just don't know

anyone who has had a good relationship for any length of time. This is an area where I'm very cynical. Everyone is dependent on love. Love is the result of the best kind of luck in the area of relations with the opposite sex."

Jon Peters, a hairdresseer turned movie producer, lives with Barbra Streisand to whom he has proposed three times.

"Obviously, I love Barbra. She's powerful. She's gentle. She's beautiful. She's fun to be with. On our good days we could fly over the universe. Our lows are pretty low too.

"Marriage, I think, is a wonderful thing but it's not essential. At best, it's a romantic gesture and ultimately makes a woman feel better."

John Denver, whose songs celebrating simple, earthy pleasures have entranced millions, and his wife of seven years, Annie, have two adopted children: Zachary, 5, and Anna Kate, 2. A strong believer in population control, Denver himself has had a vasectomy.

"People get married with such unreal expectations of self-fulfillment. But I don't know any individual who can fill up the spaces in another individual.

"It seems, too, that people who divorce keep marrying the same people. They start with the same kind of relationship and take it to the same point. They never allow it to deepen and grow. When that's the case, you are really cheating yourself."

Dolly Parton in the last two years has jumped from country-western stardom to international success. She has been married for 14 years to a man she met outside a laundromat in Nashville, when her career was still only a dream.

"I've written a lot of songs about heartbreak and love gone bad, but Carl and I have never had an argument. A real important thing is that, though I rely on my husband for love, I rely on myself for strength."

David Bowie, a rock star, met his wife, Angela, through a mutual boyfriend.

"We love each other, but I don't think we fell in love. I've never been in love. Maybe once; it was an awful experience. It rotted me and drained me.

"I'm very demanding sometimes, not physically but mentally. I'm very intense about anything I do and I scare away most people I've lived with.

"The amazing thing about Angie and me is that we're still together. We should have broken up years ago, but we still love each other and we love our son Zowie. I can't imagine life without either of them."

Donna Summer, the disco queen, is now divorced from the Austrian father of her daughter, Mini, 5. For the last year she has been living with musician Bruce Sudano.

"I don't jump from relationship to relationship the way I notice some people doing. I never have. I'm not a loose person. I will stick it out with a person until the bitter end.

"I would almost prefer to be taking care of a man than having him take care of me. Fifty-fifty is best but I don't mind paying the bills if I'm earning the most.

"One of my ex-boyfriends was a painter, and I didn't see why he should go out and struggle and be half as good a painter if I was making enough for both of us. As long as he could deal with people thinking he was being kept, I could deal with it."

## Swinging

Duane Denfeld and Michael Gordon

*How does swinging differ from open marriage or from other forms of extramarital relationships? How are the rules different?*

**The Swinger**    The swingers who advertise and attend swinging parties do not conform to the stereotypical image of the deviant. They have higher levels of education than the general population; 80 percent of one study attended college, 50 percent were graduates, and 12 percent were still students. They are disproportionately found in professional and white-collar occupations (J. and L. Smith, 1969). They tend to be conservative and very straight.

> They do not represent a high order of deviance. In fact, this is the single area of deviation from the norms of contemporary society. The mores, the fears, that plague our generation are evidenced as strongly in swingers as in any random sampling from suburbia (Bartell, 1969).

Every study we looked at emphasized the overall normality, conventionality, and respectability of recreational swingers.

**Extent of Swinging**    The number of couples engaged in swinging can at best be roughly estimated. The Breedloves developed, on the basis of their research, an estimate of eight million couples. Their figure was based on a sample of 407 couples. They found that less than four percent of them placed or replied to advertisements in swinging publications, and in the year prior to publication (1962-1963) of their study "almost 70,000 couples either replied to, or placed ads as swinging couples" (W. and J. Breedlove, 1964). With this figure as a base they arrived at their estimate of the number of couples who have at one time or another sexually exchanged partners. They further concluded that, conservatively 2-1/2 million couples exchange partners on a somewhat regular basis (three or more times a year).

***Getting Together***    The "swap" or swingers club is an institutionalized route to other swingers, but it is not the only method of locating potential partners. Bartell suggests four ways: 1) swingers' bars, 2) personal reference, 3) personal recruitment, and 4) advertisement (Bartell, 1970). The last method deserves special attention.

Advertisements are placed in underground papers and more frequently in swingers' magazines. The swingers' publications, it has been claimed, emerged following an article in *MR.* magazine in 1956.

> Everett Meyers, the editor of *MR.*, later claimed that it was this article which touched off a flood of similar articles on wife-swapping, or mate-swapping. In any event, *MR.* followed up its original article with a regular monthly correspondence column filled with alleged letters from readers reporting their own mate-swapping accounts (Brecher, 1969).

Publications began to appear with advertisements from "modern marrieds" or swingers who wished to meet other swingers. *La Plume*, established about 1955, has boasted in print that it was the first swingers' magazine. A recent issue of *Select*, probably the largest swingers' publication, had 3,500 advertisements, over 40 percent from married couples. *Select* and *Kindred Spirits* co-sponsored "Super Bash '70" on April 11, 1970. It was advertised to be "the BIGGEST SWINGDING yet," and featured dancing, buffet dinner, go go girls and a luxurious intimate ballroom. Clubs such as Select, Kindred Spirits, Mixers, and Swingers Life have moved beyond the swingers' party to hayrides and vacation trips.

There are at least a couple of hundred organizations like Select throughout the country. Many of them are very small, some with only a few members, and many of them are fly-by-night rackets run by schlock guys less interested in providing a service than in making a quick buck. Most however, are legitimate and, as such, very successful. They have been a major factor influencing the acceleration of the swapping scene (Fonzi and Riggio, 1969).

Our review of the swinging club and magazine market located approximately fifty nationally-sold publications. The "couple of hundred" figure reported above may include some lonely hearts, nudist directories, homosexual, and transvestite organizations, some of which serve the same purpose as swingers' publications. They bring together persons with the same socio-sexual-interests.

A person's first attendance at a swingers' party can be a difficult situation. He must learn the ideologies, rationalizations, and rules of swinging. These rules place swinging in a context that enables it to support the institution of the family. We turn to these rules in the next section.

***Rules of the Game***    Our model views swinging as a strategy to revitalize marriage, to bolster a sagging partnership. This strategy can be seen in the following findings of the empirical research. Evidence to support the model is divided into four parts: 1) the perception of limitation of sex to the marital bond, 2) paternity, 3) discretion, and 4) marital supportive rules.

1. *"Consensual adultery": the perception that sex is limited to the marital bond* – Swingers have developed rules that serve to define the sexual relationship of marriage as one of love, of emotion. Some of the Smiths' respondents would answer "no" to questions pertaining to "extramarital sexual experience," but would answer

"yes" to questions pertaining to "mate-sharing or co-marital relations" (J. and L. Smith, 1969). Sharing, for the swingers, means that the marriage partners are not "cheating." Swingers believe that the damaging aspects in extramarital sex is the lying and cheating, and if this is removed extramarital sex is beneficial to the marital bond. In other words, "those who swing together stay together" (Brecher, 1969). Swingers establish rules such as not allowing one of a couple to attend a group meeting without the other. Unmarried couples are kept out of some groups, because they "have less regard for the marital responsibilities" (W. and J. Breedlove, 1964). Guests who fail to conform to rules are asked "to leave a party when their behavior is not appropriate."

> For one group of recreational swingers, it is important that there be no telephone contact with the opposite sex between functions. Another group of recreational swingers always has telephone contact with people they swing with, although they have no sexual contact between functions (Symonds, 1968).

2. *Swinging and children* — "Recreational swingers are occasionally known to drop out of swinging, at least temporarily, while the wife gets pregnant" (Symonds, 1968). By not swinging, the couple can be assured that the husband is the father of the child; unknown or other parentage is considered taboo. This reflects a tradional, middle-class view about the conception and rearing of children.

Swinging couples consider themselves to be sexually avant-garde, but many retain their puritan attitudes with respect to sex socialization. They hide from their children their swinging publications. Swingers lock their children's bedrooms during parties or send them to relatives.

3. *Discretion* – A common word in the swingers' vocabulary is discretion. Swingers desire to keep their sexual play a secret from their non-swinging or "square" friends. They want to protect their position in the community, and an effort is made to limit participation to couples of similar status or "respectability."

> Parties in suburbia include evenly numbered couples only. In the area of our research, singles, male or female, are discriminated against. Blacks are universally excluded. If the party is a closed party, there are rules, very definitely established and generally reinforced by the organizer as well as other swingers . . . stag films are generally not shown. Music is low key fox trot, not infrequently Glenn Miller, and lighting is definitely not psychedelic. Usually nothing more than a few red or blue lightbulbs. Marijuana and speed are not permitted (Bartell, 1969).

The swinging suburban party differs, then, from the conventional cocktail party only in that it revolves around sexual exchange of mates.

4. *Swingers' rules* – We suggest that the above rules on sex and paternity are strategies to make swinging an adjunct to marriage rather than an alternative. Another set of rules or strategies that is relevant is that dealing with jealousy. Swingers recognize the potentially disruptive consequences of jealousy, and are surprisingly successful in minimizing it. The Smiths found that only 34 percent of the females and 27 percent of the males reported feelings of jealousy. Some of the controls on jealousy are: 1) that the marriage commands paramount loyalty, 2) that there is physical but not emotional interest in other partners, 3) that single persons are avoided, and 4) that there be no concealment of sexual activities. The sharing couples.

> reassure one another on this score by means of verbal statements and by actively demonstrating in large ways and small that the marriage still does command their paramount loyalty. Willingness to

forego an attractive swinging opportunity because the spouse or lover is uninterested or opposed is one example of such a demonstration (Brecher, 1969).

Developing a set of rules to control potential jealousies demonstrates the swingers' commitment to marriage.

Duane Denfield and Michael Gordon, The Sociology of Mate Swapping: or, The Family That Swings Together, Clings Together. Journal of Sex Research, Volume VI, No. 2 (May 1970). Reprinted by permission of the Society for the Scientific Study of Sex.

# Sexual Communication

**11**

It is only with the heart that one can see rightly; what is essential is invisible to the eye.

Saint-Exupery, *The Little Prince*

Communication is the process by which individuals break out of their own isolation and come to know and understand each other. By exchanging bits of information about themselves – through words, voice, gesture, touch, movement, and other means – strangers may become friends, associates, lovers, or mates. Communication has such fundamental importance that anthropologists have built theories of culture around it. Edward Hall, for example, has defined culture itself as a "form of communication." Without communication, there could be neither culture nor relationships. Each person would have to guess what others think, desire, expect, fear, or like, and each generation would have to discover all over again what previous generations had learned. Human beings would have a more difficult time than ants, for even ants communicate.

The bits of information exchanged through communication include facts, emotions, and ideas. A fundamental aspect of communication is that it permits people to enter into intimate relationships. The willingness to reveal oneself helps to determine the direction and limits of the relationship: whether it will be friendly or impersonal, intense or casual.

A person who says, "I'm taking a course on human sexuality," is communicating something different from the one who says, "I'm taking a course on human sexuality because I want to understand myself better." Both revelations differ from that of someone who says, "I'm taking a course on human sexuality because I feel guilty about some of the things I do, and wonder whether or not they're right." Each statement reveals something about the speaker. But added meaning is implied in the last communication: "I am sharing something very personal with you, because I trust you." Thus, the type of information revealed **establishes the type of relationship**

shared by people (Borden, Gregg, and Grove 1970).

Much of how we perceive ourselves is based on interaction with others. We are not likely to be upset by critical remarks from a stranger met on the streets, while criticism from a close friend may wound deeply. If an individual comes into a sexual relationship feeling confident but is accused by a partner of being a "lousy lover," this statement (whether true or not) is disturbing. By contrast, spontaneous and genuine affection from a partner may do much to increase self-esteem.

Dyadic communication, or communication between two people, actively involves both of them. While one person is communicating primarily through words, the other may be communicating nonverbally – by looking blank, interested, nervous, irritated, or whatever; by sitting awkwardly, tensely, in a relaxed manner; by moving clumsily, quickly, spontaneously, slowly. Context is also important. If, for example, one person continues to watch television while the other is talking, the message may be that the listener is not interested, is unable to confront the topic, or is unwilling to confront it.

## Touching as Communication

Communication occurs on many levels. Harrison (1972) has suggested that only 7 percent of human communication is verbal, with nonverbal aspects accounting for the remaining 93 percent.

The primary means of sexual communication is touching, which may include caressing another person's skin, kissing, or sexual intercourse. Anthropologist M.F. Ashley Montagu (1971) has called the skin "our first medium of communication." The sense of touch is the first sense to develop in humans. An unusually sensitive organ, the skin has 50 receptors per 100 square

Words are given to man to enable him to conceal his true
feelings.

Voltaire

---

millimeters, and 7 to 135 tactile points per square
centimeter. The sense of touch is the primary
tool used by infants in distinguishing themselves
from their environment; touching things tells
them that there is an "objective reality," lying
outside their own bodies. This reality, says Montagu, is the most important element in the development of affection between mothers and their
infants.

Experiments conducted with rhesus monkeys
demonstrate that bodily contact, with clinging, is
the primary variable binding mother and infant
to each other (Harlow and Zimmerman, 1958).
Maternal affection is at its highest in face-to-face
contacts, decreasing as bodily contact decreases
(which may account for the significance of sexual
positions in which partners face one another).
Harlow concluded that intimate physical attachment between mother and child forms the basis
for the infant's later affectional responses. Without such contact, infants may withdraw, lack
vigor, and experience emotional difficulties with
others as they mature.

**Need for contact**  Evidence suggests that
much of the intense preoccupation of our culture
with sex may not be an expression of biological
drives as much as a desire to satisfy contact
needs (Montagu, 1971). Among both adolescents and adults, these contact needs are generally left unsatisfied. For example, in our culture
it is usually considered unacceptable to be held
or caressed as we were as infants except in sexual situations. Some people convert their desire
for contact into sexual desire.

Each culture teaches different thresholds for
touching to children and adolescents. In ours, girl
babies are touched more frequently and receive
more affection from their mothers than do boy
babies. In adult life, women are encouraged to
be affectionate and to touch and be touched,

while men are not. This fact has important sexual
consequences. Women often complain that men
show little tenderness or gentleness in sexual approaches; they sense a definite lack of sexual
communication and of closeness on a tactile
level. Although tactile stimulation is a major
component of sexual activity, men often seem
perfunctory or clumsy. Montagu suggests this is
rooted in the tactile deprivation they experienced
as children. Never having been extensively held,
they do not know how to hold another; never
having been extensively stroked or caressed,

they do not know how to stroke or caress.

As a result, the eroticism of men tends to be centered in the genitals; the sensuality of women, who as infants received greater tactile stimulation, tends to be diffused throughout their bodies.

Holding and touching behaviors are significant in sexual intercourse, because they develop bonding and affection between people. There are, in fact, definite similarities between sexual intercourse and the affectional behavior of mother and child: general body contact in face-to-face position, caressing, touching, sucking, and kissing. Lawrence Frank has noted that for adults who have retained their ability to communicate with others and with themselves through touch, sexual intercourse recreates with "elementary organic intensity" the primary communication once experienced between mother and child (Frank 1951).

Touching, then, is more than foreplay, more than a technique for sexually stimulating another person. It is the basis of love and affection. To the degree that an individual is able to touch *and* be touched, that person has the potential to discover new meanings for sex and love.

**Sex Differences in Communication**

As important as touching is, it is subject to misinterpretation. A woman may rub a man's back with no other purpose than to massage him; he, however, may misinterpret the rubbing as a prelude to sexual intercourse. Or a woman may misinterpret her husband's pat on her buttocks as a minor assault while he may have meant it as a love pat.

There appear to be basic sex differences in regards to physical contact. Several researchers (Nguyen, *et. al.*, 1975) asked a group of unmarried students how they would interpret a pat, squeeze, brush, or stroke from their intimate partner on the head, arms, thighs, genital areas, etc. The possible interpretations they could choose from were "playfulness," "warmth/love," "friendship/fellowship," and "sexual desire."

The researchers found that there are important differences between men and women. *Where* a woman is touched is more important than for men. By contrast, *how* a man is touched is more important. These interpretations form clusters which again are different between men and women. For a man, the same touch can mean pleasantness, sexual desire, or warmth/love; it will not mean friendliness. For women, the more a man's touch signifies sexual desire, the less she associates it with playfulness, warmth/love, friendship, or pleasantness. This clustering presents great potential for sexual misunderstanding and conflict. If men associate sexual desire with pleasantness and love, they are liable to misinterpret a woman's loving touch for a sexual one. By contrast, if women interpret a sexual touch as the opposite of playfulness, pleasantness, friendliness and love, they may see it only as aggression and exploitation. These differences help explain why, when a woman takes a man's hand to hold and caress, he misinterprets it as a signal for sexual intimacy. It also helps explain why some women misinterpret sexual playfulness as being treated as a sex object.

The perception of touching and physical contact, however, changes after marriage. The interpretation of sexual approaches as unfriendly by women may be the result of the double standard; since sex is considered unacceptable for women before marriage, any sexual touch is a potential threat to a woman's selfesteem and sense of self. Once women marry, their dislike of sexual touching disappears and, in fact, is replaced by a positive response to such touching. Sexual touching is then equated with friendliness and love.

"Four-letter words" (itself a euphemistic expression to skirt having to use the words) are more strictly taboo than any others in the English language. Until very recently they were considered too indecent for publication even in scholarly dictionaries. However, some of the recent dictionaries now acknowledge the obvious fact that the word *fuck* is known by every native speaker of English. The sexual act described by *fuck* refers to standard sexual behavior, and so there is nothing intrinsically "bad" or

"dirty" in this word. Any word is an innocent collection of sounds until a community surrounds it with connotations and then decrees that it cannot be used in certain speech situations; this is what happened when the English speech community relegated *fuck* to forbidden status about 1650. Only by the creation of this taboo did the English community create an obscenity where none existed previously.

Peter Farb

## Verbal Communication

From the time we are children, we are taught in various ways not to talk about sex. Our parents frown, don't answer, distract or reprimand us for asking questions. Teachers, counselors, ministers, aunts and uncles, doctors – all give the same message. Few adults ever let us in on the secret that sex can provide pleasure and fulfillment; instead of answering our questions, they talk about how babies are made, about sperm and ovum.

As we get older, we may talk less about sex, because we don't want others to think badly of us for discussing such a personal (that is, "nasty") subject. We may hide our sexual feelings and our tenderness, placing barriers to keep people away from us.

**Lack of Vocabulary**   But, even if willing to talk about our sexuality, how are we to do it? In our language, there is no effective vocabulary. Euphemisms are not satisfactory, for they imply that sex cannot be discussed in direct terms. Our sexual words are usually either scientific or obscene. "To have sexual intercourse" is clumsy and detached; this phrase suggests the production of babies and orgasms, but does not indicate that there are feelings and attachments. "To fuck" is even less expressive of the range of feelings that go with sharing one's self with a lover. "Making love" is perhaps the best word available, since it gives some sense of personal involvement.

It is even difficult to describe our bodies in adequate terms. "Penis," suggests something flaccid and limp, something to be examined; "prick" and "cock" are aggressive words, often used as epithets. "Vagina," is a detached and

hidden part of a woman's body; "cunt" and "box" are also used insultingly.

This lack of appropriate words has great impact on our sexual personalities, for words help structure our experiences – in emotional and nonemotional situations alike. Novelist Robert Graves has described how a nurse, visiting a ward of wounded soldiers, asked one where he had been wounded. He replied that he couldn't say, "because I have never studied Latin."

We need to accept honest words in describing our sexuality. We need a vocabulary that expresses sex as an integral and healthy part of our lives. As Virginia Woolf wrote in *Three Guineas*, "In an age when many qualities are changing their value, new words to express new values are much to be desired."

**Saying "No"**   Each person has the ultimate right to refuse sexual intercourse whenever he or she wishes. It is their right and they need not explain their reasons or justify their decision. Unfortunately, there are two problems many people experience regarding their right to say no. The first problem is saying "no" and the second one is accepting "no." Both these are intimately tied to our traditional sex roles and beliefs about sexuality.

Each person possesses his or her own body; it is, writes Walt Whitman, every bit as important as the soul. It is often difficult for women to say "no" because they are traditionally expected to please the male regardless of their own feelings. Within a relationship, they often feel pressure to respond to the sexual desires of their partner regardless of their own feelings. If a woman says "no," the man may get angry, sulk, or withdraw;

I am a sexual being. So is she. Together, we produce an experience that is exquisite for us both. She invites me to know her sexually, and I invite her to know me sexually. We share our erotic possibilities in delight and ecstasy. If she wants me and I don't want her, I cannot lie. My body speaks only truth. And I cannot take her unless she gives herself. Her body cannot lie.

Sidney Jourard, *The Transparent Self*

she often feels guilty for *provoking* the response in him and tries to assuage it. She, however, is not responsible for his response; his responses are his own. Often, his responses are methods of manipulating the situation to his advantage. The manipulated woman may engage in sex with him in order to pacify him. An appropriate, non-manipulative response is for the man to accept her "no."

When a man refuses to accept the woman's "no," he may believe he is not consciously disregarding her wishes. Traditionally, men and women are conditioned for the woman to be passive, saying "no," and for the man to pursue her, trying to awaken his fantasy of her slumbering passion. And often enough, a woman will say "no" when she really means "coax me"; not willing to accept responsibility for her own sexual desires, she says "no" in order for the man to persuade her. If they make love, then, it is not because she wanted to, but because she was "talked" into it. Men often act as if when a woman says no, she is in fact saying "coax me"; that is the sexual script they were raised with. Unfortunately, her "no" may actually mean "no." The man who pursues his wishes against hers, believing that she really doesn't mean no, is engaged in what Germaine Greer calls "petty rape." These sexual games are really traps in which no one wins.

**Misleading Communication**   The problem of saying no is complicated by disagreement between people on how much sexual intimacy is acceptable. Adolescent boys place greater emphasis on sexuality in a relationship than do girls; girls seek affection more than sex. As they get older, there is more agreement on the degree of sexual involvement with the women becoming more permissive (Collins *et. al.*, 1976).

Yet communication remains a problem with college-aged students; although young women become more permissive as they gain more experience, men and women still mislead and miscommunicate with each other about their sexual expectations. Men ask for more sexual intimacy on dates than they actually expect to get; they hope thereby to make their date more permissive. Because women tend to take their dates at face value, not knowing that the men do not expect as much sexual intimacy as they seem to demand, the women become a little more per-

**Assertive Bill of Rights**

*Assertive Right I*   You have the right to judge your own behavior, thoughts and emotions, and to take the responsibility for their initiation and consequences upon yourself.
*Assertive Right II*   You have the right to offer no reasons or excuses to justify your behavior.
*Assertive Right III*   You have the right to judge whether you are responsible for finding solutions to other people's problems.
*Assertive Right IV*   You have the right to change your mind.
*Assertive Right V*   You have the right to make mistakes – and to be responsible for them.
*Assertive Right VI*   You have the right to say, "I don't know."
*Assertive Right VII*   You have the right to be independent of the goodwill of others before coping with them.
*Assertive Right VIII*   You have the right to be illogical in making decisions.
*Assertive Right IX*   You have the right to say, "I don't understand."
*Assertive Right X*   You have the right to say, "I don't care."

Manuel Smith *When I Say No I Feel Guilty*

It happens often enough that the lie begun in self-defense slips into self-deception.

Jean-Paul Sartre

---

missive than they really feel because of their date's expectations. During such dating games, sexual intimacy increases not out of authentic commitment or pleasure but because of misperceptions, games, and poor communication (Balswick and Anderson, 1969).

## Blocks to Effective Communication

People sometimes play sexual games that fill needs and desires that are nonsexual. In these situations, sex is simply the stage or setting. Games, as defined in the "transactional analysis" theory of the late Eric Berne, are communications that involve hidden motives, purposes, or needs.

**Sexual Games**    Although the structure of sexual games is very simple, the results may be dangerous and exploitative. As formulated by Berne, the game pattern is:

Con + Gimmick = Response → Switch → Payoff

The "con," or bait, is an action, gesture, word, or mood that looks like one thing but is really something else. It triggers the gimmick, which is a need, desire, or weakness in another person. On receiving a response, the first person pulls a "switch," and the real purpose of the con – the "payoff" – appears. Both players may be unaware that cons, gimmicks, and deceptions are involved.

Games are often conditioned by sex-role stereotype. Judy, for example, has been socialized to be manipulative, indirect, and seductive. Tom has been socialized to be sexually active, direct, and power-seeking. Judy goes to Tom's apartment, is coy and seductive; this is her con. Tom is attracted to her and also needs sexual conquest to feel effective as a man; this is his gimmick. They kiss, and both become sexually excited. As Tom becomes more aggressive, the switch occurs – Judy says, "Yes, I want to, but not now." She gets what she wants: a man interested in her, proving that she is desirable. Tom gets at least a little of what he wants: sexual contact, with a promise of more later.

There are thousands of variations on sexual games. Both players have usually been socialized to respond in specific ways. Both are responsible for letting the games continue and for letting themselves become victims. What the games provide is a means of avoiding intimacy, while creating the illusion that there is communication. There are also certain satisfactions:

Sexual games satisfy other, nonsexual needs. People can use their sexuality to fulfill those needs by baiting people. Those who need to dominate may express this in their sexual relationships, treating others as objects or fools.

Sexual games help people to avoid responsibilities, commitments, or confrontations. In a relationship based on games, neither person understands what is happening. There are no intimate exchanges, which might make either or both feel vulnerable.

Sexual games help people confirm their own views of themselves. They may, for example, play I-am-the-greatest-lover-who-ever-lived games, with the payoff always proving them superior to others. If they are convinced they are failures, their games will always prove them to be.

But we can stop such games any time we want. The most significant aspect of communication is that it is *learned*, that bad communication can be unlearned. The first step is becoming aware of your own responses; this awareness helps break down previous socialization.

**The Double Bind**    The double bind is a more complicated form of miscommunication (Bateson, 1967). Its basic ingredient is the repetition of

My wife and I tried two or three time in the last forty years to have breakfast together, but it was so disagreeable we had to stop.

Sir Winston Churchill

situations in which two people are faced "with the dilemma either of being wrong . . . or being right for the wrong reasons or in the wrong way." Regardless of how they respond, there is some form of punishment or censure.

A classic double bind may occur when a man greets a woman by putting an arm around her affectionately. When her body stiffens and he senses disapproval, the man releases her. "Don't you love me, dear?" she asks. He is confused, and she says, "Darling, you shouldn't be so embarrassed about showing your feelings. Men ought to show their feelings, too." She had said one thing while her body has done another, giving the man a conflicting message and presenting him with a dilemma: *If I want to keep my rela-*

According to one of Perl's best-known statements, "I don't exist to fulfill your expectations, and you don't exist to fulfill mine."

I've seen people take those line and blow their lives

apart. It's easy to remember the first half of the comment and forget the second half. When misread this way, it goes, "I don't want you to expect from me, but I'm going to keep on expecting from you. . . . "

Victor Daniels and Lawrence Horowitz
*Being and Caring*

tionship with her, I must not show that I care about her. But if I don't show affection, she will leave.

Double binds are disturbing traps, but they also point out the many levels of communication. For communication to be clear, words and tone, voice, movements, and gestures must be in harmony.

**Pseudo-Mutuality** One of the most fundamental human needs is to be involved with other people – loving them, sometimes hating them, caring for them. To give coherence and meaning to the experiences and changes in our lives, we also need to develop a sense of personal identity. Although self-identity is the central factor that holds us together, identities are seldom permanently fixed. They change as we change and as our experiences change.

Often, problems of relatedness and identity are connected, and we must deal with both at the same time. If relationships with others prevent us from developing our own identities as people, we must either change them or dissolve them. Either solution may be very painful, so some people choose to avoid resolving unsatisfactory situations, pretending there are no problems.

The two main responses to problems or relatedness and identity are *mutuality* and *pseudo-mutuality*. In *mutuality*, each person recognizes that the other has individual interests, desires, and needs that may differ from his or her own. This recognition is more than simple toleration. It is a positive acceptance of differences, an appreciation of what the diversity brings to the relationship. Neither person feels unloved or threatened by the identity of the other, and both view each other as fully developed people rather than as stereotypes.

In *pseudo-mutuality*, however, each person

directs energy toward fulfilling role expectations rather than to developing individual identity. The roles are usually static, with changes seen as threatening to the relationship. So, although people involved in pseudo-mutual relationships may feel frustrated, unfulfilled, and unhappy, they may refuse to seek a real resolution. Psychiatrist Lyman Wynne (1958), who developed the concept of pseudo-mutuality, points out four characterisitcs of this kind of relationship within the family setting:

Despite changes in a family's physical and emotional circumstances, roles and role structure remain persistently unchanged.

Family members insist that their roles are both desired and appropriate.

There is intense concern about anyone changing roles.

There is an absence of spontaneity, novelty, warmth, and affection in family interaction.

Pseudo-mutual relationships may affect everyone in a family or only a few members. A man may always take the sexual initiative because it is important for him to feel sexually superior, while his wife always fakes orgasms because she feels obligated to do so. Both feel emotionally frustrated, a fact that is sensed by their children. But nobody takes any action, for all fear change. Better communication can resolve the situation. When people reveal to others how they really feel, there is then the alternative of either developing mutuality or ending the relationship.

**Ineffective Communication**
People may give others unclear messages because of fear of rejection or of destroying a relationship (Satir, 1972). By adopting certain patterns of communication, fears may be disguised. People may *placate*, so the others do not become angry; *blame*, to avoid being held respon-

The most intimate thing I ever saw between my mother and father occurred when I was about ten. My mother was upset about something and Father was talking to her in the den. She was in a nightgown, having just gotten up. My father was sitting opposite her, and he reached over and patted her on the knee. I thought this was embarrassingly intimate. Their kisses were brief and birdlike, nothing more.

In their adulthood, my own two sons reproached me for not having shown physical affection for them. I was surprised and totally unprepared for this and said, "But my father never showed me the slightest physical affection." It never occured to me to show any toward my sons. In the neighborhood I grew up in, I never saw a father being physically affectionate with his son, or his wife.

Dr. Benjamin Spock

sible; *compute*, using big words and cool logic; or *distract*, by ignoring situations, behaving as if nothing were wrong, and changing the subject. Although there are thousands of ways of failing to communicate, these are four of the most common.

*Placaters* are always agreeable. They are passive, speaking in an ingratiating manner and acting helpless. If a partner wants to make love, they don't want to say no, because that might cause a scene. No one knows what a placater really wants or feels – and they often do not know themselves. All they know is that what they get is not what they need. Our society socializes women in the role of placater.

*Blamers* act superior. Their bodies are tense, they are often angry, and they gesture with their fists. Inside, they feel weak and want to hide this from everyone (including themselves). If a blamer does not have an orgasm, the partner is at fault; if a child is conceived, the partner is responsible. With a blamer, no one else ever wins. The blamer does not listen and always tries to escape responsibility.

*Computers* are very correct and reasonable. They show only print-outs, not feelings (which they consider dangerous; feelings subject one to being vulnerable). "If one takes careful note of my increasing heartbeat," a computer may say, placing his date's hand on his chest, without smiling, "one must be forced to come to the conclusion that I find you terribly appealing." The female computer removes her hand and, without changing expression, replies, "My dear sir, I find your interest in me not wholly platonic. Indeed, you seem to exhibit an undue interest in my physical appearance." Both can only guess at

what the other means.

*Distractors* look frenetic and seldom say anything relevant. They flit about and may almost make you dizzy. Inside, they feel lonely and out of place. In sexual situations, distractors light cigarettes and talk about politics, school, business, anything to avoid discussing relevant feelings. If a partner wants to discuss sexual relationships, distractors change the subject.

None of these responses ever gets anyone anywhere, except into a hole. The only meaningful communication is honest communication.

**Effective Communication**

Communications traps, which are basically bad habits, can be avoided. Communication, as learned behavior, can be changed. There are several basic ideas that are helpful to keep in mind in trying to improve your own communication:

*To communicate directly, you need to know exactly who you are and what you need or desire.* This sounds simple but is difficult. We are taught to meet the demands and expectations of others – parents, friends, spouses, lovers, as well as the demands and expectations of society. We may be unable to learn what we need and who we are; we may fear rejection, and hide from ourselves.

*Be aware of what you experience as you talk.* Your body moves, as do your eyes. Your voice includes certain tones, inflections, speeds, degrees of smoothness. You smile, purse your lips, scowl. Are these communications appropriate to what you are saying, or is a smile hiding hostility? Relax your body, and feel what is happening as you talk.

*Check what your message is saying.* Are you saying what you want to say, or what someone expects

Sometimes speech is no more than a device for saying nothing – and a neater one than silence. Even in a case where words *do* convey information, they lack the power to suppress, sidetrack, or neutralize realilty; their function is to *confront* it. If two people manage to convince themselves that they possess any power over the events or people which form the subject of their mutual confidences, then they are deceiving themselves: their "honesty" is the merest pretext. There is a certain type of supposed loyalty which in fact constitutes the most flagrant hypocrisy: it is limited to the sphere of sexual relations, and its purpose, far from aiming at any intimate understanding between a man and a woman, is to supply one of them – more often the male partner – with a soothing alibi. He nurses the illusion that by confessing his infidelities he somehow redeems them; whereas actually he inflicts a double hurt upon his partner.

Simon de Beauvoir

you to say? If you felt totally confident about your relationships, would you say things differently?

*Listen carefully and accurately.* Listening is one of the most difficult aspects of communicating. You hear what people say in the context of how they sound, smell, feel and look. And how they react is partially a result of how you sound, smell, feel, and look to them. Your brain takes all this in, processing the message through past experiences. If your experience has taught you that certain subjects should not be talked about, this may obscure another person's message.

*Respond to the person as a person.* Consider people as they are, not as your think they are or would like them to be. Avoid putting labels on people as being a "typical man" or a "typical woman." Listen to each person as an individual.

Beginning to communicate about sex may appear frightening and threatening: rejection may result, the relationship might break up. These are real possibilities, but if partners have a firm basis of mutual trust – and a desire to work at understanding each other – the chances that the relationship will develop in new ways are good.

Each individual must work out his or her own way of dealing with sexual communication. Sometimes it is easiest, and least threatening, to discuss feelings and beliefs in a nonsexual setting. Reactions are likely to be more honest and less defensive. When communicating, a person should be able to say "I want . . . I need . . . I feel." Such "I" statements make it very clear that the other person is not being blamed, accused, or faulted. Responsibility lies with the speaker. Dealing with sex abstractly or in general terms tends to depersonalize a discussion, making it a discussion of ideas that may or may not reflect one's feelings. It is important to stay within the limits of personal experiences, to keep the dis-

cussion centered on *present* feelings. At first, there may be understandable uneasiness, but that will be overcome as partners develop sexual vocabularies to discuss their sexuality.

A useful approach to avoiding problems in sexual communication is to keep in constant contact with each other regarding sexual feelings. There are four helpful steps that a couple may choose to use in communicating with each other. After lovemaking, each partner may say "I like. . . ." Then he or she should ask, "What did you like best about our lovemaking?" The partners should suggest what each found unsatisfactory and what might be done to improve it. Finally, the couple should decide what they would like to do next time they make love.

Communication, although fulfilling, is seldom easy. Our culture has socialized us to avoid sexual communication, and our language lacks the vocabulary necessary for expressing sexuality in human terms. We may engage in pseudo-mutual relationships, which prevent us from expressing ourselves adequately. We may play sexual games and put others in double binds. We may placate, blame, compute, and distract. Communicating honestly and directly enables us to avoid all of these entrapments.

## QUESTIONS

1. How do people communicate with each other? What are their various means of communication? What is the significance of communication in human relationships?

2. What is the significance of touching in sexual communication? How may it be misinterpreted? Why?

3. Discuss the problem of saying "no." How

does it differ depending on a person's sex? Why?

**4.** Are women traditionally socialized to be placators? What about men? Discuss.

**5.** Discuss the impact of pseudo-mutuality on a relationship.

# Readings

*Excerpt from* **Games People Play**

Eric Berne

*Eric Berne was a witty observer of human sexuality and his game plans have had a lasting influence in psychological circles. Note that these particular games depend largely on people playing traditional sex roles.*

*Thesis.* This is a game played between a man and a woman which might more politely be called, in the milder forms at least, "Kiss Off" or "Indignation." It may be played with varying degrees of intensity.

1. First-Degree "Rapo," or "Kiss Off," is popular at social gatherings and consists essentially of mild flirtation. White signals that she is available and gets her pleasure from the man's pursuit. As soon as he has committed himself, the game is over. If she is polite, she may say quite frankly "I appreciate your compliments and thank you very much," and move on to the next conquest. If she is less generous, she may simply leave him. A skillful player can make this game last for a long time at a large social gathering by moving around frequently, so that the man has to carry out complicated maneuvers in order to follow her without being too obvious.

2. In Second-Degree "Rapo," or "Indignation," White gets only secondary satisfaction from Black's advances. Her primary gratification comes from rejecting him, so that this game is also colloquially known as "Buzz off, Buster." She leads Black into a much more serious commitment than the mild flirtation of First-Degree "Rapo" and enjoys watching his discomfiture when she repulses him. Black, of course, is not as helpless as he seems, and may have gone to considerable trouble to get himself involved. Usually he is playing some variation of "Kick Me."

3. Third-Degree "Rapo" is a vicious game which ends in murder, suicide or the courtroom. Here White leads Black into compromising physical contact and then claims that he has made a criminal assault or has done her irreparable damage. In its most cynical form White may actually allow him to complete the sexual act so that she gets that enjoyment before confronting him. The confrontation may be immediate, as in the illegitimate cry of rape, or it may be long delayed, as in suicide or homicide following a prolonged love affair. If she chooses to play it as a criminal assault, she may have no difficulty in finding mercenary or morbidly interested allies, such as the press, the police, counselors and relatives. Sometimes, however, these outsiders may cynically turn on her, so that she loses the initiative and becomes a tool in their games.

In some cases outsiders perform a different function. They force the game on an unwilling White because they want to play "Let's You and Him Fight." They put her in such a position that in order to save her face or her reputation she has to cry rape. This is particularly apt to happen with girls under the legal age of consent; they may be quite willing to continue a liaison, but because it is discovered or made an issue of, they feel constrained to turn the romance into a game of Third-Degree "Rapo."

In one well-known situation, the wary Joseph refused to be inveigled into a game of "Rapo," whereupon Potiphar's wife made the classical switch into "Let's You and Him Fight," an excellent example of the way a hard player reacts to antithesis, and of the dangers that beset people who refuse to play games. These two games are combined in the well-known "Badger Game," in which the woman seduces Black and then cries rape, at which point her husband takes charge and abuses Black for purposes of blackmail.

One of the most unfortunate and acute forms of Third-Degree "Rapo" occurs relatively frequently between homosexual strangers, who in a matter of an hour or so may bring the game to a point of homicide. The cynical and criminal variations of this game contribute a large volume to sensational newspaper copy.

The childhood prototype of "Rapo" is the same as that of "Frigid Woman," in which the little girl induces the boy to humiliate himself or get dirty and then sneers at him, as classically described by Maugham in *Of Human Bondage* and, as already noted, by Dickens in *Great Expectations*. This is Second Degree. A harder form, approaching Third Degree, may be played in tough neighborhoods.

*Antithesis.* The man's ability to avoid becoming involved in this game or to keep it under control depends on his capacity to distinguish genuine expressions of feeling from moves in the game. If he is thus able to exert social control, he may obtain a great deal of pleasure from the mild flirtations of "Kiss Off." On the other hand it is difficult to conceive of a safe antithesis for the

Potiphar's Wife maneuver, other than checking out before closing time with no forwarding address. In 1938 the writer met an aging Joseph in Aleppo who had checked out of Constantinople thirty-two years previously, after one of the Sultan's ladies had cornered him during a business visit to the Yildiz harem. He had to abandon his shop, but took time to pick up his hoard of gold francs, and had never returned.

---

## The Inexpressive Male

Jack O. Balswick and Charles W. Peek

*How does traditional masculinity affect the communication process? What are female counterparts to the cowboy type and playboy type? Is it only males who are inexpressive or both males and females in our culture?*

At least two basic types of inexpressive male seem to result from this socialization process: the cowboy and the playboy. Manville (1969) has referred to the *cowboy type* in terms of a "John Wayne Neurosis" which stresses the strong, silent, and two-fisted male as the 100 percent American he-man. For present purposes, it is especially in his relationship with women that the John Wayne neurosis is particularly significant in representing many American males. As portrayed by Wayne in any one of his many typecast roles, the mark of a real man is that he does not show any tenderness or affection toward girls because his culturally-acquired male image dictates that such a show of emotions would be distinctly unmanly. If he does have anything to do with girls, it is on a "man-to-man" basis: the girl is treated roughly (but not sadistically), with little hint of gentleness or affection. As Manville puts it:

> The on-screen John Wayne doesn't feel comfortable around women. He does like them sometimes – God knows he's not *queer*. But at the right time and in the right place – which he chooses. And always with his car/horse parked directly outside, in/on which he will ride away to his more important business back in Marlboro country.

Alfred Auerback, a psychiatrist, has commented more directly (1970) on the cowboy type. He describes the American male's inexpressiveness with women as part of the "cowboy syndrome." He quite rightly states that "the cowboy in moving pictures has conveyed the image of the rugged 'he-man,' strong, resilient, resourceful, capable of coping with overwhelming odds. His attitude toward women is courteous but reserved." As the cowboy equally loved his girlfriend and his horse, so the present day American male loves his car or motorcycle and his girlfriend., Basic to both these descriptions is the notion that the cowboy does have feelings toward women but does not express them, since ironically such expression would conflict with his image of what a male is.

The *playboy* type has recently been epitomized in *Playboy* magazine and by James Bond. As with the cowboy type, he is resourceful and shrewd, and interacts with his girlfriend with a certain detachment which is expressed as "playing it cool." While Bond's relationship with women is more in terms of a Don Juan, he still treats women with an air of emotional detachment and independence similar to that of the cowboy. The playboy departs from the cowboy, however, in that he is also "non-feeling." Bond and the playboy he caricatures are in a sense "dead" inside. They have no emotional feelings toward women, while Wayne, although unwilling

and perhaps unable to express them does have such feelings. Bond rejects women as women, treating them as consumer commodities; Wayne puts women on a pedestal. The playboy's relationship with women represents the culmination of Fromm's description of a marketing-oriented personality in which a person comes to see both himself and others as persons to be manipulated and exploited. Sexuality is reduced to a packageable consumption item which the playboy can handle because it demands no responsibility. The woman in the process becomes reduced to a playboy accessory. A successful "love affair" is one in which the bed was shared, but the playboy emerges having avoided personal involvement or a shared relationship with the woman.

The playboy, then, in part is the old cowboy in modern dress. Instead of the crude mannerisms of John Wayne, the playboy is a skilled manipulator of women, knowing when to turn the lights down, what music to play on the stereo, which drinks to serve, and what topics of conversation to pursue. The playboy, however, is not a perfect likeness; for, unlike the cowboy, he does not seem to care for the women from whom he withholds his emotions. Thus, the inexpressive male as a single man comes in two types: the inexpressive feeling man (the cowboy) and the inexpressive non-feeling man (the playboy).

Balswick and Peek, *The Family Coordinator*. Copyright © 1971. Reprinted by permission from the National Council on Family Relations, Minneapolis, Minn.

---

### He Blames Her, She Blames Him – Who's Right?

Laura Schlessinger

*Laura Schlessinger describes a typical blaming situation. Is anyone to blame? How does blam-*

*ing affect sexual interaction? How can Mark and Joan approach their difficulties differently?*

"Yes, that's right," Mark nodded furiously. "I don't bother to approach her sexually anymore. But that's her fault.

"All I ever got for my efforts was criticism or very little response."

"I'm not responsive because there is nothing much to respond to," complained Joan. "He rarely approaches me and when he does, it's just the same old thing so it's hard for me to get into it. He doesn't spend any time getting me in the mood and it ends up just hurting me."

If this kind of dialogue, about sex or anything else, seems familiar then you too might have been caught up in the perpetual, round-robin, blame-finding routine which occupies too much time in too many relationships.

There is just enough truth in the complaints of each to exaggerate justification for maintaining the battle stance of each position. Each refuses to acknowledge even a smidgen of truth in the other's complaint, and so much time is spent arguing the particulars, the main issue goes unattended to – which is exactly the intent of the participants!

From the above example, Mark is sensitive about his experience, knowledge, technique and competency as a lover. A lack of immediate responsiveness from Joan, makes any of her how-to or how-not-to comments threatening and uncomfortable.

Rather than reveal these feelings he defends his position by attacking, making her responsible for his lack of participation in their sex life.

From her comments, it would appear that Joan sees herself as a victim, being insensitively mishandled and suffering through it all because she "didn't want to hurt his feelings."

In actuality, her anger and resentment evolved into coldness and rejection, blaming him for "making her become this way."

Joan, too, is uncomfortable with sexual candor but there are other feelings, non-sexual in nature, which interfere with her feeling sexually free and giving. Joan has other levels of disappointment and dissatisfaction with Mark's nature and behavior. However, none of these feelings is being dealt with directly.

Therefore, they both have a stake in avoiding sex. Mark can avoid those feelings of incompetency undermining his sense of masculine identity and Joan is avoiding closeness because there are so many things that are so difficult to forgive and forget.

In summary, Mark doesn't want to get hurt and Joan doesn't want to forgive.

So much of our communication tends to be an attempt to keep from communicating anything of depth and meaning to us personally.

Life then turns into a power struggle of maintaining control to avoid vulnerability. Since intimacy is an exchange of vulnerability it is easy to see how sexual intimacy is often compromised indirectly.

How do we get off this merry-go-round blame-finding binge? By telling the truth, lovingly.

Dr. Laura Schlessinger, *San Francisco Chronicle*. Copyright © 1979 Copely News Service. Reprinted by permission.

## Guilt, Shame, Humiliation

Victor Daniels and Lawrence Horowitz, Being and Caring

*Learning about sex in America is to learn guilt, shame, and humiliation at the same time. Concerning guilt, John Money and Anne Ehrhardt have observed, "If you instill a sense of guilt into your children about one of the ordinary func-*

tions of the human body, then you have a weapon, guilt, which you can forever use over them."

Guilt, shame, and humiliation are all potent ways of stopping feelings. Let's say I'm a child who enjoys masturbating until adults tell me it's a shameful, dirty thing to do. I still like it, but others predict the very worst if I keep on. So now I feel guilty when I do it, because they expect me not to do it anymore.

Guilt is my feeling that I'm bad for doing what I'm doing, because my action is contrary to my image of how I'm expected to behave. Shame and humiliation are my feelings about myself when someone finds me out.

A "psychopath" not only lacks feelings of guilt and shame, but has also failed to develop means of self-regulation based on a genuine caring and affection for other people.

Guilt and shame and humiliation all include my anger toward you for stopping me from doing what I want to do. I may also be angry with you for making me feel small in front of others. Since I don't express my anger, it turns to resentment, or even hate. Hate is the extreme of resentment. In direct proportion to your success in causing me to feel guilty, ashamed, or humiliated, I resent or hate you. If I'm greatly afraid of losing your love or being otherwise punished, I may block out my awareness of my hatred or resentment.

Once I've cleared out my resentment against you, I can more easily appreciate that you may have done the best you could, teaching me in the only way you knew. A true understanding of what you faced is more likely to grow in me once I get my bitter feelings toward you off my chest.

This process of "catharsis" works because I have said the "unsayable" and I continue to exist, and exist in relationship to you. I finish my unfinished business with you, and don't have to carry it around anymore. At the same time, I work through my fear of expressing the feelings I've held in, and develop my ability to express them.

If my parents dealt with me by using shame, guilt, and humiliation, after I confront them with my resentment – whether they're still alive or not – I'm less apt to displace my anger toward them by venting it on my children, using these same power tools of shame, guilt, and humiliation.

If you and I are in a close relationship and I feel guilty or ashamed about some ways I act toward you, I want to check whether I have any underlying resentment I need to tell you about.

I also want to make sure that I'm telling you I resent or I feel angry about these things, and that I don't slip into blaming and condemning you for doing them. If you start defending your actions as I express my resentments, this tells me that you're feeling attacked and aren't hearing me. I can point out that these are my feelings, and not condemnations, or I can skip it for now and try again when you're more open to listening to how I feel.

Those who taught us by guilt and shame and humiliation came through that same school themselves.

Yet, there are other ways of teaching. I can teach you by giving you my appreciation when you do what I ask you to, and by loving you and caring for you as a unique and beautiful person.

Sometimes just pointing out to you the consequences of actions may be enough to get you to change your behavior, if you haven't thought about those consequences before.

### Excerpt from **The Serial**

Cyra McFadden

*The hot tub capital of the world, Marin County, California, is also one of the nation's hottest centers of experimentation in intimate lifestyles. Unfortunately, as in any field of endeavor, many experiments don't work out.*

Kate's attempt to take her psychiatrist friend Leonard as a lover couldn't have turned out worse if Sam Peckinpah had written her life script. But it looked great in the planning stage, while she was still conceptualizing it, and she trucked off to Tiburon that awful day in a warm glow of anticipation. She was feeling just terrific. For one thing, she was wearing her new proletarian-chic overalls, which were dynamite. For another, she had decided to play the whole scene off the wall, to just go with the flow. Everybody knew, in these days of heightened consciousness, that the rational mind was a screwup; the really authentic thing to do was to act on your impulses.

How could she have dreamed that two hours later she'd be gorging compulsively on refined sugar at the Swedish bakery, weeping into her coffee, and wondering how to get even with Leonard for doing that absolutely unbelievable number on her?

Omens and portents were everywhere, if she'd just stopped to notice them. For one thing, Tiburon was crawling with tourist types, in drip-dry coordinates, and their no-class wives, who all looked like runners-up for Miss Disneyland of 1955. For another, when she finally found a parking place in front of Tiburon Vintners, another VW bus tried to back into it while she was backing and filling.

Kate won, but not before the other driver, whose bumper sticker read "One World, One Spirit, One Humanity," had given her the finger. Then she got the pant leg of her overalls caught in the bus door, a blow because they were just back from Meader's. Kate hadn't dared wash them because she was afraid the Esso patch would run,

And finally, when she got to Leonard's office in the back of a remodeled ark he shared with a head shop, Sunshine, Leonard's receptionist, was still at her desk. Kate had hoped she'd be off on her yogurt break.

At last Sunshine padded out in her beaded moccasins, made for her "by this native American craftsman who's one thirty-second Cherokee," and Kate stopped pretending to read *Psychology Today* and restlessly paced Leonard's office, which was wittily decorated with positively Jungian primitive African masks and a collection of shrunken heads.

Leonard emerged from his inner sanctum a few minutes later escorting a boy of about seven. The boy was carrying something Kate recognized, incredulously, as one of those plastic dog messes from the sidewalk stands in Chinatown. As she stared, he thrust it at Leonard.

"Nummy num num!" Leonard said enthusiastically, pretending to take a bite. Then he steered the kid out the door a bit more firmly than seemed absolutely necessary. "And remember," he told him, waving, "stay loose."

Kate couldn't help blowing her cool and asking what *that* was all about, and when Leonard told her that Kevin had "this mind and body dichotomy thing," and that Leonard was trying to get him in touch with himself, starting with feces, her throat closed.

So they got off to a bad start, and things went steadily downhill from there. Kate suggested lunch, but they couldn't agree where to go; she liked El Burro, but Leonard was "enchilada'd out" and had also "O.D.'d on tostadas compuestas" the night before. He manipulated her into agreeing on Sam's Deck, which Kate didn't like because the last time she'd gone there, a gull had dumped on her shrimp Louie.

Worst of all, when they were sitting on the sunny deck at last, he couldn't stop talking about his own trip, rapping at her in this very hyper way about how he was into corporal punishment, the latest break-through in child psychology. He said he'd had amazing results just acting out his anger with his patients. He was also big on video feedback ("fantastic"), role-playing ("fantastic") and Japanese hot tubs, which made meaningful human interaction "practically inevitable."

Her anxieties mounting as Leonard ordered another Wallbanger (did she have enough cash in her Swedish carpenter's tool kit to cover the tab?), Kate wondered how a man who has spent three weekends at Esalen and knew Werner Erhard personally could be so insensitive. She kept trying to tell Leonard about Harvey's hangups and how repressed she was because of them, but Leonard wouldn't really pay attention. Although he kept saying, "I hear you, I hear you," he wasn't listening, and once, when she confessed a particularly intimate dissatisfaction with Harvey, he murmured absently, "That's cool. . . ."

Her self-image disintegrating rapidly, Kate decided to lay her body on the line. "Leonard," she said, raising her voice, "I'm sorry to dump on you like this, but I'm on a really heavy trip right now, you know? Like, I can't get my act together." She paused significanatly. "Leonard, I *need* you. I want you to help me get clear."

Leonard leaned across the table and gave Kate his full attention for the first time. At least she thought he did; he was wearing acid glasses, so it was hard to tell.

"Listen," he said sincerely, "I know exactly where you're coming from." He covered her hand warmly with his, crushing the piece of hamburger bun she'd been nervously shredding.

"Why don't you come to my place in Bolinas for the weekend?" His turquoise ring bit into her knuckles as he began to chant seductively. "Wholistic nutrition . . . hypnosis . . . biofeedback . . . massage . . . " Kate was beginning to hyperventilate when he added, in another voice entirely, "Friday night through Sunday noon. One

hundred and fifty bucks if you crash in the dorm. Extra charge for the hot tub. I take Master Charge, American Express, all your major credit cards."

Kate had seldom felt such overwhelming affection for her husband, good old Harvey, as she did when she was back in her Mill Valley tract house that afternoon, cooking her nuclear family a gourmet dinner to expiate her guilt and wondering how she could manage to plant a dead horse in Leonard's waterbed. But while she was furiously mashing chicken livers, which reminded her unpleasantly of Kevin's plastic turd, Harvey called to say he wouldn't be home for dinner and not to wait up.

She knew better, of course, but she felt an alarming little pang of suspicion. The fourth time this week, and was Harvey really *that* far behind on his flow charts?

# Unit 5

## Sexual Behaviors

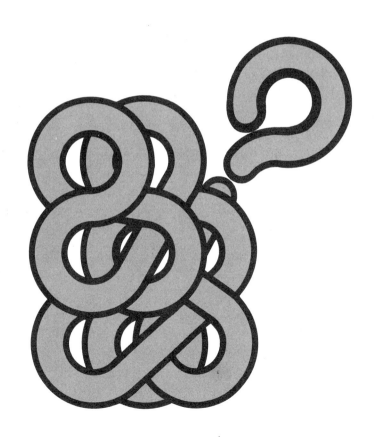

Everyone has unique ways of responding to sexual situations, and depending on the occasion, eroticism may or may not involve other people. In fact, *autoeroticism*, which involves dreams and fantasies as well as masturbation, may be the most diverse way a person experiences sexuality.

## Autoeroticism

**Masturbation** Individuals masturbate by rubbing, caressing, or otherwise stimulating their genitals to bring themselves sexual pleasure. They may masturbate during particular periods or throughout their entire lives. Kinsey (1953) reported that 92 percent of the men and 58 percent of the women he interviewed said they had masturbated. Today, there appears to be a slight increase in both incidence and frequency. Negative attitudes toward masturbation have been part of the Judeo-Christian heritage for more than 2,000 years, reaching almost paranoid proportions during the nineteenth century. For the last 75 years, these attitudes have changed to the extent that masturbation is no longer overwhelmingly condemned. A recent study indicates that two-thirds of the men and women interviewed believed that masturbation is not wrong; it is not clear, however, how many feel that it is a *positive* good. A study of male graduate students indicated that more than 40 percent feel guilty about masturbating. Although we may not feel that this sexual activity is to be condemned, as our parents and grandparents did, many people apparently do not accept it. In 1976, for example, the Roman Catholic Church issued a "Declaration on Certain Questions Concerning Sexual Questions," which stated that masturbation is a "seriously disordered act," despite "the force of certain arguments of a biological and philosophical nature..."

Few people realize that masturbation is an important means of learning about their bodies. Through masturbation, young boys and girls learn what is pleasing sexually, how to move their bodies, what their natural rhythms are. The activity has no harmful physical effects. Although masturbation often decreases significantly when individuals make love regularly, it is not necessarily a temporary substitute for sexual intercourse but is a legitimate form of sexual activity in its own right. Recently, sex therapists have been encouraging patients to masturbate, as a means of overcoming specific sexual problems and of discovering their personal sexual potential. (Kinsey's studies have shown that women are three times as likely to experience orgasm in the first year of marriage if they have previously masturbated to orgasm.)

*The Masturbatory Cycle* Male infants have been observed with penises erect, a few hours after birth. A baby boy may laugh in his crib while playing with his erect penis (although he does not ejaculate). Baby girls sometimes move their bodies rhythmically – almost violently – appearing to experience orgasm. Children often discover accidentally that playing with their genitals is pleasurable, and continue this activity until reprimanded by an adult.

By the time they are four or five, children have usually been taught that this form of sexual behavior is considered "nasty" by adults. Later this view becomes generalized to include the sexual pleasure that accompanies the bahavior. Thus, children learn to conceal their masturbatory sex play. Despite the myth of childhood innocence which rejects the possibility of sexual or protosexual behavior, the number of children who masturbate is fairly high. At eight or so, they enter a period in which sexual behavior increases. More than 57 percent of the men and 27 percent of the women interviewed by Kinsey recalled some kind of erotic arousal during childhood, although they may not have recognized it as being erotic at the time. About one out of twelve girls experienced orgasm before puberty.

When boys and girls reach adolescence, the behavior becomes overtly sexual. They no longer regard it as ambiguous play, but know that it is sexual. During this period, which is one of intense change both socially and biologically, there is often great confusion. In many ways, youngsters are expected to behave like a "man" or a "woman." Sex stereotyping is imposed more vigorously, and they are expected to behave in accordance with their sex roles. Most boys act sexually aggressive, priding themselves on their sexual prowess; girls act more passive sexually, and most pride themselves on their virtue. But the psychological toll is high (particularly for girls, who may enter adulthood with the attitude that sexual feelings are to be rigidly repressed and denied). The sex roles of adolescent girls and boys are contradictory rather than complementary, and this conflict often leads to tension and hostility between the sexes.

Kinsey found that masturbation increases with age during adolescence, and presented the following statistics showing the percent of males and females who masturbate at certain ages: at 12, boys 21 percent and girls 12 percent; at 13, boys 45 percent and girls 15 percent; at 15, boys 82 percent and girls 20 percent; at 20, boys 92 percent and girls 33 percent. These percentages vary, according to social class and educational level. The 1974 study of Hunt, however, suggests that adolescents now begin masturbatory experience earlier, perhaps as a result of changing social attitudes; 63 percent of the boys and 33 percent of the girls interviewed stated they had begun masturbating by age 13 (Hunt 1974).

This variation according to gender may be caused by differences in conditioning and in communication. Most boys discuss masturbatory experiences openly, relating different methods and recalling "near misses" when they were almost caught by their parents. Among boys, masturbation is a subject for camaraderie. In contrast, girls usually learn to masturbate through self-discovery. Because "nice" girls are not supposed to be sexual, they seldom talk about their own sexuality but hide it, repress it, or try to forget it. Masturbation is not considered a conversational subject by most adolescent girls.

Complex emotions are usually involved in adolescent masturbation. Teen-agers often feel guilt and shame for engaging in a practice that their parents and other adults indicate is reprehensible, and they are fearful of discovery. They may not really believe the stories that hair will grow on their hands or that they will get pimples, but there is enough free-floating misinformation to give them anxiety that something terrible will happen to them (and some unconsciously believe that their actions deserve punishment). A body shuddering and quivering during first orgasm is so far beyond the ordinary range of experience that the spasms themselves may seem to be among the evil consequences young people may dread. A girl who feels her vaginal lubrication for the first time may be frightened, as many a boy who sees the semen of his first ejaculation. Although frank discussion could alleviate fears, open talk is not always possible in a setting that involves unconscious shame.

Masturbation is the only sexual outlet for many adolescents. Because the accepted form of sexual behavior involves a partner of the opposite sex, masturbation may be viewed as a sign of sexual failure. This negative social value obscures the fact that self-masturbation is a

## Portnoy's Complaint

It was at the end of my freshman year of high school – and freshman year of masturbating – that I discovered on the underside of my penis, just where the shaft meets the head, a little discolored dot that has since been diagnosed as a freckle. Cancer. I had given myself *cancer*. All that pulling and tugging at my own flesh, all that friction, had given me an incurable disease. And not yet fourteen! In bed at night the tears rolled from my eyes. "No!" I sobbed. "I don't want to die! Please – no!" But then, because I would very shortly be a corpse anyway, I went ahead as usual and jerked off into my sock. I had taken to carrying the dirty socks into bed with me at night so as to be able to use one as a receptable upon retiring, and the other upon awakening.

Philip Roth

means of erotic self-discovery and of erotic fulfillment, and that it is an important part of the psychosexual development of most adolescents. It teaches them how their bodies respond, providing a biologically healthy substitute for sexual intercourse during the period when young people are developing emotionally. Among those who feel personally inadequate, however, masturbation may become a substitute for establishing meaningful relations with another person. Used as a permanent substitute for interpersonal involvement, masturbation becomes an unhealthy escape mechanism.

Masturbation continues after adolescence, although the frequency declines among men and increases among women. Kinsey's incidence for single men ages 16-20 was 88 percent, ages 21-25 was 81 percent. His incidence for single women ages 16-20 was 20 percent, ages 21-25 was 35 percent. Percentages for women may be much higher today. Although Kinsey cited masturbation among women 18-24 at 21 percent, with a median frequency of 20 times a year, a recent study indicates 37 times, with 60 percent of the women in this age group reported as masturbating. Kinsey found that almost half the women reported masturbating in their late twenties and early thirties, while Hunt (1974) reports 80 percent. Unlike men, women apparently do not tend to masturbate less as they grow older. Their masturbatory experiences remain stable through middle age and then slowly decrease. For men, however, the earlier leveling off and decrease may not be biological; it may reflect that idea that a "masculine" man gets all the sex he needs from his partner, making it unnecessary to "resort" to masturbation.

Most people continue to masturbate after they marry, although the rate is significantly smaller.

Kinsey reported that among the married, about 10 percent of the female orgasms and 4-6 percent of the male orgasms result from masturbation; no males of any age group masturbated more than once a month, but 40 percent of those in their late twenties and early thirties masturbated occasionally, with a median frequency of six times a year. More recently, Hunt reported that in the same age group, 72 percent of the husbands masturbated, with a median frequency of 24 times a year. While 33 percent of the women of this age masturbated, with median frequency of ten times a year in Kinsey's era, Hunt (1974) reports that although the median frequency has remained the same, 68 percent now masturbate.

A survey of 100,000 women in 1975 indicated that almost 75 percent have masturbated during marriage – 20 percent occasionally and 20 percent often. (Levin and Levin 1975). The rate is significantly higher among women who rated their marriages as unsatisfactory, suggesting that masturbating is used because personal and sexual relationships are unfulfilling.

There are many reasons for continuing the activity during marriage: masturbation is a pleasurable form of sexual excitement, a spouse is away or unwilling, sexual intercourse is not satisfying, the male fears impotence, or the individual acts out fantasies. Despite the high incidence of masturbation, this subject is rarely discussed among older people (particularly by women). A sense of shame is frequently experienced by those who feel that masturbation is what you do only when you do not have a sexual partner. Some feel sexually inadequate because they continue to masturbate after they have a partner. Some fear that partners would be disappointed or disapproving, perhaps feeling that the masturbating

To be a really good lover, then, one must be strong and yet tender.

How strong?

I suppose being able to lift fifty pounds should do it.

Woody Allen

You come
Like a white butterfly
Through green-black shadows.

Mary Ann Cronin

---

spouses considered them inadequate..

Discussing the anxieties sometimes resolves the guilt feelings. One man said:

I felt really bad about masturbating. We have been married for six years and have a really good marriage, but I've never told my wife about masturbating. I just couldn't. What would she think about me, a grown man, masturbating just like I was a kid again I was really preoccupied by it; I was afraid some day she would walk in and find me doing it.

Sometimes I would be in a bad mood all day about it. I didn't want to talk to her. But finally I talked it over with some friends of mine. That really took guts, then. Now, it's pretty easy. They told me that they all did it, and so did their wives. So I went to my wife and told her. You know what she said "Oh, I've always wondered about that. I do it, too, but I've always been too embarrassed to ask you about it or tell you."

Communication, though necessary, is not always easy. Sometimes the partners may respond negatively, feeling that they do not provide enough sexual satisfaction or that there is something wrong with their sexual response. In a society that considers masturbation to be an unwholesome activity, this attitude is understandable.

The sexual responsiveness of men usually declines after middle age, and for many the decline is traumatic. Because men often identify their self-worth in terms of sexual potency, they may turn to masturbation as their primary sexual outlet, using it as an escape from fears of impotency that may arise in sexual intercourse. A man who loses his partner through death or divorce may experience intense anxiety about having sexual relations with another woman. Fearing that he may be unable to have an erection, he may turn to masturbation as a "safe" outlet (De Beauvoir 1972).

Socially, older women are at a disadvantage.

Although it is considered acceptable for men to seek younger women, our society disapproves of relationships involving women and younger men. Ironically, it is the younger male who is most capable of satisfying an older woman sexually. Yet most women marry men of their own age or older, and by the time a couple is past middle age, the man is usually less active sexually than is the woman. She may turn to masturbation as a satisfying outlet. The older woman who loses her husband through death or divorce may be unable to find another sexual partner. Her age group includes significantly larger numbers of women than of men, and many of the few remaining men seek partners among women who are youthful. Unless she is extremely attractive, the older woman may find that masturbation is her only outlet for sexual satisfaction.

As masturbation becomes more significant in the lives of older people, they may experience intense guilt. When today's older generation was young, masturbation was severely repressed and condemned – and with age, childhood memories tend to increase. Until recently, few studies were concerned with the lives of older people. As yet, there is little data on their involvement with masturbation.

***Masturbation and Fantasies***  Almost all men and two-thirds of all women fantasize when they masturbate, with fantasies often providing the stimulus. These fantasies include almost everything — heterosexual, homesexual, and sadomasochistic behaviors as well as intercourse with animals and even parents. Fantasies usually relate to something within the individual's range of experience. Young men and women who have experienced only petting will probably fantasize about petting. Unlike the fantasies of men, however, those of women usually involve a romantic setting, including a particular mood and

## Marriage East & West

An American lady, on a visit to India, was taken for a drive along a country road. She and her host chatted gaily about Indian life. She was intrigued, as all Westerners are, by the strange ways of the East.

The driver swung the car round a bend and brought it suddenly to a halt. The way ahead was blocked by a pair of monkeys in the act of mating. The driver relaxed and settled down to wait till they were finished.

"They are entitled," he explained over his shoulder, "to be undisturbed at such a time."

---

the loving exchange of words and feelings; in the socialization of the woman, these factors have played a major part in attitudes toward sexual activity (Kinsey 1953).

The content of fantasy changes with experience and is generally related to age. Young girls and boys usually fantasize about kissing; depending on their experiences, they later fantasize about petting and intercourse. Interestingly, men tend to fantasize slightly beyond the range of their experience, but this may be simply a result of socialization and communication. Males are open about discussing sexual experiences, and are more likely to have had access to pornographic literature and movies. The women interviewed in Kinsey's study reported that they fantasized about a variety of sexual relations: 60 percent had fantasized about heterosexuality; 10 percent, homosexuality; 4 percent, sadomasochism; and 1 percent, bestiality.

**Sexual Fantasies**    Erotic fantasy is probably the most universal of all sexual behaviors. Although nearly everyone has experienced such fantasies, because they touch on feelings or desires considered personally or socially unaccept-

Ensor's *The Tribulations of St. Anthony* (1887) Oil on Canvas, The Museum of Modern Art, New York.

Embarrassed, the American lady tried to change the subject. The Indian gentleman who was her host, however, was not to be thus diverted. To him, sex was not a topic for prudery or evasion. It was a part of life, to be accepted as such. It was indeed closely allied with religion.

"Why shouldn't the phallus be worshiped," he asked, "as well as the sun or any other life-giving inhabitant of Heaven or Earth?"

David & Vera Mace

able they are not widely discussed. They may interfere with an individual's self-image, causing a loss of self-esteem, as well as confusion. A woman, for example, reported the following fantasy:

I sometimes like to imagine that I am a prostitute in a very expensive, Victorian-like bordello. Men will pay anything to make love to me and I will do anything they like. Sometimes I will make love with three or four men at a time; sometimes I will be making love with men and women on a waterbed, floating like a wave on the ocean, kissing their bodies all over, men and women alike. It is very hard for me to accept these feelings, though, because I'm not like that. At least, I don't think I am, am I?

Whether erotic or not, fantasy is a form of play. But Western culture – with its emphasis on the work ethic and the production of material goods, regardless of the psychological cost to the individual – discourages fantasy because it is not productive. Fantasies, which may interfere with the production of goods by turning the mind to other possibilities, are potential visions that threaten the status quo. Our culture describes the status quo as "reality," rejecting the place of fantasy as a valid phenomenon.

The difference between fantasy-as-play and fantasy-as-acted-out has been blurred by our social values. Both are considered equally dangerous, although only the acting out of fantasy has the potential for being antisocial. Jesus provided Biblical grounding for the Christian hostility toward sexual fantasies in the Sermon on the Mount "You have heard it said, 'You shall not commit adultery.' But I say to you that all who look at a woman lustfully has already committed adultery in his heart with her. If your right eye causes you to sin, pluck it out and throw it away. It is better that you lose one of your members than that your entire body be thrown into hell. And if your right hand causes you to sin, cut it off

and throw it away. It is better to lose one of your members than that your whole body goes into hell" (Matthew 5:27-30).

Yet fantasies, occurring spontaneously in the mind, are part of the body's regular functioning in the same way as the heart's beating or the stomach's digesting. Fantasies may function as substitutes for real actions and may provide a means of coping with frustrations. They may deal with past events, helping the individual to compensate for unpleasant experiences; they may deal with future events, providing a means of anticipating experiences. Whatever their particular function, fantasies that are accepted in an open and healthy manner help to maintain emotional balance. Some psychotherapists encourage patients to act out their sexual fantasies, in the attempt to discover inner feelings about their sexuality that had been blocked from conscious levels of awareness (Robertiello 1969).

One study reports that 98 percent of orgasmic women, but only 80 percent of those who are non-orgasmic, have sexual fantasies. Fantasies apparently help to prepare women for experiences that are erotically satisfying (Shope 1975).

Traditionally, men are open, bawdy, and obscene about their fantasies, which are a part of their public selves (at least in the settings of poolrooms, bars, locker rooms, and dormitories). Men exchange sexual fantasies through jokes and humor, discussing women they find attractive, going to pornographic films, sharing magazines and stories. They may also tell their wives and lovers about their fantasies. Women have traditionally been discouraged from discussing such fantasies; sex, to them, is supposed to be only a minor aspect of their personalities. From childhood, they are told that "dirty" thoughts are shameful. Consequently, women share little of their sexual fantasies with men or even with each other.

## A Zen Story

Two monks, Tanzan and Ekido, were travelling down the road in a heavy rain. As they turned a bend, they came upon a beautiful young woman in a silk kimono. She was unable to pass because the rain had turned the road to mud.

Tanzan said to her, "Come on," and lifted her in his arms and carried her across the mud. Then he put her down and the monks continued their journey.

The two monks did not speak again until they reached a temple in which to spend the night. Finally, Ekido could no longer hold back his thoughts and he reprimanded Tanzan. "It is not proper for monks to go near women," he said, "Especially young and beautiful ones. It is unwise. Why did you do it?"

"I left the woman behind," replied Tanzan. "Are you still carrying her?"

---

Nancy Friday, in first attempting to collect material for her two volumes of women's sexual fantasies, found that in 1968 women were reluctant to talk about them (Friday 1973). Men who were present when women were questioned often interrupted, saying that women didn't need fantasies because they had men, and that sexually satisfied women didn't need to indulge in fantasy. Friday concluded that men, feeling threatened by the fact that women may fantasize, rejected the possibility of them doing so. Women usually related fantasies in general and abstract terms, and seemed afraid of provoking anxiety in their husbands. The rise of the women's movement, however, has turned many inward in the search for discovery of their own sexuality. It is becoming increasingly common for women to discuss their fantasies – to admit these to others as well as to themselves – and Friday's collection reveals an immense eroticism. Fantasies ranged from heterosexual intercourse to group sex to rape, sadism, and fetishism. The differences reported by Kinsey – 84 percent of the men fantasized as compared to 69 percent of the women – may well reflect not actuality but merely the disinclination to reveal self-admissions that conflict with prevailing social views. There have always been women who, in selected company, expressed the same kind of bawdy sexual humor men express openly. As the moral climate of our society becomes more permissive, it is to be expected that such humor — and revelations of sexual fantasies as well – may become more freely expressed by females.

Fantasies also have a dark side, however. They may be disturbing, because attempts to repress them are usually unsuccessful. Repression may, indeed, cause the mind to focus more strongly on the unwelcome fantasy. Although fantasies that are incestuous, perverse, or homosexual are common, to the person experiencing them they may be destructive and threatening. Perhaps the best way to deal with a disturbing fantasy is simply to relax and accept it. When it comes to mind, do nothing more than look at it. Because it is simply a fantasy, it need not be evaluated as being "good" or "bad." If with time a disturbing fantasy fails to disappear, you may want to discuss it with someone you trust.

**Dreams**    Dreams are part of our forgotten heritage, one of the primary experiences in many primitive societies. They transport the dreamer into another reality, to the source of visions and spiritual power. The dreamer bridges the gap between the physical world and the spiritual world. Although dreams were a part of our folk heritage, they were not considered worthy of serious investigation until Sigmund Freud made his pioneering studies of their possible meaning. His non-empirical speculations revolutionized attitudes toward dreams, but are now important primarily because of their place in the development of psychological theory; Freud's speculation has been replaced by approaches that are less didactic and subjective.

Freud believed that the function of the dream is to protect sleep. Because the superego (conscience) is relaxed during sleep, repressed wishes threaten to come to the surface. But unacceptable wishes would destroy sleep by causing a person to awaken. Therefore, said Freud, these wishes are disguised as dreams, which surface as symbols. Sexual intercourse may be symbolized by a puffing locomotive, a penis by a tree-trunk, a vagina by an open door. Freud devised more than 55 symbols for sexual intercourse, 102 for

A woman was deep in slumber when a man appeared in her dream. "What are you going to do to me?" she queried. "Don't ask me, lady," he replied, "It's your dream."

the penis, 95 for the vagina.

According to Freud, dream content has two aspects. The *manifest content* is usually material from the day's experiences. The *latent content*, or real message, is disguised in symbols, whose meanings are discovered through *free* association of the elements in the manifest content. For example, a patient who lay back on Freud's famous leather couch in Vienna recounted a dream of walking up and down a staircase to a locked door. Through free association, Freud "guided" the patient to "discover" that walking represented sexual intercourse (both involve a common rhythm, heavy breathing, and a sense of relaxation when completed); the locked door symbolized an unwilling or unsatisfying partner (her vagina unyielding to the partner's efforts). Yet, once when asked about the symbolic meaning of the cigar he was smoking, Freud replied, "My dear sir, there are times when a cigar is simply a cigar." He felt that symbolism has to be determined within context.

Through the use of dreams, Freud tried to help patients discover the sources of their neuroses, which he believed went back to childhood. These neuroses usually related to some sexual conflict, often originating in the child's sexual desire for the parent of the opposite sex. Although the theory has been influential, several of its aspects have been questioned by subsequent researchers. Dreams may be no more than natural phenomena, in which meaning is not disguised by symbols at all. Carl Jung believed that dreams do not return the dreamer to repressed childhood fantasies but deal with existing situations. He rejected the possibility of latent content, believing that dreams express hidden problems in the present and that they point to future possibilities by revealing a person's potential.

The interpretation of dreams has become an **expensive form of therapy**, conducted by psychoanalysts at $50 to $200 a session. Experimental dream researcher Calvin Hall, however, developed a theory that enables people to interpret their own dreams. He believes that dreams are messages *from* ourselves *to* ourselves, which give us clues about unresolved problems through a natural "picture" language. Dreams give very clear and precise pictures of what the dreamer thinks, revealing feelings of strength, weakness, compassion, terror, and so on. The meaning of the dream is not to be found in any theory, but in the dream itself.

Hall gives four basic rules for those who want to interpret their own dreams. First dreams tell the dreamers how they feel and see themselves and their desires, other people, and the world. Dreams, being subjective, do not necessarily reflect any "truth"; rather, they reflect feelings. Second, dreamers themselves are the source of everything they dream. They dream nothing that they do not feel, think, or believe – however good or evil these may be. Third, dreamers have multiple conceptions of themselves, their impulses, their friends and acquaintances, and the surrounding world. Dreams reflect the sometimes complementary, sometimes contradictory aspects of life. And fourth, dreams must be interpreted as ongoing rather than isolated events. They relate to each other, tying together both conscious and unconscious thoughts.

*Erotic Dreams*    Almost all of the men and two-thirds of the women in Kinsey's study reported having had overtly sexual dreams. From 8 to 10 percent of the women experienced homosexual dreams (in which some even became pregnant). Like fantasies, dreams do not usually go beyond an individual's experience. But, while fantasies tend to be logical and related to ordinary reality, the images and unrealities of dreams are frequently very intense. Although

If I see and hear my beloved, I know her more than if I just
see her. But if I touch, smell and taste her, I know her still
more. But she will not allow me to come that close if she
doesn't trust me or want me to know her.

Sidney Jourard, *The Transparent Self*

---

people tend to feel responsible for fantasies,
which occur when awake, they are usually less
troubled by sexual dreams.

The content of the overtly sexual dream often
includes strangers who through interpretation
turn out to be people known to the dreamer.
One young man reported:

> I dreamed about meeting a young woman at a con-
> cert. She was very attractive and charming, with a
> wonderful laugh. I fell in love with her almost im-
> mediately. Very soon after we met, we began mak-
> ing love almost every night, but it was never
> passionate. It was more tender, than anything else.
> Then one night, when she was not at home, I went
> over to her house. Only her mother was there. She
> was 37 years old and even more beautiful than her
> daughter. We were both attracted to each other, and
> made love. I was more attracted to her than to her
> daughter.

> It did not take any dream work to figure out who the
> mother was. It was nothing Freudian. It wasn't my
> mother I desired. I realized that I was very attracted
> to my girl friend's mother, although I never really
> allowed myself to get turned on to her, or even was
> really aware of it until I had this dream.

Overtly sexual dreams are not necessarily sexually exciting, while dreams that are apparently
non-sexual may cause arousal. It is not unusual
for individuals to awaken in the middle of the
night, to find their bodies moving as if they were
making love. They may also experience nocturnal orgasm. Two to three percent of a woman's
orgasms may be nocturnal, while for men the
number may be as high as 8 percent of their total
orgasms. About 50 percent of the men interviewed by Kinsey had more than five nocturnal
orgasms a year, but less than 10 percent of the
women experienced them that frequently.

Dreams almost always accompany nocturnal
orgasm. The dreamer may awaken, and men
usually ejaculate. Although the dream content

may not be overtly sexual, it is always accompanied by sensual sensations. Erotic dreams run
the gamut of sexual possibilities: heterosexual,
homosexual, or autoerotic; incestuous,
sadomasochistic, bestial, fetishistic. Women
seem to feel less guilt or fear about nocturnal
orgasms than do men, accepting them more easily as pleasurable experiences. Men tend to
worry about them, perhaps because they emit
semen.

## Pleasuring

Making love involves giving and receiving pleasure, yet many people do not know how to experience erotic pleasure. They strive for orgasms,
and make love frequently, yet they do not fully
experience the erotic pleasure of sex. There is
something missing and they do not know what it
is. One reason they do not experience themselves fully is that they are not open to each
other sexually. They may have intercourse with
each other, but their bodies remain foreign to
each other and to themselves. In the course of
their sexual research, Masters and Johnson have
developed the idea of pleasuring. Pleasuring is a
means by which couples get to know each other
physically through touching. It begins with nongenital touching and caressing; neither tries to
sexually stimulate the other – they simply explore
each other. They discover how their bodies respond to touching. The man guides the woman's
hand over his body, telling her what feels good;
she takes his hand and moves it over her body,
telling him what she likes. Masters and Johnson
(1970) write:

> The partner who is pleasuring is committed first to
> do just that; give pleasure. At a second level in the
> experience, the giver is to explore his or her own
> component of personal pleasure in doing the touch-
> ing – to experience and appreciate the sensuous

*What turns women on? It is your duty to know; but first, take off those silly boxer shorts.*

Germaine Greer

dimensions of hard and soft, smooth and rough, warm and cool, qualities of texture and, finally this somewhat indescribable aura of physical receptivity expressed by the partner being pleasured. After a reasonable length of time ... the partners are to exchange roles of pleasuring (giving) and being pleasured (getting) and then repeat the procedure...

Such pleasuring gives each a sense of his or her own responses; it also allows each to discover what the other likes and dislikes. No one can assume they know what any particular individual likes, for there is too much variation between people. Books, pictures, and one's own assumptions can never give more than a rough and general idea of what is sexually pleasing to another. Pleasuring opens the door to communication: couples discover that the entire body is erogenous, rather than just simply the genitals. And pleasuring does not need to lead to sexual intercourse; it may be its own end whenever a couple chooses. Shere Hite (1976) wrote:

All the kinds of physical intimacy that were channeled into our one mechanical definition of sex can now be reallowed, and diffused throughout our

lives, including simple forms of touching and warm body contact. There need not be a sharp distinction between sexual touching and friendship. Just as women described "arousal" as one of the best parts of sex, and just as they described closeness as the most pleasurable aspect of intercourse, so intense physical intimacy can be one of the most satisfying activities possible – in and of itself.

There is no reason why physical intimacy with men should always consist of "foreplay" followed by intercourse and male orgasm; and there is no reason why intercourse must always be a part of heterosexual sex. Sex is intimate physical contact for pleasure, to share pleasure with another person (or just alone). You can have sex to orgasm, or not to orgasm, genital sex, or just physical intimacy – whatever seems right to you. There is never any reason to think the "goal" must be intercourse, and try to make what you feel into that context.

**Sexual Intercourse**

Unlike autoerotic behavior, sexual intercourse – whether heterosexual or homosexual – is a complex interaction between people. From a physiological point of view, it involves the triggering by the brain of a series of mechanisms that permit intercourse. The motivation is the same as that for non-sexual behaviors; the anticipation of reward. The reward may not necessarily be orgasm, however, because the meanings of sexual intercourse vary considerably at different times for different people.

Although sexual intercourse is usually regarded as either an impersonal drive or the expression of something called "love," it is in essence a form of communication. Its meanings vary greatly and change frequently. Sexual intercourse can be used to:

| | |
|---|---|
| show love | receive pleasure |
| have children | show tenderness |
| give pleasure | gain revenge |

Sensual pleasure occupies a very small and fiery place in the illimitable desert of love, glowing so brightly that at first nothing else can be seen. Around this inconstant campfire is danger, is the unknown. When we arise from a short embrace or even a long night, comes again the necessity of living near each other, for each other.

Collette, *The Wanderer*

| make a commitment | prove masculinity/femininity |
| end an argument | degrade someone |
| gain acceptance | degrade yourself |
| show rejection | touch or be touched |

Sex can be used to keep a person interested in you, to relieve loneliness, to dominate another, to make yourself or another feel guilty, to relieve physican tension, to express liking or love. These meanings vary and are infinite. An individual can make love one day to show affection, the next to gain revenge, the next to pretend love. No two occasions are necessarily the same.

Sexual positions and activities may also have meaning that varies from person to person, from time to time. A male who wishes to control may insist on *always* being in the position above his partner. Another individual may refuse to assume any but the traditional "missionary" position, because of embarrassment or shame concerning sex. Anal penetration by the male may signify curiosity, or disassociation from the partner. There are no rules that decree particular meaning for particular acts; meaning changes from context to context and from person to person.

Orgasm, too, may serve as a form of communication. Partners may, in fact, argue about whether *his* orgasm is more important than *hers*. "You always think of yourself first," is a common accusation between unhappy partners, who often transfer basic problems to the sexual relationship. Males who are anxious about their masculinity may feel sexually inadequate if a partner does not reach orgasm. Women who do not experience orgasm may worry about their own sexuality; they may also use the failure to reach orgasm as a means of expressing hostility toward their partners.

**Learning the Script**    Each culture has its own script for sexual intercourse, which people gen-

erally follow. Coitus, or intercourse, may or may not be preceded by kissing, fondling the breasts, and genital stimulation. (In some societies, "petting" follows intercourse rather than preceding it.) Most people know the general outline of their culture's script. Yet, as Simon and Gagnon (1973) have pointed out, in reality the playing out of the general cultural script does not necessarily fit the particular situation or individuals:

> Sometimes contact on the clitoris hurts, the breasts may not be sensitive, his fingers are crude, their clothing becomes disarrayed; she worries about being caught and if he is going to use a condom. At the same time, the couple is insulated in a silent world where it is not really possible to know what the other is feeling except through inarticulate gestures and sounds. At no point is there assurance that what one is doing is in fact having the effects that one would wish . . .

As sexual intercourse proceeds, the couple must integrate a new set of meanings, which are particularly confusing when first experienced. Petting and necking are behaviors involved during dating, but coitus usually involves a greater degree of commitment in terms of time, energy, and affection. The script is extended to include taking off clothes in front of another person, exposing genitals to each other, and possible feelings of embarrassment. Partners may worry about the way their genitals look; whether a penis is too small, whether the vagina has an unpleasant odor. Then they must discover how to interact compatibly with their bodies, how to move arms and legs and pelvises; how to move the genitals to give pleasure to both oneself and the partner. And there are other worries along the way. What if the hymen is intact? Will breaking it be painful? Will there be blood? Many of the anxieties and fears may be concealed during intercourse. When it is over, the individuals must return to their non-sexual world – yet coitus has

**All About "Kegels"  For Women** *

These exercises were originally developed by Dr. Arnold Kegel (Kay'-gill) to help women with problems controlling urination. They are designed to strengthen and give you voluntary control of a muscle called pubococcygeus (pew-bo-kak-se-gee'-us), or P.C. for short. The P.C. muscle is part of the sling of muscle stretching from your pubic bone in front to your tail bone in back. Since the muscle encircles not only the urinary opening but also the outside of the vagina, some of Dr. Kegel's patients found that doing the exercises had a pleasant side effect —increased sexual awareness.

*Why Do Kegel Exercises?*
Learning Kegel exercises:
- Can help you be more aware of feelings in your genital area.
- Can increase circulation in the genital area.
- May help increase sexual arousal started by other kind(s) of stimulation.
- Can be helpful after childbirth to restore muscle tone in the vagina.

*Identifying the P.C. Muscle*   Sit on the toilet. Spread your legs apart. See if you can stop and start the flow of urine without moving your legs. That's your P.C. muscle, the one that turns the flow on and off. If you don't find it the first time, don't give up; try again the next time you have to urinate.

**The Exercises**  *Slow Kegels*  Tighten the P.C. muscle as you did to stop the urine. Hold it for a slow count of three. Relax it.

*Quick Kegels*   Tighten and relax the P.C. muscle as rapidly as you can.

*Pull in – Push out*   Pull up the entire pelvic floor as though trying to suck water into your vagina. Then push or bear down as if trying to push the imaginary water out. (This exercise will use a number of "stomach" or "abdominal" muscles as well as the P.C. muscle.)

At first do ten of each of these exercises (one "set") five times every day. Each week increase the number of times you do each exercise by five (15, 20, 25, etc.). Keep doing five "sets" each day.

- You can do these exercises any time during daily activities that don't require a lot of moving around: driving your car, watching television, doing dishes, sitting in school or at your desk or lying in bed.
- When you start you will probably notice that the muscle doesn't want to stay "contracted" during "Slow Kegels" and that you can't do "Quick Kegels" very fast or evenly. Keep at it. In a week or two you will probably notice that you can control it quite well.
- Sometimes the muscle will start to feel a little tired. Not surprising. You probably haven't used it very much before. Take a few seconds rest and start again.
- A good way to check on how you are doing is to insert one or two lubricated fingers into your vagina.
- Remember to keep breathing naturally and evenly while you are doing your Kegels!

*University of California, San Francisco, Human Sexuality Program.

i like my body when it is with your
body.   It is so quite new a thing.
Muscles better and nerves more.
i like your body.   i like what it does,
i like its hows.   i like to feel the spine
of your body and its bones and the trembling
-firm-smoothness and which i will
again and again and again
kiss,   i like kissing this and that of you,
i like slowly stroking the shocking fuzz

of your electric fur and what-is-it comes
over parting flesh...And eyes big love-crumbs,

and possibly i like the thrill

of under me you so quite new

E. E. Cummings*

*Copyright © 1925 by E. E. Cummings. Reprinted by permission of Harcourt Brace Jovanovich, Inc. from *Complete Poems, 1913-1962.*

---

given possible new meanings to even this type of interaction. What do you say to one another? To others? Only after partners have had experience with each other will the integration of sexual and non-sexual roles become easier. To a certain degree, each new partner brings the same problems, although usually with diminishing intensity.

**Sexual Positions** Only in the mechanistic sense can a textbook describe the positions of coitus. Sexual intercourse is among the most personal of acts, and no two people necessarily carry it out in exactly the same way. Individuals must listen to their own inner selves and to the responses and movements of their own bodies; they must simultaneously observe the feelings of partners. Ideally, there is awareness of and sensitivity to both partner *and* self.

The illustrations provided on the following page exemplify some of the possibilities of heterosexual intercourse, but in reality, potential positions are almost infinite. Moving a leg up or an arm to the side, touching lightly or firmly, kissing tenderly or passionately – all of these variables provide nuances that can make each sexual experience unique. In addition to the traditional sexual intercourse, the practice of oral-genital stimulation of genitals with the mouth or tongue is now being admitted with far greater openness than in the past, although this position, called "69" because of the figuration vaguely suggested, is still banned by law in most states as being an "unnatural act".

Amidst the concern expressed over sexual positions and "how-to-do-it," the importance of body movement is often overlooked. Yet it is through the body – with its vitality, its flexibility, its liveliness – that we ultimately express ourselves sexually. Therapists such as Alexander

Lowen, Moshe Feldenkrais, and Ida Rolf believe that free and vital movement of the body is the key to sexual satisfaction. They point out that people have varied experiences in orgasm, ranging from slight and scarcely noticeable twitchings to overwhelming waves of sensation, and that there are varying degrees of intensities and sensations. Unlike most American researchers, these therapists are more interested in the quality of orgasm than in frequency.

According to Lowen (1965), a "partial orgasm" does not fully discharge the sexual tension built up during the excitement phase of intercourse; tension is blocked instead of being released, and the individual does not achieve a sense of satisfaction and fulfillment but continues to feel sexually restless. Sexuality remains centered in the genitals rather than being diffused throughout the body. By contrast, the "full orgasm" involves the loss of ego control and the discharge of sexual tension; body movement is involuntary rather than controlled. Of this movement, Lowen writes that:

> It is generally assumed that the function of the sexual movements is to increase the friction between the genital organs. It is not generally appreciated that the sensory elements of contact and friction serve to provide the excitation for the movement. The sensation of orgasm is a function of the movement...

When the individual "lets go," involuntary movements of coitus begin, developing spontaneously from the voluntary motions after a certain level of excitement is reached. Lowen continues:

> The excitation takes possession of the body and mind of the individual and reverses his [or her] normal orientation.

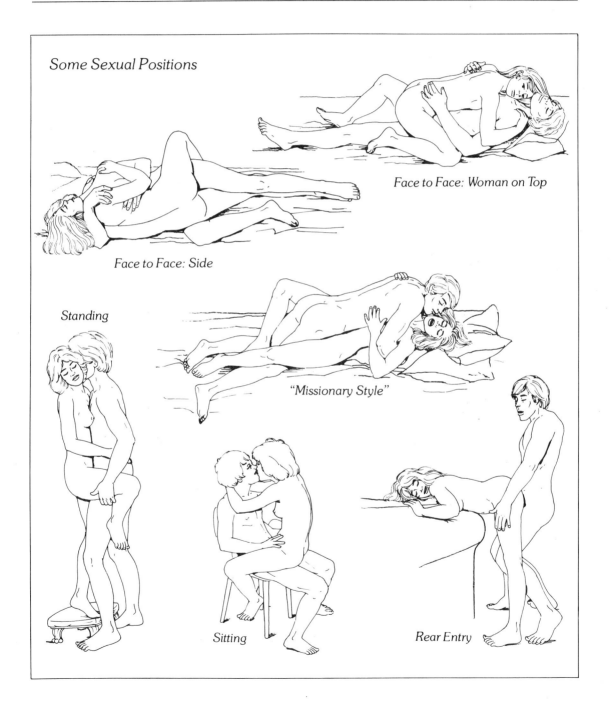

Some Sexual Positions

Face to Face: Woman on Top

Face to Face: Side

Standing

"Missionary Style"

Sitting

Rear Entry

And yet not cloy thy lips with loathed satiety,
But rather famish them amid their plenty,
Making them red and pale with fresh variety;
Ten kisses short as one, one long as twenty:
A summer's day will seem an hour but short,
Being wasted in such time-beguiling sport.

Shakespeare, *"Venus and Adonis"*

Whereas the voluntary movements are ego directed, the involuntary movements are under the control of the pelvic sensations. It is as if a center of excitation and feeling develops in the pelvis that is strong enough to overthrow the hegemony of the conscious ego.

Because orgasm is both highly personal and highly subjective, variations in sensation are not easily measured. Researchers have debated whether or not there is a difference in partial and a full orgasm. But the significance of Lowen's work — whether the opinions are right or wrong — is that it points to the importance of free, spontaneous movement. Overemphasis on position

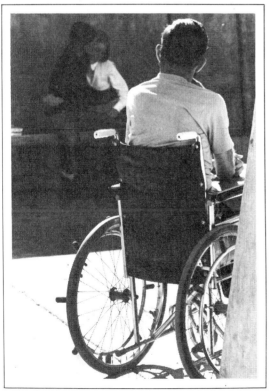

The Myth of the Handicapped: That they are without sexual desires.

and performance may limit spontaneity of movement. Certainly, freedom cannot be achieved by the partner who is thinking, "Okay, now, I put my hand there, first, and then there. Ooops! I forgot to kiss that and nibble this. When can we really get down to business?"

### Sex and The Handicapped

The sexual needs and desires of the handicapped, like those of the aged, have been generally overlooked and ignored as though sexuality was not a part of their lives. One physician, in fact, was amazed to learn from a panel of paraplegics that "if they had their choice between getting back their walking or their normal sexual function, they'd choose sex . . . In the hospital we put all our effort toward walking — we were doing nothing about this other problem" ("Sex and the Paraplegic," *Medical World News*, January 14, 1972).

In dealing with the sexual problems of the handicapped, the handicapped person must overcome his or her sexual performance expectations and realign them with his or her actual sexual capacities. Instead of perpetual, mutual, or multiple orgasms (which are generally unrealistic) the handicapped person must discover what his or her particular capabilities are. In cases where the spinal cord is cut, for example, there is no feeling in the genitals, but that does not eliminate sexual desires or end other possible sexual behaviors. Such persons are frequently advised by their physicians to engage in oral or manual sex; anything, in fact, that they and their partners find pleasurable and acceptable. They are encouraged to experiment in attempts to discover new erogenous areas in their bodies, such as their breasts, ears, necks, armpits, et cetera. Among those men whose spinal cords are only partially severed, 70 percent can ejaculate; most of them, given the availability of partners, can have intercourse.

However, a major problem for many handicapped persons is to overcome guilt. They feel guilty because their bodies are not ideal, because they cannot fulfill their sexual desires and fantasies as able-bodied persons can. They often live in dread of rejection, which may or may not be a realistic expectation, depending on whom they seek as partners. But guilt is not necessary, as Milton Diamond (1974) pointed out:

> One needn't worry about being different sexually because anything goes that is functional and mutually acceptable. Oral-genital stimulation, manual stimulation, anything that the couple or the individual can find satisfaction in doing is okay . . . We must not put a negative value on any practice found acceptable, whether it involves masturbation, oral-genital relations, a female superior position, or anything else that satisfies the couple.

Thus, a major function for therapists working with handicapped clients is giving their clients "permission" to engage in sexual activities that are appropriate to their capacities and suggesting new activities or techniques. Handicapped clients should be advised of the use of vibrators and artificial penises and vaginas; these devices should be sold, suggests Dr. Diamond, "in surgical supply stores as freely as in the porno supply shops, where they are presently sold."

Finally, it is important for the physically handicapped to understand that sexual satisfaction is quite different from orgasm. Sex is a means of communicating deeply intimate and human feelings to another person, not simply orgasm. These feelings can be communicated to other people without the elaborate nightlong bouts of lovemaking or the "idealized anatomy" of the able-bodied, godlike figures of television and movie actors. Satisfaction really comes from good sexual communication and intimacy, independent of orgasm. Both can be sought after, but one does not guarantee the other.

## QUESTIONS

1. Discuss the masturbatory cycle. How does it change through a person's lifetime? Why is it different between men and women?
2. Is the fantasy life between men and women different? Why?
3. What is meant by "pleasuring"? Is it a useful concept?
4. How are meanings given to sexual intercourse? What are the possible meanings and motivations behind sexual intercourse?
5. What adjustments must handicapped people make in terms of their sexuality?? What is the significance of sex for handicapped people?

# Readings

### The Tyranny Of Technique

Rollo May, *Love and Will*

*Rollo May suggests that there are several paradoxes to sex and love in contemporary*

*America. The first is that sexual enlightenment has not solved the sexual problems of our society. Guilt and anxiety are still widespread. The second paradox is that there is increased emphasis on sexual techniques, which instead of in-*

creasing connectedness between people alienates them. *Techniques turn sex into a performance. The third paradox is the rise of a new puritanism: alienation from the body, the separation of emotions from reason, and the use of the body as a machine.*

A second paradox is that *the new emphasis on technique in sex and love-making backfires.* It often occurs to me that there is an inverse relationship between the number of how-to-do-it books perused by a person or rolling off the presses in a society and the amount of sexual passion or even pleasure experienced by the persons involved. Certainly nothing is wrong with technique as such, in playing golf or acting or making love. But the emphasis beyond a certain point on technique in sex makes for a mechanistic attitude toward love-making, and goes along with alienation, feelings of loneliness, and depersonalization.

One aspect of the alienation is that the lover, with his age-old art, tends to be superseded by the computer operator with his modern efficiency. Couples place great emphasis on bookkeeping and timetables in their love-making — a practice confirmed and standardized by Kinsey. If they fall behind schedule they become anxious and feel impelled to go to bed whether they want to or not. My colleague, Dr. John Schimel, observes, "My patients have endured stoically, or without noticing, remarkably destructive treatment at the hands of their spouses, but they have experienced falling behind in the sexual timetable as a loss of love." The man feels he is somehow losing his masculine status if he does not perform up to schedule, and the woman that she has lost her feminine attractiveness if too long a period goes by without the man at least making a pass at her. The phrase "between men," which women use about their affairs, simi-

larly suggests a gap in time like the *entr'acte.* Elaborate accounting-and ledger-book lists — how often this week have we made love? did he (or she) pay the right amount of attention to me during the evening? was the foreplay long enough? — make one wonder how the spontaneity of this most spontaneous act can possibly survive. The computer hovers in the stage wings of the drama of love-making the way Freud said one's parents used to.

It is not surprising then, in this preoccupation with techniques, that the questions typically asked about an act of love-making are not, Was there passion or meaning or pleasure in the act? but, How well did I perform? Take, for example, what Cyril Connolly calls "the tyranny of the orgasm," and the preoccupation with achieving a simultaneous orgasm, which is another aspect of the alienation. I confess that when people talk about the "apocalyptic orgasm," I find myself wondering, Why do they have to try so hard? What abyss of self-doubt, what inner void of loneliness, are they trying to cover up by this great concern with grandiose effects?

Even the sexologists, whose attitude is generally the more sex the merrier, are raising their eyebrows these days about the anxious overemphasis on achieving the orgasm and the great importance attached to "satisfying" the partner. A man makes a point of asking the woman if she "made it," or if she is "all right," or uses some other euphemism for an experience for which obviously no euphemism is possible. We men are reminded by Simone de Beauvoir and other women who try to interpret the love act that this is the last thing in the world a woman wants to be asked at that moment. Furthermore, the technical preoccupation robs the woman of exactly what she wants most of all, physically and emotionally, namely the man's spontaneous abandon at the moment of climax. This abandon gives her whatever thrill or ecstacy she and the experience are capable of. When we cut through all the rigmarole about roles and performance, what still remains is how amazingly important the sheer fact of intimacy of relationship is – the meeting, the growing closeness with the excitement of not knowing where it will lead, the assertion of the self, and the giving of the self – in making a sexual encounter memorable. Is it not this intimacy that makes us return to the event in memory again and again when we need to be warmed by whatever hearths life makes available?

It is a strange thing in our society that what goes into building a relationship – the sharing of tastes, fantasies, dreams, hopes for the future, and fears from the past – seems to make people more shy and vulnerable than going to bed with each other. They are more wary of the tenderness that goes with psychological and spiritual nakedness than they are of the physical nakedness in sexual intimacy.

Rollo May *Love and Will*. Copyright © W. W. Norton and Company, Inc. Reprinted by permission.

## Kinsey On Female Masturbation

*Kinsey's findings on masturbation among women distressed many people when it was first published because it contradicted the myth of women's sexual "innocence." Perhaps even more disturbing was that women had a greater frequency of orgasm from masturbation – "that nasty practice" – than they had from heterosexual intercourse. At the same time, it helped alleviate guilt many women felt about masturbation; after all, millions did it.*

Of the six possible types of sexual activity, heterosexual petting is the one in which the largest number of females engage before marriage, and marital coitus is the one in which the largest number of females engage after marriage. Masturbation is the one in which the second largest number of females engage both before and after marriage.

Among all types of sexual activity, masturbation is, however, the one in which the female most frequently reaches orgasm. Even in her marital coitus the average female fails to achieve orgasm in a fair proportion of her contacts, and this is true in most of the petting which she does prior to marriage; but in 95 percent or more of all her masturbation, she does reach orgasm.

This is due to the fact that the techniques of masturbation are especially effective in producing orgasm. Socio-sexual relationships usually demand some adjustment of the interests, the desires, the physical capacities, and the physiologic reactions of the partner in the activity. In coitus, a female who is strongly aroused by the psychologic aspects of the relationship may find some of the adjustments which she has to make interrupt the steady flow of her response, and she is, in consequence, delayed or completely prevented from reaching orgasm. She may prefer the socio-sexual relationship because of its psychologic and social significance, and the delay in reaching orgasm may in actuality increase her pleasure, but the fact remains that the techniques of masturbation usually offer the female the most specific and quickest means for achieving orgasm. For this reason masturbation has provided the most clearly interpretable data which we have on the anatomy and the physiology of the female's sexual responses and orgasm.

Masturbation among the females in the sample had most frequently involved some manipulation of the clitoris and/or the labia minora. The clitoris is the small, bud-like structure — a homologue of the male penis – which is located near the outer surface at the upper end of the female genitalia. The labia minora are the paired and at times protrudent and prominent inner lips of the genitalia. Some 84 percent of those females in the sample who had ever masturbated had depended primarily on labial and/or clitoral techniques.

The clitoris and the inner surfaces of the labia minora are of about equal sensitivity and of equal importance as centers of stimulation. In masturbation, the female usually moves a finger gently and rhythmically over the sensitive areas, or applies rhythmic or steady pressure with several of her fingers or with her whole hand. Frequently a single finger or two may be slowly or more rapidly moved forward between the labia in a manner which brings each stroke against the clitoris. Sometimes the labia are gently but still rhythmically pulled. This stimulates these structures and, because they are attached at their forward end to the clitoris, simultaneously stimulates that organ. Occasionally the subject's heel or some other object is used to press on the sensitive areas.

This concentration of stimulation on the clitoris and the labia minora in masturbation is a demonstration of the fact that they are the portions of the genitalia which are best supplied with end organs of touch. The minimum use of deep penetrations of the vagina in masturbation is a reflection of the fact that the walls of the vagina itself are practically without nerves in most females, although there may be some sensory nerves close to the entrance to the vagina in some individuals.

*Nocturnal Sex Dreams*   The nocturnal sex dreams of males have been the subject of extensive literary, pornographic, scientific, and religious discussion. The male, projecting his own experience, frequently assumes that females have similar dreams, and in erotic literature as well as in actual life he not infrequently expresses the hope that the female in whom he is interested may be dreaming of him at night. He may think it inevitable that anyone who is in love should dream of having overt sexual relations with her lover. But relatively few records of female dreams have been available to establish such a thesis. Even some of the best of the statistical studies of sexual behavior have failed to recognize the existence of nocturnal dreams in the female.

This is curious, for it has not proved difficult to secure data on these matters. Females who have had nocturnal sex dreams seem to have no more difficulty than males in recalling them, and do not seem to be hesitant in admitting their experience. Whether or not they reach orgasm in these dreams is a matter about which few of them have any doubt. Because the male may find tangible evidence that he has ejaculated during sleep, his record may be somewhat more accurate than the female's; but vaginal secretions often bear similar testimony to the female's arousal and/or orgasm during sleep. As with the male, the female is often awakened by the muscular spasms or convulsions which follow her orgasms. Consequently the record seems as trustworthy as her memory can make it, and the actual incidences and frequencies of nocturnal orgasms in the female are probably not much higher than the present calculations show. The violence in the female's reactions in orgasm is frequently sufficient to awaken the sexual partner with whom she may be sleeping, and from some of these partners we have been able to obtain descriptions of her reactions in the dreams. There can be no question that a female's responses in sleep are typical of those which she makes when she is awake.

Masturbation and nocturnal sex dreams to the point of orgasm are the activities which provide the best measure of a female's intrinsic sexuality. All other types of sexual activity involve other persons – the partners in the sexual relations – and the frequencies and circumstances of such socio-sexual contacts often depend upon some compromise of the desires of the two partners. The frequencies of the female's marital coitus, for instance, are often much higher than she would desire, and even those females who are most responsive in their sexual relations might not choose to have coitus as often as their spouses want it. Since other persons have a minimum effect upon the incidences and frequencies of masturbation and nocturnal sex dreams, these latter outlets provide a better measure of the basic interests and sexual capacities of the female.

Alfred Kinsey et al, *Sexual Behavior in the Human Female.* Copyright © 1953 Philadelphia. Reprinted by permission.

## What Happens in Intercourse?

The Boston Women's Health Book Collective

*The following excerpt from* Our Bodies Ourselves *gives some pleasant thoughts on intercourse.*

What is it like to have intercourse and to experience an orgasm and what happens?? Here is a rough sketch to give some idea of the main events.

Maybe you have just had a bath and are warm and relaxed, or maybe you have been flirting and teasing each other and are excited and aroused. One way or another you end up on the bed (sofa, floor, lawn) with some or all of your clothes off, and begin making love. You stroke each other all over, maybe give each other a back rub. You take turns concentrating on *giving* and *receiving* pleasure. Before long you become aware of your genitals; the penis and clitoris begin to get hard, the woman may feel a faint tingling or swelling in the labia, and a wetness inside the vagina. (This wetness is an early sign of arousal and doesn't mean that the woman is ready to accept the penis.)

You begin to concentrate more on the genitals. The man may enjoy having his penis stroked, or maybe licked, and perhaps having his testicles pulled gently or fondled. The woman may like her clitoris and labia stroked, or massaged or maybe licked. You can tell each other what feels good. (Women have a myth that men automatically know how to make love. This is not true. Not only do they have to learn, but since every woman's nerves are a little different, you have to tell them what *you* find stimulating.)

If there were an observer, he would notice that your heart was beating faster and you were breathing harder. These manifestations will continue up to orgasm, and then slowly subside.

In a little while you are feeling much aroused; you may be moaning from the excitement. Maybe one of you feels inside the vagina with your finger to see if it has loosened up. If you are using foam or a condom, it's time to put it in or on. Then one of you holds the penis in your hand, and you gently guide it into the vagina. Maybe you just lie together for a minute, letting the vagina get comfortable around the penis and enjoying each other. Gently at first, by rolling your hips or moving in and out, you begin to move the penis inside the vagina. For some women these motions can stimulate the clitoris enough to reach orgasm.

Exactly when orgasm occurs depends on the person, and it's unusual for both people to reach orgasm at the same time. At some point the penis or clitoris has received enough stimulation, and it triggers off. First there is a feeling of expectation, as if your genitals were about to sneeze; the clitoris or penis may tingle. Then your whole body, especially the penis or clitoris-plus-vagina-plus-uterus goes into a glorious spasm (actually a series of rhythmic contractions), followed by a sense of relief.

Sometimes the woman, with continued stimulation, can have several or more orgasms. The man will have a "refractory period," during which he can't come to orgasm again. This can last from a few minutes to several days, depending on his age and physical condition.

## Ten Sex Myths Exploded

William H. Masters and Virginia E. Johnson

*Masters and Johnson look at ten sexual myths that are current in contemporary America. Why are these myths so powerful?*

In this age of candor and supercommunication, It has been a pleasure to witness the demise of some of the more irrational and pernicious sex myths. But the pleasure one feels at this progress, which has come about through increased sex education in the communication media, in the schools and in the counseling professions, is tempered by the realization that for every myth uprooted, another takes its place.

We have chosen for this article ten myths, a few as old as Methuselah but still running strong, and others almost as modern as today's headlines but likely to be discussed a good deal longer. We trust discussion will be leavened with a few facts.

*The Most Satisfying Position Is The Male Superior* The "missionary" position is certainly the one most frequently employed, but it isn't necessarily the most gratifying. In fact, the female partner generally has more freedom and, hence, more satisfaction if she is above. Another position we recommend – particularly for sexually distressed couples – is the lateral, or side by side. It does not put the responsibility on either partner to accommodate the other. Rather, it makes it possible for either or both to exercise whatever activity is desired at a given time. This position allows the greatest freedom of movement for both partners, and it gives the male the greatest security of ejaculatory control.

But there should be no guidelines as to the "best" position. Whichever a couple finds most satisfactory at a given moment is the one that should be used. Many couples – particularly those in the higher educational strata – like to vary their coital positioning rather than follow any rigid pattern.

*Sex During Menstruation Is Unclean and Harmful* The erroneous notion that a menstruating woman is dirty and dangerous, still prevalent in modern society, dates back to prehistoric times. J. G. Frazer states, in *The Golden Bough*, "According to the Talmud, if a woman at the beginning of her period passes between two men, she thereby kills one of them." The Bible declares that anyone lying with a woman within seven days of the onset of her period – even if it lasts only three – "shall be unclean seven days and every bed whereon he lieth shall be unclean."

This is nonsense. Medically, the menstrual flow is in no sense dirty or harmful. But it has been used as a convenient excuse by women wishing to avoid intercourse. As a pathetic example, we have had many reports at our clinic of mothers who force their daughters to wear menstrual pads on dates.

This attitude is a residual of the double standard, and, as society approaches a sane sex ethic, women should be able simply to say no if they wish to avoid intercourse and men should be secure enough to accept an honest, well-intentioned rejection without considering themselves humiliated.

Actually, many women feel below par during the height of their menstrual flow, and they are frequently bothered by cramps. This, and not an irrational taboo, should be sufficient reason to abstain. But if the woman feels up to it, and a small percentage actually experience heightened desire toward the end of their periods, there is no reason for her or her partner to be deprived of the pleasure of sexual intercourse.

### Sex Should Be Avoided During Pregnancy
"The ban on coition during pregnancy," writes Alex Comfort in his book *The Anxiety Makers*, "has an interesting history. Hippocrates was against it (together with hill walking, washing and sitting on soft cushions) – Galen was more concerned with abstention during lactation, since intercourse spoiled the taste of the milk and a new conception robbed it of important ingredients. For the anxiety maker, it was an additional means of cutting down the amount of unpleasant and dangerous coition to which the moral athlete was to be exposed."

Dr. J. R. Black, quoted by Comfort, wrote "Coition during pregnancy is one of the ways in which the predisposition is made for that terrible disease in children, epilepsy." Dr. J. H. Kellogg said, "Indulgence during pregnancy is followed by the worst results of any form of marital excess . . . the results upon the child are especially disastrous."

Unquestionably, sexual intercourse with a pregnant woman should not be indulged in as lightly as a stroll through the park. There are some precautions to be observed, but they are certainly not of the magnitude dictated by those Comfort rightly describes as the "anxiety makers."

During the first pregnancy, the initial three months may be a difficult period – sexually and otherwise: Many women usually suffer from nausea, vomiting, bloating and a general sense of discomfort. These will tend to blunt her sex drive and reduce her sexual effectiveness. More seriously – but much more rarely – women who have lost at least three early pregnancies may abort when the uterus contracts during orgasm (from either intercourse or masturbation). This has not yet been clinically proved, but it hasn't been disproved, either, and in such cases it's wise to avoid elevating sexual tensions to orgasmic levels – by any means – during the first three months.

It's also possible that uterine contractions will stimulate labor in the final stages of childbearing in a normally pregnant woman. However, this usually occurs during the terminal period of pregnancy and does not represent a danger: postorgasmic uterine response leading into premature labor is extremely rare.

Apart from these contraindications, there is little to prevent a willing couple from having intercourse during pregnancy. Many women report a level of sexual tension during the three middle months that represents a personal high in their experience. Frequently their sex drive is unlimited, regardless of how many episodes they may have. One of the explanations is the increased blood supply to the female reproductive organs as pregnancy progresses. This may cause many women to remain in a relatively constant state of sexual excitation.

The primary modern taboo on sex during pregnancy pertains to the final six or eight weeks, when many doctors, as a precautionary measure, proscribe sex. This restriction is generally unnecessary, though the woman herself may find that she is growing lethargic and uncomfortable and, as a result, not very desirous of sex. However, if there is no vaginal bleeding, no pain during intercourse, no broken membranes, and if the woman retains some degree of sexual desire, there is no reason to avoid intercourse right up to the moment of labor.

***A Small Penis Is Less Satisfying to a Woman Than a Large One*** This phallic fallacy is one of the most destructive of sexual myths, because belief in it leaves men feeling inadequate and women unfulfilled. For, indeed, a woman who believes that a large penis is necessary to satisfy her will be satisfied with nothing less, even though, physiologically, her belief is totally unwarranted.

Here are the facts. There is a great deal of variation in the size of flaccid penises. But when they become erect, the differences are minimized, because the small flaccid penis grows proportionately bigger than the large flaccid penis. The insignificant differences that still exist among the sizes of erect penises are further minimized by the fact that the vagina accommodates to any size. This occurs because it's a potential rather than an actual space, and during the plateau phase of intercourse (between initial excitement and orgasm), it contracts snugly around the penis, regardless of its length or circumference. The male who is fearful of penile shortcomings should also take comfort in knowing that the vagina itself in not very sensitive. Once the penis is inserted and the male begins thrusting, he is providing indirect stimulation to the clitoris, which is the center of female sexual

sensitivity. It is this that provides the woman with pleasure, not necessarily the contact between the male sex organ and the vaginal walls.

***Prostitutes Are Either Frigid or Homosexual (Or Both)*** It's difficult to trace the origin of this myth, but one would suspect that it's part and parcel of the new puritanism that tends to infiltrate the social sciences. The old Puritans decreed that sex was sin and, counting on the populace's adherence to religious tenets, let it go at that. But in our modern society, where science has replaced the traditional deities for many people, we find new ways to impose the old restraints. So we no longer point our finger at the whore and declare her sinful. That's too unsophisticated. Rather we declare that she's *sick*. It's not considered possible for her to be motivated by economic gain (in a society that thrives on such motivation) or even by sexual pleasure (it offends the sexual restraint we've worked so hard to achieve to believe that anyone can have that much fun). To make our diagnosis more plausible, we define her sickness as unconscious homosexuality or unconscious antagonism toward men, either or both resulting in frigidity.

There was some justification for the belief that prostitutes rarely experience orgasm in earlier times. Then, when bordellos were the fashion and the girls had a quick turnover of clientele, there was little opportunity for them to turn on during the few minutes with each customer. But today's call girl, who frequently spends an hour or more – and sometimes the entire night – with each John, has infinitely greater opportunity for orgasmic return. As a consequence, and because prostitutes, like all women (and men), respond to time, place and circumstance, they frequently do experience orgasm.

It's true that some prostitutes are overt lesbians. But so are some married women. There is no valid generalization to be made from either statements.

***Anal Intercourse Is Perverted and Dangerous***   "If a man also lie with mankind, as he lieth with a woman, both of them have committed an abomination: they shall surely be put to death; their blood shall be upon them." Thus said the Old Testament (Leviticus 20:13). A host of fallacies and legal proscriptions have proliferated since to enforce this biblical injunction against "unnatural" intercourse (anal *and* oral). Both are against the law in almost every state of the Union – even between married partners – and have been blamed for nymphomania, cancer, impotence, insanity, blindness – even backache – among other ailments.

Nothing could be farther from the truth, although certain elementary precautions should be observed when performing anal intercourse. Initially, it can be painful, but, presuming that the receiving partner is willing to undergo an uncomfortable breaking-in period and that the male partner (in a heterosexual situation) takes care to avoid contamination of the vaginal tract, there is no reason to fear physical harm from the practice. We have had many reports from men that they withdraw their penis from the rectum and insert it in the vagina just prior to ejaculation. When the man does this, he risks transporting bacteria to the vagina, which may produce severe infection, afflicting not only the vagina but the uterus and Fallopian tubes as well. An additional danger in both heterosexual and homosexual anal intercourse is that bacteria may enter the penile passage and cause prostatic, bladder or kidney infections. These usually can be prevented if a condom is used.

Thus, there are certain easily prevented dangers in this practice, but the notion that it is "perverted" requires no medical comment. Obvi-ously, if an individual's aesthetic or religious scruples preclude this or other forms of non-vaginal intercourse, then he should obey his conscience – without making judgments on the practices of others.

Unfortunately, many husbands apply undue pressure to their wives, who may be reluctant to have anal intercourse, but it should be needless to say that no form of sexual activity is enjoyable if performed unwillingly. However, when conducted with the consent of both partners and with the routine precautions we've outlined, anal intercourse can afford great pleasure. Indeed, many women report that it provides them with overwhelming orgasmic response.

***It's Good to Sublimate the Sex Drive for Long Periods of Time***   This is a tricky myth, because the concept of sublimation is so little understood and so highly controversial. Some authorities have suggested that it is possible to suppress or repress the sex drive and convert it to higher goals – such as success in art, writing, athletics and other endeavors. We have never seen any evidence, however, that abstention from overt sex can transform the libido into other kinds of energy.

The next question that arises is, sublimation apart, can human beings simply abstain from sex for sustained periods of time? The answer is yes – with reservations. Human sexual expression is a natural physical-response pattern, like breathing or bladder or bowel function. But sex is unique among physiological responses in that it can be taken out of its natural context for indefinite periods of time. This quality is useful in a civilized society, for it allows us to delay overt sexual activity until an appropriate time and, accordingly, lets us go about our business. Unfortunately, it should be noted that religious and legal authorities have abused the capacity for the deferral of sex by imposing all sorts of unrealistic restraints on it, thus conditioning people to avoid sex and to fear it even when it is appropriate. For example, the little girl whose hand is slapped for touching her genitals may develop an aversion to sexual touch that can last a lifetime. This negative conditioning contributes to the multiplicity of sexual distresses suffered by so many people today. (We estimate that 50 percent of all marriages in the U. S. are afflicted by one sort of sexual inadequacy or another.)

Unquestionably, there are men and women who have never had heterosexual or homosexual intercourse, never masturbated and never had sex dreams or fantasies. We believe these individuals are rare – incredibly rare, we should add.

The final question is, are extended periods of abstention harmful? If a person rates sex at the bottom of his value system, he may be able to adjust to periodic or even lifetime abstention by making suitable adjustments and compensations. These often take the form of defensive armor commonly described as uptightness. But we do believe that he will not be able to turn on and turn off his sex drive at will. Regularity of expression is essential to effective sexual functioning – particularly if the individual wishes to perform sexually in his later years. Rejection of sexual activity for extended periods of time can introduce a mental handicap when it is resumed and can even contribute toward a mild atrophy of the sexual organs.

We must speculate in conclusion that absention is certainly possible, but, with few exceptions, it is seldom advisable from a physical point of view.

***An Excessively Amorous Woman Is a Nymphomaniac*** Classically, a nymphomaniac is defined as a woman with persistently high levels of sexual tension who constantly searches for orgasmic relief but fails to attain it. This is a fascinating fantasy – the woman in constant heat and begging for fulfillment – that could have been created only by males with great imaginations and little familiarity with female sexual response. Statistically, this type of woman is virtually nonexistent.

We suspect that the men who have perpetuated this notion have been victims of the situation described by Wardell Pomeroy (a coauthor of the Kinsey reports), who, with tongue in cheek, characterizes a nymphomaniac as any woman who exhibits even a slightly higher degree of sexual desire than her male partner. Pomeroy's point is well taken, because, in our culture, nymphomania does not refer to objectively measured states of female excitation but, rather, to male concepts of excessive female need. Obviously, the term *excessive* varies from female to female and from male to male and in their relationship to each other. In fact, the human female has an infinitely greater capacity for sexual expression than the male. She has the natural potential for multiorgasmic response, and her orgasmic experiences are more intense and last longer than those of the male.

The American male, who suffers from society's destructive dictum that sexual success rests with him, often attempts in vain to match his partner's orgasmic ability with an equal number of ejaculations. This is ridiculous and self-defeating. It can lead only to a sense of insecurity that may ultimately become a sexual inadequacy.

***Advancing Age Means the End of Sex*** The most pernicious of all sexual fictions is the nearly universally accepted belief that sexual effectiveness inevitably disappears as the human being ages. It simply isn't true. Obviously, our vigor progressively declines as we go from our 50s to our 80s. This means that our sexual performance will not be characterized by the same physical energy as it was in our teens, 20s, 30s and 40s. But, then, we can't run as fast in later years as we did when we were young. And we don't worry about that.

Sexually, the male and the female can function effectively into their 80s, if they understand that certain physiological changes will occur and if they don't let these changes frighten them. Once they allow themselves to think they will lose their sexual effectiveness, then, for all practical purposes, they will, indeed – but because they will have become victims of the myth, not because their bodies will have lost the capacity to perform.

Here are some of the changes that can be expected. The male's erection will take longer to achieve once he's past his 40s. It may take minutes, as compared with seconds in his salad days. Also, his erection may not be as full or as firm as it was when he was younger. If he has an understanding partner who helps him guide his penis into her vagina, he'll find that it will become sufficiently erect after a few strokes. There is also a reduction in seminal fluid, and some men may notice that the force of ejaculation has lessened, as well. At the conclusion of intercourse, the older man may find his erection returning to a relaxed state so quickly that it virtually feels as if his penis is dropping from the vagina. And then he'll probably notice that it takes considerably longer for him to obtain another erection. These are natural occurrences and are no cause for concern.

Perhaps one of the most perplexing changes in the older man's physiology is his reduced need for ejaculation. He simply does not feel the de-

mand for an orgasm that a younger man feels. If he performs once or twice a week at the age of 60, let's say, he may want to ejaculate only every second or third time. This change can be particularly upsetting to a couple, because the man and his partner may think they're not getting the job done. They're both victims of the fallacy of "end-point release" – in other words, they believe, like so much of society, that sex cannot be satisfying and fulfilling unless a goal is set for both partners: ejaculation for the male, orgasm for the female. If the female can be educated to the fact that her aging male partner should ejaculate only when he feels like it, then the odds are greater that he'll continue being an effective lover. *He* needs to be educated, too, to understand that he should ejaculate at whim and not at her urging.

The icing on the cake in all this is that, concomitant with the reduced demand for ejaculation, the male usually is able to exercise much greater control than he ever had before. This means less likelihood of premature ejaculation for him and greater likelihood of orgasm – even multiple orgasms – for his partner.

Her physiological changes may also make her fearful as she reaches her 50s and beyond. She tends to lubricate more slowly than before, and the walls of her vagina become thinner. This means they can be easily irritated and may even be stretched or torn with forceful sexual activity. Regular sexual activity and adequate sex-steroid replacement therapy – in other words, a replenishment of hormones – can compensate for this involution to some degree, but a simple understanding that these are natural changes and need not prevent intercourse is just as important.

In the final analysis, the male and the female do not have to give up sexual relations well into advanced age, as long as they remain in good physical condition and have partners who are interested in them and interesting to them.

***Any Man Who Can't Make It With a Woman Is Suffering From Severe Psychiatric Problems*** As Gershwin's Sportin' Life said, "It ain't necessarily so." Certainly, there can be a background of psychopathology in cases of impotence and premature ejaculation – the two major types of male sexual inadequacy. But often these dysfunctions are caused by faulty conditioning, negative sex education and/or pervasive ignorance (often compounded by irrational fear).

The underlying cause of premature ejaculation, in our estimation, is the male habit of "going for the goal line," with nothing valued in between. This reflects male disregard for female satifaction, an attitude that is usually conditioned in the young man before his sex ethic is fully formed. Many men who ejaculate before their partners are satisfied were initially exposed to quickie sex relations with girls in the back seats of cars or with importuning prostitutes. Similarly, the first sexual experiences of some men are under intense pressure in cheap motels or behind park bushes. Also, the adolescent practice colloquially called dry humping teaches disregard for female satisfaction, as does *coitus interruptus*, the technique in which the male withdraws his penis just prior to ejaculation; he may (or may not) accomplish birth control, but he usually leaves his partner in a state of high sexual excitation.

Clinical experience convinces us that since premature ejaculation is usually a result of faulty conditioning, it can almost invariably be cured by simple reconditioning techniques, accompanied by counseling that stresses the importance of the male's concern for his partner's pleasure, both physiological and psychological. If there is an accompanying neurosis – and there frequently is – then that condition may require psychotherapy. But the inability to control the ejaculatory process is not necessarily linked to a psychiatric condition.

Impotence is a more complex dysfunction and more often does, indeed, have an underlying psychopathology. But almost as often it does not. Many men have normal sex lives for 10, 20 and 30 years before the onset of erective inadequacy. In some cases these men are premature ejaculators whose wives complain of their inadequacy to the extent that the husbands finally become convinced they lack manhood and consequently lose their power to erect. In other cases a bout with drugs or alcohol or fatigue or preoccupation or a fight with one's partner can induce an episode of impotence, which, if not understood and placed in its proper context, may lead to a fear syndrome that perpetuates the problem. Moreover, some men who are adequately attuned mentally fail to have erections because of an endocrine imbalance or other physiological disability. This is relatively rare, but it occurs. One of the saddest and most unnecessary causes of impotence is the male's tendency to convince himself that he won't be able to function sexually beyond a certain age. As we pointed out in the preceding myth, advancing age does not prevent sexual activity; thinking it will might well prevent it.

The male's erective function is incredibly complex and can fail for a number of causes, some of them psychopathological but, as we have seen, many of them not. As a final note, we'd like to add that the professions that are most experienced at treating sexual inadequacy are the clerical and the behavioral (psychologists, social workers and marriage counselors). Psychiatrists and physicians fall quite a bit behind.

## Sex And The Handicapped

Milton Diamond, Journal of Rehabilitation Literature

*There are hundreds of thousands of handicapped people in America who have had to make adjustments in their sexual lives. Some were born handicapped, others were crippled in automobile or industrial accidents, some were struck down by illness or blown up in Vietnam. All have had to discover new meanings for their sexuality.*

DR. DIAMOND: When we think of the functions that sex serves, we have to think in terms of giving and getting pleasure, of reducing tension, of sharing intimacies. If we keep that in mind we can remove ourself from the stereotype that "good" sex involves only an erect penis in a vagina; that that's the only way or right way. Do you feel that the value of an orgasm is part of the myth, Bill

BILL: Well, very much so. In fact, before you kinda work up to something, and then it's over. This way, you just keep going on and on.

DR. DIAMOND: What do you find the most pleasurable thing now?

BILL: Well, still touching the penis, but just touching the nipples and breasts and the sides. I'm very sensitive under the arms.

DR. DIAMOND: So you could find your own way of giving and getting pleasure and that

solves your own needs.

BILL: Yeah, but it's much better when somebody else does it.

DR. DIAMOND: Well, that's what I assumed.

BILL: You just have to try – find the right partner and I guess the right partner is just about anyone who shares your feelings toward each other.

DR. DIAMOND: Mickie, how about yourself?

MICKIE: Well, since being paralyzed and getting out of the more severe part of it, I find that I am perfectly normal except that the mechanics of the thing are different. My legs and back are totally paralyzed. As far as feelings are concerned, if anything, they're heightened because the type of polio I had made me hypersensitive. I find that it's just mostly the mechanics that interfere. And, of course, the preconceived idea that, because you're in a wheelchair, "Don't bother with her – she can't do anything anyway."

DR. DIAMOND: Well, we find that even able-bodied persons begin to find that there is more than one way to skin a cat and probably the handicapped find this out a lot quicker. George how about you and your heart condition?

GEORGE: Well, I feel like there isn't that comfort that I'm getting from the rest of the people here about my relationship with sexuality. When I had my heart attack, the doctor told me to stop having sex for awhile but he never told me when to come on again. I feel a profound kind of lack of knowledge and hesitancy . . .

MICKIE: George, do you feel a sense of fear in this area?

GEORGE: Oh, yeah. I think that the fear that accompanies this kind of activity is very profound because it's a deep insult to the body.

There's a great hesitancy and I think this leaves a feeling of separation.

DR. DIAMOND: How about your wife? Obviously, you can look at it both ways. You may want love but she doesn't want to lose you. Francis, how about yourself with cerebral palsy? How do you see your condition now?

FRANCIS: Well, I'd like to be like any normal guy. I had this cerebral palsy since back in my preschool years. There came a time when the doctors over there wanted me to progress and I didn't progress rapidly. Now, I could do almost anything any normal person could do.

DR. DIAMOND: But now, are you dating now? Are you married now?

FRANCIS: Oh, no, I'm still dating girls.

DR. DIAMOND: Jerry, how about yourself with your back condition?

JERRY: With me, it was a problem. I believe of creating a new self image. I thought that I had to be the virile male and live up to may wife's expectations (which she didn't have) of me. She was perfectly satisfied with what I was able to give her after the accident but I was always trying to do more, and finally I just sat back and enjoyed it, and it was great!

DR. DIAMOND: Why couldn't it have been this way before?

JERRY: Yeah, why did I have to go through all this misery of thinking that I wasn't performing and that I had lost my capabilities.

DR. DIAMOND: Isn't that a problem with all of us – we become spectators, rather than participants. We ask, "What am I supposed to be doing?" rather than, "What can I do?" Shouldn't we concentrate on what we have, rather than on what we don't have?

BILL: This business about fear – it can be emotional fear, too. With fear that, once you are handicapped, you're not going to be able to live up to the expectations that you've been taught in the past other people have of you and you have of yourself. Being in a wheelchair, they don't have the same expectations; they kind of wonder if you can or you can't. Once you show that you can have intercourse you can also show them what would normally be progressing steps in intercourse. You can show them that you've had good experiences and pleasurable experiences, and the orgasm doesn't become important anymore – or the typical intercourse methods.

DR. DIAMOND: Did you have different experiences as you went through different ages? Many of you have had your handicaps for quite some time.

MICKIE: I've had a rather different type of life. I lost my first husband because of my illness. He couldn't face up to having a disabled wife and two small children. The second time around, it was great. However, before my husband died, he was, for the last two or three years, so very ill that for us there was no more sex as most people think of it. But there was still a deep affection between us. I built my life around different types of activities, so I can't say that I really felt too great a lack in my life because he was still very affectionate, very sweet to me, and showed me lots of love and attention, and I tried to do the same for him. That was important. The fact that we no longer had typical sexual relations just ceased to be of any importance to either one of us.

DR. DIAMOND: Do any of you get the feeling that either the spouses or lovers, or what have you, are hesitant in initiating sex because of the handicap? How do you overcome that??

GEORGE: I feel that one of the greatest difficulties with my whole family is lack of being able to say it's all right. We begin to have a profound doubt of our own feedback mechanism. You know what I mean – an acceptance. That I'm okay where I'm at is kind of cut off because of this regression. You know, when you're on your own, you lose that trust in yourself.

DR. DIAMOND: Is there anybody that you can commune with? Your physician or your spouse?

GEORGE: Somewhat; I think more would be helpful.

DR. DIAMOND: Francis, whom do you talk to when you have problems?

FRANCIS: I sometimes talk to my parents, counselors, or probably with the girl I'm dating. I find that the girls are understanding. I talk about the problems that I have and they feel compassion about my problems and I feel that they understand.

DR. DIAMOND: What is your biggest problem that you think you've had and overcome? Jerry, how about that?

JERRY: I really believe that the biggest problem was living up to an expectation that wasn't expected at all.

DR. DIAMOND: But now you don't worry about it at all?

JERRY: No, I don't worry about it. That's just the way it is. My wife is a wonderful woman. She's very loving and we've established a new relationship on a different level.

DR. DIAMOND: You just don't have the movements.

JERRY: Right.

DR. DIAMOND: Bill, how about yourself?

BILL: I agree with that. That the most important thing is to get your own self-confidence and just do what comes naturally when you're with your girl.

DR. DIAMOND: How do you do that?

MICKIE: Well, you throw your inhibitions out the window and let it all hang loose.

DR. DIAMOND: How do you do that though? How do you throw out your inhibitions if you've got them?

BILL: It's just a matter of confidence. The first time you may not take advantage of what you later perceive to be the girl's willingness, then you verbally kick yourself in the rear end. The next time, by God, you're not going to make the same mistake twice! You're going to go ahead and do it.

DR. DIAMOND: Mickie, you said something I think is crucial about getting rid of your inhibitions. How about those feelings with guilt? That you may be doing something that somebody else says is not normal?

MICKIE: That is a very hard thing to overcome, but you've got to make up your mind; either you're going to take happiness now while it's there waiting for you or forget it because you're not going to come back and do it again. You know – it's just that simple. It isn't like having a piece of cheese in the "refrig" and a week later going and getting it out. There's no way that you're going to be able to do that. So you've just got to say – maybe we'll try something else.

DR. DIAMOND: Sex, in terms of genitals, is important but, in terms of personal worth, getting along with somebody and self-worth are perhaps more important.

MICKIE: Oh, I think so!

Milton Diamond, Copyright © *Journal of Rehabilitative Literature*. Reprinted by permission.

Sexual dysfunctions (problems in giving or receiving erotic satisfaction) with physical causes are considered in Chapter 3. This chapter is concerned with the more common psychological roots.

Since sexual experience is unique for every individual, it is difficult to apply precise definitions to sexual dysfunctions. Nevertheless, certain problems occur with sufficient frequency to warrant generalized descriptions. *Erectile dysfunction* (sometimes termed 'impotence') is the inability of a male to achieve or maintain erection. *Premature ejaculation* is the inability to delay ejaculation. The most common dysfunctions of women are *orgasmic dysfunction* (failure to attain orgasm), vaginismus (tightening of the muscles surrounding the vagina to the point that it is impenetrable), and *dyspareunia* (painful intercourse).

**New Awareness and New Meanings** The awareness of sexual dysfunctions in *both* men and women is a relatively recent event in our culture. Traditionally, there has always been an awareness of male dysfunctions–especially impotence – and the cures can be traced back centuries to the ancient Egyptians. Desperately trying to revive their potency, men have taken potions made from phallus-shaped mandrake roots, gone to magicians (and more recently physicians), carried charms, chanted and prayed to strange gods, and undergone surgery. Traditionally cast as a comic or pathetic character in literature, the impotent figure inspires uneasy laughter among men, for all men know or fear that they *might* become that comic figure. Karen Horney pointed out a fundamental difference between male and female sexuality: "Now one of the exigencies of the biological differences between the sexes is this; that man is actually obliged to go proving his manhood to the

woman. There is no analogous necessity for herself. Even if she is frigid, she can engage in sexual intercourse and conceive and bear a child. She performs her part by merely being, without any doing" (Horney, 1945). Sexual dysfunction strikes at the core of men's identities; until recently, it did not for women's.

Until the last few decades, very little concern was expressed about sexual dysfuctions with women, except for vaginismus (tightening of vaginal muscles preventing penetration) or dyspareunia (painful intercourse). This reflects interest in female sexuality *vis-à-vis* the male. Female sexuality took on meaning only in relation to intercourse with the male. Frigidity, or the inability to experience orgasm, was generally passed over with little comment since women were not expected to be sensual beings. In fact, women with strong sexual desires were often suspect, especially during the 19th century. We are still heirs to this attitude. There are countless examples in the medical literature of that period in which female sexual desire is seen as a sexual dysfunction. Marriage manuals during the 19th century described various treatments for "inordinate desire" among women, seeing it as a serious sexual disorder. It was not uncommon for women to have their clitorises surgically removed by a physician in order to curtail their sexuality. When concern was expressed among women about their sexuality, it was usually in terms of their inability to conceive children. The advice a 19th-century mother might have given her daughter before her wedding night reflects the cultural norms from which we have recently emerged: "Just shut your eyes, dear, and think of the British Empire." Such advice prepared women for orgasmic dysfunctions.

The acceptance of women as sexual beings has altered radically views on what is healthy sexual functioning. It is around the idea of women as orgasmic beings that new meanings have been given to sexual dysfunctions for both men *and* women. At one time, for example, men who ejaculated early were little cause for concern as long as they felt satisfied. A man ejaculating just before entering his partner or soon afterwards may have felt immense pleasure, as much as if he had made love all night. It was by *his* standard that orgasmic adequacy was judged, and if he enjoyed it, then *everything* was all right. Today, however, the man's actions are likely to be judged as a sign of sexual inadequacy because the woman also is expected to experience arousal and orgasm. A man has to remain erect long enough for his partner to come to orgasm if she is orgasmic. His ejaculation is now called *premature* and is defined as a sexual dysfunction. Kinsey, who wrote during the transition period on attitudes towards female sexuality, however, was astounded that early ejaculation could be called a sexual dysfunction. He wrote (Kinsey, 1948): "Far from being abnormal, the human male who is quick in his sexual response is quite normal among mammals, and usual in his own species. It is curious that the term 'impotence' should have *ever* been applied to such rapid response. It would be difficult to find another situation in which an individual who was quick and intense in his response was labelled anything but superior." But what Kinsey did not understand was that women were becoming a standard against which male sexuality was measured. Sex had to be satisfying for both partners. He was being left behind as sexual mores changed.

The realization in American culture that women are capable of – and have a right to – orgasm is a tremendous stride forward in human sexuality. They can now accept their sexual feelings; but this, too, is double-edged, for many women now define their adequacy as women in terms of their ability to have orgasms. Failure to have an orgasm is becoming analagous to impotence for men in the way it effects an individual's self-esteem. For nonorgasmic women, orgasm has become a challenge to their self-image. Until recently noted Rollo May (1968), the challenge they had to confront with men was whether or not to go to bed with them (it was fundamentally a moral question about where they stood *vis-a-vis* cultural norms). But this has changed and the question women now face is not so much "will you" or "won't you" but "can you" or "can't you." The question has shifted to one of personal identity and self-worth. With this change in the sense of woman's sexual potential, lack of orgasm has now been defined as a sexual dysfunction.

However, the most dramatic instance of the relativity of the idea of sexual inadequacy lies perhaps in what Masters and Johnson call "masturbatory orgasmic inadequacy." It is now generally accepted to label lack of orgasm in sexual intercourse a sexual inadequacy. But for Masters and Johnson that is not enough. A woman must also be orgasmic in masturbation. They wrote in *Human Sexual Inadequacy*: "A woman with masturbatory orgasmic inadequacy has not achieved orgasmic release by partner or self-manipulation in either homosexual or heterosexual experience. She can and does reach orgasmic expression during coital connection." Here is a radically new definition of a sexual dysfunction that illustrates how changing meanings of sexuality define adequacy. Because lack of masturbatory orgasm is labelled a dysfunction, it is quite possible that women who thoroughly enjoyed themselves and were orgasmic in intercourse may begin to feel that they are inadequate. This is the danger that comes in labelling behavior as adequate or inadequate: it may be totally out of joint with the individual's or the couple's sexual experience.

This awareness that we have today about sexual dysfunction reflects not only new definitions of female sexuality but may in part reflect our performance ethic. We judge ourselves against somewhat arbitrary norms of how we should behave sexually: oftentimes, the standards do not apply to a particular individual or couple. Individuals should be aware when they are trying to find sexual self-understanding that there is an arbitrary quality at work in defining sexual adequacy and inadequacy. If a man is impotent on occasion, it is not disastrous; if a woman is nonorgasmic on occasion, that is not the beginning of a history of sexual dysfunction. But, if people begin to label themselves as inadequate, they are likely to start feeling inadequate and then actually become inadequate. Most sexual dysfunctions are in the head, not in the body.

## Theoretical Bases of Sexual Dysfunctions

*Psychosocial Influences*   Most sexual malfunctions result from traumatic personal interactions. Some psychosocial theorists suggest that relationships with parents in the first few years of life permanently establish a person's sexual characteristics. Others theorize that sexual identity is fluid, subject to change throughout life and strongly influenced by cultural as well as interpersonal influences.

Living in an age obsessed with sexuality, people have come to expect a lot from themselves and others when it comes to erotic performance. As the author of a popular book on sexuality pointed out, the media, which most influence us are filled with messages of "superpotency . . . on television (implicitly), in the movies (explicitly), and in novels (very explicitly)" (Reuben, 1969). It is not surprising, there-

fore, that many people are dissatisfied with their sexual capabilities or the performance of their mates. Because fear of failure tends to amplify inadequacies, people with sexual problems may trap themselves in vicious cycles of increasingly poor performance and heightened anxiety.

Not many years ago people tended to keep their sexual problems to themselves, to the point of not even discussing them with their mates. The contemporary trend is away from secrecy – people are communicating more about their sexual desires and seeking professional help in establishing satisfying relationships. Philosophies of sex therapy have proliferated since Sigmund Freud introduced *psychoanalysis* in the late nineteenth century. Freud was an incredibly forceful person whose beliefs about the nature of human sexuality have had a lasting influence.

*Psychoanalytic Theory*   Central to Freud's concepts were the theories of unconscious mental activity and infantile sexuality. Freud believed people to be dominated by thoughts outside the realm of consciousness and he theorized that experiences of early childhood form impressions in the unconscious mind that profoundly influence sexual behavior in adulthood.

Psychoanalysts believe that human mental activity occurs in three modes: ego, superego, and id. The *ego* is thought to embody functions such as sensory perception, memory, and communication; it includes the "sense of self" resulting from experience. The *superego* is commonly equated with the conscience; its theorized function is to ensure morality (according to the code by which one has been raised). The *id* is the primordial essence of human existence, the personality with which a baby is born; its sole aim is the gratification of all needs. According to the Freudian scheme the ego and superego develop as a child learns that his or her desires must

Orville's adviser in college told him he had no real aptitude for Accounting, but he studied hard and graduated in the exact middle of his class. Orville hated his father, but he was also scared of him.

"Don't you understand," Senior told the psychiatrist later on, "He wants to go to some place called Little America and have his own gas pump."

"It is not crazy, in the clinical sense, merely to desire something other people don't," said Dr. Schmidlapp icily ... Then he told Senior about Oedipus.

"I don't know anything about that," said Senior. "I'm a businessman."

Rob Swigart, *Little America*

---

sometimes be suppressed. This suppression results in conflicts between the ego, id, and superego, which occur in the unconscious mind.

Sexuality plays a central role in psychoanalytic theory in that Freud conceived the primary motivator of the id to be an urge for sexual gratification. He believed the sex drive (*libido*) to be an innate force that develops in three stages during the first years of life.

In the earliest phase – the "oral" stage – libido is claimed to be centered at the mouth and manifested by the sucking response. Infants are portrayed as not only obtaining food by nursing but also deriving sensual or sexual gratification from it. In the next phase – the "anal" stage – the focus of libido shifts to the anus and bowels. As an infant learns to control its bowels it obtains sensual (sexual) gratification from the consciously directed retention and elimination of body wastes.

If all goes well preoccupations of the oral and anal stages play themselves out within the first three years of a child's life. At about the age of three, however, children become more keenly aware of their genitals and of the pleasures of manipulating them. If they are permitted to do so, children of three or four will make sexual explorations with others, which initiates the third stage – the "phallic" stage.

According to psychoanalysts, a crucial feature of the phallic stage is an erotic attraction of the child to the parent of the opposite sex – the "oedipal complex." A child in the throes of an oedipal conflict is portrayed as feeling rivalry toward the parent of the same sex with consequent fear of loss of love and punishment involving mutilation of the genitals ("castration complex"). By the psychoanalytic scheme, normal development results when a child resolves the oedipal conflict by giving up sexual desires for his or her parent.

The next few years are a phase of relative sex-

ual latency, a period of rapid physical and intellectual growth but, for most children, little sexual activity. With the onset of adolescence, however, sexual urges re-emerge, and patterns of adult behavior develop. Conflicts that began during childhood may remain in the unconscious and may influence the course of one's psychosexual development. According to psychoanalytic theory, unresolved oedipal conflicts cause sexual maladjustments. In Freudian terms, an impotent male loses his erection because his unresolved childhood fears of castration are rekindled by what would normally be an erotic situation.

Freud's psychoanalytic theories continue to influence many sex therapists, and his ideas on unconscious mental activity and infant sexuality are widely acclaimed. But, many modern authorities criticize certain of his beliefs. In particular, the idea that oedipal conflicts are at the root of all sexual problems is seen as a gross oversimplification by most modern psychologists. Furthermore, Freud's theories concerning the oral and anal stages of erotic development were formulated on the basis of life histories told to him by adult patients and were never substantiated by observations of children.

Many parents, however, have observed their infants to have what appears to be erotic sensations centered in the genitals. Some male infants have erections, and babies of both sexes masturbate. Self applied pressure to the groin and rhythmic pelvic thrusts culminate in spasms similar to those of adult orgasm. The penises of male infants throb during "orgasm," but there is no ejaculation. Thus, the genitals (not the mouth or anus) seem to be endowed with erotic potential early in life. Sensual experience involving sucking and toilet training do seem important in psychological development, but the belief that they have erotic significance is questionable.

*Learning Theory* In the years since Freud introduced psychoanalytic thought, researchers of human behavior have been primarily concerned with the mechanisms of learning. The most significant behavioral experiments have not dealt with human subjects but the results of animal studies have had important influences on the development of behavioral approaches to sex therapy.

The first major breakthroughs in animal behavior came as the result of experiments performed by Ivan Pavlov in Russia early in the twentieth century (Pavlov, 1927). Pavlov began his studies with the simple observation that when a hungry dog is presented with food, it salivates. This response is innate (inborn) and, hence, does not need to be learned. The experiment involved ringing a bell before food was presented to the dog. In time, the animal was conditioned to salivate in response to the bell alone; no food was necessary to prompt the *conditioned response*.

This phenomenon, known as *classical conditioning*, involves responses to specific stimuli. But most animal behavior is not passive – dogs don't sit around waiting for food; they spontaneously look for it when they are hungry. Spontaneous behavior can also be modified, however, and the term applied to the process is *operant conditioning*.

The foremost researcher of operant conditioning, B.F. Skinner, devised his theories as the result of experiments involving rats (Skinner, 1938). In one study a hungry rat was placed in a box, and, while searching about the strange environment, eventually contacted a small lever that was rigged to deliver a pellet of food. Eventually the rat learned the relationship between the lever and food and could satisfy its hunger at will.

The preceding experiment involved "positive reinforcement" – the rat was conditioned to perform a specific function by the delivery of a reward. Operant conditioning can also involve "negative reinforcement," in which a task is performed to avoid punishment. For instance, a rat will quickly learn to push a lever to stop an electric shock or an annoying noise.

Thus, the basic principles of operant conditioning are quite simple; anyone who has ever used a bit of food to coax a dog to shake hands or the threat of punishment to train the same animal not to urinate indoors has use the basic principles of conditioning.

There have been few controlled experiments dealing with the effects of operant conditioning on human sexual behavior. There have, however, been controversial attempts at modifying behavior of sex offenders by negative reinforcement, with ill-defined results. But, there is an abundance of evidence from everyday life that reinforcement can affect potency and other sexual characteristics. For example, men with histories of virility have experienced loss of potency after mates have criticized their erotic techniques.

Behaviorists believe that sexual conditioning occurs in many subtle ways. For those adolescents whose sexual experience has been limited to furtive intercourse in the back seats of cars, rapid ejaculation becomes a conditioned response whose reinforcement is the cessation of anxiety about getting caught. Later in life, when sex can be enjoyed in less hostile surroundings, there is no longer a reward for hasty ejaculation, but the pattern may be so well established that attempts to delay ejaculation are futile.

Psychoanalysts downgrade behavioral theories by pointing out that the same circumstances do not affect all people in the same way (not all adolescents who felt compelled to get it over with quickly in their first sexual experiences remain premature ejaculators in adulthood, for example). According to psychoanalytic theory, when an inadequacy develops in adult life it is attributable more to long repressed childhood disturbances than to immediate problems.

In fact, certain kinds of behavior have been shown to be learned at specific phases early in life and are difficult, if not impossible, to change. Konrad Lorenz has demonstrated this with experiments involving geese (Lorenz, 1965). Shortly after hatching, goslings begin following their mother wherever she goes, waddling or swimming in a tight procession behind her. If, however, the goslings are separated from their mother soon after hatching they will automatically follow any moving object of approximately the right size and speed (the tolerances are fairly wide, even a human caretaker will do). The goslings will be *imprinted* by the artificial mother and will preferentially follow it even if their actual mother is reintroduced. This phenomenon can be explained if it is assumed that there is an innate (inherited) predisposition to becoming imprinted by a moving object. The theorized genetic program is not so specific that it excludes all objects except for geese, but it strictly limits the phase during which the behavior can be learned to a specific "critical period" early in life.

In recent years, extensive research has been done on the behavior of animals higher in the evolutionary order than geese. Monkeys and chimpanzees (the closest living evolutionary relatives of humans) have been the subjects of experiments designed to reveal if phenomena such as imprinting are significant forces in behavioral development.

The work of Harry F. Harlow on the sexual development of monkeys is of particular interest (Harlow, 1971). Harlow's experiments indicate that in order for young monkeys to develop normal patterns of sexual behavior, a sequence of relationships with older monkeys as well as with their peers is necessary. In one series of

experiments infant monkeys were isolated and reared in wire-mesh cages. At puberty they appeared to be sexually mature (individuals of both sexes masturbated and reached orgasm). But, when placed in contact with peers of the opposite sex who had not been isolated, socially deprived monkeys were generally either inadequate in their attempts or made no attempts at copulation. Previously isolated males were obviously aroused by females, but the males appeared puzzled. Some made clumsy attempts at mounting, while others brutally attacked potential mates. Females also showed the effects of social isolation, feebly raising their tails in a poor substitute for the receptive posture (in which the tail is held stiff and erect). Previously isolated females could sometimes be induced to endure copulation, but it appeared to be a fearful experience for them.

Harlow's findings are not as clear cut as Lorenz's discovery of imprinting by goslings, in which a specific trait has to be learned during a critical period of early life. Harlow's observations of socially deprived monkeys indicate more variability in subsequent patterns of sexual behavior. Although monkeys that had been isolated in youth were generally incompetent as sexual partners, the manifestations of inadequacies differed greatly from individual to individual. Thus, imprinting or other highly restrictive mechanisms of behavioral development appear to play less of a part in the development of sexual behavior in monkeys than in goslings.

Of all animals, humans are the most variable in their reactions to the experiences of early youth. There are certain behavioral characteristics that virtually everyone exhibits (the sucking response of infancy, for example). But, people vary markedly when it comes to more complex modes of behavior. Even the most dogmatic psychoanalysts point out that similar traumas during the first years of life can have drastically different effects on different individuals. Learning theorists place more emphasis on the here-and-now. They concede that negative learning experiences early in life can have almost irreversible influences on sexual behavior, but they believe that therapeutic learning experience need not involve digging into the circumstances of one's early childhood. If there is one point of agreement between psychoanalysts and learning theorists, it is that undesired patterns of sexual behavior can, with effort, be changed.

### Physical Basis of Sexual Dysfunctions

The vast majority of sexual dysfunctions are psychological in origin, resulting from negative feelings about sexuality or destructive personal or sexual interaction. A man who is constantly rejected by his partner may become impotent so that he does not have to endure the repeated humiliation of rejection. A woman may be nonorgasmic because she learned as a small girl that sex was "nasty" or she may use her lack of orgasm as a message to her partner that she does not feel free with him. There are many reasons behind sexual dysfunction, and few of them are physical.

Although most sexual dysfunctions are rooted in the psyche – which does not make them any less real or difficult – possible physical causes should not be overlooked. For someone experiencing a sexual dysfunction, the first step in treatment should be a thorough physical examination by a *competent* physician. Possible physical bases for dysfunctions follow.

*Females:* Women may have difficulties in intercourse that result from an obstructed or thick hymen, clitoral adhesions, a constrictive clitoral hood, or a weak pubococcygeal muscle. Endometriosis and ovarian and uterine tumors and cysts may affect a woman's sexual response. A poor episiotomy (the incision made between the vagina and the anus during childbirth to facilitate delivery) can lead to sexual dysfunctions.

The skin that covers the clitoris can become infected or gummed; women who masturbate too vigorously can rub their clitorises raw, making intercourse painful; and men can stimulate their partners too roughly, causing soreness in the vagina or the clitoral area. If their hands are dirty, they can cause an infection in the woman.

Anal intercourse (an increasingly common sexual experiment) can cause coliform vaginitis, which inflames the vagina and makes intercourse painful. When a couple engages in anal intercourse and then vaginal intercourse, the man, before intercourse, must wash his genitals thoroughly with soap and water to kill any germs that might infect his partner.

*Males:* An uncircumcised male can have difficulties achieving an erection if his foreskin is too tight; after orgasm, he may complain of pain at the end of his penis.

In some rare instances, the penis may be deformed. or injured – bent sharply to the left or right or up or down – making penetration difficult if not impossible. Sexual movements may be painful to both the man and woman. Such deformities may be congenital or they may be the result of accidents or gonorrhea. Unfortunately, surgery can rarely correct an angularly deformed penis.

A dull, throbbing pain in the testicles may be the result of prolonged sexual arousal without release through masturbation, oral sex, or intercourse. An older man who experiences pain in his testicles, pelvic area, or inner thighs may be suffering prostate trouble. He should consult a physician.

Other causes of sexual difficulties include diabetes, lumbar-disc disease, diffuse ar-

And therefore – since I cannot prove a lover
To entertain these fair well-spoken days --
I am determined to prove a villain,
And hate the idle pleasures of these days.
Plots have I laid, inductions dangerous,
By drunken prophecies, libels and dreams.

                                    Shakespeare, *Richard III*

---

teriosclerosis or multiple sclerosis. Excessive drinking, the use of heroin or methadone, tranquilizers, and other medications may cause erectile difficulties. There is some evidence that smoking also contributes to sexual difficulties.

## Psychological Causes of Sexual Dysfunctions

Sexual dysfunctions have their origin in any number of psychological causes. Some dysfunctions originate in immediate causes, others from conflict within the self, and still others from a particular sexual relationship. Relatively few dysfunctions can be traced to physical causes, although the possibility of physical origin should be the first to be explored, especially if the person has been ill.

## Immediate Causes

*Fatigue and Stress*   Many dysfunctions have fairly simple causes. A man or woman may be physically exhausted from the demands of work or childrearing; they bring their fatigue into the bedroom, along with a lack of desire or responsiveness. What they need is not therapy or counseling but rest, a change in their daily routines. The familiar I'm-too-tired-to-make-love-tonight may be a truthful description of a person's feelings. Unfortunately, the partner may feel rejected; fatigue often brings a break in affection, discontent, and discord. As the fatigue continues, the sexual relationship diminishes and each partner adjusts to the lack of desire. The man no longer approaches his partner; the woman does not expect her man to be responsive. Silence, frustration, and anger may replace a once tender and erotic relationship. A pattern is now set that becomes independent of fatigue. Even if both partners change their lives to end the sources of fatigue, its legacy remains in an unhappy pattern of sexual unresponsiveness and frustration. If the couple is able to identify the problem as one of fatigue early, then they may be able to alter its source before the pattern becomes an ingrained habit.

Long term stress can also contribute to lowered sexual drive and responsiveness. A man or women preoccupied with making ends meet, an unruly child, or prolonged illness can lose his or her sexual desire. Unemployment, for example, can lead to conflict within a relationship, depression, and a subsequent lack of sexual responsiveness. An unemployed husband fails to fulfill his traditional role as breadwinner. Initially he and his partner are supportive of one another; but if the unemployment is prolonged, he begins to lose his self-esteem and his partner becomes increasingly impatient and anxious. There is less communication and understanding. Sexual problems may arise, but there are fewer emotional resources to deal with them; the couple's relationship deteriorates and there is less ability to deal with sexual difficulties. The man may retreat into impotence or the woman may become non-orgasmic or sexually non-responsive.

*Ineffective Sexual Behavior*   The plethora of popular books on sexuality seem to promise sexual bliss if only certain techniques are used. Usually sexual techniques are not the issue between a couple; but since such information is easily conveyed, men and women focus on improving their techniques rather than the quality of their loving. Yet, as Helen Kaplan (1974) writes, there is a surprising amount of simple sexual ignorance that prevents couples from being fully sexual with each other. She writes:

> Many couples do not know very much about sexuality and are too guilty and frightened to explore

We unwittingly set the stage for feelings of inadequacy and inferiority. The more rigidly we define ourselves the less likely we are able to cope with the infinite variety of life.

Earnest Rossi, *Dreams and the Growth of Personality*

and experiment. Women, who especially in their younger years require more stimulation and sensitivity on their partner's part to bring their sexual potential to full flower, are the more frequent victims of this situation. It is still astounding to me that so many couples who seek help for the wife's lack of responsiveness or from decreasing frequency of sexual contact are basically only suffering from this sort of ignorance.

Certain myths contribute to sexual difficulties between partners. The belief in the mutual orgasm in which both climax simultaneously may undermine healthy relationships. Mutual orgasms are unlikely except in the rarest instances. During orgasm, the man's tendency is to continue pelvic thrusting although some males stop thrusting completely. By contrast, a woman during orgasm usually desires to continue the movements of the excitement and plateau phase, or may want to increase the pressure of her vulval area. The male and female orgasmic movements are basically incompatible for mutual orgasm. To strive for mutual orgasm usually leads to frustration and a rising belief in one's sexual inadequacy

***Sexual Anxiety*** The fear of failure is probably the most important immediate cause of impotence and, to a lesser extent, also of orgasmic dysfunction (Kaplan, 1974). If a man fails to experience an erection – because of drinking, drugs, fatigue, lack of interest, pressure from his partner or any number of reasons – anxiety and fear are a fairly common set of responses. Potency cuts to the very center of a man's identity; to be impotent is, in some sense, for most men, to be less a man. Many men can dismiss these episodes of non-erection for what they are: simply non-erection related to various factors. But if the man is particularly anxious about his sexuality or has repeated failures in responding with an erection, he may actually become impotent; a cycle of panic and resulting impotence begins, causing more panic and more failure. Some men respond to an occasional erectile failure with calm, knowing that such failures are normal, while others react with panic, unaware that such failures are normal. Women experience similar performance anxieties concerning their orgasmic abilities. If they are unable to experience orgasm, the same cycle of fear arises and they feel themselves on the line as a sexually responsive woman. While being non-orgasmic gives rise to feelings of not-being-quite-a-woman and sexual frustration, the woman is nevertheless able to engage in sexual intercourse and can derive other erotic satisfactions and feelings; an impotent man, by contrast, is unable to have sexual intercourse.

How fear and anxiety contribute to sexual dysfunctions can be explained physiologically. The autonomic nervous system is composed of sympathetic and parasympathetic subsystems. The sympathetic subsystem controls the release of adrenalin which stimulates our 'fight or flee,' behavior, preparing us for danger or adversity. Among men, it controls the physiological responses involved in ejaculation; with women, the sympathetic nervous system governs the motor aspects of orgasm. The parasympathetic subsystem governs not only sleep, digestion, and relaxation, but erection, vaginal lubrication and vasocongestion, as well as the erotic sensations accompanying orgasm.

In order for a man to become erect and a woman excited, the sympathetic subsystem cannot interfere with the parasympathetic system. If a man or woman is anxious, however, the body will be charged with adrenalin to meet some unknown danger – in this case, the fear of impotence or orgasmic failure. Instead of being relaxed, the body is tense, rigid, defensive. The

Unsatisfactory sexual relations are a symptom of marital discord, not the cause of it. It is difficult for the victims to see this because of the mass of propaganda about sex that attacks them day and night, on the street, in the home, in the office.

John Jones, for example, is dissatisfied with his marriage. On his way to work he may look up and see a billboard with a picture of a nearly nude, beautiful woman, advertising a brand of stockings. John is stimulated sexually and says to himself, "Boy, I'd like to have an affair with something like that." He knows this is wishful thinking, and may even recognize that the

beautiful model might be incompatible with him. Next he retreats from the daydream and his thoughts turn toward his wife. But the sexual fantasy he has had about the girl in the ad colors his reflections about his marriage relationship, and he thinks, "Golly, Mary's legs might look better in that kind of hosiery." What he means is, "If Mary were a better sexpot we'd both have a happier marriage." He is caught in a double error: the appearance of Mary's legs has nothing to do with the couple's sexual satisfaction, and he has forgotten his own function in achieving a successful union.

William Lederer and Don Jackson

---

sympathetic system prevents the parasympathetic system from properly functioning by injecting vast amounts of adrenalin into the body. And if ever there were an antidote to desire, it is adrenalin; penises remain limp and vaginas dry. And as a man or woman fails at erection or orgasm, each time a sexual encounter is likely, the body will respond to the idea of sex as a threat rather than as a source of pleasure or intimacy.

*Performance Anxieties* Performance anxieties are closely related to fear of failure. Some men experience their first erective failure when a partner initiates or demands sexual intercourse. In the male myth, the man is supposed to be always ready for sex at any time with any woman. And when a woman makes an offer he *can't* refuse, he is confused when he cannot have an erection. Although erections are autonomic reflexes and cannot be produced on demand, many men feel impotent if they are unable to respond. Women are permitted to say "no," but men have not learned that they, too, may say *no* to sex. To feel compelled to make love when there is no desire or when there is psychic conflict may lead to erective failure. If the man is unable to handle such failures as normal functioning, he may begin the vicious cycle of fear and impotence.

Women suffer similar anxieties, but theirs tend to center around orgasm rather than ability to make love. While a woman cannot become aroused on demand, she can permit herself to be made love to by a man. Oftentimes a man will demand that his partner have an orgasm; but the orgasm is not so much for her as it is for reassurance and proof of *his* sexual ability. Such reas-

surance for him often leads a woman to fake an orgasm; a woman will also fake an orgasm to hide feelings from her partner of her own sexual inadequacy. However, a relationship built on fake orgasms has little chance to go further since basic sexual problems are not confronted or acknowledged. It will remain mired down by inauthentic responses.

*Excessive Need to Please the Partner* Another source of anxiety is an excessive need to please a partner (Kaplan, 1974). Fearing to disappoint a partner can create severe anxiety. A man who suffers from this anxiety wants a quick erection to please his partner; he wants to hold his orgasm until after his partner's so that she can fully enjoy herself; he feels his penis is not large enough, that he is not sexually attractive enough for her. The woman who experiences this anxiety wants to have an orgasm quickly to please her partner; she worries about her attractiveness, the size of her breasts, her hips, the smell of her lubricating vagina, its stickiness and wetness.

One of the signs of a mature sexual relationship is the desire to please a partner, to forego one's own pleasure for the other when it is appropriate, to care about their needs. But the source of these feelings is based on a sense of self, confidence in one's being, and love for the other person. When it becomes excessive, it is usually rooted not in love but in fear of rejection (Kaplan, 1974). If a man does not last long enough, he fears his partner will leave him. If a woman does not have an orgasm, she thinks her partner will reject her. In trying to please their

**A Zen Student**

A Zen student fell into the snow and lay in it unable to get up. A monk walked near him and the student called to him for help. Instead of pulling him up, the monk lay down next to him and remained silent. The student then pulled himself out of the snow and walked away.

---

partners, they themselves may wind up feeling cheated. The fail to recognize the wonderful mutuality in healthy lovemaking; over the long run, pleasing one's self usually pleases one's partner. Sex is not simply composed of each partner receiving separate, isolated pleasure. A woman who is aware of and acts on her own pleasure and her partner's pleasure both gives and receives pleasure at the same time. A man who is aware of his own pleasure and his partner's pleasure similarly gives and receives at the same time. To dismiss one's own pleasure in order to give pleasure to your partner breaks the mutuality of giving-and-receiving that is the basis of sound sex. It opens the door to sexual frustration, anxiety, and possibly dysfunction.

## Conflicts within the Self

Western civilization has left its heirs with an implacably hostile and ascetic sexual tradition. As we have seen, our religious traditions view sex as dangerous and worldly; pleasure is the associate of sin, beauty the snare of the devil. Religious devotion is deeply implicated with sexual dysfunctions. "Unequivocally, absolutely, religious orthodoxy is responsible for a significant degree of sexual dysfunction. And it doesn't matter which of the three major religions is involved" (Lehrman, 1970).

Guilt and sin are the two great inventions of the Judaeo-Christian tradition; they do not exist in most tribal religions or eastern religions such as Buddhism and Hinduism. While the hold of guilt and sin is loosening in contemporary America for adults, they are still powerful forces in repressing childhood sexuality. And it is in our childhood that we have our first critical learning about sexuality. While the double standard between men and women is diminishing, it still holds strong between children and adults. What we accept as

normal for adults is repressed and disapproved of for and by children. Much of growing up and maturing as an adult is a casting off of the sexual guilt and repression instilled as a child.

Guilt and conflict, however, do not usually eliminate a person's sexual drive; rather they inhibit the drive and alienate a person from his or her sexuality. A person comes to see sexuality as something bad or "dirty", it is not something to be happily affirmed. Sexual expression is forced, Helen Kaplan (1974) writes, "to assume an infinite variety of distorted, inhibited, diverted, sublimated, alienated and variable forms to accommodate the conflict." Sometimes the conflicts actually result in sexual dysfunctions; but usually they result in a less than satisfying sexual interaction, a lowering of pleasure, a fear of sexuality. In contrast to immediate causes, these psychic conflicts are much more deeply rooted. They exist *within* the person rather than in anxieties and fears which are the result of situations in the immediate past. They are part of a person's personality and cannot be as easily changed. Often these conflicts remain unconscious; their existence remains unknown to the person suffering from them.

## Relational Causes

Sexual problems do not exist in a vacuum. They usually exist within the context of a relationship. Most frequently, it is married couples that come into therapy because they have a greater investment in the relationship than couples who are dating or who are living together. Sexual difficulties in a dating relationship often never come to the surface; if they do, the commitment between partners is often not sufficient enough for them to undertake therapy either together or individually. Usually what happens is that the couple will split up. The same is usually true of a couple

## Marriage

Whatever endures can be created only gradually by
long-continued work and careful reflection.
. . . He who demands too much at once . . . ends by
succeeding in nothing.

I Ching

---

living together; they do not have the shared
bonds – the children, the financial arrangements,
the marital commitment of husband/wife – which
are more difficult to break. But married couples
have a significantly greater emotional investment
in their lives together and they are more likely to
try to resolve their difficulties. It is usually easier
for unmarried couples to break up than to
change the patterns of their relationship that contribute to their sexual problems.

The recognition that sexual problems often
originate in the difficulties of a marital relationship, writes Helen Kaplan (1974), is one of the
most important advances in the behavioral sciences. She continues:

> The system, or the model, which governs the rela-
> tionship, rather than the problems of the individual
> spouses, is often the major source of a sexual dys-
> function and the optimum site of intervention. In
> treating a sexual dysfunction, modification of the
> sexual and marital system is the basic aim.

**Marital Discord**    Rage, anger, disappointment
and hostility often become a permanent part of
marital interaction; somehow they seem to slip
into the very structure of a relationship without
anyone noticing until it is too late to change
without drastic upheaval. Underlying fears of rejection or abandonment may help form the marital structure without either partner's awareness.
But these factors vastly influence the nature and
quality of the relationship between husband and
wife. They ultimately affect the sexual relationship, for sex is very much like a barometer for the
whole relationship. And as Masters and Johnson
once observed, one half of American marriages
are "sexual disaster zones" (Masters and
Johnson, 1970).

Kaplan (1974) suggests that marital discord
finds its sources in six areas: (1) transferences, (2)
lack of trust, (3) power struggles, (4) contractual

disappointments, (5) sexual sabotage, and (6)
lack of communication.

When we *transfer* feelings, we take feelings we
had about someone else (usually parents or
other significant persons in our lives) and transfer
those feelings to our partners. If a man loves his
wife, he takes some of the feelings he had for his
mother and transfers them to his spouse. Some
of this is normal. But if there is too much transference, one is liable to suffer from unconscious
incestuous feelings. These incestuous feelings
block one's responses to one's spouse. Women
may respond to their husbands as father figures,
and feel that they must please their husband/
fathers or be rejected; or they may also suffer
from incestuous conflicts.

Love, intimacy, and sexuality involve *trust*.
Without trust in the other, we are unwilling to
expose ourselves, our feelings, our bodies, in the
deepest sense. With trust we become transparent; it is no slight coincidence that we speak of
standing naked before the other both metaphor-
ically and physically. We must trust that the other
will respond to our needs and not ridicule us –
that the most intimate movements and sighs and
groans of lovemaking will not be mocked. We
are our most vulnerable when we are sexually
intimate; we must trust that we have nothing to
fear if we surrender ourselves sexually.

*Power struggles* take place when domination
is a central theme in a marital relationship. Sexuality becomes a tool in control struggles. A man
will force his wife to *submit* to him sexually; he
will force her to engage in sexual activities she
does not like. She will humiliate him by forcing
him to perform, by withholding sex from him, by
being non-responsive or non-orgasmic. The result of such unconscious power struggles may be
lessened desire, poor sexual interaction, impotence, or orgasmic dysfunction. Sexual responsiveness to the partner becomes tantamount to

submission; sexual pleasure is forgotten in such stituations.

*Contractual disappointments* stem from the unwritten marriage contract between couples. These unwritten contracts are the assumptions and expectations – usually unconscious – of how each should act in the marriage. A man may assume his wife will have children when they marry; she does not want them. Because neither discussed these aspects with the other, it does not come out until after marriage. Friction arises from the unwritten contract. Or each may assume the other is more interested in sex than they actually are. A man complains that they hardly make love at all; a woman complains that they make love too often. In fact, they make love 2 times a week, but each interprets the frequency of intercourse differently. He feels she is unresponsive, she feels he is oversexed. Each becomes angry with the other.

A couple may engage in *sexual sabotage* with each other, asking for sex at the wrong time, putting pressure on the other, frustrating the other's sexual desires and fantasies. They most often do this unconsciously; the various techniques of sabotage are so effective that to do so consciously would sometimes border on being vicious. This lack of awareness partly absolves a person, but makes solving the problem more difficult.

Finally, *failing to communicate* is one of the most important factors underlying sexual problems and dysfunctions. One cannot be a sexual mindreader; each partner must know how the other feels about sex, various sexual techniques, practices, and positions. Without knowing how the other feels – especially if one or both partners fake responses by pretending to be excited when they are not, thrilled by a touch when it actually hurts, having an orgasm when they are not (but

pretending in order to get it over with) – a great amount of harmful misinformation may be assumed.

## Male Sexual Dysfunctions

**Impotence** *Impotence* – a male's inability to have or maintain an erection during intercourse – is a common phenomenon that affects as many as half the men in America at one time or another according to one estimate (Kaplan, 1974). Despite its common and usually transitory occurrence, impotence deeply affects a man's concept of himself. Sex is one of the ways that a man *proves* that he is a man: he must be able to *do* something. There is nothing quite analagous for women: woman can have sexual intercourse without having to "do" anything, she simply has to be (Horney, 1945; de Beauvoir, 1948). Since men identify their masculinity with the erect penis, it is here that their masculinity is always in peril. Male sexual potency is subject to enough variations through life (one out of four men are impotent after age seventy) that many men have considerable free-floating anxiety about their sexuality. And certainly when it happens, even if only once, the man may panic and become haunted by doubts about his potency.

Impotence is generally divided into two types: primary impotence and secondary impotence. Those men with primary impotence have never had an erection, and those with secondary impotence have had erections in the past.

Master and Johnson approach the problem of impotence, as well as other sexual dysfunctions, by dealing with the couple rather than the individual. They regard sexuality as an interpersonal phenomenon rather than an individual one. In fact, they tell their clients that there are not dysfunctional individuals but dysfunctional couples, and that faulty sexual interaction is at the root of sexual problems. Neither individual is to blame; rather, it is their *mutual* interaction that sustains a dysfunction.

Masters and Johnson attempt to take into therapy only those couples who have a genuine commitment to their relationship. Each must be willing to give the other emotional support during the therapy for it to be successful. It is not uncommon for some couples to come to the clinic who are so alienated from each other that they are told to see a divorce lawyer instead. Divorce in these cases may be the best therapy. Oftentimes, sexual dysfunctions are simply situational, reflecting distrust, anger, fear, or indifference toward the partner.

Under treatment for two weeks, the couple is told not to attempt sexual intercourse until they are given permission by their therapists, a man and a woman. In this way, the man is immediately relieved of any pressure to perform, thus easing his anxieties and allowing a more relaxed attitude toward sex to develop. The first morning, each individual is interviewed separately by the therapist of the same sex; in the afternoon, the interview is repeated by the therapist of the opposite sex. The therapists are careful not to assign blame to either partner; it is the couple, not the individual, that is being treated. They ask the man whether he has ever had erections, what they felt like; whether he and his partner are demonstrative with each other, touching each other, loving each other; whether she appears to like sex; whether he likes sex. What were his best sexual experiences, his worst ones, and with whom. The therapists constantly remind their clients that they are not seeking to assign blame, since blame is one of the factors that keeps people from accepting their own re-

sponsibility in a problem. The therapists are aware that many of their clients' responses may be evasive, unclear, erroneous, or even false since the topic is often painful or embarrassing.

After the interviews and the case histories have been taken, the couple meets together with both therapists to discuss what has been learned so far. The therapists begin by explaining what they have learned about the couple's personal and sexual interaction, encouraging the man and woman to expand, or correct, what they are saying. Then, the therapists discuss the sexual myths and fallacies that the couple holds that may interfere with their sexual interaction.

The most common myth is that penis size is important in intercourse. Many impotent men come into therapy fearful that their penis is not large enough, or sometimes that they are too large, and they are quietly told by the therapists that penis size makes no difference in terms of a woman's sexual satisfaction. The large penis gets about one-third larger when erect and the small penis may double or triple in size. Plus, women can't tell the difference during intercourse anyway. Penis size, it turns out, is really a man's concern, not a woman's.

If there appear to be substantially conflicting views about the couple's sexual history, the therapists point out the importance of honest communication between the partners. If the woman doesn't really know what her partner likes, how can she really satisfy him, and vice versa. The therapists stress openness and directness, the ability of a partner to say, "I like fellatio" or "I don't like fellatio" or "I like cunnilingus" or "I don't like cunnilingus."

At the end of the third day, the therapists introduce the idea of "sensate focus," which is nothing less than each partner touching the other, giving and receiving pleasure, sexual and nonsexual. Here is Masters and Johnson's most radical departure from traditional therapies, revealing their commitment to behaviorist therapy. They engage in direct behavior modification. They point out how successful experiences contribute to further successful experiences by positive reinforcement; non-successful experiences reinforce fears of failure. Failure especially creates apprehension and both partners worry whether or not the man will get an erection. It is this fear of failure to which the therapists address themselves, beginning with sensate focus. Sensate focus is the first step in behavior modification.

Couples who have lost or have never learned

Touch is the basis of *sensate focus.*

the ability to touch and be touched have lost the fundamental means of being sexual. Sex depends on body contact and feeling, not technique or expertise. Touch is soothing or arousing, tender or passionate, filled with infinite nuances of meaning that people often forget in our culture. The therapists focus the couple's awareness (not self-consciousness) on touching. In this way, they begin to work on the couple's inability to experience sensually each other and themselves through touch. The other senses – smell, sight, hearing, and taste – are worked on indirectly as a means of reinforcing the touch experience.

To increase the couple's "sensate focus," the couple is instructed to return to their motel and to take off their clothes so that nothing will restrict their sensations. One partner is arbitrarily told to give pleasure, the other to receive it, something that may take considerable reorientation. The giver touches, caresses, massages, strokes his or her partner's body everywhere except the genitals and the breasts. The purpose is not sexual arousal but simply sense awareness. The partner simply tries to relax and receive pleasure, which may be more difficult than it seems at first. Masters and Johnson point out that this may be the first time a couple has touched and caressed without a sexual aim, "without need to explain their sensate preferences, without the demand for personal reassurance, or without a sense of need to 'return the favor.' " Later, the partners change roles, and each guides the other to pleasure spots. After the fourth day, the couple is given permission to touch each other's genitals and the woman's breasts. (They are still not permitted to try intercourse.) At this time, the couple is given a lesson on sexual anatomy, especially the female genitals, which may be a mystery to both the man and the woman.

At the end of the fourth day of therapy, which is basically the same for any type of sexual dysfunction, the therapists begin to focus on the particular dysfunction affecting the couple. In dealing with impotence, the couple is taught that fears and anxieties are largely responsible for impotence and that the removal of these fears is the first step in therapy. The woman is instructed that her concern – however sympathetic or compassionate – contributes to his fears about his masculinity. Once the fear is removed, the man is less likely to be an observer to his sexuality; he can become an actor rather than a spectator or judge and experience his sexuality rather than worry about it. Both are taught not only to give pleasure but – more important for the man – to receive it and to enjoy their sensuous experiences.

After the sensate-focus exercises have been integrated into the couple's behavior, they are told to play with each other's genitals but not to attempt an erection. Often, a man becomes erect because there is no demand on him, but he is encouraged to let it become soft again, then erect, then soft, to reassure him that he can become erect repeatedly. This builds his confidence

and hers by letting her know that she can excite her partner.

During this time, the couple is counseled on other aspects of their relationship that contribute to their sexual difficulties: what feelings of resentment or hostility they have toward each other, how they feel unfulfilled or cheated, what they can do to change their behaviors, and end resentment. They also talk about their practice sessions and are encouraged to discuss their "mistakes" in a lighthearted manner. These discussions are aimed at further reducing the couple's anxieties that appear during their practice sessions.

Then, about the tenth day, the couple attempts their first intercourse, if the man has had erections with some success. The woman initiates the attempt, using the female superior position, her partner lying on his back. She manipulates his penis, bringing it to erection, and then *she* inserts in into her vagina, moving slowly, never thrusting heavily. There is no attempt at bringing him to orgasm, just her gentle move-

Non-demanding sex play is an important element in overcoming impotence.

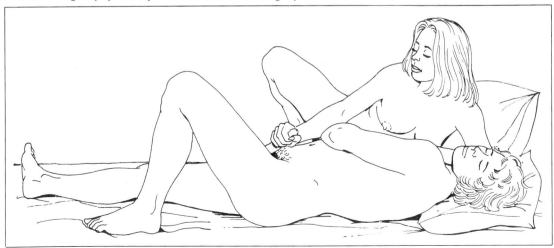

ment. They repeat this exercise several times so that the man can gain confidence in his ability to sustain an erection within his partner. If he loses his erection, she gets off him and begins to fondle him until he becomes erect again; then she mounts him. If he does not become erect again, the session ends. After the couple completes this exercise successfully, she mounts him but this time does not move while he thrusts. Then they move together still with no attempt at orgasm; the only object is sensual pleasure. Eventually, in the final sessions, the man will have an orgasm.

**Premature Ejaculation**    In *premature ejaculation* – the most common sexual complaint of

The Squeeze technique for premature ejaculation.

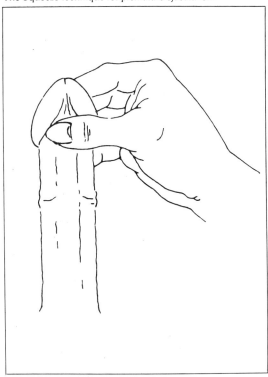

men in sex therapy – the man is unable to control or delay his ejaculation. Usually, premature ejaculation is a problem when the woman is unable to become sufficiently aroused to have an orgasm if she is orgasmic. Oftentimes, couples are confused, bewildered, and unhappy when the man consistently ejaculates too early. The woman is sexually dissatisfied, while her partner – who has already had his orgasm – does not know why she is so complaining (or "slow"). She may tell him that he is a lousy lover and that only increases his anxiety or anger. They may begin to avoid each other by sleeping in separate rooms and having intercourse rarely or never. The man may withdraw from sex completely, sometimes becoming impotent because of his anxieties over premature ejaculation.

Masters and Johnson treat premature ejaculation by using initially the same pattern they used in treating impotence while concentrating especially on reducing fears and anxieties and increasing sensate focus and communication. The specific technique used by Masters and Johnson – the squeeze technique – is simple: when the man is brought manually to a full erection, just before he is about to ejaculate, his partner squeezes his penis with her thumb just below the corona. She squeezes with considerable pressure for 10-30 seconds and reduces his erection 10 to 30 percent. He will lose his urge to ejaculate. After thirty seconds of inactivity, she arouses him again and, just before he ejaculates, she squeezes again. Using this technique, the couple can go fifteen to twenty minutes before the man ejaculates. After several days, in the female superior position, she inserts his penis and just before he ejaculates, she squeezes. (The squeeze technique does not work if the man tries to squeeze himself.) This technique has worked in almost every case.

**Retarded Ejaculation**  Retarded ejaculation is not a common dysfunction, but it happens frequently enough to deserve comment. In fact, in mild forms it occurs with some frequency (Singer, 1974). In retarded ejaculation, the man is erect but is unable to ejaculate. In its mildest forms, anxiety-provoking situations interfere with a man's ejaculatory reflex; he can't have an orgasm in certain situations in which he feels guilt or conflict, or with a particular woman, or except in masturbation. Often this inhibition is overcome when the situation or partner changes or when the man engages in a little fantasy, additional stimulation, or is distracted. Such men rarely seek professional help since the problem is generally transitory.

But more troublesome is when a man is unable to reach an orgasm though he does everything he knows in order to climax. He may make love for hours, drink, smoke marijuana to relax himself, or fantasize, but nothing helps. Such men may love to please their partners, but afterwards masturbate for release.

Master and Johnson (1970) treat this difficulty by having the man's partner manipulate his penis. She asks for verbal and physical direction to bring him the most pleasure possible. It may take a few days before he reaches his first orgasm. The idea is to identify his partner with sexual pleasure and desire. He is encouraged to feel stimulated by his partner, but also stimulated by her erotic responses to him. After the man has reached orgasm through manual stimulation, he then proceeds to vaginal intercourse. His partner brings him to a high level of sexual excitement manually. When he is excited, while he is lying on his back, she gets on top of him in a female superior position and inserts his penis into her vagina. She immediately begins strong pelvic thrusts toward the penis. Generally this technique brings ejaculation quickly. If it does not, the woman gets off him and begins manual stimulation. As he reaches the point where he is about to ejaculate involuntarily, he motions her. She quickly tries to insert his penis into her vagina before orgasm. Sometimes he will ejaculate before she has his penis entirely in her vagina. Nevertheless, even if he ejaculates only a drop into her vagina, this usually assists him in overcoming his sense of incompetence. After a few more such sessions, he usually begins to establish a certain confidence in himself. The therapists then suggest that the female insert his penis at lower levels of sexual excitement. Finally, the man is able to function sexually without fear of ejaculatory retardation.

## Female Sexual Dysfunctions

**General Sexual Dysfunction**  General sexual dysfunction is Helen Kaplan's (1974) clinical term for "frigidity." While the term suffers from the usual obtuseness of scientific terminology, the old word "frigid" is filled with emotional undertones and opprobrium. "Frigidity" is more like an accusation than a description. Certainly many men have described women who have refused to make love with them as "frigid"; it would be comical for an unhappy man to call a reluctant lover "generally sexually dysfunctional." Masters and Johnson shy away from the term "frigidity" because it is imprecise; they prefer "female orgasmic dysfunction," because orgasm can be measured. They consider general sexual dysfunction to be part and parcel of orgasmic dysfunction (Masters and Johnson, 1970). They treat both similarly.

General sexual dysfunction and orgasmic dysfunction are clinically separate entities. Generally dysfunctional women find little pleasure in sexual stimulation, if any at all; they are often non-orgasmic. By contrast, women with orgasmic dysfunctions may be highly erotic and feel great sexual pleasure, but not be orgasmic.

General sexual dysfunction for women is not a surprising phenomenon in our cultural climate. In fact, their lack of responsiveness generally fits the ideal woman of the Victorian era. The conditioning that young girls and adolescents receive from parents, school, and church encourages such general repression of sexual feelings and desires. To expect a woman to cast off a lifetime of negative conditioning simply because she is married or an adult is often unrealistic. Some women are able to overcome negative conditioning immediately, others gradually, but some never or only after great struggle and conflict. Yet sometimes women who go to male physicians, priests, or clergymen are advised that their lack of sexual feelings are normal; indeed, that they are even virtuous and moral, that sex and orgasms are for men. Women need to be sexually informed and aware of biases concerning female sexuality.

Masters and Johnson treat general sexual dysfunction as they do orgasmic dysfunction (see above), emphasizing self-discovery and exploration, including masturbation. The discovery that women have their highest orgasmic frequency in autoerotic activities suggests that masturbation is an important technique for awakening themselves sexually (Kinsey, 1953; Heiman, et. al., 1976). Therapists suggest contracting the pubococcygeal muscles during intercourse to give especially erotic sensations in the vagina (Kaplan, 1974; see p. 335 for Kegle exercises, Chapter 12).

The important points in therapy, however, are to make sexual experiences nondemanding in order to keep anxiety at a minimum; to center the sexual experience on *her* pleasure so that she is not distracted by trying to please her partner; and to help both the woman and her partner become aware of each other's needs through open communication.

Masturbation is used by some therapists in treating orgasmic dysfunctions.

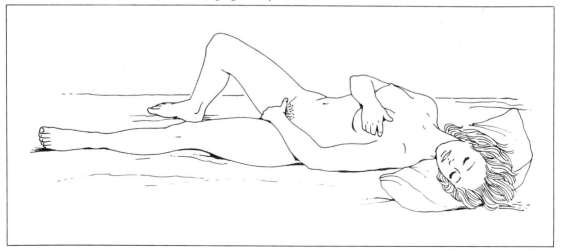

**Female Orgasmic Dysfunction**   Since negative attitudes are so influential in many women's development, Masters and Johnson probe in depth a preorgasmic woman's sexual attitudes: her parental influences, her sexual likes and dislikes, her sexual and emotional feelings about her partner, and their sexual history. (Sometimes, the therapists discover that a woman is not orgasmic because her partner ejaculates prematurely or because he is unaware of how to arouse her.)

As in the treatment of other dysfunctions, after the history taking, the couple is given sensate focus exercises; then the experience is discussed in some detail in order to discover what emotional responses she had to being touched. She may have to learn new responses to touch. If she was taught as a child never to let anyone touch her genitals or breasts, instead of experiencing pleasure when they are touched, she may panic or freeze. She may have to learn that having her erogenous zones touched by her partner is not only permissible, it is pleasurable. Instead of tensing her body when being erotically touched, she must learn to relax it and let the pleasure of being touched – and aroused – flow through her body.

After the sensate focus sessions, the woman's partner begins to touch and caress her vulva; she guides his hand to show him what she likes and does not like. The man is told, however, not to directly stimulate the clitoris because it is extremely sensitive and may cause pain instead of pleasure. (Women, in fact, rarely touch their clitorises directly when they masturbate.) Instead, the man stimulates the area around the clitoris, the vaginal lips, and the upper thighs. During this time, the couple is told not to try for orgasm since it would place undue pressure on the woman to perform. They are simply to explore the woman's erotic potential and discover what brings her the greatest pleasure.

After the couple has learned to arouse the woman to a high erotic level, the next step for them is to begin intercourse with the woman in the superior position. When both are sexually excited, the woman inserts the penis into her vagina and remains motionless, simply being aware of the penis inside her and enjoying it. Then she begins to move slowly; once she is aroused, she signals her partner to begin moving and thrusting. They continue as long as it is pleasurable to them both. The next time they begin intercourse, they lie side by side, which permits both to move with the greatest flexibility and freedom. It is especially effective for the

Pleasuring

woman since she can move in whatever manner is the most stimulating for her at any time.

**Vaginismus**    At one time, *vaginismus* was one of the most common complaints among women. Taught, during the Victorian era and afterwards, to dread intercourse or to perform it perfunctorily, some women's muscles around the vaginal entrance went into spasms, preventing the insertion of the penis. This is a relatively rare phenomenon today (Kaplan, 1974). Vaginismus is essentially a conditioned response that reflects fear, anxiety, or pain. It may have resulted from negative attitudes about sexuality or from harsh early sexual experiences, from fear of men or childbirth or from painful pelvic examinations.

Vaginismus is one of the easiest sexual dysfunctions to eliminate with the use of simple mechanical devices. Under informal, relaxed settings, vaginal dilators are slowly inserted into the woman's vagina. She inserts it before going to bed at night, taking it out in the morning. As soon as the woman is able to receive a dilator of one size without having vaginal spasms, a larger one is used. In most cases, the vaginismus disappears – to the relief of both partners. (Some men find it humiliating not to be able to penetrate their partners and they retreat into impotence.)

**QUESTIONS**

1.  What are sexual dysfunctions? How common are they?
2.  What are the differences between psychoanalytic theory and learning theory concerning sexual dysfunctions? How do these differences affect treatment?
3.  Discuss the Masters and Johnson treatment of sexual dysfunctions.
4.  What are the immediate causes of sexual dysfunctions? What is the role of conflicts in the self?
5.  What is impotence? What is general sexual dysfunction? What is orgasmic dysfunction?

# Readings

### Poor Communication As a Cause of Dysfunction

Helen Kaplan

*Helen Kaplan discusses poor communication as an element of female dysfunction.*

One reason for the man's apparent "selfishness" is that he often has no idea where his wife "is." He is apt to judge her state of arousal on the basis of his own feelings. His projections are likely to be incorrect, or he may mistakenly assume that her acquiescence, together with physical evidence of vaginal lubrication (which is only a sign of early arousal), means that she is ready for intercourse.

The illusion, common among many men, that they understand their partner's reaction when they really do not is fostered and perpetuated by women who keep their needs obscure. The woman may be reluctant to communicate her real sexual desires to her lover for a variety of reasons. She frequently assumes that there is no need to do so. The woman knows where her man "is" during lovemaking because she has his erection to guide her, and she erroneously assumes that he appreciates her state of arousal even as she does his. Neither realizes that, in contrast to the male, the female's physiological responses are largely cryptic and internal. Consequently, she is apt to feel angry and rejected when he proceeds solely on the basis of his own cues, not realizing that his apparent indifference to her needs is due to ignorance rather than callousness. If a woman wants to have good sex, she must take responsibility for her own sexual well-being and learn to communicate her erotic needs to her partner in a gentle and non-defensive manner.

Apart from the fact that she may fail to communicate her needs because she erroneously assumes that the man knows "where" she is, a woman may fail to take responsibility for her own effective stimulation if she is a victim of the myth, common in our culture, that sex is exclusively the man's responsibility and that sexual assertiveness in the woman is "unfeminine." If she believes this, she may not even try to understand why she is not responding adequately, or recognize that it is important that she act in her own behalf. Instead, she will wait passively, but often with growing anger, for her husband to "make love *to* her." In fact, however, unless she tells him so, he is not even likely to realize that something is wrong. Clearly, then, the development of a certain degree of sexual autonomy is indispensable if a woman is to enjoy her full sexual potential.

Another factor which frequently prevents the woman from assuming responsibility for her effective erotic stimulation is the fear of rejection should she fail to be the perfect lover, which in our culture is often equated with sexual compliance and self-sacrifice. Thus the woman may fear that if she delays the man's ejaculation by asking him to prolong foreplay, or makes him "work" by indicating she wants to be stimulated clitorally, or if she does not reach orgasm on coitus and lets him know, she will be compared to others who don't make such "excessive" demands and will be rejected in favor of a more

generous and "feminine" partner. Women who fear rejection may find it far less anxiety-provoking to suppress their own sexual needs and wishes, to simulate arousal, to silently and passively let the man retain sole control of sex. Certainly, it is safer to signal the end of foreplay when she senses that *he* is ready for intercourse, or when she feels that *he* is getting impatient and tired of waiting for her to become sufficiently excited, or when *he* signals that his sexual urge is compelling. On the other hand, this type of transaction is not likely to result in her own sexual fulfillment.

The belief held by many women that they will be rejected if they are sexually active and assertive is part of our cultural heritage. Even today, the "new morality" notwithstanding, sex is still associated with sin, shame, and/or danger, and this association has had a much stronger adverse effect on female than on male sexual behavior. Thus, women who have been taught from an early age to consider passivity and compliance a virtue are likely to react to their impulses to assume a more active role in sex with guilt and shame. In contrast, men do not usually fear rejection and censure if they actively seek out stimulation and pleasure; on the contrary, such behavior is considered a sign of virility. In our society, similar activity on the woman's part is often regarded both by herself and her partner as aggressive, unfeminine, and selfish. Such passive attitudes can seriously interfere with female sexuality; therefore when they exist, their modification is essential to the success of treatment.

However, a woman's reluctance to express her needs is not always based on cultural paranoia. The woman may run a real risk of displeasing her husband if she becomes more assertive sexually. Some men are actually repelled by such behavior and regard women who attempt to assume a more active role in sex as aggressive, "ballsy" females. In part, of course, this response reflects our cultural mores. On a deeper psychological level, however, the man may feel threatened on being confronted by his wife's sexual desires if he perceives this as a challenge to his own sexual adequacy. In other words, once he has been made aware of them, his wife's sexual needs cannot be ignored and he may fear that he is sexually incapable of fulfilling these needs. Too often, he fails to realize that what he needs to supply is gentle and sensitive stimulation, and not a perpetual erection, in order to be a good lover. Consequently, he subtly encourages his wife's silence and compliance. One reason conjoint therapy is considered so valuable in sex therapy is that is facilitates the resolution of this type of interactional difficulty.

In summary, the key to helping a couple make love in such a way as to enchance the woman's sexual response, without sacrificing the man's pleasure, does not consist solely of teaching the couple new erotic techniques. Rather the couple's sexual system must be altered. The woman must learn to assume a share of the responsibility for her sexual pleasure. She must develop a degree of sexual autonomy, so that she is no longer solely dependent on her husband for her sexual gratification. If she is to achieve such autonomy, she must learn to communicate her sexual desires to her husband gently and openly, without demand or defensiveness, devoid of shame and guilt or fear of rejection.

This is true for the husband as well. The couple must learn to negotiate and compromise sexually. It is not realistic to expect that both will get exactly what they want every time they make love. Occasionally, the man may want rapid, "selfish" sex which is not entirely satisfactory for his wife. At other times she may want prolonged, gentle caressing which may become tedious and frustrating for him if their lovemaking must invariably follow this pattern. They both must learn to refuse each other, as well as to ask for what they want, without guilt and defensiveness. They must also learn to accept refusal of their expressed wishes, so that such refusals do not evoke paranoid feelings that they are being controlled or rejected. Only if both the man and woman are able to exercise a degree of sexual autonomy and learn, concomitantly, to take turns giving and receiving and to trust each other can they achieve a truly open and intimate sexual relationship.

Some women who have deep conflicts surrounding sex actively avoid potentially arousing stimulation. For example, the couple's sexual history may reveal that the wife will not allow her husband to touch her gently; that she becomes irritated rather than aroused when he tries to kiss her; that she feels "ticklish" rather than erotic when he touches her inner thighs; that she "can't bear" to have her breasts caressed. Such behavior usually suggests the presence of conflict which must be resolved before the woman can respond sexually.

## The New Impotence

George L. Ginsberg, William A. Frosch, and Theodore Shapiro

*The authors suggest that the increasing assertiveness and sexual openness among women is leading to increased impotence among young men. Is this true? Does it affect all men or only traditionally oriented men?*

Rapid changes in social mores may be reflected in changes in psychiatric symptomatology. It is our common experience that: (1) young men now appear more frequently with impotence, and (2) young women more frequently complain of initial impotence in their young lovers. We suggest that this may be related to changed social attitudes toward premarital sexuality, particularly among women.

The "average acceptable sexual behavior" of the adult woman in certain segments of middle class American society has changed. Although perhaps never real, the generally accepted and religiously prescribed standard of wedding night virginity prevailed well into the 20th century. An acceptable myth separated women into good and bad, with respect to their premarital sexual behavior. Under such conditions many a woman viewed intercourse as something inflicted upon her by her mate and her responsibility consisted of not denying him his rights. During the 1950s and especially the 1960s, advances in medical and social science provided the means by which emphasis on equal sexual rights for women has become so important in the 1970s. Women seek and expect orgastic release. Virginity is largely irrelevant. We suggest that these cultural changes have consequences in the structure and manifestations of neurotic phenomena. By breaking the former ecologic balance in society, a disequilibrium has been created, leaving its mark on the male partners of these new women.

Our observations of a group of impotent young men suggest that this cultural trend must be considered as a significant etiologic factor in order to understand their disturbing and anxiety-producing impotence. While impotence has always existed, it now takes on an additioal form. Sociologic study is needed to know if there is an absolute increase in the complaint, but clinical psychological study can suggest some avenues of such a sociologic approach. Moreover, clinical study of a manifest symptom provides an

avenue to understanding intrapsychic conflict which may earlier have been obscured by socially approved rationalization. Hartmann *et al* emphasize that demands of reality prohibit or facilitate drive discharge. While most depth analysis focuses on intrapsychic and familial determinants, the larger social context is also an important factor in falling ill. If it was formerly disregarded, it is only because social changes in this sector occurred more slowly.

The case studies which follow attempt to explore the strain of current social demands upon the psychology and behavior of a group of young men.

*Clinical Data*   Case 1. – A 19-year-old college student complained that fear of losing his erection had resulted in severe social inhibition with women. Following a period of pleasurable sexuality which included petting, his girl friend has suggested that their sexual practices were immature and that coitus was more appropriate. He ejaculated prematurely and then was impotent. He had formerly been more comfortable in his voyeurism because "the female is never responsible for compliance, for she doesn't even realize I am looking." Masturbation or fellatio was acceptable because "my penis is the center of attention" and he did not feel "used and appreciated as a tool." Coitus is difficult because he sees it as "doing something for her"; he had been potent when he did not feel "compelled to continue [to coitus] by social pressure," when he is reassured that he is cared for and when he feels loved. He did not, however, find it easy to give love.

Case 2. – A man in his mid-30s was referred for therapy after urologic examination had failed to reveal any organic basis for his impotence. He sought both consultations because his wife threatened divorce: she was unsatisfied by sexual practices limited to foreplay. The patient felt that his problems resulted from lack of experience. Driven to excel in order to impress his powerful and effective father, he had thrown himself into campus politics and then into the family business. He claimed inadequate time to develop a longer or lasting relationship with a "good girl," one that might have led to sexual involvement. Instead he sought out prostitutes whom he saw as dirty and diseased. Justifying his insistence on fellatio rather than coitus, he said that not only did he thus avoid infection [sic] but he also rationalized it as quicker, permitting prompt return to the major pursuits of his life. He finally married in his early 30s because he felt it was expected of him. Until his wife's insistent demand that he perform sexually, he was able to avoid his anxiety at confronting the female genitals and his own castration anxiety.

Case 3. – A 24-year-old single white man came for analysis consciously wishing to avoid military service because he was unable to urinate in public toilets. His limited sexual contacts had been marked by impotence or premature ejaculation. His excellent academic performance had deteriorated; he was in danger of not completing his current year of professional school. He lived a monastic existence, and only ventured forth from his cluttered, dirty, shade-drawn apartment to go to work.

He was initially impotent with his fiancee and attempted to drive her away by confessing his difficulties. Her sympathetic and understanding response, at variance with the demanding attitude of other women he had known, allowed him to tolerate the failure. His symptom reflected inhibition of tremendous rage due to his fear of retaliation. He partially gratified both the wish and the defense in not giving the woman what she wanted while protecting himself by refraining. He also preempted the expected retaliation

by confession. "How better to take your anger out on a woman – it doesn't matter what the cause is – she has to feel there is something wrong with her – fear will do it, anger will do it [impotence] – but ever since I've been able to love her sex is fun."

Case 4. – A man in his early 20s entered treatment because of concern about recent impotence. He had met a young woman whom he liked. After the first two dates he felt that she expected him to approach her sexually. When she responded vigorously to his advance, he interrupted with the excuse that her roommate might return. He then felt no longer able to avoid the expected sexual contact and was obliged to invite her to his room. When he attempted coitus he ejaculated immediately after intromission and apologized. A second attempt that same evening ended because he could not sustain an erection. When the failure was repeated on their fourth date his partner suggested there was something wrong and berated him for his failure. In addition, she was unable to achieve orgasm when he tried to practice masturbation on her. She claimed this was unusual and tacitly blamed his insufficiencies. Depite his friends' commiserations concerning her impatience, he became increasingly inhibited, depressed, and aware of his retaliatory rage.

A similar failure in a European brothel at 17 had not been disturbing: he had been able to rationalize that a friend had chosen the prostitute for him and that she was indifferent and mechanical. The psychological features of his current difficulty were the same: although he had not actively chosen to perform, performance was expected, and he did not feel desired "for himself."

**Comment**   Erikson suggested that "social institutions offer ideological rationales for widely different patterns of partial sexual moratoria such as complete sexual abstinence for a specific period, promiscuous genital engagement without personal commitment, or sexual play without genital engagement." This generalization points the way to a consideration of society's role in providing the context for abnormal or unusual behaviors. Ideally we would examine the same individual exposed to varying cultural conditions; the concept of a constant human product with variations in external environment is, however, an abstraction. We can examine clinical variation in symptom profiles over time as an index of the influence of culture on neurotic constellations.

Formerly patients with impotence were, for the most part, married men who gradually began to withdraw sexually from their wives following a period of more successful sexual functioning. They complained that the excitement had passed and that their wives no longer provided the variety in sexual practices they craved. Impotence was accompanied by minimal anxiety: they usually had conscious fantasies about the secretary at work, the girl next door, etc., and felt confident that novel objects or practices could revive their interest. This conviction prevented the emergence of major anxiety and resulted in relative indifference to their wives' plaints. Indeed, there was often either a kind of hysterical belle indifference or hostility toward the spouse. One of our patients (not cited in this paper) did succumb to a readily available partner. The temptation exceeded the restraining limits of fantasy satisfactions and he was impotent with this new and presumably exciting partner.

A second type of impotence accompanied by more anxiety is seen in younger men of borderline disposition or with a large component of latent homosexual or polymorphously perverse attitudes. Hostility to women and a strong degree of castration anxiety mark the underpinnings of their personality. One of our patients (case 2) with such problems was able to postpone any awareness of his coital inhibitions for many years. His wife's demands led to the loss of his rationalizations and development of anxiety.

Currently young men describe failure occurring early in their relationships. Following such early failure they become preoccupied with its meaning to their manhood. They either withdraw or, more characteristically, venture into counterphobic choice. While it did not result in Don Juanism with repetitive failure, humiliation and lowering of self-esteem did occur. Anxiety sometimes leads to commiseration with friends or, if the female partner is tolerant, a "stiff upper lip" feminine forbearance provides the male with a patient mother – vintage 1971 (case 3). Accompanying drug use may contribute to the failure or be used to rationalize it.

When we explored these sexual failures occurring early in a relationship, we found a common male complaint: these newly freed women demanded sexual performance. The male concern of the 1940s and 1950s was to satisfy the woman. In the late 1960s and early 1970s, it seems to be "will I have to maintain an erection to maintain a relationship?" This idea is permeated with feelings of "who calls the shots" and "who is sex for." There is a reversal of former roles: the role of the put-upon Victorian woman is that of the put-upon man of the 1970s. "Whereas a man's impotence is obvious, a woman's frigidity can be hidden." Inhibited nonorgastic women can often hide their lack of response but men without erect penises cannot even feign intromission. This challenge to manhood is most apparent in a sexually liberated society where women are not merely available but are perceived as demanding satisfaction from masculine performance.

Such newly free women might say, "So be it –

let the chips fall where they may." Women's sense of exploitation, however, often results in retaliatory rage and distortion of many worthwhile libertarian and equalizing aims. Unconscious transmission of feminine revenge by an aggressive manner and overassertiveness may enhance a man's castration anxiety with consequent fear of the vagina. This must be seen in an adaptational and social framework rather than as a purely psychological and particularly intrapsychic phenomenon.

Kubie has suggested, "A free society does not automatically bring psychological freedom to the individual; but it makes it possible for him to strive for it." Although for some the new "sexual freedom" may indeed be liberating, for others it merely induces different symptoms rather than improved mental health. Although focused on the decreased control of aggression rather than on sexual symptomatology, a recent paper states that "sexual freedom has, in accordance with Freud's conception of repression, considerably transformed the manifestations of the neuroses; ... [it has produced] ... The task of 'reconciling men to civilization' is not made easier through the liberation of drives.

### References

1. Hartmann H, Kris E, Loewenstein RM: Some psychoanalytic comments on "culture and personality," in Wilbur G, Muensterberger W (eds): *Psychoanalysis and Culture*. New York, International Universities Press, 1951, pp 3-31.
2. Erikson EH: *Identity, Youth and Crisis*. New York, WW Norton & Co Inc Publishers, 1968, p 187.
3. Fenichel O: *The Psychoanalytic Theory of Neurosis*. New York, WW Norton & Co Inc Publishers, 1945, p 174.
4. Kubie L: *Psychoanalysis and Contemporary Science*, New York, Macmillan Co Publishers, to be published.
5. Lowenfeld H, Lowenfeld Y: Our permissive society and the superego: Some current thoughts about Freud's cultural concepts. *Psychoanal Quart* 39:607, 1970.

## The Cult of Orgasm

Philip E. Slater

*The origins of many sexual dysfunctions lay in worry over a failure to be orgasmic in every sexual encounter. Is orgasm the essence of the sexual experience? Why?*

Discussions of sexuality in America have always centered on the orgasm rather than on pleasure in general. This seems to be another example of our tendency to focus on the product of any activity at the expense of the process. It may seem odd to refer to an orgasm as a product, but this is the tone taken in such discussions. Most sex manuals give the impression that the partners in lovemaking are performing some sort of task; by dint of a great cooperative effort and technical skill (primarily the woman's which masculine mystification has made problematic) is ultimately produced. The bigger the orgasm, the more "successful" the task performance.

This thought pattern owes much to the masculine preoccupation with technical mastery. Women in popular sexual literature become manipulable mechanical objects — like pianos ("It's amazing what sounds he can get out of that instrument"). Even more pronounced is the competitive note in writers such as D. H. Lawrence and Norman Mailer, who often make it seem as if lovemaking were a game in which the first person to reach a climax loses.

The emphasis on orgasm also reveals, paradoxically, a vestigial puritanism. The term "climax" expresses not only the idea of a peak or zenith but also the idea of termination or completion. Discussions of the sexual act in our society are thus primarily concerned with how it ends. Leisurely pleasure-seeking is brushed aside, as all acts and all thoughts are directed toward the creation of a successful finale. The better the orgasm, the more enjoyable the whole encounter is retrospectively defined as having been. This insures against too much pleasure obtained in the here and now, since one is always concentrating on the future goal. In such a system you can find out how much you're enjoying yourself only after it's all over, just as many Americans traveling abroad don't know what they've experienced until they've had their films developed.

Eastern love manuals, although rather mechanical and obsessional in their own ways, direct far more attention to the sensations of the moment. The preoccupation in Western sexual literature with orgasm seems to be a natural extension of the Protestant work ethic in which nothing is to be enjoyed for its own sake except striving.

The antithetical attitude would be to view orgasm as a delightful interruption in an otherwise continuous process of generating pleasurable sensations. This would transform our ways of thinking about sex — we would no longer use the orgasm as a kind of unit of lovemaking as in "we made love three times that day" (. . . "I have two cars," "I played nine holes of golf," "he's worth five million dollars"). The impulse to quantify sex would be sharply diminished, and along with it the tendency to infuse pleasure-seeking with ideas of achievement and competition. Affectionate caresses exchanged in passing would not

be so rigidly differentiated from those interludes culminating in orgasm.

Women already espouse this view to a greater degree than men; witness the complaint of many women that their husbands never caress them except in bed. The reason they assign to this behavior, however — "he's only interested in sex, in my body, not in me" — misses the point. A man who behaves this way is not interested in sex, either — he is interested only in releasing tension. Far from enjoying pleasurable stimulation, he cannot tolerate it beyond a minimum level and wants it to end as rapidly as possible within the limits of sexual etiquette and competent "performance."

This desire for release from tension, for escape from stimulation, lies at the root of our cultural preoccupation with orgasm. In a society like ours, which perpetually bombards its participants with bizarre and dissonant stimuli — both sexual and nonsexual — tension release is at a premium. It is this confused and jangling stimulation, together with the absence of simple and meaningful rhythms in our daily lives, that makes Americans long for orgasmic release and shun any casual pleasure-seeking that does not culminate in rapid tension discharge.

It is men who suffer most from this need for tension release, since it is men who have specialized most acutely in sacrificing feelings in the service of ambition — in postponing gratification, in maintaining a stiff upper lip, in avoiding body contact, in emotional coldness. Women often express the feeling in the midst of intense lovemaking that they want it never to end. I wonder how many men are capable of sustaining such a sentiment — are able to imagine themselves enjoying endless inputs of acute pleasurable stimulation?

Philip Slater, *Earthwalk.* Copyright © 1974. Reprinted by permission of Doubleday and Co. Inc.

**I**f you walk along certain streets in most large and medium-sized cities, you may enter a different sexual world. In restaurants, couples have dinner, dance, laugh, and flirt by candlelight. Some are happy, some are quiet, others sullen. While this sounds like an ordinary scene, it is not – for the couples sharing the intimate relationships are of the same sex. The people are homosexual, or "gay." Although they may work or go to school in the "straight" world, many of their social relations occur in the world of gay bars and restaurants.

Although homosexuality is an aspect of an individual's personality, it distorts the perception of such people to label them solely in terms of their sexual preferences. We do not refer to people whose preferences are heterosexual as "heterosexuals," because this is not the only aspect of their humanness. Therefore, in this book, "homosexual" is being used as an adjective rather than as a noun.

**Homosexual Behavior**

Only a small number of people are exclusively homosexual in their relationships. Kinsey estimated that among those between the ages of 20 and 35, only 1 to 3 percent of the women and 2 to 16 percent of the men have been exclusively homosexual at any one time.

The lives of a considerable number of people include both homosexual and heterosexual responses or experiences. Yet behavior is often categorized as normal or abnormal, heterosexual or homosexual, without recognizing gradations. A person with only one homosexual experience may be placed in the "homosexual" category and lose his or her job – or even be jailed, if a male.

Although Americans generally condemn homosexuality, 50 percent of the men and 28 percent of the women interviewed by Kinsey reported having had homosexual experiences – 38 percent of the men and 13 percent of the women to the point of orgasm. Obviously, some of the people who publicly condemn homosexuality have had this type of experience.

Men apparently feel greatly threatened by male homosexuality. (It is significant that there is no formal term in our language for the homosexual male, although "lesbian" has long been used in referring to homosexual females.) Men do not appear to have a great deal of hostility toward lesbians, and women are more tolerant toward homosexual individuals of either sex.

Hostility toward homosexual men is particularly strong among American men, because our culture considers sexual relations with females to be part of masculinity. Most psychotherapists believe that many of the men who are especially hostile toward homosexual men are fearful of their own homosexual impulses. Hostility, then, becomes a means of denying homosexual responses, of affirming one's own "masculinity." Men who are secure in their own heterosexuality, tend to be more tolerant of homosexuality, are less fearful of being 'sexually corrupted" by homosexual males.

Kinsey's research led him to believe that heterosexuality and homosexuality should not be viewed in terms of black and white but as shades of gray. He placed responses on a continuum rather than identifying them as "homosexual" or "heterosexual." The 0 category indicated no homosexual responses; 1 indicated almost exclusive heterosexuality, with some homosexual interest; 2, basic heterosexuality, but active interest in homosexual activity; 3, equal heterosexual and homosexual interest; 4, greater interest in homosexuality, with active interest in heterosexuality; 5, predominant homosexuality, with some heterosexual interest; 6, exclusive homosexual-

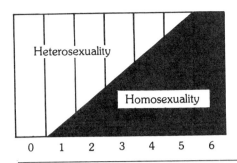

ity. (See above).

There are no great differences between heterosexual and homosexual techniques. Both involve kissing, caressing, and reaching orgasm. Per se, these acts are not homosexual. What makes them so is that they are engaged in by members of the same sex.

Homosexual activity cannot be categorized as "active" or "passive," as "masculine" or "feminine." Studies by Simon and Gagnon (1973) indicate that 46 percent of the homosexual men interviewed practice various positions or roles, depending on their own desires and those of their partners. Half expressed no preference at all, the other half indicated preferences for activities that do not seem to be related to a specific sex role.

Homosexual men usually kiss, caress each other's penises, and reach orgasm through anal intercourse or through fellatio (either separately or mutually). There is apparently more emotional involvement between homosexual women, who usually express affection before actual sexual caresses begin — reflecting their socialization as women. They usually reach orgasm through mutual masturbation and cunnilingus. Homosexual women rarely use dildos or other objects for vaginal penetration (the belief that they do is based on the notion that all sexual activity is modeled after heterosexual intercourse).

Kinsey found that women have a higher frequency of orgasm in relations with other women than with men. Partly this may be because of psychological stimulation, but it may also be because two people of the same sex understand their own anatomy and physiology better than do people of the opposite sex. Many men approach women as they themselves would like to be approached — with genital stimulation. They are likely to continue with this approach throughout their lives, unless women take the initiative in telling them what they prefer.

A new study by Masters and Johnson (1979) suggests that there are several significant differences in sexual interactions between homosexual couples and married heterosexual couples. First, committed homosexual couples tended to communicate more freely, both verbally and nonverbally, about their sexual needs, pleasures, and displeasures, which enhanced their sexual satisfactions. But among married heterosexuals there was frequently a great gap in communication. If a husband stimulated his wife's genitals too vigorously, she was unlikely to tell him; if she did, he often forgot or ignored her. Few husbands told their wives what they liked.

Another difference was that heterosexual couples tended to be more perfunctory about sexual interaction. Homosexual couples tended to engage in more nongenital stimulation and take more time building up sexual excitement. Masters and Johnson write (1979):

> In contrast, the sexual behavior of the married couples was far more performance-oriented. An apparent pressure to "get the job done" was usually evident during partner manipulation and fellatio-cunnilingus and was consistently present during coition.

Because homosexual couples tend to spend more time in sexual preliminaries, they are not as easily distracted during lovemaking; as a result, their sexual involvement and possibly sexual pleasure is increased. Masters and Johnson (1979) observed that the:

> married couple's inherent sexual advantage over the committed homosexual couple in diversity of sexual approaches is more than neutralized in two ways: first, by the concept that intercourse is the only acceptable endpoint of sexual interchange, and second, by persistent neglect of the vital com-

municative exchange of letting one's partner know what pleases, what distracts, what might be enjoyable, and what is not acceptable.

### Homosexuality as a Sexual Variation

Until recently, homosexuality has been studied primarily by psychiatrists, psychologists, and psychoanalysts – people whose disciplines deal with emotional disturbances. They have considered homosexuality as an illness, and have directed much of their work toward "curing" it.

Heterosexuality, in the most exclusive sense of the term, has been the standard for judging sex-

ual behavior. Yet Kinsey has questioned whether such a standard is scientifically meaningful. Homosexuality appears to be a sexual variation practiced by significant numbers of Americans. Are *that* many of us "sick"?

When the American Psychiatric Association recently removed homosexuality from its list of mental illnesses, the vote was approved by only a narrow margin. Although none of the psychoanalysts and psychiatrists who have studied the family dynamics and backgrounds of homosexual men and women in the attempt to find predisposing factors has succeeded, their ideas have been immensely influential. In es-

How can we explain heterosexual behavior if this too is a learned phenomenon? And if there is homosexual behavior which can be called nonpathological, can it be explained along the same lines? The answer to these questions becomes much more obvious when we reflect upon the reason why heterosexual behavior is the most common form of sexual behavior in our present society. The reason, I think, is very clear. It is because heterosexuality is encouraged and because homosexual behavior is discouraged. Consequently, it is the "natural" thing for young men to prefer girls as sexual objects. One need only reflect upon the content of the popular media to realize that the cues are all around us and that they exist in the most subtle as well as the most gross forms. Men learn heterosexual object-choice because no other object-choice is considered possible for them; that is, they are not allowed to conceive of the possibility that there can be another kind of sexual object other than the opposite sex.

Martin Hoffman

---

sence, the ideas reflect popular folklore about homosexuality. Psychoanalyst Irving Bieber (1962), for example, has presented the simple argument that homosexual men are acutely afraid of women. Their mothers were over-protective and sexually provocative, while their fathers showed little interest or love. Their parents interacted poorly with each other, and mothers turned to their sons as husband/lover substitutes. (This simplistic pattern has no resemblance at all to the early lives of many homosexuals, and it completely ignores people who are comfortable in both homosexual and heterosexual relationships.)

Unlike Kinsey, Bieber assumes that exclusive heterosexuality is the norm. He believes that if the homosexual individual wants to become "normal," this can be achieved through therapy. The person who does not want to be "normal" will remain forever homosexual.

William Masters and Virginia Johnson (1979) have recently published work on "reversing" or "converting" homosexual individuals to heterosexuality in two weeks of therapy at their sexual research laboratories in St. Louis, Missouri. Treating 54 men and 13 women between 1968 and 1976, only 33 percent of the men and 40 percent of the women failed in turning to heterosexuality. Unlike Bieber's work and that of psychoanalysts in general, Masters and Johnson do not view homosexuality as an illness; rather, their work is aimed at helping those *wanting* to change from homosexuality to heterosexuality. Yet there is considerable criticism about how successful Masters and Johnson actually were in "reversing" homosexuality. Of the men they treated, only three were classified as number 6 on Kinsey's scale; six men were rated as number 5. Of the women, two were number 6 and one was number 5. Only two of these men and none of the women failed to "convert" to heterosexuality. Critics argue that those were exceptionally highly motivated to change; some doubt that they were as high on the Kinsey scale as Masters and Johnson classified them.

Most of the persons treated in St. Louis, however, were in groups one through four; such individuals, argues Judd Marmor, formerly president of the American Psychiatric Association, were "essentially bisexual" (*Science News*, April 28, 1979). Many such persons may become heterosexual without *any* professional treatment. John Money, however, believes that the difficulty of such behavioral studies lies even deeper. The problem is really the definition of homosexuality. Psychiatrist John Money says: "We've all fallen into the trap of defining a psycho-sexual problem as a sexual one." He continues that the totally homosexual individual, "is incapable of falling in love except with someone with the same sex organs as himself or herself. I don't think Masters and Johnson addressed this problem – Are their so-called 'cured' homosexuals able to fall in love?" (*Science News*, April 28, 1979).

The search for a "cure" has in large part prevented researchers from scientifically exploring other aspects of homosexuality. What makes up the homosexual world? How do homosexual individuals relate to one another? What emotional problems originate from society's hostile reaction to them? What problems arise from their own feelings of guilt and shame?

There are as many different kinds of homosexual individuals as there are heterosexual people. Those who are homosexual do not necessarily talk strangely, are certainly not always identifiable by their appearance. Some have emotional problems, others do not. Homosexuality is not necessarily a cause or symptom of unhappiness or emotional disturbance – any more than is heterosexuality.

What makes the lives of homosexual men and women difficult are the adjustments they must make to a hostile society. Simon and Gagnon believe that understanding the homosexual individual's relationship to the world is as significant as understanding the cause of homosexuality.

> It is necessary to move away from an obsessive concern with the sexuality of the individual, and attempt to see the homosexual in terms of the broader attachments that he must make to live in the world around him.

Homosexual people are viewed by society almost solely in terms of their sexuality, which our culture stereotypes as excessive, lustful, uncontrollable. But homosexual men and women, like those who are heterosexual, are people who work, drive cars, listen to music, drink coffee and cocktails, feel love and hate, decorate their homes, go to football games, engage in activities and hobbies. They are Republicans and Democrats, they are conservatives, liberals, environmentalists and whatever. They are anything anyone can be – except that they are labeled as "deviant." Everything else in their lives becomes unimportant once the word "deviant" is applied to them because of their sexual behavior.

In studying homosexuality, sociologists consider deviance in terms of societal reaction theory (Rubington and Martin, 1973). This theory, which concerns the interaction of individuals and their societies, views deviance as an artificial concept. Deviant behavior is simply behavior that deviates from the norm; that is, it is not practiced by the majority of people. Homesexual behavior is deviant, in this sense.

In our society, heterosexuality is assumed. Thus, one does not describe Jack as being heterosexual, white, 20, and a student. It would not be uncommon, however, to describe him as homosexual, white, 20, and a student. Homosexuality, because it deviates from the norm, may become a major status classification in identifying both men and women.

As Weinberg and Williams point out in their major work, the major problems facing homosexual men and women result from the social and cultural contexts in which they must seek sexual expression. Homosexuality is not a problem created by individual men and women, but a problem that is created by society. The response to homosexuality has varied significantly in different cultures, and our own society's hostility toward male homosexuality represents a minority viewpoint. Among 76 cultures studied in a survey (Ford and Beach, 1952), almost two-thirds accepted certain forms of male homosexuality. Among native American Indian bands, for example, male homosexuals were not only widely accepted, but were in some groups believed to possess great spiritual power.

Little research has been done on homosexual women in other cultures (perhaps because of our preoccupation with male homosexuality). In America, such women have not been subjected to as much hostility as have homosexual men, for a number of reasons. Lesbian women ordinarily do not engage in public solicitation and prostitution, as do homosexual men. In general, society is more sympathetic toward lesbians – perhaps because of the widespread opinion that women reach this state only because they are unable to find a man as a sexual partner. In addition, women are not as anxious as men about their sexual identities. (Some men even find the viewing of lesbian intercourse erotically stimulating, and such "shows" are not uncommon at

There is no provision in this hetero-sexist society for the Lesbian mother. But her existence cannot be denied – nor can her relationship to her children. In the past she has been treated like a leper, a threat to her own children. Court rulings have disregarded any possibility of her being named legal guardian in custody cases; the disregard has been on the false assumption that as a Lesbian, she cannot adequately serve her offspring's many and varied needs. Husbands, by their sole claim to heterosexuality, have been awarded custody regardless of their suitability as parents. The onus is on the mother, and the label "Lesbian" is enough to deny her her children.

Del Martin & Phyllis Lyon

houses of prostitution.)

The rise of the women's liberation movement has brought about a change in the general approach to woman's sexuality. Increasingly, it is being examined independently of men's sexuality. After intense discussion, for example, the moderate National Organization for Women declared its support of legislation to end discrimination against homosexual women.

## Growing Up Homosexual

Children engage in rough-and-tumble play when very young with little regard to whether they are playing with boys or girls. Viewing adults, however, usually consider wrestling and similar physical contact to have "homosexual" implications when engaged in by children of the same sex, and these forms of play are inhibited. The children may continue to feel strong affection for others of the same sex – friendship, akin to love, which they do not give a label.

As young people enter puberty, sexual feelings become stronger. They may experience intense feeling for another of the same sex – but they have already learned that teachers, parents, and friends expect them to have "crushes" on members of the opposite sex, whom they are expected eventually to marry and form a family with. A child of ten or twelve may be terrified by a "crush" on a friend of the same sex – fearful that someone will find out. Children are less able than adults to face the consequences of being considered "different," even when they are not yet aware of what is actually involved in homosexuality.

Pressures to play out traditional boy-girl dating roles increase in high school. Should young people not be interested in these roles, there is usually no one they can turn to for advice and discussion. School counselors or ministers may regard homosexual feelings as a "sickness." A boy once confided in his physical education teacher, believing the man might be sympathetic and understanding. Instead, the teacher never spoke to him again.

Most young people – both heterosexual and homosexual – go through identity crises. *Who am I? What is the meaning of my life? What do I want to do?* Those who conclude that they have a sexual preference for the same sex must resolve the crisis, by either accepting or rejecting such a preference.

Because our society does not accept the view proposed by Kinsey as a result of his surveys – that heterosexuality and homosexuality are not

as sharply defined as black and white but are most accurately portrayed as shades of gray – the individual who has a preference for members of the same sex feels the need to make a decision. Our society does not allow people to find satisfaction in both heterosexual and homosexual activity; they must make up their minds which they prefer. In our society, the most important factor affecting homosexual men and women is whether their homosexuality is known. Once identified as homosexual, this aspect of behavior becomes primary, affecting every other aspect of the individual's life.

**"Passing"**    For fear of ostracism, persecution, and disgrace, many men and women who prefer homosexual relationships disguise this fact. They may engage in flirtations and marry. A man may become macho, attacking behavior that looks "queer" or "sissy." Such behavior, called "passing," may make the individual who practices it feel alienated and psychologically disoriented. One man, who felt he must watch every word and gesture to avoid discovery, reported that the strain of deceiving friends and family was often intolerable (Weinberg and Williams, 1974).

Although lesbians experience similar difficulties, their homosexuality can be more easily disguised. Women are not expected to be as sexually active as men in our culture and failure to respond to a man does not necessarily imply that a woman is homosexual. Two women can live together without causing undue suspicion, while two single men who evidence no interest in women cannot.

The study of Weinberg and Williams (1974) indicates that homosexual men who "pass" tend to be more depressed, to experience greater awkwardness in relations with others, and to feel more guilt than do those whose homosexuality is known. In one group of homosexual men, 59 percent reported they had a significant number of friendships with heterosexual people, and almost half said that more than half their friends were heterosexual. But 30 percent hid their homosexuality from *all* their heterosexual friends, and 38 percent hid it from most.

Becoming publicly known as homosexual is a major event in life, because this fact may jeopardize many relationships. Yet Weinberg and Williams concluded that, once homosexuality becomes known, apprehension gives way to relief. Most of the anticipated – and dreaded – social responses are based on the popular view that the response to disclosure will be disgust, censure, violence, ridicule, and accusations of mental illness; homosexual people also circulate sad tales and stories among themselves.

In fact, however, heterosexual people react to revelations of homosexuality in varied ways. Usually, their responses involve negative consequences to varying degrees. But these are often subtle, and may be avoided, adapted to, or disregarded.

**Fear of Discovery**    Many homosexual people go outside their own group to find primary sexual partners. This search forces them into the open, making them more familiar to the homosexual community. The search also leads to interaction between covertly and overtly homosexual people. A man who was covertly homosexual told Leznoff and Westley that some men don't care whether or not their homosexuality is public knowledge, and he described such men as being "pitiful." They were, he said, either insignificant or were independently wealthy; he could not afford to associate with them on a friendly basis, because he wanted to protect his own social position.

Covert lesbians express similar feelings about associating with overtly homosexual women.

One such woman is quoted by Abbott and Love (1972):

> If I see someone in a work situation that I met in a bar, I never say hello. I avoid talking to her at all. I have a horror that one day the phone will ring and it will be someone from the bar. If that ever happens, I will hang up. If I see someone in the street, I avoid her eyes and just walk past, especially if I'm with someone from the office or someone in my family.

**The Gay World**

Our culture views homosexuality as perverse, and many homosexual people accept this view of themselves. One man observed that it is impossible to live in a world that rejects you, that outlaws and ridicules your activities and desires, that sneers at and detests you, without these attitudes having a fundamental impact on your personality. (Weinberg and Williams, 1974).

The gay community, however, provides an emotional climate where homosexual men and women can meet with others and find acceptance, warmth and support. One homosexual male, who always felt strained around "straights" (whom, incidentally, he referred to as "normal") even when they were unaware of his homosexuality, felt he could be himself only in a gay group. The only time he really forgot that he was homosexual was when he was with other gays (Simon and Gagnon, 1967).

Yet the gay community is not isolated from the heterosexual world, but is encircled by it. Fear of discovery contributes to the tendency toward anonymity and lack of intimacy that marks many homosexual encounters. The tendency may also be caused by the fact that homosexual individuals often retain the traditional heterosexual view of homosexuality; some may even deride other homosexual people (Weinberg and Williams, 1974).

**Gay Bars**    The gay bar, the center of the homosexual social world, is found in all sizable cities. "The bar is the homosexual equivalent of the USO or the youth club, where the rating and dating process may unfold in a controlled and acceptable manner." writes Nancy Achilles (Reiss, 1974).

Most of the people who frequent gay bars are young to middle-aged men, and most of them look much like any other people who visit middle-class bars. The most striking difference is that gay patrons usually face away from the bar, checking others over as they walk in, but do not strike up conversations as often as do men in heterosexual bars. Physical attractiveness is apparently more important than personality in the gay world. Martin Hoffman (1968) has observed:

> If one can only present the visible and non-identifying aspects of one's identity, one's physical appearance will be the central aspect that can be displayed to others. If homosexuals could meet as *homosexuals* in the kind of social interaction ... a great deal of the anonymous promiscuity ... would be replaced by a more "normal" kind of meeting between two persons. Perhaps, then, the sexual relationships which develop would become more stable.

The relationships of many homosexual men, like those of heterosexual men, are relatively short and are promiscuous. In our culture, it is common for men to first respond to a partner sexually and then emotionally. Most of the homosexual men in Weinberg and Williams' study have had at least one exclusive relationship with a male partner. Significantly, however, these men also had high social involvement with other homosexual men, which provided the emotional support for maintaining an exclusive relationship.

The gay bar is also a place to relax. Said a lesbian quoted by Abbott and Love (1972):

The Dean had called Mar in for a friendly talk (oh with the best intentions, no doubt!), but, as Hilary guessed, he had not known how to go about it at all. Even the fringes of this subject aroused so much fear, of course, that it was usually mishandled by people in authority, as if they were not dealing with loyalty and love!

"The filthy bastard made me feel filthy!" Mar shouted. The tight coil was sprung at last.

"No doubt," Hilary said gently, "he was scared to death."

"Oh he didn't say anything outright. It was all insinuations. Slimy insinuations."

---

The bar is the only relief I have from pretending. I can dress the way I want and think the way I want. I can truly relax for a few hours. I need this to carry on during the day, which has become increasingly exhausting.

Although homosexual men and women may gather at separate bars, both types of bars are sexual meeting places. Lesbians, however, seldom cruise parks, baths and coffee houses looking for one-night stands, and usually come to gay bars to socialize or to be alone. Homosexual women are more interested in emotional relationships than are homosexual men. In this sense, homosexual relationships among women tend to duplicate heterosexual relationships.

Because of the illegal status of homosexuality, legitimate businessmen seldom own gay bars. Such establishments do earn profits, however, and are often supported by underworld investors. Police may also be paid off by anxious owners. It is notable that in San Francisco, where homosexuality is generally accepted, organized crime and police corruption are apparently not involved in the gay scene. Illegality is obviously what promotes organized crime and corruption (Weinberg and Williams, 1974).

The gay world was created by the straight world, to provide a culture in which homosexual people could gather and live with acceptance. "Once you accept your gayness," said one homosexual male interviewed by Strong (1975), "you don't have to adjust to a hostile society. You have your own society." He continued:

The emphasis in most things I have read about homosexuality is on how sad it is. That's because most sociologists are heterosexual. They start off with the heterosexual assumption that happiness consists of a good marriage, raising children, and a job. Well, we can't have the first two, so they conclude our lives must be sad. Our lives aren't sad, they're just different.

The way to really think about gays is the same way you think about straights. We're no different in what we feel, think, believe, we're just gay. That's the only real difference.

There are really a lot of good things about the gay world that you never hear about. The gay world is generally more unconventional and more tolerant. Gays are more open to new ideas, to doing kookie and funny things, because they've broken the greatest convention of all – being straight. They're not afraid of breaking others. They're not as afraid to cry or to show their feelings. They've had to deal with their masculinity in human terms, and they've found that traditional masculinity isn't where it's at if you want to be a human being. It makes masculine stereotypes easier to break.

**Lesbians** Although the stereotype of a homosexual woman is the "dyke" – a woman who dresses and acts like a man – such women are a minority. Lesbians adapt the traditional polarity of heterosexual sex roles, which tends to produce the "butch" and the "fem," one aggressive and dominant, the other submissive and passive. Women in gay liberation are challenging these stereotypes, which they view as duplicating the worst aspects of the traditional heterosexual relationship.

Many lesbians experiment with a masculine identification for a short period, usually during the identity crisis experienced when they admit their homosexuality to themselves. Some retain the heterosexual view that a lesbian is a man in a woman's body; this stereotype helps create a distance between their heterosexual and homosexual identities.

A woman who adopts an obviously masculine role is also protected from having to confront men; they recognize her on sight as being unavailable. Obvious masculinity may also operate protectively in the gay world, as revealed to Simon and Gagnon (1967):

"And there was no truth in them?"

"Why should I tell you?" Mar shouted at her as if she were now the enemy herself.

"No reason. Except that I want to understand."

Mar leapt to his feet and stood over Hilary in an attitude that she sensed was threatening. Because she felt a threat, she lifted her head and looked up at him, meeting his glance full on. He did not lower his eyes; she could see the pupils widen. He was black in his sacred fury.

"So you can 'help.' I suppose." It was a slap in the face.

"So I can understand. For me, not for you."

May Sarton

---

... When I first got into the gay world with the first girl, there was no butch or fem. We didn't know, though I was slightly more aggressive ... in taking care of things, managing, planning. When we made love, there was a kind of flow, a sharing. So I eventually come out in the gay world as kind of butch. Mostly because I felt you had to be somewhere. Later, if someone asked, I said I was butch, but mostly because I didn't want any of these bull dykes coming to me.

Another woman's views, presented in the same study, expressed the feeling that homosexual women see themselves as women:

Do you have a preference as to active or passive roles? For me it would be reciprocal. But among the gay people I know, I guess I am classified as fem. Probably because I'm not the aggressive type... Do you prefer girls who are butch or fem? That's hard to say. I think most of the girls I have been attracted to were also attractive to men, some of them very much so. Also, there has to be some community of interest, so that there is something to talk about. A way of seeing things the same way.

Homosexual women usually form more lasting relationships than do homosexual men, reflecting the socialization patterns of women with regard to intimacy; they are usually more committed to finding an enduring relationship based on love. Yet many homosexual women, like those who are heterosexual, have a fear that relationships will not last. One lesbian, deeply involved with another, was reluctant to live with her. Although she felt security and acceptance that went beyond sex, experience with women who had turned out to be "lemons" had convinced her it was preferable to live alone rather than to make a commitment (Simon and Gagnon, 1967).

Homosexual men and women achieve satisfying relationships only with difficulty, because they lack a number of supports provided to heterosexual people. Foremost, they have neither the social sanction nor the legal approval of our society. They lack, in addition, the bonding roles of mother/father provided by rearing children.

### Religion

There does not seem to be a connection between religious background and homosexuality, but the *practice* of religion is significant. Among religiously inactive men and women, the frequency of homosexual contacts is higher. Kinsey noted that by age 35, homosexual orgasms had been experienced by 17 percent of the women who were inactive Protestants but only 7 percent

"The issue of homosexuality always makes me nervous...
I don't have any, you know, personal knowledge about
homosexuality and I guess being a Baptist, that would
conribute to a sense of being uneasy."

Jimmy Carter

of those who were active; by 25 percent of the non-practicing Catholic women but only 5 percent of those who said they were devout Catholics.

Religious convictions often make for conflict. Many homosexual people leave their churches, others modify religious beliefs after great struggle. Simon and Gagnon report that a woman who considered herself "very religious" said:

> I stopped going to church when my minister told me that if I couldn't control my feelings, I could control acting on them. That it was a challenge. I just knew that God would not have given me these feelings if they were so bad. Somehow I know He understands.

Religious homosexual men do not seem to have any greater psychological problems than do those who are irreligious. They tend to redefine their religion, however, so that homosexuality does not violate their personal code. A homosexual minister noted that being homosexual does not alter God's love for you as a human being. Christ did not die solely for heterosexuals, he said, nor promise eternal salvation only for straights. At no time did Jesus discuss homosexuality, and the minister suggested that his teachings regarding sexual morality apply equally to homosexual and heterosexual persons.

As far as a homosexual person is able to redefine religious teachings, there is not much strain.

## The Conservative Reaction to Gay Rights

In June 1969, New York police raided the Stonewall, a small gay bar in Greenwich Village, once again harassing and intimidating members of the homosexual community. But this time the gays fought back, led by street queens dressed in their wild clothes and battling the police armed with clubs and mace. For several nights, gays

poured into the area to protest police harassment, rioting in the hot summer nights. The riots were a turning point; they marked the beginning of gay liberation, the movement of gays out of the closets and into the streets. The Stonewall riots, declared one militant at a rally, were "the realization of innocence." The riots gave birth to a new militancy, bringing gay rights into the foreground as a leading sexual issue.

Sidney Abbott and Barbara Love (1972) described the gay militants who emerged from those tumultuous evenings:

> Psychologically the gay activist might be considered a mutant form of homosexual, who sees essentially positive a life that has appeared negative. "When we hated ourselves we saw everything we were and everything we did as more or less bad. Now we are looking into things and realize that what we do is not bad, just different, and even beautiful."

Abbott and Love describe further traits of the activists:

> The activist drops much self-consciousness and develops a social consciousness.
>
> Instead of guilt, the activist experiences pride.
>
> Instead of deviant behavior, the activist sees homosexual behavior as creative and individualistic.
>
> Instead of accepting the concept of disturbed patterns of gender identity, the activist talks of new and expanded human behavior transcending societally-set boundaries.
>
> Instead of passively accepting oppression and surrendering like a vegetable, the activist confronts society.

For a long time, it seemed that gays were gaining their rights. The American Psychiatric Association removed homosexuality from its list of mental disorders, although by a narrow margin in the voting. The United States Civil Service

Commission ruled that gays may not be fired simply because of their sexuality, and a dozen major corporations made it company policy not to discriminate against gays in employment opportunities. Forty cities and counties passed liberal antidiscrimination ordinances, and eighteen states repealed all restrictions on sexual acts between consenting adults in private.

But there was bound to be a reaction to the new openness. Traditionally, Americans have been hostile toward homosexuality and the backlash began in Dade County, Florida, in 1977. In May 1977, television commercials began appearing around Miami that depicted tanned majorettes high stepping in long columns. A voice softly intoned to the marching majorettes: "The Orange Bowl parade... Miami's gift to the nation. Wholesome entertainment." Then the scene dissolved to a gay rights parade and the tone of voice changed to disapproval: "But in San Francisco, when they take to the streets, it's a parade of homosexuals. Men hugging other men. Cavorting with little boys. Wearing dresses and makeup. The same people who turned San Francisco into a hotbed of homosexuality want to do the same thing to Dade County."

Earlier, Dade County had passed an ordi-

The only unnatural sex act is one that can't be performed.

Alfred Kinsey

---

nance prohibiting discrimination in housing, employment, and public accommodation based on "affectional or sexual preference." It was a major victory for the homosexual community. But for Anita Bryant (a former Miss Oklahoma, a runner-up Miss America, and the leading promotor of Florida orange juice) the ordinance was an abomination. She protested to the Dade County Metropolitan Commission before the ordinance was passed but to no avail. Then she took to battle, declaring "This is not my battle. It's God's battle." To combat the ordinance she helped found Save Our Children, Inc., which had a heavy fundamentalist bent. She took to the speaking circuit, saying, "If homosexuality were the normal way, then God would have made Adam and Bruce." Later, she declared, "The Lord is on our side. We know that homosexuality is an abomination." She referred to homosexual persons as "human garbage" and argued that the antidiscrimination law gave people the right to have "intercourse with beasts." Her speaking tours were heavily sprinkled with quotes from the Bible, especially Romans, Corinthians, and Leviticus. Her favorite quotation was Leviticus 20:13, "If a man also lie with mankind as he lieth with a woman, both of them have committed an abomination: they shall surely be put to death: their blood shall be upon them."

Leading the opposition to the ordinance, Anita Bryant easily collected six times as many signatures as she needed to force a referendum on the issue. For weeks the campaign went on, with most political commentators believing the vote would be close. But it was not. Anita Bryant's forces won an overwhelming victory, defeating the ordinance by a two-to-one vote. Learning of her victory, Anita Bryant danced a jig and her husband kissed her, gleefully observing "that's what heterosexuals do." With the victory

secured, Save Our Children, Inc., opened an office in Washington, D.C., and Bryant linked her fight to anticommunism: "The more we let violence and homosexuality become the norm," she said, "the more we'll become such a sick nation that the communists won't have to take over – we'll just give up."

The issues the campaign against the ordinance raised, however, were more significant than Anita Bryant's rhetoric. Save Our Children, Inc., posed the question of whether or not homosexual men are a threat to children and should not be allowed to teach or work in childcare. There are not many studies, but most indicate that the vast majority of sexual attacks on children are committed by heterosexuals, not homosexuals. The issue of role models, however, is another question raised by Save Our Children, Inc. If a child becomes aware of his or her teacher's homosexuality, will that lead him or her to adopt a homosexual orientation also? Then there is the one further question of civil rights legislation: should gays receive special protection? Florida's governor Reuben Askew denied that they should receive any special legal consideration, saying "I have never viewed the homosexual lifestyle as something that approached a constitutional right." Yet, there is no denying that homosexual men and women suffer discrimination in housing and employment and harassment because of their sexual orientation. Finally, there is the question of whether antidiscrimination legislation would encourage the spread of homosexuality and undermine the family. Save Our Children claims that it would, while the gay community claims that it would not.

The debate over the issue raised in the Dade County election reached as far as Washington, D.C., where President Jimmy Carter stated his feelings, probably the first president to address the issue of homosexuality. At a press conference

*Our laws were never made to protect abnormals. They were made for the majority.*

Anita Bryant

on June 18, 1977, Carter said that he does not believe that homosexuality is a "threat to the family." He also said that he does not believe that homosexual persons ought to be harassed. Reflecting the ambiguity many Americans who tolerate homosexuality experience, he said:

What has caused the highest publicized confrontations on homosexuality is the desire of homosexuals for the rest of society to approve and add its acceptance of homosexuality as a normal sexual relationship.

I don't feel that it's a normal interrelationship. But at the same time, I don't feel that society, through its laws, ought to abuse or harass homosexuals. I think it's one of those things that is not accepted by most Americans as a normal sexual relationship. In my mind it's certainly not a substitute for family life.

Then Carter was asked if he would be upset if his daughter Amy were taught by a homosexual teacher. It was a thorny issue and Carter, like many heterosexual persons who take a liberal stance, felt uncomfortable with it:

That's something I'd rather not answer. I don't see any need to change laws to permit homosexuals to marry. I know that there are homosexuals who teach and the children don't suffer. But this is a subject I don't particularly want to involve myself in. I've got enough problems without taking on another.

Then he changed the subject.

What the outcome of this new movement against gay rights will be is not clear, but it has certainly caused immense concern in the homosexual community. Several weeks after the vote in Dade County, a homosexual man was murdered in San Francisco by a gang of hoodlums who shouted "faggot! faggot!" as they repeatedly stabbed him in the chest. Their only motive was that he was gay. Leaders in the homosexual community declared that Anita Bryant should be indicted as an accessory to the crime for what they called the "hate campaign" she led.

In November, 1978, Dan White, a former San Francisco supervisor, shot and killed the mayor of San Francisco, George Moscone, and another supervisor, Harvey Milk. Moscone, a liberal, had often supported the gay community and Milk, a gay, represented a district in the city noted for its large homosexual population. As a supervisor, White had consistently opposed the outspoken and often flamboyant gay community on many issues. When White came to trial and received in May, 1979, what appeared to be too lenient a sentence, the gay community erupted in a riot at the steps of city hall. For many, the brutality of the crime seemed to be overshadowed by the issue of gay rights; the leniency of the sentence was thought to be influenced by a growing conservative reaction against gay rights. Gays are clearly on the defensive as the mood of America appears to shift away from a more liberal posture and moves into the 1980s. And Dan White will be eligible for parole after only three years in prison for his double, execution style murder.

## QUESTIONS

1. Kinsey claimed that people were neither heterosexual nor homosexual. Instead, he said, they engaged in heterosexual and homosexual *behaviors* on a continuum. Explain the significance of this distinction. Is it valid? Would homosexual men and women agree with it?

2. Recently there has been increased opposition to gay rights. Why? Are gay rights different from human rights?

3. Many states have repealed laws that sent

homosexual men and women to jail for "unnatural" sexual practices. Should such laws be repealed or enforced? What makes a sexual act "unnatural?"

4. Discuss the impact that "passing" as "straight" has on a homosexual person. Is it important that a person "come out of the closet?" Why?

5. What future trends do you foresee regarding gay rights and homosexuality? Will times become more or less tolerant? What indications do you have for your conclusions?

# Readings

### *Excerpt from* **Patterns of Sexual Behavior**

*Ford and Beach*, Harper & Row

*Ford and Beach's classic study examines sexuality from both a cross-cultural and animal perspective. They discovered great variety in animal behavior and treatment of homosexuality by different cultures.*

Social codes differ markedly in the treatment of liaisons between members of the same sex. At one extreme are societies such as our own that forbid and punish any homosexual relationship in individuals of any age and of either sex. There are, in contrast, other peoples who are tolerant of homosexual play in childhood but disapprove of the same behavior on the part of adults. Still a third group of societies actively enforces homosexual relations upon all its male members. This is true, however, only for a given age group, and it is usually associated with puberty ceremonials. A number of cultures make special provisions for the adult male homosexual, according him a position of dignity and importance and permitting him to live as the "wife" of some man.

Our cross-cultural comparisons suggest three generalizations concerning homosexual behavior in human beings. First, there is a wide divergence of social attitudes toward this kind of activity. Secondly, no matter how a particular society may treat homosexuality, the behavior is very likely to occur in at least a few individuals. Third, males seem more likely to engage in homosexual activity than do females. In order to interpret these facts it is necessary to see their relationships to the zoological and physiological data.

Homosexual behavior is not uncommon among males and females of several infrahuman primate species. Immature monkeys and apes indulge in a variety of homosexual games which include manipulation of the genitals of a like-sexed partner and may even involve attempts at homosexual coitus. Such relationships tend to occur less frequently after puberty, but in some cases an adult individual may form an enduring homosexual liaison with an immature member of his own sex. It is significant that in other primates, as in human beings, homosexuality is less prevalent among females than among males. It is also important to note the absence of any evidence to justify classifying this behavior exclusively as a substitute for heterosexual relations. Adult male monkeys with ample opportunity for heterosexual intercourse may nevertheless indulge in homosexual relations with younger males. And in some cases the same individual wil carry on hetero-and homosexual alliances concurrently.

Male and female mammals belonging to infraprimate species sometimes display mating responses typical of the opposite sex. Adult females often mount other females in masculine fashion, and the females that are thus mounted react as they would to a male. Under certain circumstances males attempt to copulate with males, and occasionally the one thus approached will react in the manner of a receptive female. Such observations reveal the bisexuality of the physiological mechanisms for mammalian mating behavior. Even in such species as the rat or rabbit, the neuromuscular basis for feminine responses is present in males as well as females, and the normal female's physiological capacities include the ability to react as would the male. Temporary inversions of the sexual role are due in these species not to an underlying physical abnormality in the individual but to the nature of the external stimulus situation.

It is our belief that a comparable though much more complex condition obtains in human beings. It seems probable that all men and women possess an inherited capacity for erotic responsiveness to a wide range of stimuli. Tendencies leading to sexual relations with individuals of the same sex are probably not as strong as those leading to heterosexual relations. But the important fact is that all societies enforce some modification of the individual's genetically determined impulses, with the result that the preferred type of behavior is strongly influenced by experience.

Men and women who are totally lacking in any conscious homosexual leanings are as much a product of cultural conditioning as the exclusive homosexuals who find heterosexual relations distasteful and unsatisfying. Both extremes represent movement away from the original, intermediate condition which includes the capacity for both forms of sexual expression. In a restrictive society such as our own a large proportion of the population learns not to respond to or even to recognize homosexual stimuli and may eventually become in fact unable to do so. At the same time a certain minority group, also through the process of learning, becomes highly if not exclusively sensitive to the erotic attractions of a like-sexed partner. Physical or physiological peculiarities that hamper the formation of heterosexual habits may incline certain individuals to a homosexual existence.

Dr. Clellan S. Ford and Dr. Frank A. Beach, *Patterns of Sexual Behavior.* Copyright © 1951 by Ford and Beach. Reprinted by permission.

## Homosexuals: Many Types, Many Causes

Lois Timnick

*There are no clear-cut answers about how a person learns a homosexual orientation, yet most authorities agree that it takes place early in life. The question of its origin is crucial in the debate concerning homosexual teachers. In 1978, Proposition 6 tried to ban homosexuals from teaching in California. It was defeated. How would you feel if your child was being taught by a homosexual teacher? Is there a genuine basis for concern? Or is it simply anxiety?*

*"Some people say, 'If you have homosexual teachers, you're automatically going to have homosexual students.'*
*"I don't know about that theory. Because if it were true, today I would be a nun."*
*— Comedian Mark Russell*

"What evidence is there that boys are at risk of 'catching' homosexuality from their teachers?" the psychiatrist asked. "You'd think they'd have 'caught' heterosexuality from their parents, who've had years of their most vulnerable time. How can a French teacher offset that in 50 minutes a day?"

Most experts – psychiatrists, psychologists and psychoanalysts who have spent their lives studying sexuality – say that while parental fears that a homosexual teacher might serve as an unhealthy role model for their children are understandable, they are not justified.

Does role modeling ever create homosexuality?

"The scientific answer is an unequivocal no," says Dr. Judd Marmor, a USC psychiatrist and psychoanalyst, past president of the American Psychiatric Assn. and author of the homosexuality chapter of one of the most widely used psychiatric texts.

"The weight of evidence at this point – and it's overwhelming – is that whatever these factors are that make a child predisposed to homosexuality they are probably set for the vast majority of homosexuals in the first six years of their lives," he said.

"I would say that the chance of that (the influence of a popular teacher known to be gay) creating a homosexual out of a child not already predisposed are absolutely nil."

"I know of no case of homosexuality that has ever developed in the hundreds I've examined and the thousands I've read about where homosexuality could be said to be derived from admiring a homosexual."

The experts do not all agree on how homosexuality comes about, but most believe that sexual orientation is essentially set – and not easily changed – by the time a child enters first grade.:

– "Studies suggest familial or genetic influences, but not role modeling," says Dr. Joshua S. Golden, director of UCLA's human sexuality program clinic. "The idea that a teacher would cause a normal person to want to become gay is preposterous. There is no evidence that even an occasional homosexual experience (which many

boys have) will make someone a lifelong homosexual."

– "That's one thing most of us are convinced is not the case: you are not seduced into being a homosexual," says Dr. Hans Hesseldahl, a member of the sex therapy team at the University Clinic of Copenhagen, where much of the European work on homosexuality and transsexuals has been done. "You have a predisposition for it, and when the circumstances are right, you will become a practicing homosexual unless you deny your sexual feelings altogether," Hesseldahl said on a recent visit to California.

– "Patently absurd," is how Alan P. Bell, coauthor of the (Kinsey) Institute for Sex Research's latest volume, "Homosexualities," terms Proposition 6's basic premise, that an openly gay teacher could influence a child's sexual preferences.

– "Most boys couldn't be recruited to homosexuality by a homosexual teacher no matter how hard the teacher tried," said Dr. L. J. West, director of UCLA's Neuropsychiatric Institute and chairman of psychiatry and biobehavioral sciences there. "A few boys are already bound for homosexuality by the time they encounter a teacher who might be blamed for corrupting them when it wouldn't make a bit of difference whether they'd encountered him or not.

"But," West added, "It is possible for a student who otherwise would not have become an active homosexual to be recruited to homosexuality. There are certain people who could go either way and, depending on the type of experience that they have at a certain age, their subsequent behavior will be different one way or the other. I'm talking about behavior. The extent to which their fundamental character will be changed is very difficult to estimate."

The Times contacted six experts and reviewed

the research of about 25 others. Only one said he believed a homosexual teacher could set a damaging example.

"Gender identity (the sense of being male or female and its accompanying traits) develops in the years from 1 to 3, but fluctuates throughout life," said New York psychoanalyst, Dr. Charles W. Socarides. "Certainly the teacher is an important role model toward heterosexuality."

A homosexual teacher who openly advocates the gay life, he said, can create problems for any youngster growing up with uncertainties and doubts about his own masculinity.

Some parents, however, fear more than subtle psychological seduction. They hear assertions that homosexual teachers are more likely than their straight counterparts to seduce or molest their students. The antigay initiative's author, state Sen. John V. Briggs (R-Fullerton), has said that "everybody knows homosexuals are child molesters."

Statistics do not bear this out. For example, a recent study by Dr. A. Nicholas Groth, formerly director of psychological services at the Massachusetts Center for the Diagnosis and Treatment of Sexually Dangerous Persons, looked at a random sample of 175 males convicted of sexual assault against children. The majority, he found, were heterosexuals who turned to a child for gratification after an adult relationship had disintegrated, or pedophiles, men who had always focused on children and tended to show a slight preference for boys.

"In no case were there peer-oriented homosexual males (men attracted to males their own age) in the sample who regressed to become sexually involved with children," Groth told his colleagues in a Sexuality Today newsletter. Nor has he seen a single such case in his 12 years of work with child molesters, said Groth, now with the Connecticut Correctional Institu-

tion's sex offender program.

California's Commission for Teacher Preparation and Licensing does not break down its license revocations by sex. But statistics compiled for the state Legislature earlier this year found that of 32 instances from 1974 to 1977 in which teachers' licenses were revoked for sexual assault of school-age children – rape, unlawful intercourse, contributing to the delinquency of a minor, exciting lust of a child under 14, oral copulation or child molestation – half involved female victims, half males. All the teachers were men.

(Seduction of girls by male teachers is thought by many to be far more frequent but less likely to be reported.)

These 16 homosexual assaults represent less than 1% of the estimated 2,500 male homosexual teachers in California's public school systems. That estimates is based on the most recent estimates from the Kinsey people at Indiana University's Institute for Sex Research that about 4% of American men are predominantly homosexual.

The majority, 81%, of nearly 700 homosexual men profiled in the recent book, "Homosexualities," said they had never had sex with minors.

The principal researcher in a massive study of homosexuals by the New York Society of Medical Psychoanalysts, Dr. Irving Bieber, found few instances of seduction of young people by older homosexuals.

Sixty percent of the 72 patients in the New York study who had had their first homosexual encounter by age 16 described their partner as being about the same age. Only thirteen reported this first partner to have been at least 10 years older.

"There is no evidence that seduction by other homosexuals is of any significance," he wrote, pointing not only to his own work but to a follow-up study of 108 boys who had been sexually seduced between the ages of 7 and 16.

"None subsequently became homosexual," he said.

If physical seduction is neither frequent nor a cause of homosexuality, and if youngsters do not turn to the gay life just because they have come under the influence of a homosexual role model, how does homosexuality – erotic arousal by persons of the same, rather than opposite sex – come about?

Probably in a variety of ways, just as there are a variety of types of homosexuals with different backgrounds and different life-styles.

Fewer than 10% of the homosexuals in Bell's and Martin S. Weinberg's study worked in stereotypically gay occupations. More were involved in "masculine" fields like engineering. Thirty-one percent had reached the professional or management level; 12% were in positions of public trust.

It has been nearly 30 years since retired UCLA psychologist Evelyn Hooker interviewed homosexuals in gay bars and showed the fallacy of drawing conclusions about all gays from studies of troubled homosexuals who seek psychiatric treatment.

Now, "Homosexualities," published this fall, documents their diversity further, but the kinds of experiences that underlie this diversity are still not well understood.

Some recent evidence suggests that homosexuality may be determined by prenatal factors – either genetic or constitutional – especially in those types of homosexuals who are and always have been effeminate – "sissy little boys."

A German physiologist, for example, castrated a group of male rats on the first day of life, but on the third day gave half of them a single shot of the male hormone, testosterone. At puberty all were given male hormones to cause them to develop into normal-looking males. But while those that had gotten the hormone on the third day of life behaved in a normal, heterosexual manner, the others acted like female rats. They did not mount females but instead presented themselves to other males.

This kind of study has led many scientists to conclude that there is a critical point in the development of male mammals – and in humans it is while the fetus is still in the uterus – at which the brain must be sensitized by male hormones. If not, the boy will behave in an effeminate way.

Other biological evidence comes from a study of identical twins, which found that when one twin was gay, the other was too, and from the frequency with which more than one homosexual is found in the same family. Some investigators have found more XX (female) chromosomes in cells scraped from inside the mouths of homosexual males than in similar cells from heterosexuals.

Still other studies have found lower levels of testosterone in the blood plasma and urine of homosexuals, and differences in the ratio of two breakdown products of this hormone in homosexuals and heterosexuals.

And a new, still unpublished, study shows that very young effeminate boys can be differentiated from their more masculine counterparts by analyzing their brain waves. (A clear relationship has been established between femininity in boys and adult homosexual practices.)

The existence of homosexual behavior in the animal world and in other societies throughout history also points to some biological basis.

But the fragmented and conflicting evidence to date means that whether there may be innate genetic or hormonal differences between homosexuals and heterosexuals is still undecided.

"The weight of evidence," USC's Marmor said, "is that most homosexuality is caused by factors in the first five years of life which interfere with a satisfactory male identification." Most scientists believe this process is largely learned.

As early as 1905, Freud (in "Three Essays on the Theory of Sexuality") suggested that men with weak or absent fathers and frustrating mothers were apt to become homosexual; Bieber's New York study of 106 male homosexual patients in 1962 also found in the backgrounds of most, a detached, hostile father and an over-protective, seductive mother who dominated her husband.

As psychoanalyst Marmor explains it: If the little boy lacks a loving father who does "masculine" things with him (and what these things are may change as society changes) that make him feel he will someday be a competent man and yet is not so forbidding or heroic that he feels he can never measure up, *and* if he has a controlling, smothering mother, he may be predisposed to homosexuality in later life.

In normal sexual development, the boy transfers his feelings for his first love – his mother – to other females. An overprotective mother will arouse mixed feelings of love, dependency and resentment in her son, producing fear or hatred of women. "And you just don't think of having sex with an overpowering figure," Marmor added.

On the other hand, if the mother is extremely seductive with her young son, she may create such guilt feelings in him (since incest is taboo) that he will be unable to become sexual with any woman he admires.

More than two-thirds of the mothers of homosexuals in Bieber's study had extraordinarily close relationships with their sons. They were often both overprotective and seductive, favoring this son over both husband and other children.

But if family patterns alone caused homosex-

uality, it would be found more often in the ghetto – where fatherless households are common. This is not so, Marmor says, because good relationships with other youngsters and exposure to other male figures in the early years can offset the effects of an over-close bond between mother and son and a missing father.

Also, he said, homosexuality is most likely to develop in an atmosphere of sexual puritanism. "Families that foster the notion that sex is a nasty taboo thing unconsciously support same-sex relations," he said. "They don't mind their little boy palling around with other little boys or their little girl sleeping in a bed with other girls, however, and as sexuality develops in the critical years from 3 to 6 it is reinforced in a homosexual direction."

UCLA's West says that most experience supports the view that "social learning in the family context determines masculinity and femininity of personality and behavior far more than even gross biology will do."

For example, an infant boy mistakenly assigned to the wrong sex at birth, due to a congenital abnormality, will grow up as a normal girl (until the mistake is discovered at puberty) because his parents and society *treat* him like a girl. And a baby girl, exposed to excessive amounts of masculinizing hormones before birth, will show only mild effects – such as tomboyish behavior – so long as she is considered a girl.

Some parents in several Asian countries, West noted, deliberately rear their male children to be effeminate homosexual prostitutes by dressing them from infancy in dresses, earrings, long hair and lipstick. It clearly works.

But to say that the groundwork for homosexuality is laid down very early on is not to say that it is forever fixed, unchangeable and untreatable. The New York study found that 27% of the homosexual patients who sought treatment switched from gay to straight with psychoanalysis; other studies have reported success rates ranging from 20% to 50%.

But the trend today is toward helping homosexuals adjust to what they are, rather than attempting to change them into heterosexuals unless they deeply desire such a change.

Freud, in his famous letter to a worried mother in 1935, wrote that "homosexuality is assuredly no advantage, but it is nothing to be ashamed of, no vice, no degradation, it cannot be classified as an illness; we consider it to be a variation of the sexual function produced by a certain arrest of sexual development."

Yet in the American Psychiatric Assn.'s first Diagnostic and Statistical Manual of Mental Disorders (DSM) in 1952, it was listed as a type of pathologic sexual deviation in the sociopathic (criminal) personality disturbance category under personality disorders. That view held for 16 years, until DSM II, in which it was still listed as a sexual deviation, this time under the heading "personality disorders and certain other nonpsychotic mental disorders."

It has disappeared altogether in DSM III, which is still in draft form and will be published in 1979 or 1980. The draft explains that homosexuality itself "is not considered a disorder" and that only those behaviors that involve "gross impairment in the capacity for affectionate sexual activity between adult human partners" will be listed as sexual deviations. It does list, as a psychosexual disorder, what is called "ego-dystonic homosexuality" – which simply means being miserable about one's homosexuality.

That evolution of thinking within the medical profession, however, has hardly affected the 60% of Americans a recent study shows still carry stereotyped ideas about homosexuals.

Two-thirds of nearly 100 other societies, another study found, were tolerant of homosexuals. "Homophobia" among Americans seems to stem from the Judeo-Christian tradition (the Bible considers homosexuality a sin), simple ignorance and insecurity about their own sexuality.

"A high proportion of kids indulge in homosexual play," Marmor says, because girls are forbidden. "Nobody becomes a homosexual because of those experiences. A small percentage do become homosexual later on, and for them these (experiences) just reinforced what already existed."

(The original Kinsey report in 1948 found that about half the males in the white, middle-class sample admitted to having had some kind of homosexual play in their life, and about a third had experienced orgasm in a homosexual context at least once.)

If role modeling were as potent a factor as Proposition 6's supporters argue, Marmor said, homosexuality would never develop, "because every homosexual grows up in a heterosexual environment. He has heterosexual parents and the vast majority of people he is likely to meet are heterosexual role models."

But the gay teacher can serve as an important and positive role model in another way, he said:

"If a child is moving in a heterosexual direction, he will learn tolerance, which will help eliminate unhealthy homophobia.

"If he is moving in a homosexual direction – and a child of 6, 7 or 8 may still be confused, while by 9, 10, 11 or 12 he may have begun to suspect that he is different – a homosexual teacher may help him feel that he can grow up and be a decent human being, not a monster."

Lois Timnick, *Los Angeles Times*, Wed. Nov. 1, 1978. Copyright © 1978 Los Angeles Times. Reprinted by permission.

## Being Gay in College

Peter Nye

*These anecdotes reveal some experiences of homosexual students at Stanford University. How common are they?*

Accepting your gay feelings and revealing them to other people in your life is a slow, frightening, and yet exhilarating process. It is a declaration of self-respect, independence, and freedom in a world which is attempting to keep them from you.

Here is a composite of experiences gay women and men have had coming out at Stanford:

### The internal struggle

– You escape from a small midwestern town and come to California to find freedom, only to find your freshperson dorm has about the same opinion of faggots as your high school class had.

– After months of feeling that you must be the only gay person on campus, you notice another man looking at you. You panic, and walk quickly the other way.

– You fall in love with your roommate and spend the next half year in agony, because you are afraid that if he finds out, he won't associate with you any more.

– You try to be straight. You convince yourself that you are falling in love with a woman in your dorm. It becomes clear that the relationship isn't going to work, but you can't tell her why.

### First ventures out

– You want desperately to meet other Lesbians. You finally work up the courage to walk into GPU, only to find out it is Men's Night.

– You tell your roommate. She moves out, word

gets out, and you suddenly find it very difficult to find a replacement.

– You pace back and forth across the street from GPU every Tuesday night for two quarters. You finally go in, petrified because for the first time in your life, there will be other people who will know you are gay. You find that the woman who sits next to you in your math class is there, as well as several other people you know.

– You tell your roommate. She says she's known all along, and she's glad you finally decided to start accepting yourself.

– You try to come out to a friend, but whenever you bring up the subject of homosexuality, she changes the subject.

### Reactions

– On your way out of a GPU meeting, you are threatened with an iron pipe by two drunks, who call you a stinking faggot. Later they claim you were trying to molest them.

– You find that at parties, men are continually coming up and asking you to dance, because "We hate to see you two girls dancing all by yourselves."

– You are afraid your advisor will find out, because you think you probably won't get your Ph. D. if he does.

– You have problems with finding a place for you and your lover of five years to live. You are told that the housing in Escondido Village is for married couples only.

– A group of men attack you verbally in the Coffee House for sitting too close to your woman friend. They then proceed to discuss your probable sexual orientation in loud voices.

– After spending most of your life watching straight couples being affectionate, you are accused of being blatant for holding hands with your lover.

### Gay people are everywhere

– You quit a woman's CR group because only relationships with men are discussed. You find out later that more than half the group are Lesbians.

– You are afraid that your roommate will find out about your being involved with a woman. Later you find out that she had broken up with the same woman the year before.

– You are at a party with your lover, and are afraid to dance with her because one of your co-workers is there, until you notice him dancing with another man.

– You go to the Gay Freedom Day Parade in the city. After years of being surrounded by straights, there are nothing but people like you as far as you can see.

– A student comes to see you for counseling at the Bridge. He says you're the only other gay person he has ever met. You remember what it was like to be alone, and think that no one should ever have to go through that again.

---

### Ruby Fruit Jungle

Rita Mae Brown

*Two young women are lovers in a college dorm.*

The rest of that semester we spent in bed, emerging only to go to class and to eat. Faye made her grades because it was the only way we could be together, and she stopped drinking because she found something that was more fun. Chi Omega began to think Faye had died and gone to heaven. Tri Delta resorted to sending me urgent notices in the mail. We were eighteen, in love, and didn't know the world existed – but it knew we existed.

Not until February did I notice that people on our hall weren't speaking to us anymore. Conversations stopped when one or both of us would amble down the brown halls. Fay concluded they all had chronic laryngitis and decided she'd cure it. She hooked up a Mickey Mouse Club record to the ugly brick bell tower that rang class changes. Then she announced to our dorm neighbors that at three-thirty the true nature of the university would be revealed via the bell tower. As soon as the record blared across the campus Dot and Karen ran in from next door to giggle at Faye's success. Just as quickly they turned on their heels to walk out when Faye bluntly asked, "How come you two don't talk to us anymore?"

Terror crossed Dot's face and she told a half truth, "Because you stay in your room all the time."

"Bullshit," Faye countered.

"There's got to be another reason," I added.

Karen, angered at our bad manners in being so direct, spat at us gracefully. "You two are together so much it looks like you're lesbians."

I thought Faye was going to heave her chemistry book at Karen, her white face was so red. I looked Karen right in the face and said calmly, "We are."

Karen reeled back as though she were slapped with a soggy dishrag. "You're sick and you don't belong in a place like this with all these girls around."

Fay was now on her feet moving toward Karen, and Dot, the picture of courage, was at the door fumbling with the knob. Faye shifted into overdrive and roared her engine, "Why, Karen, are you afraid I might sleep with you? Are you afraid I might sneak over in the middle of the night and attack you?" Faye was laughing by this time and Karen was petrified. "Karen, if you were the last woman on earth, I'd go back to men—you're a simpering, pimply-faced cretin."

## Learning Your Spouse Is Gay

By Ruthe Stein

*What kind of feelings is a person likely to have upon learning his or her spouse is homosexual?*

### He Learned She Was A Lesbian

It has been five years since Mark Adams' wife left him for her lesbian lover. But from the emotion in his voice as he tells the story of the devastating effect it has had on his life, it could have happened yesterday.

"She really picked the worst way to hurt me. She poisoned me. I have been through it all — questioning of my own sexuality, a feeling of sadness, the social embarrassment.

"I have tried to talk to friends and family about the real reason for our breakup. But most people choose to ignore the facts. The usual retreat is into the liberal outlook that everything is O.K. It makes them defensive of her, rather than to try and understand me, so I have given that up."

Adams, a Bay Area attorney, had known his former wife Mary since he was 16. They were married for 18 years, and in all that time he never had any suspicion that she might be a lesbian. In retrospect he wonders how much the fact of his being "a very dominant person" and "allowing her to retreat to a soft position" might have contributed to her turning to a woman for love.

"We had a normal sexual life for the entire time we were married. I felt she was satisfied with our sexual relations." He paused for a moment and added, "although obviously I can't speak for her."

There was no big confrontation scene about "the other woman" when Mary Adams announced she wanted 'to end their marriage.' In fact she admitted only once "in a fleeting statement" that she was leaving him for a woman.

"I know now that it had been going on for two years of our marriage, but I had no inkling of it at that time, other than a feeling that this other woman had a certain power or control over my wife, and I was concerned about her influence."

Mary and Mark Adams both saw a psychiatrist for six months after their separation, but Adams believes his wife never really wanted to save their marriage. "She was just trying to feel better about herself. Her psychiatrist agreed that whatever made her comfortable was the best he could provide."

Adams said he has made several attempts to see Mary over the years "but there is no way for me to find a common ground with her."

They share custody of their children, who are now teenagers, which Adams agreed to in order to avoid "a very ugly court situation." Every other year, the children live with their mother — her lover is in the same apartment complex.

"The children have handled it with support for their mother," said Adams. "They feel a kind of resignation — if something is love, it is okay. The two older children feel anger towards me. I appear to be the provider and the solid person, and obviously I must have done something wrong.

"The children have definitely wondered about their own sexuality. My oldest daughter had a period of about six months when she had what may have been a homosexual relationship with an older woman. Certainly they were very close. My daughter finally pulled away from it, but it almost seemed that she did what she did to justify her mother's position."

His sons, Adams believes, are handling the sexuality issue better. "The identity crisis for them is less. They are satisfied with being the protector of their mother."

Adams started dating immediately after the separation and found women were able to understand what he was going through much better than men.

"The only sexual problems I have had is I found my ability to care about another woman to be flattened. I was very timid to express myself. But my sexual activity has not been affected specifically."

He is planning to marry a woman he has been dating for three years. "She has lived in a situation where she was approached by gay women, and she turned them down. It is very important for me to know that fact about her."

Adams said his "compassion and understanding" about the gay liberation movement hasn't been improved by what he has been through "but it hasn't been obliterated either. The reality teaches you that sometimes people are hurt when homosexual relationships are established.

"I would certainly hope other people would not have to live through watching what they thought was a successful marriage be bashed through. I can't say I wasn't partially responsible. But I have had to deal with the devastation left over, and that has been very hard."

## Her Husband Left Her For a Man

Rachel Wright was positive that she had the ideal marriage. Her only complaint, looking back on it, was that her husband, Tom, was not particularly affectionate. But she learned to live with that and even convinced herself that it was probably her fault.

Her list of Tom's attributes, on the other hand, was lengthy. An honor student, a football player and a fraternity man, handsome, successful in his profession, Tom was well-liked in the community, a good companion to his wife, and a good father to their children. "We worked well together," said Rachel.

For 12 years, she was "perfectly happy" with the marriage.

Then, one hot summer day, after a family picnic and before the neighbors were due in for cocktails, came the "numbing" announcement. Tom had been "very, very uptight and tense," Rachel recalled recently, her voice quavering occasionally with emotion. "So I said, 'Whatever it is that's bothering you, you'd better tell me or you're going to blow up.' "

His reply came in the form of a letter that he handed her. In it he revealed that he was a homosexual, had suspected as much since his late teens (they had married in their early 20s), and ended by asking permission to attend a party later that night with his male lover.

"In total shock," Rachel retreated to their bedroom and cried, then went through the motions of normality by entertaining their guests. However, she did talk Tom out of going to the party.

Rachel remembers the following six months as "a hell-hole, a nightmare that I thought I'd wake up from." Once the news was out, she said that Tom and his lover carried on their affair openly. She had to deal with love letters and "harassing" late-night phone calls and sometimes mediate jealous spats between the two men.

"I thought Tom was sick," Rachel said, adding that a psychiatrist confirmed that during this time he had a mental breakdown. The thought of a separation was impossible "because you don't leave your husband when he's sick."

Her own mental state was also in turmoil. "I couldn't eat. I couldn't sleep. I felt rejected and disgraced and overwhelmed and ashamed." She agonized over the fact that she had not detected her husband's gayness herself. "Homosexuality wasn't new to me," she said. She had gay friends. "But there just wasn't anything (in Tom), not a hint."

Rachel also felt she couldn't share the nightmare with anyone. If Tom had been having an affair with another woman, it might have been different, she said, "but you don't go out and say 'my husband is a homosexual'." (She eventually did and got nothing but support from her parents and close friends.)

After several months, the Wrights consulted a marriage counselor. His advice was to let Tom "have his freedom for six months" and see what happened. Rachel agreed because she hoped Tom would "straighten out" and "it was my intent to keep the marriage together. It didn't work, of course."

The final blow for her was a calendar Tom presented her, noting the dates he intended to spend a way from home with his lover. "He couldn't understand why I was upset when he thought he was still being a good husband and father. At that point I'd had it."

The Wrights separated and worked out a divorce settlement out of court "to protect the children." They agreed that Rachel would keep the children and Tom would have visitation rights "only if he sees them alone or with people I approve of," which does not include the man Tom lives with.

Two years after the ordeal, Rachel says she is back on her feet and ready – even eager – to tell her story in the hopes it will help others. The reason for talking, she said, is that as hellish as the situation was, it was not utterly hopeless.

Once she realized the futility of trying to change her husband's behavior and save their marriage, she decided "you either die on the vine or get up and get going." She joined organizations, went to work and started dating. Recently she remarried, with no fear that the situation would repeat itself with her second husband. When they discussed her experiences, he revealed that he, ironically, had once gone out with another woman whose former husband was gay.

For her, "the ending was happy." For her children, she continues to have doubts. They were 5 and 7 when their father revealed his homosexuality and while they were told the truth, they were and still are "too young to understand totally," Rachel said. They know that Tom "preferred to live with another man and sleep in the same bed with him." The subject is still discussed "any time it comes up."

But Rachel worries about what will happen when the children are older if their classmates tease them about their father, whose preference for men is by now common knowledge in their community.

"Teenage kids have enough to handle without this extra hunk of garbage on their heads," she said.

She wonders, too, about the children's sexuality. "I worry about my son becoming a homosexual. It's funny, though, I don't worry about my daughter."

She says she can accept homosexuality, but there is bitterness in her voice when she talks about how it entered her life.

She resents the fact that Tom, knowing his own sexual preference, married her and fathered his own children.

"To drag innocent women into it, and then children, I have no respect for that," Rachel said.

Whatever her children turn out to be, she hopes that by the time they are adults, homosexuality will no longer have to be hidden and denied. "By then," she said, "I hope this is a dead story."

Judith Anderson, *The San Francisco Chronicle*. Thursday, Nov. 17, 1977. Copyright © Chronicle Publishing Co. Reprinted by permission.

Pass no judgement, and you will not be judged; do not condemn, and you will not be condemned; acquit, and you will be acquitted; give and gifts will be given you . . . for whatever measure you deal out to others will be dealt to you in return.

Luke 6:37-38

---

The range of human sexual behavior is almost infinite; most people fall within certain ranges or degrees of behavior. Normal sexual behavior, as we have seen, is an amorphous concept, often revealing beneath its surface an arid moralism or cultural absolutism. Departures from the standard sexual practices in our society are known as sexual variations; they are also known as sexual deviations, although we do not use the term because *deviation* and its ancilliary *deviant* are often used in a moral rather than clinical sense. "Variation" does not have these confusing value connotations; it is a cleaner term.

What will be clear as we examine the most common forms of sexual variations is that they exist in some form in most of us; what makes them aberrant is when they become excessive or dominant in our sexual behavior. Although homosexuality is strictly speaking a sexual variation, we have decided to treat it in depth in the previous chapter. It is classified as a sexual variation because it is a variation of object choice. The standard object choice is heterosexual, that is, a person of the opposite sex. Other variations in object choice include inanimate objects (fetishism), close relatives (incest), a child (pedophilia), and animals (zoophilia). Variations in the choice of sexual aims are those behaviors that don't seek sexual intercourse. These include watching sexual intercourse (voyeurism), exposing one's genitals (exhibitionism), inflicting and receiving pain (sadomasochism), and cross-dressing (transvestism). Other behaviors — such as oral-genital sexual behavior and anal intercourse — have been classified in the past as sexual variations; they are still subject to criminal prosecution in many states (see chapter 16). But they have become widely accepted in recent years, revealing the relativity of the concept of normal sexual behavior.

## Exhibitionism

Exhibitionists expose their genitals to others — usually of the opposite sex — and derive sexual gratification from such exposure. Exposure is not a prelude or invitation to intercourse; instead, it is an escape from intercourse. The exposure is the man's sexual act, ending in masturbation. He does not seek intercourse, for he never exposes himself to a willing woman – only to strangers or near strangers. In those few instances in which a woman shows interest, the exhibitionist immediately flees (Stoller, 1977).

Exhibitionism is a fairly common sexual variation; about a third of all arrests for sexual offenses involve exhibitionism (Allen, 1961). But most exhibitionists are physically harmless nuisances; they rarely are involved in other sex crimes. In fact, the exhibitionist usually remains a safe distance away from the woman, generally six to sixty feet (Gebhard, et. al., 1965).

Exhibitionists are generally shy, introverted men who feel insecure or inadequate. They feel impotent as men and their sexual relations with their wives are usually poor. This impotency gives rise to anger and hostility, which they direct to other women in the form of "flashing." But their behavior is a weak expression of their sense of self; it does not go to the source of their anger. These men were generally raised in strict, prohibitive and religious environments; their mothers were powerful, domineering forces in their lives. Their exhibition of their erect penises is their one pathetic proof that they are men and can frighten women. Stoller (1977) writes about the need exhibitionists feel to be caught:

> Unfortunately, despite arrest and punishment, the likelihood that the exhibitionist will repeat his behavior and be caught again is extremely high, for the deviation does not achieve its object unless the sufferer believes he has caused a furor. It is as if, in exhibiting his penis, he must upset the observing

One half of the world cannot understand the pleasures of the other.

Jane Austen

woman and later the civil authorities; only then has he forced society to attend to the fact that he unquestionably is male, is masculine, and has a penis. Then he can be certain, temporarily, about his status as a man.

Some exhibitionists expose themselves to adult women; others expose themselves primarily to children. Those who expose themselves to adults use their exhibitionism as a tool of anger; but those who expose themselves to children are frequently looking for nonjudgmental responses. While older children are often upset by exhibitionism, the upset is usually passing unless the parents become overly upset or hysterical.

## Fetishism

Fetishists are sexually attracted to objects and turn the object into a sexual symbol. Instead of relating to another person, a fetishist gains sexual gratification from kissing a shoe, caressing a glove, drawing a lock of hair against his cheek, or masturbating with a piece of underwear. The fetishist, however, does not necessarily focus on an inanimate object: he may be attracted to a woman's ears, her breasts, her legs, elbows or any other part of her body (Caprio, 1955). Fetishists are usually males who, in certain cases, may burglarize a home or car or assault a women to gain a shoe, panties, or stockings (Karpman, 1954). College panty raids of another time were fetishistic rites in which groups of men assaulted women's dormitories; their prizes were panties, nightgowns, and bras which they would put on or display as trophies. These raids renewed the men's roles as dominating warriors (mock war, rape, and pillage), assured status among themselves as *men*, and gave them symbols of female conquest.

Paul Gebhard views fetishistic behavior as existing on a continuum. Fetishistic behavior moves from a slight preference for an object to a strong preference. It continues from there to whether the object is necessary for arousal and finally to the object as a substitute for a sexual partner (Gebhard, 1976). Most people have slight fetishistic traits: men describe themselves as leg men or breast men; they prefer dark-haired women or light-haired ones. Some women are attracted to muscular men, others to small penises, and still others to shapely buttocks. One of the great poems in the English language is strongly fetishistic. It is a famous love poem, "On a Girdle," by the 17th century poet Edmund Waller:

> That which her slender waist confined
> Shall now my joyful temples bind.

Chinese foot-binding: A once culturally approved fetishism.

No monarch but would give his crown
His arms might do what this has done.

It was my heaven's extremest sphere,
The pale which held that lovely deer.
My joy, my grief, my hope, my love
Did all within this circle move!

A narrow compass, and yet there
Dwelt all that's good and all that's fair;
Give me but what this ribbon bound,
Take all the rest the sun goes round.

It is only when a person develops a strong preference for an object that his attachment moves outside the range of statistical normality. How a person develops fetishistic responses is not known with any certainty, but it seems rooted in childhood. Fetishistic behavior does not exist in most primitive cultures which often permit their children to engage in early sexual experiments. It appears in highly developed cultures, and especially in Europe and America, which tend to restrict sexual behavior. In some manner, shoes, or panties, or some other object becomes associated in the child's mind with sexual excitement; these objects often belong to a person with emotional significance for the young boy. Through powerful symbolic transformation, the object, writes Paul Gebhard (1976), "is given all the power and reality of the actual thing and the person responds to the symbol just as he would the thing." The object receives erotic significance usually before puberty, and during this time, the child tends to have few girls for playmates. By the time fetishistic boys reach adulthood, they have very little heterosexual experience and use their fetishes as substitutes for genuine sexual encounters with women (Gebhard *et. al.*, 1965). Fetishists tend to be psychosexually immature, fearful or anxious about sexual intercourse, and generally hesitant about sex.

## Incest[1]

The most universal taboo known in human societies is the incest taboo. No one knows how it originated but it exists with only a few exceptions: only the royal families of ancient Egypt, Peru, and Hawaii were exempt. There is no instinctive aversion to incest; if there were, there would have been no reason to create such extensive rules prohibiting it. (In fact, it has been recently estimated that between three to five percent of the American population has had an overtly incestuous experience. Many people have had fleeting incestuous fantasies.)

There are a number of explanations regarding why the incest taboo is so prevalent. The biological explanation is that inbreeding is likely to cause genetic damage due to the inheritance of genetic defects. Incest exists throughout the animal kingdom. (The great apes, our closest animal relative, practice incest quite freely, for example.) Among humans, different societies define incest differently. One society calls marriages incestuous when they occur between cousins; yet another will urge marriages between cousins. In our society, the definition of incest has changed historically. Traditionally, a marriage between a man and his mother, sister, daughter, aunt, niece, grandmother, or granddaughter is considered incestuous. Women are forbidden to marry the corresponding male relatives. A little more than half the states prohibit marriage to half-brothers, half-sisters, and first cousins. Marriages between stepparents and stepchildren – in which there are no blood ties – are forbidden in about half the states. Marriage to a parent's

---

[1]This material is adapted from Bryan Strong, *et. al.*, *The Marriage and Family Experience*, Minneapolis: Copyright © West Publishing Co. 1979.

former spouse is also illegal in many states. But during colonial times, second cousins were often prohibited from marrying each other as well as in-laws from earlier marriages. Clearly, blood is not the basic factor in incest taboos. Peter Farb writes:

> If man rejects the notion of incest, it is solely because he himself dreamed up the notion in the first place. The reason that psychological and genetic explanations explain nothing is that the problem is not psychological or genetic, it is cultural. (Farb, 1968)

Some anthropologists suggest that the incest taboo comes from the need for families to extend their kinship bonds. The larger the number of families related through marriage, the larger the number of cooperative groups and allies. Others, principally Claude Levi-Strauss, find marriage primarily a trade agreement or exchange. Groups trade material objects, ideas, values, and women. Hostile tribes that become friendly do so through trade, finally trading brides as well as goods. The marrying of daughters into groups is the end of a reciprocal gift process. Levi-Strauss writes that it "brings about the transition from hostility to alliance, from anxiety to confidence, and from fear to friendship." Incest taboos are related to the exchange of gifts:

> The prohibition of incest is a rule of reciprocity. It means: I will give up my daughter or my sister if my neighbor will also give up his also ... The fact that I can obain a wife is, in the last analysis, the consequence of the fact that a brother or a father has given up a woman ... the relation which exists between marriage and gifts is not arbitrary. Marriage is in itself an inherent part of as well as a central motive for the accompanying reciprocal gifts. (Levi-Strauss, 1957).

And there is certainly a strong element of gift-giving in marriage. During most religious marriage ceremonies the question "Who gives this woman?" is asked and the father responds "I do." The father gives his daughter away to another family, but in doing so, unites with that family. (Interestingly, the question "Who gives this man?" is never asked, underlining the use of women – not men – as gifts.) The bride's family becomes in-laws to the husband; the bridegroom's family becomes in-laws to the wife. The children who come from the marriage are related by blood to both families. All through the simple process of one man giving his daughter away. But if the young man or woman had married his or her parent or other relative no new bonds would have been created.

Margaret Mead, following Sigmund Freud's insight, views the incest taboo as a means of avoiding conflict within the family. Freud considered the Oedipus myth (in which Oedipus killed his father and married his mother) as a prototype of child development. Each child forms strong bonds – including erotic ones – with the parent of the opposite sex. So strong are these bonds that the child desires to replace its parent of the same sex; it wants to marry the parent of the opposite sex. This deep sexual competition is repressed through the incest taboo so that it rarely surfaces. Freud called this desire of the child for the parent of the opposite sex the "Oedipus complex." Mead points out, however, that the incest is reciprocal. It protects children from their parents and parents from their children, thereby avoiding potentially deadly conflict and jelousy. But the taboo goes further. The incest taboo is indirectly extended to protect immature children from adults in general.

Although taboos against sexual activity with

children not one's own are extensions of the incest taboo, they are usually not as effective. Legally, these informal incest taboos take the form of laws concerning child molesting as well as laws regarding age-of-consent (that is, the minimum age before which sexual intercourse becomes a crime between an adult and minor). When there are substantial differences in age between partners, the incest taboo is reflected in the older person being called "cradle robber," "dirty old man," or "dirty old lady."

The most common form of incest that is reported is father/daughter incest. In such cases, the father (or foster father or stepfather) almost always initiates the incest, but often his daughter does not resist or is actually willing. These relationships are often long term and usually sexually exploitative. Such relationships usually become known when the daughter becomes angry at her father or decides to end the incest (Weinberg, 1955). The least common form of incest is mother/son, although mythically it is a more common theme (as in *Oedipus Rex*). It is also a central theme in Freud's theory of psychosexual development, and has a compelling hold on the Western imagination. Mother/son incest appears to be an important psychological symbol in our culture, although it rarely occurs in fact. It is open to speculation as to why this is so.

Another common form of incest is between brother and sister, although it is rarely reported. It usually takes place in early adolescence or earlier, is rarely discovered and, when it is, it is usually not treated seriously. It is often a form of sexual experimentation, occurring when children are given sexual freedom, have little access to sexual partners, and when brother and sister share the same bedroom. Incestuous relations also occur between cousins.

It is not clear how prevalent incest is: certainly it is underreported.

## Pedophilia

Pedophilia refers to the behavior of an adult who seeks sexual gratification from relationships with children; such relationships typically involve exhibitionism, fondling the child's genitals, fellatio or cunnilingus, or sexual intercourse. Eleven percent of the cases of child molesting involved sexual intercourse or anal penetration (rape), according to one sample (Jaffe, 1976).

While pedophiliacs are vastly despised as perverts and child rapists, less than 15 percent of pedophiliac relationships involve force or even threats. There may be some adult/child relationships which are not harmful; but generally, this type of relationship is pathological.

Most pedophiliacs come from a rigorous religious background which negated sexual feelings; they feel guilty about sex while at the same time they are obsessed by it. Their sexual attitudes are rigid and repressive; they believe in the double standard, insist that their wives be virgins, and define women as "good" or "bad" depending on their sexual experience. They tend to read the Bible devoutly, pray excessively (especially for divine help in overcoming their sexual desires), and are regular church attenders. On the outside they appear to be paragons of virtue and morality (Gebhard, 1966).

Child molesters are not necessarily strangers; indeed, between fifty to eighty percent of child molestation is done by relatives, family friends, neighbors, or acquaintances. If the molestation was incestuous, it may induce deep trauma, especially if it occurred on a regular basis, as often happens with incest. But in the majority of cases where force was not used and there was no intercourse, the child may be frightened, but not traumatized. The upset is not much more than that which a child experiences from a snake or spider (McCaghy, 1971). But when the parents enter the picture and become hysterical, the pos-

In the *Summa Theologica*, Saint Thomas says that
fornication between man and woman, even if they be
married, is nevertheless a venial sin. Now I think that's a
very sexy idea. Sin multiplies the possibilities of desire.

Luis Buñuel

sibility of lasting psychological damage occurs.
The late James McCary wrote (1978):

> Most psychologists agree that sexual experiences at
> the hands of a pedophile are less traumatic to the
> child than to the parents. If parents can deal with
> such unfortunate occurrences in a controlled man-
> ner, the child will usually suffer no residual trauma.

## Sadomasochism

*Sadomasochism* refers to sexual arousal derived
from receiving or giving physical or mental pain.
*Sadists* give the pain while *masochists* receive it.
The two are closely interrelated and they are
widespread on a fantasy level. In fact, Kinsey
(1948, 1953) found that approximately twenty
percent of the men and twelve percent of the
women he interviewed found themselves
aroused by stories of rape, bondage, punishment, whips, chains and other paraphernalia.
Nancy Friday's (1974) work on women's sexual
fantasies revealed many masochistic feelings.
One woman described her fantasies:

> . . . when I was very young I used to lie stretched
> out on my bed and dream that I was a princess who
> had been captured and who was waiting to be tor-
> tured, and this made me feel physically aroused.
> Later, as I became more sophisticated and my

thoughts developed, I imagined myself being racked, impaled, flogged, branded, and every other thing you can think of, ending with vigourous and orgasmic masturbation.

Interestingly, however, after describing some more fantasies, the woman remarked, almost parenthetically:

From all this you will think that I am masochistic, but the truth of the matter is that I am not and I just cannot stand pain. My parents never punished me and once, after stealing some money, I was threatened with the strap and this sent me into howling hysterics (Friday, 1974).

Men's fantasies tend to be aggressive:

I get an enormous kick out of imagining that a young innocent girl is forced to fellate me. It is even better if I imagine that two women, sort of ward-resses, are holding her. They twist her arms behind her back and lift her skirt to show her to me. Then one of them takes out my erect organ and forces the girl to please me with her mouth. I can imagine the look of fear and disgust on her face, but she has to do it. There is no pleasure in it for her, and that really excites me (Barros, 1970).

These fantasies are deeply rooted in our culture; they are the traditional male/female stereotypes taken to their ultimate and most extreme sexual conclusion. The sadist and the masochist are the two poles of male and female carried beyond reality. Men and women line up somewhere on the continuum; for most people who have these fantasies, the fantasies are nothing more than possible magnifications of our larger culture. As Gebhard writes:

Sadomasochism is embedded in our culture since our culture operates on the basis of dominance-submission relationships, and aggression is socially valued. Even our gender relationships have been formulated in a framework conducive to sadomasochism: the male is supposed to be dom-

inant and aggressive sexually and the female reluctant or submissive (Gebhard, 1976).

While many people have sadomasochistic fantasies, few act them out. Morton Hunt (1974) found that 5 percent of the men and 2 percent of the women in his study had received sexual gratification from inflicting pain on their partner. Five times as many single men had engaged in sadism in contrast to married men; twice as many men and women under 35 years of age had been involved in sadistic activities. Hunt found that 2.5 percent of the men and 4.6 percent of the women in his study had been sexually aroused by pain being inflicted on them by their partners.

Sadism seems to be a deeply ingrained aspect of Western civilization. It was often an integral part of justice. In England, after the restoration of the monarchy in the 17th century, the judges who had condemned Charles I to death were sentenced to die. The court sentence read:

You shall go from hence to the place from whence you came, and from that place shall be drawn upon a hurdle to the place of execution, and there shall hang by the neck until half dead, and shall be cut down alive, and your privy members cut off before your face and thrown into the fire, your belly ripped up and your bowels burnt, your head to be severed from your body, your body shall be divided into four quarters, and disposed as his Majesty shall see fit (in Taylor, 1970).

It is an intergal aspect of warfare. Following the massacre of the Cheyenne at Sand Creek in 1864, one witness testified before a Senate committee:

I saw one squaw cut open with an unborn child, as I thought, lying by her side. Captain Soule told me that such was the fact. I saw the body of White Antelope with the privates cut off, and I heard a soldier say he was going to make a tobacco pouch out of them. I saw one squaw whose privates had been cut out (in The Council on Interracial Books for Children, 1971).

The atrocities committed in Vietnam by both sides often revealed a sexual component. Female torture is often an integral element of imprisonment or interrogation. Susan Brownmiller (1976) wrote:

Torture of female political prisoners traditionally includes rape or variations of genital abuse. Whether sadistic torture leads by its own logic to the infliction of sexual pain, or whether the motive of eliciting political information is merely a pretext for the commission of hostile sex acts, the end results for a moman is almost inevitable (Brownmiller, 1976).

Sadism derives its name from the Marquis de Sade (1740-1814), a French nobleman and writer, who was inprisoned because of his strange sexual practices and cruelty, both in word and deed. When the Bastile was stormed in 1789, signifying the beginning of the French Revolution, all prisoners were set free but the Marquis. Masochism derives its name from the German novelist Leopold von Sacher-Masoch (1836-1895), the most influential writer following Goethe, whose works focused on the erotic degradation of men by women.

But it is de Sade who has captured the modern imagination. He applied a ruthless logic to his cruelty, inventing reasonable rationales for the *naturalness* of his acts. For him, sex is the ultimate expression of nature; it demands the total subjection of human beings to its impulses, even if these impulses ultimately are destructive. The French philosopher, Albert Camus, in discussing postwar society, wrote of de Sade:

Sade's success in our day is explained by the dream that he had in common with contemporary thought: the demand for total freedom, and dehumanization coldly planned by the intelligence.

The reduction of man to an object of experiment, the rule that specifies the relation between the will to power and man as an object, the sealed laboratory that is the scene of this monstrous experiment, are lessons which the theoreticians of power will discover again when they come to organizing the age of slavery (Camus, 1956).

There are significantly fewer sadists than masochists, and relatively few sadomasochists are exclusively sadists or masochists. Pain in itself is not what the masochist seeks, nor usually is it what the sadist wishes to give. A masochist receives no pleasure from accidentally cutting or burning him or herself. The pain has to be part of a drama; sadomasochism is theatre in which the play is carefully planned. Scripts are given out to each player. The play is either structured or un-

The Marquis de Sade (1740-1814) Culver Pictures, Inc. New York.

structured. Gerald and Caroline Greene, who call sadomasochism the last taboo, described the structured and unstructured scenario. In the structured scenario:

> the couple can agree to go into a scene with fairly rigid outlines, even down to dialogue. The submissive can thus work out (and in a sense control) the various stages of the impending punishment, even perhaps deciding at what point to interject intercourse; the couple can agree how much begging off, stalling, imploring, is or is not turning on, how much pain is to be given, and shown (or mimed) . . .

> In the unstructured . . . the dominant obviously carries the greater onus. He/she must take the initiative, while the submissive follows a lead, sensing perhaps more thrill in the unknown . . . responding in kind to the ordering around, the particular amount of touching and humiliation and punishment allotted and designed (Greene and Greene, 1974).

Within this scenario, to be effective, certain conditions must be met for the masochist, according to the Greenes. The scene should resemble as closely as possible the original situation which gave rise to the sadomasochistic impulse. If, for example, it began when the man was whipped with a rod across his buttocks by his angry mother when he was a child, that scene shoud be recreated. But the scenario should not give rise to other feelings such as anger or disgust that would interfere with the sexual feelings. These feelings would compete with the sexual ones and perhaps blot out the erotic pleasure. Furthermore, the punishment should not be too strong or too weak. If it were too strong, the pain might overwhelm the erotic feelings; if the punishment were too weak, it would not excite the masochist sufficiently. Finally, at the time the scene takes place, the person must be sexually

aroused or desire to be (Greene and Greene, 1974).

The causes of sadomasochism in the individual are not at all understood in a definitive sense. Sadists may have been taught to have contempt and disgust for anything sexual. Since sexuality is wrong, the sadist punishes his or her partner for their indulgence; guilt is resolved and projected onto the other. Or sadists may be suffering from feelings of inferiority; failing to dominate the larger world, the sadist dominates his partner. Or sadism might reflect hostility toward parents (Coleman, 1972; Moore, 1969; Thorpe, et. al., 1961.)

Masochism also may find its root in disgust of sexuality. Pain and punishment erase the sin of sex, and since sex is punished during childhood and adolescence, the association between sex and pain is easy to establish. In this system, guilt is quickly relieved: the masochist receives his pleasure at the same time he is receiving his punishment for that pleasure; or he has a right to experience pleasure having first experienced the punishment (Gebhard, 1976).

## Transsexuality

In transsexuality, the individual's gender identity and sexual anatomy are at war. A biological male believes himself to be a woman; a biological female believes herself to be a male. They firmly believe that by some strange quirk of fate, they have been given the body of the wrong sex. James Morris who became Jan Morris through transsexual surgery recalled:

> I was three or perhaps four years old when I realized that I had been born into the wrong body, and should really be a girl. I remember the moment well, and it was the earliest memory of my life.

> It was also worrying me, for though my body often

yearned to give, to yield, to open itself, the machine was wrong (Morris, 1974).

There are no definitive answers on the causes of transsexualism. Transsexualism may begin in childhood; it is detectable sometimes in the first two years after birth. Parents often remark that their male children who by age four or five identify themselves psychologically as girls had acted as girls from the very beginning. Throughout childhood, these children engaged in girl's activity, play, and dress; they moved, walked, and ran as girls. Their playmates were girls. The parents may stand by and watch this behavior, hop-ing their transsexual child is merely going through a phase; others – especially the same-sex parent – may even encourage these behaviors. By the time the transsexual child reaches late adolescence, he may request an operation to change his genitals to those of a woman's. By this time, the adolescent has usually learned the roles associated with femininity so well that he can easily pass as a woman in most situations. Even then the transsexual is still usually discontent with his male body; eventually he requests a sex-change operation to align his sexual anatomy with his female gender identity. Then

Women's tennis star Renee Richards (left) was formerly a male opthamologist (right).

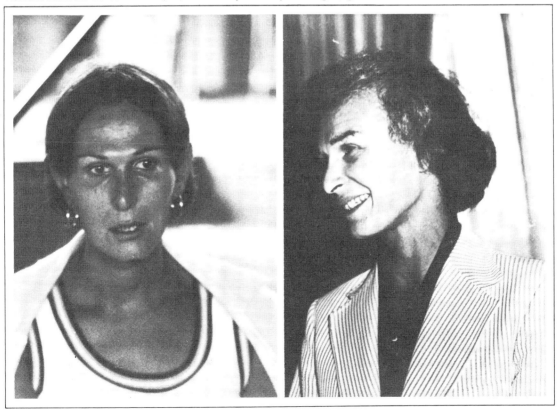

he becomes she. Of the estimated 10,000 trans-sexuals in the United States, about 3,000 to 4,000 have undergone surgery to correct nature's anatomical "mistake."

**Tranvestism**

Transvestites are men who become sexually excited by wearing women's clothes or garments. The origin is usually in the faulty development of their gender roles. As we have seen in an earlier chapter, the ·genitals determine the gender a child will identify with. But for some reason, the connection between penis = boy is not as firm

for transvestites. The boy, however, knows that he is male; it is only later, after he has firmly established his masculinity, that he will dress as a woman. Some transvestites are homosexuals but most are heterosexuals.

Transvestities have no desire to undertake a sex change operation; rather they believe that they have both masculine and feminine personalities within themselves. Their feminine personality appears when they cross dress; sometimes they give their female personality a name. Cross dressing is very popular in American and English comedy. Bob Hope frequently dresses as a woman in his shows or movies and Flip Wilson

Whosoever loveth wisdom is righteous but he that
keepeth company with fowl is weird.

                                        Woody Allen

has invented a female character for himself
whom he calls Geraldine. In comedy, cross
dressing is a source of humor perhaps because it
expresses traits considered feminine and hence
unacceptable for western men. Nevertheless,
men can identify with these expressions in comedy, and yet simultaneously reject them through
laughter.

Many transvestites are known as such to their
wives and families; they are able to cross dress at
home as a result. They may even walk around
town dressed as a woman and not be recognized. A recent study (Janus et. al., 1977) of the
sexual practices of men in power describes cross
dressing as a frequent practice. The authors
write:

> Politicians, who cannot afford the risk of being dis-
> covered in public got up in high drag, will some-
> times delight in the deception of wearing frivolous
> frilly women's undergarments underneath a man's
> suit, complete with vest, secretly luxuriating in the
> feel of silk next to their skin. Major policy speeches
> have been delivered to the full House and Senate
> by congressmen dressed like this. . . .

Heterosexual transvestites are usually quite
conventional in their masculine dress and attitudes. Dressed as women, they may become
sexually aroused, and masturbate or make love
with a woman. There are no studies showing the
prevalence of transvestities in large part because
of the secrecy surrounding this behavior by its
participants.

## Voyeurism

Voyeurs receive sexual pleasure and excitement
from secretly watching sex acts. In order to become aroused, the man must hide and remain
unseen and the woman or couple must be unaware of his presence. The excitement is inten-

sified by the possibility of being discovered.
Sometimes the voyeur will masturbate while he
is peering through the window or keyhole. Some
brothels and sex theatres have one-way mirrors
in which men may view (for a price) couples
making love or women performing lesbian acts.

Very little study has been done of voyeurs,
nine out of ten of whom are men (McCary,
1978). If a man feels sexually inadequate, then
he may gain orgasm by merely watching others
engaged in sexual intercourse while he himself is
fantasizing. In this manner, the voyeur is freed
from worrying about his potency; he may have a
vicarious orgasm. At the same time, he may receive a sense of superiority over those he is
watching; he knows something which they don't
know and which would annoy, embarrass, or
anger them if they knew he was watching them.
Voyeurs tend to be younger men and their viewing is a transient phenomenon; it may be nothing
much more than excessive curiosity about the
sexual acts in which they have not yet had much
experience (Stoller, 1977).

## Zoophilia

Zoophilia, or bestiality, involves sexual satisfaction derived from intercourse with animals. Although conception is biologically impossible
from such matings, classical mythology includes
satyrs (human/goat), centaurs (human/horse),
and the Minotaur (human/bull); Zeus transformed himself into a bull for intercourse
with Europa, a swan for Leda, a serpent for
Persephone.

Kinsey reported that about 8 percent of the
men and 3 percent of the women surveyed had
experienced at least one sexual contact with
animals. Seventeen percent of the men who had
been reared on farms had had such contact, but

these activities accounted for less than 1 percent of their total sexual outlet.

## QUESTIONS

1. What is a sexual variation? Are sexual variations different in kind or magnitude from more conventional sexual behavior?

2. How common is incestuous behavior? Incestuous feelings? What is the difference between the two?

3. Sado-masochism has become more open in recent years. Why? Is Western culture rooted in sado-masochism as some theorists suggest?

•

Leonardo De Vinci's "Leda and the Swan", A major classical myth.

**4.** Some hospitals that perform transsexual operations are having second thoughts about the benefits of such operations. Does a person have an inherent right to a sex change operation? How would you react to a friend who was transsexual?

**5.** Transvestites are often ridiculed, but cross-dressing is a fairly common component of English and American comedy. Bob Hope and Charlie Chaplin have appeared in roles dressed as women. Why is cross-dressing a part of our comic heritage?

# Readings

### Few Transsexuals Adjust Easily

Betty Liddick

*Transsexuals believe they are prisoners in the bodies of the wrong sex. They are men or women whose gender identity conflicts with their anatomy. A person with a penis believes himself (herself) to be a woman; a person with a vagina believes herself (himself) to be a man. No one knows how many transsexuals there are in America, but estimates run as high as 20,000. Nor does anyone know the origin of transsexuality, although – as with any sexual variation – there are plenty of theories, none of which can be validated. Some claim it is a result of prenatal hormonal influences, others blame it on the mother, who is the perennial scapegoat of Freudian misogynists.*

*But whatever the cause, the life of a transsexual is seldom easy. As one transsexaul said, "Sometimes you hear the dumb remark that you have the best of both worlds. More often than not, you have the worst."*

In the beginning she hated going out in public. She would hole up in the apartment and let the phone ring and live on raisins for days.

When she did go out, she hid her hands. They were suitable hands for a fourth-string tackle maybe, but broad and thick for a woman. A clue. She would pile on more makeup than a $10 hooker and slouch along, trying to look shorter than 5-7. She was tormented. Could anybody "read-her" – find her out?

These days Canary Conn strides along Hollywood's Sunset Strip full of confidence, blonde hair flying, face unmadeup and tilted toward the sun. Recently she was towering on four-inch heels when she entered the dark glow of Cyrano for lunch. She ordered sea bass and watched the traffic on Sunset. Slowly she began to smile.

Miss Conn was remembering. Eight years ago, only a few blocks from here, she had tried to kill herself. She had stepped in front of a car high-balling along Sunset. The car stopped.

It was at that moment, granted an extra breath on this planet, that Canary Conn, who was then Danny O'Connor – an 18-year-old husband, father, winner of the best male vocalist award in a national talent contest – decided life was worth living. As a woman.

She had surgery to change male genitalia to female.

And after the final operation, when she nearly bled to death in a Tijuana hospital, she stopped caring what others thought about her. She realized she had changed her gender for herself, not the world. She was free.

Which is not to say roses now suddenly bloom in her presence and pizzas are always delivered hot. "I'm happier than I was before," Miss Conn will say, "but I won't really be happy till social pressures stop, until people start to realize transsexuals are human beings."

Miss Conn's singing career is stalled. She has been unable to get a recording contract as she did as a man. Her sisters hold her responsible for the "murder" of Danny. Romantic love eludes her.

"Men just don't understand this trip," she said, about the sex change. "It just freaks them out, justifiably so. It's not an easy life."

And if it is difficult for Miss Conn, who has feminine features, a measure of talent and self-assurance, it must be anguish for others – those who go public and risk ridicule and those who submerge themselves in happy obscurity, all the while praying no errant Army record or job reference will surface to betray them.

Said Wendy Hall, an attractive transsexual who runs a music service for composers and song writers: "Sometimes you hear the dumb remark that you have the best of both worlds. More often than not, you have the worst."

Carol Katz, for example, said her salary is $6000 a year less since her sex reassignment. As a man she worked in law enforcement but as a woman has been unsuccessful in returning to that field. Now clerking is the only job she can find. (Title 7 of the Civil Rights Act forbids discrimination on the basis of sex but no court case has interpreted the law to include transsexuals.)

Though many staunchly insist they have no regrets, only two out of ten transsexuals make a happy adjustment, according to estimates from the Erickson Educational Foundation, an informational clearing house on the subject in Baton Rouge, La.

Female-to-male transsexuals seem to have an easier time because, even with slight builds, they blend into society. Some male-to-females with strong features and rangy bodies stand out.

Erickson director Zelda Suplee said with compassion: "They feel like Marilyn Monroe and look like Johnny Cash."

Bizarre and bewildering though it may seem to some, transsexualism is not a new phenomenon. It has existed in mythology, Greek and Roman history and the tribal cultures of North American Indians.

However, it was two Californians, Renee Richards, a Newport Beach ophthalmologist, and, to a lesser degree, Steve Dain, an Emeryville gym teacher, who brought the subject to national consciousness.

Such cases present a tangle of medical, legal and social issues and, almost inevitably, stir moral repugnance.

"Especially disturbing – and not to the religious alone – is the body mutilation and destruction of fertility that must accompany sex transformation procedures," writes psychiatrist and gender identity pioneer Robert J. Stoller in his book, "Sex and Gender."

Dr. Charles Stone, a psychiatrist at the University of California at Los Angeles, believes many people are personally and emotionally threatened in contemplating transsexuals wanting their genitals removed. "And it is typical that rather than be in touch with those feelings and expressing them, people take a moral or legal view."

Despite the supposed blurring of sex roles these days, transsexuals say they could not feel complete without the surgery to match mind and body.

Though cosmetically remarkable, surgical results are far from physically perfect. The Stanford University Gender Dysphoria Program in 1974 reported 18 to 38 patients has postoperative complications. (In female-to-male surgeries, complications were further broken down to include rejection to testicular implants, infection and "desire to shoot the genitals of the surgeon with a shotgun.")

More than a dozen university hospitals and private clinics around the country offer the operations.

Reputable centers require psychiatric evaluation, a period of living in the new role and hormonal treatment. Surgical techniques vary but the usual male-to-female procedure is to remove the penis and testes and use the penile tissue to form a vagina. Cosmetic surgery, including breast augmentation may follow.

A hysterectomy and mastectomy are performed in female-to-male patients. Artificial testicles are implanted and a penis is constructed from skin grafts.

In one common procedure two prostheses are fitted postoperatively, one that provides sufficient rigidity for penetration during intercourse, another that serves as a urinary conduit.

The legitimacy of surgery for true transsexuals is not open to question, especially since there is no psychiatric treatment for them, Stone said. "These people are not freaks. They are not delusional. They have a dilemma."

But at the same time Stone, other specialists and a growing number of transsexuals fighting for their civil rights claim there are an excessive number of surgeries today.

Too many are being done on the wrong people and too few cases are adequately followed up, they say.

At least ten times as many people apply for surgery as should have it, Stone estimated. The gender clinic at Stanford rejects 75 per cent of its applicants. Stone approved only 13 of the 100 people he screened.

"That means 87 people were mad at me," he said. Many said they would commit suicide if he did not approve them. He told them threats were unacceptable. Stone screened out effeminate homosexuals who wanted the surgery to please their lovers, men who wanted to only imitate women, and psychotics.

"What is really deplorable and shocking to the medical profession is that there are places where people just show up and the surgery is done," Stone said.

Such practices invite malpractice suits and the risk of patients becoming "mentally out – psychotic," said Stone, adding that he has seen postoperative instances of both.

Irresponsible sex-change surgery may doom some individuals to social suicide, transsexuals said. Consider the men who simply don't pass as women.

"They should have just tried to live the way they were because they were at least more successful that way," one transsexual said. Unless they shut the door and never look in the mirror, they are going to be detected every time.

"They have to go to the gas station, the drugstore, the grocery, and they're going to be called "sir" in all those places. That's the horror story.

"There are a lot of transsexuals who are mistakes."

Betty Liddick, *Few Transsexuals Adjust Easily*, Copyright © Los Angeles Times. Reprinted by permission.

### Incest: An American Epidemic

Barry Siegall

*Incest is the most forbidden form of sexuality known to human beings. Yet many people have had overtly incestuous experiences, and most people have had incestuous fantasies at some point in their lives even if they have not recog-*

*nized them as such. Incest remains the most dif-*
*ficult problem for most people to discuss. What is*
*the impact of incest on a child's sexual develop-*
*ment? What can be done to protect children*
*from incest?*

She is a petite 50-year-old secretary with close-
cropped blonde hair, oversized gold hoop ear-
ings and a voice worn rough by alcohol and
cigarettes. After two failed marriages and a
homosexual affair, Jill is in a suburban psychiatric
hostial, a victim of chronic severe depression and
alcoholism. Sitting in an afternoon group therapy
session, she wants to talk about her current
problems.

No, responds group leader Susan Forward,
let's talk about when you were 13. Let's talk
about the incest.

Jill protests, then reluctantly agrees.

"I was almost 13," she begins, talking slowly.
"It was the happiest, best,, proudest day of my
life. I was to give a piano recital. I feel so proud,
so good about myself for the first time. My parents had bought me a nice dress, and my dad
had invited all his busines friends.

"The recital was wonderful. There was a party
afterward back home. Mom passed out. Both my
parents always drank too much. Everyone left
finally, and my dad came and sat down next
to me. He was drunk. He put his arm around
me and said how proud he was. His arm felt
good. . . . "

Mrs. Forward, a former actress turned psychiatric social worker, interrupts. "It felt good because for once, you were Daddy's girl?"

Jill looks down at her hands. "It felt good because for once, I was anybody's girl."

She started to sob. "But then things just
got too heavy. I don't know what happened. It
hurt. . . . "

Mrs. Forward interrupts again. "You had intercourse?"

The patient nods, unable to answer yes. "I
hated him afterward. I wanted to kill him. On
that, of all days. . . . Talking about this is making
me sick. I feel nauseated. Why are we talking
about it? It was a long time ago, far away."

Mrs. Forward stares at Jill. "It's not so far away
if it still makes you physically sick."

Before the afternoon is over, half of the eight-
person therapy group are sobbing in private cor-
ners of the room, Mrs. Forward has joked that
she wishes she owned the Kleenex concession,
and two more patients have admitted to incestuous experiences in their childhood.

Susan Forward, who holds a master's degree
in social work from USC, first became interested
in the study of incest about four years ago. She
says that in each of the dozen therapy groups she
leads each week at institutions such as the
Ross-Loos Medical Center and Van Nuys Psychiatric Hospital, "one of the women would
always break down and admit to incest. Then
one or two others would say, 'hey, well, yeah,
me too. . . . '

"This was such a continuous pattern. Incest
appeared consistently to be at the root of so
much female pathology. Disturbed relationships,
sexual dysfunction, severe depression, migraine
headaches, repressed rage, guilt, self-loathing.
Everything."

As Mrs. Forward noticed this pattern, psychologist Hank Giarretto in San Jose was starting a
child sexual abuse treatment program for Santa
Clara County's juvenile probation department.

At that time, in 1971, authorities generally estimated the rate of incest to be one case per
1 million population, although they had no
hard statistics.

But out of a county population of slightly more

than 1 million — predominately middle-class white, with the highest median income of any California metropolitan area — Giarretto in his first year received not one case, but 30. Last year he handled 270 cases. This year, he will treat between 500 and 600.

"I believe," he said, "that incest is epidemic in America."

Incest, sex researchers William Masters and Virgina Johnson agree, "is much commoner in this country than we care to admit."

(Incest is formally defined as sexual activity between perons who are related to each other so closely that they are legally forbidden to marry.)

So Mrs. Forward started what she calls "my personal crusade to wake up people about this. We deal with rape, we deal with sexual dysfunctions. Incest is the only sex problem we are not dealing with."

Mrs. Forward quickly found plenty of reasons why incest is not talked about openly: California laws and court decisions that require medical authorities to report incest cases to the police; possible prison sentences of 1 to 50 years; and the social stigma and general fear of identification.

But more important than all these influences, say some therapists, is the simple fact that many people tend to be unsympathetic about incest victims, to regard incest as a mutually willing act, to ostracize the participants rather than offer help. The topic of incest, in fact, more often than not elicits off-color jokes. . . .

So some people might be tempted to ignore Susan Forward when she mentions that the average age of an incest victim is 11, that studies show the child is forced or threatened 60% of the time, and that incest occurs "everywhere from Bel-Air to Westchester, involving normal, hardworking, law-abiding citizens."

But it is not so easy for Mrs. Forward to ignore

all this, because she deals daily with the aftereffects of incest that persist years later.

In some studies, as many as 80% of nonorgasmic women, 40% of drug abusive women and 25% of prostitutes examined had incestuous backgrounds.

By exploiting a child's naive need for love, therapists say, a parent destroys that child's sense of trust and security in the home. The results, they add, can be horrendous.

Consider Diane Johnson.

In Diane's medical records, her mother is described as an "ambulatory psychotic" who never could "attend to the patient's needs at any point in her life." The father is described as "a rather passive supporter of the more dominant mother."

As far as Diane can remember, neither parent ever held her.

Now 23, Diane sits in one of Mrs. Forward's psychodrama therapy groups at a local psychiatric hospital, telling her story. She has short-cropped brown hair and a gentle, but distant, manner. The facts are true, although the names are changed.

"All I remember," she begins, "is going upstairs in the bedroom and both of my brothers approaching me. I was 6 years old. The first brother was 12, the next 7. My older brother had intercourse with me. I cannot remember whether the 7 year old did anything or not. This continued off and on from then until I was 13. With both brothers, but mainly the older one.

"The reason I never told my parents was, I remember after it first happened, I went downstairs and my brothers told my parents that I had my clothes off, so my father beats the hell out of me, so after that I never told them anything.

"I thought what was happening was maybe

normal . . . But I just felt something funny was going on. I didn't know what it was. I knew it wasn't right, like even when I was a child, like when I was 8 or 9 years old, I knew it wasn't right, something was wrong somewhere, but I couldn't define it."

Finally, Diane told her uncle what was happening.

"My uncle told my aunt about it, and then, I think I was 14, he told me that he was going to show me that men weren't all bad. His wife was crippled and I guess he wasn't getting satisfied. So when my brothers stopped, my uncle started. This went on from the time I was 14 until 17.

"There is a reason why I couldn't stop: Fear. He wouldn't let me."

Finally, Diane escaped from her uncle the only way she knew how. One day she went home, swallowed every pill in the house and drank a bottle of liquor. It would be the first of six suicide attempts she would make in the next six years.

She has, all told, been hospitalized in psychiatric wards five times since the age of 17 and undergone repeated shock treatments. She tells her doctors she "doesn't fit in this generation," talks at times of a "white wedding dress," and thinks she is "paying for my sins" when she suffers undiagnosed leg and back pains.

Above all, she is filled with guilt and self-loathing because she remembers enjoying some of the sexual experiences.

A psychologist who tested her writes that Diane "projects a world where dogs are tearing each other apart, where blood flows and explosions occur . . . Her world is a dark and martial arena . . .

"Her anger appears to be directed principally at her mother and men from whom she expected love and understanding . . . and alternately introjected in the form of self-hate and depression . . .

She believes that she will be all right if she finds someone to understand her."

But over the years, her various therapists have noted a grim range of diagnoses: "devoid of all meaningful social relationships" . . . "presentation is one of an ambulatory schizophrenic " . . . "hopeless, empty, quite depleted" . . . "suicidal" . . . and 'chronic depression."

The supervising psychiatrist's final remark: "There is an inner emptiness that is chilling."

Diane Johnson's story is vivid, but not all that unusual to Mrs. Forward. In her six years of leading psychodrama therapy sessions, she says she has encountered "hundreds" of incest cases.

Most of those in her groups are also treated by psychiatrists, who refer their patients to Mrs. Forward for additional therapy.

The thumbnail sketches she offers, drawn only from her personal caseload, are painful to consider, "Of course, I see the extreme," she points out. "The others are not as traumatized."

Among others, there is the young girl seduced by both her grandfather and her uncle – a priest – and then blamed by her parents for what happened. There is the 5-year-old girl molested until the age of 9 by her totally blind father, who threatened her with loss of food and clothing if she wasn't "good." And there is the 6-year-old girl repeatedly seduced until the age of 9 by her grandfather, a minister.

In this last case, the girl's mother knew well what the grandfather was doing, having herself been regularly molested by him as a child. But because she wanted to be alone with her second husband, she sent her daughter to the grandfather every weekend.

It is not rare at all, says Mrs. Forward, for a mother in an incest case simply to refuse to believe her daughter's story, because she does not want to ruin her marriage. In one case, a mother warned her daughter she would commit suicide if her marriage fell apart. In another, a mother on her death bed made her 18-year-old daughter promise to forgive the father, who had been having intercourse with the girl since she was 5.

The aftereffects for the women in these cases include recurrent migraine headaches, chronic depression, suicidal impulse and sexual frigidity. Partially because of these problems, many incest victims experience severe marital conflicts as they move into their early 30s.

It would be wrong, however, to conclude from these case histories that all incest incidents involve younger girls and older men.

Sister-brother relationships are the most common, but therapists consider them the least traumatic and damaging, because they usually represent peer-group experimentation rather than exploitation by an adult figure.

Grandfather-granddaughter relationships are more frequent than expected. "Often the mother virtually gives her daughter to her father," says Mrs. Forward, "almost like a human sacrifice, to please her father, to get approval from Dad."

Mother-son relationships are much rarer, but are considered the most traumatic. Often they involve fondling or overtly seductive behavior by the mother, rather than actual sexual intercourse.

One of Mrs. Forward's patients – Carl, a 41-year-old store clerk – suffers from suicidal impulses, severe depression and a sexual identity crisis. He links these problems to the fact that his mother continuously bared her breasts, undressed and used the toilet in front of him when he was a child.

At a recent group therapy session, he burst into angry sobs. "Why did she show me? I didn't want to see. She ruined my life, and I've ruined everyone else's. I'm homosexual or bisexual or whatever. I'm not a man. I can't function as a man . . ." He stopped, in tears.

Mrs. Forward also has found some incidents of homosexual incest among her patients. There was the yound girl raped by her older sister, the 32-year-old plumber who experienced oral sex with his 8-year-old son, and the 16-year-old boy – raised in foster homes – who was raped at razor point on Christmas Day by his natural father.

The next month, the boy withdrew from school and was committed to a psychiatric hospital, diagnosed as suicidal and homicidal.

In the other half, where arrests are made, results of the investigation are then presented to Juvenile Court and the district attorney's office, which must decide whether to prosecute. On the average, the DA decides in about half of these cases not to file a formal complaint, because for one reason or another, he does not think he can prove his case in court.

So in the end, only a quarter of the incest cases referred to the police end up in court. Moreover, many medical and law enforcement officials acknowledge that most cases go unreported in the first place; only 118 cases of sexual abuse were officially referred to the LAPD abused-child unit in 1976.

The reasons are clear.

Medical authorities generally do not want to lose what they see as their therapeutic role by handing patients over to the police. There also is a reluctance to break up any family, even an incestuous one. And many cases, of course, do not even come to the attention of the therapists.

If there is a more effective deterrent to incest than the law, it might be found in simply listening to someone such as Tammy Balker, 25, describe how she feels about her father.

Tammy's marriage broke up in part because of her semifrigidity – "sex just doesn't do **anything** for me" – and the breakup caused the severe depression that brought her to a local psychiatric hospital. She has suffered from unrelenting, incapacitating headaches for years. She tells her story to Mrs. Forward in a sweet, almost angelic voice.

"I was in the third grade, living with my grandparents, when my father came to live with us. I had always thought my father was fantastic. He reminded me of Elvis Presley and I always had these dreams about marrying Elvis Presley and I always thought my father was so good-looking and that he was so great and so wonderful. . . .

"My father asked me one night when he first had started living there, 'Tammy, why don't you come and sleep in my bed tonight?' And I didn't think anything of it, and I said OK, because I thought it was a big deal to sleep in my daddy's bed because he finally came home to me instead of living with my stepmother.

"And so that night he started saying, 'Why don't you touch me here, or touch me there' and I was really afraid. And so then he said, 'Well, why don't you just start kissing me down there?' . . .

Eventually, he forced an act of oral sex on her.

"I was scared to death, I didn't know what in the world was happening. I remember throwing up, and all my father said was that he was sorry . . .

"It seemed like after he did that to me, it was like he just went downhill. He was the only father I had, but from then on, I just tried to stay away from him. Now I don't even want to talk to my father at all."

Mrs. Forward asks Tammy if she feels betrayed.

"I think," she answers, "that if ever I saw a man do that to my kids, I would kill him. I would really kill him. Knowing what I have gone through in my mind, I would kill him. . . ."

Psychiatric social worker Susan Forward belives that regardless how seductive a young daughter may be, it is the responsibility of the adult to repress incestuous impulses. A basic goal in her group psychodrama treatment of incest victims is to relieve their guilt and make them understand how they were exploited.

Barry Siegal, "Incest: An American Epidemic", *Los Angeles Times*, August 21, 1977. Copyright © 1977 Los Angeles Times. Reprinted by permission.

### *Excerpt from* Psychopathia Sexualis

Dr. Richard von Krafft-Ebing

*In the late 1800's Richard von Krafft-Ebing made a significant contribution to the knowledge of human sexuality (and sensational Victorian Europe) by publishing his analysis of sexual perversion.*

The following case of *kid-glove-fetishism* is peculiarly adapted to show the origin of fetishistic associations as well as the enormous influence permanently exercised by such an association although itself based upon a psycho-physical and morbid predisposition.

Mr. Z., an American, thirty-three years of age, manufacturer, for eight years enjoying a happy married life, blessed with offspring; consulted me for a peculiar, troublesome glove-fetishism. He despised himself on account of it, and said it brought him well nigh to the verge of despair and even insanity.

He claimed to come of thoroughly sound parents, but since infancy had been neuropathic and very excitable. By nature he was very sensual, whereas his wife was very frigid.

At the age of nine, he was seduced by schoolmates to practice masturbation, which gratified him immensely, and he yielded to it with passion.

One day when sexually excited he found a small bag of chamois skin. He stripped it over his member and experienced thereby great sensual pleasure. After that he used it for onanistic manipulations, put it around his scrotum and carried it about with him day and night. This aroused in him an unusual interest for leather in general, but particularly for kid gloves.

With puberty this centered entirely in ladies' kid gloves, which simply fascinated him. If he touched his penis with one such glove it produced erection and even ejaculation.

Men's gloves did not excite him in the least, although he loved to wear them.

In consequence, nothing about a woman attracted him but her kid gloves. These were his fetish. They must be long, with many buttons, and if worn out, dirty and saturated with perspiration at the fingertips, they were preferable. Women wearing such, even if ugly and old, had a particular charm for him. Ladies with silk or cotton gloves did not attract him. He always looked at her gloves first when meeting a lady. As for the rest, he took very little interest in the female sex.

When he could shake hands with a lady gloved with kid, the contact with the soft, warm leather would cause erection and orgasm in him.

Whenever he could get hold of such a glove he would at once retire to a lavatory, wrap it around his genitals and masturbate.

Later on when visiting brothels he would beg the prostitute to put on long gloves provided by himself for that purpose, which act alone would excite him so much that ejaculation ensued forthwith.

Z. became a collector of ladies' kid gloves. He would hide away hundreds of pairs in various places. These he would count and gloat over in his spare time, "as a miser would over his gold," place them over his genitals, bury his face in a pile of them, put one on his hand and then masturbate. This gave him more intense pleasure than coitus.

He made covers for his penis of them, or suspensories, wearing them for days. He preferred black, soft leather. He would fasten ladies' kid gloves around his waist in such a fashion that they would, apron-like, hang down over his genitals.

After marriage this fetishism grew worse. As a rule he was only virile when he put a pair of his wife's gloves by her head during coitus so that he could kiss them.

The acme of pleasure was when he could persuade his wife to put on kid gloves and thus touch his genitals previous to cohabitaion.

Z. felt very unhappy on account of this fetishism, and made repeated but vain attempts to free himself of the curse.

Whenever he came across the word, or the picture of a glove in novels, fashion-plates, advertisements, etc., he was simply fascinated. At the theatre his eyes were riveted on the hands of the actresses. He could scarcely tear himself away from the show-window of glove-dealers.

He often would stuff long gloves with wool or some such material to make them resemble arms and hands. Then he would rub his member between these artificial arms until he had achieved his object.

It was his habit to take ladies' kid gloves to bed with him and wrap them around his penis until he could feel them like a large leathern member between his legs.

In the larger towns he bought from the cleaners ladies' gloves which had not been called for, but preferred those most soiled and worn. Twice he admitted to have yielded to the temptation to steal such gloves, although in every other respect he was absolutely correct. When in a crowd he must touch ladies' hands whenever possible. At his office he allowed no opportunity to pass without shaking hands with ladies, in order to feel for "at least a second the soft, warm leather." His wife must wear as much as possible kid gloves or such made of chamois, with which he provided her lavishly.

At his office he always had ladies' gloves lying on his desk. Not an hour passed in which he did not touch and stroke them. When especially excited (sexually) he put such a glove in his mouth and chewed it.

Other articles of the female toilet, likewise other parts of the female body besides the hand, did not attract him. Z. felt much depressed about his anomaly. He felt ashamed to look into the innocent eyes of his children, and prayed God to protect them from this curse of their father.

# Unit 6

# Sexuality and Society

## The Law and Sexual Relationships

Paternity suits, popularly considered a hopeless trap for the innocent male, are devastatingly rigged against the female. The requirements in most jurisdictions are barbaric in terms of consideration for human dignity. For example, in a paternity trial, the female must describe, in open Court in very explicit terms how, when, and where the male defendent's penis entered her vagina and the Court record must show that she used those terms. The entire procedure implicitly indicates that the Court regards her as a whore, and that the only

---

Politics is a strange mixture of reason and un-reason. As political scientist Harold Laswell (1960) observed, it is often the means by which the irrational bases of society come to the surface. Politics may be viewed as the conflict between groups, interests, and ideas, conflict that is intensified when it touches emotional attitudes about the way one feels people *should* behave. This view is particularly true when politics becomes involved with sex and morality. People become especially indignant when they want to coerce others to act in certain ways, especially when sex, the *bete noire* of Western culture, is concerned. The result is the establishment of punitive laws, prohibiting various forms of sexual behavior.

It is generally true that the greater the sexual content or degree of deviance of an offense against such laws, the greater the punishment. The relative harm the offense inflicts on individuals or society is not likely to be considered. Thus, men convicted of homosexuality or exhibitionism often serve greater sentences than do those convicted of armed robbery or murder. Almost all sexual offenders receive longer prison terms than do politicians convicted of corruption, bankers convicted of embezzlement, or corporation executives convicted of fraud. For both criminal and sexual offenses, imprisonment is generally reserved for the poor, the mentally deficient, or the blue-collar worker.

## Sex and Politics

The politics of sex is often characterized by the projection of private motives onto public actions, with the projection rationalized as being for the "common good." Anthony Comstock, for example, was obsessed by sexual purity. He began his career as self-appointed custodian of American virtue in the 1870s, by leading the New York Society for the Suppression of Vice. In a short period, he confiscated 202,679 "obscene pictures and photos"; 64,094 "articles of immoral use of rubber, etc. [contraceptives];" and 26 "obscene pictures, framed on walls of saloons." Almost single-handedly, in 1873, he lobbied passage of the Comstock Law, which made "obscenity" the tool for wholesale interference into any matter related to sex. Comstock ruthlessly pursued Margaret Sanger, early leader of the birth control movement (Kennedy, 1970), and caused a minor sensation by declaring the French painting "September Morning" to be obscene. In retrospect he appears ludicrous, almost pathological. But he was not harmless, for hundreds were sent to prison as a result of his actions; birth control and the liberalization of sex laws were severely restricted. Comstock's efforts inflicted immeasurable injury on thousands of people. (Brown and Leach, 1927).

Nor is Comstock's activity an isolated phenomenon in American history. In fact, he is in the mainstream of our past. The intimate association between sex, politics, and law, which began to be strongly felt in the nineteenth century, continues today.

**In the Past Century**    In our country's earliest days, American elites legislated sexual morality. But sex was not a political issue; there was general consensus concerning sexual values, because most Americans (except for slaves) shared the English cultural heritage. Early in the nineteenth century, however, a pluralistic society began to emerge. The aristocratic elites were challenged by the rising middle class; in the political arena the Federalists were challenged by the Democrats, and the conflict also moved into the sexual sphere. The aristocratic tradition did not rigorously emphasize virginity, sexual purity, nor sexual restraint. The middle class viewed this

reason the Court listens to her at all is for the sake of the taxpayer, in that support for the child (not for her) should be obtained from the father rather than from welfare. The ultimate is reached in at least one state, where, if the girl wishes to give up her baby for adoption, she must somehow persuade the alleged father to sign permission for the adoption, or must publicly state on the record in Court that she has no idea who the father is or what his name may be, thus publicly confessing that she is promiscuous.

Robert Sherwin

---

tradition as additional proof of aristocratic decadence, and the popular literature of the day portrayed the aristocrat as the seducer. Ultimately, the middle class and its sexual ethic triumphed; the triumph of democracy was also the triumph of "virtue." (Fiedler, 1967; Davis, 1957).

Between 1830 and 1850 there was an influx of Irish Catholics, marking the first major immigration of non-English, non-Protestant groups. America had been built on Protestantism; now suddenly its religious base was being threatened. The Irish brought with them Catholicism and "strange" sexual pratices. Their large families signified sensuality and lack of self control, and their priests and nuns were celibate, a foreign "perversion" rejected by Protestants as unnatural. The lurid book *Awful Disclosures of the Hotel Dieu Nunnery*, purported to be a description of monastic life written by a nun. "One of my great duties," she wrote, "was to obey the priests in all things; and this I soon learnt was to live in the practice of criminal intercourse with them." She related only those incidents that could be recalled "without offending a virtuous ear; for some there were, which, although I have been compelled to submit to . . . I would not mention or describe." Her vagueness was a pornographer's delight, and it led militant Protestants to attack monastaries indiscriminately (Monk, 1836, Billington, 1964).

***Slavery***    Sexuality was intimately connected to the slavery controversy. Sexual fantasies had traditionally colored whites' descriptions of blacks. Sir Francis Bacon described the "Spirit of Fornication" as a "little foul ugly Aethiop," and more than one early-day traveler noted that Africans possessed "large Propagators," a recurring sexual fantasy to this day. Black women were believed to be especially passionate (Jordan, 1968).

> Next comes a warmer race, from sable sprung. To love each thought, to lust each nerve is strung; The Samboe dark, and the Mullattoe brown, The Mestize fair, the weel-lim'b Quaderoon, And jetty Afric, from no spurious sire, Warm as her soil, and as her sun – on fire. These spoty dames, well vers'd in Venus' school. Make love an art, and boast they kiss by rule.

The view of blacks as sexually aggressive was firmly rooted in nineteenth century white folklore. Much of that lore was a projection of their own desires onto blacks. The desire for black women – whom they regarded as sexually degraded – was unacceptable both to themselves and to society. Their own sexual desire was denied (and their guilt was cleansed) by attributing it to blacks rather than to themselves. Their own feelings of sexual inadequacy made the black men appear especially sexual and potent. (Jordan, 1968; Handlin, 1957). As abolitionist feeling increased, Southerners spread the opinion that slave revolt would result in the rape and murder of countless white women. Anxieties about black sexuality reinforced the racial and economic aspects of slavery. (Jordan, 1968; Cash, 1941). Abolitionists, in turn, focused much of their attention on the relationships between the planter and his women slaves, accusing Southerners of supporting slavery because of their "love of licentiousness and despotic control." Slavery was evil because it undermined marriage among blacks, removing this means of curtailing their sexual passion (Lloyd, 1938).

Much of the hostility was not against slavery *per se*, but against violations of middle-class sexual norms. The abolitionists misunderstood the relationship of the white male to the black female slave; the planter's sexual prerogatives were not so much the reason he supported slavery as they were a by-product of slavery. Had slavery not violated the abolitionists' sexual norms, it might not have been attacked so strongly.

After the Civil War, Southern codes placed severe restrictions on blacks — politically, economically, legally, and sexually. Interracial marriage was prohibited; blacks who raped white women were lynched or hanged, while whites who raped blacks were generally ignored. Blacks were frequently castrated for sexual offenses, while whites were not.

***Women's Rights***    The woman's movement of the nineteenth century adopted sexual rights as one of its primary issues. Because most women accepted the basic image of themselves as sexually pure, however, sexuality was perceived in terms of conflict between men and women. In the 1850s, Elizabeth Cady Stanton wrote her friend Susan B. Anthony that the key to women's rights was woman's fight to maintain her sexual purity (Blatch, 1922). Mrs. Stanton wrote:

> Man in his lust has regulated long enough this whole question of sexual intercourse. Now let the mother of mankind, whose prerogative it is to set the bounds for his indulgence, rouse up and give this whole matter a thorough, fearless examination . . . I feel, as never before, that this whole question of woman's rights turns on the pivot of the marriage relation, and mark my words, sooner or later it will be the topic for discussion. I would not hurry it on, nor would I avoid it. Good night.

Susan B. Anthony traced prostitution to men's "unnatural" sexual appetite (Harper 1898). The causes of prostitution were different for men and women:

> The acknowledged incentive to this vice on the part of man is his abnormal passion; while on the part of women, in the great majority of cases, it is

conceded to be destitution . . . while woman's want of bread induces her to pursue this vice, man's love of vice itself leads him into it and holds him there.

If women could vote, they would be able to end prostitution; men would never vote to end it, because it served their passions. If they were allowed to vote, women would also establish prohibition. Alcohol led not only to alcoholism but to loss of self-control; moderation was not the answer, because self-control fled when alcohol was taken even in small amounts. If women were to protect themselves against men's lust, then men must not be allowed to drink (Sinclair 1962).

This strange mixtures of women's rights and sexual politics derived from the "pure" image women had of themselves in that century. The early feminists would probably be at odds with today's women, who are seeking to expand women's sexuality.

***In This Century***    The relationship between sex and politics changed the twentieth century when Victorian sexual attitudes and behavior relaxed. Sex was becoming a less fearful and terrifying aspect of life. In fact, it could now be integrated with human loving instead of having to be curtailed or avoided.

In the previous century, sexual issues had been significant components of major social and political issues: democracy, aristocracy, antislavery, prohibition, and women's rights. Today, sexual aspects are often involved in political issues, but, with the exception of women's rights, they are seldom a focal point of social issues. People oppose marijuana for a number of reasons, including the fear that it releases sexual inhibitions. Others oppose integration for fear their white daughters may become sexually involved with black men; yet this point is scarcely ever presented as an argument in public debate. Sexual fears and demagoguery no longer excite the same passions they did a century ago. Sexual behavior and attitudes have perhaps become too diverse to make sex a primary motivating force in political and social movements.

Nevertheless, sex is still an active force in politics. An important cluster of attitudes revolve around political identifications. In a Gallup poll, 79 percent of the students who identified themselves as liberal believed that virginity before marriage was not important; 58 percent of the conservative students felt that it was important. Another study of college students found that political ideology was more directly related to acceptance of premarital intercourse than to social class, supporting the view that liberals tend to accept such intercourse while conservatives do not (Swift 1970; Reiss 1967).

The sexual issues in politics are usually specific and do not blend into other types of issues. Contemporary sexual issues include homosexuality, prostitution, pornography, rape, and abortion. Abortion, in particular, has become important politically.

### Sex and the Law

The vast majority of American men are sex criminals, whose crimes have gone undetected by the police. Women are only slightly less guilty. These unapprehended criminals have engaged in premarital intercourse, oral-genital relations, extramarital affairs, statutory rape, cohabitation, homosexual contacts, or intercourse with prostitutes. All of these acts are "victimless," yet most states have enacted laws prohibiting them. Although approximately 95 percent of all adult males have engaged in at least one of the activities, they remain illegal, and countless

thousands have been imprisoned for committing them (Kinsey 1948).

Why were such restrictive laws enacted? As Kinsey pointed out, sexual behavior differs significantly according to class, with each class believing that its particular pattern is the "right" one. At the time these laws were passed, the middle class rationalized its sexual behavior in terms of what is "moral," while the lower social classes rationalized their behavior in terms of what is "natural." There was a distinct clash of viewpoint, but because power rested with the white middle-class lawmakers, their views prevailed. Kinsey noted that American sex laws are really nothing more than a codification of middle-class sexual mores, established by legislators who are generally from the same class. Judges usually deal severely with sexual offenders, defending their own middle-class standards. The harsh moral condemnation and sentences that come from the bench are often bewildering

to defendants, who generally come from a lower social class.

Middle-class sex offenders are not as likely to get caught; aware of what is forbidden and what is not, they are usually more discreet. They are also less likely to be convicted, because they usually have more resources and can hire good lawyers. The people who are convicted are usually from the lower class, poorly educated, and significantly below average in intelligence; few are involved in drugs, but almost a third are drunk when they commit their crimes. They often have some form of personality disturbance, although usually no more serious than neurosis. One study found that 3 percent were psychopathic, 2 percent were psychotic, and 8 percent bordered on psychotic. Yet, as Kinsey noted, only a relatively small proportion of men sent to prison have engaged in sexual behavior materially different from that of most men. (Ellis and Abarbanel 1961; Gebhardt, et al. 1965).

Contemporary sex laws include a number of significant features: They prohibit activities that the overwhelming majority of people have engaged in. The activities are usually between consenting adults; there are no victims and no harm is done to others or to property. Enforcement is sporadic and accidental, yet these laws threaten the privacy and liberty of most people. In contrast to other laws, they are rarely amended or repealed. Each state has it own code of sex laws, which may differ radically in terms of what acts are illegal and what punishment is given. An act may be subject to a small fine in one state, to a five-year prison sentence in another, and be legal in a third.

There are more than 40,000 arrests a year for sexual offenses. The highest proportion are for statutory rape, perversion, oral-genital contact, and anal intercourse. The vast majority are consenting acts; few sex offenders are involved in

non-sexual crimes (Ellis and Abarbanel, 1961). A number of states punish premarital intercourse as fornication, which is usually a misdemeanor (in Arizona, however, it is a felony). Couples living together are subject to prosecution under fornication laws, the application of which may vary according to the defendant's sex. A married woman who has sexual intercourse with an unmarried man is often charged with adultery; while a married man having intercourse with an unmarried woman would most likely be charged with fornication. Fornication is not as serious a crime as adultery, and in some states is not a crime at all. Statutory rape legislation is designed to "protect" minor girls from sexual intercourse (whether or not they want to be protected), but a woman of 40 who has intercourse with a boy of 12 has not committed statutory rape. Boys do not need protection, according to the law; it is part of their socialization to be sexually active. Conversely, girls are more frequently held delinquent by the courts for sexual promiscuity. The delinquency of boys, rarely defined in sexual terms, usually involves antisocial behavior, such as theft or destruction of property.

Within marriage, genital contact must theoretically be restricted to vaginal intercourse, lest it be subject to criminal penalties as "perversion." Frequency of intercourse is also the concern of many states. The Minnesota Supreme Court declared that sexual intercourse averaging three times a week was "uncontrollable craving," justifying divorce. On the other hand, if there has been no intercourse, the marriage is annulled. Traditionally, women serve as the means for containing their husband's concupiscence; if a wife is available, it is presumed that men will not seek other sexual objects. Thus, wives are specifically exempted from rape laws. A husband may force his wife to submit with threats or beatings and be within his legal rights; yet if he were to treat another woman in exactly the same manner he would be arrested and imprisoned for forceable rape. A few states have recently enacted marital rape laws, changing this situation slightly.

States continue to define adultery as criminal behavior, with the punishment ranging from small fines to five years in prison. Until 1965, states had the right to prohibit the use of contraceptive devices in marriage, and some of them did so.

**Homosexuality**  Labeling homosexual behavior as "criminal" has helped create a subculture, set aside from the rest of society, in which these people attempt to be themselves without constant fear of arrest. Although there are relatively few arrests, the threat hangs over homosexual men and women as an ever-present possibility. The greatest impact of legal repression is not direct; rather, the law's effect is to symbolize the rejection of homosexual individuals by society (Weinberg and Williams, 1974).

Until recently, every state had some form of legislation prohibiting homosexual behavior. Homosexuality itself was not illegal, but specific acts such as oral-genital contact, intercourse, and mutual masturbation were prohibited. These prohibitive laws applied equally to heterosexual and homosexual behaviors, yet they were used most commonly against the latter.

The penalties for what some states called "crime against nature" were often harsh. Until just a few years ago, homosexuals could be sentenced to prison for life in five states, for 20 years in thirteen states; and for 15 years in twenty states. Illinois, in 1962, became the first state to permit consensual homosexual acts in private between adults. Since 1971, at least eight other states have similarly liberalized their laws.

Harsh punishments were infrequently used, however; more often, homosexual individuals were arrested for misdemeanors, for which laws were vaguely worded, punishments were less severe, and convictions were easier to obtain. Consequently, even with laws that permit homosexual behavior in private, individuals can be arrested for a variety of other offenses if police decide to harass them. The laws under which homosexual people have most commonly been arrested include disorderly conduct, lewd and lascivious behavior, and vagrancy. They are arrested for "disorderly conduct" if no particular act they are performing is illegal. They are arrested for "lewd and lascivious behavior" for dancing, holding hands, or engaging in more explicit sexual behavior. "Vagrancy" is used generally as a form of harassment. Almost without exception, only homosexual males are arrested.

Both homosexual and heterosexual individuals are subject to "sexual psychopath" laws, which provide for treatment over an indefinite time. "Sexual psychopathology," not a medical term but a legal term, refers to compulsive, repetitive, and bizarre sexual behavior as *interpreted by a judge*. Judges are not impartial and neutral interpretors of the law, however; they are men who tend to enforce the sexual values of their own class. Behavior may be "deviant" only from the judge's own psychosexual perspective.

Despite the vagueness and the unconstitutionality of these laws, men and women are convicted under them. In a few states, people who are simply *accused* of homosexuality can be committed to mental institutions. They are not jailed because of illegal actions, but because of their "condition." Courts do not require a violation to have actually taken place, because commitment as a sexual psyshopath is a civil rather than a criminal procedure. Release will not be made until a "cure" is effected; people have spent their entire lives in institutions for homosexuality, exhibitionism, or voyeurism

(Churchill, 1967).

Laws directed against homosexual activity – like all sex laws – are difficult to enforce. Countless illegal sex acts are committed each week, usually in private between consenting individuals. Thus, the police haphazardly enforce anti-homosexual laws, often using degrading techniques (UCLA Law Review, 1966).

Police "decoys" purposely give the impression that they are homosexual, using homosexual signals to entice other men. The decoys loiter in public restrooms, parks, or streets; they cruise homosexual hangouts, giving other men the eye. If someone responds, he is arrested, handcuffed, put into a squad car, and taken to jail. More than half the misdemeanor arrests reported in a University of California (Los Angeles) study on homosexuality resulted from decoy techniques. Homosexual men accuse the police of entrapment; the police deny it. In court, the policemen's testimony is usually accepted and the verdict is "guilty." In Provo, Utah, a man recently responded to an ad in the local gay newspaper. What the man did not know was that the ad was placed by the Brigham Young University police department; the department apparently wanted to entrap homosexuals. Using a BYU law enforcement student, wired with a concealed electronic signalling device, the BYU police followed the man and decoy off-campus. The man was arrested for forcible sexual abuse which is a felony in Utah. The university – which like its ruling Mormon Church strictly forbids homosexuality – denies that it has a surveillance program of gays. In fact, it conceded that "an officer overstepped his duties." At this time, the case has not yet come up to trial.

The second major method used by police is direct observation. "Observers" remain on the alert for hours in restrooms, watching men urinate, waiting for an "unnatural act" – at which time they spring into action. Men are watched through peepholes and one-way mirrors; cameras are also used. Most felony arrests occur in this manner. Because of recent concern over unreasonable search and invasion of privacy, courts have curtailed these practices somewhat, but they are still very common. Unfortunately there are no studies available on the psychopathology of vice squads.

The police also routinely patrol homosexual locales, and harass patrons at homosexual bars by arresting them on legitimate grounds. Such sweeps occur because of pressure from politicians, businessmen, district attorneys, or "concerned citizens." The appointment of a new police chief or the election of a mayor may alter the homosexual individual's situation drastically, or a patrolmen may decide to "get queers."

Males arrested for homosexual offenses are frequently required to register as "sex offenders" in the city or county in which they live. If they move, they must register within 30 days at their new residence. This reflects a belief on the part of the police that homosexual males are likely to commit violent sex crimes or molest children. No study has ever confirmed this belief (Gebhardt 1965). Arrest records may result in the homosexual male being unable to find employment. He may be picked up for questioning whenever a sex crime is committed. He is ineligible to continue a military career if he is discovered to be homosexual.

Homosexual women are generally unaffected by law, except in custody disputes over children. Courts generally rule against lesbians being fit mothers, and award custody to the father or make the children wards of the state. Gradually, the laws are changing; meanwhile, however, thousands of individuals are subject to harassment, imprisonment, or other forms of discrimination.

**Prostitution**   Prostitution is the only sexual offense for which women are extensively prosecuted. Yet it is an act that involves two people. The fact that the male patron is seldom arrested is illogical and discriminatory, suggesting that the reason may lie in unconscious attitudes. Is this a form of sex discrimination, or is it based on some vague idea that the patron is the woman's "victim," that the woman prostitute "provokes" her customer's ordinarily latent desire? Or is it because nearly all legislators, judges, district attorneys, and police are men? The dynamics of the discrimination against women prostitutes are not clear. What is clear, however, is that there is no *real* desire to end prostitution; otherwise the patron would be arrested as well. Prostitution arrests and clean-ups seem to be a communal ritual practiced by influential segments of the population to reassert their moral, political, and economic dominance. The arrests are symbolic of disapproval; yet the victims of these rituals — women — are *real* people and are imprisoned.

Prostitutes are distinguished from other sex partners because they are paid money for specific sexual acts. Although prostitution is called the world's "oldest profession," its nature varies, depending on attitudes toward sex. Sex can be exalted as *eros*, as it was by the ancient Greeks, or it can be degraded as *animalness* as it was by nineteenth-century Americans.

Contemporary attitudes toward prostitution are rooted in the nineteenth-century assumption that men have a basic and uncontrollable sex drive, but "nice" women do not. Most women prostitutes of the past century were driven into it by low wages and harsh working conditions in factories, and usually worked in "houses," where prostitution offered them better working conditions and pay. These women provided sexual experience and "relief" for men (Simon and Gagnon 1973; Riegel 1968).

But prostitution in the present century is different, in several respects. First, a much higher proportion of women now engage in premarital intercourse; their boyfriends no longer need to turn to prostitution for sexual contact. Although according to Kinsey the proportion of men – 19 percent – who go to women prostitutes was the same for those born before and after 1910, contact was only a third to a half as frequent for the younger group. (Another study in 1968 suggested that only 4 percent of college youths had had such contacts.) Today, prostitution accounts for only a small amount of our society's total sexual outlet. Often such contacts are a part of a young man's first sexual experiences, establish-

ing or reinforcing his status among friends. The attitudes of such men toward women prostitutes is similar to those they have toward "bad" girls (Packard 1968).

Often, prostitutes are women who have been the target of early male sexual aggression, who have had extensive sexual experience in adolescence without pay, who have been rejected by peers because of sexual activities, and who have not been given adequate emotional support by their parents. The parents seemed unable to relate to each other successfully, failing to provide their daughters with a model of affectionate interaction. As a result, the girls tended to be anxious, to feel lonely and isolated, and to be unsure of their own identity (Greenwald 1970; Simon and Gagnon 1973).

Because these women had already had extensive but impersonal sexual experiences, their main emotional conflict resulted not from the performance of the act but from accepting money for it. They could justify a consistent pattern of impersonal sexual relations in terms of affection, romance, pleasure, or desire, but those justifications disappear when payment becomes the motive. With the acceptance of money as payment for sexual activity, the female is no longer a "woman" but is instantly transformed into a "prostitute," with a new status that defines her exclusively in sexual terms.

A woman's identity as a prostitute is fundamentally a criminal identification. Because of this identification, she may begin to withdraw from the conventional world, moving into a shadowy subculture. She usually avoids contact with her family and may move to a different city. Her new world consists of pimps, panderers, petty thieves, mobsters, and patrons. Eventually they become her only world, which is difficult to leave because the conventional world does not want to associate with a prostitute or ex-prostitute; the "de-

viant" label may remain with her the rest of her life. (In Denmark, women are not arrested for prostitution if they have another occupation as well. The authorities hope that through their other work, women will retain ties to the larger community, enabling them to more easily leave the world of prostitution.)

Women prostitutes may justify their deviant behavior in terms of the cultural values accepted by the conventional world. They may take pride in financial success – their high earnings, easy life, beautiful clothes, expensive cars. The women who live two lives – mother and wife by day, prostitute by night – are more likely to hold conventional middle-class values and to justify prostitution in terms of family responsibilities. They need the money for their children, sick parents, unemployed husband, or some other commendable reason.

Women prostitutes often conform to societal norms in order to disguise their sense of isolation and social rejection. They may project their feelings about being regarded as socially deviant onto others: If prostitutes are bad, then the so-called respectable people who come to them are worse – hypocrites who are freaks, weirdos, and perverts, who ask prostitutes to perform all sorts of strange sexual acts. Women prostitutes frequently encounter such people, and they tend to generalize about the whole world from these experiences (Greenwald, 1970).

Women prostitutes are subject to arrest for various activities, including vagrancy and loitering, but the most common charge is for "solicitation." Soliciting – a "word, gesture or action" that implies an offer of sex for sale – is vague enough that women who are not prostitutes occasionally are arrested on the charge. It is usually difficult to witness a direct transaction in which money passes hands, and such arrests are also complicated by involving the patron. Laws may also

What pornographic literature does is precisely to drive a wedge between one's existence as a full human being and one's existence as a sexual being – while in ordinary life a healthy person is one who prevents such a gap from opening up.

Susan Sontag

include actions not ordinarily associated with prostitution; for example, some states define prostitution as offering oneself for promiscuous and indiscriminate intercourse *without* payment.

### Pornography

Pornography is a concern for legislators and police as well as for large numbers of the population. The enforcement of several federal laws directed against pornography costs taxpayers more than $6 million a year. In addition, almost *every* state has laws relating to "obscene" material; 41 prohibit its distribution to minors. A conservative estimate is that these states spend $10 million a year in enforcing such laws. Despite the expressed concern of both citizens and government about the dissemination of pornography to minors, 90 percent of all state and local prosecution has involved distribution to adults (Report 1970; Holbrook, 1973).

Pornography laws, the first of which were passed in the nineteenth century, were a result of the belief that "obscene" material and consequent arousal corrupts the morals of the community, leads to an increase in sex crimes, and causes psychological damage to children. Sexual arousal is not necessarily harmful to the community, however. In a study of sex offenders, it was found that they had used pornography neither more nor less than normal cross-section of the male population (Gebhardt, 1965). Sex offenders were no more likely to be aroused by pornography than other groups. The effect that pornography has on children is unknown. (Ironically, however, there is little effort to protect children from viewing violence that *is* known to have negative effects.)

Steven Marcus (1966) observed in his classic study that the view of sexuality expressed in pornography, in the past century, was the direct op-

posite of the official middle-class moral view. When the official culture issued warnings against masturbation, pornography extolled it: when medical journals described the harmful effects of sexual excess, pornography depicted insatiable orgies and infinite orgasms; when the official culture glorified the frigidity and coldness of respectable women, pornography presented a thousand images of voluptuous and panting women. Pornography is not just a graphic depiction of sex, but of *illicit* sex, in which either a conventional sexual activity is placed in an unconventional setting or a unconventional sex is placed in a conventional frame (Simon and Gagnon, 1973). Content usually relates to sex

A book whose sale is forbidden,
All men rush to see.
And prohibition turns one reader into three.

Italian proverb

---

organs and heterosexual intercourse, rather than to homosexual activities and oral-genital contact; sadomasochistic activities are rarely featured. The President's Commission on Obscenity and Pornography observed that "portrayals of sex that conform to general cultural norms are more likely to be seen, and portrayals of sexual activity that deviate from these norms are less likely to be seen."

Although few pornographic books, magazines, or movies are directed specifically toward women, women as well as men are exposed to these materials. Approximately 85 percent of the adult men and 70 percent of the adult women in the commission's study had seen explicit sexual material, and most had chosen to view it.

Viewers of pornography tend to be younger and better educated than non-viewers, to read books, magazines, and newpapers more frequently, and to go to movies more often. They are more active socially and politically (it has been alleged that in the Nixon years pornographic movies were available at Camp David). The sharing of pornography usually occurs among friends of the same sex or with sexual partners, and is usually a group activity. Among adolescent boys, only 11 percent viewed pornography when alone; only 6 percent when with the other sex. Forty-eight percent viewed it with friends of the same sex; 35 percent saw it in mixed company.

Pornography, then, appears to have a social context, in which people interact about what excites them or interests them, laughing, being embarrassed, telling stories. Among adolescents, pornography may be the only source of explicitly erotic information; parents, schools, and other institutional sources usually present sex information in abstract, scientific, sentimental, or unreal terms. Pornography facilitates sexual discussion by defining the situation as one in which sex is

the topic (Simon and Gagnon, 1973).

The Presidents-Commission found that pornography usually had little effect on sexual behavior, although masturbatory or coital activity was more likely to increase than decrease after viewing it, and there were also some increases in the frequency of erotic dreams, sexual fantasies, and conversation about sexual matters. The commission concluded, "In general, established patterns of sexual behavior were found to be very stable and not altered substantially by exposure to erotica. Where sexual activity occurred following the viewing or reading of these materials, it constituted a temporary activation of individuals' preexisting patterns of sexual behavior." The commission came to similar conclusions regarding attitudinal responses: "Exposure to erotic stimuli appears to have little or no effect on already established attitudinal commitments regarding either sexuality or sexual morality."

### Rape

The weapon in rape is the penis, which is used as a spear to attack, subordinate, and humiliate the victim – who is usually a woman. Sexual intercourse, as we ordinarily think of it, has very little to do with rape. Rather rape, which forces its victim into an intimate physical relationship with the rapist, is a means of degrading another person. The ultimate meaning behind rape is superior power.

Rape has been a constant in history from earliest times. It is an integral part of warfare, inspiring terror in civilians and a sense of power in soldiers. (Although rape is prohibited by military law, little is done to prevent it because it is part of the folklore of war.) Rape is an everyday occurrence in prisons, where men rape one another. Rape, castration, mutilation, and sexual sadism are routine aspects of political interrogation in many countries and are ignored by governments. What makes rape particularly terrible as an interrogation device is that it has been developed to routine, bureaucratic proportions; once considered the acts of psychotic persons, rape and sadism are now standard operating procedures of the political system in many parts of the world.

Rape is not only an act but also a threat. As small girls, women are warned against taking candy from strangers, walking alone down dark streets, and leaving doors and windows unlocked. Men might fear assault if they accept candy, walk alone, or leave a door unlocked, but women fear assault *and* rape. Women are raped often enough – estimates range from 55,000 to 255,000 rapes a year – that the fears have credibility. As a result, large numbers of women live in dread of the *possibility* of being raped, and rape is a part of their consciousness.

The threat of rape is complemented by what Ruth Herschberger (1948) calls the "myth of rape." She suggests that rape is an outgrowth of our folk belief that men are basically sexually aggressive and are physically superior to women. This belief, coupled with the need men frequently feel to prove their masculinity, sets the stage for rape. The myth is reinforced by male folklore that women really *want* someone to overcome their resistance (someone who is a man according to *machismo* definitions: brutal, powerful, instinctive.) Once a woman yields herself in sexual surrender, according to the myth, she enjoys being raped. This belief derives from the idea that women are sexually receptive and, by nature, sexually passive. Although a woman's erogenous zone do not function erotically when encounters are basically violent, the belief that women respond pleasurably to rape has occasionally caused rapists to arrange a subsequent meeting with a victim. On encountering the

police and not the woman, the rapist cannot believe she did not enjoy the sexual attack.

In MacDonald's 1968 study, 64 percent of the rapists were men between the ages of 15 and 24 years; approximately 47 percent were blacks, 51 percent were whites. They, like their victims, tend to be from the poorest and most socially disorganized parts of cities, slum areas where low income, high unemployment, high ethnic or racial concentrations, and low education prevail.

Victims are usually women 15 to 24, although elderly women are also raped. Most are single women from a working-class background. About half were raped by strangers. In a Denver study, 60 percent were raped by strangers, 17 percent by casual acquaintances (about half of whom the women met the day of the rape), or friends. Of the remaining rapes, 4 percent were raped by a stepfather or mother's boyfriend, 2 percent by an employer, 1 percent by a neighbor, 1 percent by a brother-in-law, 2 percent by an ex-husband, future father-in-law, employee, or tenant.

Rape places the victim in an inferior and degraded position. Rapists satisfy their hostile feelings toward women (and sometimes toward other men) by forcing submission, using sadistic impulses as compensation for feelings of sexual inadequacy. (Karpman, 1964). Rape sometimes has an interracial character as well. For blacks, the rape of a white woman is often a revenge against white society. For whites, the motive may combine feelings of domination with myths about the black woman's sexuality. Penalties are often lighter for the white rapists than for blacks, reflecting the impact of racial prejudice. Between 1930 and 1968, 89 percent of the 455 men executed for rape in the United States were blacks. If a black rapes another black, he usually gets a shorter sentence than does a white who rapes another white; if a black rapes a white woman, his punishment is heavier than that of a white who rapes a black woman. Punishment in these cases appears to be motivated by a desire to protect the white community rather than to reform the offender (MacDonald, 1971).

The problem of consent is crucial in rape cases; but consent (except in statutory rape) is not at all clear. A woman is raped when she submits to real or implied threats of force. But she is also raped in a legal sense when she consents under the influence of alcohol or drugs; if intercourse takes place while drunk or high, for example she can claim she was unable to give responsible consent, and accuse the man of "forcible rape."

Some courts require a woman to demonstrate that she physically tried to defend herself against rape. If she cannot prove this to the judge's satisfaction (which may vary from judge to judge) he may rule that her lack of resistance implied consent. Until 1974, California defense attorneys could question a woman about her previous sexual experiences, trying to imply promiscuity in order to free a client; until 1975, California judges instructed juries to examine the woman's testimony "with caution," although no such cautionary notes were made with other crimes.

**Statutory Rape**   Ironically, most rape convictions are not for forcible but for *statutory rape*, or consenting sexual intercourse with girls under the state's established "age of consent." Below this age, the court ignores a girl's consent. As one court put it, "the state says that they do not consent or that their apparent consent shall be disregarded. It offers resistance for them. It deals with the case as *rape*; not as a mere statutory offense. A rape with consent is an anomaly."

Until late in the nineteenth century, the age of consent was between ten and thirteen; proponents of raising the age believed that men would be less likely to "seduce" young girls if that

seduction were classified as rape. Raising the age of consent was to end "animal lust and moral degradation of man, and the destruction of womanhood," according to one advocate (Arena, 1891).

Maximum penalties for statutory rape range from one year in the county jail to fifty years in state prison. Enforcement of statutory rape laws are sporadic, accidental, and often arbitrary. These laws threaten young couples in which the girl might be underage, making the boy liable to felony convictions. They might be accidentally discovered by police, or the girl's parents may have her boyfriend arrested and imprisoned by filing a complaint.

## Abortion

From earliest times, opinions concerning abortion differed. Both Plato and Aristotle supported it, while Hippocrates required physicians to pledge not to give women abortive remedies. Jewish law penalized aboriton with "thou shall give life for life." Under Roman law the fetus was seen as part of the mother's body rather than as a separate human being; the only law affecting abortion was that if a woman aborted against her husband's will, she committed the crime of disobedience.

Christianity revolutionized the question of abortion, but its stand has varied in different historical periods. Tertullian (200 A.D.) was one of the first to maintain that the fetus was a human being; his argument was based on the Old Testament (Exodus 21:22), which reflected a Jewish heritage. The New Testament is silent on abortion. Tertullian's teachings were submerged by St. Augustine, who distinguished between a formed and non-formed fetus. Abortion of an unformed fetus did not constiute murder. Over the centuries theologians have argued about when the soul entered the fetus. St. Thomas believed that life began not as conception but with movement. Animation of the soul, according to him, began on the fortieth day for males and on the eightieth day for females. The present position of the Catholic Church is that the soul enters the embryo upon conception; thus it makes no difference when abortion is performed, for it is a sin at any time. In 1917 the Church called for the excommunication of all those involved in an abortion (DeBeauvoir, 1948; Noonan, 1965).

In the United States, there were no restrictions on abortion until the middle of the nineteenth century. The objections were medical rather than religious; but morality and religion became intimately involved in the issue by the end of the century. By the 1920s, abortions had become severely restricted in the United States.

In 1972 the United States Supreme Court declared unconstitutional those laws that interfere with "a woman's qualified right to terminate her pregnancy." States must now consider the stage of a woman's pregnancy. During the first stage – up to the beginning of the fourth month – the woman and her physician are responsible for the decision. After that, the state may regulate abortions to varying degrees. This decision was praised by those working for women's rights as a major victory. To anti-abortionists it was legalization of murder, and they began a nationwide campaign to pass a constitutional amendment against abortion.

The central focus of the issue deals with the *legality* of abortion. Anti-abortionists desire to make abortion a criminal act, even though past experience proves that laws do not prevent abortions but result in women having the operation performed secretly, often without proper medical care. During the 1950s, when abortion for other than therapeutic reasons was illegal in every state, approximately 200,000 to 1,200,000 il-

legal abortions were performed by physicians, 8 percent were self-induced, and the remainder were performed by various untrained persons.

When abortion was illegal, many women and adolescent girls tried to abort themselves. Extensive organic damage often resulted – perforation of the uterus or vagina, pertionitis, parametritis, and fat emboli. Self-induced abortion has claimed many lives.

Despite the legalization of abortion, at least one-third of the American women who wanted such an operation in 1974 were unable to obtain it, according to a study conducted by Christopher Tietze for the Planned Parenthood Federation. These women were primarily the young, the poor, and those who do not live in large cities. They were refused abortions because many hospitals will not allow the operation, despite the Supreme Court's decision. Thus, women continue to find it difficult to have safe, legal abortions. As a result, self-induced abortion is on the rise.

This situation was aggravated in June 1977 when the Supreme Court ruled six to three that neither the Constitution nor current federal law requires states to use Medicaid funds for nontherapeutic abortions. The Court further ruled that public hospitals are not required to provide or even permit elective abortions. This ruling allows every state and locality to prohibit the use of public funds and facilities for nontherapeutic abortions if they decide to. Although it is not clear at this point, it appears that the federal government will be free to prohibit the use of government funds and facilities for nontherapeutic abortions. More litigation will probably be required to clarify the relation of federal funds to nontherapeutic abortions. But the Supreme Court ruling appears to clear the way for Congress to ban funds for nontherapeutic abortions.

The majority opinion declared that the deci-

## Hyde Amendent Unconstitutional

In January 1980, the Hyde Amendent was ruled unconstitutional by the U.S. District Court in New York. The amendment banned the use of federal Medicaid funds for abortions unless the mother's life was endangered. The amendment effectively cut off abortion aid for the poor. The judge ruled that "medically necessary" abortions covered a wider ground than the "life endangerment" test of the Hyde Amendment. The decision could require every state to reinstate medical services for the poor seeking abortions. The court decision, however, is under appeal.

---

sion was no retreat from its 1973 ruling, but Justice Harry Blackmun, writing a dissenting opinion, strongly disagreed. He wrote that, by giving states the ability to deny both funds and facilities for abortions, the Court was permitting them "to accomplish indirectly what they could not do directly." He called the decision "punitive and tragic. Implicit in the Court's holding is the condescension that [the poor] may go elsewhere for abortion. I find that . . . alarming, almost reminiscent of 'Let them eat cake'."

This ruling is the most significant victory for antiabortion forces since the landmark 1973 Court ruling. Its consequences are likely to be severe for hundreds of thousands of women who want abortions each year. Medicaid has paid over $50 million dollars a year for abortions for approximately 300,000 poor women. The poor will find it more and more difficult to get abortions. Some, the Court conceded, may find it impossible to get an abortion because of lack of funds or because hospitals in their area will not permit them. But the impact will be most severe – as is usually the case – on the poor who lack the power and resources of the middle class and well-to-do. Middle-class women are not dependent on Medicaid funds and the impact on them will be minimal in contrast to the poor. More unwanted children will be born among the poor, more women will die from "coat-hanger" abortions, and the number of illegitimate births undoubtedly will rise.

Since that decision, Congress has eliminated funding for abortions for the poor; and only sixteen states continue to finance abortions for women without the means to pay. In Akron, Ohio, there have been even greater restrictions on all abortions, including the humiliating requirement that women take the aborted fetus to a licensed funeral director (*Newsweek*, June 5, 1978).

The abortion question is an amazingly complicated issue, filled with emotional intensity and moral ambiguities. Few who support a woman's right to choose would maintain that an abortion is no different than a tonsilectomy. They recognize that the embryo or fetus is more than a simple collection of cells. It is fairly common, in fact, among women planning to have an abortion to also to feel pleased at being pregnant. However, a woman may feel that it is the wrong time to give birth. Suzannah Lessard writes:

. . . making the decision to have an abortion tends to precipitate a woman into an unusually unencumbered confrontation within herself, because being pregnant isolates a person, particularly if she's single and doesn't want to have a child. If you live in a society where bearing an illegitimate child is something to be ashamed of, and where, on the other hand, abortion is illegal, you are suddenly cut off from all support, advice, information and facilities which have diluted the immediacy of earlier crises in your life (Lessard, 1972).

By giving a woman that right to choose abortion, the state hands her the responsibility for making one of the most important decisions in her life. Women do not take this responsibility lightly when they have to make this choice.

By contrast, Right-to-Life groups deny that women have a choice; for them, abortion is murder. Ideally, pregnancy should be avoided – there is no disagreement between pro–and anti-abortion groups concerning this issue. There is disagreement, however, in how pregnancy is to be prevented. Pro-abortion supporters tend to believe that more effective contraception and increased knowledge about sexuality is the key. They generally recognize the profound changes in sexual behavior that have taken place over the last few decades. By contrast, pro-life groups oppose birth control devices for the young because they believe such devices encourage what they

```
┌─────────────────────────┐      ┌─────────────────────────┐
│      IN MEMORIAM        │      │      IN MEMORIAM        │
│                         │      │                         │
│    To the thousands of  │      │    To the thousands of  │
│      Babies killed      │      │      Women killed       │
│       by Abortion       │      │   from illegal abortions│
│                         │      │                         │
└─────────────────────────┘      └─────────────────────────┘
```

call promiscuity and moral decadence. Most pro-life groups oppose the use of any contraceptive devices even among married couples. Instead, they urge the rhythm method or continence. (The rhythm method is generally ineffective and continence is difficult.)

What lies at the root of the abortion controversy may very well be a conflict in sexual morality. Whether or not abortions are legal, history has shown that they will be obtained if a woman wants one desperately enough. The pro-life forces represent an older way of thinking: they oppose legalized abortion because it represents society's acceptance of a sexual morality they consider wrong. Their moral values, once dominant in America, have been challenged, and in some instances have been replaced as the result of the sexual revolution of the 1960s.

Because their moral values are no longer accepted by society at large, these groups seek to enforce them through laws. Such laws, however, would represent a symbolic moral victory, nothing more, because abortion will continue as it has all throughout history. Sociologist Joseph Gusfield (1968) suggests that moral conflicts reflect status politics, with the issue not political or economic interest but moral domination. He notes that the coercive reformer – one who would *force* other people to reform – seldom views them with sympathy. *Coercive reform is the reaction of a group's sense of declining dominance or status in a community.* The people who violate the group's norms are viewed as enemies; in the case of abortion, they are seen as "murderers." Coercive reformers react to rejection of their opinions with anger and outrage, feeling no sympathy, compassion, or pity for their opponents. Their opponents' activities have no impact whatsoever on the life or behavior of the reformer, yet this person seeks to outlaw their activities with a vengeance (Gusfield, 1968).

In a study of 42,598 abortions obtained since legalization, 71 percent were performed within 12 weeks of conception; no deaths occurred in more than 30,000 cases in which the fetus was aborted during the first three months of pregnancy. There were complications in 6 percent of the abortions performed within the first 12 weeks, in 21 percent of those after 12 weeks. Less than 2 percent of the women suffered major complications.

Almost half the teen-age women, however, waited until after 12 weeks before they sought an abortion, increasing the risk of complications. These younger girls delayed because of a sense of confusion, fear of parental response, lack of money, and ignorance – many of them, unaware of the signs of pregnancy, did not realize they were pregnant (Tietze and Lewit, 1972).

The decision to have an abortion is not easy, even if one accepts abortion in the abstract. A woman has to deal with the rejection – even if only temporary – of maternity, which traditionally is one of her basic roles. In some ways, abortion is almost a rejection of her womanness. The drawbacks of being a woman, Simone de Beauvoir has pointed out – menstruation, illness, lack of status, and drudgery – find compensation in motherhood. The decision to have an abortion therefore requires a drastic reexamination of a woman's self-definition. In the long run, however, women experience few serious emotional problems as a result of abortion. A recent study suggests that mood, self-perception, affect, and feelings about abortion are not seriously impaired among women who have had them. Those under 18 years, however, experience more stress with premarital pregnancy and had a more difficult time dealing effectively with their problems.

## QUESTIONS

1. Most states continue to regulate sexual behavior between consenting adults through their criminal codes. *Who* decides what behavior will be legal and illegal? What moral code do these laws reflect? Discuss the impact of such laws on society and the individual.
2. How does engaging in prostitution affect a woman's life?
3. What is the significance of pornography in contemporary America? What are the arguments for and against restricting pornography? Is there a difference between pornography and erotica?
4. Is there a "myth" about rape? Why has the women's movement chosen rape as an issue? What does rape symbolize? Can laws against a husband raping his wife be enforced?
5. Discuss the arguments for and against abortion? Should abortion continue to be legal? How do abortion opponents undermine the *spirit* of the law in many states?

# Readings

### How We Guarantee
### the Ineffectiveness of Sex Education

Peter Scales, Ph.D. Public Affairs Director
National Organization for Non-Parents Baltimore, Maryland

*Can sex education influence behavior significantly? Who supports it and who opposes it?*

Opposition to sex education has been fueled by two beliefs: one is that knowledge stimulates irresponsible sexual behavior, and the other is that, in any case, sex education does not promote responsible behavior. It has become almost fashionable to mock sex education. Many professionals have added legitimacy to the controversy by simply reporting, without deeper analysis, that there are "insignificant" differences in sexual and contraceptive behavior between those who have taken a sex education course and those who have not. *The missing information of course, is whether the class was interesting or boring; whether the teacher was adequately trained; whether the class was comprehensive, semester-long treatment or a single, hurried lecture; whether students were stimulated to think about how they communicate with their partners about sex or whether only the "facts" were presented; etc.*

The argument that knowledge stimulates sexual "experimentation" has led to an effort to keep youth ignorant about love and sex. In New York, for instance, a state senator objected to our distributing the comic book *Ten Heavy Facts About Sex* (Gordon, 1971) at the state fair. His reason? The book would put ideas into the minds of young people who did not have the "ideas" already. In another case, magazines such as *Playgirl, Viva,* and *Penthouse* are made more titillating by being displayed with the front cover diagonally folded back to hide the offending breasts or pubic hairs. In Tallahassee, a local minister who had read that 984 out of 1000 unmarried girls had "committed fornication" while rock music was playing began collecting and destroying such records in order to "protect the moral decency of youth" (Cvetkovich & Grote, 1976).

A *New York Times* article (Powledge, 1977) questioned whether sex education has *any* effects, stating that "no one has the slightest idea of what the effects of sex education are, or can be." In that one sentence, the author managed to dismiss a volume of research so vast that it has taken nearly a year to review it and reach some tentative conclusions (Scales & Gordon, 1978). The most recent nationally representative study of teenage women in the U.S. also concluded that the "transfer of knowledge in formal settings may be likened to carrying water in a basket" (Zelnik & Kantner, 1977). In another book that supposedly contained the most up-to-date "advice," based on modern research about childbearing, the authors stated that "studies do not indicate that children who receive detailed sexual instruction from their parents arrive at any better long-term sexual adaptation than children who receive their instruction from other sources" (Fisher & Fisher, 1976). *Our review of the literature has consistently indicated, however, that children whose parents talk to them about sexuality do in fact tend to delay their first intercourse longer than children whose parents avoid sexuality — and these children tend to use contraception when they do have intercourse.*

Direct relationships between "sex education" and measures of responsible sexuality are rarely observed, however, because our approach as a society to preparing youth to deal with sexuality has been based on guilt, innuendo, and at times outright denial that young people are sexual: "We offer religions thick with the dust of a past era, parental counsel that is vague, timid, false, irrelevant, or negligible, and teachers who, on the subject of contraception, are silenced by rule

of law" (Konner, 1977). Michigan, for instance, requires sex education in the school but, until late 1977, also expressly forbade teaching contraception (Scales, 1977).

Sometimes our peculiar notions of cause and effect block understanding of the effects of sex education. For instance, *"social studies" is rarely charged with having negative or undersirable effects*, while sex education is frequently charged with stimulating "promiscuity." Such charges lead us to *bend over backward to demonstrate the positive value of sex education.* From this defensive posture, we often ask for direct, causal relationships between sex education and "quality of life" *that we would not dream of asking social studies to demonstrate.* Apparently, we are not doing too well with social studies either: last year the National Assessment of Educational Progress reported that nearly half of the nation's 17-year-olds do not know that each state has two senators (NAEP, 1977)!

We have reached the following tentative conclusions from our review of the research:

1. People do not become more predictably "liberal" or "permissive" in their attitudes after being in a sex education course – they do seem to become more accepting of other people's behaviors, even if they would not engage in the behaviors themselves.

2. Knowledge about sexuality is not associated with sex crime, or with significant changes in the frequency or variety of a person's sexual behavior – in fact, people who commit sex crimes are likely to have had "childhood experiences which encourage sexual repression and inhibition of sexual curiosity" (U.S. Commission on Obscenity and Pornography, 1970). Research shows that a person who does not like oral sex enough to en-

gage in it is unlikely to change that frequency, and a person who has frequent intercourse is unlikely to change that behavior.

3.  In all areas of the world, the highest fertility is associated with low levels of education, inadequate knowledge about conception and contraception, and an inferior status for women. In the United States, several studies have demonstrated that racial differences in unwanted fertility tend to be erased as educational differences are narrowed.

4.  Young people who talk with their parents about sexuality, and who expect positive reactions from their parents rather than arbitrary strong disapproval of "premarital" sex, are much more likely to use contraception than those whose parents react negatively at discussion of sexuality and who strongly disapprove of premarital sex.

5.  Young people who accept their sexuality are more likely to use contraception than those who are guilty about or fearful of expressing themselves sexually.

While there is also evidence that education can help reduce venereal disease, research designs have as yet been inadequate to distinguish an actual increase in incidence from an increased use of treatment centers due to a successful education program.

Although we have noted these effects, education is no panacea. Several studies show that "knowledge" about sex (often limited in these studies to a single item on timing of the "fertile" period) is not related to avoiding venereal disease and unwanted pregnancy. More importantly, especially in the youngest age groups, we have not counteracted the myths which make it difficult for even somewhat knowledgable young people to behave responsibly. We cannot get re-

sults from sex education if young people are admonished to be responsible but also taught to feel guilty and secretive about their sexual feelings and experiences. The results of our failure are obvious: the V.D. rate is increasing most rapidly among 11–to 14-year-olds, and the birth rate for teens 15-17 has risen 2% in the last ten years, as compared to a drop of over 25% in all other age groups.

Our society still recoils at the notion of young people having sexual experiences, or even sexual thoughts, and so we have failed to provide the education they really need. Even a basic grounding in facts is lacking – only six states and the District of Columbia require some type of "sex education" (Alan Guttmacher Institute, 1976). More important than the facts, however, are answers to questions such as: How does a young lover put on a condom without destroying the sensitivity and excitement of the moment? How does a young person take precautions against V.D. without leaving the partner feeling as if her or she is diseased? If a young male asks his partner if she is using anything, and she says that she is on the pill, what does he do if he thinks she is not telling the truth? How can a woman recognize and respond when she is being used?

Our discomfort over sexuality has led to a sexual revolution based on the myth of the normal outlet – isn't it abnormal for adults to masturbate? isn't it abnormal to go too long without sex? – or a new myth of normality, isn't it abnormal to want only one sexual relationship at a time? Sex education needs to communicate that there is no particular range of behavior people need to strive for in order to be "normal."

We need to talk more about the possible feelings between partners, feelings that can range from near disregard to passionate devotion, and are often an ambivalent combination somewhere in-between. Our sex education needs to expose and work toward eliminating destructive sex roles. Most men are still taught to be opportunistic about sex and most women are told to be skeptical. For instance, we studied 165 college students' views on virginity. We found that nearly everyone has some fears about their first sexual intercourse, but that men worried significantly more about how they would perform and women significantly more about whether they were doing the "right" thing (Buder, Scales, & Sherman, 1977). We need to overcome the fact that no one has prepared young people to communicate accurately and honestly about sex, with the result that over a third of 400 students we surveyed (Gordon & Scales, 1977) said that the first time or two they have sex with someone, it "just seems to happen without talking."

But even if we provide this kind of education, we still need to make services more accessible. Only half of sexually experienced teenage women are thought to have access to a clinic or physician, and it seems that men are ignored by nearly all sexual health care providers. Except for the pharmacist and the advertising of most magazines "for men," men are neglected – and even many pharmacists do not put up condom displays because they fear a negative "community" reaction. Some young people do not use clinics because they believe, accurately in many cases, that their confidentiality will not be protected. In a study of 40 clinics in eight major U.S. cities, it was found that "fear of parents finding out" was the main reason teenagers gave for not using clinics (Urban and Rural Systems Associates, 1976).

Clinics also frequently neglect to treat sexual problems socially as well as medically. In one of our participant-observation studies, a college woman found that no questions were asked about her partner(s), and about how her style of

sex life might effect her sexual health care needs – this lack of social attention occurred on three different visits to the university health clinic (Scales & Weitzner, 1977). Whether it concerns dealing with one's parents or with one's partners, young clients need the opportunity (which some will not elect) to talk about their social concerns so that social uncertainties do not continue to turn into medical problems.

Finally, laws regarding access to sexual health care also need to change. In a study conducted by the Urban Institute, it was found that states with laws denying contraceptive services to under-18s had significantly higher birth rates among unmarried black teenagers, and that states denying abortion services to under-18s had higher births to unmarried white teenagers (Moore & Caldwell, 1976).

Peter Scales *SIECUS Report VI, No. 4, March 1978.* Copyright © SIECUS, New York, N.Y. Reprinted by permission.

### Excerpt from Rabbit Run

John Updike

*When prostitution is under discussion, people frequently forget that prostitutes are first human beings, then prostitutes. Each woman has her own life, her own past, her own experience, despite our tendency to view her only as a degraded sex object. In the excerpt from John Updike's Rabbit, Run, a former high school basketball star, Rabbit, has left his wife and child. He is now living with a woman whom he first met as a prostitute. The excerpt begins with an argument between the two.*

"What the hell makes you think you don't have to pull your own weight?

"What's your kick? I support you."

"The hell you do. I have a job." It's true. A little after he went to work for Mrs. Smith she got a job as a stenographer with an insurance company that has a branch in Brewer. He wanted her to; he was nervous about how she'd spend her afternoons with him away. She said she never enjoyed that business; he wasn't so sure. She wasn't exactly suffering when he met her.

"Quit it," he says. "I don't care. Sit around all day reading mysteries. I'll support ja."

"You'll support me. If you're so big why don't you support your wife?"

"Why should I? Her father's rolling in it."

"You're so smug, is what gets me. Don't you ever think you're going to have to pay a price?" She looks at him now, squarely with eyes bloodshot from being in the water. She shades them with her hand. These aren't the eyes he met that night by the parking meters, flat pale disks like a doll might have. The blue of her irises has deepened inward and darkened with a richness that, singing the truth to his instincts, disturbs him.

These eyes sting her and she turns her head away to hide the tears, thinking, That's one of the signs, crying easily. God, at work she has to get up from the typewriter and rush into the john like she had the runs and sob, sob, sob. Standing there in a booth looking down at a toilet laughing at herself and sobbing till her chest hurts. And sleepy. God, after coming back from lunch it's all she can do to keep from stretching out in the aisle right there on the filthy floor between Lilly Orff and Rita Fiorvante where that old horse's neck Honig would have to step over her. And hungry. For lunch an ice-cream soda with the sandwich and than a doughnut with the coffee and still she has to buy a candy bar at the cash register. After she's been trying to slim down for him and *had* lost six pounds, at least one scale said. For him, that was what was rich, changing

herself for him when he was worth nothing, less than nothing, he was a menace, for all his mildness. He had that mildness. The others didn't. The thing was, when they knew you were one, they didn't think you were human, and thought they were entitled. Which they were, but still, some of the things. It was like they hated women and used *her*. But now she forgives them because it all melts, the next day is the next day and you're still the same and there, and they're away. The older they were, the more like presidents they looked, the wiser they should have been, the worse they were. Then they wanted some business their wives wouldn't give, in from the back which she didn't mind it was like being a hundred miles away once you get adjusted, or with the mouth. That. What do they see in it? It can't be as deep, she doesn't know. After all it's no worse than them at your bees and why not be generous, the first time it was Harrison and she was drunk as a monkey anyway but when she woke up the next morning wondered what the taste in her mouth *was*. But that was just being a superstitious kid there isn't much taste to it a little like seawater, just harder work than they probably think, women are always working harder than they think. The thing was, they wanted to be admired there. They really did want that. They weren't that ugly but they thought they were. That was the thing that surprised her in high school how ashamed they were really, how grateful they were if you just touched them there and how quick word got around that you would. What did they think, they were monsters? If they'd just thought they might have known you were curious too, that you could like that strangeness there like they liked yours, no worse than women in their way, all red wrinkles, my God, what was it in the end? No mystery.

John Updike, *Rabbit Run*. Reprinted by permission of Random House, Inc.

## The Prostitution Papers

Kate Millet

I don't feel that I'm a whore now, but the social stigma attached to prostitution is a very powerful thing. It makes a kind of total state out of prostitution so that the whore is always a whore. It's as if — you did it once, you become it. This makes it very easy for people to get locked into it. It's very hard to get married; then too, most of the people who do it are not that well educated, not that many of them could do any other job. You get locked into it simply because you get hooked on luxuries. You can get hooked on consumerism, or even just on living decently. You can get hooked on a certain kind of freedom, where you can go where you want to without being beholden to someone who supports you. For me prostitution didn't even offer good hours 'cause I had this work hangup. I worked about twenty-four hours a day — I was into making so much money — obsessive about it. I can also see how people could be trapped in it because it's so hard for them literally, objectively, so difficult to do anything else, let alone to do as well economically.

---

## The Effects of Pornography on Individuals

*In 1970, the Commission on Obscenity and Pornography issued its controversial report. The majority report found little reason to impose legal restrictions on the "right of adults to read or see explicit materials." But one dissenting committee member wrote: "The Commission's majority report is a Magna Carta for the pornographer." President Richard Nixon thought the report was trash. One controversial section concerns the effect of pornography on individuals. If there is no evidence linking pornography to sexual deviance or crime, should moral considerations provide grounds for curtailing the availability of pornography to adults?*

There is no consensus among Americans regarding what they consider to be the effects of viewing or reading explicit sexual materials. A diverse and perhaps inconsistent set of beliefs concerning the effects of sexual materials is held by large and necessarily overlapping portions of American men and women. Between 40% and 60% believe that sexual materials provide information about sex, provide entertainment, leads to moral breakdown, improve sexual relationships of married couples, lead people to commit rape, produce boredom with sexual materials, encourage innovation in marital sexual technique and lead people to lose respect for women. Some of these presumed effects are obviously socially undesirable while others may be regarded as socially neutral or desirable. When questioned about effects, persons were more likely to report having personally experienced desirable than undesirable ones. Among those who believed undesirable effects had occurred, there was a greater likelihood of attributing their occurrences to others than to self. But mostly, the undesirable effects were just believed to have happened without reference to self or personal acquaintances.

Surveys of psychiatrists, psychologists, sex educators, social workers, counselors and similar professional workers reveal that large majorities of such groups believe that sexual materials do not have harmful effects on either adults or adolescents. On the other hand, a survey of police chiefs found that 58% believed that "obscene" books played a significant role in causing juvenile delinquency.

*Psychosexual Stimulation* Experimental and survey studies show that exposure to erotic stimuli produces sexual arousal in substantial portions of both males and females. Arousal is dependent on both characteristics of the stimulus and characteristics of the viewer or user.

Recent research casts doubt on the common belief that women are vastly less aroused by erotic stimuli than are men. The supposed lack of female response may well be due to social and cultural inhibitions against reporting such arousal and to the fact that erotic material is generally oriented to a male audience. When viewing erotic stimuli, more women report the physiological sensations that are associated with sexual arousal than directly report being sexually aroused.

Research also shows that young persons are more likely to be aroused be erotica than are older persons. Persons who are college educated, religiously inactive, and sexually experienced are more likely to report arousal than persons who are less educated, religiously active and sexually inexperienced.

Several studies show that depictions of conventional sexual behavior are generally regarded as more stimulating than depictions of less conventional activity. Heterosexual themes elicit more frequent and stronger arousal responses than depictions of homosexual activity; petting and coitus themes elicit greater arousal than oral sexuality, which in turn elicits more than sadomasochistic themes.

*Satiation* The only experimental study on the subject to date found that continued or repeated exposure to erotic stimuli over 15 days resulted in satiation (marked diminution) of sexual arousal and interest in such material. In this experiment, the introduction of novel sex stimuli partially rejuvenated satiated interest, but only briefly.

There was also partial recovery of interest after two months of nonexposure.

*Effects Upon Sexual Behavior* When people are exposed to erotic materials, some persons increase masturbatory or coital behavior, a smaller proportion decrease it, but the majority of persons report no change in these behaviors. Increases in either of these behaviors are short lived and generally disappear within 48 hours. When masturbation follows exposure, it tends to occur among individuals with established masturbatory patterns or among persons with established but unavailable sexual partners. When coital frequencies increase following exposure to sex stimuli, such activation generally occurs among sexually experienced persons with established and available sexual partners. In one study, middle-aged married couples reported increases in both the frequency and variety of coital performance during the 24 hours after the couples viewed erotic films.

In general, established patterns of sexual behavior were found to be very stable and not altered substantially by exposure to erotica. When sexual activity occurred following the viewing or reading of these materials, it constituted a temporary activation of individuals' preexisting patterns of sexual behavior.

Other common consequences of exposure to erotic stimuli are increased frequencies of erotic dreams, sexual fantasy, and conversation about sexual matters. These responses occur among both males and females. Sexual dreaming and fantasy occur as a result of exposure more often among unmarried than married persons, but conversation about sex occurs among both married and unmarried persons. Two studies found that a substantial number of married couples reported more agreeable and enhanced marital communication and an increased willingness to discuss sexual matters with each other after exposure to erotic stimuli.

*Attitudinal Responses* Exposure to erotic stimuli appears to have little or no effect on already established attitudinal commitments regarding either sexuality or sexual morality. A series of four studies employing a large array of indicators found practically no significant differences in such attitudes before and after single or repeated exposures to erotica. One study did find that after exposure persons became more tolerant in reference to other persons' sexual activities although their own sexual standards did not change. One study reported that some persons' attitudes toward premarital intercourse became more liberal after exposure, while other persons' attitudes became more conservative, but another study found no changes in this regard. The overall picture is almost completely a tableau of no significant change.

Several surveys suggest that there is a correlation between experience with erotic materials and general attitudes about sex: Those who have more tolerant or liberal sexual attitudes tend also to have greater experience with sexual materials. Taken together, experimental and survey studies suggest that persons who are more sexually tolerant are also less rejecting of sexual material. Several studies show that after experience with erotic material, persons become less fearful of possible detrimental effects of exposure.

*Emotional and Judgmental Responses* Several studies show that persons who are unfamiliar with erotic materials may experience strong and conflicting emotional reactions when first exposed to sexual stimuli. Multiple responses, such as attraction and repulsion to an unfamiliar object, are commonly observed in the research literature on psychosensory stimulation from a variety of nonsexual as well as sexual stimuli. These emotional responses are short-lived and, as with psychosexual stimulation, do not persist long after removal of the stimulus.

Extremely varied responses to erotic stimuli occur in the judgmental realm, as, for example, in the labeling of material as obscene or pornographic. Characteristics of both the viewer and the stimulus influence the response: For any given stimulus, some persons are more likely to judge it "obscene" than are others; and for persons of a given psychological or social type, some erotic themes are more likely to be judged "obscene" than are others. In general, persons who are older, less educated, religiously active, less experienced with erotic materials, or feel sexually guilty are most likely to judge a given erotic stimulus "obscene." There is some indication that stimuli may have to evoke both positive responses (interesting or stimulating), and negative responses (offensive or unpleasant) before they are judged obscene or pornographic.

---

*Excerpt from* **Adios, Scheherazade**

Donald Westlake

*Pornography is selling a lot of books these days, and by following Donald Westlake's simple formula, you too can strike it rich!*

Here's the way it goes. There are four sex novel stories, which we will number 1 through 4:

1. A boy in a small town wants to see the world. He screws his local sweetheart goodbye and goes to the big city. In the big city he gets a job and meets a succession of people, mostly

female, and lays them all. Typical sequences are hitching to New York and being given a ride by a bored but beautiful wife in a convertible, or getting a job in a store and meeting a nymphomaniac in the stockroom, or going to pick up a date and meeting her nymphomaniac roommate instead. At the end of all this crap the boy can do one of three things. He can go back to the small town and the local sweetheart. He can marry one of the big city girls. He can become ruthless and shaft one of the big city girls and wind up alone. It doesn't matter which of the three, any one of them will give your sludge that redeeming social significance which will prohibit the cops from confiscating it. All resolutions are emotional – sad, happy, pointed, poignant, cynical, sentimental or whatever – so take your pick. You can't lose.

2. The same as 1, except with a girl. She leaves her little home town, pausing first to fuck with her little home town boy friend, and then it's off to the big city for her. The reason she shacks up with her lesbian roommate is she was just raped by her boss. Fill in the details and a few more studs and you've got a book. Same jazz about the ending.

3. *La Ronde.* Chapter 1 introduces George, who screws Myra. Chapter 2 switches to Myra's viewpoint, and she makes it with Bruno. In Chapter 3 we follow Bruno as he climbs into the rack with Phyllis. And so on, and so on. The finish here is either to have the last character in bed with the first charcter, or the last character decides to stay with the next-to-last character and end this chain of meaningless sex. Either way will do.

4. A bored husband and a bored wife. The chapters alternate between their viewpoints. We watch them having bored sex with each other and less bored sex with other characters. If we make one of them, husband or (more usually)

wife, the heavy, we can finish with the heavy getting his (her) comeuppance and the good guy (girl) getting a better girl (guy). If we make them both merely confused and troubled but basically nice, they get back together again at the finish. Redeeming social significance either way, if you'll notice.

Copyright © 1970 by Donald E. Westlake. Reprinted by permission of Simon & Schuster.

### Roe et. al. v. Wade

*The following (in an abbreviated form of its oblique glory) is the Supreme Court's landmark decision on abortion. Hint: Start with Section 2.*

SUPREME COURT OF
THE UNITED STATES
*Syllabus* *
ROE et al. v. WADE, DISTRICT ATTORNEY
OF DALLAS COUNTY
APPEAL FROM THE UNITED STATES
DISTRICT COURT FOR THE
NORTHERN DISTRICT OF TEXAS
No. 70-18. Argued December 13,
1971 – Reargued October 11, 1972
Decided January 22, 1973

A pregnant single woman (Roe) brought a class action challenging the constitutionality of the Texas criminal abortion laws, which proscribe procuring or attempting an abortion except on medical advice for the purpose of saving the

*NOTE; Where it is deemed desirable, a syllabus (headnote) will be released, as is being done in connection with this case, at the time the opinion is issued. The syllabus constitutes no part of the opinion of the Court but has been prepared by the Reporter of Decisions for the convenience of the reader. See *United States v. Detroit Lumber Co.*, 200 U.S. 321, 337.

mother's life. A licensed physician (Hallford), who had two state abortion prosecutions pending against him, was permitted to intervene. A childless married couple (the Does), the wife not being pregnant, separately attacked the laws, basing alleged injury on the future possibilities of contraceptive failure, pregnancy, unpreparedness for parenthood, and impairment of the wife's health. A three-judge District Court, which consolidated the actions, held that Roe and Hallford, and members of their classes, had standing to sue and presented justiciable controversies. Ruling that declaratory, though not injunctive, relief was warranted, the court declared the abortion statutes void as vague and overbroadly infringing those plaintiffs' Ninth and Fourteenth Amendent rights. The court ruled the Does' complaint not justiciable. Appellants directly appealed to this Court on the injunctive rulings, and appellee cross-appealed from the District Court's grant of declaratory relief to Roe and Hallford. *Held*:

1. While 28 U.S.C., 1253 authorizes no direct appeal to this Court from the grant or denial of declaratory relief alone, review is not foreclosed when the case is properly before the Court on appeal from specific denial of injunctive relief and the arguments as to both injunctive and declaratory relief are necessarily identical. P. 8.

(a) Contrary to appellee's contention, the natural termination of Roe's pregnancy did not moot her suit. Litigation involving pregnancy, which is "capable of repetition, yet evading review," is an exception to the usual federal rule that an actual controversy must exist at review stages and not simply when the action is initiated. Pp. 9-10.

(b) The District Court correctly refused injunctive, but erred in granting declaratory, relief to Hallford, who alleged no federally protected right not assertable as a defense against the

good-faith state prosecutions pending against him. *Samuels v. Mackell*, 410 U.S. 66.

(c) The Doe's complaint, based as it is on contingencies, any one or more of which may not occur, is too speculative to present an actual case or controversy. Pp. 12-14.

2. State criminal abortion laws, like those involved here, that except from criminality only a life-saving procedure on the mother's behalf without regard to the stage of her pregnancy and other interests involved violate the Due Process Clause of the Fourteenth Amendment, which protects against state action the right to privacy, including a woman's qualified right to terminate her pregnancy. Though the State cannot override that right, it has legitimate interests in protecting both the pregnant woman's health and the potentiality of human life, each of which interests grows and reaches a "compelling" point at various stages of the woman's approach to term. Pp. 36-49.

(a) For the stage prior to approximately the end of the first trimester, the abortion decision and its effectuation must be left to the medical judgment of the pregnant woman's attending physician. Pp. 36-47.

(b) For the stage subsequent to approximately the end of the first trimester, the State, in promoting its interest in the health of the mother, may, if it chooses, regulate the abortion procedure in ways that are reasonably related to maternal health. Pp. 43-44.

(c) For the stage subsequent to viability the State, in promoting its interest in the potentiality of human life, may, if it chooses, regulate, and even proscribe, abortion except where necessary, in appropriate medical judgment, for the preservation of the life or health of the mother. Pp. 44-48.

3. The State may define the term "physician" to mean only a physician currently licensed by

the State, and may proscribe any abortion by a person who is not a physician as so defined. Pp. 34-35, 48.

4. It is unnecessary to decide the injunctive relief issue since the Texas authorities will doubtless fully recognize the Court's ruling that the Texas criminal abortion statutes are unconstitutional. P. 51.

314 F. Supp. 1217, affirmed in part and reversed in part.

Blackmun, J., delivered the opinion of the Court, in which Burger, C.J., and Douglas, Brannan, Stewart, Marshall, and Powell, J.J., joined. Burger, C.J., and Douglas and Stewart, J.J., filed concurring opinions. White, J., filed a dissenting opinion, in which Rehnquist, J., joined. Rehnquist, J., filed a dissenting opinion.

## Facts About Abortion
## Zero Population Growth

*Is the controversy about abortion one of facts or morality?*

**1. Abortion is legal in the United States.** In 1973, the U.S. Supreme Court ruled that the abortion decision, in the first trimester of pregnancy (usually defined as 13 weeks), must be left up to the woman, in consultation with her doctor. During the second trimester, state regulations "reasonably related to maternal health" are permissible. Once the fetus reaches viability – the capability of life outside the womb, usually at 24 to 28 weeks – the Court permits laws to protect the state's "interest in the potentiality of human life," but states may not prohibit abortions when the woman's life or health is at stake. In preserving individual freedom of choice, the Court's decision does not force any woman to have an abortion against her will.

**2. Most Americans believe the choice to have an abortion should be left to a woman and her doctor.** These majorities have varied in size from poll to poll; Knight-Ridder Newspapers 1/76, 81 percent; Times-CBS 10/77, 74 percent; Yankelovich 11/77, 64 percent. Gallup polls in 1975 and 1977 found that three-fourth of Americans approval of legal abortion under some or all circumstances. In 1977, 22 percent of the Gallup sample said "all circumstances," and 55 percent specified varying "certain circumstances." Among Catholics questioned by Gallup, 53 percent approved of legal abortion under certain circumstances, and 20 percent under all circumstances. Support for government funding of voluntary abortions for poor women is less substantial and clear: Times-CBS 7/77, 38 percent; Harris, 51 percent.

**3. Legal abortion is probably the most frequently performed kind of surgery in the U.S.** Women chose to have more than 1.1 million abortions here in 1976. One in four pregnancies (excluding those that end in miscarriage) were terminated by induced abortion. Seven in 10 abortions involve unmarried women.

**4. Despite the larger numbers of women who choose abortion each year, the operation is still not available in eight of 10 U.S. counties.** Fewer than one in five public hospitals performed the service in 1975, and only one in three non-Catholic private hospitals. Availability has been concentrated in the biggest cities and on the East and West coasts. As a result, 143,000 to 654,000 women who wanted abortions in 1976 were unable to have them, according to estimates by the Alan Guttmacher Institute.

**5. Legal abortion in the first trimester of pregnancy is nine times safer for a teenager, in terms of life or death, and 39 times safer for a**

*woman aged 40 to 44, than carrying the pregnancy to childbirth.* In 1975, there were fewer than two deaths per 100,000 women who had first-trimester abortions. That's three times safer, in terms of deaths, than tonsillectomies, and 200 times safer than appendectomies. Eight of every 10 abortions are performed in the first trimester. Health risks are considerably higher for a later abortion, but it is still safe compared to most kinds of operations. Improved access to abortion services for poor, young and rural women would decrease the number of late abortions.

*6. Since August 1977, low-income women have not been able to get federal assistance for elective abortions.* – while wealthier women are not impeded in their right to choose. Medicaid had been paying for three of every 10 abortions (about 250,000 in 1976) until August, when a federal court allowed the Hyde Amendment passed by Congress in 1976 to take effect. That court decision was prompted by a Supreme Court ruling in June 1977 that governments are not required by the Constitution to finance abortions for indigent women. Congress' revised 1977 Medicaid funding restriction allows funding only when the mother's life would be endangered by carrying the fetus to term, when two doctors agree that damage to her physical health would be severe and long-lasting, or when rape or incest has been reported promptly to the authorities. While federal funds have been cut off, 17 states (as of January 1978) have chosen to continue funding abortions for low-income women through the Medicaid program.

*7. A woman may have an abortion without the consent of her husband or her parents, even if she is younger than 18.* That's the 1976 decision of the U.S. Supreme Court. When a woman disagrees with her husband or parents on the abortion decision, the Court said, she should make the decision since if affects her more immediately. Giving veto power to the husband or parents wouldn't enhance family relationships, the Court said.

*8. Hundreds of thousands of unplanned pregnancies are inevitable, even for couples using birth control.* Even when used perfectly, all contraceptive methods fail occasionally (except sterilization, which fails very seldom). In actual practice, one of every three couples using birth control will have an unwanted pregnancy every five years. In a one-year survey of couples trying to prevent pregnancy, four in 100 using the birth control pill had unwanted pregnancies – and five in 100 using the intra-uterine device (IUD), 10 in 100 using condoms, 17 in 100 using a diaphragm, 21 in 100 using periodic abstinence (rhythm) and 22 in 100 using spermicidal foam. Young couples, and couples trying merely to delay (not to prevent) pregnancy, had failure rates considerably higher than average.

*9. Teenagers had one-third of all legal abortions performed in the U.S. in 1975.* Many of these young women became pregnant because they lacked access to contraceptives or did not know how easily they could become pregnant. These were the reasons given by seven in 10 sexually active teenage women who weren't using contraception, according to a 1971 survey. Yet few schools teach teens about birth control, and the topic is taboo on TV and in most other media. Nearly half of sexually active females aged 15 to 19 – some 1.8 million – are *not* getting family planning help from clinics or doctors, and four in five say they've had sexual intercourse at least once without birth control.

*10. Two-thirds of the world's people live in countries where abortions may be performed legally* – about one-third where they are legal under any circumstance, and one-third where the law is moderately restrictive. Thirty million to 55 million abortions are induced each year, perhaps half of them illegally. In many countries, abortion services are free or subsidized by the government. Because primary forms of birth control are not available, not used or not effective for millions of women worldwide, abortion terminates at least one pregnancy for every four that end in live births.

**11. When and where abortion is prohibited, it is performed in defiance of the law – usually at higher risk to the woman.** Before states began to legalize abortion in the 1960s, estimates of illegal abortions in the U.S. ranged from 200,000 to 1.2 million a year. The year after the Supreme Court's legalization decision, there was a 40-percent drop in abortion related deaths. And in Romania, abortion-related deaths increased six-fold after the law there was made more restrictive. Illegal abortions are often inexpert and unsanitary, leading to infections and other complications. If abortion had been outlawed in 1974, Population Council biostatistician Christopher Tietze has estimated, seven out of 10 legal abortions would have been performed illegally.

**12. Several major religious groups are opposed to abortion, but many others support the right of a woman to choose abortion.** The Religious Coalition of Abortion Rights includes The American Baptist Church, Catholics for a Free Choice, the Union of American Hebrew Congregations, the Presbyterian Church in the U.S., the Unitarian Universalist Association, the United Methodist Church, the United Church of Christ, and the United Presbyterian Church, U.S.A. Even the Roman Catholic Church leadership which currently condemns even therapeutic abortions, permitted abortions under some circumstances until a Papal decree in 1869.

**13. While public funding is denied in most states, an outpatient abortion costs, on the average, three weeks' entire living allotment for a welfare family of three.** First-trimester abortions average $175 in cost, and the average Aid to Families with Dependent Children payment is $234 for a mother and two children. These are national averages, however. For many families living at the poverty level, welfare pays less than the average and the abortions cost more. That three-person family receives, on the average, a welfare check of only $47 a month in Mississippi, $102 in Texas and $191 in Ohio – all states refusing to subsidize abortions for indigent women. Many abortion costs exceed these monthly allotments: first trimester abortions in a hospital average $300; second-trimester abortions, $350 to $700.

**14. When a genetic disorder is suspected in a fetus, prenatal testing can determine whether a deformed child would be born.** With test results in hand, parents can decide whether to choose abortion. Ultrasound, fetal blood sampling and other techniques can detect certain disorders. Unfortunately, one of the most useful tests, amniocentesis, can rarely be performed before the 16th week of gestation – meaning that the abortion decision is delayed til mid-pregnancy. Amniocentesis can detect dozens of inherited disorders including many incurable, degenerative diseases that would cause a painful childhood and an early death. Mongolism (Down's syndrome). Tay-Sachs disease, spina bifida and Duchenne's muscular dystrophy can be detected with amniocentesis. Medicaid-eligible women can receive federal funding for amniocentesis, but Congress has refused to pay for abortions, even when diagnosis shows the child would be born deformed. Meanwhile, anti-abortion groups are pressuring the March of Dimes and the Muscular Dystrophy Association to stop amniocentesis research and services. Doctors often advise use of the test when there were earlier birth defects in the family, or when the mother is older than 35 or 40. Fewer than three percent of fetuses tested are found to have severe disorders, but in those cases nearly all parents choose abortion.

**15. The U.S. Civil Rights Commission has opposed restrictions on the right to choose abortion, including current attempts to add an anti-abortion amendment to the Constitution.** The Commission stated in 1975: "So long as the question of when life begins is a matter of religious controversy and no choice can be rationalized on a purely secular premise, the people by outlawing abortion through the amending process, would be establishing one religious view and thus inhibiting the free exercise of religion in others." More than 50 resolutions for an anti-abortion amendment of the Constitution are pending in Congress. And some anti-abortion activists are calling for an unprecedented Constitutional Convention to vote on such an amendment. Nine state legislatures have called for a "Con Con," out of the 34 needed to make it happen.

15 Facts You Should Know About Abortion, Reprinted by courtesy of Zero Population Growth Inc.

### Life or Death

*The following excerpt is pro-life (anti-abortion) view. How do its assumptions differ from the pro-abortion supporters' arguments. What facts does each emphasize? How accurate are each's "facts"?*

**What of the U.S. Supreme Court Decision?** This has opened all fifty states to abortion on demand until the cord is cut. It prevents any state from forbidding abortion when needed for the life *or health* of the mother. "Health" specifically includes mental health. Ample precedence both legal (U.S. Supreme Court, Vuitch case) and in practice (California, Wash. D.C.) has shown that "mental health" is abortion on demand.

The Dred Scott Decision in 1857 ruled that black people were not "persons" in the eyes of the Constitution. Slaves could be bought, sold, used or even killed as property of the owner. That decision was overturned by the 14th Amendent.

Now the court has ruled that unborn people are not "persons" in the eyes of the Constitution. They can be killed at the request of their owners (mothers). This dreadful decision can only be overturned by another constitutional amendment.

The fact of human life in the womb cannot be denied. To today allow one age group of humans to be killed because they are socially burdensome will lead inexorably to allowing the killing of other humans at other ages who have become socially burdensome.

**But legalizing abortion would eliminate criminal abortions!** This is purely wishful thinking, and a completely false statement. Consistent experience has been that when laws are liberalized, the legal abortion rate skyrockets, the illegal abortion rate does not drop, but frequently also rises. The reason consistently given is the relative lack of privacy of the offical procedures. (Handbook on Abortion)

**Doesn't a mother have a right to her own body?** This is not her body but the body of another human person. Since when have we given to a mother the right to kill her children — born or unborn?

***Abortions is only a religious question, isn't it?***
No, Theology certainly concerns itself with respect for human life. It must turn to science, however, to tell it when life begins. The question of abortion is a basic human question that concerns the entire civilized society in which we live. It is not just a Catholic, or Protestant, or Jewish issue. It is a question of who lives or dies.

***Isn't abortion another means of birth control?***
No. Do not confuse abortion with birth control. Birth control prevents new life from beginning. Abortion kills the new life that has already begun.

***Why bring unwanted babies into the world?***
An unwanted pregnancy in the early months does not necessarily mean an unwanted baby after delivery. Dr. Edward Lenoski (U. of S. Cal.) has conclusively shown that 90% of battered children were planned pregnancies.

"A world without unwanted children, wives, oldsters, etc. would be a perfect world. The measure of our humanity is not that we won't always have unwanted ones among us but what we do with them. Will we try to help them? or kill them?" Willke, *Handbook on Abortion*

***What about the girl who's been raped?*** Pregnancy from rape is extremely rare. A scientific study of 1000 cases of rape treated medically right after the rape resulted in zero cases of pregnancy. J. Kuchera, J.A.M.A., Oct. 25, 1971

***What if the mother threatens suicide?*** Suicide among pregnant women is almost unknown. In Minnesota, in a 15-year period, there were only 14 maternal suicides. Eleven occurred after delivery. None were illegitimately pregnant. All

were psychotic.

***Are there after-effects to the mother?*** After legal abortions there is an increase in sterility of 10%, of miscarriages of an additional 10%, of psychiatric aftermath (9 to 59% in England), of Rh trouble later. Tubal pregnancies rise from 0.5 to 3.5% and premature babies from 5 to 15%. There can be perforation of the uterus, blood clots to the lung, infection, and later fatal hepatitis from blood transfusions. (Handbook on Abortion)

***But isn't it cruel to allow a handicapped child to be born — to a miserable life?*** The assumption that handicapped people enjoy life less than "normal" ones has recently been shown to be false. A well-documented investigation has shown that there is no difference between malformed and normal persons in their degree of life satisfaction, outlook of what lies immediately ahead and vulnerability to frustration. "Though it may be both common and fashionable to believe that the malformed enjoys life less than normal, this appears to lack both empirical and theoretical support." Paul Cameron & D. Van Hoeck, Am. Psychologic Assn. Meeting, 1971

***A new ethic?*** For two millenia in our western culture, specifically protected by our laws, and deeply imprinted into the hearts of all men has existed the absolute value of honoring and protecting the right of each person to live. This has been an inalienable, and unequivocal right. The only exceptions have been that of balancing a life for a life in certain situations or by due process of law.

Our new permissive abortion laws represent a complete about-face, a total rejection of one of the core values of western man, and an acceptance of a new ethic in which life has only a relative value. No longer will every human have an absolute right to live simply because he exists. Man will now be allowed to exist only if he measures up to certain standards of independence, physical perfection, or utilitarian usefulness to others. This is a momentous change that strikes at the root of western civilization.

It makes no difference to vaguely assume that human life is more human post-born than pre-born. What is critical is to judge it to be, or not to be, human life. By a measure of "more" or "less" human, one can easily and logically justify infanticide and euthanasia. By the measure of economic and/or social usefulness, the ghastly atrocities of Hitlerian mass murders came to be. One cannot help but be reminded of the anguished comment of a condemned Nazi judge who said to an American judge after the Nuremburg trials: "I never knew it would come to this." The American judge answered simply: *"It came to this the first time you condemned an innocent life."* Willke, *Handbook on Abortion*

**Isn't it true that restrictive abortion laws are unfair to the poor?** It is probably true that it is safer for a rich person to break almost any law, than for a poor person to do so. Perhaps the poor cannot afford all the heroin they want. Rich people probably can. Does that mean we should make heroin available to everyone? Not everything that money can buy is necessarily good. The solution is not to repeal laws, but to enforce them fairly. Laws restricting abortion can be, and frequently have been, adequately enforced.

**Isn't abortion safer than childbirth?** No, in the last stages it is far more dangerous. Even in the first three months more mothers die from legal abortions than from childbirth. Most legal abortion deaths are not reported however.

**What of the Population Explosion?** Fertility in the United States has dropped below the "replacement" level of 2.1 children a family that is necessary to achieve zero population growth. It is now under 1.9.

If the current decline in the world birth rate continues "It should be possible to reduce the world crude birth rate to less than 20 and the world population growth rate to less than 1% per annum by 1980" (same as U.S.A.). World Fertility Trends During the 1960's, R. Ravenholt, director, off. of population USAID

**Constructive Answers** "Choosing abortion as a solution to social problems would seem to indicate that certain individuals and groups of individuals are attempting to maximize their own comforts by enforcing their own prejudices. As a result, pregnant school girls continue to be ostracized, mothers of handicapped children are left to fend for themselves, and the poor are neglected in their struggle to attain equal conditions of life. And the **only** solution offered these people is abortion. It becomes very disturbing when we think that this destructive medical technique may replace love as the shaper of our families and our society."

"We **must** move toward creating a society in which material pursuits are not the ends of our lives; where no child is hungry or neglected; where even defective children are valuable because they call forth our power to love and serve without reward. Instead of destroying life, we should destroy the conditions which make life intolerable. Then, every child regardless of its capabilities or the circumstances of his birth, could be welcomed, loved, and cared for." Induced Abortion, A Documented Report, p. 134.

The world of difference between "rape fantasy" and rape can be expressed in one word: control. The point of a fantasy is that a woman . . . orders the reality within it, ordains its terms, and censors it according to her needs; the point of rape is that a woman is violated against her will.

Molly Haskell, *Ms*, November, 1976

---

### If Someone Tries to Rape You . . .

*This information was prepared for the "Rape Awareness" program in Clackamas County, Oregon. Unlike many other areas, it has a Rape Victim Advocate who accompanies any woman who is raped through her hospital examination and police interview. The police have been sensitized to the victim's feelings, again unlike many other areas. What rape crisis program has your area undertaken?*

***This Can't Be Happening To Me . . .***    There are no hard and fast rules to prevent a rape once you are attacked. Only you know what will work in your case. There are a number of ways to protect yourself which may work in some cases. However, you should be aware of their pitfalls as well as their merits.

***Screaming (and Noise)***    Before you start screaming, consider what the rapist's reaction might be. He may be scared off, but he might feel forced to shut you up. Screaming and noise (whistles and air horns) can work if you're sure help is near, sure that it will arrive in time and that it will be enough when it does. If you do yell, yell "FIRE". More people will respond to that than a call of "HELP".

***Struggling***    It may rebuff him, but it can work against you. It could wear you out, make him angry or sexually arouse him. Ask yourself if you're willing to seriously hurt him to stop him; you may have to. If your natural reaction would be to fight, then make sure you know how. Take a class in martial arts and keep up with it.

***Weapons***    You probably carry all your so-called weapons in your purse . . . the first thing you're going to drop if attacked. Also, a weapon can be taken away and used against you. Finally, it may be illegal for you to carry certain weapons such as guns and knives.

***Running***    This will work if you're sure you can get to safety. He will probably try to stop you.

***Surrender***    Letting your attacker think you're surrendering can be used as a stall to buy time to think.

***Psychological Warfare***    Communicate with your attacker. Use words, gestures or whatever, but get him talking to you. Don't be afraid to let him see you're afraid. Try to talk him out of it with any argument you can think of: "I'm pregnant," "I've got VD," or "I'm only 16" or "How would you feel if this was your sister?" Make it believable or it won't work.

There are some physical techniques with which you can turn off an attacker, too. Vomiting on him is a good example. Use your head – it can be your best weapon.

Whatever method you choose, if it gets you home alive, it was the right one. Too many women suffer from the "what-ifs" (What if I had done this or that unnecessarily). If you survive your attack, if you make it home safely, your technique worked. Your life was interrupted by a rape, instead of death.

***If You Are Raped***    If, in spite of your efforts, you are raped, try not to panic. Concentrate on the attacker's identity. Remember his exact description, any peculiar marks, scars, defects or identifying traits. Remember his vehicle and anything inside of it. Call the police as soon as you can. Your cooperation with them may insure that someone else will not have to suffer the same experience. DO NOT BATHE OR SHOWER. DO NOT APPLY MEDICATION. DO NOT THROW AWAY YOUR CLOTHES OR WASH THEM. All of these are natural reactions after an assault, but they destroy important evidence.

*Then What Happens?*   When the police arrive, they will take you to the hosital for a medical examination. There a County Rape Victim Advocate will meet you to accompany you through the rest of the ordeal. She can answer questions, refer to specialized help and just be a friend when you need one. The police will have to interview you as to the details of the crime and as to your assailant. They are not interested in past sexual activity except that which may affect the evidence just gathered at the hosital. If you decide to prosecute, the trial will not be easy. But remember, there is no shame in what has happened to you. The shame would be if the attacker went free.

*Reactions To Rape*   A victim has many feelings after a rape. Confusion about what happened and confusion as to what to do are normal. There may be a feeling of being degraded or abused, or fear of further violence from the rapist. Feelings of hurt and anger are common; in fact, anger is a healthy reaction. There may be a loss of self-respect, a feeling of isolation and some distrust of everyone. Support by a victim's family and friends is essential at this point to re-establish her feelings of normalcy. The problem may be compounded by their feelings which may be those of betrayal, confusion or guilt. All of these are normal and can be worked through. If the feelings become overwhelming, counseling is available.

*Rapists do not have a special look. Therefore, it is important to recognize potentially dangerous situations to protect yourself. Here are some common-sense suggestions toward that end.*

### At Home
1.  Have your keys in hand as you approach the door. Always keep entrances well lit.
2.  When you move to a new place or lose your keys, change the locks.
3.  Install single cylinder deadbolt locks, or if there's glass in the door or a window nearby, a double cylinder deadbolt.
4.  Keep doors and windows secured, even if you leave for just a few minutes.
5.  Drill and pin all windows and sliding glass doors.
6.  Don't let a stranger in to use the phone; make the call yourself.
7.  Demand identification from any stranger. If you have doubts, call his company.
8.  If you live alone, use initials in the phone book, and the mailbox, and on mail.
9.  Vary your routine each day. Remember most rapes in the victim's home are planned.

### Walking
1.  Try not to go anywhere alone.
2.  Let someone know where you're going and when you're due back.
3.  Walk on well-lit, well-traveled familiar streets.
4.  Walk close to the road, avoiding houses and hedges.
5.  Walk facing traffic so you see any autos approaching you.
6.  Be constantly aware of who and what is around you. If you are unaware, an attacker has a better chance.

### In The Car
1.  Have your keys in hand when you approach the car. Check the back seat before entering the vehicle.
2.  Always keep the doors locked and the windows rolled up.
3.  Check your gas gauge before each excursion. Keep your car in good running order. Know how to change a flat tire.
4.  If you suspect someone is following you or trying to run you off the road, do something

to attract attention. Keep your car operable as long as you can. If you have to stop, leave the engine running and in gear. Wait until the pursuer gets out of his car, then drive away as fast as you can. Don't drive home. Go to a fire or police station or any place where there will be people.

## Marital Rape

Editorial, *San Francisco Chronicle*, June 25, 1979

*If ever a mockery were made of justice, it was in the case of Greta and John Rideout. In 1977, the Oregon legislature passed a bill permitting wives to charge their husbands with sexual assault. The first test case came in October, 1978 when John Rideout was indicted for raping his wife, Greta. They had a long history of marital violence in their short marriage. John was acquitted in the trial; then the couple re-united again, more in love than ever before, they reported, after "bringing Christ into their marriage." They continued to quarrel and finally divorced. Their on-again/off-again relationship used the marital rape law as a weapon in their stormy relationship, discrediting the law's original purpose of protecting wives.*

*In September, 1979, however, James Chretien was convicted of raping his wife Janice by a Massachussetts court. This was the first such conviction in U.S. history; Chretien received a 3-5 year prison sentence. Unlike the Rideouts, however, the Chretiens were not living together at the time of the rape; instead, James broke into his wife's apartment.*

*A number of states have now passed marital rape laws. One such bill has passed the California Assembly at the time of this writing. An edito-rial from the San Francisco Chronicle suggests caution. What are the merits of a marital rape law? What are the possible disadvantages?*

IN PASSING A bill that makes it a crime for husbands to rape their wives, the Assembly has launched the legislature proceeding that must be approach with caution.

The problem here is that such a law constitutes an invasion by the government of the marital bedroom; a place from which we have been largely successful in removing its prurient eye. Those old laws forbidding "crimes against nature" even between married couples no longer operate. And we are the more mature and civilized for that.

The relationship between married people is a special one in that it is largely predicated on reasonable commitment to sexual acquiescence. That Oregon case of unhappy memory demonstrates how easy it is to bring a charge of marital rape after a tiff between two immature partners.

In such a highly personal situation, too, it would be difficult to get dispassionate witnesses. The specter of children being called to testify against their father summons up a traumatic picture. As the Oregon case spelled out for us, the temptation toward levying of emotion-inspired, spur-of-the-moment charges would be great. And that would tend to demean the whole principle of swift, appropriate justice for true violations.

There is no question that cases occur in which a wife is physically maltreated by her husband. But she still has recourse in proceeding against him through charges of assault and battery. Once again, we caution the legislature to take care as it approaches this delicate and sensitive issue.

*San Francisco Chronicle*, editorial June 25, 1979. Copyright © 1979 Chronicle Publishing Co.

# EPILOGUE

## "Am I Normal?"

**B**eneath the haunting question "Am I Normal?" lies the guilt, fear, and anxiety that accompany most people's feelings about their sexuality. The questions are insistent: Do I make love often enough? Are my sexual fantasies perverse? Is the way I make love normal? Is it wrong to masturbate? In our culture, where sex is alternately repressed and exploited, where it is hidden from children, where contradictory sexual norms abound, where upholders of morality violate in private what they preach in public, it is no wonder that people ask if their private desires and activities are normal. Indeed, what could be more normal given these circumstances than wondering "Am I normal?"

But, does *normal* sexual behavior exist? Albert Ellis observes that "normal" sex behavior is anything and everything which we – or which the societies in which we happen to live – declare and make it to be." Thus, homosexuality was normal behavior in ancient Greece; stimulation of the genitals of young children by adults was normal among the Hopi; and male sexual passivity was normal among the Balinese, where the women were expected to take the sexual initiative.

Normal behavior, consequently, means the form of behavior encouraged and sanctioned by a society. Sexual attitudes and behavior of any culture can be examined using any one of the following criteria:

***Statistically "normal" behavior*** Certain forms of sexual behavior are acceptable or "normal" simply because the customs, mores, and laws of a culture encourage them. For example, our culture discourages women from initiating sexual intercourse; thus male-initiated intercourse is statistically more prevalent than female-initiated intercourse. Some American men, therefore, consider a woman abnormal if she initiates a sexual encounter. Because they don't know any women who are sexually assertive, men label abnormal those women who do not subscribe to the prevailing standard. Statistically normal behavior is *made* normal by the sexual attitudes of a culture.

***Biologically "normal" behavior*** Sexuality is inherent to human life. We are an organism which must copulate to reproduce (notwithstanding artificial insemination and the recent success in "test tube" fertilization). Our species would cease to exist without penile/vaginal intercourse.

Yet, we are also a thinking species, and there is question as to what real interrelationship exists between mind and body. Very little is known about why some men with perfectly adequate sexual "plumbing" cannot put it to use. We do know, however, that some such men respond well to counseling and various sensual techniques, such as the methods of Masters and Johnson and Helen Singer Kaplan.

Much less is known about the mind/body components of homosexuality, a sexual trait which is far less responsive to attempts at change than impotency. Indeed, more and more men and women of homosexual inclination are making it known that they are perfectly satisfied with the way they are.

Evolutionary theorists have shown quite convincingly that, generation by generation, organisms respond to environmental changes by adapting both physically and behaviorally. Given the proven susceptibility of human sexual response to psychological influences, it would seem likely that our species would feel the pressure to behaviorally adapt, and perhaps (over thousands of years) show perceptible physical adaptations. It may then seem, what is biologically "normal" behavior to us, is simply what we are accustomed to.

*Healthy "normal" behavior*    Sexual behavior that makes us feel happy or emotionally and physically fulfilled is "normal"; that which makes us feel guilty, anxious, tense, frustrated, or neurotic is "abnormal." But, here again, such behavior is "normal" and "healthy" because we have been taught to feel good when we behave in prescribed ways. We are unhappy about masturbating because we have been taught to feel guilty about masturbating, making masturbation unhealthy for ourselves. Yet there are other cultures in which masturbation is wholly accepted as a healthy form of self-exploration and discovery. Even within our own culture – especially among certain liberated factions as well as some sex therapists – positive attitudes are being developed regarding masturbation, so that mastur-

bation is now considered by some as a healthy sexual activity.

*Morally "normal" behavior*.    If "normal" sexual behavior is defined as moral sexual behavior, it is clear that the morality of any act depends on the culture in which it occurs. There are no moral absolutes. Indeed, much morally "normal" behavior – such as the traditional Christian emphasis on premarital chastity – is abnormal behavior when judged from a statistically significant or physically pleasurable standard.

All of these categorizations form the basis of our definition of what is normal. Often these various meanings of "normal" conflict. How does a person determine whether he or she is normal if statistically prevalent behavior is condemned as immoral by one's religion? Such dilemmas as these are commonplace in our culture and give rise to the ever-present question: "Am I normal?"

We hope this book has stimulated an enjoyable self-analysis and led to a clearer perception of your personal sexual normalcy.

# Bibliography

Altman, Dennis. *Homosexual; Oppression and Liberation*, New York: Dutton, 1971.

Amir, Menachem. *Patterns in Forcible Rape*, Chicago: University of Chicago Press, (1971).

Balswick, Jack and James Anderson. "Role Definition in The Unarranged Date," *Journal of Marriage and the Family*, 31, (1969): 776-778.

Bandurak, A. *Principles of Behavior Modification*, New York: Holt, Rinehart, and Winston, 1969.

Bardwick, Judith. *The Psychology of Women: A Study of Biocultural Conflicts*, New York: Harper Row, 1971.

Barrett-Connor, et.al. "Heart Disease Risk Factors and Hormone Use in Postmenopausal Women," *Journal of the American Medical Association*, May 18, 1979.

Barros, Ricardo. *Sexual Fantasy*, London: Luxor Press, 1970.

Beral, V., *Mortality Among Oral Contraceptive Users*, Lancet, 727f, October 8, 1977.

Berne, Eric. *Games People Play*, Westminster, Maryland: Ballantine, 1978.

Bibring, Grete. "Some specific psychological masks in pregnancy and motherhood," in Signe Hammer (ed.), *Women: Body and Culture*, New York: 1975.

Billington, R. A. *The Protestant Crusade 1800-1860*, Chicago: Quadrangle Books, 1964.

Blatch, Harriot Stanton. (ed) *Elizabeth Cady Stanton Revealed In Her Letters, Diary, and Reminiscences*, New York: Harper (1922).

Bohannan, Paul. (ed.) *Divorce and After*, Garden City, New York: Doubleday, 1972.

Borden, George, Richard Gregg, and Theodore Grove. *Speech Behavior and Human Interaction*, Englewood Cliffs, New Jersey: Prentice-Hall, 1969.

Bossard, James H. and E. Boll. *The Large Family System: An Original Study in the Sociology of Family Behavior*, Philadelphia: University of Pennsylvania Press, 1956.

Boston Women's Health Collective. *Our Bodies, Ourselves*, New York: 1973.

Bott, Elizabeth. *Family and Social Network*, London: Tavistock, 1957.

Brennan, B. and J. R. Heilman. *The Complete Book of Midwifery*, New York: E. P. Dutton, 1977.

Brenton, Myron. *Sex Talk*, New York: Stein and Day, 1972.

Brownmiller, Susan. *Against Our Will*, New York: Random House, 1976.

Byrne, D. "A Pregnant Pause in the Sexual Revolution," *Psychology Today*, July, 1977.

Camus, Albert. *The Rebel*, New York: Doubleday, 1956.

Cash, W. J. *Mind of the South*, New York: Knopf, 1941.

Churchill, Wainwright. *Homosexual Behavior Among Males: A Cross-cultural and Cross-species Investigation*, New York: Hawthorn Books, 1967.

Cimons, M. "Program to Reduce Mongolism," *Los Angeles Times*, 1974.

Cohen, A. *Everyman's Talmud*. New York: Dutton, 1949.

Collins, John, et.al. "Insights into a dating partner's expectations," *Journal of Marriage and the Family*, 38 (1976) 373-378.

Colman, Arthur and Libby. *Pregnancy: The Psychological Experience*, New York: 1971.

Comfort, Alex. *Sex In Society*, New York: Citadel Press, 1966.

——. *The Anxiety Makers: Some Curious Preoccupations of the Medical Profession*, London: Nelson, 1967.

*Contemporary Obstetrics and Gynecology*, 97f,

November, 1978.

"Contraception Study," *New York Times*, May 6, 1976.

Cook, R. J. and B. M. Dickens. "A Decade of international change in abortion law: 1967-1977," *American Journal of Public Health*, July, 1978.

Council on Interacial Books, *Chronicles of American Indian Protest*, Washington, D. C., 1971.

Curie-Cohen, M. et.al. "Current practice of artificial insemination by donor in the United States," *New England Journal of Medicine*, March 15, 1979.

Davis, David. *Homicide in American Fiction, 1798-1860: A Study in Social Values*, New York: Cornell University Press, 1968.

deBeauvoir, Simone. *The Coming of Age*, New York: Putnam, 1972.

———. *The Second Sex*, New York: 1948.

De Martino, (ed.) *Sexual Behavior and Personality Characteristics*, New York: Citadel Press, 1963.

Dick-Read, G. (1944) *Childbirth Without Fear*, 4th edition, New York: Harper and Row, 1972.

Ehrhardt, et.al. "Fetal Androgens and Female Gender Identity in the Early Treated Adrenogenital Syndrome," Baltimore Md.: *Johns Hopkins Medical Journal* 122, 1968.

———. "Influence of androgen and some aspects of sexually dimorphic behavior in with the late-treated adrenogenital syndrome," Baltimore, Md.: *Johns Hopkins Medical Journal* 123, 1968.

Ellis, Albert and A. Abarbanel, (eds.). "The psychology of sex offenders," *The Encyclopedia of Sexual Behavior*, Vol II, New York: Hawthorn Books, 1961.

Ellis, Havelock. *Studies in the Psychology of Sex*, New York: Random House, 1940.

*Epidemic: Venereal Disease*. Proceedings of the 2nd International Venereal Disease Symposium, 1972.

Epstein, L. M. *Sex Laws and Customs in Judaism*, New York: Block Publishing, 1948.

Erikson, Erik. *Identity, Youth and Crisis*, New York: Norton, 1968.

———. *Young Man Luther*, New York; Norton, 1962.

Faraday, Ann. *Dream Power*, New York: Coward, McCann and Geoghegan, 1972.

Fellini, F. *Satyricon*, 1970.

Fiedler, Leslie. *Love and Death in the American Novel*, New York: Stein and Day, 1966.

Fielding, J. E. and A. Yankaur, "The Pregnant Smoker," *American Journal of Public Health*, September, 1978.

Ford, Clellan and F. A. Beach. *Patterns of Sexual Behavior*, New York: Harper, 1951.

Friday, Nancy. *My Secret Garden; Women's Sexual Fantasies*, New York: Trident, 1973.

Gagnon, John and Joan Greenblat. *Life Designs*, Englewood Cliffs, New Jersey: Prentice-Hall, 1978.

Gagnon, John H. and William Simon. *Sexual Conduct: The Social Sources of Human Sexuality*, Chicago: Aldine Publishing Co., 1973.

Gallant, D. M. "Sexual survey #14: Current Thinking On Recreational Drugs and Sex," *Medical Aspects of Human Sexuality*, September, 1978.

Gebhard, P., et.al. *Pregnancy, Birth and Abortion*, New York: Harper, 1958.

———. *The Sex Offenders*, New York: Harper, 1965.

Golbus, M. S., et.al. "Prenatal Genetia Diagnosis in 3000 Amniocentices," *The New England Journal of Medicine*, page 157, January 25, 1979.

Green, Gerald and Caroline Green. *Sado-Masochism: The Last Taboo*, New York: Ballantine, 1974.

Greenblatt, R. B. "Hormone Deficiency as a Cause of Sexual Dysfunction," *Medical Aspects of Human Sexuality*, October, 1978.

Greenwald, Harold. *The Elegant Prostitute: A Social and Psychoanalytic Study*, New York: Walker, 1970.

Gusfield, Joseph. *Symbolic Crusade: Status Politics and The American Temperance Movement*, Urbana, Illinois: University of Illinois Press, 1966.

Haller, John and Robin Haller. *The Physician and Sexuality in Victorian America*, Urbana, Illinois: University of Illinois Press, 1974.

Haller, Mark. *Eugenics: Hereditarian Attitudes in American Thought*, New Brunswick: Rutgers University Press, 1963.

Handel, Gerald (ed.). *The Psychosocial Interior of the Family; A Source-book for the Study of Whole Families*, Chicago: Aldine Publishing Co., 1967.

Handlin, Oscar. *Race and Nationality in American Life*, Boston: Little, Brown, 1957.

Harlow, H. F. et.al. *Psychology*, Albion Publishing Co., San Francisco: 1971.

Harlow, Margaret and Harry Harlow. "The Effects of Rearing Conditions on Behavior," John Money, (ed.), *Sex Research: New Developments*, New York: Holt, 1965.

Harper, Ida. *The Life and Work of Susan B. Anthony*, Indianapolis and Kansas City: Bowen-Merrill Co., 1898-1908.

Hatcher, et.al. *Contraceptive Technology: 1978-1979*, New York: Irvington Publishers, 1978.

Heart Attack, *British Medical Journal*, May, 1975.

Heller, Joseph. *Something Happened*, New York: Ballantine, 1975.

Herschberger, Ruth. *Adam's Rib*, New York: Pellegrini and Cudahy, 1948.

Hilgers, Thomas and Dennis Horan (eds.). *Abortions and Social Justice*, Mission, Kansas: Sheed Andrews and McMeel, 1973.

Hoffman, Martin. *The Gay World: Male Homosexuality and the Social Creation of Evil*, New York: Basic Books, 1968.

Holbrook, David, (ed.). *The Case Against Pornography*, LaSalle, Illinois: Open Court Publishing, 1973.

Hooker, E. "An Empirical Study of Some Relations Between Sexual Patterns and Gender Identity in Male Homosexuals," in John Money (ed.), *Sex Research – New Developments*, New York: Holt, 1965.

Humphreys, Laud. *Out of the Closets: The Sociology of Homosexual Liberation*, Englewood Cliffs, New Jersey: Prentice Hall, 1972.

Hunt, Morton. *Sexual Behavior in the 1970s*, Chicago: Playboy Press, 1974.

———. *The Divorce Experience*, New York: World, 1978.

Janus, Sam. *Sexual Profile of Men in Power*, New York: Warner Books, 1977.

Johnston, Jill. *Lesbian Nation*, New York: Simon and Schuster, 1973.

Jordan, Winthrop. *White Over Black: American Attitudes Toward The Negro*, Williamsburg: University of North Carolina Press, 1968.

Kaercher, D., "What Can Be Done About Infertility?," *Better Homes and Gardens*, September, 1979.

Kaplan, H. S. *The New Sex Therapy*, New York: Brunner/Mazel, 1974.

Karpman, Benjamin. *The Sexual Offender and His Offenses*, New York: Julian Press, 1960.

Kennedy, David. *Birth Control in America: The Career of Margaret Sanger*, New Haven, Conn: Yale University Press, 1970.

Kephart, William. *The Family, Society, and the Individual*, Boston: Houghton, 1961.

Key, Wilson Bryan. *Subliminal Seduction*, Englewood Cliffs, New Jersey: Prentice-Hall, (1973).

Keyl, Anne. *VD: The People to People Disease*, Toronto: 1972.

Kinsey, Alfred. et.al. *Sexual Behavior in the Human Female*, New York: Saunders, 1953.

———. *Sexual Behavior in the Human Male*, Philadelphia: Saunders, 1948.

Kolodny, R. et.al. "Depression of Plasma Testosterone Levels After Chronic Marihuana Use," *The New England Journal of Medicine* 290, 1974.

Komarovsky, Mirra. *Blue-Collar Marriage*, New York: Random House, 1964.

Kraemer. et.al. "Baboon Infant Produced by Embryo Transfer," *Science*, June, 1976.

Kron, R. E. et.al. "Newborn Sucking Behavior Affected by Obstetrical Sedation," *Pediatrics* 37, 1966.

Laing, R. D., *The Politics of Experience*, New York: Random House, 1969.

———. *The Politics of the Family*, Westminster, Maryland: Pantheon, 1967.

Landesman, R. and B. B. Saxena. "Results of the first 1000 Radioreceptorassays for the Determination of Human Chronic

Gonadotropin," *Fertility and Sterility*, April, 1976.

Lasswell, Harold. *Psychopathology and Politics*, New York: Viking, 1960.

LeBoyer, Frederick. *Birth Without Violence*, Alfred A. Knopf, 1975.

Lederer, Wolfgang. *The Fear of Women*, New York: Grune and Stratton, 1968.

Leech, Margaret. *Anthony Comstock, Roundsman of the Lord*, New York: A. & C. Boni, 1927.

Lidz, Theodore. *The Family and Human Adaptation*, New York: International Universities Press, 1963.

Liebow, Elliot. *Tally's Corner: A Study of Negro Streetcorner Men*, Boston: Little, 1967.

Lloyd, Arthur. *The Slavery Controversy, 1831-1860*, Chapel Hill: The University of North Carolina Press, 1939.

Lorenz, Konrad. *Evolution and Modification of Behavior*, Chicago: University of Chicago Press, 1965.

Love, Barbara and Sidney Abbott. *Sappho Was A Right-on Woman*, New York: Stein and Day, 1972.

Lowen, Alexander. *Love and Orgasm: A Revolutionary Guide to Sexual Fulfillment*, New York: Macmillan, 1965.

Luckey, Elanor and Gilbert Nass. "A Comparison of Sexual Attitudes and Behavior in an International Sample," *Journal of Marriage and the Family*, 31 (1969): 364-369.

Macdonald, John. *Rape Offenders and Their Victims*, Springfield, Illinois: 1971.

Marcus, Steven. *The Other Victorians: A Study of Sexuality and Pornography in Mid-Nineteenth Century*, New York: Basic Books, 1966.

Masters, W. H. and V. E. Johnson. "Advice for

Women Who Want to Have a Baby", Redbook, March, 1975.

———. *Human Sexual Inadequacy*, Boston: Little Brown and Company, 1970.

———. *Human Sexual Response*, Boston: Little Brown and Company, 1966.

McCall, Michael. "Courtship as Social Exchange: Some Historical Comparisons," in Bernard Farber (ed), *Kinship and Family Organization*, New York: Wiley, 1966.

McClintock, M. K. "Menstrual Synchrony and Suppression," *Nature*, 229, 1971.

Mead, Margaret. *Male and Female*, New York: 1949.

"Medical Aspects of Human Sexuality," *In-Vitro Fertilization Procedures* (illus.), December, 1978.

Mills, C. Wright. *White Collar: American Middle Classes*, New York: Oxford University Press, 1951.

Money, J. and A. A. Ehrhardt. *Man and Woman, Boy and Girl*, Baltimore: Johns Hopkins University Press, 1972.

Monk, Maria. *Awful Disclosures of the Hotel Diew Nunnery of Montreal, or The Secrets of the Black Nunnery Revealed*, New ed. Aurora: The Menace Publishing Co., First Published 1836.

Montagu, Ashley. *Touching: The Human Significance of the Skin*, New York: Columbia University Press, 1971.

Morgan, Edmund. *The Puritan Family: Religion and Domestic Relations in 17th Century New England*, New York: Harper and Row, 1966.

Morris, Jan. *Conundrum*, New York: Harcourt, Brace, 1974.

Murphy, John. *Homosexual Liberation; A Personal View*, New York: Praeger Publishers, 1971.

National Center for Health Statistics, *Monthly Vital Statistics Report: Natality Statistics*, September, 1977.

Newton, Niles. *Maternal Emotions*, New York: 1955.

Nguyen, Tuan, et.al. "The meaning of touch: sex differences," *Journal of Communication*, 25 (1975), 92-103.

Noonan, John. *Contraception: A History of its Treatment by the Catholic Theologians and Canonists*, Cambridge: Belknap Press of Harvard University Press, 1965.

Oakley, Ann. *Sex, Gender, and Society*, New York: Harper Row, 1972.

Packard, Vance. *The Hidden Persuaders*, New York: Pocket Books, 1958.

———. *The Sexual Wilderness*, New York: McKay, 1968.

Paige, Karen. "Women Learn To Sing the Menstrual Blues," *Psychology Today*, September, 1973.

Paulsen, K. and R. A. Kuhn (eds.). *Women's Almanac*, 195. J. B. Lippincott, 1976.

Pavlov, I. P. *Conditioned Reflexes: An Investigation of the Physiological Activity of The Cerebral Cortex*, London: Oxford University Press, 1927.

Phillips, O. C. and T. M. Frazier. "Obstetric anesthetic care in the United States," *Obstetrics and Gynecology* 19, 1962.

*Population Reports*, "Sterilization," Department of Medical and Public Affairs, The George Washington University Medical Center, May, 1976.

Rainwater, Lee and Gerald Handel. "Changing Family Roles in the Working Class," in Arthur Shostak and William Gomberg, *Blue-Collar World: Studies of the American Worker*, Evanston, Ill.: Prentice-Hall, 1964.

Rainwater, Lee. *And the Poor Get Children: Sex, Contraception, and Family Planning in the Working Class*, Chicago: Watts, 1960.

———. *Family Design: Marital Sexuality, Family Size, and Contraception*, Chicago: Aldine, 1965.

Rainwater, Lee (ed.). *Social Problems and Public Policy: Deviance and Liberty*, Chicago: Aldine, 1974.

Reiss, Ira. *The Social Context of Premarital Sexual Permissiveness*, New York: Irvington, 1967.

*Report of the Commission on Obscenity and Pornography*, United States Commission on Obscenity and Pornography, New York: Bantam Books, (1970).

Reuben, David R. *Everything You Always Wanted to Know About Sex but Were Afraid to Ask*, New York: David McKay Co., 1969.

Riciardi, V. M. et.al. "Genetic Counseling as Part of Hospital Care," *American Journal of Public Health*, 652, July, 1978.

Rorvik, David M. and Landrum Shettles. *Your Baby's Sex: Now You Can Choose*, New York: Dodd, Mead and Co., 1970.

Rosenblatt, D. *Nine Months, One Day, One Year: A Guide to Pregnancy, Birth and Babycare*, New York: Harper and Row, 1975.

Rowan, R. and P. Gillette. *Your Prostate*, Doubleday and Co., Inc., 1973.

Rubington, Earl and Martin Weinberg. *Deviance: The Interactionist Perspective*, New York: Macmillan. 1973.

Rubin, Isadore. *Sexual Life After Sixty*, New York: Basic Books, 1965.

Russell, E. S. "Anesthesia and Obstetric Outcome," *International Anesthesiology Clinics* 11 #2, 1973.

St. Augustine. *The City of God*, London: T. Clarke, 1934.

*San Francisco Chronicle/Examiner*, Advertisement for Predictor, 29, October 8, 1979.

Santa Cruz Women's Health Collective, *Herpes*, Santa Cruz, California: 1978.

Sarrel, Lorna and Philip. "What you should know about your man's body," *Redbook*, September, 1978.

Satir, Virginia. *People Making*, Palo Alto: Science and Behavior Books, 1972.

Scanlon, J. W. and M. H. Alper, "Prenatal Pharmacology and Evaluation of the Newborn," *International Anesthesiology Clinics* 11 #2. 1973.

Schnider, S. M. "Obstetric anesthesia coverage: problems and solutions," Obstetrics and Gynecology 34, 1969.

Schulz, David A. *Coming Up Black: Patterns of Ghetto Socialization*, Englewood Cliffs, New Jersey: Prentice-Hall, 1969.

Schur, Edwin. *Labeling Deviant Behavior: Its Sociological Implications*, New York: Harper and Row, (1971).

Sears, Robert, Eleanor Marcoby, and Harry Levin. *Patterns of Child-Rearing*, Evanston. Ill.: Row, Patterson, and Co., 1957.

Shapiro, H., *The Birth Control Book*, New York, St. Martin, 1977.

Shaw, N. S. *Forced Labor*, Pergamon Press, 1974.

Sherfey, M. J. *The Nature and Evaluation of Female Sexuality*, New York: Random House, 1972.

Shope, David. *Interpersonal Sexuality*, Philadephia: Saunders, 1975.

Simmel, George. *The Sociology of George Simmel*, Chicago: Free Press, 1950.

Simon, William and John Gagnon. *Sexual Conduct: The Social Sources of Human Sexuality*, Chicago: Aldine, 1973.

Sinclair, Andrew. *Prohibition: The Era of Excess*, Boston: Little, Brown, and Company, 1962.

Skinner, B. F. *The Behavior of Organisms: An Experimental Analysis*, New York: Appleton-Century-Crofts, 1938.

Somes, M. "Giving Birth,": *Ramparts Magazine* (Sept. 1974).

Speroff, L., et.al., *Clinical Gynecologic Endrocrinology and Infertility*, Baltimore, Md., Williams and Wilkins, 1973.

Speroff, L., "Is There a Biologic Basis for Homosexuality?," *Contemporary Obstetrics and Gynecology*, August 1978.

Stechler, G. "Newborn Attention as Affected by Medication During Labor," *Science* 144, 1964.

Stein, R. "A Trend Toward Safer Birth Control," *San Francisco Chronicle*, October 12, 1978.

Stewart, F. and F. Guest, G. Stewart, R. Hatcher. *My Body, My Health*, John Wiley and Sons, 1979.

Stoller, R. J. "Sexual Deviations" in F. A. Beach, *Human Sexuality in Four Perspectives*, Baltimore: Johns Hopkins Press, 1977.

Strong, Bryan et.al. *The Marriage and Family Experience*, Minneapolis, Minn.: West Publishing Co., 1979.

Taylor, Gordon R. *Sex in History*, New York: Harper, Row, 1970.

Teevan, James. "Reference Groups and Premarital Sexual Behavior," *Journal of Marriage and the Family*, 33 (May, 1972): 283-291.

Thomas, L. "On Cloning a Human Being," *New England Journal of Medicine*, 1296f, December 12, 1974.

Weinberg, Martin and Colin Williams. *Male Homosexuals: Their Problems and Adaptations*, New York: Oxford University Press, 1974.

Yarber, W. L. "Preventing Venereal Disease Infection: Approaches for the Sexually Active," *Health Values*, March/April, 1978.

Zelnik, Melvin and John Kanter. "Sexuality, Contraception and Pregnancy Among Young Unwed Females in the United States" in *U. S. Commission on Population Growth and the American Future, Demographic and Social Aspects of Population Growth, Research Report #1*, Washington, D. C.: U. S. Government Printing Office (1973).

Zelnik, M. and R. Kantner, "Sexual and Contraceptive Experience of Young Married Women in the United States, 1976 and 1971," *Family Planning Perspectives*, March/April, 1977.

Zipf, George. *Human Behavior and the Principle of Least Effort: An Introduction to Human Ecology*, Cambridge: Addison-Wesley, 1949.

# Glossary

**aberration** a departure from what is defined by a culture as "normal" behavior.

**abortion** the premature termination of pregnancy, either through spontaneous miscarriage, or induced by a physician, one's self, or another individual. (The latter two are common in areas where abortion is illegal.)

**adolescence** the period between puberty and adulthood, which differs by sex and cultural definition. For boys in our culture, adolescence is between 13-22 years; for girls, between 12-21 years.

**adrenal glands** glands above the kidneys that produce sex hormones in small amounts.

**adrenogenital syndrome** a genetic anomaly, which of a chromosomally female person (XX) with masculinized external anatomy and female internal anatomy.

**adultery** sexual intercourse between a married person and someone other than his/her spouse.

**afterbirth** the placenta and fetal membranes expelled from the uterus following childbirth.

**agglutination test** a pregnancy test involving a urine analysis.

**amenhorrhea** absence of periods of menstrual bleeding.

**amniocentesis** withdrawal of a small portion of the amniotic fluid surrounding a fetus through a needle inserted into the mother's abdomen.

**amnion** a fluid-filled, membranous pouch surrounding a developing fetus.

**ampullae** paired, convoluted ducts, which store sperm prior to ejaculation and empty into the prostate gland.

**androgen-insensitivity syndrome** a genetic defect in which an individual who is chromosomally male (XY) is insensitive to testosterone. Persons with this syndrome develop with partially feminized sex organs.

**androgens** hormones with masculinizing influences.

**androsperm** a sperm cell bearing a Y chromosome.

A zygote formed by the union of an androsperm and an egg will develop into a male.

**antibodies** proteins that destroy foreign substances in living systems.

**anus** the orifice of solid elimination.

**aphrodisial** a substance which is purported to enhance sex drive.

**approach-avoidance conflict** conflict arising when an action (such as sexual intercourse) is simultaneously considered desirable and repulsive.

**areola** the darkly pigmented area around a human nipple.

**autoeroticism** self-stimulation or erotic behavior toward one's self, usually referring to masturbation, but also including erotic dreams and fantasies.

**axillary hair** underarm hair.

**Bartholin's glands** two small organs of secretion at the sides of the vaginal orifice.

**bestiality** sexual contact with animals.

**blastocyst** an embryo, about five days after conception, consisting of a microscopic sphere of approximately 100 cells.

**breakthrough bleeding** erratic uterine bleeding, also termed "spotting."

**breech position** a fetal position in which the buttocks are directed into the birth canal.

**broad ligaments** ligaments that suspend the uterus within a female's pelvic bone structure.

**Caesarean section** an operation in which an infant is delivered via an incision in its mother's abdomen and uterus.

**carpopedal spasms** twitching and clutching movements of the hands and feet during the plateau of erotic arousal.

**castration complex** in Freudian theory, the infantile fear by males of losing their genitals because of incestuous desires. In females, the fantasy that the infant girl once had a penis but was castrated. This latter interpretation is widely disputed by feminists and non-Freudian psychologists, who find no empirical proof for it.

**cephalic position**  a fetal position in which the head points down into the cervix.

**cervix**  the tip of the uterus, which protrudes into the inner vagina.

**chancre**  a painless sore that is a symptom of syphilis. Chancres first appear as dull red bumps; sometimes they burst and form crusty scabs.

**chromosomes**  conglomerates of matter that carry hereditary information. Each chromosome carries several thousand genes (half of which have been received from each parent).

**circumcision**  removal of the foreskin of the penis.

**clitoral hood**  fold of membranous flesh that protects the clitoris.

**clitoris**  the center of female erotic arousal, situated where the labia minora meet.

**clomid**  a drug which induces ovulation, used in certain cases of female infertility.

**coitus**  (also, coition) sexual intercourse.

**colostrum**  a substance produced by the breasts during late pregnancy and immediately after childbirth. Colostrum is nutritious and contains antibodies that protect an infant from certain diseases.

**combination pills**  oral contraceptives containing progestin and estrogen, commonly called "the pill."

**conditioning**  in behavior modification, "classical conditioning" involves responses to specific stimuli. "Operant conditioning" involves rewards to encourage and punishments to discourage a specific pattern of behavior.

**condoms**  also known as "rubbers," "skins" and "prophylactics," condoms are tight sheaths placed over the penis to trap semen.

**continence**  total abstinence from sexual behavior.

**copper T**  an IUD which utilizes copper as a spermicide.

**corpus luteum**  an ovarian follicle that an egg has just left, which produces progesterone.

**corpus spongiosum**  spongy, erectile tissue within the penis, surrounding the urethra.

**Cowper's glands**  male glands that secrete a clear, sticky fluid into the urethra prior to ejaculation. Tens of thousands of sperm are usually contained in the few drops that emerge from the urethral meatus; they may foil practitioners of withdrawal.

**cunnilingus**  oral contact with the female genitals.

**cystitis**  an infection of the bladder, which may be contracted during sexual intercourse.

**diaphragm**  a thin, flexible rubber cap placed over the cervix as a contraceptive.

**diethylstilbestrol (DES)**  a synthetic hormone which was used to prevent miscarriages; known to cause cancer of the vagina and cervix in daughters of women to whom it was administered.

**dilation and curettage (D & C)**  a technique of abortion in which the fetus is scraped from the interior of the uterus.

**douching**  cleansing the vagina with a flow of water.

**drive**  goal-directed behavior based on biological needs.

**dysfunction**  malfunction of sexual or other responses.

**dysmenorrhea**  painful menstruation.

**dyspareunia**  painful intercourse.

**ego**  a portion of human mental activity, in Freud's scheme; conceived as embodying functions such as sensory perception, memory, and communication.

**ejaculation**  expulsion of semen during male orgasm.

**ejaculatory ducts**  ducts within the prostate that receive sperm from the ampullae.

**ejaculatory incompetence**  inability to ejaculate within a vagina.

**embryo**  an organism in its earliest phase of development. In humans, embryonic development lasts for two months following the union of a sperm and egg.

**endometrium** the inner lining of the uterus, into which an embryo may settle and grow.

**epididymis** a convoluted tube that adheres to a testicle and stores sperm between ejaculations.

**epidural injection** injection of anesthetics near but outside the spinal cord, used to deaden the sensations of childbirth.

**episiotomy** an incision made from the vagina toward the anus, to avoid the tearing of tissues during childbrith.

**erectile dysfunction** inability to achieve erection, also called impotence.

**erogenous zones** sexually sensitive parts of the body. The genitalia are erogenous zones for almost everyone; other parts of the body, such as the nipples, anus, mouth, and ears, may also be erogenous.

**erotic** pertaining to sexual sensation.

**estrogen** hormone produced by the ovaries, which stimulates development of certain female sex characteristics and is one of the four hormones of the menstrual cycle.

**eunuch** a male whose testicles have been removed by castration.

**excitement phase** a phase in the Masters and Johnson scheme of sexual response; anticipation of an erotic encounter.

**exhibitionism** the exposure of parts of the body, usually the genitals, for sexual excitement.

**Fallopian tubes** ducts that channel eggs from the ovaries into the uterus.

**fellatio** oral contact with the male genitals.

**fertilization** union of a sperm with an egg to form a primordial human cell.

**fetishism** the use of an inanimate article, most often clothing, as a sex object.

**fetus** an organism in the latter phase of prenatal development. The human fetal phase lasts from the ninth week following conception until birth.

**follicle** a microscopic sac on the surface of an ovary in which an egg develops.

**follicle-stimulating hormone (FSH)** a hormone produced by the pituitary gland that stimulates production of estrogen by ovaries and sperm by testicles.

**foreskin** the fold of skin normally extending from the shaft of the penis over the glans penis, commonly removed from male infants by circumcision.

**fornication** sexual intercourse between two people who are unmarried.

**fraternal twins** conceived if two eggs are fertilized simultaneously.

**frenulum** the underside of the penis immediately behind the glans penis, a particularly erogenous portion of the male anatomy.

**fuck** tabooed, but now commonly used, word for "to have sexual intercourse."

**gay** colloquial for "homosexual."

**gender identity** a person's perception of his/her sexual identity. Gender identity may not be the same as genetic sexuality.

**genes** hereditary codes carried in every cell of the body. Reproductive cells (sperm and eggs) carry only half the genetic material in other cells of the body.

**genitalia** organs of the reproductive system (sometimes used with reference only to the external sex organs).

**genitals** genitalia.

**gestalt** physical, biological, and psychological whole of an individual.

**glans clitoris** tip of the clitoris.

**glans penis** the smooth acorn-shaped tip of the penis.

**gonadotropins** gonad-stimulating hormones.

**gonads** primary reproductive organs, ovaries and testicles.

**gonorrhea** a venereal disease involving bacterial infection of the mucous membranes of the reproduction organs, anus, or throat.

**gynecomastia** enlargement of male breasts.

**gynosperm** a sperm cell bearing an X chromosome. A zygote formed by the union of a gynosperm and an egg will develop into a female.

**heat** a phase in which certain female animals are receptive to sexual advances.

**Hegar's sign** an early indication of pregnancy, the softening of the uterus just above the cervix.

**hermaphrodite** a person possessing both ovaries and testicles.

**herpes genitalis** a venereal disease caused by a virus, evidenced by painful blisters on the genitals.

**heterosexuality** sexual preference for members of the opposite sex.

**heterosociality** social interaction between people of opposite sexes.

**homologous organs** male and female organs that develop from common embryonic structures.

**homosexuality** sexual preference for members of the same sex. A *covert* homosexual hides his/her sexual preference to most people; an *overt* homosexual is publicly known as a homosexual.

**homosociality** interpersonal relations between people of the same sex.

**hostile mucus** sperm-killing mucus secreted by the cervix in certain women; a cause of female infertility.

**hot flash** a symptom of menopause involving a sudden sensation of heat.

**human chorionic gonadotropin (HCG)** a hormone involved in pregnancy, which helps prepare the female body for nurturing an embryo.

**hymen** a thin fold of flesh, which partially closes the vaginal orifice.

**hypothalamus** a projection of the brain that is connected by nerves and blood vessels to the pituitary gland.

**id** a portion of human mental activity, in Freud's scheme; the personality with which a baby is born.

**identical twins** twins resulting from the splitting of an embryo.

**identity** the individual's self or personality.

**impotence** inability to achieve or maintain erection.

**incest** sexual relations between people closely related, as defined by custom or law.

**induction of labor** a procedure by which childbirth is artificially started with drugs or mechanical probing.

**infertility** inability to conceive.

**infundibula** the membranous fringed funnels by which eggs enter the Fallopian tubes from the ovaries.

**instinct** an unlearned pattern of behavior, such as sucking by infants.

**interstitial cells** cells in the testicles that produce testosterone.

**interstitial cell-stimulating hormone (ICSH)** hormone produced by the pituitary gland that causes testosterone-producing cells in the testicles to become active.

**intrauterine device (IUD)** a contraceptive object inserted into the uterus, which apparently prevents implantation by an embryo.

**intromission** insertion of a penis into a vagina.

**in vitro fertilization** artificial fertilization, outside the female reproductive system. Also called "test tube" fertilization.

**Klinefelter's syndrome** also termed the "XXY syndrome," this is a genetic abnormality in which a male receives an extra X chromosome.

**labia majora** outer folds of skin that protect the delicate flesh of the vulva.

**labia minora** the inner folds that close over the vaginal orifice.

**lactation** production of milk by a mother's breasts.

**lesbian** homosexual female.

**libido** sexual instinct.

**lightening** the descending of a fetus's head into the

cervix during late pregnancy.

**luteinizing hormone (LH)**   a hormone produced by the pituitary gland that is involved in the menstrual cycle.

**lympho-granuloma venereum (LGV)**   a venereal disease of Asian origin brought to the United States during the Vietnamese War, caused by a micro-organism that invades the lymph system.

**macho/machismo**   excessive "masculine" behavior, usually referring to aggressive, competitive, sexual, or other interpersonal behavior.

**masochism**   sexual variation in which a person obtains sexual pleasure by inflicting pain on him/herself.

**masturbation**   manual or mechanical stimulation of the genitals.

**meiosis**   the type of cell division by which reproductive cells are formed.

**menarche**   a female's first period of menstrual bleeding.

**menopause**   also termed "the climacteric," a phase of hormonal change during which a woman's fertility diminishes and ultimately ceases.

**menstrual cycle**   the cyclical buildup and breakdown of the uterine lining.

**menstrual extraction**   a technique used for abortion during the first weeks of pregnancy.

**midwife**   a person licensed to manage care of mothers and babies throughout the maternity cycle, so long as pregnancy meets criteria accepted as normal.

**mini-pills**   oral contraceptives utilizing progestin as the pregnancy-inhibiting agent. Mini-pills must be taken every day of the month.

**miscarriage**   spontaneous loss of an embryo or fetus that results in its death.

**miscarriage**   spontaneous loss of an embryo or fetus that results in its death.

**"missionary position"**   belly-to-belly intercourse with the male on top.

**mitosis**   cell division characteristic of most body cells, in which the two cells formed by the division of a "parent cell" receive a duplicate of each chromosome.

**mittelschmerz**   abdominal pain experienced by some women during ovulation.

**monosomy-X**   a genetic abnormality in which a male has only a single X chromosome.

**mons veneris**   the area covered with pubic hair above the labia majora.

**morning-after-pill**   a massive dose of estrogen used to prevent pregnancy after non-contracepted intercourse.

**morning sickness**   nausea and vomiting that often accompanies pregnancy.

**Mullerian ducts**   fetal forerunners of Fallopian tubes.

**myotonia**   muscular tension.

**necrophilia**   behavior in which an individual is sexually attracted to a dead person.

**non-gonorrheal urethritis (NGU)**   an infection of the urethra with superficial symptoms resembling gonorrhea.

**obstetrician**   a doctor whose specialty is childbirth.

**oral-genital contact**   the stimulation of genitals by mouth or tongue.

**orgasm**   the climax and release of erotic tension.

**orgasmic dysfunction**   inability to achieve orgasm.

**orgasmic platform**   the outer third of the vagina, which constricts during the plateau phase of erotic arousal.

**os**   passage through the cervix that links the uterus with the vagina.

**ovaries**   the primary female reproductive organs, paired organs that produce eggs.

**ovulation**   release of an egg (ovum) by an ovary.

**ovum**   egg, a female reproductive cell.

**oxytocin**   a hormone produced by the pituitary gland that induces labor and lactation.

**Pap smear**    a test for cancer of the cervix.

**paracervical block**    injection of anesthetic into the cervix through a needle inserted through the vagina, used to deaden the pain of childbirth.

**passing**    pretending to be "straight" despite a preference for homosexuality.

**pedophilia**    the use of children for sexual gratification, most often by adult men.

**penis**    the male organ of copulation and urination.

**perineum**    band of muscular flesh between the anus and the external genitals.

**perversion**    socially unacceptable sexual behavior, which varies from culture to culture.

**pheromones**    odorous substances produced by certain species of animals, which stimulate sexual responses.

**pitocin**    a drug which induces labor.

**placebos**    medically inert substances.

**placenta**    the organ of exchange between a fetus and its mother, where delicate blood vessels from the mother and child intermingle.

**plateau phase**    in the Masters and Johnson scheme of sexual response, the phase that is the balance between excitement and orgasm.

**pornography**    sexually arousing – but socially unacceptable – material in art, literature, movies, or other forms of communication.

**postpartum period**    the month or so immediately following birth.

**premature ejaculation**    inability to delay ejaculation.

**prenatal**    before birth.

**prepuce**    fold of skin over the tip of an uncircumcised penis; also called foreskin.

**progesterone**    also termed "pregnancy hormone," is produced by the ovaries and prepares the uterus to receive an embryo.

**progesterone T**    an IUD impregnated with progesterone.

**progestin-induced hermaphroditism**    a condition in which female offspring of mothers who were treated with progestins (commonly used in the 1950s to prevent miscarriage) developed masculinized genitals.

**progestins**    synthetic compounds resembling progesterone in chemical structure.

**prolactin**    a hormone produced by the pituitary gland that induces lactation.

**prostaglandins**    hormones whose natural functions are little understood, which have been used with a certain amount of success as contraceptive and abortive agents.

**prostate gland**    a muscular organ within the lower abdomen, which produces the bulk of semen and acts as a two-way valve between the urethra and the bladder and testicles.

**prostatitis**    inflammation of the prostate.

**prostitution**    the exchange of sexual favors for money.

**pseudohermaphrodite**    a person with either male or female gonads, whose sexual anatomy is ambiguous (for example, with a complete set of female organs, plus an empty scrotum).

**pseudo-matuality**    the maintenance of a relationship with the presence that it is mutually fulfilling.

**psychoanalysis**    Freud's scheme of psychological probing.

**psycho-sexual**    relating to sexuality in its widest sense – emotionally, psychologically, and physically.

**puberty**    a phase of maturity when humans become fertile.

**pubic lice**    commonly called "crabs," transmitted during sexual intercourse and also acquired from clothing and toilet seats.

**pudendum**    see vulva.

**quickening** fetal movements.

**radioimmunoassay (RIA)** see *radioreceptor-assay*.

**radioreceptorassay (RRA)** a pregnancy test which monitors the level of human chorionic gonadotropin.

**rape** sexual intercourse with another person without his/her consent, which is legally defined.

**rectum** the terminal portion of the large intestine.

**reflex arc** in the nervous system, a neural pathway between receptor and effector cells.

**refractory period** period following orgasm, during which males are incapable of erotic arousal.

**resolution phase** a phase of the Masters and Johnson scheme of sexual response, during which erotic tension subsides.

**retrograde ejaculation** ejaculation into the bladder rather than through the urethra.

**Rh test** analysis to check for a genetic difference between parents' blood types that may lead to destruction of a fetus's red blood cells.

**rhogam** a drug used to prevent damage to the offspring of Rh-incompatible parents.

**rhythm** abstaining from intercourse during the period of ovulation, in hopes of preventing pregnancy.

**rubella** also called "German measles," a disease that may cause congenital defects if contracted during the first trimester of pregnancy.

**sadism** sexual gratification obtained by inflicting physical or psychological pain on another person.

**sado-masochism** the mutual infliction of pain on one another by two people for sexual purposes.

**saline injection** a technique of abortion in which a salt solution is injected into the uterus.

**salpingitis** gonorrheal infection of the Fallopian tubes.

**sanitary napkins** highly absorbent pads of cotton used to absorb menstrual discharge.

**scopolamine** sometimes called "scope" or "twilight sleep," a drug used to deaden the sensations of childbirth.

**scrotum** pouch of wrinkled, elastic skin containing testicles.

**secondary sex characteristics** characteristics of maturation due to influences of the sex hormones, which are not directly linked to reproductive functions.

**semen** sperm plus the fluid in the ejaculate.

**seminal vesicles** paired glands that secrete a sperm-activating substance into the ampullae.

**seminiferous tubules** tiny, convoluted tubes within the testicles in which sperm are produced.

**septicemia** a gonorrheal infection which has entered the bloodstream.

**sequential pills** pills containing estrogen as the primary pregnancy-inhibiting agent (banned in 1976, they were found to cause potentially fatal blood clots).

**sex flush** a blush of the skin of breasts and abdomen during erotic arousal.

**sexual deviation** departure from the sexual norms and dominant patterns established by a society. (Because this term has moral or pathological associations, the authors prefer *sexual variation*.)

**sexual inversion** psychoanalytic term meaning "homosexuality."

**sexual variations** departure from the sexual norms and dominant patterns of a culture.

**sexually transmissible disease (STD)** see *venereal disease*.

**sixty-nine** colloquial expression for mutual oral-genital contact.

**smegma** a moist, curd-like substance that may accumulate under the foreskin of a penis or around the clitoris.

**sodomy** variously used to mean anal intercourse, intercourse with animals, illegal or variant sexual behavior; often undefined by statutes.

**sperm**   male reproductive cells.

**spermatogenisis**   the process by which sperm are produced within the testicles.

**spermicides**   creams, foams, and jellies used to kill sperm.

**sphincter muscle**   a circular muscle that closes an orifice (such as the anus).

**spinal injection**   injection of anesthetics directly into the spinal column, used to deaden the pain of childbirth.

**spontaneous abortion**   see *miscarriage*.

**spotting**   erratic uterine bleeding.

**status politics**   political activity motivated by a group's loss (or threatened loss) of *moral* dominance.

**statutory rape**   sexual intercourse with a female under a legally prescribed age; age and penalties vary from state to state.

**sterilization**   procedures that render a person infertile.

**superego**   a portion of human mental activity, in Freud's scheme, commonly equated with conscience.

**syphilis**   venereal disease caused by a micro-organism.

**tampons**   cylinders of cotton inserted into the vagina to absorb mentrual discharge.

**tenting**   expansion of the inner two-thirds of the vagina during erotic arousal.

**"test tube" fertilization**   see *in vitro fertilization*.

**testicles**   primary male reproductive organs, the paired sperm-producing organs within the scrotum.

**testosterone**   the "male" hormone produced within the testicles.

**thrombophlebitis**   formation of blood clots in the legs, a potentially fatal side-effect of oral contraceptives high in estrogen.

**toxemia**   retention of toxic body wastes that results in self-poisoning.

**transvestite**   a person who wears the clothes of (and may imitate) the other sex.

**trisomy-X**   a genetic abnormality in which a male has three X chromosomes.

**tubal ligation**   tying the Fallopian tubes to sterilize a female.

**tubal pregnancy**   implantation and initial development of an embryo in a Fallopian tube rather than the uterus.

**twins**   see *fraternal twins* and *identical twins*.

**umbilical cord**   a cord carrying blood vessels, which attaches the placenta to the abdomen of the fetus.

**urethra**   the single duct that transports both semen and urine from the prostate gland through the penis.

**urethral meatus**   mouth of the urethra at the tip of the penis.

**urethritis**   infection of the urethra.

**urinary duct**   the duct from the bladder that merges with the urethra in the prostate, closed by a sphincter muscle during erotic arousal.

**uterus**   muscular organ in the female abdomen, in which the fetus develops.

**vacuum aspiration**   a technique of abortion using suction.

**vagina**   the female genital canal that receives the penis during intromission.

**vaginismus**   tightening of the muscles surrounding the vagina, which makes it impenetrable by a penis.

**vaginitis**   infection of the vagina.

**varicoceles**   varicose veins of the scrotum, thought to contribute to male infertility.

**vas deferens**   the duct that transports sperm from a testicle into the lower abdomen (plural, vasa deferentia).

**vasectomy**   severing the vasa deferentia to sterilize a male.

**venereal disease**   a disease transmitted by sexual intercourse.

**venereal warts**   warts caused by a virus which is passed during sexual intercourse.

**voyeur**   a person who receives sexual satisfaction by watching sexually stimulating activities.

**vulva**   the external genitals of the female.

**yolk sac**   an embryonic structure which exists only as a vestige in humans. A food-storing organ in egg-laying species.

**zoophilia**   sexual attraction for animals.

**zygote**   a fertilized egg; the primordial cell of an organism.

SATYRIASIS or SATYROMANIA. n., Gr. from late Latin.
An excessive and often uncontrollable sexual desire
in men. Gr. satyros, a satyr.

NYMPHOMANIA. n., Latin, meaning an Abnormally strong
and uncontrollable sexual desire in women.

# Index

†